MEET THE *SOUTHERN LIVING* FOODS STAFF

On these pages we present the *Southern Living* Foods Staff (from left in each photograph).

Peggy Smith, Assistant Test Kitchens Director;
Kaye Mabry Adams, Associate Foods Editor

Susan Dosier, Foods Editor; Andria Scott Hurst,
Assistant Foods Editor; Denise Gee, Assistant Foods Editor

Charles Walton IV, Senior Foods Photographer;
Elle Barrett, Executive Editor; Karen Brechin, Editorial
Assistant

Patty Vann, Test Kitchens Director; Julia Dowling, Test
Kitchens Home Economist; Susan J. Reynolds, Recipe Editor

Susan Hawthorne Nash, Editorial Coordinator;
Dana Adkins Campbell, Associate Foods Editor

Test Kitchens Home Economists: Judy Feagin (seated),
Diane Hogan, and Vanessa Ward

Jodi Jackson Loe, Editorial Assistant; Jane Cairns, Test
Kitchens Home Economist; Jackie Mills, Assistant
Foods Editor

Tina Evans, Photographer; J. Savage Gibson, Photographer;
Ashley S. Johnson, Photo Stylist; Leslie Byars, Photo Stylist

3

Southern Living®

1994 ANNUAL RECIPES

Oxmoor House®

Library of Congress Catalog Number: 79-88364
ISBN: 0-8487-1403-2
ISSN: 0272-2003

Manufactured in the United States of America
First printing 1994

Cover: *Chocolate-Orange Roulage (page 314), Toffee-Pecan Roulage (page 312)*
Back Cover: *Christmas Crostini (page 318), Almond-Bacon-Cheese Crostini (page 318), Mozzarella Crostini (page 319)*
Page 1: *Best-Ever Lemon Meringue Pie (page 208), Raspberry Cream Pie (page 209), Coffee Cream Pie (page 209)*
Page 4: *Cameo Cake (page 58)*

Southern Living®

Foods Editor: Susan Dosier
Associate Foods Editors: Kaye Mabry Adams,
    Dana Adkins Campbell
Assistant Foods Editors: Denise Gee, Andria Scott Hurst,
    Jackie Mills, R.D.
Contributing Editors: Elle Barrett, Susan Hawthorne Nash
Recipe Editor: Susan Reynolds
Test Kitchens Director: Patty Vann
Assistant Test Kitchens Director: Peggy Smith
Test Kitchens Staff: Jane Cairns, Julia Dowling,
    Judy Feagin, Diane Hogan, Vanessa McNeil Ward
Editorial Assistants: Karen Brechin, Jodi Jackson Loe
Senior Foods Photographer: Charles Walton IV
Photographers: Tina Evans, J. Savage Gibson
Photo Stylists: Leslie Byars, Ashley S. Johnson
Photo Services: Tracy Underwood
Production Manager: Kenner Patton
Assistant Production Manager: Vicki Weathers
Production Assistant: Stephanie L. McGuire

Oxmoor House, Inc.

Editor-in-Chief: Nancy J. Fitzpatrick
Senior Editor, Editorial Services: Olivia Kindig Wells
Art Director: James Boone

Southern Living® *1994 Annual Recipes*

Senior Foods Editor: Susan Carlisle Payne
Assistant Foods Editor: Whitney Wheeler Pickering
Copy Editor: Donna Baldone
Editorial Assistant: Keri Bradford
Production and Distribution Director: Phillip Lee
Production Manager: Gail Morris
Associate Production Manager: Theresa L. Beste
Production Assistant: Marianne Jordan
Editorial Consultant: Jean Wickstrom Liles
Indexer: Mary Ann Laurens
Designer and Illustrator: Carol Middleton

TABLE OF CONTENTS

If your tastebuds are tingling and you're not sure which type of food will satisfy them, turn to the versatile and cross-referenced indexes in the back of this cookbook. They'll put the year's worth of recipes and food ideas at your fingertips.

The chapters of this cookbook are arranged like the pages of the magazine each month – right on target to meet the needs of the seasons and your multifaceted lifestyle.

For example, when the weather cools down, turn up the heat with our Cajun versus Creole debate and the spicy flavors that simmer in October's main story. You'll find ideas personalized for the winter holidays by flipping through the last two chapters of this book.

OUR YEAR AT SOUTHERN LIVING®

In almost every letter I receive from readers, they talk about how busy they are.

Here at *Southern Living*, our staff definitely identifies with those readers struggling to balance careers or volunteer commitments, time with friends, and time with family. These challenges inspired us to make some changes in our recipes this year.

We worked to improve the way we write our recipes. We sent samples of a proposed recipe format to 508 readers who subscribe to our magazine and use it in the kitchen. Of that group, 501 responded saying they found the new format simpler and easier to read. A guide on page 12 explains this recipe "tune-up." We hope you like it.

When you write, you also tell us you're trying to eat healthier.

Several of you asked why we don't offer a nutrient analysis with every recipe. If we included the analysis with every recipe, we'd have less room to publish new recipes. Knowing your interest in nutrition, however, we redesigned and renamed our section of light and healthy recipes. Now known as "Living Light," these pages provide some of the best tasting recipes we've ever published. The flavor is so good, no one believes they're low in calories and fat.

And that's not surprising, considering that our Registered Dietitian, Jackie Mills, has also worked as a chef. Her love of good food has made our "Living Light" pages very popular. You can use those recipes and know you won't feel cheated. I give you my word on it.

That's what SOUTHERN LIVING food is all about – making food a joy, making it something to savor and celebrate.

The opportunity to prepare meals for our families is a privilege, and cooking for those you love is a special gift and a tradition worth keeping.

I read in food magazines last year that more recipes for mashed potatoes were published than any other type of potato recipe. What fun! Some traditions are just too good to lose. That's like *Southern Living® Annual Recipes*, a tradition we're delighted to share with you once again. Even though you're busy, we hope you'll find this cookbook a valuable guide and companion in your kitchen.

Let us hear from you. And thank you for all of the recipes, cards, and notes you've sent us this year. We look forward to more in the coming year.

Susan Dosier

1994's Top-Rated Recipes

....

Fifteen Foods professionals scrutinize each of our recipes at taste-testing every day, and yes, we do have our favorites.

Each recipe must be prepared, tasted, retested, if necessary, and "passed" before being published. After a recipe gets our stamp of approval, we assign it an in-house rating. It's rare for a recipe to receive our highest rating – a three – but when it does, it's extra special. We'd like to share four recipes that received our highest rating this year. You won't want to miss them as you use this cookbook.

GRILLED VEGETABLE SALAD
recipe, page 203; photograph, page 186

Grilled Vegetable Salad, with its blend of molasses and white balsamic vinegar, is the best light recipe we've tried in years. Submitted by Margaret Jordan of Birmingham, Alabama, the recipe can be made ahead up to a couple of days. Just let the vegetables soak up flavor from the vinegar mixture 30 minutes, and then cook them on the grill in a grill basket until they're tender. Return them to the vinegar mixture to stop the cooking process and concentrate the flavor even more. They're best when chilled at least 8 hours. This recipe packs a lot of flavor into its 103 calories per serving.

ROASTED CHILES RELLENOS WITH TOMATILLO SAUCE
recipe, page 203

With enough protein to be a meatless main dish and tipping the calorie count at just over 300, here's the other light recipe we really flipped for. Roasted Chiles Rellenos With Tomatillo Sauce are stuffed with black beans and reduced-fat Monterey Jack cheese and then battered and fried in an ever-so-slight amount of vegetable oil. Even after topping with the spicy tomatillo sauce, this Tex-Mex tempter will help keep you heart-healthy. You'd never guess, but only 23% of its calories come from fat. It's a recipe you'll be eager to splurge on – and you can.

THUNDERBOLT POTATOES
recipe, page 213; photograph, page 259

Executive Editor Elle Barrett gets accolades for this recipe. She developed Thunderbolt Potatoes in her home kitchen one day during one of her favorite culinary pastimes – cranking up the flavor in typically bland potatoes. Chili powder gives the potatoes a rosy color and corn kernels add an unexpected texture that sent the test kitchen rating to its peak when the recipe was evaluated. If there are leftovers, follow directions to turn the mashed potatoes into Thunderbolt Potato Patties. The jolt of flavor the dish contains inspired the name for these potatoes as well as the thunderbolt-shaped garnish of chile powder sprinkled on top of the dish with the aid of a simple stencil cut from paper.

APRICOT-PECAN STUFFED PORK LOIN
recipe, page 274

Elle was home working in her kitchen again when she created Apricot-Pecan Stuffed Pork Loin. As with many of her recipes, Elle doesn't measure ingredients or record what she does. But she worked closely with Test Kitchens Staff Member Julia Dowling, who duplicated the dish and kept detailed notes to make the recipe accessible to readers (and to other staff members who wanted to take the recipe home with them right away). If you make this recipe, be sure to follow directions about flaming the bourbon sauce before you bake the pork. It's a simple but important step; without it, the pork may ignite in your oven. Don't let this step intimidate you, however. It's easy to flame the sauce, and the flavor is definitely worth it.

A CHANGE OF STYLE

With each new year come resolutions. The Foods Staff always has the same – to meet your needs by publishing top quality recipes with high standards. One of our most exciting changes this year involves modifications in our recipe format that make it easier than ever to follow directions.

We added bullets (•) to highlight each step and **boldfaced** terms to help you follow recipe procedures. In addition, we often offer helpful hints and cooking tips. You'll find these just below the recipe title, before the ingredients.

Now we offer you an option to reduce calories, fat, or sodium when you see a heart-shaped symbol (♥) with a note following recipes. Each version is tested so we know the lightened one compares to the original. The heart symbol also highlights the nutritional analysis on "Living Light" recipes.

We hope keeping your resolutions will be a breeze with our new easy-to-follow recipes and emphasis on healthful options.

Bullets (•) highlight the separation of paragraphs.

A heart-shaped symbol gives healthier alternatives to lighten up selected recipes and also highlights the nutritional analysis on "Living Light" recipes.

GINGER DIP

Stir these ingredients together in less than 20 minutes. Chilling overnight thickens the consistency.

Frequently, we'll suggest helpful hints and cooking tips.

1 **cup mayonnaise**
1 **(8-ounce) carton sour cream**
1 **(8-ounce) can whole water chestnuts, drained and chopped**
¼ **cup grated onion**
¼ **cup finely chopped fresh parsley**
3 **tablespoons chopped crystallized ginger**
1 **clove garlic, minced**
1 **tablespoon soy sauce**
Dash of hot sauce

Boldfaced terms help you quickly read the steps in the recipe.

• **Combine** all ingredients; cover and chill at least 8 hours.
• **Serve** as a dip with fresh vegetables.
Yield: 3 cups.

Shorter paragraphs group the directions for each step.

♥ To reduce fat and cholesterol, substitute fat-free mayonnaise and nonfat sour cream alternative.

JANUARY

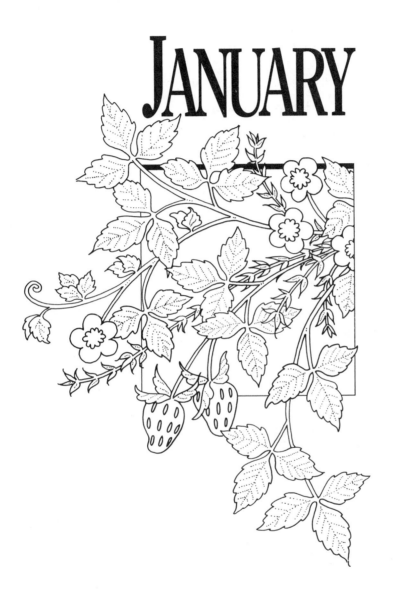

Afternoon Tea

The whole point of afternoon tea is to relax for a while.

Why, then, does it make many people so nervous? The fear of chipping

a piece of china or using the wrong fork brings sweat to many

brows (which, heaven knows, shouldn't be wiped with a linen napkin).

Just sit back and savor a spot of tea and these recipes from

the Victorian Room in Shreveport, Louisiana. For tips on brewing the

perfect cup, see "From Our Kitchen to Yours" beginning on page 17.

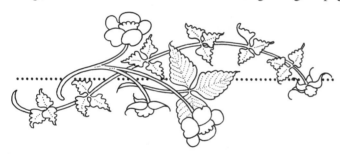

VEAL-VERMICELLI SOUP WITH QUENELLES

4 pounds boneless lamb
1 pound boneless veal
1 pound boneless Boston butt pork roast
5 quarts water
1 leek
1 bay leaf
6 white peppercorns, crushed
3 sprigs fresh parsley
1 cup chopped celery
1 tablespoon salt
1 tablespoon Worcestershire sauce
2 cups broken vermicelli
3 large eggs, lightly beaten
2 cups soft breadcrumbs
2 tablespoons chopped parsley
¼ teaspoon dried thyme
¼ teaspoon ground white pepper
Vegetable oil
Garnish: chopped fresh parsley

●**Trim** fat from meats, and cut into 1-inch cubes. Place in a large Dutch oven; add water. Bring to a boil; reduce heat, and simmer 1 hour.

●**Remove** roots and tough outer leaves from leek. Cut two 2-inch pieces from leek top. (Reserve bottom for another use.) Place leek pieces and next 3 ingredients on a 4-inch square of cheesecloth; tie with string.

●**Add** cheesecloth bag, celery, salt, and Worcestershire sauce to meat mixture; cover and simmer 10 minutes. Remove 2 cups meat, and set aside.

●**Add** vermicelli to Dutch oven; cook 5 to 7 minutes. Remove and discard cheesecloth bag. Keep soup warm.

●**Finely** chop 2 cups meat mixture. Add eggs and next 4 ingredients. Shape into 1-inch balls.

●**Pour** oil to depth of 3 inches into a small Dutch oven; heat to 375°. Fry meatballs, a few at a time, 2 to 3 minutes or until golden brown. Drain on paper towels, and keep warm.

●**Ladle** soup into individual bowls, and add meatballs (quenelles); garnish, if desired. **Yield:** 6½ quarts.

CUCUMBER SANDWICHES

1 (8-ounce) package cream cheese, softened
1 (3-ounce) package cream cheese, softened
¼ cup mayonnaise
1 tablespoon chopped green onions
⅛ teaspoon ground red pepper
⅛ teaspoon hot sauce
1 or 2 drops of red or green liquid food coloring
1 cup peeled, seeded, and grated cucumber
48 slices white sandwich bread
Garnishes: cucumber wedges, fresh dillseed

●**Combine** first 6 ingredients in a large bowl; beat at medium speed with an electric mixer until smooth. Stir in food coloring. Set aside.

●**Drain** grated cucumber on paper towels, gently squeezing out excess moisture. Fold into cream cheese mixture, and set aside.

●**Cut** bread into desired shapes, using a 2- to 3-inch cutter. Spread bread shapes with filling; garnish, if desired. **Yield:** 4 dozen.

DEVILED CHICKEN TARTS

2 cups chopped leeks (1 bunch)
1 tablespoon white vinegar
1 teaspoon ground white pepper
Brown Sauce
3½ cups finely chopped cooked chicken
2 tablespoons butter or margarine
2½ teaspoons Dijon mustard
2½ teaspoons Worcestershire sauce
⅛ teaspoon ground red pepper
3½ cups all-purpose flour
1 cup butter or margarine
¾ cup cold water
2 to 3 tablespoons soft breadcrumbs
Garnishes: sour cream, chopped fresh parsley

●**Combine** first 3 ingredients in a large skillet; cook over medium heat 3 to 5 minutes, stirring often.

● **Add** Brown Sauce, and cook over low heat 10 minutes, stirring often. Stir in chicken and next 4 ingredients; set aside.
● **Place** flour in a large bowl; cut in 1 cup butter with pastry blender until mixture is crumbly. Sprinkle cold water (1 tablespoon at a time) evenly over surface; stir with a fork until dry ingredients are moistened. Shape into a ball.
● **Roll** pastry to ⅛-inch thickness on a lightly floured surface. Cut with a 3½-inch round cutter; place circles into 24 (3-inch) fluted tart pans.
● **Spoon** chicken mixture into pastry; sprinkle evenly with breadcrumbs.
● **Bake** at 350° for 20 to 25 minutes or until lightly browned. Cool slightly, and garnish, if desired. **Yield:** 2 dozen.

Note: Jumbo (3¼-inch) muffin pans may be substituted for tart pans. Place dough circles in bottom of muffin cups, pressing ½ inch up sides with a spoon or tart tamper.

Brown Sauce

¼ cup butter or margarine
1 carrot, scraped and sliced
1 medium onion, sliced
⅓ cup all-purpose flour
2 cups chicken broth
¼ teaspoon salt
¼ teaspoon pepper

● **Melt** butter in a heavy saucepan over medium heat; add carrot and onion. Cook, stirring constantly, until tender.
● **Add** flour, stirring constantly. Cook over medium heat, stirring constantly, until flour is browned (10 minutes). Gradually stir in broth.
● **Bring** to a boil; reduce heat, and simmer 10 minutes, stirring occasionally. Add salt and pepper. Skim off fat, if necessary.
● **Position** knife blade in food processor bowl; add sauce. Process until smooth. **Yield:** 2 cups.

"There's a mystique for Americans about the whole ceremony of tea. Maybe that's what's special about it."
— *Sharon McCullar*
Owner, the Victorian Room
Shreveport, Louisiana

The English have been "taking tea" for eons, but not Americans. At the Victorian Room, you're not supposed to be an expert. You're just supposed to enjoy.

Sharon McCullar makes sure her guests do just that at her tearoom, which is surprisingly found tucked into a corner of the Shreveport drugstore she and her husband operate. Both tourists and first-time locals utter a common plea: "I can't wait to have tea, but you'll have to show me what to do."

She seats them around dining tables in the cozy room, and gives them a minute to drink in the atmosphere. Her heirloom collection sets the mood: mixed patterns of china and sterling, her grandmother's linens, antique clothes and whatnots, and the source of her recipes – Victorian cookbooks shrouded in the pale, musty scent of time gone by.

After talking about the ritual and history of tea, Sharon and her hostesses bring in the freshly brewed beverage and explain the menu they'll be serving; then she leaves her guests to relish the magic of the next hour or so in privacy.

CHESHIRE CLARET CHEESE-AND-HAM STRIPED TEA SANDWICHES

8 slices whole wheat bread
8 slices white sandwich bread
4 slices pumpernickel bread
5 ounces cooked ham
2 teaspoons Dijon mustard
1½ tablespoons mayonnaise
⅛ teaspoon ground red pepper
4 ounces Cheddar cheese with claret, shredded and softened
2 tablespoons butter or margarine, softened

• **Remove** crust from bread with a serrated or electric knife; set aside.
• **Position** knife blade in food processor bowl; add ham. Pulse until finely chopped. Transfer ham to a bowl; stir in mustard, mayonnaise, and red pepper. Set aside.
• **Position** knife blade in food processor bowl; add cheese and butter. Process until smooth, stopping once to scrape down sides. Set aside.
• **Spread** 1 tablespoon ham mixture on each of 4 wheat bread slices; top each with 1 slice of white bread, and spread with 1 tablespoon cheese mixture. Place 1 pumpernickel slice on top of each sandwich, and spread evenly with remaining cheese mixture. Top with remaining slices of white bread; spread evenly with remaining ham mixture, and top with remaining slices of wheat bread.
• **Cut** each sandwich lengthwise into 3 portions. **Yield:** 1 dozen.

Note: To keep Cheshire Claret Cheese-and-Ham Striped Tea Sandwiches fresh as if they had been made that morning, wrap uncut stacks in plastic wrap, place in a deep container, and cover with a damp kitchen towel; refrigerate. Unwrap and slice just before serving.

VICTORIA SANDWICHES

1 cup butter or margarine, softened
1½ cups all-purpose flour
¼ teaspoon salt
1 cup sugar
4 large eggs
1 tablespoon almond extract
½ to ¾ cup peach preserves or nectarine jam
Sifted powdered sugar
Garnishes: sweetened whipped cream, mandarin oranges

• **Beat** butter at high speed with an electric mixer until creamy. Combine flour, salt, and sugar; add to butter, mixing well. Add eggs and almond extract; beat at medium speed 10 minutes. Spoon batter into a greased 15- x 10- x 1-inch jellyroll pan.
• **Bake** at 350° for 18 minutes or until a wooden pick inserted in center comes out clean. Cool in pan on a wire rack 10 minutes. Remove from pan, and cool completely.
• **Cut** cake with a 2-inch heart-shaped cutter.
• **Spread** 1 to 2 teaspoons preserves on half of hearts; top with remaining hearts. Sprinkle with powdered sugar. Garnish, if desired. **Yield:** 15 to 18 sandwiches.

HAZELNUT SCONES

2 cups all-purpose flour
2 teaspoons baking powder
¼ teaspoon salt
½ cup sugar
⅓ cup butter
½ cup chopped blanched hazelnuts
2 large eggs, lightly beaten
½ cup whipping cream
1½ tablespoons Frangelico or other hazelnut-flavored liqueur
1 tablespoon sugar
18 whole hazelnuts

• **Combine** first 4 ingredients in a large bowl; cut in butter with pastry blender until mixture is crumbly. Stir in chopped hazelnuts; make a well in center of mixture, and set aside.
• **Combine** eggs, whipping cream, and liqueur; add to dry ingredients, stirring just until moistened.
• **Roll** dough to ¾-inch thickness on a lightly floured surface. Cut with a 2½-inch daisy-shaped cutter, and place on baking sheets. Sprinkle tops evenly with 1 tablespoon sugar, and place a hazelnut in each center.
• **Bake** at 350° for 15 minutes. Serve with Hazelnut Whipped Cream, Lemon Honey, butter, and strawberry jam. **Yield:** 1½ dozen.

HAZELNUT WHIPPED CREAM

1 cup whipping cream
¼ cup sifted powdered sugar
1 tablespoon Frangelico or other hazelnut-flavored liqueur
½ to 1 teaspoon grated lemon rind

• **Beat** whipping cream at medium speed with an electric mixer until foamy; gradually add powdered sugar, beating at high speed until soft peaks form. Gently stir in liqueur and lemon rind. Serve with Hazelnut Scones. **Yield:** 2 cups.

LEMON HONEY

4 large eggs
2 egg yolks
2 cups sugar
1 tablespoon grated lemon rind
½ cup lemon juice
¼ cup butter

• **Combine** all ingredients in a heavy saucepan; cook over low heat, stirring constantly, 10 minutes or until thickened. Let cool. Serve with Hazelnut Scones. **Yield:** 2½ cups.

These sweets from the Victorian Room bring the perfect ending to afternoon tea. If you don't have the luxury and leisure for a four-course tea, enjoy one of these desserts for a spectacular New Year's finale.

DIPPED STRAWBERRIES

1 quart medium strawberries
12 ounces vanilla-flavored candy coating, divided
2 or 3 drops of red liquid food coloring

● **Rinse** strawberries; dry thoroughly (candy coating will not stick to wet berries). Set aside.
● **Break** 7 ounces candy coating into small pieces, and place in a heavy saucepan. Cook over low heat until coating melts, stirring often. Stir in food coloring.
● **Dip** strawberries into melted coating; place on wax paper, and let stand until coating hardens.
● **Melt** remaining 5 ounces candy coating as directed above, omitting food coloring. Dip coated ends of berries into melted coating, barely coating tips. Place on wax paper; let stand until coating hardens. **Yield:** 3 dozen.

CREAMED APPLE TART

3 medium Granny Smith apples, peeled, cored, and finely chopped
½ cup water
⅓ cup butter or margarine, softened
⅓ cup sugar
3 large eggs
⅓ cup soft breadcrumbs
1 tablespoon grated lemon rind
2 tablespoons lemon juice
½ teaspoon ground cinnamon
¼ teaspoon ground nutmeg
⅛ teaspoon ground cloves
Common Paste Pastry
1 medium Granny Smith apple, peeled, cored, and thinly sliced
1 egg white, lightly beaten
2 tablespoons sugar
⅛ teaspoon ground cinnamon

● **Combine** chopped apple and water in a small heavy saucepan. Bring to a boil; cover, reduce heat, and simmer 20 minutes. Cool slightly. Drain, if necessary.
● **Beat** butter at medium speed with an electric mixer until creamy; gradually add ⅓ cup sugar, beating well. Add apples, beating well. Add eggs, one at a time, beating after each addition. Stir in breadcrumbs and next 5 ingredients. Pour into prepared Common Paste Pastry.
● **Arrange** apple slices in a circle over filling; brush with egg white.
● **Combine** 2 tablespoons sugar and ⅛ teaspoon cinnamon; sprinkle evenly over apples.
● **Bake** at 400° for 55 to 60 minutes. (Cover loosely with aluminum foil the last 15 minutes to prevent overbrowning, if necessary.) Cool on a wire rack. Cover and chill at least 2 hours. **Yield:** 1 (7½-inch) tart.

Common Paste Pastry

1 cup all-purpose flour
2 tablespoons sugar
⅓ cup butter, softened
3 to 4 tablespoons cold water

● **Combine** flour and sugar; cut in butter with pastry blender until mixture is crumbly. Sprinkle cold water (1 tablespoon at a time) over surface; stir with a fork until dry ingredients are moistened. Shape into a ball.
● **Roll** pastry to ⅛-inch thickness on a lightly floured surface. Place in a 7½-inch tart pan (1¾ inches deep with removable bottom); trim off excess pastry along edges. Line pastry with aluminum foil, and fill with pie weights or dried beans.
● **Bake** at 400° for 5 minutes; remove from oven, and gently remove weights and foil. Prick bottom and sides of pastry with a fork. Bake for 5 additional minutes. **Yield:** 1 (7½-inch) pastry.

FROM OUR KITCHEN TO YOURS

For a variation on a birthday party theme, how about a tea party? Recipes for savories from the Victorian Room and lifelong friends in attendance would make a birthday special. Entertaining with an afternoon tea is easy because you can make most of the preparations ahead. Just follow our timetable and tips for a hassle-free afternoon for the honoree and her dearest friends.

TWO WEEKS BEFORE
Prepare and freeze Victoria Sandwiches and Deviled Chicken Tarts.
Tip: Count on extra time if you have only one jumbo muffin pan or six tart pans. If transporting, thaw sandwiches in the car; place chicken tarts in cooler to thaw. If you're at home, thaw sandwiches at room temperature and chicken tarts in the refrigerator.

THREE DAYS BEFORE
Make the fillings for Cucumber Sandwiches and Cheshire Claret Cheese-and-Ham Striped Tea Sandwiches; cover and refrigerate.

TWO DAYS BEFORE
Bake Hazelnut Scones; cool and store in an airtight container. If you face time constraints, choose a favorite creamed soup to replace the Veal-Vermicelli Soup With Quenelles. Prepare soup; cover and refrigerate.

ONE DAY BEFORE
Assemble Cheshire Claret Cheese-and-Ham Striped Tea Sandwiches, and cut bread rounds for the Cucumber Sandwiches; wrap and refrigerate.
Tip: Lightly butter half of bread rounds on one side; top with remaining bread rounds before storing.

DAY OF PARTY
Assemble Cucumber Sandwiches, and prepare Hazelnut Whipped Cream;

refrigerate. Slice striped tea sandwiches. Prepare whipped cream and drain mandarin oranges. Garnish sandwiches, if desired, and refrigerate. Heat soup; cover scones and chicken tarts with aluminum foil, and bake at 350° until thoroughly heated. Garnish tarts, if desired.

YOUR CUP OF TEA

In the mood for some soothing hot tea? Here's how to brew the perfect cup.

■ Bring water to a boil in a teakettle; then pour into the teapot to rinse and warm it. Discard water.

■ Place a heaping teaspoon of loose tea leaves for each person and one more "for the pot" into the teapot. (Loose tea is often thought to be of finer quality than tea bags.)

■ Bring more water to a boil in teakettle, and pour into the teapot.

■ Brew 3 to 6 minutes, depending on the type of tea you're using. (The package may give you a precise time – usually the larger the leaf, the longer the brewing.)

■ Stir the pot just a little; then pour through tiny strainer into cups.

■ Serve with milk (not cream, as it may curdle), if desired. Pour the milk in first; then add tea. (The English insist on pouring tea first; then milk. Either way would be acceptable, unless you're entertaining the Queen.)

■ If you're brewing just a cup of tea, you can put leaves into a tea ball – a pierced stainless steel ball with a lid and chain. Place the tea ball into the cup, and pour boiling water directly into the cup.

A Taste of The Tropics

The winter weather forecast looks bleak. You can't bring summer any closer, but you *can* treat your taste buds to the tropics right now.

Next to the apples and pears at the supermarket, brilliant-green limes and sunshine-yellow lemons beckon. Sometimes you can find papaya, carambola (or star fruit), and kiwifruit, as well. They may be a little expensive, but, hey, they're cheaper than a ticket to the Bahamas. So make reservations in your own kitchen with these recipes. Turn on some reggae, take a bite, and you're there in spirit.

TROPICAL BREEZE BRIE

1 kiwifruit, peeled and cut in half crosswise
1 small papaya, peeled, seeded, and cut in half lengthwise
1 carambola, cut in half crosswise
1 teaspoon peeled, grated gingerroot
1 tablespoon honey
1 tablespoon lime juice
1 (15-ounce) mini Brie
1½ tablespoons flaked coconut, toasted
Garnish: twisted lime slice

●Chop half of fruit; set aside.
●Cut remaining fruit into ¼-inch slices; set aside.
●Combine chopped fruit, gingerroot, honey, and lime juice; set aside.
●Remove rind from top of cheese, cutting to within ½ inch of outside edges. Place on a microwave-safe dish. Microwave at HIGH 1½ minutes or until softened but not melted.
●Spoon fruit mixture on cheese; sprinkle with coconut. Garnish, if desired. Serve with sliced fruit and gingersnaps or shortbread cookies. **Yield:** 12 to 15 appetizer servings.

PAPAYA-PINEAPPLE ROLL

2 cups water
1½ cups sugar
½ cup butter or margarine
½ cup shortening
1½ cups self-rising flour
⅓ cup milk
1¼ cups finely chopped papaya
1¼ cups finely chopped fresh pineapple

●Combine first 3 ingredients in a saucepan; bring to a boil, stirring until sugar dissolves. Set aside.
●Cut shortening into flour with pastry blender until mixture is crumbly. Add milk; stir with a fork until dry ingredients are moistened.
●Roll dough into a 12-inch square on wax paper. Spoon fruit evenly over pastry, leaving a ¼-inch border; roll up dough jellyroll fashion.
●Cut into 1-inch-thick slices, and place slices, cut side down, into a 13- x 9- x 2-inch pan. Pour sugar mixture over rolls.
●Bake at 350° for 45 minutes. Serve warm with ice cream, if desired. **Yield:** 12 servings.

Mrs. T. L. Trimble
Pensacola, Florida

HOT BUTTERED LEMONADE

3 cups water
½ cup sugar
2 tablespoons butter or margarine
1 teaspoon grated lemon rind
½ cup fresh lemon juice (about 4 lemons)
Garnish: thin lemon slices

●Combine first 4 ingredients in a saucepan; bring to a boil, stirring until sugar dissolves.
●Stir in lemon juice; pour into mugs. Garnish, if desired. **Yield:** 3½ cups.

Marie Davis
Charlotte, North Carolina

Out of Our League

You could say that *Out of Our League* is in a cookbook league of its own. In addition to having nearly 350 pages devoted to recipes, this Junior League cookbook recommends menus for each month as well as for special occasions. It also offers gifts from the kitchen and ideas for keeping the kids busy and happy.

Since its first printing in 1978, the Junior League of Greensboro, North Carolina, has sold more than 100,000 copies of *Out of Our League*. Proceeds help fund community projects.

CHICKEN PIQUANT

1 pound fresh mushrooms, sliced
1 (3-pound) broiler-fryer, cut up and skinned
2 tablespoons cornstarch
¼ cup water
2 tablespoons olive oil (optional)
¾ cup rosé wine
¼ cup soy sauce
1 clove garlic, pressed
2 tablespoons brown sugar
¼ teaspoon dried oregano
Hot cooked rice

• **Place** sliced mushrooms in a lightly greased 13- x 9- x 2-inch baking dish. Arrange chicken over mushrooms.
• **Combine** cornstarch and water in a small bowl, stirring until smooth. Stir in olive oil, if desired, and next 5 ingredients; pour over chicken.
• **Bake,** uncovered, at 350° for 1 hour or until chicken is done. Serve with rice. **Yield:** 4 servings.

GINGER DIP

1 cup mayonnaise
1 (8-ounce) carton sour cream
1 (8-ounce) can whole water chestnuts, drained and chopped
¼ cup grated onion
¼ cup finely chopped fresh parsley
3 tablespoons chopped crystallized ginger
1 clove garlic, minced
1 tablespoon soy sauce
Dash of hot sauce

• **Combine** all ingredients; cover and chill at least 8 hours.
• **Serve** as a dip with fresh vegetables. **Yield:** 3 cups.

♥ To reduce fat and cholesterol, substitute fat-free mayonnaise and nonfat sour cream alternative.

PEPPERMINT ROUNDS

1 cup butter or margarine, softened
½ cup sugar
1 large egg
1 teaspoon vanilla extract
2½ cups all-purpose flour
½ teaspoon salt
1 cup regular oats, uncooked
⅓ cup hard peppermint candy, crushed
Powdered sugar
Frosting

• **Beat** butter at medium speed with an electric mixer until creamy; gradually add sugar, beating well. Add egg and vanilla, beating well.
• **Combine** flour and salt; add to butter mixture. Stir in oats and candy. Cover and chill 1 hour.
• **Divide** dough in half. Roll each portion to ⅛-inch thickness on a surface dusted with powdered sugar. Cut with a 2½-inch cookie cutter; place on greased, foil-lined baking sheets.
• **Bake** at 350° for 8 minutes; remove to wire racks to cool.
• **Spread** cookies with white frosting. Before frosting sets, drizzle lines of pink frosting across top of each cookie. Carefully draw a wooden pick through lines for a scalloped pattern. **Yield:** 4 dozen.

Frosting

4 cups sifted powdered sugar
¼ to ½ cup half-and-half
Dash of salt
1 teaspoon peppermint extract
Red liquid food coloring

• **Combine** first 4 ingredients, stirring until smooth. (Add additional half-and-half for desired consistency.)
• **Remove** ¼ cup frosting, and stir in 1 or 2 drops red food coloring for pink frosting. **Yield:** 1½ cups.

GO AHEAD AND SAY "YES"

Now that we've tasted the lower fat versions of these longtime favorites,

we may never use the original recipes again. There's so much flavor in these

slimmed-down dishes, we didn't even notice that the fat was missing.

Saying "yes" has never been so easy.

CHICKEN-AND-SAUSAGE GUMBO

*This low-fat gumbo uses a
fat-free roux alternative that browns
all-purpose flour in the oven.*

¾ cup all-purpose flour
½ pound 80% fat-free smoked
 sausage, cut into ¼-inch
 slices
Vegetable cooking spray
6 (6-ounce) skinned chicken breast
 halves
1 cup chopped onion
½ cup chopped green pepper
½ cup sliced celery
2 quarts hot water
3 cloves garlic, minced
2 bay leaves
2 teaspoons reduced-sodium
 Cajun seasoning
½ teaspoon dried thyme
1 tablespoon low-sodium
 Worcestershire sauce
1 teaspoon hot sauce
½ cup sliced green onions
4 cups cooked rice (cooked
 without salt or fat)

●**Place** flour in a 13- x 9- x 2-inch pan. Bake at 400° for 15 minutes or until the color of caramel, stirring flour every 5 minutes.
●**Brown** sausage in a Dutch oven coated with cooking spray over medium heat. Drain and pat dry with paper towels; wipe drippings from Dutch oven.
●**Brown** chicken; drain and pat dry. Wipe drippings from Dutch oven.

●**Cook** onion, green pepper, and celery in Dutch oven coated with cooking spray until tender; sprinkle with browned flour. Gradually stir in water; bring to a boil. Add chicken, garlic, and next 5 ingredients. Reduce heat; simmer, uncovered, 1 hour.
●**Remove** chicken; let cool. Add sausage, and cook gumbo, uncovered, 30 minutes. Stir in green onions; cook, uncovered, 30 additional minutes.
●**Bone** chicken, and cut into strips. Add to gumbo, and cook until heated. Remove and discard bay leaves; serve gumbo over rice. **Yield:** 2 quarts.

Note: For reduced-sodium Cajun seasoning, we used Tony Chachere's More Spice Less Salt Cajun blend of spices.

♥ Per serving (1 cup gumbo with ½ cup rice):
Calories 336 (24% from fat)
Fat 8.8g (3.4g saturated) Cholesterol 69mg
Sodium 200mg Carbohydrate 35.1g
Fiber 1.6g Protein 27.4g

BISCUITS AND SAUSAGE GRAVY

2½ cups reduced-fat baking mix
1 teaspoon sugar
1 cup nonfat buttermilk
Vegetable cooking spray
Sausage Gravy

●**Combine** baking mix and sugar in a large bowl; add buttermilk, stirring until dry ingredients are moistened.
●**Turn** dough out onto a lightly floured surface, and knead lightly 4 or 5 times.
●**Roll** dough to ½-inch thickness; cut with a 2-inch round cutter. Place on a baking sheet coated with cooking spray.
●**Bake** at 450° for 10 minutes. Split biscuits, and serve with Sausage Gravy. **Yield:** 9 biscuits.

♥ Per serving (1 biscuit with ⅓ cup gravy):
Calories 243 (32% from fat)
Fat 8.6g (2.3g saturated) Cholesterol 20.4mg
Sodium 826mg Carbohydrate 32.3g
Fiber 0.2g Protein 10.8g

Sausage Gravy

½ pound ground 60% fat-free
 pork-and-turkey sausage
¼ cup reduced-calorie margarine
⅓ cup all-purpose flour
3¼ cups skim milk
¼ teaspoon salt
½ teaspoon pepper
⅛ teaspoon Italian seasoning

●**Brown** sausage in a large nonstick skillet, stirring until it crumbles. Remove sausage from skillet, and drain on paper towels. Wipe pan drippings from skillet.
●**Melt** margarine in skillet; add flour, stirring until smooth. Cook, stirring

---

ADD FLAVOR, NOT FAT

To add pork flavor to foods without adding extra calories, wash ham hocks, and place in a large saucepan with enough water to cover. Bring to a boil; cover and simmer 30 minutes or until tender. Remove and discard ham hocks. Strain broth, and chill overnight or until fat rises to the surface and hardens. Remove the fat, and discard. Use this liquid to add flavor – but few calories – to greens, vegetables, and beans.

constantly, 1 minute. Gradually add milk; cook over medium heat, stirring constantly, until thickened and bubbly. Stir in seasonings and sausage. Cook, stirring constantly, until thoroughly heated. **Yield:** 3 cups.

♥ Per serving: Calories 115 (50% from fat)
Fat 6.3g (1.6g saturated) Cholesterol 20mg
Sodium 431mg Carbohydrate 8.8g
Fiber 0.2g Protein 7.1g

CHICKEN POT PIE

1 (3½-pound) broiler-fryer
2 quarts water
½ teaspoon salt
½ teaspoon pepper
1 stalk celery, cut into 2-inch
     pieces
1 medium onion, quartered
1 bay leaf
3½ cups peeled and cubed
     potato (1½ pounds)
1 (16-ounce) package frozen
     mixed vegetables
1 cup skim milk
½ cup all-purpose flour
¾ teaspoon salt
1 teaspoon pepper
½ teaspoon poultry seasoning
Butter-flavored cooking spray
5 sheets frozen phyllo pastry,
     thawed

●**Combine** first 7 ingredients in a large Dutch oven; bring to a boil. Cover, reduce heat, and simmer 1 hour or until chicken is tender.
●**Remove** chicken, reserving broth in Dutch oven; discard vegetables and bay leaf. Let chicken cool; skin, bone, and cut into bite-size pieces.
●**Remove** fat (oily liquid) from chicken broth, reserving 3½ cups broth.
●**Bring** reserved broth to a boil in Dutch oven. Add potato and mixed vegetables; return to a boil. Cover, reduce heat, and cook about 8 minutes or until vegetables are tender.
●**Combine** milk and flour in a jar; cover tightly, and shake vigorously. Gradually add milk mixture in a slow, steady stream to broth mixture, stirring constantly. Cook, stirring constantly, 1

minute or until thickened. Stir in ¾ teaspoon salt, 1 teaspoon pepper, poultry seasoning, and chicken.
●**Spoon** mixture into a 13- x 9- x 2-inch baking dish coated with cooking spray; set aside.
●**Place** 1 phyllo sheet horizontally on a flat surface, keeping remaining sheets covered with a slightly damp towel until ready for use. Coat sheet with cooking spray. Layer remaining 4 sheets on first sheet, coating each with cooking spray. Place on top of baking dish, loosely crushing edges around the dish.
●**Bake** at 400° for 20 minutes. **Yield:** 8 servings.

Note: Remove fat by chilling broth and removing congealed fat or by pouring broth through a large fat separator.

♥ Per serving: Calories 249 (21% from fat)
Fat 5.5g (1g saturated) Cholesterol 50mg
Sodium 465mg Carbohydrate 25.9g
Fiber 3.1g Protein 21.5g

BLACK FOREST CHEESECAKE

¾ cup teddy bear-shaped
     chocolate graham cracker
     cookies, crushed
Butter-flavored cooking spray
2 (12-ounce) packages fat-free
     cream cheese product,
     softened
1½ cups sugar
¾ cup egg substitute
1 cup semisweet chocolate morsels,
     melted (6 ounces)
¼ cup unsweetened cocoa
1½ teaspoons vanilla extract
1 (8-ounce) carton nonfat sour
     cream alternative
1 (21-ounce) can reduced-calorie
     cherry pie filling
¾ cup reduced-calorie frozen
     whipped topping, thawed

●**Spread** cookie crumbs on bottom of a 9-inch springform pan coated with cooking spray; set aside.
●**Beat** cream cheese at high speed with an electric mixer until fluffy; gradually add sugar, beating well. Gradually add egg substitute, mixing well. Add melted

chocolate, cocoa, and vanilla, mixing until blended. Stir in sour cream. Pour into prepared pan.
●**Bake** at 300° for 1 hour and 40 minutes. Remove from oven; run a knife around edge of pan to release sides. Let cool completely on a wire rack; cover and chill at least 8 hours.
●**Remove** sides of pan; spread cheesecake with cherry pie filling. Dollop each serving with 1 tablespoon whipped topping. **Yield:** 12 servings.

Note: For a creamy-textured cheesecake, bake at 300° for 1 hour and 20 minutes.

♥ Per serving: Calories 300 (20% from fat)
Fat 6.7g (3g saturated) Cholesterol 10mg
Sodium 407mg Carbohydrate 47.3g
Fiber 0.2g Protein 12.7g

SKINNY TIPS FOR SUPER BOWL DIPS

Instead of the usual array of chips and dip during the annual game, stir up these healthy low-fat dips.

Yogurt Dip: Combine 1⅓ cups plain nonfat yogurt, ¼ cup no-sugar-added apricot fruit spread, and ¼ teaspoon ground cinnamon in a small bowl. Serve with fresh fruit.

Onion Dip: Combine ½ cup chopped green onions, ½ cup fat-free cream cheese, ½ cup reduced-calorie mayonnaise, ½ teaspoon garlic powder, and ½ teaspoon hot sauce in a small bowl. Serve with fresh vegetables.

CORNMEAL: FROM STAPLE TO STAR

Swept along by years of tradition, the South's granular staple continues to surprise us. Unassuming cornmeal displays true grit in polenta peppered with salsa and also in waffles with three toppings. Rediscover cornmeal in these recipes. Its wholesome goodness offers nourishment and enjoyment.

CORNMEAL WAFFLES
(pictured on pages 38 and 39)

A trio of toppings, from sweet to savory, makes these waffles a warming choice for breakfast, lunch, or supper.

1½ cups self-rising cornmeal
1½ cups self-rising flour
¼ cup sugar
3 large eggs, lightly beaten
1½ cups milk
¼ cup butter or margarine, melted
Peach Topping, Chili Topping, or Turkey-Vegetable Topping

•Combine first 3 ingredients in a large bowl; make a well in center of mixture.
•Combine eggs, milk, and butter; add to dry ingredients, stirring just until moistened.
•Bake in a preheated, oiled waffle iron. Serve hot with desired topping. **Yield:** 3 (8-inch) waffles.

Peach Topping

1 (21-ounce) can peach pie filling
1 teaspoon lemon juice
¼ teaspoon ground cinnamon
Slivered almonds, toasted (optional)

•Combine first 3 ingredients in a small saucepan; cook over low heat until thoroughly heated, stirring often. Spoon over waffles, and sprinkle with almonds, if desired. **Yield:** 1¾ cups.

Chili Topping

1 (15-ounce) can reduced-fat chili with beans
1 (10-ounce) can diced tomatoes and green chiles, undrained
1 (15-ounce) can red kidney beans, drained
1 (8¾-ounce) can whole kernel corn, drained
1 cup (4 ounces) shredded reduced-fat sharp Cheddar cheese
3 green onions, sliced

•Combine first 4 ingredients in a large saucepan; cook over medium heat until thoroughly heated, stirring often. Spoon over waffles, and sprinkle with cheese and green onions. **Yield:** 6 cups.

Turkey-Vegetable Topping

1 (10-ounce) package frozen mixed vegetables
1 (23.5-ounce) jar creamy chicken sauce with mushrooms
3 cups chopped cooked turkey or chicken

•Cook frozen mixed vegetables according to package directions, and drain vegetables well.
•Combine vegetables, creamy chicken sauce with mushrooms, and turkey in a saucepan; cook over low heat until thoroughly heated, stirring often. Serve over waffles. **Yield:** 5 cups.

CORN FRITTERS

These crisp Corn Fritters are great served with a vegetable dinner.

2½ cups cornmeal mix
¼ teaspoon ground red pepper
¼ teaspoon black pepper
¼ cup finely chopped onion
2 tablespoons finely chopped green pepper
1 (2-ounce) jar diced pimiento, drained
1 (8-ounce) can cream-style corn
½ cup boiling water
Vegetable oil

•Combine first 7 ingredients in a large bowl; stir in boiling water. Let stand 10 minutes.
•Pour oil to depth of ¼ inch in a large skillet. Using a tablespoon dipped in hot water, drop cornmeal mixture into hot oil. Fry over medium heat 1 minute on each side or until golden. Drain on paper towels. **Yield:** 2 dozen.

SKILLET POLENTA SQUARES

Serve this enhanced version of polenta as a first course or side dish.

2 cups water
2 cups chicken broth
1 cup white cornmeal
½ cup whipping cream
1 cup (4 ounces) shredded Monterey Jack cheese with peppers
White cornmeal
Vegetable oil
Commercial salsa
Garnish: fresh cilantro

- **Bring** water and broth to a boil in a saucepan; using a wire whisk, gradually stir in 1 cup cornmeal. Return to a boil; reduce heat, and cook, stirring constantly, 5 minutes.
- **Add** whipping cream, and cook 20 minutes, stirring often. Stir in cheese.
- **Spoon** mixture into a lightly greased 9-inch square pan. Cover and chill at least 2 hours or until firm.
- **Cut** into 3-inch squares, and dredge in cornmeal.
- **Pour** oil to depth of ½ inch into a large heavy skillet. Fry squares in hot oil over medium heat 2 minutes on each side or until golden. Drain on paper towels. Serve immediately with salsa. Garnish, if desired. **Yield:** 9 servings.

Spread a Little Sunshine

. . . .

Slice open a lime and it resembles the sun with rays of tart, bright flavor bursting from its center. We've captured this tropical treasure in a homemade jelly and refreshed traditional canning with a new twist – of lime.

LIME JELLY

6 to 8 medium limes
1¾ cups water
4 cups sugar
Green liquid food coloring
 (optional)
1 (3-ounce) package liquid fruit
 pectin

- **Grate** rind from enough limes to measure 2 tablespoons; set aside.
- **Squeeze** juice from enough limes to measure ¾ cup; pour lime juice through a wire-mesh strainer, discarding seeds and pulp.
- **Combine** rind, juice, and water in a 4-quart saucepan. Stir in sugar.

- **Bring** mixture to a full rolling boil over high heat, stirring constantly. Add 1 or 2 drops food coloring, if desired. Quickly stir in fruit pectin. Return mixture to a full rolling boil, and boil, stirring constantly, for 1 minute. Remove from heat; skim off foam with a metal spoon.
- **Quickly** pour jelly into hot, sterilized jars, filling to ¼ inch from top; wipe jar rims. Cover immediately with metal lids, and screw on bands. Process jars in boiling water bath 5 minutes. Cool on wire racks. **Yield:** 5 half pints.

Helen Black
Woodbridge, Virginia

JAM-UP JELLY IDEAS

. . . .

Try Lime Jelly first on your favorite biscuit; then experiment with these adventurous suggestions.

■ Heat jelly with a little fruit juice, and serve warm over ice cream.

■ Top a block of cream cheese with jelly for an instant appetizer that's great on crackers, gingersnaps, and shortbread cookies.

■ Stir a little fruit juice into ½ cup jelly, and use as a basting sauce for chicken or pork tenderloin.

■ Bake a commercial cake mix in a jellyroll pan, and cut into small shapes with assorted cookie cutters. Spread jelly on one cutout and top with a matching cutout to make tea sandwiches. Dust cutouts with powdered sugar.

Just Say Cheese

. . . .

On cold winter evenings, welcome guests into the cozy warmth of your home with this rich appetizer. No one will be able to resist the savory treats. These tantalizing tidbits can be made ahead and frozen.

SPINACH-CHEESE BITES

1 (10-ounce) package sliced
 pepperoni
1 (10-ounce) package frozen
 chopped spinach, thawed and
 drained
2 cups ricotta cheese
1½ cups freshly grated Parmesan
 cheese
1⅓ cups finely chopped fresh
 mushrooms
¼ cup finely chopped onion
1 teaspoon dried oregano
½ teaspoon salt
2 large eggs, lightly beaten
¼ cup sour cream

- **Place** 1 pepperoni slice in bottom of each lightly greased miniature (1¾-inch) muffin cup; set aside. Cut remaining pepperoni slices into 48 wedges; set wedges aside.
- **Combine** spinach and next 7 ingredients in a large bowl; spoon mixture into muffin cups.
- **Bake** at 375° for 20 to 25 minutes or until lightly browned. Cool 10 minutes; gently remove to serving plate. Top each with a dollop of sour cream and a pepperoni wedge. Serve warm. **Yield:** 4 dozen.

Note: Baked Spinach-Cheese Bites and 48 pepperoni wedges may be frozen up to three months. To serve, thaw in refrigerator, and bake Spinach-Cheese Bites at 350° for 10 minutes or until thoroughly heated. Top each with a dollop of sour cream and a pepperoni wedge.

Sandra Russell
Gainesville, Florida

POP THE CORK

Begin the year in style with a New Year's toast; then pour any

leftover bubbly into these classy recipes. Even flat champagne can be used.

(After cooking, the champagne isn't bubbly anyway.) When adding

sparkle to recipes, consider the champagne a cooking liquid and flavor

booster. It's the same concept as cooking a pot roast with

Burgundy or other dry red wine.

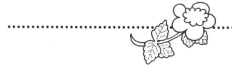

CHAMPAGNE-POACHED CHICKEN WITH CREAMY MUSTARD SAUCE

1 cup champagne or sparkling wine
½ cup chicken broth
4 skinned and boned chicken breast halves
1 cup whipping cream
1 to 2 teaspoons stone-ground mustard
¼ teaspoon ground red pepper

• **Combine** champagne and broth in a large heavy skillet; bring to a boil. Add chicken; cover, reduce heat, and simmer 10 to 12 minutes or until tender.
• **Remove** chicken from skillet; set aside.
• **Stir** whipping cream and remaining ingredients into skillet. Cook over medium heat 8 to 10 minutes or until thickened, stirring occasionally.
• **Add** chicken to skillet, and cook until thoroughly heated. **Yield:** 4 servings.

SPARKLING MUSHROOMS

1 (8-ounce) package small whole mushrooms
2 tablespoons olive oil
½ teaspoon dried rosemary
⅛ teaspoon salt
⅛ teaspoon pepper
½ cup champagne or sparkling wine
Garnish: chopped fresh parsley

• **Cook** mushrooms in olive oil in a skillet over medium-high heat, stirring constantly, 1 to 2 minutes.
• **Add** rosemary, salt, and pepper; cook 1 minute.
• **Stir** in champagne; reduce heat, and simmer 5 minutes. Garnish, if desired. **Yield:** 2 servings.

MIMOSA ICE

¾ cup sugar
1½ cups water
¾ teaspoon grated fresh lemon rind
¼ cup orange juice
1 (750-milliliter) bottle champagne or sparkling wine

• **Combine** all ingredients, stirring until sugar dissolves.

• **Pour** mixture into an 8-inch square pan, and freeze just until firm.
• **Break** frozen mixture into chunks, and place in a large mixing bowl. Beat at low speed with an electric mixer until smooth.
• **Return** mixture to pan, and freeze until firm. Let mixture stand at room temperature 10 minutes before serving. **Yield:** 5¼ cups.

A DRINK FOR ALL SEASONS

New Year's Tomato Bouillon is a great beverage for ringing in the New Year. Enjoy it either hot or cold. For another option, try serving it as a soup.

This beverage recipe comes from *Mountain Measures,* one of the winners in the *Southern Living* Community Cookbook Hall of Fame.

NEW YEAR'S TOMATO BOUILLON

3 cups tomato juice
½ small onion, sliced
1 stalk celery, sliced
1 bay leaf
4 whole cloves
1 (10½-ounce) can beef consommé, undiluted
½ cup Burgundy or other dry red wine
⅛ teaspoon salt
⅛ teaspoon pepper
Garnish: lemon slices studded with whole cloves

• **Combine** first 5 ingredients in a large saucepan; bring to a boil. Cover, reduce heat, and simmer 20 minutes.
• **Pour** mixture through a large wire-mesh strainer into a bowl, discarding solids.
• **Return** mixture to saucepan; add consommé and next 3 ingredients. Serve hot or cold. Garnish, if desired. **Yield:** 4½ cups.

February

MYSTIQUE IN THE MESQUITE

A mystique surrounds the vast King Ranch in Kingsville, Texas. There, six generations are linked by a rich heritage and a dedication to the land. One of the most notable parts of the ranch culture is the cuisine that ranges from simple, hearty fare of meat smoked over a mesquite-fueled fire to the house specialty, King Ranch Chicken. If you're hankering for the taste of mesquite flavor, take a gander at these ranch recipes.

MIGAS

2 (6-inch) corn tortillas, cut into
    1-inch squares
2 tablespoons canola or vegetable
    oil, divided
¼ cup chopped onion
¼ cup chopped tomato
2 tablespoons chopped green
    pepper
4 large eggs, lightly beaten
½ teaspoon salt
½ teaspoon pepper

• **Cook** corn tortilla squares in 1 tablespoon hot oil in a nonstick skillet, stirring constantly, until crisp; remove tortillas from skillet.
• **Add** onion, tomato, and green pepper to skillet, and cook until tender, stirring occasionally; remove vegetables from skillet.
• **Combine** eggs, salt, and pepper. Cook in remaining 1 tablespoon oil in hot skillet, without stirring, until eggs begin to set on bottom. Draw a spatula across bottom of pan to form large curds.
• **Add** tortilla squares and cooked vegetables to eggs; cook until eggs are firm but still moist. Serve immediately. **Yield:** 4 servings.

❤ To reduce fat and cholesterol, use 1 cup egg substitute to replace the 4 large eggs.

KING RANCH CHICKEN

1 (3½- to 4-pound) broiler-fryer,
    cut up
1 (10-ounce) package corn
    tortillas, cut into quarters
1 large onion, thinly sliced or
    chopped
1 large green pepper, chopped
2 cups (8 ounces) shredded
    Cheddar cheese
1½ teaspoons chili powder
½ teaspoon garlic salt
1 (10¾-ounce) can cream of
    chicken soup, undiluted
1 (10¾-ounce) can cream
    of mushroom soup,
    undiluted
1 (10-ounce) can diced tomatoes
    and green chiles, undrained

• **Cook** chicken in a Dutch oven in boiling water to cover 45 minutes or until tender. Remove chicken, reserving 3 cups broth in pan. Let chicken cool; skin, bone, and cut into bite-size pieces. Set aside.
• **Bring** broth to a boil; dip tortillas in broth 5 seconds to soften. Set aside.
• **Place** half of tortillas in a lightly greased 13- x 9- x 2-inch baking dish. Layer with half each of chicken, onion, and green pepper. Repeat layers.
• **Sprinkle** top with cheese, chili powder, and garlic salt.
• **Combine** soups, and spread over cheese; top with tomatoes. (Mixture will be wet on top.)
• **Bake** at 350° for 45 minutes or until mixture is thoroughly heated. **Yield:** 6 to 8 servings.

Variation 1: 2 cups (8 ounces) Monterey Jack cheese may be substituted for Cheddar cheese. Decrease chili powder to 1 teaspoon, and add 1 teaspoon ground cumin.

Variation 2: 6 skinned chicken breast halves may be substituted for broiler-fryer. Add 1 large sweet red pepper, chopped, to green pepper.

Variation 3: 2 cups (8 ounces) Monterey Jack cheese may be substituted for Cheddar cheese. Add 1 large sweet red pepper, chopped, and cook with onion and green pepper in 2 tablespoons butter or margarine.

BARBECUED BEEF TENDERLOIN

Mesquite or hickory chips
1 (3½- to 4-pound) beef
    tenderloin, trimmed
½ teaspoon salt
½ teaspoon pepper
1 cup Barbecue Sauce

• **Soak** mesquite chips in water 30 minutes.
• **Prepare** charcoal fire in smoker; let burn 20 minutes. Place mesquite chips on coals. Place water pan in smoker; fill with water.

- **Sprinkle** tenderloin with salt and pepper. Place on food rack. Cover with smoker lid. Cook 30 minutes.
- **Baste** tenderloin with 1 cup Barbecue Sauce. Cover and cook 1½ to 2 hours or until a meat thermometer registers 150° or to desired degree of doneness. Serve with additional Barbecue Sauce. **Yield:** 12 servings (8 to 10 cowboy servings).

Barbecue Sauce

2 (16-ounce) cans tomato
    sauce
1¼ cups ketchup
½ cup steak sauce
¼ cup lemon juice
¼ cup honey

- **Combine** all ingredients in a large saucepan.
- **Bring** to a boil; reduce heat, and simmer 30 minutes, stirring occasionally. Store remaining sauce in refrigerator up to 1 week or freeze up to 1 month. **Yield:** 5 cups.

SANTA GERTRUDIS PAN DE CAMPO

4 cups all-purpose flour
1 tablespoon plus 2 teaspoons
    baking powder
2 teaspoons salt
¾ cup shortening
1½ cups milk
1 tablespoon shortening

- **Combine** first 3 ingredients in a large bowl; cut in ¾ cup shortening with pastry blender until mixture is crumbly. Add milk, stirring just until dry ingredients are moistened. Let dough stand 5 minutes.
- **Heat** 2 (10-inch) cast-iron skillets in a 400° oven for 5 minutes.
- **Divide** dough in half; roll each half into a 10-inch circle on a lightly floured surface.
- **Remove** skillets from oven, and add 1½ teaspoons shortening to each, rotating to coat. Place dough in skillets.
- **Bake** at 400° for 15 minutes or until golden. **Yield:** 2 (10-inch) loaves.

> *"... the cowboys are still cowboys there....*
> *Their legs are still clothed in leather....*
> *Their hats are still cocked on the sides of their heads,*
> *their skins still burned by the sun,*
> *their hearts still wedded to the saddle."*
>
> — *Frank Goodwyn*
> Life on the King Ranch

Deep in South Texas is King Ranch, one of the largest and most famous ranches in the world. Sprawling across 825,000 acres, the ranch has endured since 1853. The story of King Ranch is surprisingly straightforward: It's the progress of a piece of earth from untamed wilderness to productive pastures.

Recognized as the birthplace of the American ranching industry, King Ranch established itself early on as a leader in livestock and range management, borrowing the best from the cultures on either side of the Rio Grande. The ranch's business standards and technology are decidely American. The sense of family, loyalty, and methods of working cattle, are characteristically Mexican.

Ancestors of King Ranch founder, Richard King, still work the ranch today and are known as *los Kineños*, the people of King Ranch. The Kineño culture has left its mark in the cuisine suited to the needs of the ranch and cow camps. Food is generally simple, plentiful, and flavorful.

SPANISH RICE

3 tablespoons vegetable oil
2 cups long-grain rice,
    uncooked
2 large green peppers,
    chopped
2 large celery stalks, chopped
2 medium onions, finely chopped
2 teaspoons cumin seeds,
    crushed
1 to 1½ teaspoons salt
½ teaspoon pepper
¼ teaspoon garlic powder
6 cups water
1 (8-ounce) can tomato sauce

- **Heat** oil over medium-high heat in a heavy Dutch oven; add rice and next 7 ingredients, and cook until rice is browned, stirring often.
- **Stir** in water and tomato sauce; bring to a boil. Reduce heat to medium; cover and cook 25 minutes or until rice is tender. **Yield:** 8 to 10 servings.

COW CAMP PINTO BEANS

2½ cups dried pinto beans
7 to 8 cups water
¾ teaspoon salt

• **Sort** and wash beans; place in a Dutch oven.
• **Cover** with water 2 inches above beans; let soak 8 hours.
• **Drain** beans, and return to Dutch oven. Add 7 cups water.
• **Bring** to a boil; cover, reduce heat, and cook 2 hours or until tender. (Add extra water, if necessary.)
• **Stir** in salt. **Yield:** 6 to 8 servings.

KLEBERG HOT SAUCE

6 to 8 ounces chile piquíns *
¼ cup coarsely chopped onion
2 cloves garlic
1 (28-ounce) can whole tomatoes, undrained
2 tablespoons white vinegar
¼ teaspoon salt
⅛ teaspoon pepper

• **Combine** all ingredients in container of an electric blender; pulse 3 or 4 times or until finely chopped. Store sauce in refrigerator up to 1 week or freeze up to 1 month. **Yield:** 4½ cups.

* 10 ounces serrano chiles may be substituted.

CHILE PIQUÍN JELLY

¼ cup red or green chile piquíns *
1 medium-size sweet red or green pepper
6½ cups sugar
1½ cups white vinegar (5% acidity)
2 (3-ounce) envelopes liquid pectin (6-ounce package)
Red or green liquid food coloring (optional)

• **Wash** peppers; pat dry. Seed peppers, and remove veins. Cut into quarters, and set aside.

• **Position** knife blade in food processor bowl. Add peppers; pulse 3 or 4 times or until peppers are finely chopped.
• **Combine** peppers, sugar, and vinegar in a Dutch oven; bring to a boil. Boil 2 minutes. Remove from heat, and cool 5 minutes.
• **Add** liquid pectin to pepper mixture; return to a boil, and boil 1 minute, stirring constantly. Remove from heat, and skim off foam with a metal spoon. Add food coloring, if desired.
• **Quickly** pour jelly into hot sterilized jars, filling to ¼ inch from top; wipe jar rims. Cover at once with metal lids, and screw on bands.
• **Process** in boiling water bath 5 minutes; cool and store in pantry or refrigerator. **Yield:** 6 half pints.

* Serrano chiles may be substituted.

Note: When working with hot peppers, such as chile piquíns or serranos, always wear rubber gloves. If a translucent jelly is desired, pour mixture through a wire-mesh strainer into a Dutch oven before adding pectin, and discard solids.

NUTTY FUDGY FROZEN DESSERT
(pictured on page 40)

32 cream-filled chocolate sandwich cookies
½ cup butter or margarine, melted
½ gallon vanilla ice cream, softened
2 (1-ounce) squares unsweetened chocolate
1½ cups sugar
1⅓ cups evaporated milk
½ cup butter or margarine
Garnishes: pecan halves, toasted chopped pecans

• **Position** knife blade in food processor bowl; add half of cookies. Process until finely crushed. Transfer crumbs to a large bowl. Repeat procedure with remaining cookies.
• **Combine** crumbs and ½ cup melted butter; firmly press crumb mixture in bottom and 2 inches up sides of a 9-inch springform pan.

• **Freeze** 1 hour.
• **Spread** ice cream evenly into prepared pan; cover and freeze until firm.
• **Combine** chocolate and next 3 ingredients in a heavy saucepan; cook over medium heat, stirring constantly, until mixture comes to a boil. Reduce heat to low, and cook 8 minutes or until a candy thermometer reaches 210°. Remove from heat, and cool completely.
• **Spread** half of chocolate mixture over ice cream; freeze until firm. Spread with remaining chocolate mixture; garnish, if desired. Freeze until firm. **Yield:** 8 to 10 servings.

EMPANADAS DE CALABAZA (PUMPKIN EMPANADAS)

2 (16-ounce) cans pumpkin
2 cups sugar
1 (2-inch) stick cinnamon
2 teaspoons ground cinnamon
½ teaspoon ground nutmeg
½ teaspoon ground ginger
3 cups all-purpose flour
1½ teaspoons salt
1 cup shortening
¾ cup beer

• **Combine** first 6 ingredients in a large heavy saucepan; bring to a boil, stirring constantly. Reduce heat, and simmer 1 hour or until thickened, stirring often. Remove and discard cinnamon stick; let pumpkin mixture cool.
• **Combine** flour and salt; cut in shortening with pastry blender until mixture is crumbly. Make a well in center of mixture.
• **Add** beer, stirring with a fork until dry ingredients are moistened. Shape into a ball. Flour hands, and shape into 1½-inch balls; roll or flatten to ½-inch thickness on a lightly floured surface. Let stand 30 minutes.
• **Roll** each dough round into a 4-inch circle. Place about 3 tablespoons pumpkin mixture in center of each circle, and fold pastry in half. Moisten edges with water, and press with a fork to seal. Place on ungreased baking sheets.
• **Bake** at 400° for 18 to 20 minutes or until edges are lightly browned. **Yield:** 1½ dozen.

FROM OUR KITCHEN TO YOURS

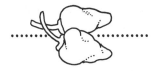

When East meets West, exotic ingredients merge with Southern ones. Taste buds tingle from the spiciness of fresh gingerroot seasoning our Far Eastern wok dishes (beginning on page 32). And they positively dance to the hot chile piquín in the King Ranch cuisine (beginning on page 26). To help you prepare the fare, here's an introduction to the unusual ingredients, along with cooking lessons and tips.

EAST

■ Underneath a buff-colored skin lies the juicy pale-yellow flesh of fresh **gingerroot.** Bursting with a pungent, spicy-hot flavor, it has overpowering strength; use it with discretion. Fresh gingerroot provides a sharp contrast to the more subtle ground version.

Cooking Lesson: Fresh gingerroot has a tough skin that must be carefully removed. For small amounts, slice off a knob or piece as needed; peel the knob with a vegetable peeler or a small paring knife, and then mince, slice, or grate. A handy gadget to have is a ginger grater; its ceramic "teeth" quickly shred the pulp.

Choose one of three storage methods for leftover gingerroot.

1. Slice off amount needed; place remaining unpeeled root, wrapped in a white paper towel, in a plastic bag, and refrigerate up to three weeks.

2. Seal an unpeeled piece in a zip-top plastic bag, and freeze up to one month. To use, slice amount needed off the unthawed root, and return remainder to freezer.

3. Place peeled slices of gingerroot in a jar, cover with dry white wine or dry sherry, and refrigerate up to six months. Use ginger-flavored wine or sherry in salad dressings or stir-fry recipes, and replace used portion with additional wine to keep gingerroot immersed.

Kitchen Tip: An irregularly shaped gingerroot, called a "hand," can have any number of bulging knobs growing at odd angles. The smaller knobs radiating from the main root have a more delicate flavor. Look for rock-hard pieces with smooth, plump, shiny skin. Check for a fresh, spicy fragrance.

Ginger Math: 1 tablespoon grated fresh gingerroot equals ⅛ teaspoon ground ginger.

■ The French technique called **chiffonade** (shihf-uh-NAHD) translates into "made of rags." With this classic preparation, lettuce or greens are cut into thin strips or shreds. The vegetable rags are either cooked or used raw for garnishing.

Cooking Lesson: To use the chiffonade technique to cut **turnip greens** or collards into thin strips for Stir-Fried Greens (on page 33), stack three or four leaves together, and roll tightly. Cut into ¼-inch strips.

Kitchen Tip: Turnip greens or collards wilt quickly. Select young, tender leaves, avoiding ones with brown or yellow patches. Larger leaves are sometimes too bitter. Store up to two days in the refrigerator.

WEST

■ **Nopales** (noh-PAH-lays), or cactus leaves, are the fleshy oval pads grown on the prickly pear cactus. An ingredient in many Southwestern dishes, cactus pads have a slightly tart flavor that's similar to green beans.

Cooking Lesson: Scrape off the "eyes" or prickles with a vegetable peeler or paring knife, if necessary; trim off any dry or fibrous areas. Rinse thoroughly, removing any remaining tiny airlike spines as well as any sticky fluid weeping from the leaves. Cut into thin strips or small pieces. Nopales must be cooked; steam, cook, or boil about 5 minutes or until tender. Add to dishes like salads and soups.

Kitchen Tip: Nopales are available at large supermarkets carrying specialty items. Choose small young leaves or pads with a pale green color and firm texture. Store in a plastic bag in the refrigerator up to one week. Freezing isn't recommended.

■ The heat of the **chile piquín** (also called tepín or chiltepín) is known as rapid because its intensity diminishes quickly. On a heat index scale ranging from 1 (mild) to 10 (hot), the chile piquín rates 8 to 8.5. This small round pepper grows wild and is difficult to classify because only small amounts are cultivated. The domesticated variety is called piquín. Because we couldn't find these peppers in our area, we substituted serrano chiles for the recipes and did not notice a change in flavor. The **serrano** chile, a 1½-inch-long and ¾-inch-wide pepper with a tapered, rounded end, has a hot, savory flavor. Scoring 7 on the heat index scale, this pepper has an intense, biting heat with a slightly delayed reaction. Bright green and red serranos are interchangeable, although the red will be somewhat sweeter. They can be purchased fresh, dried, or pickled.

Cooking Lesson: Store peppers in the crisper section of the refrigerator up to four days. (Don't wrap in plastic bags.) Freeze whole peppers up to 10 months. Because thawed peppers lose their crispness, they are best used for cooking.

Kitchen Tip: If seeding chiles isn't specified, remember that removing the seeds reduces the heat by about half; you may wish to use additional seeded chiles.

Chile Math: 1 chile piquín equals 1 serrano chile.

Take Care! Protect your hands from capsaicin, the chemical responsible for heat in chiles. When you prepare hot peppers, wear rubber gloves, don't touch your eyes or face, and afterward wash your hands well. If your hands still sting, wash them in a mixture of 2 cups water and 1½ teaspoons bleach.

CUMIN: A WORLDLY SPICE COMES HOME

Cooks from Mexico to India use cumin seeds like a fireman uses a hose – to cool down the heat. The earthy-tasting seeds balance the fire of chiles and curry, making them palatable for even tentative tasters. Cumin's pungent smell and musty taste are frequently paired with oregano, cilantro, red pepper, and chili powder in Tex-Mex dishes.

MEXI-CHICKEN CASSEROLE

1 large onion, chopped
1 tablespoon vegetable oil
3 medium tomatoes, peeled and chopped
2 cups chopped cooked chicken
½ cup ready-to-serve chicken broth
2 teaspoons chili powder
1 teaspoon salt
1 teaspoon dried oregano
1 teaspoon ground cumin
6 corn tortillas, cut into fourths and divided
1 cup (4 ounces) shredded sharp Cheddar cheese, divided

•**Cook** chopped onion in oil in a Dutch oven over medium-high heat, stirring constantly, until tender; add tomato and next 6 ingredients. Bring chicken mixture to a boil; reduce heat, and simmer 5 minutes.
•**Layer** half each of chicken mixture, tortillas, and cheese in a lightly greased 11- x 7- x 1½-inch baking dish. Repeat procedure with remaining chicken mixture and tortillas; cover with foil.
•**Bake** at 350° for 25 minutes.
•**Uncover** and sprinkle with remaining cheese; bake 5 additional minutes. **Yield:** 6 servings.

Barbara Nibling
San Angelo, Texas

CHICKEN CHIMICHANGAS

3 (5-ounce) cans 98% fat-free chicken, drained
⅓ cup sliced green onions
¾ teaspoon ground cumin
½ teaspoon dried oregano
¼ teaspoon salt
1 (16-ounce) jar salsa or picante sauce, divided
8 (8-inch) flour tortillas
1 (8-ounce) package shredded Monterey Jack or Cheddar cheese, divided
Vegetable cooking spray
Nonfat sour cream alternative

•**Combine** first 5 ingredients in a large saucepan; stir in ⅔ cup salsa. Cook over medium heat 5 minutes, stirring often. Spoon about 2 tablespoons chicken mixture just below center of each tortilla; sprinkle tortillas evenly with half of cheese.
•**Fold** left and right side of tortillas to partially enclose filling. Fold up top and bottom edges of tortilla (making a square). Place folded side down in a 13- x 9- x 2-inch baking dish coated with cooking spray. Repeat procedure with remaining tortillas. Bake at 475° for 13 minutes.
•**Heat** remaining salsa in a small saucepan; pour over tortillas, and sprinkle evenly with remaining cheese. Top each serving with a dollop of sour cream alternative. **Yield:** 8 servings.

Sharla Sparhawk
Knoxville, Tennessee

ROASTING CUMIN

You can buy cumin seeds whole or ground. Roasting enhances the flavor of whole seeds. To roast, heat in a dry skillet until the seeds are more fragrant and lightly browned. After cooking, use whole or grind, using a mortar and pestle, spice mill, electric blender, or coffee grinder.

TACO SAUCE

½ teaspoon cumin seeds
1 (16-ounce) can whole tomatoes, undrained
2 jalapeño peppers, seeded
1 small onion, sliced
1 clove garlic, peeled
1 teaspoon salt
1 teaspoon pepper
Garnish: seeded jalapeño pepper slices

•**Place** a small skillet over medium-high heat until hot; add cumin seeds, and cook, stirring constantly, until seeds are more fragrant and lightly browned. Let seeds cool.
•**Combine** cumin seeds and next 6 ingredients in container of an electric blender or food processor; process until blended. Pour into a medium saucepan.
•**Bring** to a boil; reduce heat, and simmer 5 minutes. Garnish, if desired. **Yield:** 2 cups.

Becky Holzhaus
Castroville, Texas

MEXICAN PINTO BEANS

1 pound dried pinto beans
5 cups water
6 slices bacon, finely chopped
1 large onion, chopped
½ green pepper, chopped
1½ tablespoons ground cumin
1 tablespoon chili powder
1½ teaspoons salt
1 teaspoon pepper

•**Sort** and wash beans; place in a Dutch oven. Cover with water 2 inches above beans; bring to a boil. Boil 1 minute. Cover, remove from heat, and let stand 1 hour.
•**Drain** and return pinto beans to Dutch oven.
•**Add** 5 cups water and remaining ingredients. Bring to a boil; cover, reduce heat, and simmer 1½ hours or until beans are tender. Serve with a slotted spoon. **Yield:** 7 cups.

Nancy Sloan
Lake Village, Arkansas

QUICK & EASY

SURE-BET OMELETS

Whipping up an omelet may seem daunting to cooks who have never successfully done it. But a few secrets (see box below) make creating one easy.

For cholesterol-conscious cooks, each recipe offers an alternative.

OMELET OLÉ

½ cup sour cream
⅓ cup commercial salsa
4 large eggs
1 tablespoon milk
2 teaspoons butter or margarine, divided
¼ cup cooked and crumbled bacon, divided
¼ cup chopped tomato
¼ cup chopped green chiles, drained
1 slice process American cheese, finely chopped
Avocado slices

• **Combine** sour cream and salsa in a small saucepan; cook over low heat until thoroughly heated. Keep warm.
• **Whisk** together eggs and milk; set aside. Heat a 6-inch omelet pan or heavy skillet over medium heat. Add 1 teaspoon butter, and rotate pan to coat. Add half of egg mixture. As mixture starts to cook, gently lift edges of omelet with a spatula, and tilt pan so uncooked portion flows underneath.
• **Sprinkle** with half each of bacon, tomato, green chiles, and cheese; fold in half, and transfer to a serving plate. Repeat procedure.
• **Serve** with sour cream mixture and avocado slices. **Yield:** 2 servings.

❤ To reduce fat and cholesterol, low-fat sour cream, 1 cup egg substitute and 1 egg white, skim milk, reduced-calorie margarine, chopped lean ham, and

reduced-fat process American cheese may be substituted for sour cream, eggs, milk, butter, bacon, and cheese.
Barbara T. Sherrill
Sheffield, Alabama

FAMILY-SIZE POTATO OMELET

3 tablespoons vegetable oil, divided
1 large onion, chopped
½ cup chopped green pepper
2 cups finely chopped cooked potato
1 teaspoon salt
½ teaspoon coarsely ground pepper
6 large eggs
3 tablespoons water
Sour cream
Chopped fresh or frozen chives

• **Heat** 1 tablespoon oil in a 12-inch nonstick skillet over medium heat. Add onion and next 4 ingredients; cook until onion and green pepper are crisp-tender.
• **Whisk** together eggs and water in a bowl. Stir in vegetable mixture.
• **Wipe** skillet with a paper towel.
• **Heat** skillet over medium heat; add remaining 2 tablespoons oil, and rotate pan to coat bottom. Add egg mixture. As mixture starts to cook, gently lift edges of omelet with a spatula, and tilt pan so uncooked portion flows underneath. Cover and cook 5 additional minutes to allow uncooked portion on top to set.
• **Cut** into fourths, and serve immediately with sour cream and chives. **Yield:** 4 servings.

❤ To reduce cholesterol, 1½ cups egg substitute may be substituted for eggs.
Gwen Louer
Roswell, Georgia

SHRIMP-AND-CHEESE OMELET

2 large eggs
1 tablespoon water
1 tablespoon butter or margarine
3 tablespoons shredded Monterey Jack cheese
¼ cup coarsely chopped cooked shrimp
1 tablespoon sliced green onions
2 teaspoons chopped fresh parsley
Garnishes: whole shrimp, green onion

• **Whisk** together eggs and 1 tablespoon water; set aside.
• **Heat** an 8-inch omelet pan or nonstick skillet over medium heat. Add butter, and rotate pan to coat. Add egg mixture. As mixture starts to cook, gently lift edges of omelet with a spatula, and tilt pan so that uncooked portion flows underneath.
• **Sprinkle** half of omelet with cheese and next 3 ingredients; fold in half. Transfer to a serving plate; garnish, if desired. Serve immediately. **Yield:** 1 serving.

❤ To reduce fat and cholesterol, ½ cup egg substitute and 1 egg white, vegetable cooking spray, and reduced-fat Monterey Jack cheese may be substituted for eggs, butter, and cheese.

OMELET TIPS

■ Always begin with eggs at room temperature.

■ Omelets cook quickly, so have all ingredients ready. (It should take longer to eat the omelet than to make it.)

■ Begin with a heated nonstick omelet pan or skillet.

■ Don't overcook the omelet.

TAKE A WOK

Created in China a thousand years ago, the wok is the perfect vessel for health-conscious Southern cooks of the nineties. Foods prepared with rapid-fire wok cooking retain their nutrition, taste, color, and crispness.

SCALLOP STIR-FRY

1 tablespoon sesame oil
1 tablespoon peanut oil
1 pound fresh bay scallops
1 (8-ounce) package fresh
   mushrooms, sliced
1 (8-ounce) can sliced water
   chestnuts, drained
1 medium-size sweet red pepper,
   cut into strips
2 small carrots, scraped and
   diagonally sliced
2 green onions, sliced
½ cup chicken broth
2 tablespoons cornstarch
3 tablespoons dry sherry
3 tablespoons soy sauce
1 to 2 tablespoons peeled, grated
   gingerroot
2 cloves garlic, pressed
1 (6-ounce) package frozen snow
   pea pods, thawed and drained
Hot cooked rice

• **Pour** sesame and peanut oils around top of a preheated wok, coating sides; add scallops, and cook 3 minutes, stirring constantly.
• **Add** mushrooms and next 4 ingredients; cook, stirring constantly, 3 to 4 minutes or until tender.
• **Combine** broth and next 5 ingredients; stir into scallop mixture. Add snow peas, and cook 1 to 2 minutes or until mixture thickens. Serve over hot cooked rice. **Yield:** 4 servings.

Joy Garcia
Bartlett, Tennessee

TANGY HONEYED SHRIMP

1½ pounds unpeeled large fresh
   shrimp
3 tablespoons peanut oil
2 teaspoons minced garlic
1 teaspoon peeled, minced
   gingerroot
1 (10½-ounce) can condensed
   chicken broth, undiluted
1 tablespoon cornstarch
2 tablespoons honey
2 tablespoons ketchup
1 tablespoon white vinegar
1 tablespoon rice wine or dry
   sherry
1 tablespoon soy sauce
⅛ teaspoon dried crushed red
   pepper
1 tablespoon sesame oil
2 green onions, cut into 1-inch
   lengths and shredded
1 teaspoon chopped fresh cilantro
Rice Timbales
Garnish: fresh cilantro

• **Using** a small knife, cut back of shrimp along vein line under running water; remove shell and vein, keeping the tail intact. Drain shrimp on paper towels.
• **Pour** peanut oil around top of a preheated wok, coating sides; heat at high 1 minute. Add shrimp, garlic, and gingerroot. Cook shrimp mixture, stirring constantly, about 8 minutes or until shrimp turn pink.
• **Combine** broth and next 7 ingredients, stirring until smooth. Add to shrimp mixture, stirring constantly.

• **Bring** mixture to a boil; cook 1 minute. Stir in sesame oil, green onions, and cilantro; cook until thoroughly heated. Serve immediately with Rice Timbales. Garnish, if desired. **Yield:** 3 to 4 servings.

Rice Timbales

2 cups water
½ teaspoon salt
1 cup long-grain rice, uncooked

• **Combine** water and salt in a heavy saucepan; bring to a boil. Gradually add rice, stirring constantly. Cover, reduce heat, and simmer 20 minutes or until rice is tender and water is absorbed.
• **Press** hot rice into 4 oiled 6-ounce custard cups. Immediately invert onto serving plates. Keep warm. **Yield:** 4 servings.

> *"When you put something moist in that hot oil, it dances a jig."*
>
> — *Patty Vann*
> *Test Kitchens Director*
> Southern Living *magazine*

....

It's the presizzle preparation that counts in wok cooking. Dice, slice, mince, grate, or shred all your ingredients *first*. Then fire up the wok, drop in the vegetables, and hear them hiss.

These wok recipes feature some favorite Southern ingredients. Try Stir-Fried Greens (on facing page) with apples for a quick, tasty, colorful alternative to traditional, slow-cooked collards.

CHICKEN CHINESE

(pictured on page 37)

2 skinned and boned chicken
  breast halves, cut into thin
  strips
2 cloves garlic, minced
½ teaspoon peeled, grated
  gingerroot
2 tablespoons peanut oil,
  divided
1 medium-size sweet red pepper,
  cut into thin strips
1 medium onion, cut into thin
  strips
1 cup broccoli flowerets
1 (13¾-ounce) can ready-to-serve,
  fat-free, reduced-sodium
  chicken broth
1½ tablespoons cornstarch
2 tablespoons plum sauce
1 tablespoon Worcestershire
  sauce
1 tablespoon soy sauce
Chow mein noodles

• **Combine** first 3 ingredients; cover and chill 30 minutes.
• **Pour** 1 tablespoon peanut oil around top of a preheated wok, coating sides; heat at high 1 minute. Add chicken; cook, stirring constantly, 3 minutes. Remove chicken from wok; set aside.
• **Pour** remaining 1 tablespoon peanut oil into wok. Add red pepper, onion, and broccoli; cook, stirring constantly, 2 minutes. Remove from wok; set aside.
• **Combine** broth and next 4 ingredients, stirring until smooth. Pour into wok. Bring to a boil, stirring constantly. Boil 1 minute, stirring constantly. Add chicken and vegetables. Cook until thoroughly heated. Serve with noodles. **Yield:** 2 servings.

Kitty Ebner
Annapolis, Maryland

STIR-FRIED GREENS

2 pounds fresh collard or turnip
  greens
½ pound bacon, chopped
½ cup chicken broth
1 tablespoon sugar
½ teaspoon salt
1 tablespoon balsamic vinegar
2 medium-size Winesap or Rome
  apples, cored and cut into thin
  wedges

• **Remove** tough outer stems from greens. Wash thoroughly, and drain. Stack 3 or 4 leaves together, and roll tightly. Cut rolled greens into ¼-inch strips. Repeat with remaining greens. Set aside.
• **Cook** chopped bacon in a preheated wok at high until crisp; remove bacon, reserving drippings in wok. Set bacon aside.
• **Add** chicken broth and next 3 ingredients to wok; cook until bubbly. Add greens; cook, stirring constantly, 10 minutes or until tender. Stir in bacon and apples; serve immediately. **Yield:** 6 servings.

PASTA POTPOURRI

4 ounces penne or rigatoni,
  uncooked
1 teaspoon sesame oil
1½ tablespoons olive oil
1½ tablespoons sesame oil
1 small purple onion, chopped
2 medium carrots, scraped and
  diagonally sliced
2 medium zucchini, halved
  lengthwise and sliced
2 cloves garlic, pressed
1½ teaspoons peeled, grated
  gingerroot
½ teaspoon dried crushed red
  pepper
2 tablespoons soy sauce
2 teaspoons rice wine vinegar
1 tablespoon freshly grated
  Parmesan cheese
2 teaspoons chopped fresh cilantro

• **Cook** pasta according to package directions; drain and toss with 1 teaspoon sesame oil. Set aside.

WOK TALK

· · · · · · · · · · · · ·

■ The wok's shape permits even heating and constant stirring and tossing. But it's not essential to use a wok to stir-fry – a good heavy skillet will do.

■ Round-bottomed woks, with a ring insert, are suitable for gas ranges; flat-bottomed woks, without ring inserts, are designed for electric ranges.

■ Stir-frying is the primary method of cooking in a wok, but a wok is also perfect for boiling, steaming, deep-fat frying, or braising food.

■ Vegetable oil and peanut oil are our oils of choice for stir-frying. Both can be heated to a high temperature without smoking, and the tastes are not overpowering. Never substitute butter or margarine for oil in stir-frying.

■ If vegetables are too wet they will not stir-fry well. Pat dry on paper towels before cooking.

• **Pour** olive oil and 1½ tablespoons sesame oil around top of a preheated wok, coating sides; heat at high 1 minute. Add onion and carrot; cook, stirring constantly, 2 minutes or until onion is tender.
• **Add** zucchini and next 3 ingredients; cook 1 minute, stirring constantly.
• **Stir** in cooked pasta, soy sauce, and vinegar; cook 1 minute or until thoroughly heated.
• **Transfer** to a serving dish; sprinkle with cheese and cilantro. **Yield:** 4 to 6 servings.

Note: For a quick main dish, add leftover chopped cooked chicken or beef.

Nan Rasor
San Antonio, Texas

CHINESE VEGETABLE POUCHES

1 tablespoon peanut oil
1 large carrot, chopped
1 pound cabbage, chopped
2 green onions, chopped
2 tablespoons soy sauce
2 tablespoons dry sherry
½ teaspoon sugar
¼ teaspoon ground ginger
1 clove garlic, pressed
¼ cup chopped roasted cashews
1 tablespoon cornstarch
2 tablespoons water
1 teaspoon hoisin sauce (optional)
1 (16-ounce) package egg roll
      wrappers
12 to 36 fresh chives
3 cups peanut oil
Garnishes: green onion fan, finely
      chopped carrot

●**Pour** 1 tablespoon peanut oil around
top of a preheated wok, coating sides;
heat at high 1 minute. Add carrot, and
cook 1 minute, stirring constantly. Add
cabbage, and cook, stirring constantly,
5 minutes or until tender. Stir in green
onions and next 6 ingredients.
●**Combine** cornstarch, water, and hoisin
sauce, if desired, stirring until smooth;
add to cabbage mixture. Cook, stirring
constantly, 1 minute or until thickened.
Let cool.
●**Spoon** mixture evenly into centers of
egg roll wrappers; moisten edges with
water. Bring ends to the middle, pressing together in center, and pull ends up
and out to resemble a pouch. Tie chives
around centers. Set aside.
●**Pour** 3 cups peanut oil into a wok;
heat to 375°. Fry pouches 4 minutes or
until lightly browned, turning, if necessary. Drain on paper towels. Garnish, if
desired. **Yield:** 12 pouches.

MARVELOUS MUFFULETTAS

What's so special about a muffuletta? Well, this Italian sandwich

created at the turn of the century in New Orleans has the usual meats

and cheeses, and the bread is always round. But the key ingredient –

"olive salad" – makes the big difference. Central Grocery in New Orleans

gets the unofficial patent on the invention of this Crescent City classic,

but you can find wonderful variations at other eateries.

■ You might say that **Fertitta's Deli-
catessen** in Shreveport is Louisiana's
"Central Grocery, North." It's a small,
family-owned Italian market and deli.
Original owner Sam Fertitta created his
version of the muffuletta more than 30
years ago and passed the recipe on to
his daughter, Agatha Wiley, when she
took over the store in 1980.

The olive salad and the round loaf
stay true to the original theme, but he
adds mustard, bologna, and turkey to
his recipe. And way back when Sam or-
dered the neon sign advertising his specialty, he shortened the name to just
"Muffy" to lower the cost.

FERTITTA'S "MUFFY" SANDWICH

3 tablespoons prepared mustard
1 (8-inch) round loaf Italian
      bread, cut in half horizontally
½ cup (2 ounces) shredded
      Cheddar cheese
½ cup (2 ounces) shredded
      mozzarella cheese
½ cup (2 ounces) shredded
      provolone cheese
2 to 3 ounces sliced ham
2 to 3 ounces sliced Genoa salami
2 to 3 ounces sliced bologna
2 to 3 ounces sliced turkey
1 to 1½ cups Muffy Salad Mix

●**Spread** mustard on bread.
●**Combine** cheeses; place on bottom
half of bread. Arrange meat on both
halves; place on a baking sheet.
●**Bake** at 350° for 15 minutes or until
thoroughly heated. Spread chilled Muffy
Salad Mix on bottom half; cover with
top half. Cut into quarters, and serve
immediately. **Yield:** 2 to 4 servings.

Muffy Salad Mix

1½ cups pimiento-stuffed olives,
      drained
1 cup ripe olives, drained
1 cup coarsely chopped celery
1 cup mixed pickled garden
      vegetables, drained
6 cloves garlic
1 to 1½ teaspoons dried basil
1 to 1½ teaspoons dried
      oregano
⅓ cup olive oil
⅓ cup white wine or white wine
      vinegar

●**Position** knife blade in food processor bowl; add all ingredients.
●**Process** 20 seconds or until finely
chopped.
●**Cover** and chill. Store remaining
salad mix in refrigerator up to 1 week.
Yield: 3 cups.

■**Napoleon House,** an historic French Quarter eatery, has been open almost as long as Central Grocery. The Napoleon House heats the muffulettas for an extra special touch.

NAPOLEON HOUSE MUFFULETTA

2 slices ham (about 2 ounces)
3 slices Genoa salami (about 2½ ounces)
2 slices pastrami (about 2 ounces)
¼ cup Italian Olive Salad
1 slice provolone cheese
1 slice Swiss cheese
1 (5-inch) sandwich bun with sesame seeds

● **Layer** first 6 ingredients on bottom half of bun; top with remaining bun half, and wrap in aluminum foil.
● **Bake** at 350° for 20 minutes or until sandwich is thoroughly heated. **Yield:** 1 serving.

Italian Olive Salad

4 cups pimiento-stuffed olives, drained and coarsely chopped
1 cup canned mixed vegetables, drained
1 (14-ounce) can artichoke hearts, drained and coarsely chopped
1 (15-ounce) can chick-peas, drained and coarsely chopped
1 (7¾-ounce) jar cocktail onions, drained and coarsely chopped
¼ cup capers, drained
⅔ cup pickled vegetables, drained and coarsely chopped
1 large green pepper, chopped
3 stalks celery, chopped
2 cloves garlic, minced
1 cup olive oil
½ cup red wine vinegar
1½ tablespoons dried oregano
½ teaspoon pepper

● **Combine** all ingredients; cover and chill 8 hours.
● **Store** remaining salad in refrigerator up to 1 week. **Yield:** 12 cups.

MAKE IT A MUFFULETTA-THON

A couple of these recipes make more olive salad than you can use in a few days, but we'll bet you could find a group of friends for an impromptu *muffuletta-thon.* (Just multiply the sandwich ingredients to feed the extra folks.) Or put the leftover salad into decorative jars and give to friends. Be sure to attach a recipe for the sandwich.

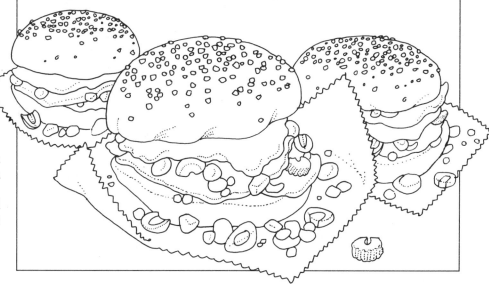

■ When Jerry Harris and his New Orleans bride moved to Birmingham, Alabama, they brought with them an addiction to Louisiana cooking. Determined to have the best of both worlds, he opened a fun restaurant – **Doodles** – featuring muffulettas, po' boys, red beans and rice, and more.

He imports authentic muffuletta loaves from New Orleans, but is keeping the source under his hat. You can substitute a round Italian loaf from your grocery store.

DOODLES MUFFULETTA

¼ pound thinly sliced ham
¼ pound sliced Genoa salami
4 slices Swiss cheese
1 (6-ounce) package sliced provolone cheese
1 (10-inch) round loaf Italian bread, cut in half horizontally
1½ cups Doodles Olive Salad

● **Layer** first 4 ingredients on bottom half of bread; place bread halves on a baking sheet.

● **Bake** at 350° for 20 to 30 minutes or until thoroughly heated.
● **Top** cheese with chilled Doodles Olive Salad and remaining bread half; cut sandwich into quarters. **Yield:** 2 to 4 servings.

Doodles Olive Salad

3 (10-ounce) jars pimiento-stuffed olives, drained and coarsely chopped
3 stalks celery, chopped
2 carrots, scraped and grated
2 cloves garlic, finely chopped
1 (4-ounce) jar diced pimiento, drained
3 tablespoons capers, drained
½ cup olive oil
¼ cup red wine vinegar

● **Combine** all ingredients; cover and chill. Store remaining salad in refrigerator up to 1 week. **Yield:** 7 cups.

CAMOUFLAGED CARROTS

Is getting your family to eat carrots like trying to get a proper Southern lady to eat fried chicken with her fingers? If it is, give these recipes a try. We think they'll come begging for more. (And you'll be able to forget the "but, they'll help you see in the dark" spiel.)

CLASSY CARROTS

1 pound carrots, scraped and sliced
½ cup sugar
2 tablespoons all-purpose flour
¼ cup butter or margarine
3 large eggs
1 cup milk
1½ teaspoons ground cinnamon
Pecan Topping
Unsweetened whipped cream (optional)

● **Cook** carrot in boiling salted water to cover 8 to 10 minutes or until tender; drain.
● **Position** knife blade in food processor bowl; add carrot. Process 20 seconds. Add sugar and next 5 ingredients; process until smooth, stopping once to scrape down sides.

● **Pour** into 6 (8-ounce) lightly greased baking dishes. Place on a baking sheet, and cover with aluminum foil.
● **Bake** at 350° for 15 minutes. Remove from oven; uncover and sprinkle with Pecan Topping. Bake 20 additional minutes. Serve with whipped cream, if desired. **Yield:** 6 servings.

Pecan Topping

½ cup chopped pecans
½ cup firmly packed brown sugar
⅓ cup all-purpose flour
2 tablespoons butter or margarine

● **Combine** first 3 ingredients in a small bowl, and cut in butter with pastry blender until mixture is crumbly. **Yield:** 1⅓ cups.

Leslie Genszler
Roswell, Georgia

CRISPY FRIED CARROTS

¾ cup cornmeal
¾ cup all-purpose flour
1 teaspoon onion powder
1 teaspoon Old Bay seasoning
½ teaspoon salt
½ teaspoon ground white pepper
2½ tablespoons chopped fresh parsley
1 egg white
⅔ cup buttermilk
½ teaspoon hot sauce
4 large carrots, scraped and cut into thin strips
Vegetable oil

● **Combine** first 7 ingredients; set aside.
● **Beat** egg white until foamy; stir in buttermilk and hot sauce.
● **Dip** carrot in buttermilk mixture; drain off excess mixture, and dredge in cornmeal mixture.
● **Pour** oil to depth of 1 inch into a Dutch oven; heat to 350°. Fry carrots 2 minutes or until lightly browned. Serve immediately. **Yield:** 4 servings.

John Fleer, Executive Chef
The Inn at Blackberry Farm

CHEESE SCALLOPED CARROTS

2 pounds carrots, sliced
2 tablespoons butter or margarine
½ cup finely chopped celery
¼ cup finely chopped onion
2 tablespoons all-purpose flour
¼ teaspoon salt
¼ teaspoon dry mustard
Dash of pepper
1½ cups milk
1 cup (4 ounces) shredded Cheddar cheese
1 cup soft breadcrumbs
2 tablespoons butter or margarine, melted
2 tablespoons chopped fresh parsley

● **Cook** carrot in boiling salted water to cover 8 to 10 minutes or until tender; drain, and set aside.
● **Melt** 2 tablespoons butter in a heavy saucepan over low heat. Add celery and onion; cook until tender, stirring often. Add flour and next 3 ingredients, stirring until blended. Cook 1 minute, stirring constantly. Gradually add milk; cook over medium heat, stirring constantly, until mixture is thickened and bubbly. Stir in cheese and carrot; spoon mixture into a lightly greased 1½-quart casserole.
● **Combine** breadcrumbs, 2 tablespoons butter, and parsley; sprinkle over carrot mixture.
● **Bake** at 350° for 25 minutes. **Yield:** 6 to 8 servings.

Hilda Marshall
Front Royal, Virginia

CARE TO GET THE MOST OUT OF CARROTS?

■ The best carrots are young, slender, and smooth. The darker the orange color of carrots, the greater the amount of vitamin A.

■ Remove tops before refrigerating. They drain carrots of moisture.

■ Cut carrots into equal pieces so they'll cook evenly. Be aware: The more you cut them, the more nutrients carrots lose during cooking.

■ Cook carrots in as little water as possible to minimize nutrient loss.

A confetti of jade and ruby vegetables, Chicken Chinese (recipe, page 33), delights all of the senses, not just the tastebuds.

Cornmeal, a Southern classic, is like the sands of time – it shifts to form an unexpected image: Cornmeal Waffles with (from left) Turkey-Vegetable Topping, Chili Topping, and Peach Topping. (Recipes begin on page 22.)

A cooling ice cream treat, Nutty Fudgy Frozen Dessert (recipe, page 28), disarms the aftermath of hot and spicy foods.

DINNER WITHOUT RESERVATIONS

With our easy entrées, dinner reservations won't be necessary. So light a fire in the fireplace and head for the kitchen. By the time the flames are going, you'll be ready to relax by the fire and enjoy a low-fat supper.

MUSTARD MARINATED SIRLOIN

2 tablespoons Dijon mustard
2 tablespoons Burgundy or other dry red wine
1 teaspoon coarsely ground pepper
2 cloves garlic, minced
1 pound lean, boneless sirloin steak, trimmed
Vegetable cooking spray
1 cup sliced fresh mushrooms
1½ tablespoons all-purpose flour
1 cup reduced-sodium, fat-free beef broth
½ cup Burgundy or other dry red wine
¼ teaspoon salt
¼ teaspoon pepper

• **Combine** first 4 ingredients. Coat steak on both sides with mustard mixture, and place in a shallow dish. Cover and refrigerate 8 hours.
• **Place** steak on a rack coated with cooking spray; place rack in a broiler pan. Broil 3 inches from heat (with electric oven door partially opened) 4 to 5 minutes on each side or until desired degree of doneness. Let stand 5 minutes. Thinly slice steak diagonally across grain; keep warm.
• **Coat** a nonstick skillet with cooking spray; add mushrooms, and cook, stirring constantly, over medium heat until tender. Add flour; cook 1 minute, stirring constantly. Gradually add beef broth and ½ cup Burgundy; cook, stirring constantly, until thickened. Stir in salt and pepper. Serve evenly over meat. **Yield:** 4 servings.

♥ Per serving: Calories 213 (31% from fat)
Fat 6.8g (2.4g saturated) Cholesterol 80mg
Sodium 435mg Carbohydrate 6.5g
Fiber 0.5g Protein 28.2g

FRUIT-TOPPED PORK CHOPS

1 tablespoon reduced-calorie margarine
¼ cup chopped celery
2 tablespoons chopped onion
1 cup herb-seasoned stuffing mix
3 (0.9-ounce) packages mixed dried fruit
2 tablespoons raisins
6 (4-ounce) lean, boneless center-cut loin pork chops (¾ inch thick)
¼ teaspoon salt
¼ teaspoon pepper
¼ cup all-purpose flour
Vegetable cooking spray
½ cup Chablis or other dry white wine

• **Melt** margarine in a large skillet; add celery and onion; cook, stirring constantly, until tender. Add stuffing mix, mixed dried fruit, and raisins; toss gently. Set aside.
• **Sprinkle** pork chops with salt and pepper; dredge in flour. Set aside.
• **Coat** a large nonstick skillet with cooking spray; add chops, and brown on both sides over medium heat.
• **Arrange** chops in an 11- x 7- x 1½-inch baking dish coated with cooking spray; top each with fruit mixture. Add wine to dish. Cover and bake at 350° for 40 to 45 minutes or until done. **Yield:** 3 servings.

♥ Per serving: Calories 302 (27% from fat)
Fat 9.1g (2.8g saturated) Cholesterol 80mg
Sodium 346mg Carbohydrate 26g
Fiber 0.9g Protein 28.2g

CHICKEN À LA KING

1 tablespoon reduced-calorie margarine
3 (4-ounce) skinned and boned chicken breast halves, cut into bite-size pieces
¼ cup chopped onion
¼ cup sliced mushrooms
¼ cup all-purpose flour
2 cups skim milk
¼ cup frozen English peas, thawed
1 (2-ounce) jar diced pimiento, drained
½ teaspoon salt
½ teaspoon pepper
4 slices wheat bread, trimmed and toasted
¼ teaspoon paprika

• **Melt** margarine in a large nonstick skillet over medium heat. Add chicken and onion; cook, stirring constantly, 3 to 5 minutes or until chicken is browned. Add mushrooms; cook 1 minute.
• **Stir** in flour and cook 1 minute, stirring constantly. Gradually add milk and next 4 ingredients; cook over medium heat, stirring constantly, until mixture is thickened and bubbly.
• **Cut** each slice of bread into 4 triangles; serve chicken mixture with 4 toast triangles; sprinkle with paprika. **Yield:** 4 servings.

Mrs. T. W. Talcott
Louisville, Kentucky

♥ Per serving: Calories 254 (14% from fat)
Fat 4g (0.6g saturated) Cholesterol 53mg
Sodium 573mg Carbohydrate 26.4g
Fiber 1.7g Protein 28g

PEPPERED SNAPPER WITH CREAMY DILL SAUCE

4 (4-ounce) snapper fillets
2 teaspoons olive oil, divided
2 tablespoons coarsely ground pepper
Vegetable cooking spray
2 cups hot cooked rice (cooked without salt or fat)
Creamy Dill Sauce

• **Brush** snapper on both sides with 1 teaspoon olive oil; sprinkle with pepper, and gently press into fish. Cover and let stand 15 minutes.
• **Coat** a large nonstick skillet with cooking spray; add remaining 1 teaspoon olive oil, and place over medium heat. Cook fillets on both sides 3 to 5 minutes or until fish flakes easily when tested with a fork. Remove from heat; keep warm.
• **Spoon** rice evenly onto serving plates; top each with a fillet and sauce. Serve immediately. **Yield:** 4 servings.

♥ Per serving (1 fish fillet with ½ cup rice and ¼ cup sauce): Calories 389 (28% from fat)
Fat 11.9g (6.8g saturated) Cholesterol 72mg
Sodium 1825mg Carbohydrate 33.9g
Fiber 1.3g Protein 31.7g

Creamy Dill Sauce

1 (10-ounce) container refrigerated reduced-calorie Alfredo sauce
2 tablespoons Chablis or other dry white wine
1 teaspoon dried dillweed

• **Combine** all ingredients in a small heavy saucepan; cook, stirring constantly, over medium heat until thoroughly heated. Remove from heat; keep warm. **Yield:** 1 cup.

♥ Per ¼-cup serving: Calories 114 (59% from fat)
Fat 7.5g (6g saturated) Cholesterol 30mg
Sodium 1381mg Carbohydrate 5.5g
Fiber 0mg Protein 5.3g

VEGETABLE-CHEESE ENCHILADAS

8 (6-inch) corn tortillas
1 medium zucchini, cut into ½-inch cubes
1 cup (4 ounces) shredded reduced-fat Monterey Jack cheese, divided
1 cup cooked brown rice (cooked without salt or fat)
¼ cup chopped green onions
⅓ cup low-fat sour cream
¼ teaspoon salt
¼ teaspoon pepper
Vegetable cooking spray
2 (10-ounce) cans chopped tomatoes and green chiles, undrained

• **Wrap** tortillas in aluminum foil, and bake at 350° for 7 minutes.
• **Cook** zucchini in boiling water to cover 2 minutes; drain and pat dry with paper towels.
• **Combine** zucchini, half of cheese, and next 5 ingredients. Spoon mixture evenly down center of each tortilla; fold opposite sides over filling, and roll up tortillas. Place, seam side down, in an 11- x 7- x 1½-inch baking dish coated with cooking spray.
• **Pour** chopped tomatoes and green chiles over tortillas.
• **Bake** at 350° for 15 minutes; sprinkle with remaining cheese, and bake 5 additional minutes. **Yield:** 4 servings.
Madeline Gibbons
North Little Rock, Arkansas

♥ Per serving: Calories 343 (27% from fat)
Fat 9.9g (4.9g saturated) Cholesterol 26mg
Sodium 1031mg Carbohydrate 47.3g
Fiber 4.3g Protein 14.1g

TIPS FOR LIVING LIGHT

Skinny Tips

■ Don't fry. Sear meats with no added fat when you use a heavy nonstick pan. Use a light coating of vegetable cooking spray to sauté vegetables. Coat fish or chicken with seasoned breadcrumbs, and bake instead of fry.
■ Use a small amount of wine as a cooking liquid for baked meats. Much of the alcohol evaporates, leaving flavor but few calories.
■ Use marinades containing wine, lemon juice, yogurt, or vinegar. The acids in these ingredients will tenderize lean cuts of beef.
■ Serve low-fat fish, like snapper, catfish, swordfish, or ocean perch.

Healthy Hints

■ Food awareness, not dieting, is a program for life. Cut down on sweets, and you'll often eliminate a lot of fat. When you crave a sweet, have a graham cracker, some dried fruit, or perhaps a few gingersnaps.
■ Take smaller portions; you'll find you don't need to eat as much as you think. Order grilled meat and a green salad when you eat out. Skip the salad dressing, and enjoy the flavor of fresh raw vegetables.
■ Give in once in awhile without feeling guilty.

Quick Tips

■ Make weeknight meals easy. Serve entrées that cook quickly on the cooktop or bake in the oven while you prepare vegetables and a salad.
■ Toss a salad in a flash when you wash enough lettuce and prepare and slice enough raw vegetables for several days' salad makings. Stored in plastic bags in the vegetable bin of the refrigerator, the produce will stay fresh for as long as five days.
■ Prepare crisp-tender vegetables as fast as possible by cooking them in your microwave.
■ Cook rice, pasta, or potatoes ahead of time, and refrigerate up to three days. You'll shave minutes from preparation time when these staples are already prepared.

BRAND-NEW RAGOUTS

Call them ragouts, call them stews, or in Kentucky, call them

burgoos. Whatever you name them, these slowly simmered dishes use

inexpensive ingredients to deliver wholesome, invigorating tastes.

Serve them with a crisp green salad, and supper is complete.

LAMB STEW WITH POPOVERS

3 tablespoons olive oil
2 pounds boneless lamb, cut into 1-inch cubes
1 medium onion, chopped
1 clove garlic, pressed
2 tablespoons all-purpose flour
1½ cups chicken broth
½ cup Chablis or other dry white wine
2 tablespoons lemon juice
1½ teaspoons salt
¼ teaspoon dried marjoram
¼ teaspoon dried rosemary
⅛ teaspoon pepper
1 bay leaf
12 pearl onions
6 to 8 small new potatoes, peeled and cut into ¼-inch slices (about 1 pound)
3 carrots, scraped and sliced diagonally into 1-inch pieces
Popovers
Garnish: fresh rosemary sprigs

• **Heat** olive oil in a Dutch oven over medium heat; add lamb, and cook until browned, stirring often. Remove lamb, reserving 2 tablespoons drippings.
• **Add** onion and garlic to drippings; cook over medium heat, stirring constantly, 3 minutes or until tender.

Return lamb to Dutch oven, and sprinkle with flour, stirring well. Stir in broth and next 7 ingredients.
• **Bring** to a boil; cover, reduce heat, and simmer 30 minutes.
• **Add** pearl onions, potatoes, and carrots; cover and simmer 20 to 30 minutes or until vegetables are tender. Remove and discard bay leaf. Serve stew in popovers. Garnish, if desired. **Yield:** 7 cups.

Popovers

1 cup all-purpose flour
¼ teaspoon salt
1 cup milk
2 large eggs, lightly beaten

• **Combine** all ingredients in a mixing bowl; beat at low speed with an electric mixer just until smooth.
• **Place** well-greased 3½-inch muffin pans or popover pans in a 450° oven for 3 minutes or until a drop of water sizzles when dropped in them. Remove pans from oven; fill them half full with batter.
• **Bake** at 450° for 15 minutes. Reduce heat to 350°, and bake 20 to 25 additional minutes. Serve immediately. **Yield:** 6 popovers.

Lynn Abbott
Southern Pines, North Carolina

VEAL-AND-ARTICHOKE RAGOUT

3 tablespoons all-purpose flour
1 teaspoon paprika
½ teaspoon salt
½ teaspoon dried basil
½ teaspoon dried rosemary
¼ teaspoon pepper
2 pounds lean boneless veal stew meat, cut into 1-inch cubes *
¼ cup vegetable oil, divided
½ pound fresh mushrooms, sliced
1 (14½-ounce) can ready-to-serve chicken broth
1 cup Chablis or other dry white wine
1 (14-ounce) can artichoke hearts, drained and quartered
Hot cooked noodles

• **Combine** first 6 ingredients in a bowl or zip-top plastic bag; add veal, tossing to coat. Set aside.
• **Heat** 2 tablespoons oil in a Dutch oven over medium heat; add half of veal. Cook until browned, stirring often. Remove veal. Repeat procedure with remaining oil and veal, reserving remaining flour mixture. Remove veal, and set aside.
• **Add** mushrooms to Dutch oven, and cook until tender, stirring often. Stir in reserved flour mixture; cook 1 minute, stirring constantly. Stir in chicken broth, wine, and veal.
• **Bring** to a boil. Cover, reduce heat, and simmer 1 hour.
• **Add** artichokes; cover and cook 10 to 15 minutes, stirring occasionally. Serve in individual bowls over noodles. **Yield:** 6 cups.

* Two pounds boneless pork may be substituted.

Jeanne S. Hotalings
Augusta, Georgia

CHICKEN RAGOUT WITH CHEDDAR DUMPLINGS

2 cups diagonally sliced carrot
1 cup sweet red pepper strips
3 tablespoons butter or
    margarine
¼ cup all-purpose flour
2 cups chicken broth
1 cup milk
1 tablespoon lemon juice
½ teaspoon salt
½ teaspoon pepper
3 cups chopped cooked chicken
1 cup frozen English peas, thawed
    and drained
2 cups biscuit mix
⅔ cup milk
¾ cup (3 ounces) shredded
    Cheddar cheese
1 (2-ounce) jar diced pimiento,
    drained

●**Arrange** sliced carrot and sweet red pepper strips in a steamer basket; place over boiling water. Cover; steam 8 minutes or until vegetables are crisp-tender; set aside.
●**Melt** butter in a large heavy saucepan over low heat; add flour, stirring until mixture is smooth. Cook 1 minute, stirring constantly. Gradually add chicken broth and 1 cup milk; cook over medium heat, stirring constantly, until mixture is thickened and bubbly. Remove from heat.
●**Stir** in lemon juice, salt, and pepper. Add chicken, steamed vegetables, and peas, stirring gently. Spoon into a lightly greased 11- x 7- x 1½-inch baking dish; set aside.
●**Combine** biscuit mix and ⅔ cup milk, stirring until dry ingredients are moistened. Stir vigorously 30 seconds. Turn out onto a lightly floured surface, and knead 4 or 5 times.
●**Roll** dough into a 12- x 9-inch rectangle. Sprinkle with cheese and pimiento, leaving a ½-inch border; roll up jellyroll fashion, starting with a long side, and turn seam side down. Cut into 1-inch-thick slices, and place over chicken mixture.
●**Bake** at 400° for 30 minutes or until golden brown. **Yield:** 6 servings.

Sue Deck
Ellenwood, Georgia

PANCHO VILLA STEW

2 pounds pork loin, cut into
    1-inch cubes
¼ cup all-purpose flour
2 tablespoons vegetable oil
2 (4-ounce) chorizo sausages, cut
    into ½-inch slices
3 (14½-ounce) cans ready-to-serve
    chicken broth
1 (14½-ounce) can whole
    tomatoes, drained
3 (4-ounce) cans diced green
    chiles, undrained
1 large purple onion, sliced into
    rings
3 cloves garlic, pressed
2 teaspoons ground cumin
2 teaspoons cocoa
1 teaspoon dried oregano
¼ teaspoon salt
1 (2-inch) stick cinnamon
2 (15-ounce) cans black beans,
    rinsed and drained
1 (15½-ounce) can white hominy,
    rinsed and drained
1 (10-ounce) package frozen
    whole kernel corn
½ cup beer or tequila
Flour tortillas

●**Dredge** pork in flour; set aside.
●**Heat** oil in a large Dutch oven over medium heat; add pork, and cook until browned, stirring often. Add sausage, and cook 2 minutes, stirring often. Add broth and next 9 ingredients.
●**Bring** to a boil; reduce heat, and simmer 1 hour.
●**Stir** in black beans and next 3 ingredients; simmer 30 minutes. Remove cinnamon stick. Serve with buttered flour tortillas. **Yield:** 3 quarts.

Judith Hartley
Signal Mountain, Tennessee

LET'S DO THE TWIST: MACARONI, THAT IS

If Yankee Doodle could spoon into these surprising macaroni dishes, he'd pronounce them dandy. Every recipe is worth the time it takes to make real macaroni and cheese from scratch.

MACARONI AND BLUE CHEESE

2 quarts water
1 teaspoon salt
1 (8-ounce) package elbow
    macaroni
¼ cup butter or margarine
¼ cup all-purpose flour
2 cups milk
1 (4-ounce) package crumbled
    blue cheese
1 large egg, lightly beaten
1 (2-ounce) jar diced pimiento,
    drained
½ cup soft breadcrumbs
½ cup walnuts, finely chopped
Garnish: fresh parsley sprig

●**Bring** water and salt to a boil in a large Dutch oven; stir in macaroni. Return to a rapid boil, and cook 8 to 10 minutes or until tender; drain. Rinse with cold water; drain.
●**Melt** butter in Dutch oven over low heat; add flour, stirring until smooth. Cook 1 minute, stirring constantly. Gradually add milk; cook over medium heat, stirring constantly, until thickened. Add blue cheese, stirring until melted. Stir about one-fourth of hot mixture into beaten egg; add to remaining hot mixture, stirring constantly.
●**Stir** in macaroni and pimiento; spoon into a greased 2-quart shallow baking dish. Sprinkle with breadcrumbs and walnuts.
●**Bake** at 350° for 35 minutes. Garnish, if desired. **Yield:** 6 servings.

JACK-IN-THE-MACARONI BAKE

2 quarts water
1 teaspoon salt
1 (8-ounce) package elbow
   macaroni
2 tablespoons butter or margarine
¼ cup chopped onion
¼ cup chopped sweet red pepper
2 cups (8 ounces) shredded
   Monterey Jack cheese with
   peppers
1 (10¾-ounce) can cream of
   celery soup, undiluted
½ cup sour cream
Chili powder
Garnish: celery leaves

• **Bring** water and salt to a boil in a
large Dutch oven; stir in macaroni. Return to a rapid boil, and cook 8 to 10
minutes or until tender; drain. Rinse
with cold water; drain.
• **Melt** butter in a Dutch oven; add
onion and red pepper. Cook over
medium heat, stirring constantly, until
crisp-tender. Remove from heat.
• **Stir** in cheese, soup, and sour cream.
Stir in macaroni; spoon into a greased
shallow 2-quart casserole. Sprinkle
with chili powder.
• **Bake** at 350° for 30 minutes. Garnish, if desired. **Yield:** 6 servings.

CREAMY MACARONI AND CHEESE

2 quarts water
1 teaspoon salt
1 (8-ounce) package elbow
   macaroni
4 cups (16 ounces) shredded
   Cheddar or Jarlsberg cheese
1 (8-ounce) carton sour cream
1 cup mayonnaise
2 tablespoons chopped onion
1 cup cheese crackers, crushed
Garnish: green onion fan

• **Bring** water and salt to a boil in a
large Dutch oven; stir in macaroni. Return to a rapid boil, and cook 8 to 10
minutes or until tender; drain. Rinse
with cold water; drain.
• **Combine** macaroni and next 4 ingredients. Spoon into a lightly greased
11- x 7- x 1½-inch baking dish; sprinkle with crushed crackers.
• **Bake** at 325° for 30 to 35 minutes,
and garnish, if desired. **Yield:** 6 to 8
servings.

♥ To reduce fat and calories, substitute
nonfat sour cream alternative, fat-free
mayonnaise, and reduced-fat Cheddar
cheese.

Nat Holland
Columbia, South Carolina

CAULIFLOWER POWER

....

Cauliflower's lunarlike landscape is
nicely crusted and surrounded by
sautéed cherry tomatoes in this rendi-
tion. The taste combination will eclipse
your expectations.

CAULIFLOWER WITH CHINESE MUSTARD GRATIN

1 large cauliflower
½ cup mayonnaise
¼ cup commercial hot Chinese
   mustard
½ cup (2 ounces) shredded Swiss
   cheese
2 tablespoons fine, dry
   breadcrumbs
Sautéed Cherry Tomatoes
Garnish: chopped fresh parsley

• **Remove** outer leaves and stalk, leaving cauliflower head whole. Place in
boiling water to cover; cover and cook
10 to 15 minutes or until tender. Drain
and place in a 9-inch square pan.
• **Combine** mayonnaise and mustard;
spread over cauliflower.
• **Combine** cheese and breadcrumbs;
sprinkle over mustard mixture.
• **Broil** 5½ inches from heat (with electric oven door partially opened) 3
minutes. Serve with Sautéed Cherry
Tomatoes, and garnish, if desired. **Yield:**
6 servings.

Sautéed Cherry Tomatoes

1 pint cherry tomatoes, cut in half
2 tablespoons vegetable oil
¼ teaspoon salt
¼ teaspoon garlic powder

• **Cook** tomatoes in oil in a small
saucepan over medium-high heat, stirring constantly, 3 minutes or until hot.
Stir in salt and garlic powder. **Yield:**
about 2 cups.

Nanette Wesley
Jackson, Georgia

SUBSTITUTES GIVE ANOTHER TWIST TO MACARONI

....

■ If you favor lots of different cheeses, try substituting them in Creamy
Macaroni and Cheese; the recipe is basic enough to accommodate most
cheese flavors.

■ By using new low-fat products on the market, you can lighten Creamy
Macaroni and Cheese considerably. The traditional one still tasted best, but
we thought the lightened version gave it a *good* run for the money.

■ Reduce the amount of sodium in any pasta dish by cooking the pasta in
unsalted water.

FINE FARE FOR A TWOSOME

While other couples flock to crowded restaurants on Valentine's Day, treat your sweetheart to a quiet dinner – at home. Light the candles and raise your glasses to valentine romance and a beautiful menu from the heart.

VALENTINE'S DAY DINNER
Serves Two

Insalata Balsamico
Filet Mignon Tarragon
Zesty Stuffed Potatoes
Chocolate Soufflé

INSALATA BALSAMICO

1 cup torn escarole
1 cup torn Bibb lettuce
1 green onion, chopped
1 slice pancetta or bacon, cut into small pieces
2 teaspoons olive oil
2 tablespoons balsamic vinegar
¼ teaspoon salt
¼ teaspoon freshly ground pepper

●**Combine** first 3 ingredients in a large bowl; set aside.
●**Cook** pancetta in olive oil in a large skillet until crisp. Remove with a slotted spoon, reserving drippings in skillet. Drain pancetta on paper towels, and sprinkle over salad greens.
●**Add** vinegar, salt, and pepper to drippings in skillet; bring to a boil, stirring constantly. Pour over salad; toss gently. Serve immediately. **Yield:** 2 servings.

FILET MIGNON TARRAGON

¼ cup Burgundy or other dry red wine
2 tablespoons low-sodium soy sauce
¼ teaspoon dried tarragon
2 (4-ounce) beef tenderloin steaks, trimmed
Vegetable cooking spray

●**Combine** first 3 ingredients in an 8-inch square dish; add steaks. Cover and refrigerate 3 hours, turning steaks occasionally.
●**Remove** steaks from marinade, discarding marinade. Place steaks on a rack coated with cooking spray; place rack in a shallow roasting pan. Broil 6 inches from heat (with electric oven door partially opened) 5 minutes on each side or to desired degree of doneness. **Yield:** 2 servings.

ZESTY STUFFED POTATOES

2 large baking potatoes (about 1½ pounds)
¼ cup sour cream
¼ cup (1 ounce) shredded Cheddar cheese
¼ teaspoon salt
¼ teaspoon pepper
1 green onion, chopped
1 tablespoon chopped pecans
1 tablespoon commercial real bacon bits (optional)

●**Scrub** potatoes, and prick several times with a fork. Place potatoes 1 inch apart on a microwave-safe rack or paper towels.
●**Microwave** at HIGH 10 to 12 minutes, turning and rearranging once; let stand 2 minutes.
●**Cut** a 1-inch lengthwise strip from top of each potato. Carefully scoop out pulp, leaving shells intact.
●**Mash** potato pulp; stir in sour cream and next 4 ingredients. Spoon into shells.
●**Combine** pecans and bacon bits, if desired; sprinkle on potatoes. Place on a microwave-safe plate.
●**Microwave** at HIGH 1 minute or until potatoes are thoroughly heated. **Yield:** 2 servings.

CHOCOLATE SOUFFLÉ

Butter or margarine
2 tablespoons butter or margarine
1 (1-ounce) square unsweetened chocolate
2 tablespoons all-purpose flour
½ cup milk
Dash of salt
2 large eggs, separated
¼ cup sugar
½ teaspoon vanilla extract
Mocha Cream

●**Coat** bottom and sides of a 2-cup soufflé dish or 2 (10-ounce) custard cups with butter. Set aside.
●**Melt** 2 tablespoons butter and chocolate in a saucepan over medium heat. Add flour; stir until smooth. Cook 1 minute, stirring constantly. Gradually

add milk; cook over medium heat, stirring constantly, until thickened and bubbly. Stir in salt; remove from heat.

● **Beat** yolks and sugar at medium speed with an electric mixer until thick and pale. Stir in vanilla. Gradually stir about one-fourth of hot chocolate mixture into yolk mixture; beat at medium speed with electric mixer until blended. Gradually add remaining hot chocolate mixture, mixing constantly.

● **Beat** egg whites until soft peaks form. Gently fold about one-fourth of egg whites into chocolate mixture; fold remaining egg whites into chocolate mixture. Carefully spoon mixture into prepared soufflé dish or custard cups.

● **Bake** at 325° for 35 minutes or until puffed and set. Serve soufflé immediately with Mocha Cream. **Yield:** 2 servings.

Mocha Cream

½ cup whipping cream
1 tablespoon sugar
1½ teaspoons unsweetened cocoa
½ teaspoon instant coffee granules

● **Combine** all ingredients. Beat at high speed with an electric mixer until stiff peaks form; chill. **Yield:** 1 cup.

Note: Mocha Cream may also be used to flavor coffee.

Lee Robinson
Oak Ridge, Tennessee

GREENS: ALL WRAPPED UP

You've seen these familiar greens in salads, slaws, and stews. But here we present *bundled* greens that wrap up oodles of flavor. Crinkly Swiss chard softens as it cloaks a rich cheese filling. Zesty grape leaves are enriched with an *avgolemono*, one of the favorite sauces in Greek cooking.

For easy and fun party fare, treat your guests (and yourself) to Thai Lettuce Folds. They're adventurous as a finger food, or try them served with a fork as a "folded salad." Either way, you won't be disappointed with the furl of delicate Asian flavors.

HUNGARIAN CABBAGE ROLLS

1 large leafy cabbage
1 pound lean ground beef
½ cup long-grain rice, uncooked
1 small onion, grated
2 large eggs
1 teaspoon salt
¼ teaspoon pepper
1 large onion, sliced
1 (28-ounce) can tomatoes, undrained
1 (8-ounce) can tomato sauce
1 clove garlic, minced
½ cup firmly packed brown sugar
3 tablespoons lemon juice
¾ teaspoon salt
⅛ teaspoon pepper

● **Remove** 12 outer leaves from cabbage, and place leaves in a large Dutch oven. Add boiling water to cover; let stand 30 to 40 minutes. Drain well, and set aside.
● **Coarsely** chop remaining cabbage, and place in bottom of large Dutch oven. Set aside.
● **Combine** ground beef and next 5 ingredients. Place about 2 tablespoonfuls mixture in center of each cabbage leaf; fold left and right sides over mixture, and roll up, beginning at bottom. Arrange cabbage rolls, seam side down, in Dutch oven. Top with sliced onion.
● **Combine** tomatoes and remaining ingredients, and pour tomato mixture over cabbage rolls.
● **Cover** and cook over medium heat 1 hour or until cabbage rolls are tender. **Yield:** 4 to 6 servings.

Margaret Watts
Charleston, West Virginia

THAI LETTUCE FOLDS

2 tablespoons peanut oil
2 cloves garlic, minced
4 skinned and boned chicken breast halves, cut into ¼-inch cubes
⅓ cup chicken broth
2 green onions with tops, finely chopped
1 tablespoon chopped fresh mint leaves
1 tablespoon chopped fresh cilantro
1 tablespoon lime juice
½ teaspoon ground red pepper
¼ teaspoon ground ginger
16 Bibb lettuce leaves
½ pound bean sprouts
Cucumber Dipping Sauce

● **Heat** peanut oil in a large skillet over medium-high heat 1 minute. Add garlic and chicken; cook, stirring constantly, 3 to 5 minutes. Add broth, and cook over medium heat until most of liquid evaporates. Stir in green onions and next 5 ingredients.
● **Spoon** 2 tablespoons chicken mixture onto each lettuce leaf; sprinkle with bean sprouts, and fold over. Serve with Cucumber Dipping Sauce. **Yield:** 16 appetizer servings.

Cucumber Dipping Sauce

½ cup water
¼ cup sugar
¼ cup rice wine vinegar
1 tablespoon plum sauce
¼ teaspoon dried crushed red pepper
⅛ teaspoon salt
½ cup finely chopped cucumber
1 tablespoon chopped fresh cilantro
1 tablespoon chopped fresh mint leaves

● **Combine** first 6 ingredients in a small saucepan.
● **Bring** to a boil; reduce heat, and simmer 3 minutes. Remove from heat, and let cool.
● **Stir** in cucumber and remaining ingredients. **Yield:** about 1 cup.

SWISS CHARD BUNDLES

1 (15-ounce) container ricotta
    cheese
⅓ cup freshly grated Parmesan
    cheese
1 clove garlic
2 egg whites
¼ teaspoon salt
¼ teaspoon pepper
⅛ teaspoon ground nutmeg
¼ cup oil-packed dried
    tomatoes, drained and
    chopped
1 (14½-ounce) can ready-to-serve
    chicken broth
½ pound Swiss chard

• **Position** knife blade in food processor bowl; add first 7 ingredients. Process until blended. Stir in tomatoes.
• **Bring** broth to a boil in a large saucepan. Add chard leaves, one at a time, and cook each leaf 15 seconds; remove and drain.
• **Line** each of 4 (4-ounce) greased custard cups with 1 chard leaf, allowing leaf to overhang. Spoon cheese mixture evenly into cups, and fold over edges of leaves. Place any remaining leaves on top to thoroughly cover cheese mixture, if desired. Place cups in a 13- x 9- x 2-inch baking dish; add hot water to pan to depth of ½ inch; cover pan with aluminum foil.
• **Bake** at 350° for 35 to 40 minutes. Unmold bundles before serving. **Yield:** 4 servings.

STUFFED GRAPE LEAVES

1 (16-ounce) jar grape leaves,
    drained
1 cup long-grain rice,
    uncooked
1 pound lamb stew meat, finely
    chopped
2 tablespoons butter or margarine,
    melted
1 teaspoon salt
½ teaspoon pepper
¼ teaspoon ground cinnamon
2 lamb bones
¼ cup lemon juice
Avgolemono Sauce

• **Place** grape leaves in a large bowl; add hot water to cover, and let stand 10 minutes. Drain and set aside. Repeat procedure 2 times.
• **Place** rice in a bowl; add hot water to cover, and let stand 10 minutes. Drain.
• **Combine** rice and next 5 ingredients; set aside.
• **Place** 1 grape leaf, right side down, on a flat surface; remove and discard stem. Place about 1 tablespoon rice mixture near bottom of leaf; fold left and right sides over, and roll up, beginning at bottom. Repeat procedure with remaining rice mixture and grape leaves, reserving any remaining grape leaves.
• **Place** lamb bones in a Dutch oven; layer reserved grape leaves over bones, and arrange stuffed grape leaves on top. Add water to cover, and place an ovenproof plate on top of stuffed leaves.
• **Bring** to a boil; cover, reduce heat, and cook 30 minutes. Add lemon juice, and cook 5 additional minutes. Remove stuffed grape leaves, and drain on paper towels. Serve with Avgolemono Sauce. **Yield:** about 2½ dozen.

Avgolemono Sauce

1 cup chicken broth
3 large eggs
⅓ cup lemon juice
½ teaspoon salt
1 tablespoon chopped fresh mint
    (optional)

• **Heat** chicken broth in a small saucepan.
• **Combine** eggs and remaining ingredients in container of an electric blender. With blender on high, gradually add broth in a slow, steady stream. Return mixture to saucepan. Cook over low heat, stirring constantly, just until thickened. Serve warm. **Yield:** 3½ cups.

Priscilla Carbonie
Birmingham, Alabama

COFFEE CAKE... TO GO!

It's a great feeling to have food on hand when you're celebrating a special event or juggling a busy schedule. Here are four coffee-cake occasions and packaging suggestions.

■ **Wedding mania:** Offer to take breakfast to a friend who is entertaining wedding guests. Take coffee cake, fresh fruit, and a carafe of juice in a big basket. They're set!

■ **Housewarming:** Welcome a new neighbor with homemade coffee cake. Include a package of gourmet coffee.

■ **New baby:** New parents will find early mornings more bearable with your gift of homemade coffee cake. Bake in a recyclable aluminum pan; wrap with colored plastic wrap, and secure with a rattle or toy.

■ **Brunch for a crowd:** Serve Cherry Coffee Cake with your favorite egg-and-sausage casserole and a fruit compote.

APRICOT LATTICE COFFEE CAKE

1 package active dry yeast
¼ cup warm water (105° to 115°)
⅔ cup butter or margarine,
    softened
⅓ cup sugar
4 large eggs
4 cups all-purpose flour
1 teaspoon salt
¾ cup half-and-half
½ cup butter or margarine,
    softened
½ cup sugar
½ cup apricot preserves *
½ cup sliced almonds
¼ cup all-purpose flour

- **Combine** yeast and warm water in a 1-cup liquid glass measuring cup; let stand 5 minutes.
- **Beat** ⅔ cup butter at medium speed with an electric mixer until creamy; gradually add ⅓ cup sugar, beating until soft and fluffy. Lightly beat eggs in a small bowl, and reserve 2 tablespoons; add remaining eggs to butter mixture, beating well.
- **Combine** 4 cups flour and salt; add to butter mixture alternately with half-and-half and yeast mixture. Reserve 1 cup batter. Spread remaining batter evenly into 2 well-greased, 9-inch round cakepans.
- **Combine** ½ cup butter, ½ cup sugar, and preserves; divide in half, and spread each portion evenly over batter. Sprinkle each with almonds.
- **Combine** reserved 1 cup batter and ¼ cup flour; divide into 12 portions. With floured hands, roll each portion into a 9-inch strip. Carefully arrange half of strips in a lattice design over filling in each pan, and brush with reserved 2 tablespoons egg.
- **Cover** and let rise in a warm place (85°), free from drafts, 1 hour or until almost doubled in bulk.
- **Bake** at 350° for 20 to 25 minutes. **Yield:** two 9-inch coffee cakes.

* Equal amounts of other fruit preserves may be substituted.

Ibby Fulkerson
Birmingham, Alabama

CHERRY COFFEE CAKE

1 (18.25-ounce) package yellow cake mix, divided
1 cup all-purpose flour
1 package active dry yeast
⅔ cup warm water (120° to 130°)
2 large eggs
1 (21-ounce) can cherry pie filling *
⅓ cup butter or margarine
Glaze

- **Combine** 1½ cups cake mix, flour, and yeast in a bowl; add warm water, stirring until smooth. Stir in eggs.

- **Spoon** batter into a greased 13- x 9- x 2-inch pan. Spoon pie filling evenly over batter; set aside. Cut butter into remaining cake mix with pastry blender or fork until mixture is crumbly. Sprinkle over pie filling.
- **Bake** at 350° for 25 to 30 minutes. Cool in pan on a wire rack. Drizzle with Glaze, and cut into squares. **Yield:** 15 to 18 servings.

* Any 21-ounce can fruit pie filling may be substituted.

Glaze

1 cup sifted powdered sugar
1 tablespoon light corn syrup
1 tablespoon water

- **Combine** all ingredients; drizzle over cake. **Yield:** ⅓ cup.

Sandy Brauer
St. Louis, Missouri

PINEAPPLE-COCONUT COFFEE CAKE

2 (15¼-ounce) cans crushed pineapple, undrained
½ cup butter or margarine, softened
1 cup sugar
1 cup firmly packed brown sugar
2 large eggs
2½ cups all-purpose flour
1 teaspoon baking powder
1 teaspoon baking soda
¼ teaspoon salt
1 (3½-ounce) can flaked coconut
1 cup chopped pecans
1 teaspoon vanilla extract
2 cups sifted powdered sugar
¼ cup flaked coconut, toasted
¼ cup chopped pecans, toasted

- **Drain** pineapple, reserving ¼ cup juice; set aside.
- **Beat** butter at medium speed with an electric mixer until creamy; gradually add sugar and brown sugar, beating mixture well. Add eggs, one at a time, beating after each addition.
- **Combine** flour and next 3 ingredients; add to butter mixture, mixing well. Stir

in pineapple, 3½-ounce can coconut, 1 cup pecans, and vanilla.
- **Spoon** batter into 2 greased and floured 8½- x 4½- x 3-inch loafpans.
- **Bake** at 350° for 55 minutes or until a wooden pick inserted in center comes out clean. Cool in pans on wire racks 10 minutes; remove from pans, and let cool completely on wire racks.
- **Combine** powdered sugar and reserved juice; drizzle over cakes. Sprinkle with coconut and pecans. **Yield:** 2 coffee cakes.

Ann Boyle
Duluth, Georgia

FIND FRUIT IN FEBRUARY

You've decided to try to eat more fruit *every* day. But maybe you're feeling uninspired, even discouraged. The fresh blueberries and cherries aren't in yet. Watermelons are just a sweet memory. Don't worry! Following are four recipes to enjoy that will have you eating always-available, delicious fruit at breakfast, lunch, and dinner.

PINEAPPLE SLAW

3 cups shredded cabbage
1 (8-ounce) can pineapple tidbits, drained
1 cup miniature marshmallows
¼ cup raisins
⅓ cup mayonnaise or salad dressing
⅛ teaspoon salt

- **Combine** all ingredients; cover and chill. **Yield:** 4 to 6 servings.

Robert Moy, Jr.
Floresville, Texas

APPLE OMELET STACK

1 cup firmly packed brown sugar
2 tablespoons cornstarch
⅔ cup milk
⅓ cup butter or margarine, melted
5½ cups peeled, coarsely chopped cooking apples (about 2 pounds)
Baked Omelets
Sour cream

• **Combine** brown sugar and cornstarch in a large saucepan; stir in milk and melted butter. Cook mixture over medium heat until thickened; stir in chopped apple, and cook 8 minutes or until tender.
• **Place** 1 omelet on serving plate, browned side up; spread with ⅓ of apple mixture. Repeat procedure layering remaining omelets and apple mixture. Cut into quarters; top each portion with a dollop of sour cream. **Yield:** 4 servings.

Baked Omelets

2 large eggs
½ cup all-purpose flour
¼ teaspoon salt
1 cup milk
Vegetable cooking spray
3 tablespoons butter or margarine, divided

• **Combine** eggs, flour, salt, and milk in a medium bowl, and beat until smooth.
• **Heat** 3 (9-inch) round cakepans at 450° for 5 minutes or until hot. Remove pans from oven, and coat with cooking spray. Add 1 tablespoon butter to each pan to coat; rotate pan. Pour batter evenly into pans.
• **Bake** at 450° for 7 minutes. Reduce heat to 350°, and bake 5 additional minutes or until browned. (Omelet will puff as it bakes and settle as it cools.) **Yield:** three 9-inch omelets.

BAKED PRUNE COMPOTE

1 (12-ounce) package pitted prunes
1 cup raisins
⅓ cup firmly packed brown sugar
⅔ cup water
Grated rind and juice of 1 lemon
Grated rind and juice of 1 orange
Pinch of salt
1 (3-inch) stick cinnamon
Sweetened whipped cream (optional)

• **Combine** first 8 ingredients in a 2-quart baking dish; cover.
• **Bake** at 325° for 1 hour. Let cool; remove cinnamon stick.
• **Cover** and chill at least 2 hours. Serve with sweetened whipped cream, if desired. **Yield:** 6 to 8 servings.

Marge Killmon
Annandale, Virginia

CRÈME DE MENTHE PEARS

10 ripe pears (about 4 pounds)
1½ cups sugar
2 cups water
¾ cup green crème de menthe
1 tablespoon lemon juice
3 or 4 drops green liquid food coloring

• **Peel** pears, and remove core from bottom end, leaving stem end intact.
• **Combine** sugar and remaining ingredients in a large Dutch oven; bring to a boil, stirring until sugar dissolves. Place pears, stem end up, in pan; cover, reduce heat, and simmer 15 to 20 minutes or until tender, occasionally spooning syrup over pears. Remove pears with a slotted spoon, and let cool.
• **Cover** pears, and chill at least 2 hours. Serve with ham or turkey or as a dessert with whipped cream. **Yield:** 10 servings.

Lu Allen
New Braunfels, Texas

BROWNIES: BASIC AND BEYOND

If you're looking for that sweet taste of chocolate, stop right here. We've scoured our files for readers' favorite recipes and discovered a chocolate smorgasbord. An array of nuts, mint patties, frostings, and commercial mixes transforms these brownies from "ho-hum" into "Oh, yum!"

PISTACHIO-MINT BROWNIES

2 (1-ounce) squares semisweet chocolate
⅓ cup butter or margarine
1 cup sugar
2 large eggs
1 teaspoon vanilla extract
¾ cup all-purpose flour
¼ teaspoon salt
½ cup chopped pistachios or pecans
1 (8¾-ounce) package chocolate mint patties, unwrapped (26 mints)
2 tablespoons chopped pistachios or pecans

• **Combine** chocolate and butter in a heavy saucepan; cook over low heat until chocolate melts, stirring often. Remove from heat.
• **Stir** in sugar, eggs, and vanilla. Add flour and salt, stirring until blended. Stir in ½ cup pistachios. Spoon into a greased 8-inch square pan.
• **Bake** at 350° for 22 minutes. Top with mint patties.
• **Bake** 2 additional minutes.
• **Cover** with aluminum foil; let stand 5 minutes. Uncover and spread melted mint patties over top. Sprinkle evenly with 2 tablespoons pistachios; cool on a wire rack. Cut into squares. **Yield:** 16 squares.

Mrs. E. W. Hanley
Palm Harbor, Florida

GERMAN CHOCOLATE CHESS SQUARES

1 (18.25-ounce) package German chocolate cake mix with pudding
1 large egg, lightly beaten
½ cup butter or margarine, melted
1 cup chopped pecans
1 (8-ounce) package cream cheese, softened
2 large eggs
1 (16-ounce) package powdered sugar, sifted

• **Combine** first 4 ingredients in a large bowl, stirring until dry ingredients are moistened. Press into bottom of a greased 13- x 9- x 2-inch pan; set aside.
• **Combine** cream cheese, 2 eggs, and 1 cup powdered sugar; beat at medium speed with an electric mixer until blended. Gradually add remaining powdered sugar, beating after each addition. Pour over chocolate layer, spreading evenly.
• **Bake** at 350° for 40 minutes. Cool on a wire rack, and cut into squares. **Yield:** 4 dozen.

Barbara Sutton
Portsmouth, Virginia

MACADAMIA-FUDGE DESIGNER BROWNIES

2½ cups sugar
1½ cups butter or margarine
5 (1-ounce) squares unsweetened chocolate
6 large eggs, lightly beaten
2 cups all-purpose flour
1 cup coarsely chopped macadamia nuts or almonds
Fudge Frosting
Garnish: chopped macadamia nuts

• **Combine** sugar, butter, and chocolate in a large saucepan; cook over low heat until chocolate melts, stirring often. Remove from heat; cool 10 minutes.
• **Stir** in eggs, flour, and nuts. Pour into a greased and floured 13- x 9- x 2-inch pan.
• **Bake** at 350° for 30 to 35 minutes. Cool on a wire rack.
• **Pour** Fudge Frosting over top; chill 15 minutes, and cut into squares. Garnish, if desired. **Yield:** 4 dozen.

Fudge Frosting

1 cup whipping cream
12 (1-ounce) squares semisweet chocolate

• **Heat** whipping cream in a medium saucepan over medium heat; add chocolate, stirring until smooth. Remove from heat, and cool to room temperature. **Yield:** 2½ cups.

Daisy Cook
Tyler, Texas

BISCUIT MIX BROWNIES

1 (12-ounce) package semisweet chocolate morsels
¼ cup butter or margarine
1 (14-ounce) can sweetened condensed milk
1 large egg, lightly beaten
2 cups biscuit mix
1½ cups chopped pecans
1 (16-ounce) container ready-to-spread chocolate fudge frosting (optional)

• **Combine** chocolate morsels and butter in a microwave-safe bowl; microwave at HIGH 2 minutes, stirring once.
• **Stir** in condensed milk and next 3 ingredients. Spoon into a greased 13- x 9- x 2-inch pan.
• **Bake** at 350° for 25 to 30 minutes. Cool slightly on a wire rack. Spread chocolate frosting on warm brownies, if desired. Cut into squares. **Yield:** about 3 dozen.

Sharla Sparhawk
Knoxville, Tennessee

MAKE A BROWNIE VALENTINE

....

What could be sweeter than a little remembrance from your favorite junior cook? Help your child surprise a relative or sitter with this easy, edible valentine.

1. Bake Biscuit Mix Brownies (at right), but do not frost them. After letting the brownies cool, remove the uncut brownies, and place on a sheet of wax paper.

2. Cut out heart-shaped brownies with a cookie cutter (larger cutters work best).

3. Spray vegetable cooking spray on your child's hand, and dust his or her hand with cocoa.

4. Let your child press his or her hand onto a large paper plate to make a handprint. Ask him or her to write "I" and "U." Place a heart-shaped brownie between the letters to complete the message.

PUT ON A HAPPY FACE…

Planning a party isn't always easy, but these whimsical cakes lighten your load and brighten any event. In addition to the usual cake-baking gear, you'll need the following equipment: scissors and a ruler. Just follow the directions, and add a few of your own extra special touches. The rest will be child's play!

RAINY DAY FUN AND GAMES

Party Tips: Create a whole party using games as your theme. Give each guest a game card with a checklist of activities from computer-generated games to relays; ask adult friends to man each game station. For party favors, award each participant a medal.

TIC-TAC-TOE CAKE

1 (19.8-ounce) package fudge brownie mix
1 (16-ounce) container vanilla-flavored, ready-to-spread frosting
1 cherry-flavored chewy fruit roll by the foot
3 peppermint patties

• **Prepare** brownie mix according to package directions; bake in a greased and floured 8-inch square pan. Cool in pan on a wire rack. Remove from pan; place on a plate. Spread top and sides with frosting.
• **Cut** fruit roll into 2 (7-inch-long) strips and 1 (1½-inch-long) piece. Cut each 7-inch-long strip lengthwise in half, and place 2 strips horizontally on cake. Place remaining 2 strips vertically on cake. Cut the 1½-inch-long piece lengthwise evenly into 6 thin strips, and place on cake to form X's. Use peppermint patties for O's. **Yield:** one 8-inch cake.

CLOWNING AROUND BIRTHDAY PARTY

Party Tips: Try a circus theme to keep kids entertained. Buy clown noses and party hats for each guest, and play "Pin the Nose on the Clown." Invite a real clown or magician to entertain. Consider face painting, too – call your local arts group to learn how.

CLOWNING AROUND BIRTHDAY CAKE

1 (18.25-ounce) package yellow cake mix
2 (16-ounce) containers vanilla-flavored, ready-to-spread frosting
½ to 1 teaspoon green liquid food coloring
1 party hat
3 cherry-flavored chewy fruit rolls by the foot, divided
3 grape-flavored chewy fruit rolls by the foot
1 (12-inch) piece string licorice
2 gumdrops
1 red gumball

• **Prepare** cake mix according to package directions; bake in a greased and floured 13- x 9- x 2-inch pan. Cool in pan on a wire rack 10 minutes; remove from pan, and cool completely on wire rack. Spread top and sides of cake with 1 container of frosting.

• **Combine** one-half of remaining container of frosting and food coloring. (Reserve remaining frosting for another use.) Pipe frosting around edges of cake.
• **Cut** 1 party hat lengthwise in half; place on cake. Unroll 1 cherry fruit roll; remove plastic, and reroll into a 2-inch loop (see diagram). Holding loop at 1 end, insert scissors, and cut through top fold. From top, cut lengthwise into thin strips, cutting almost to opposite side, to make a pom-pom. Place under top of hat, spreading out strips.

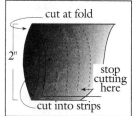

cut at fold

2"

stop cutting here

cut into strips

• **Make** 3 pom-poms for hair, with 3 grape fruit rolls, following same procedure as cherry fruit roll; place cut grape fruit rolls under hat and around face, reserving 1 grape strip for mouth.
• **Outline** face with licorice. Using 1 cherry fruit roll, cut 2 (1-inch) pieces for eyes and 1 (3-inch) oval for mouth; reserve remaining fruit roll for ruffle. Place pieces on face, adding gumdrops for eyes and grape fruit strip on mouth. Place gumball in center for nose.
• **Make** S-shaped folds for ruffle using 1 cherry fruit roll and reserved cherry fruit roll; place under face, pressing slightly into cake. **Yield:** 1 cake.

Note: To make a cake platter, cover cardboard with wrapping paper, and decorate with stickers.

Clowning Around Birthday Cake

Tic-Tac-Toe Cake

MARCH

ALL HANDS IN THE KITCHEN

Thank goodness Margaret Jones, a Birmingham, Alabama, interior designer, planned her kitchen with plenty of workspace because when her cooking club gets together, everyone gets into the act. The idea for the club, named "Dishes and Dates," arose about a year ago when Margaret became aware of two young men's dilemma: They longed for good food but didn't have the space to do "real cooking." Margaret invited them to her roomy kitchen, and the club began.

A GATHERING OF COOKS
Serves 12

Hawaiian Shrimp With Curry Sauce
Mushroom Soup
Hearts of Palm Salad With Basil-and-Garlic Dressing
Marinated Rack of Lamb
Carrot-and-Sweet Potato Puree   Masala Vegetable Medley
Soufflé au Chocolat Cointreau

HAWAIIAN SHRIMP WITH CURRY SAUCE

36 unpeeled, medium-size fresh shrimp (about 1 pound)
½ cup lemon juice
1 tablespoon curry powder
1 teaspoon salt
½ teaspoon ground ginger
2½ cups all-purpose flour, divided
2 teaspoons baking powder
1⅓ cups milk
2 cups flaked coconut
Vegetable oil
Curry Sauce

• **Peel** and devein shrimp; place in a shallow dish or a heavy-duty, zip-top plastic bag.
• **Combine** lemon juice and next 3 ingredients. Pour ¼ cup lemon juice mixture over shrimp; reserve remaining lemon juice mixture. Cover dish or seal bag, and refrigerate 1 hour, turning shrimp occasionally.
• **Combine** 2 cups flour and baking powder; stir in milk and reserved lemon juice mixture to make batter.
• **Remove** shrimp from marinade, discarding marinade. Coat shrimp in remaining ½ cup flour; dip into batter, and coat lightly with coconut.

• **Pour** oil to depth of 2 to 3 inches into a Dutch oven, and heat to 375°. Fry shrimp, a few at a time, in hot oil until golden, turning once. Drain on paper towels. Serve with Curry Sauce. **Yield:** 12 appetizer servings.

Curry Sauce

¼ cup butter or margarine
½ cup chopped onion
½ cup chopped celery
1 clove garlic
½ cup peeled, chopped Granny Smith apple
2 ounces baked ham, chopped
1 small bay leaf
1½ teaspoons finely chopped fresh parsley
⅛ teaspoon dry mustard
1 tablespoon all-purpose flour
1 teaspoon ground mace
¾ teaspoon curry powder
1 cup chicken broth

• **Melt** butter in a saucepan over medium heat. Add onion and next 7 ingredients. Cook, stirring often, 8 minutes.
• **Stir** in flour, mace, and curry powder; cook 4 minutes. Gradually add broth, stirring constantly. Reduce heat, and simmer 1 hour, stirring occasionally. Remove and discard bay leaf. **Yield:** 1½ cups.

MUSHROOM SOUP

You won't believe this recipe, filled with homemade flavor, is made from canned soups. It's good with the sherry, but we liked it even more without it.

½ cup unsalted butter
2 (8-ounce) packages fresh mushrooms, stems removed
1 large onion, sliced
2 (10¾-ounce) cans cream of mushroom soup, undiluted
2 (10½-ounce) cans beef consommé, undiluted
¼ cup dry sherry (optional)

• **Melt** butter in a large saucepan over medium-high heat. Add mushrooms

and onion; cook 5 minutes or until onions are tender, stirring often.
• **Stir** in mushroom soup and remaining ingredients, stirring often.
• **Bring** to a boil; reduce heat, and simmer 25 minutes. **Yield:** 8 cups.

HEARTS OF PALM SALAD WITH BASIL-AND-GARLIC DRESSING

2 (14-ounce) cans hearts of palm, drained and cut into ½-inch slices
2 sweet red or yellow peppers, cut into thin strips
1 pint cherry tomatoes
1 medium-size purple onion, sliced and separated into rings
5 to 6 heads Bibb lettuce
Basil-and-Garlic Dressing

• **Combine** first 4 ingredients; toss gently, and set aside.
• **Arrange** lettuce in bottom of a salad bowl or evenly on individual plates; top with vegetable mixture, and drizzle with Basil-and-Garlic Dressing. **Yield:** 12 servings.

Basil-and-Garlic Dressing

½ cup white wine vinegar
¼ cup lemon juice
8 fresh basil leaves
3 cloves garlic
¼ teaspoon salt
¼ teaspoon pepper
¾ cup olive oil

• **Combine** first 6 ingredients in container of an electric blender. With blender on high, gradually add olive oil in a slow, steady stream. Process 2 minutes. Cover and refrigerate at least 8 hours, if desired; process again before serving. **Yield:** 1½ cups.

"The best part is having someone say, 'Wait, wait! What did you put in that dish?' "
—*Madelyn Buggs*
"Dishes and Dates" member
Birmingham, Alabama

"Dishes and Dates" cooking club is a recipe for success because it's streamlined. Three couples offer their homes as locations. The host couple prepares the entrée and plans a skeleton menu. Others bring designated side dishes, and then the group experiments with wine, appetizers, and dessert.

Some of the cooks bring recipes, selecting their ideas from magazines and cookbooks. Fresh ingredients, from farmers markets, specialty food shops, or Madelyn Buggs's garden, are shown off like prized possessions.

"We're all at the same culinary level – no *real* gourmets, but nobody is a fledgling cook, either. We're all learning the same kinds of things…it's an adventure, a chance to try something new," explains Madelyn.

MARINATED RACK OF LAMB

Helen Shores Lee of Birmingham, Alabama, says her family wouldn't eat lamb until she started marinating it. Her mixture of vermouth and Dale's seasoning sauce works like magic.

4 (6- to 8-rib) lamb rib roasts, trimmed (about 8 pounds)
1 cup dry white vermouth
1 cup Dale's seasoning sauce *
3 tablespoons garlic powder
2 tablespoons dry Italian seasoning
Garnish: fresh parsley sprigs

• **Place** lamb in a large shallow dish or large, heavy-duty, zip-top plastic bags.
• **Combine** vermouth and next 3 ingredients; pour 1 cup marinade over lamb. Reserve remaining marinade; refrigerate. Cover dish or seal bags, and refrigerate 8 hours, turning lamb frequently.
• **Remove** meat from marinade, discarding marinade. Place lamb, fat side up, on a rack in a shallow roasting pan.
• **Bake** at 325° for 1 hour and 15 minutes or until a meat thermometer registers 150° (medium-rare), basting often with reserved marinade. Garnish, if desired. **Yield:** 12 servings.

* 1 cup any brand of soy sauce-based marinade may be substituted.

Note: Remove lamb from oven at 160° if you desire medium doneness.

CARROT-AND-SWEET POTATO PUREE

This colorful vegetable casserole offers an excellent reason to try fresh sweet potatoes in the spring. You can make it ahead, too.

6 large sweet potatoes (about 5¾ pounds)
1½ pounds carrots, scraped and cut into 1-inch pieces
½ cup butter or margarine, divided
1½ cups water
2 tablespoons sugar
½ teaspoon salt
½ teaspoon freshly ground black pepper
½ cup lemon low-fat yogurt
½ cup nonfat sour cream alternative
¾ teaspoon ground nutmeg
¼ teaspoon ground red pepper
Garnish: fresh mint leaves

• **Scrub** sweet potatoes, and pat dry. Prick sweet potatoes several times with a fork.
• **Microwave** at HIGH 35 to 40 minutes or until tender, rotating sweet potatoes at 10-minute intervals. Let cool to touch; peel and cut into chunks.
• **Position** knife blade in food processor bowl. Add half of sweet potatoes, and process until smooth. Transfer sweet potatoes to a large bowl, and repeat procedure. Set aside.
• **Combine** carrot, 1 tablespoon butter, and next 4 ingredients in a medium saucepan.
• **Bring** to a boil, and cook 10 to 15 minutes or until carrot is tender and liquid evaporates.
• **Position** knife blade in food processor bowl. Add carrot, remaining butter, yogurt, sour cream, nutmeg, and red pepper; process until smooth. Stir carrot mixture into sweet potatoes. Reserve 2 cups sweet potato mixture.
• **Spoon** remaining sweet potato mixture into a lightly greased 3-quart shallow casserole; pipe or dollop reserved sweet potato mixture around edges of casserole.

• **Bake** at 350° for 30 minutes or until thoroughly heated. Garnish, if desired. **Yield:** 12 to 14 servings.

Note: To make ahead, assemble casserole; cover and refrigerate. Remove from refrigerator, and let stand 30 minutes. Bake at 350° for 45 minutes or until thoroughly heated.

MASALA VEGETABLE MEDLEY

This dish's name comes from the Indian spice blend garam masala, made from spices, including black pepper, cinnamon, cloves, coriander, cumin, mace, nutmeg, and dried chiles.

1 bunch broccoli, cut into flowerets
1 small yellow squash, sliced
1 small zucchini, sliced
1 sweet red pepper, sliced
1 large onion, sliced
2 tablespoons basil-flavored olive oil or olive oil
2 tablespoons lemon juice
2 teaspoons garam masala seasoning *
½ teaspoon salt
¼ pound fresh snow pea pods, trimmed (about 1 cup)

• **Cook** first 5 ingredients in oil in a Dutch oven over medium-high heat 2 minutes, stirring often.
• **Stir** in lemon juice and remaining ingredients. Cover, reduce heat, and cook 5 to 8 minutes or until vegetables are tender. **Yield:** 12 servings.

* 2 teaspoons curry powder may be substituted.

SOUFFLÉ AU CHOCOLAT COINTREAU

Bill Gilchrist of Birmingham, Alabama, prefers to whip egg whites by hand, but this recipe works just fine with a mixer, too. You can cut this recipe in half to serve six.

Butter or margarine
2 tablespoons sugar
¼ cup butter or margarine
1 (12-ounce) package semisweet chocolate morsels
¼ cup Cointreau or other orange-flavored liqueur
12 large eggs, separated
1½ cups sifted powdered sugar
1 teaspoon ground cinnamon
1 teaspoon cream of tartar
Powdered sugar
Chocolate Cream
Garnish: orange rind strips

• **Cut** a piece of aluminum foil long enough to fit around a 2¾-quart soufflé dish or straight-sided casserole, allowing a 1-inch overlap; starting from 1 long side, fold foil into thirds. Lightly butter 1 side of foil and dish. Wrap foil around outside of dish, buttered side against dish, allowing it to extend 3 inches above rim to form a collar; secure with string or masking tape. Add 2 tablespoons sugar, tilting prepared dish to coat sides. Set aside.
• **Combine** ¼ cup butter and chocolate morsels in top of a double boiler; bring water to a boil. Reduce heat to low; cook until chocolate and butter melt, stirring often. Remove from water; cool 5 minutes. Stir in Cointreau. Set aside.
• **Beat** egg yolks; gradually add powdered sugar, beating until mixture is thick and pale. Stir in cinnamon and chocolate mixture. Set aside.
• **Beat** egg whites and cream of tartar in a large mixing bowl at high speed with an electric mixer until stiff peaks form. Gently stir 1½ cups egg white mixture into chocolate mixture.
• **Fold** remaining egg white mixture into chocolate mixture. Pour into prepared dish.
• **Bake** at 375° for 50 to 55 minutes. Sprinkle with powdered sugar, and

remove collar. Serve immediately with Chocolate Cream. Garnish, if desired. **Yield:** 12 servings.

Chocolate Cream

1 cup whipping cream
1 tablespoon sifted powdered sugar
1½ teaspoons cocoa

● **Beat** all ingredients at medium speed with an electric mixer until soft peaks form. **Yield:** 2 cups.

NEW POSSIBILITIES WITH PORK

When pork tenderloin steps in to replace veal cutlets in these quick-to-make familiar entrées, dinner is as easy on the pocketbook as it is on the cook. You'll delight your family and friends with these classic Italian-style dishes that cost a fraction of their traditional veal counterparts.

PORK SCALOPPINE MARSALA

2 (¾-pound) pork tenderloins
½ cup all-purpose flour
¼ cup butter or margarine, divided
1⅓ cups dry Marsala *
2 teaspoons beef-flavored bouillon granules
⅛ teaspoon freshly ground pepper
Hot cooked rice

● **Cut** each tenderloin into 6 (2-ounce) medaillons. Place cut side down, between 2 sheets of heavy-duty plastic wrap; flatten to ¼-inch thickness, using a meat mallet or rolling pin.
● **Dredge** pork in flour. Cook half of pork medaillons in 2 tablespoons

butter in a large skillet over medium heat about 2 minutes on each side or until pork medaillons are lightly browned. Remove from skillet; keep warm. Repeat procedure with remaining butter and pork medaillons. Pour off excess butter, if necessary, leaving pan drippings.
● **Add** Marsala, bouillon granules, and pepper to skillet. Simmer mixture 3 to 4 minutes.
● **Return** pork medaillons to skillet; cover and simmer 2 minutes. Serve with rice. **Yield:** 6 servings.

* 1¼ cups dry white wine plus 2 tablespoons brandy may be substituted.

Mike Singleton
Memphis, Tennessee

EASY PORK PARMIGIANA

1 large egg
1 tablespoon water
2 tablespoons grated Parmesan cheese
⅓ cup Italian-seasoned breadcrumbs
4 (1¼-inch-thick) slices pork tenderloin (about 8 ounces)
2 tablespoons vegetable oil
1 cup commercial spaghetti sauce
½ cup (2 ounces) shredded mozzarella cheese

● **Combine** egg and water; set aside.
● **Combine** Parmesan cheese and breadcrumbs; set aside.
● **Place** each piece of pork between 2 sheets of heavy-duty plastic wrap; flatten to ¼-inch thickness, using a meat mallet or rolling pin.
● **Dip** pork in egg mixture, and dredge in crumb mixture.
● **Cook** pork slices in oil in a large skillet over medium heat just until browned, turning once. Arrange pork in a lightly greased 8-inch square baking dish; top with spaghetti sauce.
● **Bake** at 350° for 25 minutes; top with mozzarella cheese. Bake 5 additional minutes. **Yield:** 4 servings.

Linda H. Sutton
Winston-Salem, North Carolina

PORK PICCATA

2 (¾-pound) pork tenderloins
½ cup all-purpose flour
½ teaspoon salt
¼ teaspoon pepper
3 tablespoons olive oil
½ cup Chablis or other dry white wine
½ cup lemon juice
3 tablespoons butter or margarine
¼ cup chopped fresh parsley
1½ tablespoons capers
Hot cooked fettuccine
Garnishes: lemon slices, fresh parsley sprigs

● **Cut** each tenderloin into 6 (2-ounce) medaillons. Place, cut side down, between 2 sheets of heavy-duty plastic wrap; flatten to ¼-inch thickness, using a meat mallet or rolling pin.
● **Combine** flour, salt, and pepper; dredge pork in flour mixture.
● **Cook** half of pork in 1½ tablespoons olive oil in a large skillet over medium heat about 2 minutes on each side or until lightly browned. Remove from skillet; keep warm. Repeat procedure.
● **Add** wine and lemon juice to skillet; cook until thoroughly heated. Add butter, chopped parsley, and capers, stirring until butter melts.
● **Arrange** pork over pasta; drizzle with wine mixture. Garnish, if desired. Serve immediately. **Yield:** 6 servings.

PORK NOTES

■ Overcooking pork is not necessary to ensure its wholesomeness. Pork is best cooked to an internal temperature of 160°.

■ Cut pork and other meats diagonally across the grain for tenderness and appearance.

■ Wash meat grinders and cutting boards thoroughly after each use to prevent cross-contamination.

CAMEO CAKE: A CLASSIC CREATION

If ever there was a cake so irresistible, so rich and creamy, and,

oh, so good, it's this one. White chocolate and toasted pecans mix

together for a dessert that looks as if it requires hours in the

kitchen, but it doesn't. To delight the eye, as well as the taste buds, accent

your cake with homemade crystallized violas, shaved white chocolate,

or pecans. We tell you how to create these easy, festive looks suitable for any

occasion in "From Our Kitchen to Yours" on facing page.

top and sides of cake. Store in refrigerator. Garnish, if desired. **Yield:** one 3-layer cake.

White Chocolate-Cream Cheese Frosting

1 (4-ounce) bar white chocolate *
1 (8-ounce) package cream cheese, softened
1 (3-ounce) package cream cheese, softened
⅓ cup butter or margarine, softened
6½ cups sifted powdered sugar
1½ teaspoons vanilla extract

• **Melt** chocolate in a heavy saucepan over low heat, stirring constantly. Remove from heat; cool 10 minutes, stirring occasionally.
• **Beat** cream cheese and butter at medium speed with an electric mixer until creamy. Gradually add chocolate, beating constantly until blended. Gradually add powdered sugar, beating until smooth. Stir in vanilla. **Yield:** about 5 cups.

* For the white chocolate, we used Ghirardelli.

CAMEO CAKE
(pictured on page 4)

1½ cups butter
¾ cup water
1 (4-ounce) bar white chocolate, broken into pieces *
1½ cups buttermilk
4 large eggs, lightly beaten
1½ teaspoons vanilla extract
3½ cups all-purpose flour, divided
1 cup chopped pecans, toasted
2¼ cups sugar
1½ teaspoons baking soda
White Chocolate-Cream Cheese Frosting
Garnishes: crystallized violas with leaves, shaved white chocolate, or toasted chopped pecans

• **Combine** butter and water in a medium saucepan; bring to a boil over medium heat, stirring occasionally. Remove from heat. Add white chocolate, stirring until chocolate melts. Stir in buttermilk, eggs, and vanilla; set aside.
• **Combine** ½ cup flour and 1 cup pecans, stirring to coat; set aside.
• **Combine** remaining 3 cups flour, sugar, and soda in a large bowl; gradually stir in white chocolate mixture. Fold in pecan mixture. (Batter will be thin.) Pour into 3 greased and floured 9-inch round cakepans.
• **Bake** at 350° for 20 to 25 minutes or until a wooden pick inserted in center comes out clean. Cool in pans on wire racks 10 minutes; remove from pans, and let cool completely on wire racks.
• **Spread** White Chocolate-Cream Cheese Frosting between layers and on

WHITE CHOCOLATE TIPS

. . . .

■ Use quality, well-known brands of white chocolate for your recipes. Traditionally, white chocolate contains cocoa butter but no cocoa solids; however, at the present time, there isn't an official labeling standard.

■ Melt white chocolate over low heat, stirring constantly.

■ Caution: Overheating white chocolate may cause loss of flavor and a coarse, grainy texture.

FROM OUR KITCHEN TO YOURS

The need for a simple cake with quick decorating ideas led us to develop our Cameo Cake (on facing page).

Why use a cake mix if you can make a cake from scratch in almost the same time? We deviated from the standard cake-making method and simplified the procedure.

To top off this cake, we created easy, fabulous finishes. Our techniques produced such great results that we also designed a wedding cake from the classic recipe (beginning on page 124).

CHOPPED PECAN COATING

To coat the sides of cake with chopped pecans, place the first layer on a 9-inch cardboard cake circle covered with frosting. Spread frosting between layers, and place 3 long wooden picks or skewers into cake to hold layers together. Frost sides; chill 30 minutes. Spread toasted chopped pecans on wax paper. Carefully hold cake on the top and bottom, and roll frosted sides in pecans, being careful not to rest cake on pecans. (Frosting may stick to wax paper.) Remove wooden picks, and spread frosting on top. (Pecans may also be added by scooping nuts into the palm of your hand and pressing them up against the sides of the cake, allowing the excess to fall.)

CRYSTALLIZED FLOWERS

To crystallize edible flowers, such as violas or roses, brush petals lightly with lemon juice. Using a small wire-mesh strainer, sprinkle petals with superfine sugar. (Superfine sugar is more finely granulated than regular sugar.) Let flowers dry, and store at room temperature up to 8 hours. Do not refrigerate. (Crystallized flowers, such as violets and pansies, can be purchased ready-made; however, they are easy to make for a fraction of the cost.)

SHAVED WHITE CHOCOLATE

To achieve the white chocolate shavings pattern, use this stencil technique. Cut 4 strips of wax paper longer than the width of the cake. Frost cake on top and sides, and arrange the wax paper strips at evenly spaced intervals across the top of the cake; set aside. Prepare shavings by drawing a vegetable peeler across the long edge of a white chocolate bar. Sprinkle shavings onto exposed frosting on top of cake; carefully remove wax paper strips.

MOTHER NATURE'S YEAR-ROUND FRUIT TREATS

This time of year when your favorite fruits aren't in season, here's a solution to this unseasonal dilemma: dried fruits.

As snacks, they deliver a burst of concentrated flavor. And in these recipes, most of the fruits reconstitute to a product similar to fresh. Until apricots and cherries ripen again, these will do just fine.

DRIED CHERRY MUFFINS

½ cup unsalted butter or margarine, softened
¾ cup sugar
2 large eggs
2 teaspoons grated lemon rind
2 tablespoons lemon juice
2 cups all-purpose flour
1 teaspoon baking soda
½ teaspoon salt
1 cup buttermilk
⅔ cup chopped dried cherries
½ cup chopped walnuts

● **Beat** butter at medium speed with an electric mixer until creamy; gradually add sugar, beating well. Add eggs, one at a time, beating after each addition. Stir in lemon rind and juice.
● **Combine** flour, soda, and salt; add to butter mixture alternately with buttermilk, beginning and ending with flour mixture. Stir just until blended after each addition. Gently stir in cherries and walnuts.
● **Spoon** batter into lightly greased muffin pans, filling three-fourths full.
● **Bake** at 400° for 20 minutes or until lightly browned. Remove from pans immediately. **Yield:** 15 muffins.

Gwen Louer
Roswell, Georgia

MIXED FRUIT CUP

1 (11-ounce) can mandarin
   oranges, drained
1 Red Delicious apple, finely
   chopped
1 cup golden raisins
⅔ cup pitted prunes, cut into
   quarters (14 prunes)
½ cup dried apricot halves, cut
   into quarters (14 halves)
⅓ cup orange juice
¼ cup apricot brandy (optional)
¼ cup honey
2 tablespoons lemon juice
¼ teaspoon ground cinnamon

• **Combine** first 5 ingredients in a
medium bowl; set aside.
• **Combine** orange juice and remaining
ingredients; pour over fruit. Cover and
refrigerate 8 hours. **Yield:** 6 to 8
servings.

Charlotte Moret
St. Louis, Missouri

ORANGE-DATE CAKE

1 cup butter or margarine,
   softened
2 cups sugar
4 large eggs
4 cups all-purpose flour, divided
1 teaspoon baking soda
½ teaspoon salt
1⅓ cups buttermilk
1½ tablespoons grated orange
   rind, divided
1 cup chopped pecans
1 cup chopped dates
1 cup sugar
½ cup orange juice

• **Beat** butter at medium speed with an
electric mixer about 2 minutes or until
creamy. Gradually add 2 cups sugar,
beating at medium speed 5 to 7 minutes. Add eggs, one at a time, beating
just until yellow disappears.
• **Combine** 3¾ cups flour, soda, and
salt; add to butter mixture alternately
with buttermilk, beginning and ending
with flour mixture. Mix at low speed
just until blended after each addition.
Stir in 1 tablespoon orange rind.

• **Combine** pecans, dates, and remaining ¼ cup flour; stir into batter.
• **Spoon** batter into a greased and
floured 10-inch tube pan.
• **Bake** at 325° for 1½ hours or until a
wooden pick inserted in center comes
out clean.
• **Combine** 1 cup sugar, orange juice,
and remaining ½ tablespoon orange
rind in a small saucepan; cook over
medium heat, stirring constantly, until
sugar dissolves.
• **Pour** glaze over warm cake; cool in
pan on a wire rack 15 minutes. Remove from pan; let cool completely on
wire rack. **Yield:** one 10-inch cake.

Mrs. Carl W. Terry
Huntsville, Alabama

APRICOT-APPLE CRUMB TART

2 (6-ounce) packages dried
   apricot halves
1 (8-ounce) package dried apples *
3 cups water
¼ cup sugar
1 tablespoon all-purpose flour
½ (15-ounce) package refrigerated
   piecrusts
1 teaspoon all-purpose flour
½ cup all-purpose flour
½ cup sugar
¼ cup butter or margarine
Ice cream or sweetened whipped
   cream

• **Combine** first 3 ingredients in a large
saucepan; bring mixture to a boil. Reduce heat, and simmer 30 minutes.
Drain well.
• **Combine** ¼ cup sugar and 1 tablespoon flour; stir into fruit mixture. Set
aside.
• **Unroll** pie crust, and press out fold
lines. Fit into bottom and up sides of a
9-inch tart pan, sprinkle with 1 teaspoon flour. Spoon fruit mixture into
prepared pastry shell.
• **Combine** ½ cup flour and ½ cup
sugar; cut in butter with pastry blender
until mixture is crumbly. Sprinkle mixture over tart.
• **Bake** at 425° for 10 minutes; reduce
temperature to 350°, and bake 35
minutes or until lightly browned.

Serve within 12 hours with ice cream
or sweetened whipped cream, if desired. **Yield:** one 9-inch tart.

* 1 (6-ounce) package dried apricot
halves may be substituted for a tarter
dessert.

Mrs. Carl M. Schmieg
Annandale, Virginia

PEANUT BUTTER-FRUIT PIZZA

1 (20-ounce) package refrigerated
   sliceable peanut butter cookie
   dough
1 (8-ounce) container cream
   cheese with pineapple
1 (5.4-ounce) package dried fruit
   snack mix
½ cup flaked coconut
1½ cups miniature marshmallows

• **Press** cookie dough evenly into an
ungreased 12-inch pizza pan.
• **Bake** at 350° for 20 to 22 minutes or
until done. Cool 5 minutes.
• **Spread** crust gently with cream
cheese, and sprinkle with fruit mix, coconut, and marshmallows.
• **Bake** 8 additional minutes or until
marshmallows are lightly browned.
Cool on a wire rack. **Yield:** 1 (12-
inch) pizza.

■ Fried pies made from dried or
fresh fruits are as Southern as fried
chicken. The Fried Apple Pies recipe is
traditional, while the recipe for Special
Apricot Pies is an easy baked version.

SPECIAL APRICOT PIES

1 (6-ounce) package dried apricot
   halves
¾ cup water
½ teaspoon ground nutmeg
½ teaspoon vanilla extract
½ cup butter or margarine,
   softened
4 ounces cream cheese, softened
1½ cups all-purpose flour
½ teaspoon salt
Glaze

- **Position** knife blade in food processor bowl; add apricots. Process until finely chopped.
- **Combine** apricots and next 3 ingredients in a small saucepan; cook over medium heat, stirring constantly, 5 minutes. Set aside.
- **Beat** butter and cream cheese at medium speed with an electric mixer until creamy. Add flour and salt, beating mixture at low speed until dough forms a ball.
- **Roll** dough to ⅛-inch thickness on a lightly floured surface. Cut into 2½-inch circles.
- **Place** about 1 teaspoon apricot mixture on half of each circle. Moisten edges with water; fold dough over apricot mixture, pressing edges to seal. Crimp edges with a fork, and prick top of each pie; place on ungreased baking sheets. Bake pies at 350° for 18 minutes or until lightly browned. Remove to wire racks; brush with Glaze. **Yield:** 3 dozen.

Glaze

1 cup sifted powdered sugar
1½ tablespoons milk
½ teaspoon vanilla extract
¼ teaspoon butter-flavored extract

- **Combine** all ingredients in a small bowl. **Yield:** ⅓ cup.

Carol Barclay
Portland, Texas

FRIED APPLE PIES

1½ cups sliced dried apples
2 cups water
1 tablespoon butter or margarine
½ cup sugar
¾ teaspoon ground cinnamon
½ teaspoon ground nutmeg
2 cups all-purpose flour
½ teaspoon salt
½ cup shortening
¼ to ½ cup milk
Vegetable oil
Sifted powdered sugar

- **Combine** apples and water in a medium saucepan; bring to a boil.

Reduce heat, and simmer, uncovered, 30 minutes or until apples are soft and liquid evaporates.
- **Mash** mixture with a fork. Stir in butter and next 3 ingredients; set apple mixture aside.
- **Combine** flour and salt; cut in shortening with pastry blender until mixture is crumbly. Sprinkle milk, 1 tablespoon at a time, evenly over surface; stir with a fork until dry ingredients are moistened.
- **Divide** pastry into 6 portions. Roll each portion to ⅛-inch thickness on a lightly floured surface, and cut each into a 6-inch circle.
- **Spoon** one-sixth of apple mixture on half of each circle. Moisten edges with water; fold dough over apple mixture, pressing edges to seal. Crimp edges with a fork.
- **Pour** oil to depth of ½ inch into a large heavy skillet. Fry pies in hot oil over medium-high heat until golden brown, turning once. Drain well on paper towels. Sprinkle with powdered sugar. **Yield:** 6 pies.

Mrs. Denver W. Anderson
Eva, Tennessee

APPLAUDING THE ARTICHOKE

You've seen artichokes in the produce bins: cactus green globes with scaly leaves and prickly tips. But this formidable vegetable is only *dressed* in one of nature's scariest disguises. Cooked artichoke leaves are soft and sweet. And deep inside the jagged exterior lies a soft heart with a nutty sweetness.

WHOLE COOKED ARTICHOKES

4 artichokes
Lemon wedge
3 tablespoons lemon juice

- **Hold** artichokes by stem, and wash by plunging them up and down in cold water. Cut off stem end, and trim about ½ inch from top of each artichoke. Remove any loose bottom leaves. With scissors, trim approximately one-fourth off the top of each outer leaf, and rub top and edges of leaves with lemon wedge to prevent discoloration.
- **Place** artichokes in a large stainless steel Dutch oven; cover with water, and add lemon juice.
- **Bring** to a boil; cover, reduce heat, and simmer 35 minutes or until lower leaves pull out easily. Drain and serve with desired sauce. **Yield:** 4 servings.

BAKED ARTICHOKE-CHEESE BOTTOMS

4 large Whole Cooked Artichokes (see recipe)
2 tablespoons olive oil
1 (4-ounce) container garlic-and-herb soft spreadable cheese
3 tablespoons whipping cream
2 tablespoons Italian-seasoned breadcrumbs

- **Remove** outer leaves of artichokes. (Reserve leaves for another use.) Gently spread leaves apart to reach center; scrape out fuzzy thistle (choke) with a spoon and discard. Remove remaining leaves, and place artichoke bottoms in a small bowl and drizzle with olive oil, turning to coat. Drain artichoke bottoms, reserving olive oil.
- **Combine** cheese and whipping cream. Spoon equally on artichoke bottoms; sprinkle with Italian-seasoned breadcrumbs. Place in a small baking dish. Drizzle with reserved olive oil. Bake at 450° for 10 minutes or until hot. **Yield:** 4 appetizer servings.

Ivy Trippeer
Germantown, Tennessee

SHRIMP STUFFED ARTICHOKES

4 large Whole Cooked Artichokes
   (see recipe on page 61)
3 tablespoons red wine vinegar
½ teaspoon prepared mustard
¼ teaspoon pepper
5 cups water
1 pound unpeeled, medium-size
   fresh shrimp
⅓ cup whipping cream
3 tablespoons mayonnaise
2 tomatoes, chopped
Endive
Garnishes: hard-cooked egg
   wedges, sweet red pepper strips

• **Spread** artichokes leaves apart to reach center; scrape out fuzzy thistle (choke) with a spoon, and discard. Place artichokes in a shallow dish; set aside.
• **Combine** red wine vinegar, mustard, and pepper; spoon into center of artichokes, and refrigerate 30 minutes.
• **Bring** 5 cups water to a boil; add shrimp, and cook 3 to 5 minutes or until shrimp turn pink. Drain well; rinse with cold water. Peel shrimp, and devein, if desired; cut each in half, and set aside.
• **Beat** whipping cream at medium speed with an electric mixer until soft peaks form; gradually add mayonnaise, beating until stiff peaks form.
• **Drain** vinegar mixture from artichokes, reserving vinegar mixture; fold vinegar mixture into whipped cream mixture. Fold in shrimp and tomato. Spoon into center of artichokes, and place on endive-lined plates. Garnish, if desired. **Yield:** 4 servings.

Mike Singleton
Memphis, Tennessee

HERBED CAPER BUTTER

½ cup butter
2 tablespoons chopped capers
½ teaspoon dried Italian seasoning

• **Melt** butter in a small saucepan over low heat; stir in capers and Italian seasoning. Serve warm with cooked artichokes. **Yield:** ½ cup.

CHIVE-CHEESE DIP

1 (8-ounce) container soft cream
   cheese with chives and onions
¼ cup grated Parmesan cheese
¼ cup milk
1 tablespoon lemon juice

• **Position** knife blade in food processor bowl. Add all ingredients, and process 30 seconds or until smooth, stopping once to scrape down sides. Serve with cooked artichokes **Yield:** 1½ cups.

ARTICHOKE CREAM SOUP

6 artichokes
1 lemon, sliced
1 teaspoon salt
1 quart chicken broth
½ cup butter or margarine
1 onion, finely chopped
½ cup chopped celery
1 tablespoon minced garlic
2 cups Chablis or other dry white
   wine
1 quart whipping cream
⅛ teaspoon seasoned salt
¼ teaspoon freshly ground
   pepper
Garnishes: Pumpernickel Croutons,
   peeled tomato strips

• **Wash** artichokes by plunging them up and down in cold water. Cut off stem end, and trim about ½ inch from top of each artichoke. Remove and discard any loose bottom leaves.
• **Place** artichokes in a large stainless steel Dutch oven; cover with water, and add lemon and 1 teaspoon salt.
• **Bring** to a boil; cover, reduce heat, and simmer 35 minutes. Drain well.
• **Remove** outer green leaves from artichokes; set aside. Gently spread remaining yellow leaves apart to reach center; remove fuzzy thistle (choke) with a spoon, and discard. Cut off yellow leaves, leaving artichoke bottoms intact. Set aside leaves, and finely chop artichoke bottoms; set chopped artichoke bottoms aside.
• **Combine** green and yellow artichoke leaves and chicken broth. Bring to a

boil; cover, reduce heat, and simmer 40 minutes.
• **Pour** broth mixture through a large, fine wire-mesh strainer into a container, discarding solids; set artichoke stock aside.
• **Melt** butter in a Dutch oven over medium-high heat; add onion, celery, and garlic, and cook, stirring constantly, 10 minutes or until tender.
• **Add** chopped artichoke bottoms and wine; cook over medium heat about 2 minutes. Add artichoke stock, and cook over low heat 20 minutes, stirring occasionally.
• **Pour** half of broth mixture into container of an electric blender; process until smooth, stopping once to scrape down sides. Pour mixture into a large bowl. Repeat procedure with remaining mixture; return all mixture to Dutch oven. Add whipping cream, seasoned salt, and pepper; cook over low heat until thoroughly heated. Garnish, if desired. **Yield:** 9 cups.

Pumpernickel Croutons

4 slices dark pumpernickel bread

• **Cut** bread into desired shapes; place on a baking sheet.
• **Bake** at 325° for 20 minutes or until crisp. **Yield:** 1 cup.

ARTICHOKE TIPS

■ Purchase fresh artichokes at their peak – from March through May. Size is not an indication of quality.

■ Select artichokes with tightly closed leaves. Avoid buying artichokes that have brown leaves or show signs of mold. Leaves that are separated are a sign of age and will be tough and bitter.

■ Do not cook artichokes in aluminum pots as they tend to turn the pots a grayish color.

SASSY SPINACH SALADS

As a Southern salad mainstay, fresh spinach is certainly an esteemed green.

These leafy emeralds glisten with exceptional yet simple dressings, from robust chili-lime to gentle apricot. Crunch comes from toasted nuts, crisp bacon, and icy jicama. So toss them, serve them up, and enjoy.

SPINACH SALAD WITH CHILI-LIME DRESSING

1 pound fresh spinach or
   1 (10-ounce) package fresh
   spinach
1 avocado, peeled and cubed
1 small jicama, peeled and cut into
   thin strips (optional)
¼ cup safflower or vegetable
   oil
2 tablespoons lime juice
2 cloves garlic, minced
1 teaspoon chili powder
½ teaspoon sugar
¼ teaspoon salt
¼ teaspoon ground cumin
½ cup sunflower kernels

• **Remove** stems from spinach; wash leaves thoroughly, and pat dry. Tear into bite-size pieces.
• **Combine** spinach, avocado, and jicama strips, if desired, in a large bowl; set aside.
• **Combine** oil and next 6 ingredients in a jar; cover tightly, and shake mixture vigorously.
• **Drizzle** dressing over salad, and toss gently to coat; sprinkle with sunflower kernels. Serve immediately. **Yield:** 6 to 8 servings.

Note: Sprinkle cut avocado with lemon juice or lime juice to prevent browning.

MINTED SPINACH SALAD

1 pound fresh spinach or 1 (10-
   ounce) package fresh spinach
1 (11-ounce) can mandarin
   oranges, drained
½ cup loosely packed edible
   nasturtiums or snapdragons
2 tablespoons lemon juice
2 tablespoons lime juice
2 tablespoons mint jelly
2 tablespoons vegetable oil
1½ tablespoons brown sugar
¼ teaspoon grated lemon rind

• **Remove** stems from spinach; wash leaves thoroughly, and pat dry. Tear into bite-size pieces.
• **Combine** spinach, oranges, and flowers in a large bowl; set aside.
• **Combine** lemon juice and next 5 ingredients in a jar; cover tightly, and shake vigorously.
• **Drizzle** dressing over salad, and toss gently. Serve immediately. **Yield:** 6 servings.

Kate Perry
Baton Rouge, Louisiana

A BOUQUET FOR THE SALAD BOWL

Edible flowers rest as rightfully as carrots in produce markets today. There's no real trick to serving pretty flowers as colorful garnishes as in the spinach salad above, but here are a couple of pointers.

■ Common edible flowers include nasturtiums, snapdragons, rose petals, pansies, violets, pinks, honeysuckle, and daylilies.

■ Be sure the edible flowers haven't been sprayed with any chemicals. Select flowers in the produce section of supermarkets labeled edible or use those grown in your own garden.

SPINACH-APRICOT SALAD

1 cup boiling water
1 (6-ounce) package dried
   apricot halves
1 pound fresh spinach or 1
   (10-ounce) package fresh
   spinach
3 tablespoons cider vinegar
3 tablespoons apricot
   preserves
½ cup vegetable oil
¾ cup coarsely chopped
   macadamia nuts, toasted

• **Pour** boiling water over apricots; let stand 30 minutes. Drain well; set aside.
• **Remove** stems from spinach; wash leaves thoroughly, and pat dry. Tear into bite-size pieces. Set aside.
• **Combine** vinegar and preserves in container of an electric blender; process until smooth, stopping once to scrape down sides. With blender on high, gradually add oil in a slow, steady stream.
• **Combine** spinach, half of apricots, half of nuts, and dressing, and toss gently. Sprinkle with remaining apricots and nuts. Serve immediately. **Yield:** 8 servings.

SPINACH-RICE SALAD

1 cup long-grain rice,
   uncooked
½ cup Italian salad dressing
1 tablespoon soy sauce
½ teaspoon sugar
2 cups shredded fresh spinach
½ cup sliced celery
½ cup sliced green onions
6 slices bacon, cooked and
   crumbled

• **Cook** rice according to package directions; rinse and drain. Set aside.
• **Combine** salad dressing, soy sauce, and sugar in a large bowl. Stir in rice. Cover and chill 2 hours.
• **Stir** spinach and remaining ingredients into rice mixture. Serve immediately. **Yield:** 6 to 8 servings.

Nancy Bremer
Fallston, Maryland

MARINARA MAGIC

Make the Marinara Sauce in half an hour tonight, and you'll have a head start on two nights' quick meals, plus leftover sauce to use in other recipes. For added variety, try the versatile sauce in appetizers and chicken dishes.

MARINARA SAUCE

½ cup chopped onion
2 cloves garlic, pressed
1 tablespoon olive oil
4 (14½-ounce) cans tomatoes, drained and chopped
2 tablespoons lemon juice
1 tablespoon dried Italian seasoning
2 bay leaves

● **Cook** onion and garlic in olive oil in a Dutch oven over medium-high heat, stirring constantly, until tender. Add tomatoes and remaining ingredients.
● **Bring** mixture to a boil; reduce heat to medium, and cook 20 minutes or until most of liquid evaporates, stirring occasionally.
● **Remove** and discard bay leaves. **Yield:** 5 cups.

NIGHT 1

BOW-TIE WITH MARINARA

4 to 8 ounces bow-tie pasta, cooked
1 to 2 cups Marinara Sauce (see recipe)
Freshly grated Parmesan cheese

● **Combine** pasta and sauce; sprinkle with cheese. **Yield:** 2 servings.

NIGHT 2

GRILLED CHICKEN-PASTA SALAD

4 ounces bow-tie pasta, cooked without salt
½ cup Italian salad dressing, divided
2 skinned and boned chicken breast halves
½ small cucumber
1 cup Marinara Sauce, chilled (see recipe)

● **Combine** pasta and 2 tablespoons salad dressing in a bowl, and toss gently. Cover pasta mixture, and chill at least 8 hours.
● **Place** chicken in a small baking dish; drizzle with remaining salad dressing, turning to coat. Cover and chill 2 hours.
● **Cut** cucumber half crosswise into 2 equal portions. Peel and chop 1 portion of cucumber; cut remaining portion into thin strips, and set aside. Stir chopped cucumber into Marinara Sauce, and set aside.
● **Drain** chicken breasts; cook, without grill lid, over hot coals (450° to 500°) for 5 to 7 minutes on each side or until chicken is done.
● **Arrange** pasta on individual salad plates; spoon sauce over pasta, and top with chicken breasts and cucumber strips. **Yield:** 2 servings.

A LITTLE LEFT OVER...

HOMEMADE COWBOY CAVIAR
(pictured on page 75)

1 medium eggplant, peeled and cubed
2 tablespoons olive oil
1½ cups Marinara Sauce (see recipe)
1 (16-ounce) bottle chunky picante sauce (1½ cups)

● **Cook** eggplant in oil in a nonstick skillet over medium-high heat 10 minutes, stirring often.
● **Stir** in Marinara Sauce and picante sauce; cook until heated. Serve chilled or at room temperature with corn chips. **Yield:** 4 cups.

Fran Pointer
Kansas City, Missouri

MARINARA VINAIGRETTE

1 cup chilled Marinara Sauce (see recipe)
1 clove garlic, minced
⅓ cup red wine vinegar
⅓ cup olive oil

● **Combine** all ingredients in container of an electric blender; process until smooth, stopping once to scrape down sides. Cover and chill. Serve with salad greens. **Yield:** 1¾ cups.

QUICK SPAGHETTI AND MEAT SAUCE

½ pound ground beef
1½ cups Marinara Sauce (see recipe)
Hot cooked spaghetti or linguine
2 tablespoons grated Parmesan cheese

● **Brown** beef in a skillet, stirring until it crumbles. Drain; return to skillet.
● **Stir** in Marinara Sauce; cook over medium heat 5 minutes. Serve over pasta, and sprinkle with cheese. **Yield:** 2 servings.

Nora Henshaw
Okemah, Oklahoma

CHICKEN PARMIGIANA SANDWICH

4   skinned and boned chicken
        breast halves
½   cup milk
⅓   cup Italian-seasoned
        breadcrumbs
2   tablespoons olive oil
4   slices mozzarella cheese
2   cups Marinara Sauce (see recipe
        on facing page)
4   (6- to 7-inch) French bread rolls,
        sliced lengthwise and toasted

• **Dip** chicken in milk; dredge in bread-crumbs. Set chicken aside.
• **Heat** oil in a skillet over medium heat until hot; add chicken, and cook 4 minutes on each side or until golden brown. Remove skillet from heat.
• **Top** each chicken breast with a slice of mozzarella cheese; cover, and let stand 5 minutes or until cheese melts.
• **Cook** Marinara Sauce in a saucepan until thoroughly heated.
• **Place** chicken breasts on bottom halves of rolls; spoon half of sauce over chicken, and place top halves of rolls over sauce. Serve with remaining sauce. **Yield:** 4 servings.

BAKED ZITI

1   (16-ounce) package ziti
1   pound mild Italian sausage
½   pound ground beef
½   cup chopped onion
3   cups Marinara Sauce (see recipe
        on facing page)
1   (16-ounce) package sliced
        mozzarella cheese
¼   cup grated Parmesan cheese

• **Cook** pasta according to package directions; drain and set aside.
• **Remove** sausage from casing. Cook sausage, beef, and onion in a skillet over medium heat, stirring until meat crumbles. Drain and return to skillet.
• **Stir** Marinara Sauce and ziti into meat mixture. Layer half each of ziti mixture and mozzarella cheese in a lightly greased 13- x 9- x 2-inch baking dish. Spoon remaining ziti mixture over mozzarella cheese; cover with foil.

• **Bake** at 350° for 15 minutes. Remove foil; add remaining mozzarella cheese, and sprinkle with Parmesan cheese. Bake 10 additional minutes. **Yield:** 8 to 10 servings.

Nancy Banks
Atlanta, Georgia

FOCUS ON FOCACCIA

....

Focaccia (foh-CAH-chee-ah), a fragrant bread that's the kissing cousin to pizza, is rising in popularity. Dried Tomato Focaccia is so good that we prepared it several ways.

DRIED TOMATO FOCACCIA

10   pieces dried tomatoes
         (about ⅓ cup)
½   cup boiling water
1   cup milk
2   tablespoons butter or margarine
3½ to 4 cups bread flour, divided
2   packages active dry yeast
2   tablespoons sugar
2   teaspoons salt
1   large egg
3   tablespoons dried chopped
         chives *
¼   cup olive oil
¼   teaspoon dried oregano *
¼   teaspoon dried rosemary *

• **Combine** tomatoes and boiling water in a small saucepan; let stand 30 minutes.
• **Remove** tomatoes, reserving liquid; finely chop tomatoes, using kitchen shears, and set aside.
• **Stir** milk and butter into reserved liquid, and heat until mixture reaches 120° to 130°.
• **Combine** 1½ cups flour and next 3 ingredients in a large mixing bowl. Gradually add liquid mixture to flour mixture, beating at low speed with an electric mixer. Add egg, and beat 3

minutes at medium speed. Stir in tomatoes, chives, and enough remaining flour to make a soft dough.
• **Turn** dough out onto a floured surface, and knead 5 minutes. Place in a well-greased bowl, turning to grease top. Cover and let rise in a warm place (85°), free from drafts, 1 hour or until doubled in bulk.
• **Combine** olive oil, oregano, and rosemary; set aside.
• **Punch** dough down. For round loaves, divide dough in half; shape each portion into a 10-inch round. For sandwich buns, divide dough into 12 balls, and shape each portion into a 3-inch round. Place on lightly greased baking sheets; flatten dough slightly, and brush with half of olive oil mixture. Cover and let rest 10 minutes.
• **Bake** at 350° for 15 minutes. Brush with remaining olive oil mixture, and bake 5 to 10 additional minutes or until lightly browned and bread sounds hollow when tapped. Cool on wire racks. **Yield:** two 10-inch loaves or 12 sandwich buns.

* ¼ cup chopped fresh chives, ¾ teaspoon chopped fresh oregano, and ¼ teaspoon chopped fresh rosemary may be substituted for dried herbs.

Eva Royal
Evening Shade, Arkansas

FOCACCIA VERSUS PIZZA

The thickness of the dough and the toppings are the basic differences between pizza and focaccia. Traditionally, olive oil and salt are drizzled into finger-marked little wells on focaccia, allowing flavor to seep into the bread rather than overpowering it with sauces and cheeses. Bakeries sprinkle on fennel seeds, herbs, olives, and Parmesan or Romano cheese. Restaurants slit the dough; then stuff in eggplant, potato, caramelized onions, anchovies, or blue cheese.

COOKING AT THE SPEED OF LIGHT

Just because you need to cook fast doesn't mean you have to sacrifice flavor.

For a day of light and easy menus, we offer recipes for a nearly instant

breakfast, a hearty lunch, and a dinner you'd never guess is low in fat.

A DAY IN THE LIGHT
Serves Four

BREAKFAST
Breakfast on a Bagel
Hot Herbal Tea

LUNCH
Smoked Turkey-Roasted Pepper Sandwiches
Potato-Corn Chowder   Fresh Fruit
Fruit Juice

DINNER
Asparagus Salad
Baked Catfish
Cauliflower Sauté

BREAKFAST ON A BAGEL

2 plain bagels, split and toasted
4 (1-ounce) slices Canadian bacon
4 (½-inch-thick) tomato slices
½ cup (2 ounces) shredded
    reduced-fat Cheddar cheese

• **Place** bagel halves, cut side up, on a baking sheet; layer each with Canadian bacon, a tomato slice, and 2 table-spoons shredded cheese.
• **Broil** 3 inches from heat (with elec-tric oven door partially opened) 1 to 2 minutes or until cheese melts. **Yield:** 4 servings.

❤ Per serving: Calories 179 (27% from fat)
Fat 5.2g (2.3g saturated) Cholesterol 23mg
Sodium 679mg Carbohydrate 18.8g
Fiber 0.9g Protein 13.6g

SMOKED TURKEY-ROASTED PEPPER SANDWICHES

Smoked turkey breast is soaked in a salt solution before smoking. If you're watching your sodium, substitute roasted turkey breast for the smoked.

2 tablespoons fat-free cream
    cheese product, softened
1 tablespoon reduced-fat
    mayonnaise
1 tablespoon spicy brown mustard
⅛ teaspoon pepper
¼ cup chopped commercial
    roasted red peppers, drained
2 tablespoons sliced green onions
8 slices pumpernickel bread
¾ pound sliced smoked turkey
    breast
¼ cup alfalfa sprouts

• **Combine** first 4 ingredients; stir in red peppers and green onions.
• **Spread** mixture evenly on one side of bread slices. Layer turkey and alfalfa sprouts on 4 slices of bread; top with remaining bread slices. Cut in half.
• **Serve** immediately or wrap each sandwich in heavy-duty plastic wrap, and refrigerate. **Yield:** 4 sandwiches.

❤ Per serving: Calories 280 (9% from fat)
Fat 2.9g (0.1g saturated) Cholesterol 44mg
Sodium 1057mg Carbohydrate 36.3g
Fiber 4.1g Protein 29.1g

POTATO-CORN CHOWDER

¾ cup chopped green pepper
⅓ cup chopped onion
Vegetable cooking spray
2¾ cups fat-free chicken broth
1½ cups finely chopped potato
1 teaspoon salt
¼ teaspoon pepper
¼ cup cornstarch
2¼ cups skim milk
2¼ cups frozen whole kernel corn
1 (2-ounce) jar chopped pimiento,
    undrained

• **Cook** green pepper and onion in a saucepan coated with cooking spray

SKIM MILK MAKES A DIFFERENCE

If you regularly drink 8 ounces of milk a day, switching from whole milk to skim will decrease calories enough that you'll be 6 pounds lighter in a year. Substitute skim milk for whole in cooking, too. You'll save 64 calories and 7 grams of fat every time you replace 8 ounces of whole milk with an equal amount of skim. If you can't convert overnight, first change to 2% for a month, then try 1%, and finally switch to skim milk.

over medium heat, stirring constantly, 5 minutes or until tender. Stir in broth, potato, salt, and pepper.

●**Bring** to a boil; reduce heat, and simmer 5 to 7 minutes or until potato is tender.

●**Combine** cornstarch and milk, stirring until smooth. Gradually add to potato mixture, stirring constantly. Stir in corn and chopped pimiento.

●**Bring** to a boil over medium heat, stirring constantly; cook, stirring constantly, 1 minute or until thickened. Serve immediately or pour into a thermos. **Yield:** 6 cups.

Mary Wade
Southside, Alabama

❤ Per 1½-cup serving: Calories 230 (3% from fat)
Fat 0.7g (0.2g saturated) Cholesterol 3mg
Sodium 380mg Carbohydrate 47.9g
Fiber 4g Protein 9.5g

ASPARAGUS SALAD

1 pound fresh asparagus spears
¼ cup lemon juice
2 tablespoons honey
1 tablespoon vegetable oil
8 lettuce leaves

●**Snap** off tough ends of asparagus. Remove scales from stalks, if desired. Arrange asparagus in a steamer basket; place over boiling water. Cover and steam 8 minutes or until crisp-tender.

●**Plunge** asparagus into ice water to stop the cooking process; drain and chill.

●**Combine** lemon juice, honey, and oil in a jar; cover tightly, and shake vigorously. Chill.

●**Arrange** lettuce leaves on individual plates; top with asparagus, and drizzle with dressing. **Yield:** 4 servings.

❤ Per serving: Calories 97 (30% from fat)
Fat 3.7g (0.7g saturated) Cholesterol 0mg
Sodium 6mg Carbohydrate 16g
Fiber 2.7g Protein 3.1g

QUICK TIPS

■ Cleanup will be a breeze if you line baking pans with foil and spray broiler racks with cooking spray before use.

■ Perk up the flavor of winter tomatoes by sprinkling them with fresh lemon juice, and be sure to serve them at room temperature. You might also try the more flavorful Roma tomatoes during the winter months.

■ If you prefer to make your salad dressing, prepare enough for a week at a time, and store it in the refrigerator. To save time, buy fat-free commercial salad dressing.

BAKED CATFISH

¼ cup yellow cornmeal
¼ cup all-purpose flour
¼ cup grated Parmesan cheese
1 teaspoon paprika
½ teaspoon salt
½ teaspoon ground black pepper
⅛ teaspoon ground red pepper
1 egg white
2 tablespoons skim milk
4 (4-ounce) catfish fillets
Butter-flavored cooking spray
½ teaspoon sesame seeds
Lemon wedges

●**Combine** first 7 ingredients; set aside.

●**Whisk** together egg white and milk. Dip fillets in milk mixture, and dredge in cornmeal mixture.

●**Place** fillets on a foil-lined baking sheet coated with cooking spray.

●**Sprinkle** with sesame seeds, and coat each fillet with cooking spray.

●**Bake** at 350° for 30 minutes or until fish flakes easily when tested with a fork. Serve with lemon wedges. **Yield:** 4 servings.

Wanda Bishop
Little Rock, Arkansas

❤ Per serving: Calories 196 (28% from fat)
Fat 5.9g (1.9g saturated) Cholesterol 55mg
Sodium 460mg Carbohydrate 13.4g
Fiber 0.9g Protein 20.9g

CAULIFLOWER SAUTÉ

2 cups fresh cauliflower flowerets
½ cup sliced onion
1 clove garlic, minced
1 tablespoon olive oil
1 cup fresh or frozen snow pea pods
1 sweet red pepper, cut into strips
½ cup sliced fresh mushrooms
1 teaspoon dried oregano
¼ teaspoon salt

●**Arrange** cauliflower in a steamer basket; place over boiling water. Cover and steam 8 minutes; drain and set aside.

●**Cook** onion and garlic in olive oil in a large nonstick skillet over medium heat, stirring constantly, until tender. Add cauliflower, snow peas, and remaining ingredients; cook, stirring constantly, until heated. **Yield:** 4 (1-cup) servings.

Fay M. Russell
Doraville, Georgia

❤ Per serving: Calories 69 (45% from fat)
Fat 3.7g (0.5g saturated) Cholesterol 0mg
Sodium 157mg Carbohydrate 7.8g
Fiber 2.7g Protein 2.3g

BAY LEAVES

What would a trip to Panama City, Florida, be without dinner at Captain Anderson's restaurant? Thanks to *Bay Leaves* cookbook, you can prepare Grand Lagoon Stuffed Flounder, one of the restaurant favorites, at home.

A fund-raising project of the Junior Service League of Panama City, Florida, this cookbook contains more than 800 Florida favorites, in addition to Captain Anderson's specialty. The book has raised more than $100,000 since its first printing in 1975.

SPICED PEACH SALAD

4 oranges
1 (22-ounce) jar pickled peaches, undrained
1 (16½-ounce) can pitted sweet Royal Ann cherries, undrained
1 (6-ounce) package lemon-flavored gelatin
1 cup boiling water
1 cup chopped pecans
Lettuce leaves

• **Peel** and section oranges over a bowl, reserving any juice. Chop orange sections; set aside.
• **Drain** peaches and cherries, reserving juices. Remove pits from peaches; chop peaches and cherries, and set aside.
• **Combine** reserved fruit juices; add enough water to make 3 cups liquid. Set aside.
• **Combine** gelatin and boiling water in a large bowl, stirring until gelatin dissolves (about 2 minutes). Add fruit juice mixture, and chill until the consistency of unbeaten egg white.
• **Fold** fruit and chopped pecans into gelatin mixture. Spoon mixture into a lightly oiled 7-cup mold. Cover and chill until firm.

• **Unmold** gelatin salad onto a lettuce-lined plate for serving. **Yield:** 14 to 16 servings.

GRAND LAGOON STUFFED FLOUNDER

Crabmeat Stuffing
6 (1-pound) whole flounder, dressed
⅓ cup butter or margarine, melted
3 tablespoons lemon juice

• **Spoon** Crabmeat Stuffing evenly into each fish cavity. Place fish in a lightly greased 15- x 10- x 1-inch jellyroll pan.
• **Combine** butter and lemon juice; drizzle over fish.
• **Bake** at 350° for 25 minutes or until fish flakes easily when tested with a fork. **Yield:** 6 servings.

Crabmeat Stuffing

1 green pepper, finely chopped
½ cup finely chopped onion
2½ tablespoons finely chopped celery
½ (16-ounce) package saltine crackers, crushed
½ pound fresh crabmeat, drained and flaked
1½ teaspoons salt
1½ teaspoons pepper
2 large eggs
1 cup mayonnaise or salad dressing
¼ cup Worcestershire sauce
¼ cup prepared mustard
2 tablespoons lemon juice

• **Combine** first 7 ingredients in a large bowl; set aside.
• **Combine** eggs and remaining ingredients; stir into crabmeat mixture. **Yield:** 5 cups.

Note: Leftover Crabmeat Stuffing may be used to stuff jumbo shrimp and baked as directed for flounder, or it may be shaped into croquettes and browned in hot oil.

STRAWBERRIES ROMANOFF

1 cup whipping cream
1 pint vanilla ice cream, softened
2 tablespoons lemon juice
¼ to ½ cup Cointreau or other orange-flavored liqueur
2 quarts strawberries, hulled and halved
¼ cup sifted powdered sugar

• **Beat** whipping cream in a large mixing bowl at high speed with an electric mixer until soft peaks form; set aside.
• **Beat** ice cream in a medium mixing bowl until smooth. Gently fold in whipped cream. Stir in lemon juice and liqueur; set aside.
• **Combine** strawberries and powdered sugar; serve with sauce. **Yield:** 12 servings.

Note: Romanoff sauce can be refrigerated up to three days. Sauce will separate; stir before serving.

APRIL

NEW WAVE FARE

What's so great about crab cakes? Just about *everything*. One taste

of them and you're hooked. Just about every coastal region of the South

boasts its own special version. If you're lucky enough to live in

one of these fertile seafood areas, more than likely you've already

tucked back *several* crab cake recipes. Accompanied by a sauce or

simply crowned with a generous squeeze of lemon, crab cakes

can perform as appetizers, entrées, or even salads.

CRAB CAKES WITH TOMATO CREAM

2   tablespoons unsalted butter or
      margarine
½   cup finely chopped onion
½   cup finely chopped celery
¼   cup plain yogurt
1   teaspoon baking soda
1   teaspoon seafood seasoning
1   teaspoon Dijon mustard
¼   teaspoon salt
¼   teaspoon freshly ground black
      pepper
1   tablespoon finely chopped fresh
      parsley
1   pound fresh lump crabmeat,
      drained
1   cup round buttery cracker
      crumbs
Tomato Cream

● **Melt** butter in a medium skillet over low heat; add onion and celery, and cook, stirring constantly, until tender. Transfer mixture to a large bowl; cool.
● **Stir** yogurt and next 7 ingredients into vegetable mixture.

● **Shape** into 12 (2½-inch) patties; coat each with cracker crumbs. Place on a lightly greased baking sheet.
● **Bake** at 450° for 10 minutes; turn and bake 10 additional minutes or until done. Serve with Tomato Cream. **Yield:** 6 servings.

Tomato Cream

½   cup chopped dried tomatoes
1   cup boiling water
2   cups half-and-half
1   shallot, finely chopped
¼   teaspoon salt
⅛   teaspoon ground white pepper

● **Combine** tomatoes and water in a saucepan; let stand 20 minutes. Bring tomato mixture to a boil over medium heat; boil 1 minute. Drain well.
● **Combine** half-and-half and shallot in a heavy 2-quart saucepan; bring to a boil over medium heat, stirring often. Boil until mixture is reduced to 1 cup, stirring often. Stir in tomatoes, salt, and pepper; cook just until heated, and serve immediately. **Yield:** 1⅓ cups.

CATFISH CAKES

Those of you who are landlocked may find fresh crab a bit pricey for everyday consumption, so take a look at this recipe for crab cakes. It offers an affordable and delicious alternative.

1½ pounds farm-raised catfish
      fillets *
1   large egg, lightly beaten
2   tablespoons mayonnaise or salad
      dressing
1   tablespoon prepared mustard
1   tablespoon butter or margarine,
      melted
1   teaspoon chopped fresh parsley
¾   teaspoon salt
½   teaspoon dry mustard
½   teaspoon ground black pepper
¼   teaspoon garlic salt
⅛   teaspoon ground red pepper
¾   cup crushed cornflakes cereal
Vegetable oil
Garnishes: lemon wedges, fresh
      flat-leaf parsley sprig
Commercial tartar sauce or cocktail
      sauce

● **Arrange** catfish in a lightly greased 13- x 9- x 2-inch baking dish; cover with aluminum foil, and bake at 400° for 20 minutes or until fish flakes easily when tested with a fork. Drain and flake.
● **Combine** egg and next 9 ingredients in a large bowl. Stir in fish.
● **Shape** into 8 (2½-inch) patties; coat with crushed cereal. Place patties on paper towels; refrigerate 1 hour.
● **Pour** oil to depth of ½ inch into a large skillet. Fry patties in hot oil over medium heat about 2 minutes on each side or until golden. Drain on paper towels. Garnish, if desired. Serve with commercial sauce. **Yield:** 4 servings.

* 1½ pounds trout may be substituted for catfish.

Decca Hodge
Bonham, Texas

GULF COAST CRAB CAKES
(pictured on page 73)

1 tablespoon butter or margarine
1 clove garlic, minced
1 tablespoon finely chopped sweet
   red pepper
2 teaspoons finely chopped onion
1½ teaspoons finely chopped
   green pepper
1½ teaspoons finely chopped
   sweet yellow pepper
1½ tablespoons all-purpose flour
⅓ cup whipping cream
1 pound fresh lump crabmeat,
   drained
1¼ cups soft breadcrumbs,
   divided
½ finely chopped serrano chile
1 egg yolk
2 teaspoons chopped fresh chives
1 teaspoon dry mustard
1 teaspoon stone-ground mustard
1 teaspoon lemon juice
½ teaspoon salt
¼ teaspoon pepper
¼ cup butter or margarine
Vegetable oil
1 corn tortilla, cut into thin strips
Lime-Saffron Sauce
Mango Slaw
Garnish: fresh cilantro

• **Melt** 1 tablespoon butter in a large skillet over medium heat; add garlic and next 4 ingredients, and cook 3 minutes, stirring often. Stir in flour; cook 3 minutes, stirring constantly. Gradually add whipping cream; cook, stirring constantly, until thickened.
• **Stir** in crabmeat, ¼ cup breadcrumbs, and next 8 ingredients. Cover and chill 3 to 4 hours.
• **Shape** into 10 (2-inch) patties; coat with remaining 1 cup breadcrumbs.
• **Melt** 2 tablespoons butter in a large skillet over medium heat; cook half of patties on each side until golden. Drain on paper towels. Repeat procedure with remaining butter and patties. Set aside.
• **Wipe** skillet with paper towels.
• **Pour** oil to depth of 1 inch into skillet. Fry tortilla strips in hot oil over medium-high heat until golden. Drain on paper towels. Set aside.
• **Spoon** Lime-Saffron Sauce onto plates, and arrange crab cakes and

Mango Slaw on sauce. Top with tortilla strips, and garnish, if desired. **Yield:** 5 servings.

Lime-Saffron Sauce

1 cup Chablis or other dry white
   wine
Pinch of saffron
½ teaspoon butter or margarine
1 small shallot, finely chopped
3 tablespoons lime juice
2 tablespoons whipping cream
½ cup butter
¼ teaspoon salt

• **Combine** wine and saffron in a saucepan; bring to a boil. Remove from heat; let stand 30 minutes.
• **Melt** ½ teaspoon butter in a large skillet over medium heat; add shallot, and cook, stirring constantly, until tender. Add wine mixture and lime juice; cook over medium heat until mixture is reduced to ¼ cup.
• **Stir** in whipping cream; cook until mixture is reduced to ¼ cup. Remove from heat; stir in ½ cup butter and salt. **Yield:** about ¾ cup.

Mango Slaw

1 cup finely shredded red cabbage
1 cup peeled and chopped mango
1 medium tomato, chopped
1 serrano chile, finely chopped
1 green onion, chopped
⅓ cup chopped fresh cilantro
3 tablespoons lime juice
1 teaspoon olive oil
⅛ teaspoon salt
⅛ teaspoon pepper

• **Combine** all ingredients; cover and chill at least 2 hours. Serve with a slotted spoon. **Yield:** 3 cups.

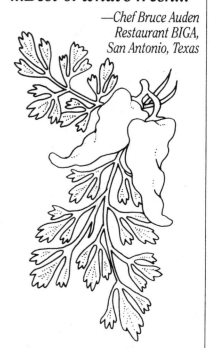

"...Best of what's fresh..."
—*Chef Bruce Auden
Restaurant BIGA,
San Antonio, Texas*

That's how Chef Bruce Auden characterizes the menu at his Restaurant BIGA in San Antonio, Texas. Bruce, whose establishment features many diverse, original dishes, almost always lists crab cakes on the menu. "With plenty of Gulf Coast seafood at our back door, crab cakes are definitely one of our most requested dishes," says Bruce, originally from England. At the restaurant, you're likely to find the crab cakes appearing as either an appetizer served on a bed of fresh pasta or in miniature as a garnish for a seafood entrée.

Bruce pairs the sweet, distinctive flavor of fresh crab with locally grown peppers, fresh herbs, and spices in his Gulf Coast Crab Cakes (on this page). You'll notice that this recipe's ingredient list is longer than most of the ones we offer, and its method is a bit more complex than some others. But we think you'll agree that it's definitely worth the extra effort.

Simply Delicious

Wonderful food does not have to begin with a bewildering grocery list.

Sometimes great taste lies in the easy combination of just a few ingredients.

Here we honor simplicity. Each of these recipes uses five or fewer

ingredients (excluding seasonings, oil or butter, and flour). But the

ingredients are carefully chosen to both intensify taste and enhance eye

appeal. Keep a handful of these ingredients in your pantry

and you won't find your hands full at dinnertime.

MEDITERRANEAN CHICKEN

4 skinned and boned chicken
   breast halves
3 tablespoons all-purpose flour
2 tablespoons olive oil
1 (14½-ounce) can ready-to-serve
   chicken broth
¼ cup sliced ripe olives
2 tablespoons capers
⅛ teaspoon pepper
1 (14-ounce) can whole artichoke
   hearts, rinsed and halved

● **Dredge** chicken in flour; set aside.
● **Heat** olive oil in a large skillet over
medium-high heat. Add chicken, and
cook 3 minutes on each side or until
lightly browned.
● **Add** chicken broth and next 3 ingredients. Bring to a boil; reduce heat, and
simmer 20 minutes or until thickened
and bubbly.
● **Stir** in artichoke halves, and cook until mixture is thoroughly heated. **Yield:**
4 servings.

RED CABBAGE CITRUS SALAD

2 cups shredded red cabbage
4 large oranges, peeled and
   sectioned
½ cup coarsely chopped pecans,
   toasted
¼ cup chopped green onions
Commercial poppy seed salad
   dressing or sweet-and-sour
   salad dressing

● **Arrange** cabbage evenly on individual
salad plates; place orange sections in center. Sprinkle with pecans and green
onions. Serve with dressing. **Yield:** 4 to
6 servings.

Cassandra Golden
Birmingham, Alabama

BAKED RANCH TOMATOES

2 tomatoes, cut in half
Vegetable cooking spray
¼ teaspoon dried Italian seasoning
1½ tablespoons commercial
   Ranch-style dressing
Garnish: fresh flat-leaf parsley

● **Place** tomato halves in an 8-inch
square pan. Coat top of halves with
cooking spray.
● **Bake** tomato halves at 350° for 16 to
20 minutes.
● **Sprinkle** with Italian seasoning, and
top evenly with dressing.
● **Broil** 3 inches from heat (with electric
oven door partially opened) 2 to 3 minutes or until tomatoes begin to brown.
Garnish, if desired. **Yield:** 4 servings.

Dorothy Cordell
Gadsden, Alabama

TOFFEE SAUCE

5 (1.4-ounce) toffee-flavored
   candy bars
¾ cup sugar
½ cup whipping cream
¼ cup light corn syrup
2 tablespoons butter or margarine
Fresh strawberries
Sour cream
Garnish: fresh mint sprig

● **Position** knife blade in food processor bowl; add candy bars. Process until
finely crushed. Set aside.
● **Combine** sugar, whipping cream,
corn syrup, and butter in a heavy
saucepan.
● **Cook** over medium heat, stirring
constantly, until sugar dissolves. Bring
mixture to a boil, and cook 2 minutes.
● **Remove** from heat; add crushed
candy, stirring until smooth.
● **Serve** sauce with strawberries and
sour cream. Garnish, if desired. **Yield:**
1⅔ cups.

Note: For a thinner sauce, stir in additional whipping cream.

Judy Laramy
Austin, Texas

Right: *Crispy fried tortilla "ribbons"
add flourish to the Mango Slaw that
accompanies Gulf Coast Crab Cakes
(recipe, page 71).*

Above: *Give your favorite recipe pizzazz with a delicious topper: (clockwise from top left) Fiesta Onion Salsa, Tomato-Avocado Salsa, Hot Kiwifruit Salsa, Mediterranean Sauce, Zesty Sauce, Teriyaki Glaze, Easy Mustard Sauce, and Papaya-Basil Relish. (Recipes begin on page 82.)*

Left: *Round up your friends for an impromptu gathering. Make-ahead Marinara Sauce is the foundation for the quick and easy appetizer, Homemade Cowboy Caviar (recipes, page 64).*

Far left: *Just a bit of blue cheese hikes the flavor of Blue Cheese Chicken Salad (recipe, page 81).*

Healthy eating is almost too good to be true when you serve Grilled Orange Scallops With Cilantro-Lime Vinaigrette (recipe on facing page).

LIGHT & EASY

SOUTHERN COOKS LIGHTEN UP

We asked three readers from around the South to share their favorite low-fat recipes, calorie-trimming

tips, and kitchen shortcuts. They are all talented cooks who know how to eliminate calories without losing flavor.

Revamping favorite recipes and creating new ones, these folks have discovered a healthier way to cook.

COASTAL COOK WITH A BUSY SCHEDULE

Penny Caughfield fills her days caring for her son, Andy, and returning to school to take classes in speech therapy at the University of Central Florida in Cocoa. Her favorite recipes reflect her busy schedule; they're quick and easy without skimping on flavor.

GRILLED ORANGE SCALLOPS WITH CILANTRO-LIME VINAIGRETTE
(pictured on facing page)

1 cup orange juice
3 tablespoons chopped fresh basil
18 sea scallops *
1 head Bibb lettuce
4 cups mixed baby lettuces
Cilantro-Lime Vinaigrette
30 yellow pear tomatoes
30 red pear tomatoes
2 cucumbers, cut into thin strips
Garnishes: fresh basil sprigs, thin orange rind strips

• **Combine** orange juice and basil in a dish; add scallops, tossing to coat.
• **Cover** dish, and refrigerate mixture about 1 hour. Uncover and drain, discarding marinade.

• **Cook** scallops, covered with grill lid, over hot coals (400° to 500°) 3 to 5 minutes on each side or until done.
• **Combine** lettuces in a bowl; drizzle with Cilantro-Lime Vinaigrette, and toss gently.
• **Arrange** lettuces on individual plates, and top with scallops, tomatoes, and cucumbers. Garnish, if desired. Serve immediately. **Yield:** 6 servings.

* 30 large shrimp, peeled, with tails intact, can be substituted for sea scallops.

Note: Scallops may be grilled directly on grill rack or, if rack openings are too large, in a grill basket or threaded on skewers.

♥ Per serving: Calories 324 (29% from fat)
Fat 11g (1.5g saturated)   Cholesterol 52mg
Sodium 272mg   Carbohydrate 28.6g
Fiber 3.6g   Protein 29.4g

Cilantro-Lime Vinaigrette

¼ cup sugar
¼ cup extra-virgin olive oil
2 tablespoons lime juice
2 tablespoons rice wine vinegar
1 clove garlic, minced
1 shallot, minced
1½ teaspoons fresh cilantro leaves, finely chopped

• **Combine** all ingredients in a jar. Cover jar tightly, and shake mixture vigorously. **Yield:** ¾ cup.

♥ Per 2 tablespoons: Calories 115 (70% from fat)
Fat 9g (1.2g saturated)   Cholesterol 0mg
Sodium 0mg   Carbohydrate 9.2g
Fiber 0g   Protein 0.1g

> *"When we eat light, we see a dramatic energy increase."*
> —*Penny Caughfield*
> *Cocoa, Florida*

When Penny's husband, Roy, found out that he had high cholesterol five years ago, she started cooking healthier meals. They'll tell you it made a big difference in their energy level.

Penny takes advantage of fresh Florida seafood. Her recipes will send you speeding to the seafood counter at your supermarket.

HOT SPICY GROUPER

4 (4-ounce) grouper or snapper
    fillets
¼ cup lemon juice
2 tablespoons water
2 tablespoons hot sauce
1 tablespoon vegetable oil
2 teaspoons grated fresh
    gingerroot
½ teaspoon salt
Vegetable cooking spray
1 tablespoon sesame seeds,
    toasted
1 tablespoon chopped fresh
    parsley

• **Place** grouper in a shallow dish; set aside.
• **Combine** lemon juice and next 5 ingredients; divide in half. Cover and refrigerate 1 portion. Pour remaining portion over fish, turning to coat. Cover with aluminum foil.
• **Refrigerate** fillets 1 hour, turning fish occasionally.
• **Remove** fish from marinade, discarding marinade.
• **Arrange** fish in a single layer in a grill basket coated with cooking spray. Cook, covered with grill lid, over hot coals (400° to 500°) 5 minutes on each side or until fish flakes easily when tested with a fork, basting with remaining marinade.
• **Transfer** fish to a serving plate; sprinkle with sesame seeds and parsley. **Yield:** 4 servings.

♥ Per serving: Calories 155 (35% from fat)
Fat 5.9g (0.4g saturated) Cholesterol 42mg
Sodium 393mg Carbohydrate 2.1g
Fiber 0.2g Protein 22.5g

SIMPLE BUT ORIGINAL IN THE BLUE RIDGE

When **Jasmin and Peter Gentling** married in 1965, she couldn't fry an egg. Today, in her no-nonsense style of cooking, she creates her own low-fat recipes and makes everything from scratch, including vanilla extract and granola. "I use recipes the first time I make

something," Jasmin says; then she allows herself to improvise.

She keeps busy with her job as a wellness educator at a health education facility in Asheville, North Carolina. And – just for fun – she is working on a master's degree in liberal arts at the University of North Carolina in Asheville.

Jasmin's inspiration for healthy cooking came from her mother, who always cooked simply with an abundance of fresh garden vegetables.

VEGGIE PIZZA

1 medium zucchini, thinly
    sliced
1 yellow squash, thinly
    sliced
1 cup sliced fresh mushrooms
½ cup chopped onion
½ cup chopped green pepper
Vegetable cooking spray
1 (8-ounce) can no-salt-added
    tomato sauce
1½ teaspoons dried Italian
    seasoning
¼ teaspoon salt
Whole Wheat Crust
½ cup freshly grated Parmesan
    cheese
2 cups (8 ounces) shredded part-
    skim mozzarella cheese
4 Roma tomatoes, sliced

• **Cook** first 5 ingredients in a large nonstick skillet coated with cooking spray, covered, over medium-high heat 8 to 10 minutes or until crisp-tender. Drain and set aside.
• **Combine** tomato sauce, Italian seasoning, and salt; spread mixture evenly over Whole Wheat Crust, and layer with cooked vegetables, cheeses, and sliced tomatoes.
• **Bake** at 450° for 20 minutes or until cheese melts and crust is browned around edges. **Yield:** 4 servings.

♥ Per serving: Calories 466 (32% from fat)
Fat 16.7g (8.3g saturated) Cholesterol 41mg
Sodium 624mg Carbohydrate 54.3g
Fiber 4g Protein 25.9g

Whole Wheat Crust

½ cup warm water (105° to 115°)
1 tablespoon sugar
1 tablespoon olive oil
1½ teaspoons active dry yeast
¾ cup whole wheat flour
¾ cup all-purpose flour
Vegetable cooking spray

• **Combine** first 4 ingredients in a bowl; gradually add flours, mixing well after each addition.
• **Turn** dough out onto a lightly floured surface, and knead until smooth and elastic. Place in a bowl coated with cooking spray. Cover and let rise in a warm place (85°), free from drafts, 1 hour or until dough is doubled in bulk.
• **Punch** dough down, and pat evenly into a 12-inch pizza pan coated with cooking spray.
• **Bake** at 450° for 5 minutes. **Yield:** one 12-inch pizza crust.

♥ Per ¼ whole crust: Calories 216 (16% from fat)
Fat 3.8g (0.5g saturated) Cholesterol 0mg
Sodium 1mg Carbohydrate 39.3g
Fiber 1.3g Protein 5.3g

JALAPEÑO CORNBREAD

1 cup cornmeal
2 teaspoons baking powder
¼ teaspoon salt
2 large eggs
3 tablespoons nonfat sour cream
1 (8¾-ounce) can cream-style
    corn
1 (4.25-ounce) jar pickled,
    chopped jalapeño peppers,
    drained (5 tablespoons)
1½ teaspoons vegetable oil
Vegetable cooking spray

• **Heat** an 8-inch cast-iron skillet in a 400° oven for 5 minutes.
• **Combine** first 3 ingredients in a large bowl; make a well in center of mixture. Set aside.
• **Combine** eggs and next 4 ingredients; add mixture to dry ingredients, stirring until moistened.

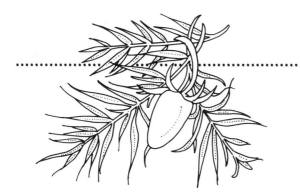
■ Remodel your favorite recipes. Why not try using less fat and sugar? You probably won't even notice a difference.

■ If you're watching your cholesterol, substitute scallops for shrimp. You'll get about 100 fewer grams of cholesterol per 3-ounce serving.

■ Try mixing nonfat products with their regular counterparts if the flavor of nonfat foods doesn't appeal to your taste buds.

■ To add flavor when you steam vegetables, toss herbs into the water you use for steaming. For even more flavor, sprinkle vegetables with butter-flavored granules after cooking.

■ Use bouillon cubes or canned chicken broth to season dried beans. Add onions and peppers during cooking for even more flavor.

JALAPEÑO CORNBREAD

1 cup cornmeal
2 teaspoons baking powder
¼ teaspoon salt
2 large eggs
3 tablespoons nonfat sour cream
1 (8¾-ounce) can cream-style corn
1 (4.25-ounce) jar pickled, chopped jalapeño peppers, drained (5 tablespoons)
1½ teaspoons vegetable oil
Vegetable cooking spray

LOW-CALORIE ENTERTAINING FROM THE CRESCENT CITY

Juggling four children and working out of her New Orleans, Louisiana, home as a graphic designer, leaves little time for **Sally Koch** to spend in the kitchen. But she finds herself cooking daily because she knows that her low-fat cooking gives her family more energy.

But don't let Sally fool you into thinking she never gives in to an occasional treat. Living in New Orleans, a city known for its great food, makes temptation hard to resist. What does Sally do when her cravings are too strong? She eats. "Pastry is my weakness," Sally says. "We're surrounded by pastry in this city, and when I crave it, I don't think twice about having it."

TARRAGON ROASTED CORNISH HENS WITH VEGETABLES

2 (1¼-pound) Cornish hens, skinned and split
1 teaspoon olive oil
1 tablespoon minced garlic
3 to 4 tablespoons chopped fresh tarragon
1 tablespoon cracked black pepper
½ teaspoon salt
8 Roma tomatoes, halved
4 carrots, cut into 2-inch slices
2 medium onions, quartered
12 ounces fresh mushrooms
1 teaspoon olive oil
½ teaspoon ground white pepper
1 cup Chablis or other dry white wine
1 cup fat-free, reduced-sodium chicken broth
1 teaspoon reduced-sodium Worcestershire sauce
2 dashes of hot sauce

●**Rub** hens with olive oil and minced garlic; place in a large roasting pan; set aside.
●**Combine** tarragon, black pepper, and salt; sprinkle over hens.
●**Combine** tomato and next 5 ingredients; toss mixture gently, and place in roasting pan.
●**Bake** hens and vegetables at 350° for 45 minutes; keep warm.
●**Combine** pan juices, wine, and remaining ingredients; bring mixture to a boil. Reduce heat, and simmer 20 minutes or until mixture is reduced to 1 cup. Transfer hens and vegetables to individual serving plates. Serve sauce with hen halves and vegetables. **Yield:** 4 servings.

♥ Per serving: Calories 335 (20% from fat) Fat 7.4g (1.7g saturated) Cholesterol 117mg Sodium 474mg Carbohydrate 27.1g Fiber 6.9g Protein 41g

GRILLED FLANK STEAK WITH BLACK BEAN- AND-CORN SALSA

1　pound flank steak
½　cup Burgundy or other dry red wine
3　cloves garlic, pressed
2　tablespoons chopped shallots
2　tablespoons Worcestershire sauce
¼　cup lemon juice
1½　teaspoons pepper
½　teaspoon garlic powder
½　teaspoon pepper
　　Black Bean-and-Corn Salsa
½　avocado, peeled and sliced

●**Place** steak in a large shallow dish or heavy-duty, zip-top plastic bag, and set aside.
●**Combine** wine, garlic, shallot, Worcestershire sauce, lemon juice, and 1½ teaspoons pepper; pour over steak. Cover dish or seal bag, and refrigerate 8 hours, turning steak occasionally.
●**Drain** steak, discarding marinade. Sprinkle with garlic powder and ½ teaspoon pepper.
●**Cook,** without grill lid, over hot coals (400° to 500°) 7 minutes on each side or until meat is desired degree of doneness. Slice steak diagonally across grain into thin slices, and serve steak with Black Bean-and-Corn Salsa and avocado slices. **Yield:** 4 servings.

♥ Per serving: Calories 371 (33% from fat) Fat 13.9g (1.4g saturated) Cholesterol 59mg Sodium 378mg Carbohydrate 32.7g Fiber 5.3g Protein 30.8g

Black Bean-and-Corn Salsa

1½　cups fresh corn, cut from cob *
1　cup canned black beans, rinsed
1　sweet red pepper, chopped
1　jalapeño pepper, seeded and finely chopped
1　clove garlic, pressed
2　tablespoons lime juice
2　teaspoons chopped fresh cilantro
¼　teaspoon salt
¼　teaspoon pepper

●**Cook** corn in a small amount of boiling water 4 minutes or until corn is crisp-tender; drain and cool.
●**Combine** corn and remaining ingredients. **Yield:** 4 cups.

* 1½ cups frozen whole kernel corn may be substituted.

♥ Per 1-cup serving: Calories 136 (7% from fat) Fat 1.2g (0.2g saturated) Cholesterol 0mg Sodium 137mg Carbohydrate 28.6g Fiber 4.6g Protein 6.3g

---

QUICK TIPS

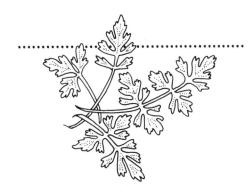

■ Chop peppers, onions, and garlic, and freeze them separately in plastic bags or small containers. You'll be ahead of the game when it's time to make dinner. After freezing, the peppers and onions will be soft, so plan to use the vegetables in cooked dishes only.

■ With this simple grilling trick you can add flavor and eliminate the messy job of washing a basting brush. Tie bundles of fresh herbs onto disposable wooden chopsticks or bamboo skewers with string to make an herb brush. The flavor of the herbs will be released when you brush on your marinade. When you're finished, toss the brush on the fire and the burning herbs will release even more flavor to whatever you're grilling.

■ Keep frequently used ingredients near where you cook. A small tray can hold salt, pepper, spices, vegetable cooking spray, flour, and vinegar. You'll save time if you don't have to look through crowded cupboards for items that you use everyday.

■ When you don't have a lot of time, keep meals simple. Broiled fish or chicken, vegetables cooked in the microwave, and a tossed salad with fat-free commercial dressing make an easy low-fat meal.

A LITTLE GOES A LONG WAY

. . . .

Call them flavor boosters: ingredients that, in small measure, rocket a dish to new heights.

The key is in the quantity. In these recipes, we've used caloric giants – blue cheese and bacon – but we've used them sparingly. Small doses can indeed deliver big tastes.

BLUE CHEESE CHICKEN SALAD

(pictured on page 74)

4 (4-ounce) skinned and boned
 chicken breast halves
Vegetable cooking spray
2 teaspoons dried dillweed
¼ teaspoon salt
¼ teaspoon ground white pepper
6 cups romaine lettuce, torn
1 medium cucumber, thinly sliced
1 small green pepper, cut into thin
 rings
2 slices purple onion, separated
 into rings
2 tablespoons olive oil
1 tablespoon Dijon mustard
1 tablespoon balsamic vinegar
1 tablespoon grated onion
2 medium tomatoes, cut into
 eighths
2 tablespoons crumbled blue
 cheese
Garnish: carrot curls

• **Coat** both sides of chicken with cooking spray; sprinkle evenly with dillweed, salt, and white pepper.
• **Place** a seasoned cast-iron skillet over high heat until hot; add chicken, and brown on both sides. Place skillet in a 350° oven, and bake 10 minutes. Cut chicken into thin diagonal slices.
• **Combine** lettuce and next 3 ingredients; set aside.
• **Combine** olive oil and next 3 ingredients; pour over lettuce mixture, and toss gently. Divide onto plates.
• **Arrange** chicken slices and tomato wedges evenly on lettuce. Sprinkle evenly with blue cheese. Garnish, if desired. **Yield:** 4 servings.

♥ Per serving: Calories 252 (46% from fat)
Fat 12.8g (3.9g saturated) Cholesterol 59mg
Sodium 525mg Carbohydrate 9.6g
Fiber 3.4g Protein 24.7g

SUBSTITUTE AND SAVE

■ Use canned evaporated skimmed milk instead of whipping cream. If the milk is well chilled, you can whip it like whipping cream, as long as you use it immediately.

■ Substitute pretzels or air-popped popcorn for fried snack chips. To add butter flavor to plain popcorn, spray it with a butter-flavored cooking spray after popping.

■ Treat yourself to frozen fruit sorbets, ice milk, or nonfat frozen yogurt instead of ice cream.

■ Use egg whites or fat-free egg substitute instead of whole eggs to reduce calories, fat, and cholesterol.

■ Use skim milk instead of whole milk for drinking and cooking.

SPINACH-AND-BACON STUFFED PORK TENDERLOIN

½ cup finely chopped
 onion
1 clove garlic, minced
Vegetable cooking spray
1 cup sliced fresh mushrooms
1 (10-ounce) package frozen
 chopped spinach, thawed and
 drained
4 slices bacon, cooked and
 crumbled
1 tablespoon Dijon mustard
¼ teaspoon salt
¼ teaspoon pepper
2 (¾-pound) pork tenderloins,
 trimmed
2 tablespoons Dijon mustard
2 teaspoons dried rosemary,
 crushed
1 teaspoon dried oregano
1 teaspoon dried thyme
1 teaspoon pepper
¼ teaspoon salt
½ cup Chablis or other dry
 white wine

• **Cook** onion and garlic in a large non-stick skillet coated with cooking spray over medium heat, stirring constantly, until vegetables are tender. Add mushrooms; cook, stirring constantly, 3 minutes. Stir in spinach and next 4 ingredients; set aside.
• **Slice** each pork tenderloin lengthwise down center, cutting to, but not through, bottom. Place between sheets of heavy-duty plastic wrap; pound into a 12- x 8-inch rectangle.
• **Spoon** half of spinach mixture over 1 tenderloin; spread to within ½ inch of sides. Roll tenderloin, jellyroll fashion, starting with short side. Tie with heavy string at 1½-inch intervals. Repeat procedure with remaining tenderloin and spinach mixture.
• **Combine** 2 tablespoons mustard and next 5 ingredients; spread evenly over tenderloins. Place seam side down in a shallow baking pan coated with cooking spray. Add wine to pan.
• **Bake** at 325° for 45 minutes. Let stand 10 minutes; remove strings. Cut into ½-inch slices. **Yield:** 6 servings.

♥ Per serving: Calories 227 (33% from fat)
Fat 7.6g (2.4g saturated) Cholesterol 88mg
Sodium 504mg Carbohydrate 6g
Fiber 2.2g Protein 29.4g

TOP THIS

Give chicken or fish fillets a wake-up call with a flavorful low-fat topping. Some of these recipes can also be used as a dip for chips or as a sandwich spread. You'll find our assortment of dishes, sauces, and salsas simply unbeatable.

HOT KIWIFRUIT SALSA
(pictured on page 75)

1 cup peeled, finely chopped kiwifruit
⅓ cup finely chopped green onions
⅓ cup finely chopped fresh tomatillo
⅓ cup seeded, finely chopped Anaheim chile
2 tablespoons chopped fresh cilantro
½ teaspoon unseeded, finely chopped red or green jalapeño pepper
¼ cup rice vinegar
1 tablespoon unsweetened pineapple juice
1½ teaspoons sugar

• **Combine** all ingredients in a medium bowl; cover and chill. Serve over fish or chicken. **Yield:** 2 cups.

♥ Per 1 tablespoon: Calories 8 (9% from fat)
Fat 0.1g (0g saturated) Cholesterol 0mg
Sodium 0mg Carbohydrate 1.7g
Fiber 0.4g Protein 0.2g

PAPAYA-BASIL RELISH
(pictured on page 75)

2 papayas, peeled and seeded
1 jalapeño pepper, seeded and finely chopped
2 tablespoons chopped fresh basil

• **Cut** 1 papaya into large pieces, and place in container of an electric blender; process until smooth, stopping once to scrape down sides.
• **Chop** remaining papaya, and place in a small bowl. Stir in papaya puree, jalapeño pepper, and chopped basil. Cover and chill. Serve over fish or chicken. **Yield:** 1½ cups.

♥ Per 1 tablespoon: Calories 8 (0% from fat)
Fat 0g (0g saturated) Cholesterol 0mg
Sodium 1mg Carbohydrate 1.9g
Fiber 0.3g Protein 0.1g

ZESTY SAUCE
(pictured on page 75)

1 cup reduced-fat mayonnaise
½ cup chili sauce
⅓ cup finely chopped green pepper
¼ cup finely chopped green onions
2 tablespoons capers, mashed
2 tablespoons prepared horseradish
1 clove garlic, minced
½ teaspoon pepper
½ teaspoon hot sauce

• **Combine** all ingredients; cover and chill. Serve with fish, chicken, or shrimp, or as a sandwich spread. **Yield:** 2 cups.
Joy Knight Allard
San Antonio, Texas

♥ Per 1 tablespoon: Calories 26 (68% from fat)
Fat 2g (0g saturated) Cholesterol 2mg
Sodium 156mg Carbohydrate 1.9g
Fiber 0.1g Protein 0.3g

FIESTA ONION SALSA
(pictured on page 75)

1 cup chopped sweet onion
¾ cup chopped tomato
3 tablespoons sliced ripe olives
1 (4.5-ounce) can chopped green chiles, drained
2 tablespoons white wine vinegar
¼ teaspoon salt
⅛ teaspoon pepper
⅛ teaspoon ground cumin
¼ teaspoon Worcestershire sauce
⅛ teaspoon hot sauce

• **Combine** all ingredients; cover and chill at least 2 hours. Serve with vegetables, fish, chicken, or tortilla chips. **Yield:** 2 cups.

♥ Per 1 tablespoon: Calories 15 (20% from fat)
Fat 0.3g (0g saturated) Cholesterol 0mg
Sodium 193mg Carbohydrate 2.4g
Fiber 0g Protein 0.6g

TERIYAKI GLAZE
(pictured on page 75)

¼ cup unsweetened pineapple juice
¼ cup reduced-sodium soy sauce
¼ cup dry sherry *
2 tablespoons brown sugar
2 teaspoons cornstarch
1 teaspoon ground ginger
1 clove garlic, minced

• **Combine** ingredients in a saucepan.
• **Bring** to a boil; reduce heat, and cook 1 minute, stirring constantly, until thickened. Serve over chicken or fish. **Yield:** ¾ cup.

* ¼ cup unsweetened pineapple juice may be substituted for sherry.
Michelle Ettenger
Alpharetta, Georgia

♥ Per 1 tablespoon: Calories 19 (1% from fat)
Fat 0g (0g saturated) Cholesterol 0mg
Sodium 162mg Carbohydrate 3.3g
Fiber 0g Protein 0.3g

TOMATO-AVOCADO SALSA

(pictured on page 75)

3 cups finely chopped tomatoes
1 cup finely chopped avocado
¼ cup finely chopped purple
 onion
¼ cup lime juice
1 jalapeño pepper, seeded and
 finely chopped
1 tablespoon fresh cilantro,
 minced
1 clove garlic, minced
¼ teaspoon salt

•**Combine** all ingredients in a large bowl; cover and chill. Serve with fish or chicken. **Yield:** 4 cups.

♥ Per 1 tablespoon: Calories 6 (50% from fat)
 Fat 0.4g (0g saturated) Cholesterol 0mg
 Sodium 10mg Carbohydrate 0.7g
 Fiber 0.2g Protein 0.1g

EASY MUSTARD SAUCE

(pictured on page 75)

⅓ cup fat-free mayonnaise
⅓ cup plain low-fat yogurt
2 tablespoons spicy brown
 mustard
1 teaspoon dried thyme
¼ teaspoon salt

•**Combine** all ingredients; cover and chill. Serve over fish, chicken, or broccoli. **Yield:** ⅔ cup.

Rebecca A. Cathey
Eutaw, Alabama

♥ Per 1 tablespoon: Calories 15 (20% from fat)
 Fat 0.3g (0g saturated) Cholesterol 0mg
 Sodium 193mg Carbohydrate 2.4g
 Fiber 0g Protein 0.6g

MEDITERRANEAN SAUCE

(pictured on page 75)

½ cup chopped onion
½ cup chopped green
 pepper
1 clove garlic, minced
Vegetable cooking spray
1 large tomato, chopped
½ cup Chablis or other dry white
 wine
4 ripe olives, chopped
⅛ teaspoon hot sauce
¼ cup (2 ounces) crumbled feta
 cheese

•**Cook** onion, green pepper, and garlic in a nonstick skillet coated with cooking spray over medium heat, stirring constantly, until tender. Add tomato and next 3 ingredients; cook 5 minutes or until thickened. Sprinkle with feta cheese, and serve over chicken or fish. **Yield:** 1 cup.

Ann Elsie Schmetzer
Madisonville, Kentucky

♥ Per 1 tablespoon: Calories 18 (50% from fat)
 Fat 1g (0.6g saturated) Cholesterol 3mg
 Sodium 62mg Carbohydrate 1.4g
 Fiber 0.3g Protein 0.7g

VERSATILE VINEGARS

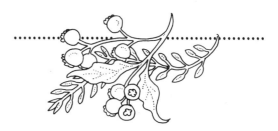

■ Vinegar can be stored in a cool, dry place up to six months.

■ Balsamic vinegar is so exceptional you can use it alone as a calorie-free salad dressing. Try balsamic vinegar sprinkled over fresh strawberries for an unusual twist.

■ Herb vinegars add flavor to foods. Sprinkle over cooked green beans, broccoli, or cauliflower, or add to vegetable soups. Give fruit salads a lift with a sprinkle of mint vinegar.

■ Commercial vinegar with green chiles is made by steeping the hot peppers in vinegar to extract their fiery flavor. Look for it in the condiment section of your grocery store. A few drops add zip to salsas, soups, and tomato-based pasta sauces – anywhere you need a touch of heat.

■ Fruit-flavored vinegars – blueberry, raspberry, or strawberry – add so much punch to vinaigrette dressings that you can use just half of the usual amount of oil. Give a new dimension to chilled fruit soups by adding a few teaspoons of fruit-flavored vinegar.

A LIGHT FETTUCCINE ALFREDO?

The ultimate splurge is fettuccine Alfredo – pasta smothered in a thick, creamy Parmesan cheese sauce. Until now, this dish has been, as one writer recently said, "a heart attack on a plate."

We've changed all that. With our reduced-fat and low-calorie Alfredo Sauce and four main-dish variations, you can enjoy it whenever you like.

ALFREDO SAUCE

2   cups nonfat cottage cheese
3   tablespoons grated Parmesan cheese
2   tablespoons butter-flavored granules
½   cup evaporated skimmed milk
½   teaspoon chicken-flavored bouillon granules
½   teaspoon dried basil
¼   teaspoon ground black pepper
Dash of ground red pepper

● **Combine** all ingredients in container of an electric blender; process until smooth, stopping once to scrape down sides.
● **Pour** into a small saucepan; cook sauce over low heat, stirring constantly, until thoroughly heated. **Yield:** 2¾ cups.

♥ Per 3½-ounce serving: Calories 86 (8% from fat)
Fat 0.8g (0.5g saturated)   Cholesterol 6mg
Sodium 495mg   Carbohydrate 6.8g
Fiber 0g   Protein 13.1g

HAM-AND-ASPARAGUS FETTUCCINE

If you're watching your sodium, substitute reduced-sodium ham for regular ham. It will reduce the total sodium content by about one-fourth.

1   pound fresh asparagus
3   cups chopped, cooked lean ham
Vegetable cooking spray
1   recipe Alfredo Sauce (see recipe)
1   (12-ounce) package fettuccine, cooked without salt or fat

● **Snap** off tough ends of asparagus. Remove scales from stalks with a knife or vegetable peeler, if desired. Cut diagonally into ½-inch slices.
● **Cook** asparagus in a small amount of boiling water 3 minutes. Drain well, and set aside.
● **Cook** ham in a large nonstick skillet coated with cooking spray over medium heat, stirring constantly, until thoroughly heated.
● **Stir** in Alfredo Sauce; add fettuccine and asparagus, and toss gently before serving. **Yield:** 6 servings.

♥ Per serving: Calories 430 (15% from fat)
Fat 7.3g (0.7g saturated)   Cholesterol 46mg
Sodium 1469mg   Carbohydrate 53g
Fiber 3g   Protein 37.5g

SHRIMP FETTUCCINE

1½ pounds unpeeled, medium-size fresh shrimp
1   cup sliced green onions
1   clove garlic, minced
Vegetable cooking spray
2   tablespoons chopped fresh parsley
1   recipe Alfredo Sauce (see recipe)
1   (12-ounce) package fettuccine, cooked without salt or fat

● **Peel** and devein shrimp; set aside.
● **Cook** green onions and garlic in a large nonstick skillet coated with cooking spray over medium heat, stirring constantly, 1 minute.

● **Add** shrimp; cook, stirring constantly, until shrimp turn pink.
● **Stir** in parsley and Alfredo Sauce; add fettuccine, and toss gently. Serve immediately. **Yield:** 6 servings.

♥ Per serving: Calories 379 (6% from fat)
Fat 2.3g (0.6g saturated)   Cholesterol 175mg
Sodium 722mg   Carbohydrate 50.5g
Fiber 1.9g   Protein 37g

FAJITA FETTUCCINE

1   tablespoon fajita seasoning
1½ pounds skinned and boned chicken breast halves
Vegetable cooking spray
1   large onion, cut into thin strips (2 cups)
½   large sweet red pepper, cut into thin strips
½   large green pepper, cut into thin strips
1   recipe Alfredo Sauce (see recipe)
1   (12-ounce) package fettuccine, cooked without salt or fat
2   tablespoons chopped fresh cilantro

● **Sprinkle** fajita seasoning on chicken breasts.
● **Coat** a large nonstick skillet with cooking spray; place over medium heat until hot. Add chicken, and cook 3 to 5 minutes on each side or until done. Remove chicken from skillet, and let cool. Cut into thin strips.
● **Add** onion and pepper strips to skillet; cook over medium heat, stirring mixture constantly, until vegetables are crisp-tender.
● **Stir** in Alfredo Sauce; add chicken and fettuccine, and toss gently. Sprinkle with cilantro, and serve immediately. **Yield:** 6 servings.

♥ Per serving: Calories 450 (11% from fat)
Fat 4.3g (1.5g saturated)   Cholesterol 77mg
Sodium 563mg   Carbohydrate 52g
Fiber 2.3g   Protein 46.6g

LIGHT & EASY

FIGURING OUT THE FAT

Most major health organizations recommend that 30% or less of total daily calories should come from fat. How can you figure this out if you're not a mathematical genius? Here's a simple three-step way to help you calculate the maximum number of fat grams you can have in a day and keep within the 30% recommendation.

· ·

■ **First, identify your Activity Factor.**

Low (sedentary) = 1.2
Moderate (1 hour of exercise, 3 days a week) = 1.4
High (1 hour of exercise, 7 days a week) = 1.6

■ **Using your Activity Factor, calculate your Daily Calorie Needs.**

The University of Texas Southwestern Medical Center at Dallas uses this formula:
Men [900 + (4.5 x weight)] x Activity Factor = Daily Calorie Needs
Women [800 + (3.1 x weight)] x Activity Factor = Daily Calorie Needs

Note: If your weight is more than ideal, you'll either need to consume 500 fewer calories a day, or increase your activity level to burn an additional 500 calories a day. At this rate, you can safely lose one pound each week. It's better to lose weight through a combination of exercising more and eating less.

■ **Using your Daily Calories Needs, figure your fat grams.**

(Daily Calorie Needs) x .30 ÷ 9 = maximum fat grams that you can have in a day to maintain 30% of your daily calories from fat

Note: Don't apply the 30% rule to individual foods or meals. Instead, consider it a guideline for meals eaten over an entire day.

DRESSED UP, SLIMMED DOWN CAKE MIX

· · · · · · · · · · · · · · · ·

Bake your cake and eat it, too – and without the guilt. We've added a few ingredients to give low-fat cake mixes a touch of from-scratch flavor.

STRAWBERRY YOGURT LAYER CAKE

1 (18.25-ounce) package 97% fat-free white cake mix
3 egg whites
1¾ cups water
Vegetable cooking spray
½ gallon nonfat frozen strawberry yogurt, softened
3 cups reduced-fat frozen whipped topping, thawed
Garnish: fresh strawberries

●**Combine** first 3 ingredients in a large mixing bowl; beat at high speed with an electric mixer 2 minutes. Pour batter into 2 (9-inch) round cakepans coated with cooking spray.
●**Bake** at 350° for 25 minutes or until a wooden pick inserted in center comes out clean. Cool in pans on wire racks 15 minutes; remove from pans, and cool completely on wire racks.
●**Split** each layer horizontally into 2 equal layers.
●**Place** 1 layer on a serving plate; spread top with one-third of yogurt. Repeat procedure with 2 layers and remaining yogurt; top with remaining layer. Cover and freeze until firm.
●**Spread** top and sides of cake with whipped topping; freeze. Garnish, if desired. **Yield:** 14 servings.

♥ Per serving: Calories 289 (11% from fat)
Fat 3.7g (0g saturated) Cholesterol 0mg
Sodium 451mg Carbohydrate 57.2g
Fiber 0g Protein 8.2g

FETTUCCINE PRIMAVERA

1 small onion, chopped
Vegetable cooking spray
1 (10-ounce) package frozen snow pea pods, thawed
1 sweet red pepper, cut into thin strips
1 cup fresh broccoli flowerets
½ cup sliced fresh mushrooms
1 recipe Alfredo Sauce (see recipe on facing page)
1 (12-ounce) package fettuccine, cooked without salt or fat

●**Cook** onion in a large nonstick skillet coated with cooking spray over medium heat, stirring constantly, until tender. Add snow peas and next 3 ingredients; cook, stirring constantly, until vegetables are crisp-tender.
●**Stir** in Alfredo Sauce; add fettuccine, and toss gently. Serve immediately. **Yield:** 6 servings.

♥ Per serving: Calories 339 (5% from fat)
Fat 2.1g (0.7g saturated) Cholesterol 6mg
Sodium 509mg Carbohydrate 57.1g
Fiber 4.2g Protein 23.3g

CHOCOLATE MINT TORTE

Vegetable cooking spray
1 (18.5-ounce) package 97%
      fat-free devil's food cake mix
3 egg whites
1¾ cups water
1 (2.6-ounce) package whipped
      topping mix
⅔ cup skim milk
2 tablespoons green crème de
      menthe

• **Coat** a 15- x 10- x 1-inch jellyroll pan with cooking spray; line with wax paper, and coat with cooking spray.
• **Combine** cake mix, egg whites, and water in a large mixing bowl; beat at high speed with an electric mixer 2 minutes. Pour batter into prepared pan.
• **Bake** at 350° for 18 to 20 minutes or until a wooden pick inserted in center comes out clean.
• **Cool** in pan on a wire rack 10 minutes. Invert onto wire rack.
• **Carefully** remove wax paper (cake will be very tender); cool completely. Cut cake crosswise into thirds.
• **Combine** 2 envelopes whipped topping mix, milk, and crème de menthe in a mixing bowl; beat at high speed with an electric mixer 4 minutes or until stiff peaks form.
• **Spread** topping between layers, reserving ½ cup. Pipe or dollop reserved topping on top of cake. Chill at least 2 hours, or freeze, if desired. **Yield:** 12 servings.

♥ Per serving: Calories 204 (14% from fat)
Fat 3g (0g saturated) Cholesterol 0mg
Sodium 319mg Carbohydrate 38g
Fiber 0.2g Protein 4.7g

SPICE LAYER CAKE WITH COFFEE FROSTING

1 (18.5-ounce) 97% fat-free
      yellow cake mix
3 egg whites
1¾ cups water
1 cup fat-free mayonnaise
1 teaspoon ground cinnamon
½ teaspoon ground allspice
½ teaspoon ground ginger
⅛ teaspoon ground nutmeg
Vegetable cooking spray
Coffee Frosting

• **Combine** first 4 ingredients in a large mixing bowl; beat at low speed with an electric mixer until blended. Add cinnamon and next 3 ingredients, and beat at high speed 2 minutes. Pour batter into 2 (9-inch) round cakepans coated with cooking spray.
• **Bake** at 350° for 25 to 35 minutes. Cool in pans on wire racks 10 minutes. Remove from pans, and cool completely on wire racks.
• **Spread** Coffee Frosting between layers and on top and sides of cake. **Yield:** 14 servings.

♥ Per serving: Calories 259 (7% from fat)
Fat 1.9g (0g saturated) Cholesterol 3mg
Sodium 635mg Carbohydrate 57.1g
Fiber 0.9g Protein 4g

Coffee Frosting

1½ cups firmly packed brown
      sugar
½ cup water
⅛ teaspoon cream of tartar
1 teaspoon instant coffee
      granules
3 egg whites
Pinch of salt

• **Combine** first 3 ingredients in a heavy 2-quart saucepan. Cook over medium heat until mixture begins to boil and sugar dissolves, stirring often. Cook until mixture reaches soft ball stage or candy thermometer reaches 240°, stirring often. Remove mixture from heat, and add coffee granules, stirring until granules dissolve.

• **Beat** egg whites at medium speed with an electric mixer until foamy. Continue to beat, slowly adding syrup mixture in a thin stream.
• **Add** salt, and beat at high speed until stiff peaks form and frosting is thick. **Yield:** 4 cups.

♥ Per 4½ tablespoons: Calories 92 (0% from fat)
Fat 0g (0g saturated) Cholesterol 0mg
Sodium 42mg Carbohydrate 23g
Fiber 0g Protein 0.7g

WHY EXERCISE?

....

Exercise...
■ Burns up calories
■ Increases your heart rate
■ Increases your good cholesterol (HDL)
■ Improves your cardiovascular fitness
■ Improves muscle strength
■ Gives you a rosy glow
■ Strengthens bones
■ Improves muscle flexibility
■ Increases your range of motion
■ Increases oxygen supply to your brain
■ Increases bone mass
■ Gives you more energy
■ Strengthens your lungs
■ Helps you sleep better
■ Lowers blood pressure
■ Improves circulation
■ Allows you to eat more calories without gaining weight
■ Improves your posture
■ Strengthens heart muscles
■ Relieves stress
■ Keeps you away from the refrigerator
■ Boosts your self-esteem
■ Gives you a chance to enjoy the great outdoors
■ Improves endurance
■ Clears your mind

TOOLING THE LOW-FAT KITCHEN

Light-and-easy cooking will be a breeze when you add some fat-fighting tools

and keep several tried-and-true pantry staples on hand in your kitchen. Here are several tools

and ingredients we recommend.

TOOLS

■ The Top-of-Stove Broiler is actually a skillet in which, after seasoning it, you can cook firm-flesh fish, scallops, shrimp, steaks, chicken, and vegetables without using any fat. The ridges on the pan will sear foods quickly, much like an outdoor grill. The grilled flavor is not as good as outdoor cooking, but it's better than oven broiling. The skillet is 11¼ inches in diameter and 2 inches deep.

■ Teapot-shaped fat strainers are essential to low-fat cooking. The spout opening is at the bottom of the strainer, allowing you to pour off the broth and leave the fat behind. Use the 4-cup soup strainer for removing the fat from stocks and soups, and the 1½-cup gravy strainer for smaller jobs.

■ Meat loaf is an all-time favorite, and you can make your best recipe lower in fat when you use the 9- x 4½- x 2-inch lean loafpan. The pan is fitted with an insert that has holes in the bottom for fat to drain through, making it a boon to fat-conscious meat loaf lovers.

■ For a thicker, creamier yogurt, use a yogurt cheese strainer. Strain low-fat yogurt overnight in the refrigerator in a cheese strainer. You can substitute it for sour cream or cream cheese, or you can use the strained yogurt plain on baked potatoes or as an ingredient in dips, desserts, and spreads.

■ Simmering soups and stews the low-fat way calls for a strainer ladle. The fat flows through the slots on top and collects in the ladle bottom. Spooning off calories has never been so easy.

STAPLES

■ Keep a stash of lemons and limes on hand. Their juices will add extra zip to salads, wake up the flavor of broiled fish or chicken, brighten bottled salsas, and perk up low-calorie sodas.

■ Freshly grated Romano or Parmesan cheese packs a big flavor punch. For just 23 calories per tablespoon, you can sprinkle rich flavor on plain rice, soups, green salads, cooked pasta, or steamed vegetables.

■ Pastas, grains, and rice are low-calorie time-savers. When cooked, they can be served as a filling side dish, added to soups, turned into bountiful salads, or mixed with vegetables and a bit of low-fat shredded cheese for a casserole. The big bonus is that many of these starchy staples can easily be cooked in 15 minutes or less.

■ Chicken and beef broths are must-haves for the cook. Make sure you buy fat-free broth, or buy regular canned broth and chill it in the refrigerator. When the regular canned broth is cold, open the can by removing the entire lid, and spoon off the solidified fat. Broths are flavor boosters when used as the cooking liquid for vegetables, pasta, and rice. They're also great as a fat-free starting point for creating a number of soups.

FULL SPEED AHEAD:
TWO TIMESAVING MENUS

"What's for dinner?" This age-old question finds its answer in these two menus – a casual one for the family and another elegant enough for company. Both are easy and boast their own timesaving tips. We serve them to you in style, complete with foolproof plans that take you from start to finish.

DINNER AT EIGHT
Serves Four

Avocado-Endive Salad
Grilled Pork Tenderloin
Steamed Vegetables With Garlic-Ginger Butter Sauce
Commercial Rolls
Almond-Raspberry Brie

DINNER COUNTDOWN

THE NIGHT BEFORE
■ Marinate pork.

6:30 p.m.
■ Wash endive and cut up avocado for salad; dip avocado in extra lemon juice to prevent discoloration. Chill ingredients.
■ Make dressing for Avocado-Endive Salad.

6:45 p.m.
■ Prepare the asparagus, carrots, and potatoes for steaming.
■ Combine ingredients for Garlic-Ginger Butter Sauce in saucepan.

7:10 p.m.
■ Assemble the Brie.

7:20 p.m.
■ Assemble Avocado-Endive Salad on salad plates, and place on table.
■ Steam vegetables according to recipe.
■ Place pork on grill.
■ Heat Garlic-Ginger Butter sauce.
■ Heat rolls.

7:50 p.m.
■ Seat guests.
■ Arrange vegetables and pork on dinner plates, and serve.
■ Microwave Brie just before serving it.

AVOCADO-ENDIVE SALAD

3 tablespoons vegetable oil
1 tablespoon fresh lemon juice
1 tablespoon red wine vinegar
1 tablespoon Dijon mustard
½ teaspoon salt
¼ teaspoon pepper
4 heads Belgian endive
1 avocado, peeled and sliced

● **Combine** first 6 ingredients in a jar. Cover tightly; shake vigorously.
● **Rinse** endive; pat dry and trim ends. Arrange endive and avocado on individual salad plates; drizzle with dressing. Serve immediately. **Yield:** 4 servings.
Adelyne Smith
Dunnville, Kentucky

GRILLED PORK TENDERLOIN

½ cup soy sauce
½ cup dry sherry or orange juice
2 tablespoons brown sugar
1 teaspoon ground ginger
2 cloves garlic, pressed
2 (¾-pound) pork tenderloins

DINNER IS SERVED

■ If you forget to marinate the pork tenderloin, don't worry. Just double the marinade ingredients, prick each tenderloin two or three times with a fork, and chill for two hours, turning often. You'll still get plenty of flavor.

■ Steaming is a timesaving technique that also lends itself to easy cleanup. If you don't have a steamer basket, use a fish poacher. Or make your own steamer basket, using a metal colander. Place vegetables in colander, and set over boiling water in a Dutch oven. Cover vegetables, and steam according to recipe directions.

- **Combine** first 5 ingredients in a shallow dish or heavy-duty, zip-top plastic bag. Add tenderloins; cover dish or seal bag, and refrigerate 8 hours, turning pork often.
- **Remove** tenderloins from marinade, discarding marinade.
- **Cook,** covered with grill lid, over hot coals (400° to 500°) 12 to 15 minutes or until a meat thermometer inserted in thickest portion of tenderloins registers 160°, turning once.
- **Cut** tenderloins into slices. **Yield:** 4 to 6 servings.

Cathy Robinson
Columbia, South Carolina

STEAMED VEGETABLES WITH GARLIC-GINGER BUTTER SAUCE

1 pound small fresh asparagus
3 carrots, scraped and cut into thin strips
3 small red round potatoes, sliced
Garlic-Ginger Butter Sauce
Chopped fresh parsley
Garnish: orange rind

- **Snap** off tough ends of asparagus. Remove scales with a vegetable peeler or knife, if desired. Set aside.
- **Arrange** carrots and potatoes in a steamer basket; place over boiling water. Cover and steam 5 minutes.
- **Add** asparagus; cover and steam 5 minutes or until crisp-tender.
- **Arrange** vegetables on plates; drizzle with Garlic-Ginger Butter Sauce, and sprinkle potatoes with parsley. Garnish, if desired. **Yield:** 4 servings.

Garlic-Ginger Butter Sauce

⅓ cup butter or margarine
1 tablespoon brown sugar
½ teaspoon ground ginger
¼ teaspoon orange rind
1 clove garlic, minced

- **Combine** butter, brown sugar, ginger, orange rind, and minced garlic in a saucepan. Cook mixture over medium heat, stirring until sugar dissolves. **Yield:** ⅓ cup.

ALMOND-RASPBERRY BRIE

1 (12-ounce) wedge Brie
2 tablespoons seedless red raspberry jam
1 tablespoon Chambord or other raspberry-flavored liqueur (optional)
1½ teaspoons brown sugar
3 tablespoons sliced almonds
1 tablespoon honey

- **Slice** Brie in half horizontally. Place bottom half of Brie on a microwave-safe serving plate.
- **Combine** jam and Chambord, if desired; spread on cheese, leaving a 1-inch margin around edge; top with remaining cheese half.
- **Sprinkle** with brown sugar and almonds, and drizzle with honey.
- **Microwave** at HIGH 1 minute or just until soft. Serve immediately with wafer cookies or gingersnaps. **Yield:** 4 to 6 servings.

SUPPER AT 6:30
Serves Six

Ham-and-Grits Crustless Quiche
Green Beans Vinaigrette
Chocolate Mousse Parfait

SUPPER COUNTDOWN

5:00 p.m.
- Make mousse parfait; freeze.

5:20 p.m.
- Prepare Green Beans Vinaigrette, and refrigerate.

5:40 p.m.
- Mix and bake quiche. Set the table; sit down and relax.

6:30 p.m.
- Serve supper.

HAM-AND-GRITS CRUSTLESS QUICHE

½ cup water
¼ teaspoon salt
⅓ cup quick-cooking yellow grits, uncooked
1 (12-ounce) can evaporated milk
1½ cups chopped, cooked ham
1 cup (4 ounces) shredded sharp Cheddar cheese
3 large eggs, lightly beaten
1 tablespoon chopped fresh parsley
1 teaspoon dry mustard
1 to 2 teaspoons hot sauce
Garnish: fresh parsley sprig

- **Bring** water and salt to a boil in a large saucepan; stir in grits. Remove from heat; cover and let stand 5 minutes (mixture will be thick).
- **Stir** in milk and next 6 ingredients. Pour into a lightly greased 9½-inch quiche dish or a 9½-inch deep-dish pieplate.
- **Bake** at 350° for 30 to 35 minutes. Let stand 10 minutes before serving.
- **Cut** into wedges. **Yield:** 6 servings.

SUPPER IS SOLVED

- If you don't have time to make mousse on a weeknight, layer ice cream and vanilla wafer crumbs into parfait glasses or custard cups, and freeze.

- Ham-and-Grits Crustless Quiche saves time because you don't have to wrestle with a piecrust. Serving bread is optional because the recipe has grits (a starch) in it. If your family wants bread, use commercial rolls or breadsticks.

- Supper doesn't have to be a hassle. To serve 12 for supper, make two quiches and double all the other recipes.

GREEN BEANS VINAIGRETTE

1 (16-ounce) package frozen
    French-cut green beans
½ cup finely chopped onion
¼ cup sliced ripe olives
1 clove garlic, minced
¼ cup olive oil
2 tablespoons cider vinegar
¾ teaspoon dried tarragon
¼ teaspoon dried basil
¼ teaspoon salt
¼ teaspoon pepper
2 to 4 tablespoons freshly grated
    Parmesan cheese
Sliced tomatoes

•Cook green beans according to package directions; drain. Plunge into ice water to stop cooking process. Drain and set aside.
•Combine onion and next 8 ingredients in a bowl; add beans, tossing to coat. Cover. Chill 45 minutes to 1 hour.
•Sprinkle with Parmesan cheese. Serve with tomatoes. **Yield:** 6 servings.

Note: If you don't have a steamer basket, you can steam vegetables in a fish poacher or place a metal colander inside a large saucepan of steaming water.

Laura Morris
Bunnell, Florida

CHOCOLATE MOUSSE PARFAIT

1 cup (6 ounces) milk chocolate
    morsels
¼ cup whipping cream
2 tablespoons water
2 teaspoons vanilla extract
1½ cups whipping cream,
    whipped
1 cup vanilla wafers, crushed

•Combine first 3 ingredients in a heavy saucepan; cook over low heat, stirring constantly, until chocolate melts. Cool.
•Stir in vanilla, and gently fold in whipped cream.
•Layer mousse and vanilla wafer crumbs evenly into 6 (4-ounce) parfait glasses. Cover.

•Freeze at least 1 hour or up to 2 days. Let stand 10 to 15 minutes before serving. **Yield:** 6 servings.

Note: For an easier dessert, prepare first two steps as directed; chill. Serve with your favorite cookie.

APPETIZER SOUP: A GRACIOUS BEGINNING

....

Guests will feel pampered by this delightful first course. Serving our elegant soups is also a way to show off your pretty soup bowls. If you don't have ones that match your china, clear glass bowls are versatile, inexpensive alternatives that can be used with any china pattern.

It's best to serve these soups before a light main course. When planning the rest of the menu, avoid recipes with cream sauces or flavors similar to the soup. If you're serving your guests a heavier entrée, a clear broth or consommé is a better choice.

CUCUMBER VICHYSSOISE

2 tablespoons butter or
    margarine
1 small onion, chopped
2 cups chicken broth
3 medium potatoes, peeled and
    finely chopped (about 2 cups)
1 teaspoon salt
¼ teaspoon ground white
    pepper
2 medium cucumbers, peeled,
    seeded, and chopped (1½
    cups)
2 cups milk
1 cup half-and-half
¼ cup sour cream
Garnish: shreds of cucumber peel

•Melt butter in a large saucepan over medium heat; add onion. Cook, stirring constantly, until tender. Add chicken broth and next 3 ingredients.
•Bring to a boil; cover, reduce heat, and simmer 12 minutes.
•Add chopped cucumber and milk; simmer, uncovered, 7 minutes.
•Stir half-and-half and sour cream into cucumber mixture.
•Pour one-third of soup mixture into container of an electric blender; process until smooth, stopping once to scrape down sides. Repeat procedure twice with remaining soup mixture.
•Chill at least 2 hours. Garnish, if desired. **Yield:** 7 cups.

POTATO-PEA SOUP

3 leeks (about 1 pound)
3 tablespoons butter or
    margarine
1 medium onion, chopped
3 tablespoons all-purpose flour
1 (49½-ounce) can ready-to-serve
    chicken broth
3 large potatoes, peeled and thinly
    sliced (about 1½ pounds)
1 (10-ounce) package frozen
    English peas
4 cups milk, divided
¼ to ½ teaspoon ground white
    pepper

•Remove roots, tough outer leaves, and green tops from leeks; discard. Wash leeks thoroughly, and chop coarsely.
•Melt butter in a Dutch oven over medium heat; add leeks and onion, and cook, stirring constantly, until vegetables are tender.
•Add flour, stirring until blended. Cook 1 minute, stirring constantly. Gradually stir in chicken broth. Add potatoes, and bring to a boil. Reduce heat, and simmer 30 minutes.
•Cool 45 minutes.
•Cook peas according to package directions; drain and set aside.
•Pour one-third of potato mixture into container of an electric blender; process until smooth, stopping once to scrape down sides. Repeat procedure twice with remaining potato mixture.

- **Combine** 4 cups potato puree, 2 cups milk, and pepper in a saucepan; cook, stirring constantly, over low heat until thoroughly heated. Set aside.
- **Combine** 2 cups potato puree and peas in container of an electric blender; process until smooth, stopping once to scrape down sides.
- **Combine** pea mixture, remaining 2 cups potato puree, and 2 cups milk in a Dutch oven. Cook, stirring constantly, over low heat until thoroughly heated.
- **Pour** both mixtures at the same time into soup bowls, and swirl. Serve immediately. **Yield:** 13 cups.

Caroline Wallace Kennedy
Newborn, Georgia

SAVORY TOMATO SOUP

1 large potato, peeled and thinly
   sliced
1½ cups water
2 (14-ounce) cans Italian
   tomatoes, undrained
½ cup dry white wine
3 tablespoons butter or margarine
3 tablespoons all-purpose flour
1 (10¾-ounce) can Italian tomato
   puree
1 cup water
½ cup finely chopped onion
1 teaspoon chopped fresh parsley
1 to 2 tablespoons brown sugar
1 tablespoon vegetable-flavored
   bouillon granules
½ teaspoon dried thyme
½ teaspoon salt
¼ teaspoon pepper
1 bay leaf

- **Combine** potato slices and 1½ cups water in a medium saucepan; cook over medium-low heat 25 to 30 minutes or until potato mixture is reduced to 1 cup, stirring occasionally. Remove from heat, and set aside.
- **Drain** and chop tomatoes, reserving juice; set tomatoes aside.
- **Combine** reserved juice and wine; set aside.
- **Melt** butter in a large heavy saucepan over low heat; add flour, stirring until smooth. Cook 1 minute, stirring constantly. Gradually stir in juice mixture.

- **Combine** tomato puree and 1 cup water; gradually stir into soup mixture. Stir in chopped tomatoes, onion, and next 7 ingredients; cook mixture over low heat 5 minutes.
- **Add** 1 cup potato mixture, and simmer about 15 minutes, stirring occasionally. Remove and discard bay leaf. **Yield:** 8 cups.

Linda DeJongh
Chapel Hill, North Carolina

HOMEMADE PIZZA THAT DELIVERS

·············

Even though pizza from your own oven is better than what zooms to your doorstep in a cardboard box, most people don't take the time to make it. This version skips the slow process of a yeast-based crust and uses sheets of phyllo instead. So hang up the phone, and grab the phyllo.

PHYLLO PIZZA

8 sheets frozen phyllo pastry,
   thawed
Butter-flavored cooking spray *
10 unpeeled, large fresh shrimp
1 tablespoon olive oil
1 tablespoon lemon juice
¼ teaspoon salt
⅛ teaspoon pepper
1 (8-ounce) package cream cheese,
   softened
1 (4-ounce) package feta cheese
1 teaspoon dried tarragon
3 cherry tomatoes, cut into
   wedges
½ small green pepper, cut into
   thin strips
½ small sweet red pepper, cut into
   thin strips
¼ cup sliced ripe olives
2 tablespoons butter, melted
1 teaspoon minced garlic

- **Place** 1 phyllo sheet on a flat surface; keep remaining phyllo covered with a slightly damp towel until ready to use. Coat phyllo sheet with cooking spray. Layer remaining phyllo sheets on first sheet, spraying each with cooking spray. Place phyllo sheets into a 15- x 10- x 1-inch jellyroll pan coated with cooking spray; roll phyllo edges toward center, forming a 15- x 7-inch rectangle. Spray edges of phyllo with cooking spray, and prick bottom of crust with a fork.
- **Bake** phyllo at 400° for 5 minutes. Remove from oven, and gently press down center; bake 5 additional minutes, and cool.
- **Peel** shrimp, and devein, if desired; slice in half lengthwise. Cook shrimp in olive oil in a skillet over medium heat, stirring constantly, 1 minute. Add lemon juice, salt, and pepper. Set aside.
- **Combine** cheeses; spread on phyllo crust, and sprinkle with tarragon. Top with shrimp, tomatoes, pepper strips, and olives. Combine butter and garlic; drizzle over pizza.
- **Bake** at 400° for 10 minutes. Serve hot. **Yield:** 4 to 6 servings.

* ⅔ cup melted butter may be substituted for cooking spray. Brush on phyllo pastry sheets.

FRAGILE PHYLLO

■ Handle phyllo pastry carefully. Thaw it in the package as directed on the label. Beware: If the pastry is used before completely thawed, it will tear. In Phyllo Pizza (on this page), it doesn't matter if you accidentally tear the delicate pastry. These imperfections won't show once it's topped with cheeses, shrimp, and fresh vegetables.

■ Work with only one sheet of phyllo at a time; keep the remainder covered with a damp towel to keep it from drying out.

FROM OUR KITCHEN TO YOURS

Simply cooked and dressed with complementary seasonings, spring vegetables burst with freshness and flavor. The length of time required for cooking a given vegetable cannot be stated exactly. Times will differ depending on your texture preference, as well as the variety, maturity, and size of the vegetable.

VEGETABLE COOKING CHART

VEGETABLE	MINUTES FOR COOKING		SEASONINGS
	Boiling	Steaming	
Asparagus	2 to 5	5 to 8	Tarragon, dill, lemon, vinaigrette
Beans, green	10 to 20	15 to 25	Basil, dill, thyme, mint, oregano, savory, tarragon
Beets (whole)	30		Allspice, ginger, orange, lemon
Broccoli (spears) (flowerets)	6 to 8 / 3 to 5	10 to 15 / 8 to 10	Dill, tarragon, lemon, vinaigrette
Cabbage (wedges) (shredded)	7 to 10 / 3 to 10	15 / 8 to 12	Caraway, tarragon, savory, dill
Carrots (slices or thin strips)	5 to 8	10 to 15	Ginger, nutmeg, caraway, cinnamon, dill, lemon, mint, orange
Cauliflower (flowerets)	8 to 12	10 to 20	Caraway, dill, mace, tarragon, Parmesan cheese
Eggplant (slices or cubes)	5 to 8	10 to 15	Marjoram, sage, oregano, basil, Parmesan cheese
Greens Spinach and beet Kale and Swiss chard Mustard Arugula and watercress	3 to 8 / 10 to 15 / 20 to 45 / 1 to 3		Basil, chives, oregano, dill, tarragon, nutmeg, rosemary, Parmesan cheese, lemon
Peas, green	5 to 12	10 to 20	Mint, chervil, marjoram, rosemary, garlic, tarragon
Potatoes, new (whole)	10 to 15	20 to 30	Lemon, parsley, vinaigrette, chives, dill, basil, thyme
Squash (slices)	8 to 12	10 to 12	Basil, garlic, rosemary, dill, thyme, oregano

To boil: Bring a small amount of water or broth to a boil. Add vegetables; reduce heat, and cook as recommended.
To steam: Arrange vegetables in a steamer basket; place over boiling water. Cover and steam for time given or until crisp-tender.

CHICKEN

Drumsticks – those prized pieces of a chicken – always seem to disappear fast, if not first, at family dinners. Today, there are plenty to go around your table because individual chicken parts are often packaged separately and sold by the pound with prices to fit any weekly food budget. So if everyone in your family wants legs, it's no problem. No matter which chicken part you prefer, you'll love these easy-to-prepare recipes.

CREOLE CHICKEN

1 medium onion, sliced
8 cloves garlic, minced
¼ cup olive oil
½ cup orange juice
⅓ cup fresh lime juice
3 tablespoons Chablis or other dry white wine *
1 teaspoon sugar
1 teaspoon salt
¼ teaspoon pepper
1 teaspoon white vinegar
1 (3- to 3½-pound) broiler-fryer
Garnishes: lime slices, orange slices, fresh cilantro

● **Cook** onion and garlic in olive oil in a small saucepan over medium-high heat 2 minutes. Add orange juice and next 6 ingredients.
● **Bring** mixture to a boil. Remove from heat, and cool. Reserve ¼ cup marinade, and refrigerate.
● **Place** chicken in a shallow dish or a heavy-duty, zip-top plastic bag. Pour remaining marinade over chicken. Cover or seal, and refrigerate 8 hours, turning chicken occasionally.
● **Remove** chicken from marinade, and discard marinade. Pat chicken dry with a paper towel. Place chicken on a lightly greased rack, and place rack in a broiler pan.
● **Bake** at 400° for 15 minutes; reduce heat to 350°, and bake 1 hour to 1 hour and 15 minutes, basting with reserved ¼ cup marinade.
● **Cover** chicken with aluminum foil after 1 hour to prevent excessive browning. Place chicken on a large serving platter, and garnish, if desired. **Yield:** 4 servings.

* 3 tablespoons chicken broth may be substituted.

Juanita Plana
Coral Gables, Florida

CHICKEN IN FOIL

1 (2½-pound) broiler-fryer, skinned and quartered
¼ teaspoon garlic salt
⅛ teaspoon paprika
1 large onion, cut into 4 slices
1 large potato, cut into 8 slices
2 carrots, scraped and cut into ¾-inch pieces
2 stalks celery, cut into ¾-inch pieces
1 (4-ounce) can sliced mushrooms, drained
1 (10¾-ounce) can cream of chicken soup, undiluted

● **Cut** 4 (24- x 18-inch) pieces of heavy-duty aluminum foil.
● **Place** a chicken quarter in center of each piece of foil; sprinkle with garlic salt and paprika.
● **Top** chicken evenly with onion and next 4 ingredients.
● **Spoon** soup evenly over each portion. Seal bundles, and place on a 15- x 10- x 1-inch jellyroll pan.
● **Bake** at 400° for 1 hour and 15 minutes or until chicken is done. **Yield:** 4 servings.

Margaret Jahns
Tarpon Springs, Florida

THE PRICE IS RIGHT

■ To stretch food dollars, buy a whole fryer cut up and substitute the pieces in recipes calling for legs and thighs.

■ Cut up broiler-fryer at home or ask a butcher to cut it into quarters. Either way you save money.

■ Compare prices carefully at your local grocery. A 3-pound chicken will provide approximately 1 pound 5 ounces of boneless meat. It may be less expensive to buy a whole chicken than boneless parts.

JALAPEÑO OVEN-FRIED CHICKEN LEGS

¼ cup olive oil
1 teaspoon chili powder
½ teaspoon salt
¼ teaspoon garlic powder
¼ teaspoon ground thyme
¼ teaspoon dried marjoram
¼ teaspoon dried rosemary, crushed
6 chicken legs
1¼ cups crushed jalapeño crunchy potato chips *
Vegetable cooking spray

• **Combine** first 7 ingredients in a shallow dish; set aside.
• **Skin** chicken, if desired, and place in dish, turning to coat. Cover and refrigerate 2 hours, turning chicken every 30 minutes. Drain.
• **Dredge** chicken in potato chip crumbs; place on a rack coated with cooking spray. Place rack in a broiler pan.
• **Bake** at 400° for 15 minutes; turn chicken. Reduce heat to 350°, and bake 20 minutes. **Yield:** 3 servings.

* 1½ cups crushed hot-and-spicy potato chips may be substituted.

H. W. Asbell
Leesburg, Florida

BARBECUED CHICKEN LEGS AND THIGHS

4 chicken legs, skinned
4 chicken thighs, skinned
¾ cup ketchup
⅓ cup firmly packed brown sugar
3 tablespoons Worcestershire sauce
2 tablespoons orange juice
1 tablespoon dried onion flakes
1 tablespoon prepared mustard
½ teaspoon garlic powder

• **Place** chicken in a greased 13- x 9- x 2-inch baking dish; set aside.
• **Combine** ketchup and remaining ingredients, and pour over chicken.
• **Bake** at 350° for 1 hour, turning chicken once. **Yield:** 8 servings.

HOT-AND-SPICY CHICKEN DINNER

2 cups quick-cooking rice, uncooked
2 (10-ounce) cans diced tomatoes and chiles, undrained
1 (11-ounce) can Cheddar cheese soup, undiluted
1 small onion, chopped
1 teaspoon dried basil
½ teaspoon salt
⅛ teaspoon pepper
2 pounds chicken legs and thighs, skinned

• **Combine** first 7 ingredients; pour into a greased 11- x 7- x 1½-inch baking dish. Arrange chicken in dish; cover loosely with wax paper.
• **Microwave** at HIGH 15 minutes. Turn chicken pieces over. Microwave at HIGH, uncovered, 11 to 15 minutes or until chicken is done. **Yield:** 4 to 6 servings.

Note: Casserole may be baked at 350° for 45 minutes.

Hettie Morgan
Shreveport, Louisiana

FOOD SAFETY QUESTIONS?

Look for a label similar to this on meat and poultry packages.

Safe Handling Instructions

THIS PRODUCT WAS PREPARED FROM INSPECTED AND PASSED MEAT AND/OR POULTRY. SOME FOOD PRODUCTS MAY CONTAIN BACTERIA THAT COULD CAUSE ILLNESS IF THE PRODUCT IS MISHANDLED OR COOKED IMPROPERLY. FOR YOUR PROTECTION, FOLLOW THESE SAFE-HANDLING INSTRUCTIONS.

KEEP REFRIGERATED OR FROZEN. THAW IN REFRIGERATOR OR MICROWAVE. KEEP RAW MEAT AND POULTRY SEPARATE FROM OTHER FOODS. WASH WORKING SURFACES (INCLUDING CUTTING BOARDS), UTENSILS, AND HANDS AFTER TOUCHING RAW MEAT OR POULTRY. COOK THOROUGHLY. KEEP HOT FOODS HOT. REFRIGERATE LEFTOVERS IMMEDIATELY OR DISCARD.

THE THICK & THIN OF IT

Have you ever purchased barbecue sauce with big plans for a fine feast, and then discovered that the sauce wasn't what you expected? Well, no more surprises. We've tested lots of sauces, picked the best, and named them to suit their taste.

Barbecue sauces are both savored as condiments at the table and used to add flavor and keep the meat moist as it cooks. Baste with the thicker, sweet sauces only during the last few minutes of grilling because the sweet ingredients (including ketchup) burn easily and can cause the fire to flare up if they drip on the coals.

THIN AND TASTY BARBECUE SAUCE

1 (8-ounce) bottle ketchup
1 cup cider vinegar
¼ cup water
1½ tablespoons pepper
1 tablespoon paprika
1½ teaspoons chili powder
½ teaspoon salt
½ teaspoon dry mustard
1½ teaspoons Worcestershire sauce
1½ teaspoons hot sauce

●Combine all ingredients in a bowl.
●Divide sauce into separate containers for basting and serving at the table. (Basting brushes used on raw food should not be dipped in table sauce.) Use as a basting sauce during last 10 minutes of cooking time for burgers, chicken, or ribs.
●Refrigerate leftover table sauce, and discard any remaining basting sauce. Yield: 2⅔ cups.

Mrs. P. D. Moore
Roanoke, Virginia

THICK AND ROBUST BARBECUE SAUCE

¾ cup cider vinegar
½ cup ketchup
¼ cup chili sauce
¼ cup Worcestershire sauce
2 tablespoons chopped onion
1 tablespoon brown sugar
1 tablespoon lemon juice
½ teaspoon dry mustard
Dash of ground red pepper
1 clove garlic, minced

●Combine all ingredients in a saucepan; bring to a boil over medium heat, stirring occasionally. Reduce heat, and simmer, uncovered, stirring occasionally, 40 minutes.
●Divide sauce into separate containers for basting and serving at the table. (Basting brushes used on raw food should not be dipped in table sauce.) Use as a basting sauce during last 10 minutes of cooking time for steak, pork, or burgers.
●Refrigerate leftover table sauce, and discard any remaining basting sauce. Yield: 1¾ cups.

WHITE BARBECUE SAUCE

1½ cups reduced-calorie mayonnaise
½ cup water
¼ cup white wine vinegar
¼ cup lemon juice
2 tablespoons sugar
2 tablespoons freshly ground pepper
2 tablespoons white wine Worcestershire sauce

●Combine all ingredients in a large bowl; stir with a wire whisk to blend thoroughly.
●Divide sauce into separate containers for basting and serving at the table. (Basting brushes used on raw food should not be dipped in table sauce.) Use as a basting sauce and condiment for chicken. Be sure to refrigerate leftover table sauce, and discard any remaining basting sauce. Yield: 2½ cups.

THICK AND SWEET BARBECUE SAUCE

½ cup chopped onion
1 clove garlic
¼ cup vegetable oil
1 (8-ounce) can tomato sauce
¼ cup firmly packed brown sugar
1½ teaspoons grated lemon rind
¼ cup lemon juice
2 tablespoons Worcestershire sauce
2 tablespoons prepared mustard
1 tablespoon chopped fresh parsley

●Cook onion and garlic in oil in a skillet over medium heat, stirring constantly, until tender. Add tomato sauce and remaining ingredients. Reduce heat, and simmer, uncovered, 20 minutes, stirring often.
●Divide sauce into separate containers for basting and serving at the table. (Basting brushes used on raw food should not be dipped in table sauce.) Use as a basting sauce during last 10 minutes of cooking time for burgers, chicken, or ribs. Refrigerate any leftover table sauce, and discard any remaining basting sauce. Yield: 1 cup.

Ruth Sherrer
Fort Worth, Texas

BARBECUE BASICS

When using sauce to baste meat *and* to serve on the side, follow one of these recommended procedures for safety.

■ Before basting, pour off a portion of the sauce to save for serving on the side.

■ After basting the meat, bring remaining sauce to a boil to destroy any bacteria that may have been transferred from raw meat to the basting brush.

BUENOS DÍAS BRUNCH

After a Saturday morning walk (or workout), wake up your taste buds with this zesty Tex-Mex entrée. Soothe the hot, spicy flavors of peppers, sausage, and chili powder with the refreshing tastes of fresh fruit and cilantro. (If desired, substitute fresh mint for the cilantro.) A blend of sweetened chocolate, cinnamon, and coffee makes a delicious finale.

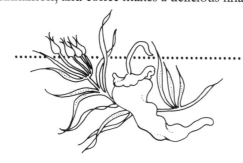

MEXICAN BRUNCH MENU
Serves Six

Mexicali Quiche With Avocado Topping
Fruit Salad With Citrus-Cilantro Dressing
Commercial Cinnamon Rolls
Mexican Coffee

TIMESAVING TIPS

■ Cook sausage mixture for quiche up to a day ahead, and chill until ready to mix the filling.

■ Cut up fruit, except for berries, and prepare dressing for the fruit salad up to a day ahead; chill in separate containers. An hour before serving, mix fruit, berries, and dressing.

■ To save time as well as calories, serve the quiche with commercial salsa rather than the Avocado Topping. If you're really pressed for time, purchase a jar of unsweetened fresh fruit salad available in the produce department of your supermarket. Drain the fruit, and add fresh berries; toss with Citrus-Cilantro Dressing. Serve a gourmet cinnamon and chocolate coffee blend in place of Mexican Coffee.

MEXICALI QUICHE WITH AVOCADO TOPPING

6 (6-inch) corn tortillas
½ pound ground hot pork sausage
¼ cup finely chopped onion
1 tablespoon chili powder
1 teaspoon ground cumin
3 large eggs, lightly beaten
1 (4.5-ounce) can chopped green chiles, divided
1½ cups half-and-half
½ teaspoon salt
⅛ teaspoon pepper
1½ cups (6 ounces) shredded Monterey Jack cheese, divided
Avocado Topping

● **Pour** water to depth of 2 inches in skillet. Bring to a boil; remove from heat.

● **Dip** each tortilla in water to soften; drain on paper towels. Place tortillas in 6 lightly greased 10-ounce custard cups; set aside.

● **Cook** sausage and next 3 ingredients in skillet over medium heat until meat is browned, stirring until it crumbles; drain and set aside.

● **Combine** eggs, half of green chiles, and next 3 ingredients in a large bowl; stir in sausage mixture.

● **Spoon** half of egg mixture evenly into tortilla shells; sprinkle with half of cheese. Pour remaining egg mixture evenly over cheese.

● **Bake** at 350° for 20 minutes. Sprinkle with remaining cheese, and bake 5 additional minutes.

● **Remove** from oven, and let stand 5 minutes. Remove from custard cups, and sprinkle with remaining green chiles. Serve with Avocado Topping. **Yield:** 6 servings.

Avocado Topping

1 avocado, peeled and mashed
1 tomato, peeled, seeded, and chopped
1 clove garlic, minced
1 to 2 tablespoons lime juice

● **Combine** all ingredients in a small bowl. **Yield:** 1½ cups.

Note: To make Mexicali Quiche in a 9-inch deep-dish pieplate, soften 8 corn tortillas in boiling water, as directed; place in lightly greased pieplate, overlapping and extending tortillas about ½ inch over edge. Spoon half of egg mixture into shell; sprinkle with half of cheese, and spoon remaining egg mixture over cheese. Bake at 350° for 30 minutes. Sprinkle with remaining cheese, and bake an additional 5 minutes. Remove from oven, and let stand 5 minutes. Sprinkle with remaining green chiles. Serve with Avocado Topping. **Yield:** one 9-inch quiche.

FRUIT SALAD WITH CITRUS-CILANTRO DRESSING

3 cups fresh pineapple chunks or
   1 (20-ounce) can pineapple
   chunks in juice, drained
2 cups pink grapefruit sections
   (about 3 grapefruit)
2 cups fresh strawberry slices
1 mango, peeled and sliced
Citrus-Cilantro Dressing
1 tablespoon chopped fresh
   cilantro

● **Combine** pineapple chunks, grapefruit, strawberry, and mango in a bowl; toss with Citrus-Cilantro Dressing, and sprinkle with cilantro.
● **Cover** mixture, and chill 1 hour. Serve salad with a slotted spoon. **Yield:** 6 to 8 servings.

Citrus-Cilantro Dressing

⅓ cup orange juice
⅓ cup fresh lime juice
3 tablespoons chopped fresh
   cilantro
2 tablespoons honey

● **Combine** orange juice, lime juice, and cilantro in a small saucepan.
● **Bring** to a boil; reduce heat, and simmer 5 minutes.
● **Pour** mixture through a wire-mesh strainer into a bowl; discard cilantro. Stir in honey. **Yield:** about ½ cup.

MEXICAN COFFEE

½ cup ground dark roast coffee
1 tablespoon ground cinnamon
¼ teaspoon ground nutmeg
5 cups water
¼ cup firmly packed dark brown
   sugar
⅓ cup chocolate syrup
1 cup milk
1 teaspoon vanilla extract
Sweetened whipped cream
Garnish: ground cinnamon

● **Place** coffee in coffee filter or filter basket; add ground cinnamon and nutmeg. Add water to coffeemaker, and brew.

● **Combine** brown sugar, chocolate syrup, and milk in a large heavy saucepan. Cook over low heat, stirring constantly, until sugar dissolves. Stir in coffee and vanilla. Serve immediately with a dollop of whipped cream; garnish, if desired. **Yield:** 6½ cups.

PUT OUT THE FIRE WITH DESSERT

....

The next time you're in the mood to serve something distinctive, try a Southwestern dessert.

These sweets make a perfect ending to a fiesta. Each dessert is simple, hearty, and able to stand up to the strong flavors and personalities of spices and hot chiles.

MEXICAN APPLE PIE

1½ cups sugar
2 cups water
½ cup butter or margarine,
   melted
4 cups peeled and chopped Golden
   Delicious apples (about 1½
   pounds)
2 teaspoons ground cinnamon
10 (6-inch) flour tortillas
Whipped cream
Ground cinnamon (optional)

● **Combine** sugar and water in a small saucepan; cook over medium heat, stirring constantly, until sugar melts. Set aside.
● **Place** butter in a 13- x 9- x 2-inch baking dish; set aside.
● **Combine** apples and 2 teaspoons cinnamon, stirring to coat.
● **Place** about ½ cup apple mixture down center of each tortilla. Roll up, and place, seam side down, in baking

dish. Pour sugar mixture over top of tortillas, and cover with aluminum foil.
● **Bake** at 350° for 30 minutes.
● **Uncover** and bake 25 to 30 minutes. Let stand 10 minutes. Serve warm with whipped cream; sprinkle with additional cinnamon, if desired. **Yield:** 10 servings.

Diane Dawson Martin
Summerville, Georgia

BANANA RUM SALSA

2 medium-size ripe bananas,
   peeled
2 tablespoons sugar
2 tablespoons dark rum
2 teaspoons butter, melted
½ teaspoon ground
   cinnamon
½ teaspoon vanilla extract
Vanilla ice cream
Tortilla Baskets
Garnish: cinnamon sticks

● **Cut** bananas lengthwise in half; place on a rack, and place rack in a broiler pan. Sprinkle bananas evenly with sugar.
● **Broil** 5½ inches from heat (with electric oven door partially opened) 5 minutes or until brown and bubbly. Coarsely chop bananas; place in a bowl.
● **Add** rum, butter, cinnamon, and vanilla to bananas; toss gently. Scoop ice cream into Tortilla Baskets. Top with banana mixture; garnish, if desired. **Yield:** 4 servings.

Tortilla Baskets

4 (6-inch) flour tortillas
Vegetable cooking spray
6 ounces chocolate-flavored candy
   coating, melted

● **Brush** tortillas with water on both sides. Place each inside an 8-ounce custard cup coated with cooking spray.
● **Bake** at 350° for 10 to 12 minutes. Cool baskets in cups on a wire rack.
● **Dip** edges of baskets in melted candy coating, and let stand until firm. (Reserve remaining coating for another use.) **Yield:** 4 baskets.

Mildred Bickley
Bristol, Virginia

CREATE EASTER MEMORIES

Pleasant memories weave in and out of our lives like ribbons,

letting us feel the joy of special times, over, and over, and over....

Why not relive the wonderful memories of the Easter cakes that

your mother prepared? We've recreated those cakes for you to try.

We hope they'll not only remind you of your childhood, but that they'll

help create special future memories for your family as well.

EASTER EGG CAKE

1 (16-ounce) package pound cake
    mix
¾ cup milk
¾ cup chocolate syrup
2 large eggs
½ teaspoon vanilla extract
Seven-Minute Frosting
Ribbon (optional)

●**Combine** first 5 ingredients in a large mixing bowl; beat at medium speed with an electric mixer 4 minutes. Pour 2 cups batter into a deep ovenproof 3-cup bowl; set aside remaining batter.
●**Bake** at 325° for 55 to 60 minutes or until a wooden pick inserted in center comes out clean. Cool in bowl on a wire rack 10 minutes. Remove cake from bowl; cool completely on wire rack.
●**Repeat** baking procedure with additional 2 cups batter.
●**Spoon** remaining batter into 5 paper-lined muffin cups, and bake at 350° for 16 to 18 minutes. Remove from pan immediately.
●**Spread** ¼ cup Seven-Minute Frosting on flat side of 1 cake; insert 4 wooden picks, and join to flat side of second cake, forming an egg shape. Cut ½ inch from 1 side of egg to prevent rolling, and place on a piece of foil-covered cardboard or a serving plate.

●**Spread** remaining frosting on top and sides of egg cake, and on top of cupcakes. Tie fabric ribbon around egg, if desired. Decorate cupcakes, if desired. **Yield:** 1 cake and 5 cupcakes.

Seven-Minute Frosting

1½ cups sugar
¼ cup plus 1 tablespoon cold
    water
2 egg whites
1 tablespoon light corn syrup
Dash of salt
1 teaspoon vanilla extract
Red liquid food coloring (optional)

●**Combine** first 5 ingredients in top of a large double boiler. Beat at low speed with an electric mixer 30 seconds or just until blended.
●**Place** over boiling water; beat constantly at high speed 7 minutes or until stiff peaks form. Remove from heat.
●**Add** vanilla, and beat 2 minutes or until frosting is thick enough to spread. Tint frosting with red food coloring, if desired. **Yield:** 4¼ cups.

Note: For other occasions, this cake can be decorated as a football for a birthday or team celebration.

BUNNY CAKE

Red liquid food coloring
½ teaspoon water
1 (14-ounce) package flaked
    coconut, divided
1 (18.25-ounce) package white
    cake mix
Seven-Minute Frosting
3 pink jelly beans
Red string licorice
Pink ribbon (optional)

●**Combine** 1 drop food coloring and water in a plastic bag or jar; add ½ cup coconut. Seal and shake until evenly tinted. Set aside.
●**Prepare** cake mix according to package directions; spoon batter into 2 greased and floured 9-inch round cakepans.
●**Bake** at 350° for 27 minutes or until a wooden pick inserted in center comes out clean. Let cool in pans on wire racks 10 minutes; remove from pans, and let cool completely on wire racks.
●**Cut** a 5½-inch circle in center of 1 layer (see A); cut outer edge into 8 equal parts. Place 5½-inch circle on a 12- x 9-inch foil-covered board for the head. Cut a 6-inch square in center of remaining layer (see B); place square on board for body. For each bunny paw, stack 2 of the remaining 8 small pieces (from A). Arrange remaining 4 pieces (from B) to form ears (see C).

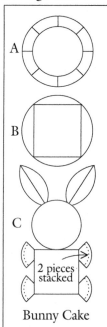

Bunny Cake

●**Spread** Seven-Minute Frosting over top and sides of cake; sprinkle pink coconut in center of face, down center of ears, and in center of bottom paws. Pat remaining coconut around sides and top. Position pink jelly beans for eyes and in center of pink coconut for nose. Use red string licorice to outline eyes and to make mouth and toes on top paws. Add a ribbon bow, if desired. **Yield:** 1 cake.

Seven-Minute Frosting

1½ cups sugar
¼ cup plus 1 tablespoon cold
    water
2 egg whites
1 tablespoon light corn syrup
Dash of salt
1 teaspoon vanilla extract

●**Combine** first 5 ingredients in top of a large double boiler. Beat at low speed with an electric mixer 30 seconds or just until blended.
●**Place** over boiling water; beat constantly at high speed 7 minutes or until stiff peaks form. Remove from heat.
●**Add** vanilla, and beat 2 minutes or until frosting is thick enough to spread. **Yield:** 4¼ cups.

EASTER RABBIT CAKE

The cake mix makes two layers. If you want to make two Easter Rabbit Cakes, double the frosting and remaining ingredients. Or you can freeze the second layer for later.

1 (18.25-ounce) package white
    cake mix
Vanilla Buttercream Frosting
1 (3½-ounce) can flaked coconut
2 pink jelly beans
1 red jelly bean
6 yellow plastic picks
1 (12- x 9-inch) sheet pink
    construction paper
1 (12- x 9-inch) sheet white
    construction paper

●**Prepare** cake mix according to package directions; spoon batter into 2 greased and floured 8-inch round cakepans.
●**Bake** according to package directions until a wooden pick inserted in center comes out clean. Cool in pans on wire racks 10 minutes; remove from pans. Cool completely on wire racks.
●**Cut** 1 layer in half crosswise, forming 2 half-circles. (Freeze the other layer for later or make 2 Easter Rabbit Cakes.)
●**Spread** ½ cup Vanilla Buttercream Frosting on bottom (flat side) of one

half-circle; top with second half-circle (flat sides together). Stand layers upright on cut edge on a piece of foil-covered cardboard or a platter.
●**Cut** a notch (see A) to shape bunny; then shape reserved cutout portion to form tail (see B), and attach with frosting.
●**Spread** remaining frosting on cake, rounding out sides; sprinkle with coconut. Position pink jelly beans for eyes and red jelly bean for mouth. Attach plastic picks on sides of mouth for whiskers. Cut out 2 pink and 2 white paper ears (about 5½- x 1½-inches); trim pink

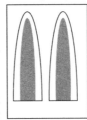

pieces ⅛ inch smaller than white. Glue pink pieces to white pieces; crease lower half of ears, and attach to cake. **Yield:** 1 cake.

Vanilla Buttercream Frosting

1½ cups butter or margarine,
    softened
4 cups sifted powdered
    sugar
2 tablespoons milk
1 teaspoon vanilla extract

●**Beat** butter at medium speed with an electric mixer until creamy; gradually add powdered sugar, beating mixture until light and fluffy. Add milk and vanilla, beating until spreading consistency. **Yield:** 3 cups.

CREATE YOUR OWN CAKE SETTING

We surrounded these cakes with commercial plastic grass. For a different effect, use tinted green coconut. To tint coconut, combine a drop or two of green liquid food coloring and ½ teaspoon water in a plastic bag or glass jar. Add coconut; seal and shake until the color is distributed evenly. Repeat procedure for darker grass.

Kids' eyes will light up when they discover that the Easter Bunny has hidden jelly beans and small marshmallow chicks in the surrounding grass.

Easter Rabbit Cake

Bunny Cake

Easter Egg Cake

FORECAST: EXPECTING SHOWERS

Shower (SHAU-er): n **1: a.** a sudden, abundant flow of gifts, usually pink and blue **b.** a party given to help expectant parents prepare for their new arrival.
Good idea.
2: a casual gathering that centers around a group of good friends, good food, and a good time.
Great idea!
What better reason for celebrating and sharing with friends than an anticipated beginning.

PARENTS-TO-BE PICNIC
Serves Eight

Apple Berry Sparkler
Commercial Dip With Assorted
Fresh Vegetables
Grilled Chicken Quarters
Baked Beans Quintet
Dill-and-Sour Cream Potato Salad
Herbed French Bread
Chocolate Chip Pound Cake

APPLE BERRY SPARKLER

1 (6-ounce) can frozen apple juice concentrate, thawed and undiluted
1 (12-ounce) can frozen cranberry juice concentrate, thawed and undiluted
6 cups sparkling mineral water, chilled
Garnish: lemon slices

• **Combine** apple juice and cranberry juice concentrates; chill.
• **Stir** in chilled mineral water. Serve over ice, and garnish, if desired. **Yield:** 2 quarts.

BAKED BEANS QUINTET

6 slices bacon
1 cup chopped onion
1 clove garlic, minced
1 (16-ounce) can butterbeans, drained
1 (17-ounce) can lima beans, drained
1 (15-ounce) can pork and beans
1 (15-ounce) can red kidney beans, drained
1 (19-ounce) can chick-peas, drained
¾ cup ketchup
½ cup molasses
¼ cup firmly packed brown sugar
1 tablespoon Worcestershire sauce
1 tablespoon prepared mustard
¼ teaspoon pepper

• **Cook** bacon in a large skillet until crisp; remove bacon, reserving drippings in skillet. Crumble bacon, and set aside.
• **Cook** onion and garlic in drippings, stirring constantly, until tender; drain.
• **Combine** bacon, onion mixture, butterbeans, and next 4 ingredients in a large bowl. Stir in ketchup and remaining ingredients. Spoon mixture into a lightly greased 2½-quart bean pot or baking dish; cover with aluminum foil.
• **Bake** at 375° for 1 hour. **Yield:** 8 to 10 servings.

Carolyne M. Carnevale
Ormond Beach, Florida

DILL-AND-SOUR CREAM POTATO SALAD

3 pounds unpeeled new potatoes
⅔ cup mayonnaise
1 (8-ounce) carton sour cream
1 tablespoon chopped fresh dill
2 teaspoons chopped fresh parsley
½ teaspoon salt
½ teaspoon pepper
Garnish: fresh dill sprig

• **Cook** unpeeled potatoes in boiling, salted water to cover 15 minutes or until tender; drain and let potatoes cool to touch.
• **Cut** potatoes into eighths, leaving skins on. Place in a large bowl.

• **Combine** mayonnaise and next 5 ingredients. Add to potatoes, toss gently.
• **Cover** and chill 8 hours. Garnish, if desired. **Yield:** 8 servings.

Prissy Grozinger
Shreveport, Louisiana

CHOCOLATE CHIP POUND CAKE

1 (18.25-ounce) yellow cake mix with pudding
1 (3.9-ounce) package chocolate instant pudding mix
½ cup sugar
¾ cup vegetable oil
¾ cup water
4 large eggs
1 (8-ounce) carton sour cream
1 cup semisweet chocolate morsels
Sifted powdered sugar

• **Combine** first 3 ingredients, stirring with a wire whisk to remove large lumps. Add oil and next 3 ingredients, stirring until smooth. Stir in chocolate morsels. Pour batter into a greased and floured 12-cup Bundt pan.
• **Bake** at 350° for 1 hour or until a wooden pick inserted in center comes out clean.
• **Cool** cake in pan on a wire rack 10 minutes; remove from pan, and cool completely on wire rack.
• **Sprinkle** with sifted powdered sugar. **Yield:** one 10-inch cake.

Becky DeWare
Houston, Texas

SHOWER THEM WITH THE UNEXPECTED

Traditional shower gift? Not this time. Invite guests to help build a culinary "layette" by bringing their favorite casseroles, frozen. During the party, store the entrées in a disposable, plastic foam cooler. Cap the festivities by sending the soon-to-be parents home with meals they can enjoy after the baby arrives.

MAY

Soups From The Sea

The aroma immediately snags your senses. Whether the seafood soup is delicate and creamy or rich and hearty, reassuring wafts from the pot deliver a beguiling sense of place. Who can resist a sip?

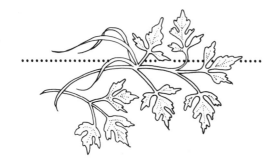

SPICY THAI LOBSTER SOUP
(pictured on page 109)

This soup hints of faraway places with a serendipitous blend of coconut milk, red pepper, and ginger.

2 fresh lobster tails *
1 tablespoon ground ginger
½ teaspoon ground red pepper
1 tablespoon peanut oil
5 cups chicken broth
1 tablespoon coarsely grated lime rind
⅓ cup long-grain rice, uncooked
1 cup unsweetened coconut milk
6 large fresh mushrooms, sliced
½ cup chopped onion
1 tablespoon chopped fresh cilantro
2 tablespoons lime juice
Garnishes: chopped green onions, fresh cilantro sprigs

● **Remove** lobster from shell; slice. Set aside.
● **Cook** 1 tablespoon ground ginger and ½ teaspoon ground red pepper in peanut oil in a large saucepan over medium heat 1 minute. Add chicken broth and lime rind.
● **Bring** mixture to a boil. Stir in rice; cover, reduce heat, and simmer 15 to 20 minutes.
● **Add** coconut milk, sliced mushrooms, ½ cup chopped onion, and chopped cilantro; cook 5 minutes, stirring mixture occasionally.
● **Add** lobster; cook 3 to 5 minutes. Remove from heat, and stir in lime juice. Spoon into bowls; garnish, if desired. **Yield:** 6½ cups.

* 1 pound unpeeled, medium-size fresh shrimp may be substituted. Peel shrimp, and devein, if desired.

Heather Riggins
Nashville, Tennessee

GULF COAST CIOPPINO
(pictured on page 109)

Plump clams and inky-shelled mussels are cradled in this rich, colorful, tomato-based soup.

20 fresh mussels
20 fresh clams
¼ cup butter or margarine
1 tablespoon olive oil
2 cups chopped celery
2 cups chopped green pepper
1 cup chopped green onions
2 cloves garlic, pressed
1 (16-ounce) can crushed tomatoes, undrained
1 (15-ounce) can tomato sauce
1 to 1½ tablespoons dried Italian seasoning
1 to 1½ teaspoons ground red pepper
1½ teaspoons paprika
1 teaspoon sugar
1 teaspoon salt
½ teaspoon ground black pepper
2 (14½-ounce) cans ready-to-serve chicken broth
1 pound grouper, amberjack, or sea bass fillets, cut into bite-size pieces

● **Scrub** mussels with a brush, removing beards. Wash clams. Discard any opened mussels and clams. Set aside.
● **Melt** butter in a large Dutch oven. Add olive oil and next 4 ingredients; cook, stirring constantly, 5 minutes or until tender.
● **Stir** in tomatoes and next 7 ingredients; cook mixture 2 to 3 minutes, stirring occasionally. Stir in broth.
● **Bring** tomato mixture to a boil; reduce heat, and simmer for 45 minutes, stirring occasionally.
● **Stir** in mussels, clams, and fish; cook 3 to 4 minutes, stirring occasionally. (Mussels and clams should open during cooking. Discard any unopened shells.) Serve immediately. **Yield:** about 3 quarts.

Malana Clark
Birmingham, Alabama

SHRIMP ENCHILADA SOUP

If you love the taste of Tex-Mex, then this bowl's for you.

5   cups chicken broth
4   ounces tortilla chips (3 cups)
1   pound unpeeled, medium-size fresh shrimp
2   (4.5-ounce) cans chopped green chiles
1   (10-ounce) can diced tomatoes and green chiles
2   tablespoons butter or margarine
1   medium onion, chopped
2   cloves garlic, minced
1   cup sour cream
¼   cup chopped fresh cilantro
Shredded mozzarella cheese
Shredded Cheddar cheese

•**Bring** chicken broth to a boil in a large Dutch oven.
•**Add** tortilla chips. Remove from heat, and let stand 10 minutes.
•**Peel** shrimp, and devein, if desired. Set shrimp aside.
•**Position** knife blade in food processor bowl; pour in half of broth mixture. Process until smooth, stopping once to scrape down sides. Transfer mixture to another container. Repeat procedure with remaining mixture.
•**Return** blended broth mixture to Dutch oven; stir in green chiles and tomatoes. Set aside.
•**Melt** butter in a large skillet over medium-high heat. Add shrimp, onion, and garlic; cook, stirring constantly, 3 to 4 minutes or until shrimp turn pink.
•**Stir** shrimp mixture into broth mixture; cook over medium heat until thoroughly heated (do not boil).
•**Stir** in sour cream and cilantro. Serve soup immediately. Sprinkle each serving with mozzarella and Cheddar cheeses. **Yield:** 2 quarts.

Laurie McIntyre
Houston, Texas

Seafood loves to become soup. Most varieties blend beautifully with a wide sweep of flavors and textures. The aura may be complex, but the effort isn't.

Unlike some main courses, seafood soups feed a crowd without rocking your budget. Sensational seafood concoctions are often dictated by availability, so let yourself be inspired by the fresh catch of the day.

CURRIED SEAFOOD CHOWDER

Curry powder paints this soup the color of the afternoon sun.

1   pound unpeeled, medium-size fresh shrimp
3   tablespoons butter or margarine
3   tablespoons all-purpose flour
1   tablespoon curry powder
2   cups chicken broth
2   (8-ounce) bottles clam juice
2   cups half-and-half
4   medium potatoes, peeled and coarsely chopped (about 4 cups)
1   pound grouper or amberjack fillets, cut into bite-size pieces

•**Peel** shrimp, and devein, if desired; set shrimp aside.

•**Melt** butter in a large Dutch oven over medium heat; add flour and curry powder, stirring constantly, until mixture is smooth. Cook 1 minute, stirring constantly. Gradually add chicken broth, stirring until smooth. Stir in clam juice, half-and-half, and chopped potatoes.
•**Bring** to a boil; cover, reduce heat, and simmer 20 minutes or until potatoes are tender.
•**Add** fish and shrimp; cook 5 minutes or until shrimp turn pink. Serve immediately. **Yield:** 3½ quarts.

Kay C. Regnier
Winterville, North Carolina

CRAB-AND-LEEK BISQUE

Delicate ingredients bring a blush of fragile flavors to this creamy soup.

3 leeks (about 1½ pounds)
½ cup butter or margarine
1 clove garlic, minced
½ cup all-purpose flour
4 cups chicken broth
½ cup Chablis or other dry white wine
2 cups half-and-half
½ pound fresh crabmeat, drained and flaked
¼ teaspoon salt
¼ teaspoon ground white pepper
Garnish: sliced leeks

● **Remove** roots, tough outer leaves, and green tops from leeks. Split white portion of leeks in half, wash, and cut halves into thin slices.
● **Melt** butter in a Dutch oven over medium-high heat. Add leeks and garlic, and cook, stirring constantly, 3 minutes or until tender.
● **Add** flour, stirring until smooth. Cook 1 minute, stirring constantly. Gradually add broth and wine; cook over medium heat, stirring constantly, until mixture is thickened (about 4 minutes).
● **Stir** in half-and-half and next 3 ingredients. Garnish, if desired. **Yield:** 2 quarts.

Ian Tarica
Atlanta, Georgia

FISH TALES

■ The Gulf of Mexico harbors some of the the richest shrimp beds in the world. In the United States, shrimp is the most popular of all crustaceans, followed by crab and lobster.

■ If you see "Brushwood Shrimp" on a Chinese menu, you'd better think twice about ordering: It means grasshoppers.

■ The lobster's eyes are mounted on long, wispy reeds, permitting it to see in all directions, yet it's still quite dim-sighted, often "bumping into" its dinner.

■ Lobsters have one very large claw used for crushing prey, and a small one for cutting. Lobsters can be either "right or left clawed," with the big claw sometimes on the left and other times on the right.

■ The very word "soup" is thought to be imitative of the sound of slurping hot liquid from a spoon.

■ When told that the phosphorous in fish improves the brain, Mark Twain once suggested that some folks he knew should "eat a couple of whales."

CLAM-AND-SAUSAGE CHOWDER

Clams and sausage deliver full-bodied flavors to this robust chowder.

2 dozen fresh clams
2 pounds smoked Polish sausage, thinly sliced
1 medium onion, chopped
2 cloves garlic, minced
2 tablespoons olive oil
1½ pounds potatoes, cubed
1 (10-ounce) package frozen whole kernel corn, thawed
4 (8-ounce) bottles clam juice
2 cups water
1 teaspoon fennel seeds, crushed
½ to 1 teaspoon ground red pepper
2 (16-ounce) cans crushed tomatoes, undrained
½ cup fresh parsley, chopped

● **Wash** clams thoroughly, discarding any opened shells. Set aside.
● **Brown** sausage in a Dutch oven over medium heat; drain on paper towels, and set aside.
● **Cook** onion and garlic in olive oil in a Dutch oven over medium-high heat, stirring constantly, until tender. Add potatoes and next 5 ingredients.
● **Bring** to a boil; cover, reduce heat, and simmer 15 minutes or until potatoes are tender. Stir in tomatoes.
● **Remove** 2 cups potato mixture, and pour into container of an electric blender. Process until smooth, stopping once to scrape down sides. Return mixture to Dutch oven.
● **Bring** to a boil. Add clams; cover, reduce heat, and simmer 4 to 5 minutes or until clam shells open. (Discard any unopened shells.)
● **Stir** in sausage and parsley; cook until thoroughly heated. **Yield:** 3 quarts.

NAVIGATING THE WATERS

....

■ The key to a delicious seafood soup is quality seafood. Buy only the best – fresh or fresh frozen.

■ Trust your nose: Good-quality fresh fish has the aroma of the sea – not the boat bottom.

■ Make the fish market your last stop. Fish should go straight home to the bottom shelf or the meat keeper of your refrigerator, where temperatures are coldest.

■ Immediately discard fish wrapping, bones, and shells in a sealed plastic bag in your outside garbage can.

■ Keep seafood refrigerated until just before you cook it, and use it within a day.

■ To avoid cross-contamination, don't cut raw and cooked seafood on the same surface. Always wash cutting board after each use to avoid contamination of the next food.

■ If a fish bone gets caught in your throat, eat a piece of bread. As you swallow, it will take the bone with it.

For more tips on seafood safety, see "From Our Kitchen to Yours" on this page.

FROM OUR KITCHEN TO YOURS

A trip to the beach isn't complete without bringing back a souvenir – the fishermen's catch of the day from the local seafood market. Here's how to haul your "catch" home.

CHARTING A SAFE COURSE

Fish and shrimp: Remove heads and entrails from fish; remove scales and fillet, if desired. Remove heads from shrimp, if purchased whole. Wrap dressed fish and shrimp in heavy-duty plastic wrap, and mix together crushed ice and table or rock salt using ½ pound salt for every five pounds of ice.

Place a rack in the bottom of a well-insulated cooler to keep seafood out of any water that accumulates from melting ice. Line the bottom of the cooler with three to four inches of salted ice mixture, and layer fish in cooler, covering each layer with the salted ice mixture. Top the fish layers with a generous layer of ice, and close securely. Place inside the car, not in the trunk. For overnight trips, drain off melted water at night, and add more salted ice mixture.

Clams: Place three to four inches of ice in bottom of cooler. Cover with waxed cardboard or plastic foam that has several air holes punched in it. Place clams on the cardboard and leave the lid slightly ajar for air circulation. Maintain a temperature between 35° to 40°. Keep traveling time to one to two days. Discard any open shells.

Mussels: Place on top of ice to keep temperature just under 45°. Don't place ice on top of the shells. Keep traveling time to one to two days. Discard any gaping shells or ones that don't snap shut when tapped.

Lobsters: Fill the bottom of a cooler with a layer of ice packs or zip-top plastic bags filled with ice; layer with a ½-inch thickness of wet newspapers (sea water is best). Place lobsters on top, and

SAVANNAH SNAPPER GUMBO

Savor the flavors of the Lowcountry in this Georgian gumbo.

3 tablespoons vegetable oil
2 tablespoons all-purpose flour
1 medium green pepper, chopped
1 stalk celery, chopped
1 medium onion, chopped
1 (14½-ounce) can stewed tomatoes, undrained
1 (14½-ounce) can ready-to-serve chicken broth
1 (10-ounce) package frozen sliced okra
1 (10-ounce) package frozen whole kernel corn
1 cup water
1 tablespoon Worcestershire sauce
½ teaspoon salt
¼ teaspoon ground red pepper
⅛ teaspoon dried thyme
1 bay leaf
12 ounces fresh red snapper fillets, cubed
Hot cooked rice

● **Combine** oil and flour with a wire whisk in a large Dutch oven; cook over medium heat, stirring constantly, 10 to 15 minutes or until roux is the color of chocolate.
● **Stir** in green pepper, celery, and onion. Cook over medium heat, stirring occasionally, about 10 minutes or until vegetables are tender.
● **Add** tomatoes and next 9 ingredients.
● **Bring** to a boil; reduce heat, and simmer 10 minutes.
● **Stir** in fish; cook 5 minutes. Remove and discard bay leaf. Serve with hot cooked rice. **Yield:** 2 quarts.

Lilann Taylor
Savannah, Georgia

cover with another layer of wet newspapers. Leave the lid slightly ajar for air circulation. Keep traveling time to one to two days.

Crabs and oysters: Place three to four inches of ice in bottom of the cooler. Cover with waxed cardboard or plastic foam that has been punched with air holes. Place crabs or oysters on cardboard, and cover with damp burlap or folded cheesecloth. Leave the cooler lid slightly ajar for air circulation. Maintain a temperature between 40° to 50° for crabs and between 35° to 40° for oysters. Limit traveling time to one day. Cook only crabs that show movement of the legs.

SEAFOOD SHENANIGANS

If you can't capture fresh flavor at the seaside, look for these seafood characteristics at your nearby landlocked supermarkets.

Fish: Bright, clear, full, and often protruding eyes; bright-red or pink gills; firm, elastic flesh which springs back when gently pressed with a finger; shiny skin; firmly attached scales; fresh, mild odor; fresh-cut appearance for fillets.

Shrimp: Mild odor; firm, not slippery, flesh; head closely attached to tail section; shell and flesh free of black spots.

Clams, mussels, and oysters: Tightly closed shells or shells that snap shut when tapped; no gaping shells.

Crabs and lobsters: Show movement of legs. Lobster tail curls under the body when picked up.

ROMAINES OF THE DAY: EASY CAESARS

The Caesar salad was a vehicle to stardom for the emperor of lettuces – romaine. But traditional Caesar salads call for anchovies, which many people don't like, and for uncooked eggs, which the U.S. Department of Agriculture recommends be eliminated from everyone's diet. Our Caesar lineup soars past the Parmesan-dusted prototype.

SOUTHERN CAESAR SALAD

Caesar comes to Dixie in this stately salad, dressed in the flavors of the South.

⅓ cup peanut oil
3 tablespoons cider vinegar
2 tablespoons egg substitute *
2 tablespoons honey mustard
¼ teaspoon pepper
4 ounces thinly sliced country ham, cut into ¼-inch strips
1 tablespoon peanut oil
1 large head romaine lettuce, torn
¾ cup pecans, toasted and coarsely chopped
Honeyed Cornbread Croutons

• **Combine** first 5 ingredients, and mix well with a wire whisk. Cover and chill at least 1 hour.
• **Cook** ham in peanut oil in a skillet over medium-high heat, stirring constantly, until browned. Drain on paper towels.
• **Combine** lettuce, pecans, and ham in a large bowl; add dressing, tossing gently.

Sprinkle with Honeyed Cornbread Croutons. **Yield:** 6 servings.

* For egg substitute, we used either Egg Beaters or Second Nature.

Honeyed Cornbread Croutons

1 (11.5-ounce) package refrigerated cornbread twists
¼ cup butter or margarine, melted
1 tablespoon honey

• **Unroll** dough; separate at perforations to form 16 strips. Place on an ungreased baking sheet.
• **Combine** butter and honey; brush on strips.
• **Bake** at 375° for 11 minutes. Remove to wire racks to cool.
• **Cut** each strip diagonally into ½-inch slices, and place on an ungreased baking sheet.
• **Bake** at 225° for 20 minutes, stirring every 5 minutes. Cool.
• **Store** in airtight container up to 1 month. **Yield:** 4 cups.

ORIENTAL CAESAR SALAD

With a bow to the flavors of Japan, plum sauce gently sweetens the rice wine vinaigrette polishing this elegant salad.

⅔ cup soybean or safflower oil
¼ cup egg substitute *
¼ cup rice wine vinegar
2 tablespoons commercial plum sauce
1 tablespoon soy sauce
1 tablespoon sesame oil
1 head romaine lettuce, torn
1 (11-ounce) can mandarin oranges, drained
1 (8-ounce) can sliced water chestnuts, drained
1 teaspoon sesame seeds
Sesame Egg Roll Fan

● **Combine** soybean oil, egg substitute, rice wine vinegar, plum sauce, soy sauce, and sesame oil in a small bowl; mix well with a wire whisk. Cover and chill.
● **Combine** lettuce, oranges, and water chestnuts in a large bowl; add dressing, tossing gently.
● **Arrange** salad on individual plates, and sprinkle evenly with sesame seeds. Serve with Sesame Egg Roll Fan. **Yield:** 4 servings.

* For egg substitute, we used either Egg Beaters or Second Nature.

Sesame Egg Roll Fan

4 (8-inch) egg roll wrappers
1 egg white
1 tablespoon soy sauce
1 teaspoon sesame seeds

● **Place** each egg roll wrapper on cutting board, and cut into ¼-inch strips, cutting to within 1 inch of opposite edge. Cut off ends of strips diagonally to form points. Set aside.
● **Combine** egg white and soy sauce; brush on egg roll wrappers, and sprinkle with sesame seeds. Fold bottom edge of each wrapper to form a fan shape. Place fans carefully on a lightly greased baking sheet.
● **Bake** at 350° for 5 to 8 minutes or until lightly browned. **Yield:** 4 fans.

CAESAR MARGARITA SALAD

A frosty salted rim frames this Caesar salad inspired by the margarita.

Lime wedges (optional)
Kosher salt (optional)
1 large head romaine lettuce, torn
1 cup (4 ounces) shredded Monterey Jack cheese
¼ cup finely chopped fresh cilantro
1 sweet red pepper, cut into thin strips
Margarita Dressing
Tortilla Triangles
Garnish: lime wedges

● **Rub** rims of 6 chilled salad plates with lime wedges, if desired; place salt in saucer, and roll rim of each plate in salt. Set aside.
● **Combine** lettuce and next 3 ingredients in a large bowl; add Margarita Dressing, tossing gently.
● **Arrange** salad on plates, and sprinkle with Tortilla Triangles. Garnish, if desired. **Yield:** 6 servings.

Margarita Dressing

⅓ cup canola or safflower oil
¼ cup lime juice
2 tablespoons egg substitute *
1½ tablespoons tequila
1½ teaspoons Triple Sec or other orange-flavored liqueur
1 clove garlic, minced
1 serrano chile, seeded and finely chopped
¼ teaspoon salt
¼ teaspoon ground cumin

● **Combine** all ingredients in a small bowl; mix well with a wire whisk. Cover and chill. **Yield:** 1 cup.

* For egg substitute, we used either Egg Beaters or Second Nature.

Tortilla Triangles

6 (6-inch) corn tortillas, cut into small triangles
½ cup canola or vegetable oil
Kosher salt

● **Fry** tortilla triangles in hot oil in a small skillet until golden brown; drain on paper towels, and immediately sprinkle with kosher salt. **Yield:** 1½ cups.

MAUI CAESAR SALAD

The breezy tastes of the islands wreathe this lush salad.

⅓ cup peanut oil
2 tablespoons rice wine vinegar
2 tablespoons pineapple juice
2 tablespoons egg substitute *
2 tablespoons ground ginger
¼ teaspoon salt
1 large head romaine lettuce, torn
1 (3½-ounce) jar macadamia nuts, coarsely chopped and toasted
Hawaiian Bread Croutons
1 cup banana chips (optional)

● **Combine** first 6 ingredients, and mix well with a wire whisk. Cover and chill dressing at least 1 hour.
● **Combine** lettuce and nuts in a large bowl; add dressing, tossing gently. Sprinkle with Hawaiian Bread Croutons and banana chips, if desired. **Yield:** 6 servings.

* For egg substitute, we used either Egg Beaters or Second Nature.

Hawaiian Bread Croutons

½ tablespoon butter or margarine, softened
2 (¾-inch-thick) slices Hawaiian bread
1 teaspoon ground ginger, divided

● **Spread** butter on both sides of bread slices; sprinkle evenly with ginger.
● **Cut** bread into ¾-inch cubes; place in a 15- x 10- x 1-inch jellyroll pan.
● **Bake** at 350° for 15 to 20 minutes or until browned and crisp, stirring every 5 minutes. **Yield:** 3 cups.

Katherine Nelson
Birmingham, Alabama

SOUTHERN ACCENT

It takes lots of testing and tasting to put together an award-winning cookbook.

The Junior League of Pine Bluff, Arkansas, did just that with *Southern Accent*. The 750-recipe cookbook

covers everything from casual backyard barbecues to elegant candlelight dinners.

Southern Accent is one of the original cookbook inductees in the Walter S. McIlhenny Cookbook Hall of Fame. The Junior League members of Pine Bluff who compiled the cookbook attest that the recipes for the fund-raising project were triple tested. We applaud their efforts, and we think you will, too.

ARMENIAN THIN BREAD

1 package active dry yeast
1 cup warm water (105° to 115°)
3¼ to 3¾ cups all-purpose flour, divided
1½ teaspoons salt
1 teaspoon sugar
¼ cup butter or margarine, melted

●**Combine** yeast and warm water in a 2-cup liquid measuring cup; let stand 5 minutes.
●**Combine** yeast mixture, 2 cups flour, and remaining ingredients in a large mixing bowl; beat at medium speed with an electric mixer until smooth. Stir in enough remaining flour to make a stiff dough.
●**Turn** dough out onto a floured surface, and knead until smooth and elastic (about 8 minutes). Place in a

well-greased bowl, turning to grease top. Cover and let rise in a warm place (85°), free from drafts, 1 hour or until doubled in bulk.
●**Punch** dough down, and divide into fourths; roll and stretch each portion into a 14- x 10-inch rectangle. Place on ungreased baking sheets.
●**Bake** at 350° for 15 to 20 minutes or until golden brown. Break into pieces. **Yield:** 4 bread sheets.

POPPY SEED CHICKEN

12 bone-in chicken breast halves, skinned
2 (10¾-ounce) cans cream of chicken soup, undiluted
3 (8-ounce) cartons sour cream
¼ cup sherry
½ teaspoon salt
½ teaspoon pepper
1½ cups crushed round buttery crackers (35 to 40 crackers)
2 tablespoons poppy seeds
⅓ cup butter or margarine, melted

●**Place** chicken breasts in a large Dutch oven and add water to cover; bring to a boil over high heat. Reduce heat, and simmer 45 minutes or until tender. Remove chicken from broth, and cool chicken to touch. (Reserve

broth for another use.) Bone chicken; chop into bite-size pieces.
●**Place** chicken in a lightly greased 13- x 9- x 2-inch baking dish. Set aside.
●**Combine** soup and next 4 ingredients; pour over chicken.
●**Combine** cracker crumbs and poppy seeds; sprinkle over soup mixture, and drizzle with butter.
●**Bake** at 350° for 30 minutes. **Yield:** 12 servings.

♥ To reduce fat and sodium, substitute reduced-fat cream of chicken soup, nonfat sour cream, low-salt round buttery cracker crumbs, and butter flavored cooking spray for butter.

Note: To make ahead, assemble recipe omitting cracker crumb topping; cover and refrigerate up to 24 hours. Remove from refrigerator, and let stand 30 minutes. Add cracker crumb mixture and butter, and bake at 350° for 40 minutes.

Above: *Unlike some main courses, rich Gulf Coast Cioppino (recipe, page 102) feeds a crowd without rocking your budget.* Inset: *Spicy Thai Lobster Soup (recipe, page 102) is your passport to seafood at its best.*

Left: *Enjoy an early summer evening with our Dinner Under the Stars menu:* (from top) *Peppered Goat Cheese and Roasted Peppers With Balsamic Vinaigrette served with French baguette slices; Grilled Sirloin Salad; and Frozen Fruit Cream crowned with Fresh Plum Sauce. (Recipes begin on page 128.)*

A lavish dessert can be easy; just drop spoonfuls of batter onto a baking sheet to make the cookies for Berry Napoleons (recipe, page 120).

MEET ME IN ST. LOUIS FOR A MILK SHAKE

St. Louis, Missouri, is known as the "Gateway to the West." But to some, the city's famous arch symbolizes "Gateway to the Best" – milk shakes, that is. So grab a straw and sip away summer's sizzle with these cooling treats.

Where have the locals in Missouri's river city sipped and savored summer for decades? Most recall hot days spent at one of three family-owned businesses, each with more than 60 years – and thousands of shakes – under their belts: Crown Candy Kitchen, Ted Drewes Frozen Custard, and The Velvet Freeze Ice-Cream Company. Here's the scoop on them:

CROWN CANDY KITCHEN

Don't let the name fool you. Although Crown Candy has made wonderful candy since 1913, their shakes are the main attraction here at the city's oldest soda fountain.

Owners Andy and Mike Karandzieff grew up behind the counter here in their grandfather's (and later their father's) shop. Today, the brothers still serve the old-fashioned shakes just the way regulars remember them – just good homemade ice cream, milk, and your choice of syrups – at a whopping 1,100 calories each. And if you want a "malted," they'll add a little malt powder on request.

PINEAPPLE MILK SHAKE

3 cups vanilla ice cream
1 (8-ounce) can crushed
    pineapple, undrained
½ cup milk

● **Combine** all ingredients in container of an electric blender; process just until smooth, stopping once to scrape down sides. **Yield:** 3 cups.

STRAWBERRY MILK SHAKE

3 cups vanilla ice cream
¾ cup fresh or frozen sliced
    strawberries, thawed
¼ cup strawberry-flavored
    syrup
¾ cup milk

● **Combine** all ingredients in container of an electric blender; process just until smooth, stopping once to scrape down sides. **Yield:** 5 cups.

CHOCOLATE-BANANA MILK SHAKE

3 cups vanilla ice cream
⅓ cup chocolate syrup
1 banana, sliced
½ cup milk
2 tablespoons malt-flavored drink
    mix (optional)

● **Combine** first 4 ingredients in container of an electric blender; process just until smooth, stopping once to scrape down sides. Stir in drink mix, if desired. **Yield:** 3¾ cups.

TED DREWES FROZEN CUSTARD

A St. Louis household name since 1929, Ted Drewes's shop is known for the thickest shake in town. So thick, you can hold it upside down – spoon, straw, and all – without spilling it. So thick, it really won't "shake." So instead, he calls it a "concrete." And your server often wears a hard hat.

■ This treat was created in honor of the Fox Theater, which was built the same year as Ted Drewes Frozen Custard.

FOXTREAT "CONCRETE"

½ cup fresh or frozen raspberries,
    thawed and drained
¼ cup commercial fudge sauce
3 cups vanilla ice cream, softened
½ cup coarsely chopped
    macadamia nuts

● **Combine** first 3 ingredients in container of an electric blender; process just until smooth, stopping once to scrape down sides (mixture will be thick). Add macadamia nuts; process a few seconds, just until blended. **Yield:** 3½ cups.

■ The St. Louis Cardinals baseball team is the inspiration for this winning Drewes concoction.

CARDINAL SIN "CONCRETE"

1 (16-ounce) can pitted sour red
    cherries, drained
4 cups vanilla ice cream
⅓ cup commercial fudge sauce

● **Freeze** cherries until firm.
● **Position** knife blade in food processor bowl; add half each of cherries, ice cream, and fudge sauce. Process just until smooth, stopping once to scrape down sides (mixture will be thick). Remove mixture, and repeat procedure. **Yield:** 4¾ cups.

■ Drewes dreamed up the Abaco Mocha, a tropical treat, after a vacation to the Bahama island of Abaco.

ABACO MOCHA "CONCRETE"

3 cups vanilla ice cream
¼ cup cold espresso *
½ teaspoon rum extract
¼ cup commercial fudge sauce

● **Combine** all ingredients in container of an electric blender; process mixture just until smooth, stopping once to scrape down sides. (Mixture will be thick.) **Yield:** 3½ cups.

* ¾ teaspoon instant espresso granules dissolved in ¼ cup cold water or ¼ cup cold strong coffee may be substituted.

AN EXTRA SCOOP: THE VELVET FREEZE ICE CREAM COMPANY

....

In 1932, the Velvet Freeze Ice Cream Company opened its doors. It has ebbed and flowed with the economic tide, resulting in today's 15 stores, plus an ice cream manufacturing plant owned by the John McGuinness family.

Customers can choose from more than 40 "homemade" flavors. They can even request a milk shake made to order.

John loves chatting with customers, even – no, especially – after all these years. "I still have so many who come in for a shake and say, 'You know, my grandfather used to work here.' " He hopes that his son will someday take the reins and hear that same comment from locals for years to come. So does the rest of St. Louis.

■ The "All Shook Up" shake gets its name from Elvis's favorite snack combination of peanut butter and banana.

ALL SHOOK UP "CONCRETE"

3 cups vanilla ice cream
⅔ cup miniature peanut butter sandwich cookies
1 banana, sliced

● **Combine** all ingredients in container of an electric blender; process just until smooth, stopping once to scrape down sides of container (mixture will be thick). **Yield:** 3½ cups.

A TASTE FOR THE BLUES

Blue seems to be the stylish color for cornmeal these days. You see it popping up on more and more restaurant menus. And in many cities around the South, blue cornmeal now resides on supermarket shelves next to its more conventional family members, yellow and white cornmeal.

Southwesterners will proudly tell you that blue corn has been part of their lives for well over a thousand years. American Indians first cultivated the colorful kernels for food and used them in ceremonial dances honoring the regeneration of Mother Earth. Today, blue corn is still grown by American Indians, and it remains a defining ingredient in most New Mexican cooking.

Don't let the soft-blue, powdery appearance fool you. Its nutty, earthy flavor is bold enough to stand up to the heat of even the hottest chile in Serrano Chile Blue Cornbread, yet subtle enough to form a heavenly partnership with the taste of fresh blueberries and oranges in Blue Cornmeal-Blueberry Pancakes.

BLUE CORN MUFFINS

1 cup all-purpose flour
1 cup blue cornmeal
1 tablespoon baking powder
1 (4.5-ounce) can chopped green chiles, drained
¾ cup (3 ounces) shredded Monterey Jack cheese, divided
2 large eggs, lightly beaten
1 cup milk
¼ cup butter or margarine, melted
2 tablespoons honey
Vegetable cooking spray

● **Combine** first 3 ingredients in a large bowl; stir in chiles and ½ cup cheese. Make a well in center of mixture. Set aside.
● **Combine** eggs and next 3 ingredients; add to dry ingredients, stirring just until moistened.
● **Place** paper baking cups in muffin pans, and coat with cooking spray; spoon batter into cups, filling three-fourths full. Sprinkle with remaining ¼ cup cheese.
● **Bake** at 400° for 17 minutes or until golden. Remove from pans immediately. **Yield:** 1½ dozen.

SERRANO CHILE BLUE CORNBREAD

1¼ cups blue cornmeal
1 cup all-purpose flour
1 tablespoon baking powder
1 teaspoon salt
⅛ teaspoon baking soda
2 tablespoons sugar
2 tablespoons butter or margarine
3 to 4 serrano chiles, unseeded and finely chopped
3 cloves garlic, minced
1 sweet red pepper, finely chopped
1 green pepper, finely chopped
2 large eggs, lightly beaten
1 cup buttermilk
⅓ cup butter or margarine, melted
⅓ cup shortening, melted
2 tablespoons plain low-fat yogurt
1 (11-ounce) can white corn, drained
3 tablespoons chopped fresh cilantro

- **Combine** first 6 ingredients in a large bowl; make a well in center of mixture. Set aside.
- **Melt** butter in a large skillet; add serrano chiles and next 3 ingredients. Cook over medium heat 2 to 3 minutes or until vegetables are tender. Set aside.
- **Combine** eggs and next 5 ingredients; add to dry ingredients, stirring just until moistened. Stir in vegetable mixture and cilantro.
- **Place** a well-greased 10-inch cast-iron skillet in a 450° oven for 4 minutes or until hot. Remove from oven; spoon batter into skillet.
- **Bake** at 450° for 25 minutes or until cornbread is lightly browned. **Yield:** 8 to 10 servings.

Kelli Silliman
Dallas, Texas

BLUE CORNMEAL-BLUEBERRY PANCAKES

2 cups blue cornmeal
2 cups all-purpose flour
1½ teaspoons baking soda
½ teaspoon salt
3 large eggs, lightly beaten
2½ cups buttermilk
⅓ cup honey
3 tablespoons vegetable oil
1½ cups fresh or frozen
   blueberries, thawed
2 tablespoons sugar
Garnishes: fresh blueberries, sifted
   powdered sugar
Orange Butter

- **Combine** cornmeal, flour, soda, and salt in a large bowl; make a well in center of mixture.
- **Combine** eggs, buttermilk, honey and vegetable oil in a small bowl; add to dry ingredients, stirring just until moistened. Let stand 10 minutes.
- **Sprinkle** 1½ cups blueberries with sugar, and stir into batter.
- **Pour** ¼ cup batter for each pancake onto a hot, lightly greased griddle or skillet. Cook pancakes until tops are covered with bubbles and edges look cooked; turn and cook other side. Garnish, if desired. Serve with Orange Butter. **Yield:** 24 (4-inch) pancakes.

Orange Butter

1 cup butter or margarine,
   softened
2 tablespoons honey
1 tablespoon grated orange rind

- **Beat** butter at medium speed with an electric mixer until creamy. Stir in honey and orange rind. **Yield:** 1 cup.

FAJITAS ARE WHAT YOU MAKE THEM

. . . .

Folks across the South have discovered the fun and flavor of these delicious sizzlers. Little by little, the word "fajita" has come to refer not only to the beef steak, but also to the technique of marinating any meat, grilling or searing it, and serving the strips of meat wrapped in a tortilla.

PLUM GOOD FAJITAS

1 (16-ounce) can purple plums in
   heavy syrup, undrained
½ cup butter or margarine
1 large onion, chopped
1 (6-ounce) can frozen lemonade
   concentrate, thawed and
   undiluted
½ cup chili sauce
¼ cup soy sauce
1 tablespoon dry mustard
1 teaspoon ground ginger
1 teaspoon Worcestershire sauce
2 drops of hot sauce
8 (8-inch) flour tortillas
1 sweet red pepper, cut into strips
1 green pepper, cut into strips
1 large onion, sliced
2 (1-pound) flank steaks
Sliced green onions
Sour cream or guacamole
Garnish: fresh cilantro sprigs

- **Drain** plums, reserving syrup; remove pits from plums. Place plums and syrup in container of an electric blender; process until smooth, stopping once to scrape down sides. Set plum puree aside.
- **Melt** butter in a saucepan over medium-high heat; add onion, and cook, stirring constantly, until tender. Stir in puree, lemonade concentrate, and next 6 ingredients. Bring sauce to a boil; reduce heat, and simmer 15 minutes.
- **Heat** tortillas according to package directions; keep warm.
- **Place** peppers and onion in a greased grill basket. Place basket and steaks on food rack; baste with sauce. Cook, without grill lid, over hot coals (400° to 500°), 10 minutes on each side or until desired degree of doneness, basting often.
- **Cut** steaks diagonally across grain into thin strips.
- **Serve** steak and grilled vegetables in tortillas; top with green onions and sour cream or guacamole. Garnish, if desired. **Yield:** 8 servings.

Mary Tom Harper
Corpus Christi, Texas

FAJITAS: A BITE OF HISTORY

Back in the old days out on the range, "fajita" (fah-HEE-tuh), Spanish for "little skirt" or "sash," referred to the thin, well-marbled flank muscle from a beef hindquarter. Inventive chuckwagon cooks discovered that when seared quickly over hot coals and wrapped in flour tortillas burrito-style, what was once considered a throw-away portion of beef soon had cowboys clamoring for more.

FAJITA CRÊPES

1½ pounds sirloin steak
1½ cups green pepper strips
1 medium onion, cut into strips
5 large mushrooms, sliced
1 (0.9-ounce) envelope fajita marinade mix
2½ tablespoons fajita seasoning mix
¼ cup water
¼ cup lime juice
¼ cup vegetable oil
Vegetable cooking spray
8 Crêpes
1 (8-ounce) carton sour cream, divided
Picante Sauce, divided
Guacamole
Sliced green onions
Shredded Cheddar cheese

• **Partially** freeze steak; slice diagonally across grain into ¼-inch strips, and place in a large shallow dish. Add green pepper strips, onion, and sliced mushrooms; set aside.
• **Combine** fajita marinade mix, fajita seasoning mix, ¼ cup water, lime juice, and vegetable oil. Pour marinade over beef mixture; cover and refrigerate 4 to 6 hours.
• **Remove** beef and vegetables from marinade, discarding marinade.
• **Cook** half each of beef and vegetables in a large skillet coated with cooking spray over medium-high heat, stirring constantly, until beef browns on both sides. Remove from skillet, and repeat procedure with remaining half of beef and vegetables.
• **Spoon** beef and vegetables evenly down center of spotty side of each Crêpe; top each with 1½ teaspoons sour cream and 1½ teaspoons Picante Sauce. Fold sides over, and place, seam side down, in a lightly greased 13- x 9- x 2-inch baking dish. Spread remaining sour cream down center of folded Crêpes, and cover with aluminum foil.
• **Bake** at 350° for 30 minutes or until thoroughly heated. Uncover and top with remaining Picante Sauce. Serve fajitas with Guacamole, green onions, and shredded Cheddar cheese. **Yield:** 4 to 6 servings.

Crêpes

3 large eggs
1½ cups milk
1⅓ cups all-purpose flour
½ teaspoon salt
1½ tablespoons vegetable oil
Vegetable cooking spray

• **Combine** first 5 ingredients in electric blender; process 1 minute, scraping down sides once. Chill 1 hour.
• **Coat** bottom of an 8-inch crêpe pan or nonstick skillet with cooking spray; place over medium heat just until hot, not smoking.
• **Pour** 3 tablespoons batter into pan. Quickly tilt pan in all directions so batter covers pan in a thin film; cook 1 minute or until crêpe can be shaken loose from pan. Flip crêpe, and cook about 30 seconds. Place crêpe on a towel to cool.
• **Repeat** procedure with remaining batter. Stack crêpes between layers of wax paper to prevent sticking. Place in an airtight container; refrigerate up to 3 days, if desired. **Yield:** 12 (8-inch) crêpes.

Picante Sauce

1 small onion, quartered
4 jalapeño peppers, partially seeded
2 cloves garlic
2 (16-ounce) cans whole tomatoes, drained

• **Position** knife blade in food processor bowl; add onion, jalapeño peppers, and garlic. Pulse 3 or 4 times or until mixture is chopped. Add tomatoes, and process until blended. **Yield:** 2½ cups.

Guacamole

2 large avocados, peeled and mashed
1½ teaspoons lemon juice
1½ teaspoons garlic powder
1 teaspoon onion powder
1 teaspoon chili powder
2 tablespoons Picante Sauce (see recipe)

• **Combine** ingredients. **Yield:** 1½ cups.
Dee Buchfink
Oologah, Oklahoma

CHEESE SOUFFLÉ: HERE'S THE SECRET

Complicated and risky? Not this soufflé. This easy recipe begins with a cheese-flavored white sauce, thickened with egg yolks, and lightened by folding in stiffly beaten egg whites. Hot air, trapped during baking, puffs the mixture to inviting heights.

There's no secret to serving this soufflé with confidence for brunch, lunch, or supper – just follow our tips (on the facing page).

CHEESE SOUFFLÉ

3 tablespoons butter or margarine
¼ cup all-purpose flour
1¾ cups milk
1 teaspoon salt
¼ to ½ teaspoon ground red pepper
2 teaspoons prepared mustard
½ teaspoon Worcestershire sauce
1½ cups (6 ounces) shredded sharp Cheddar cheese
6 large eggs, separated
Butter or margarine

• **Melt** butter in a heavy saucepan over low heat; add flour, stirring until smooth. Cook 1 minute, stirring constantly. Gradually add milk and next 4 ingredients; cook over medium heat, stirring constantly, until thickened and bubbly. Add cheese, stirring until it melts. Remove from heat, and cool slightly (about 10 minutes).
• **Beat** egg yolks until thick and pale. Gradually stir about one-fourth of hot mixture into yolks; add to remaining hot mixture, stirring constantly.

- **Beat** egg whites until stiff but not dry; fold into cheese mixture.
- **Pour** into a lightly buttered 2-quart soufflé dish.
- **Place** soufflé dish into a 13- x 9- x 2-inch pan. Add hot water to pan to depth of 1 inch.
- **Bake** at 300° for 1½ hours. Serve immediately. **Yield:** 6 servings.

Note: The top will be slightly firm to the touch when done.

Beverley Dunn
Birmingham, Alabama

HERE ARE THE SECRETS TO GREAT SOUFFLÉS

Smoothing Secrets
- Prevent lumps by stirring flour into melted butter with a wire whisk; then gradually add the milk while stirring constantly.
- Cook sauce mixture over medium heat; high heat can cause the mixture to curdle.

"Eggsclusive" Secrets
- Carefully separate cold eggs.
- Stirring a small amount of hot mixture into beaten egg yolks warms them. This step – called tempering – prevents the egg yolks from coagulating (lumping).

Puffing Secrets
- Even the smallest amount of fat, including that in a drop of egg yolk, keeps egg white from beating properly.
- Avoid using wooden or plastic bowls when beating whites; they tend to absorb fat.
- Stiff, but not dry, means egg whites no longer slip when the bowl is tilted.

- To fold in beaten egg whites, use a down-across-up-and-over motion with a rubber spatula to cut through the cheese mixture. Fold just until there aren't any remaining streaks. Don't stir – it forces out the air in the beaten whites.

Substitute Secrets
- Dish size is important; if the container is too small, the mixture may run over. If the container is too large, the mixture won't rise to the rim and have its traditional appearance.
- Use a straight-sided casserole dish if you don't have a traditional soufflé dish.

Baking Secrets
- Baking the soufflé in a water bath surrounds the delicate mixture with gentle heat and promotes even cooking.
- Place soufflé in a preheated oven immediately after mixing.
- Don't peek; opening the oven door will cause a soufflé to collapse.

A PASSION FOR PEPPER

....

Once you've discovered the fresh ground flavor from a pepper mill, you'll happily go back to the grind – again and again. Freshly ground pepper adds a sharp, lively flavor to food. (For pointers on pepper, see next page.)

STEAK IN PEPPER CREAM

¼ teaspoon salt
2 (12-ounce) New York strip
   steaks, trimmed
1½ tablespoons green
   peppercorns in liquid,
   drained *
2 tablespoons steak sauce
2 tablespoons water
1 cup whipping cream
¼ teaspoon black pepper

- **Place** a 10-inch cast-iron skillet over medium heat until hot; sprinkle salt in skillet. Place steaks over salt; cook 1 to 2 minutes on each side or until browned. Remove from skillet.
- **Combine** peppercorns, steak sauce, and water in hot skillet; cook over medium heat, stirring constantly, to loosen browned food particles on bottom of skillet. Stir in whipping cream and black pepper.
- **Bring** to a boil; reduce heat, and simmer, stirring constantly, 3 to 4 minutes, or until slightly thickened.
- **Add** steak; simmer 5 minutes or until desired degree of doneness, stirring occasionally. **Yield:** 4 servings.

* Dried green peppercorns may be substituted.

Sandi Pichon
Slidell, Louisiana

LEMON-GARLIC OLIVES

1 (10-ounce) jar pimiento-stuffed
   olives, undrained
4 sprigs fresh oregano
3 cloves garlic, pressed
2 lemon slices
10 black peppercorns
3 tablespoons lemon juice

● **Drain** olives, reserving liquid.
● **Layer** half each of olives, oregano, garlic, lemon slices, and peppercorns in olive jar; repeat layers.
● **Pour** 3 tablespoons lemon juice into the olive jar; add just enough of the reserved olive liquid to fill the olive jar. Screw lid on jar.
● **Chill** olive mixture at least 8 hours. Store in refrigerator up to 2 weeks. **Yield:** about 32 appetizer servings.

Fran Baker
Rockledge, Florida

PEPPERED CHEESE BALL

2 (8-ounce) packages cream
   cheese, softened
1 bunch green onions with tops,
   finely chopped
¼ teaspoon garlic powder
2 teaspoons black peppercorns,
   coarsely cracked
2 teaspoons pink peppercorns,
   coarsely cracked
2 teaspoons white peppercorns,
   coarsely cracked

● **Combine** first 3 ingredients; shape mixture into a 5-inch ball.
● **Combine** cracked peppercorns; roll cheese ball in mixture until evenly coated. Wrap in heavy-duty plastic wrap, and chill until firm. Serve with assorted crackers. **Yield:** one 5-inch cheese ball.

Fran Walker
Broken Arrow, Oklahoma

living *light*

LIFE IN THE *FAST* LANE

....

Whether you plan ahead for drive-thru dinners or you need to improvise in a hurry, these recipes will keep you on the fast track. Even the most cautious calorie counters have an occasional craving for their favorite fast food. But don't merge these high-fat entrées with the accompanying French fries or fried pies.

Give the red light to driving under the influence of fat. Speed on home, and serve your take-away entrées with these almost-quicker-than-"drive-thru" side dishes, salads, and desserts. You'll pass up fat and sodium and feel better about your indulgence.

PEPPER POINTERS

....

■ You'll find pepper mills and assorted whole peppercorns at a gift or kitchen shop, or perhaps your grocery. Choose a pepper mill that's easy to fill and holds enough to avoid too-frequent refilling.

■ You can either choose just one color of peppercorn – black, white, green, or pink – or combine several in a clear acrylic mill for a rainbow of color and flavor.

■ Black, green, and white peppercorns are actually berries of the same plant. They're just harvested and dried at various stages of growth, thus the different colors. Each has its own flavor, black being strongest, white the mildest.

■ When a recipe calls for cracked peppercorns instead of ground, it's easiest to use a mortar and pestle or to put them in a plastic bag and crack the peppers with a rolling pin.

■ You may be aware of the safety scare over pink peppercorns a few years ago, but there's no need to worry. The ones you find now at your grocer have been approved by the Food and Drug Administration.

FREEZER SALAD

1 cup white vinegar
1 cup water
¾ cup sugar
½ teaspoon celery seeds
4 cups broccoli flowerets
4 cups cauliflower flowerets
1 large carrot, scraped and
   shredded
½ cup chopped green pepper
½ cup chopped sweet red pepper
1 medium onion, finely chopped
1 teaspoon salt

● **Combine** first 4 ingredients in a saucepan; bring to a boil, stirring occasionally. Boil 1 minute. Cool.
● **Combine** broccoli and remaining ingredients in a large bowl. Add vinegar mixture; toss.
● **Pack** into 4 (1-pint) freezer containers, filling to ½ inch from top. Cover, label, and freeze up to 1 month. To serve, thaw in refrigerator 8 hours. **Yield:** 8 cups.

♥ Per 1-cup serving: Calories 116 (3% from fat)
Fat 0.4g (0g saturated) Cholesterol 0mg
Sodium 317mg Carbohydrate 28.5g
Fiber 3.5g Protein 2.8g

CHEESY SUMMER VEGETABLES

1 (10-ounce) package frozen sliced
   okra
1 (10-ounce) package frozen
   whole kernel corn
2 (10-ounce) cans diced tomatoes
   and green chiles
1 (15-ounce) can black beans,
   drained and rinsed
½ teaspoon garlic powder
½ teaspoon pepper
1 cup (4 ounces) shredded
   reduced-fat Cheddar cheese

● **Combine** first 6 ingredients in a large saucepan. Cover and cook over medium heat 8 minutes, stirring occasionally.
● **Sprinkle** with shredded cheese before serving. Serve with a slotted spoon. **Yield:** 6 cups.

❤ Per 1-cup serving: Calories 177 (22% from fat)
Fat 4.2g (2.2g saturated) Cholesterol 12mg
Sodium 540mg Carbohydrate 24.1g
Fiber 2.9g Protein 10.6g

POTATO WEDGES

4 (5-ounce) baking potatoes
1 tablespoon water
1 teaspoon paprika
½ teaspoon garlic powder
1½ teaspoons vegetable oil
½ teaspoon browning-and-
   seasoning sauce
1 teaspoon dried parsley flakes
¼ teaspoon salt

● **Cut** each potato into 8 wedges.
● **Combine** water and next 4 ingredients in an 8-inch square baking dish. Add potato wedges, tossing to coat. Cover with wax paper. Microwave at HIGH 8 minutes or until tender, stirring after 4 minutes. Sprinkle with parsley flakes and salt. **Yield:** 4 servings.
Wanda Bishop
Little Rock, Arkansas

❤ Per serving: Calories 123 (14% from fat)
Fat 1.9g (0.3g saturated) Cholesterol 0mg
Sodium 157mg Carbohydrate 24.2g
Fiber 2.4g Protein 3.3g

FAST FOOD DOESN'T HAVE TO BE FATTENING FOOD

Instant Additions

■ For a quick salad, halve fresh mushrooms and drizzle with fat-free Italian salad dressing. Add a sprinkling of freshly grated Parmesan cheese.

■ For an easy and quick dessert, combine ¼ cup reduced-fat sour cream and ¼ cup reduced-fat frozen whipped topping in a small bowl; add 2 tablespoons brown sugar and 2 tablespoons fruit-flavored liqueur. Serve with fresh strawberries.

■ Unpeeled and quartered new potatoes cook in 8 to 10 minutes in boiling water and are a low-fat alternative to fries. Drain cooked potatoes and toss with a little reduced-calorie margarine. Add fresh chives, freshly ground pepper, and salt.

Healthy Hints

■ Because fast food is high in sodium, reduce salt for breakfast and lunch when you know dinner will be from the "drive-thru."

■ For a healthier carryout dinner for two, order one Chinese entrée and a double serving of rice.

■ There are no "bad" foods. Don't feel guilty about enjoying a burger or taco. Just make sure it's the exception, not the rule. If your fast-food fling sends you over your fat allotment for the day, eat low-fat meals the next day and get in some extra exercise.

■ Prepare for snack attacks. Keep vegetables washed, cut up, and ready to eat with fat-free dips. Section citrus and store covered in the refrigerator.

■ Lighten up casserole recipes with reduced-fat versions of canned soup, sour cream, and cheese.

■ Exercise every day. It's the key to keeping the pounds off.

■ Minimize temptation. Don't stock your cupboards with high-calorie foods.

FROZEN STRAWBERRY SALAD

1 (8-ounce) package fat-free cream
   cheese product, softened
½ cup sugar
1 (8-ounce) container reduced-fat
   frozen whipped topping,
   thawed
2 cups frozen no-sugar-added
   whole strawberries, thawed
   and halved
1 (15¼-ounce) can unsweetened
   crushed pineapple, undrained
1½ cups sliced banana (2 medium)

● **Beat** cream cheese at medium speed with an electric mixer until creamy; gradually add sugar, beating until smooth.
● **Fold** in whipped topping and remaining ingredients; spoon into a 13- x 9- x 2-inch dish. Cover with aluminum foil.
● **Freeze** until firm. **Yield:** 12 servings.
Linda S. Zachry
Dallas, Texas

❤ Per serving: Calories 138 (17% from fat)
Fat 2.6g (0g saturated) Cholesterol 4mg
Sodium 128mg Carbohydrate 25.9g
Fiber 1g Protein 3.7g

CHILI VEGETABLE SOUP

2 (16-ounce) cans ready-to-serve, fat-free, reduced-sodium chicken broth
2 (16-ounce) cans reduced-sodium stewed tomatoes
4 (8-ounce) cans no-salt-added tomato sauce
2 large onions, chopped
2 medium-size green peppers, chopped
2 stalks celery, sliced
1 (16-ounce) can chili hot beans, undrained
2 zucchini, cut in half lengthwise and sliced (1 pound)
2 yellow squash, cut in half lengthwise and sliced (½ pound)
1 (1¼-ounce) package taco seasoning

● **Combine** chicken broth, stewed tomatoes, tomato sauce, chopped onions, chopped green peppers, and sliced celery in a large Dutch oven; bring mixture to a boil over high heat. Reduce heat, and simmer 30 minutes, stirring occasionally.
● **Add** chili beans and remaining ingredients; bring to a boil. Reduce heat, and simmer 10 to 15 minutes. **Yield:** 4½ quarts.

♥ Per 1½-cup serving: Calories 115 (11% from fat) Fat 1.5g (0g saturated) Cholesterol 0mg Sodium 180mg Carbohydrate 22g Fiber 2.2g Protein 5.4g

DECEPTIVE CONFECTIONS

Looks are deceiving – these show-off desserts are easy. A lavish dessert doesn't have to be hard to make, though. These dazzling napoleons are merely sweet fillings sandwiched between layers of cookies or flaky puff pastry. The next time dinner calls for an elegant dessert, but your schedule calls for ease, try these stacked sweets for a perfect ending.

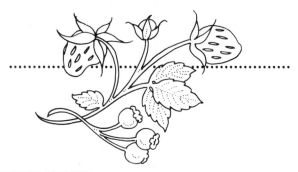

BERRY NAPOLEONS
(pictured on page 112)

Edged with a pool of Strawberry Sauce or served plain, Berry Napoleons are the perfect finish to a summer meal.

Vegetable cooking spray
1½ cups quick-cooking oats, uncooked
½ cup butter or margarine, melted
¾ cup sugar
1 teaspoon all-purpose flour
1 teaspoon baking powder
1 large egg, lightly beaten
½ cup chopped pecans
1 teaspoon vanilla extract
¾ cup semisweet chocolate morsels
1½ tablespoons Chambord or other raspberry-flavored liqueur
1 tablespoon butter or margarine
2 cups whipping cream
¼ cup sifted powdered sugar
1 pint fresh blackberries or raspberries
Garnish: fresh berries
Strawberry Sauce (optional)

● **Cover** baking sheets with aluminum foil, and coat with cooking spray. Set aside.
● **Combine** oats and ½ cup melted butter in a bowl; stir in sugar, flour, and baking powder. Add egg, pecans, and vanilla, stirring until blended.
● **Drop** mixture by rounded teaspoonfuls 2 inches apart into 36 mounds onto prepared baking sheets.
● **Bake** at 325° for 12 minutes or until lightly browned. Allow to cool completely on baking sheets. Remove from foil, and place cookies on wax paper.
● **Combine** chocolate morsels, liqueur, and 1 tablespoon butter in a small saucepan; cook over low heat, stirring constantly, until chocolate melts.
● **Spoon** mixture into a heavy-duty, zip-top plastic bag; seal. Snip a tiny hole in 1 corner of bag, and gently squeeze bag to drizzle chocolate over cooled cookies. Let stand until chocolate is firm.
● **Beat** whipping cream until foamy; gradually add powdered sugar, beating until soft peaks form. Set aside ¾ cup whipped cream.
● **Place** 1 cookie on each serving plate. Pipe or dollop ½-inch layer of whipped cream onto each cookie, and top with berries. Top each with a second cookie,

and repeat procedure. Top with remaining cookies. Pipe or dollop with reserved ¾ cup whipped cream; top each with a berry. If desired, spoon about 1 tablespoon Strawberry Sauce around 1 side of napoleon. Garnish, if desired. **Yield:** 12 servings.

Strawberry Sauce

1 (10-ounce) package frozen
   strawberries
1 tablespoon cornstarch

● **Puree** strawberries in blender.
● **Pour** mixture through a wire-mesh strainer into a small saucepan; press with back of spoon against sides of strainer to squeeze out juice. Discard seeds remaining in strainer.
● **Add** cornstarch. Bring mixture to a boil over medium heat, stirring constantly. Boil 1 minute. Cool before serving. **Yield:** 1 cup.

Mrs. Carl W. Terry
Huntsville, Alabama

PEANUT BUTTER-AND-CHOCOLATE NAPOLEONS

1 cup creamy peanut butter
1 (8-ounce) package cream cheese,
   softened
½ cup sugar
1 teaspoon vanilla extract
½ cup whipping cream, whipped
24 chocolate wafers
3 (1-ounce) squares semisweet
   chocolate, melted
¼ cup milk
Chocolate Sauce

● **Beat** first 4 ingredients in a large mixing bowl with an electric mixer; fold in whipped cream. Reserve ½ cup peanut butter mixture.
● **Pipe** or spoon one-fourth of remaining peanut butter mixture evenly onto 6 chocolate wafers. Top each with a second chocolate wafer; pipe or spoon another fourth of peanut butter mixture evenly onto the wafers. Repeat procedure with a third wafer and another fourth of peanut butter mixture, and top with remaining wafers. Pipe or dollop

with remaining fourth of peanut butter mixture; refrigerate.
● **Spoon** melted chocolate into a heavy-duty, zip-top plastic bag; seal. Snip a tiny hole in 1 corner of bag. Pipe melted chocolate to form an overlapping leaf design onto 6 plates. Chill plates until chocolate is firm. For each chocolate garnish, pipe remaining melted chocolate onto wax paper in overlapping leaf designs; chill until chocolate is firm.
● **Combine** ½ cup reserved peanut butter mixture and milk.
● **Spoon** peanut butter mixture and Chocolate Sauce inside piped design on prepared plates. Use a wooden pick to spread sauces to edges of the leaves.

Arrange napoleons on plates. Top each napoleon with a chocolate garnish. Serve immediately. **Yield:** 6 servings.

Chocolate Sauce

½ cup whipping cream
2 tablespoons sugar
3 (1-ounce) squares semisweet
   chocolate
½ teaspoon vanilla extract

● **Combine** whipping cream and sugar in a small saucepan over low heat. Add chocolate, and cook, stirring until it melts. Remove from heat, and stir in vanilla. **Yield:** ¾ cup.

NAPOLEON KNOW-HOW

Peanut Butter-and-Chocolate Napoleons use commercial cookies, so you don't even have to turn on the oven. To make the cookies for Berry Napoleons, just drop spoonfuls of batter onto a baking sheet and bake. Blueberry-Lemon Napoleons (on next page) use frozen puff pastry, which is as easy to bake as canned biscuits.

To make the decorated plates for Peanut Butter-and-Chocolate-Napoleons, pipe melted chocolate to form overlapping leaves on individual serving plates. Spoon small amounts of Chocolate Sauce and peanut butter mixture inside the leaf designs. Then use a wooden pick to spread the sauces to the edges of the leaves.

For the chocolate garnish on top, pipe three small overlapping leaf designs onto wax paper. Chill the designs for a few minutes, and peel away the paper.

BLUEBERRY-LEMON NAPOLEONS

1 (17¼-ounce) package frozen
   puff pastry sheets, thawed
Blueberry Sauce
Lemon Filling

• **Unfold** pastry sheets, and cut into 9 (3-inch) rounds. Place on an ungreased baking sheet.
• **Bake** at 400° for 10 minutes or until lightly browned. Remove to a wire rack to cool. Split each round in half crosswise forming 18 rounds.
• **Spoon** Blueberry Sauce evenly onto 6 plates; place 1 pastry round in center of each. Spoon or pipe half of Lemon Filling evenly onto pastry rounds; top each with a second pastry round and remaining filling. Top with remaining rounds. Serve immediately. **Yield:** 6 servings.

Blueberry Sauce

2 cups fresh blueberries
¼ cup sifted powdered sugar

• **Position** knife blade in food processor bowl; add blueberries and sugar. Process until pureed.
• **Pour** through a wire-mesh strainer, discarding solids. **Yield:** about 1 cup.

Lemon Filling

1 (14-ounce) can sweetened
   condensed milk
1 (8-ounce) package cream cheese,
   softened
¼ cup lemon juice
½ teaspoon vanilla extract

• **Combine** all ingredients in a small mixing bowl; beat at medium speed with an electric mixer until smooth.
• **Cover** and chill 1 hour or until thickened. **Yield:** 1¾ cups.

HOST A PAINT PARTY

Need a little help with that paint job? Invite friends over and bribe them with some munchies. These quick-and-easy recipes make planning a party while you paint about as easy as whistling while you work.

You won't have to do anything to the area you're painting; cover furniture, clear a corner, and take advantage of our clever serving ideas to host a party with (shall we say "minimalist"?) style. Assemble the items from this equipment checklist, and you're ready to go.

A PAINTING PARTY
Serves 15 to 20

Can-Can Fruit Punch
Creamy Horseradish Dip
Herb-Seasoned Popcorn
Beer Cheese Spread
Assorted Vegetables
Bagel Chips

CAN-CAN FRUIT PUNCH

2 (6-ounce) cans frozen orange
   juice concentrate, thawed and
   undiluted
2 (6-ounce) cans frozen lemonade
   concentrate, thawed and
   undiluted
2 (46-ounce) cans red fruit
   punch
2 (1-liter) bottles ginger ale

• **Combine** first 3 ingredients in a large plastic container; cover and refrigerate. Stir in ginger ale, and serve over ice. **Yield:** 5 quarts.
Pam Scarbrough
Albertville, Alabama

EQUIPMENT CHECKLIST

You'll need...
■ a large container to mix punch
■ quart-size, heavy-duty, zip-top plastic bags
■ knife and cutting board
■ measuring cups
■ mixing spoons
■ measuring spoons
■ plastic resealable containers
■ cups and napkins
■ spreader
■ large bowl
■ can opener
■ cup for serving punch
■ colorful tissue paper
■ new paint roller tray
■ small gift bags or paper sacks

CREAMY HORSERADISH DIP

1 (8-ounce) package cream cheese,
   softened
½ cup mayonnaise or salad
   dressing
½ cup finely chopped cooked ham
½ cup finely chopped green
   pepper
¼ cup commercial horseradish
   sauce
2 tablespoons finely chopped
   onion

• **Combine** all ingredients, stirring vigorously with a spoon until blended. Cover and chill at least 3 hours.
• **Serve** with vegetables. **Yield:** 2 cups.
Janice M. France
Louisville, Kentucky

HERB-SEASONED POPCORN

4 (3.5-ounce) packages butter-
   flavored microwave popcorn
2 teaspoons dried basil
2 teaspoons dried chervil
2 teaspoons dried thyme
2 (12-ounce) cans mixed salted
   nuts

- **Prepare** popcorn, 1 package at a time, according to package directions; carefully open each bag, and add ½ teaspoon of each herb. Close bag, and shake; pour into containers.
- **Add** nuts, and toss gently. **Yield: 9 quarts.**

BEER CHEESE SPREAD

1 (8-ounce) package shredded Colby and Monterey Jack cheeses, softened
1 (8-ounce) package shredded sharp Cheddar cheese, softened
½ cup beer
1 teaspoon garlic powder
½ teaspoon dry mustard
⅛ teaspoon salt
2 teaspoons Worcestershire sauce
¼ teaspoon hot sauce

- **Combine** all ingredients in a heavy-duty, zip-top plastic bag; push air out of bag, and seal.
- **Knead** plastic bag with hands until mixture is blended and spreading consistency. Serve spread with bagel chips. **Yield: 2¼ cups.**

Janice M. France
Louisville, Kentucky

SPREADABLE VEGETABLES

. . . .

Fresh from the garden or sprung from the can, vegetables themselves are easily transformed into a satiny spread for crackers or bread.

Once-crisp green, sweet yellow, or sweet red peppers paint a creamy, pale landscape in Roasted Pepper Spread. And hummus, the Middle Eastern spread traditionally made with garbanzo beans, is brushed in down-home warmth with black-eyed peas as the main ingredient.

NUTTY CARROT SPREAD

1 (8-ounce) package reduced-fat cream cheese, softened
½ teaspoon grated orange rind
3 to 4 tablespoons orange juice
1 cup shredded carrot
¾ cup (3 ounces) shredded Cheddar cheese
½ cup chopped pecans, toasted
¼ cup raisins

- **Combine** first 3 ingredients in a medium mixing bowl, and beat at medium speed with an electric mixer until blended.
- **Stir** in carrot and remaining ingredients; cover and chill. **Yield: 2 cups.**

Betty Huffcut
Pensacola, Florida

BLACK-EYED PEA HUMMUS

3 green onions, sliced
1 clove garlic
1 jalapeño pepper, halved and seeded
4 sprigs fresh cilantro
1 (15-ounce) can black-eyed peas, rinsed and drained *
½ cup commercial tahini
3 tablespoons lemon juice
½ teaspoon salt
¼ teaspoon ground cumin
2 tablespoons olive oil

- **Position** knife blade in food processor bowl; add first 4 ingredients. Process 20 seconds, stopping once to scrape down sides.
- **Add** black-eyed peas and next 4 ingredients; process until smooth.
- **Pour** olive oil gradually through food chute with processor running; process until combined. Cover and chill, if desired. **Yield: 1¾ cups.**

* 1 (16-ounce) can black beans, rinsed and drained, may be substituted for black-eyed peas.

Note: Tahini is a thick paste made from sesame seeds. This product may be found in the peanut butter section of large supermarkets.

ROASTED PEPPER SPREAD

2 large sweet red, sweet yellow, or green peppers
1 jalapeño pepper
1 small onion, unpeeled
1 clove garlic, unpeeled
1 (3-ounce) package cream cheese, softened
1 teaspoon salt

- **Place** sweet peppers and jalapeño pepper on an aluminum foil-lined baking sheet.
- **Bake** at 500° for 5 to 10 minutes or until skin looks blistered, turning once. Add onion and garlic, and bake 10 minutes. Set onion and garlic aside.
- **Place** peppers immediately into a heavy-duty, zip-top plastic bag; seal and let stand 10 minutes to loosen skins. Peel peppers, and remove and discard seeds.
- **Peel** onion and garlic; cut onion into quarters.
- **Place** onion, garlic, and peppers in container of an electric blender; process until smooth. Add cream cheese and salt; process until smooth, stopping once to scrape down sides. **Yield: 1½ cups.**

Katharine Jones
Greeneville, Tennessee

TOMATO SPREAD

20 oil-packed dried tomatoes, drained
1 (12-ounce) jar roasted sweet red peppers, drained
5 fresh basil leaves
1 tablespoon balsamic vinegar
½ teaspoon salt
¼ teaspoon sugar

- **Combine** all ingredients in container of an electric blender; process until smooth, stopping once to scrape down sides. **Yield: 1¾ cups.**

Helen Dowling
Birmingham, Alabama

TIERS OF JOY

You can bake this multitiered cake (and eat it, too) for your own wedding.

Or if not for your own, then maybe for your daughter's reception

or even your parents' anniversary.

You'll find this cake is reasonable in cost and simple in design. Just a few inexpensive specialty items, such as cakepans and cardboard cake circles, are needed. Preparing it requires no special skills – just time and patience. And if it's your first time to make a tiered cake, our tips will guide you through each step.

TROUBLESHOOTING

■ It's difficult to find a flat serving tray for large cakes, so plan ahead. We used a broken piece of scrap marble from a tile-and-marble company. A mirror or a ¼-inch-thick piece of plywood covered with decorative foil or fabric also works well.

■ To avoid transportation disasters, stack the cake tiers and garnish the cake at the reception site. Place cake tiers in separate sturdy boxes; place a damp towel underneath each box to prevent sliding.

■ Buy pans and cardboard circles from cake decorating supply stores.

Here's why: To support the weight of the next cake tier, wooden sticks or nonflexible plastic straws are vital.

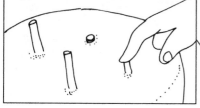

CAMEO WEDDING CAKE

2 recipes Tiered Cameo Cake (see recipe on facing page)
2 (6-inch) cardboard cake circles
1 (8-inch) cardboard cake circle
1 (12-inch) cardboard cake circle
2 recipes White Chocolate-Cream Cheese Tiered Cake Frosting
8 wooden craft sticks or non-flexible straws
Garnishes: ribbon, roses, maidenhair fern

• **Prepare** and bake 1 recipe of Tiered Cameo Cake. Repeat procedure with remaining recipe. Refrigerate or freeze, if desired.
• **Cover** 2 (6-inch), 1 (8-inch), and 1 (12-inch) sturdy cardboard cake circles with aluminum foil.
• **Cut** domed top off each layer, using a serrated knife.
• **Prepare** 1 recipe of White Chocolate-Cream Cheese Tiered Cake Frosting. Repeat procedure.
• **Spread** a small amount of frosting on 1 side of 12-inch circle.
• **Place** 1 (12-inch) layer on top. Spread top of cake with about 1 cup frosting, leaving a ½-inch border. Place remaining 12-inch layer on top. Spread sides with a paper-thin layer of frosting; spread with a heavier layer of frosting, swirling, if desired.
• **Insert** 4 wooden craft sticks (cut to match the depth of 12-inch cake tier) vertically into 12-inch layers about 3 inches from sides. Press down so the

Here's why: Prepare recipes for Tiered Cameo Cake separately; only 1 recipe will fit into a typical home mixer bowl.

Here's why: Using the cardboard bases adds support to each tier and makes it easier to transfer. For this cake, the circles should be the same size as the cakepans.

Here's why: For appearance and to prevent layers from sliding, cake layers must be perfectly flat when the tiers are stacked.

Here's why: 1 tablespoon of frosting, spread on each cardboard circle, holds cake layers in place.

Here's why: Thick frosting spread between cake layers can cause the top layer to slip. Too much frosting and failure to leave a ½-inch border will cause frosting to ooze out the sides of cake due to weight of tiers. Spreading the sides of cake first with a paper-thin layer of frosting seals in crumbs.

tops of sticks are level with the top of cake. Spread top of cake with frosting.
- **Refrigerate** up to 2 days or freeze up to 2 months.
- **Assemble** 2 (8-inch) layers on cardboard base as previously described; refrigerate or freeze.
- **Assemble** 2 (6-inch) tiers on cardboard bases as previously described, omitting wooden sticks and completely frosting top of both tiers; refrigerate or freeze.
- **Position** 8-inch tier in center of 12-inch tier, and place 1 (6-inch) tier on 8-inch tier.
- **Garnish** up to 2 hours before serving, if desired. Do not place in direct sun or in warm areas.
- **Garnish** and package remaining 6-inch tier, if desired. **Yield:** about 125 servings and 1 (6-inch) 2-layer cake.

Tiered Cameo Cake

3 cups butter
1½ cups water
2 (4-ounce) bars white chocolate, broken into small pieces
3 cups buttermilk
8 large eggs, lightly beaten
1 tablespoon vanilla extract
7 cups all-purpose flour, divided
2 cups chopped pecans, toasted
4½ cups sugar
1 tablespoon baking soda

- **Grease** and flour 1 (6-inch, 8-inch, and 12-inch) round cakepan; set aside.
- **Combine** butter and water in a large saucepan; bring to a boil over medium heat, stirring occasionally. Remove pan from heat.
- **Add** white chocolate, stirring until chocolate melts. Stir in buttermilk, eggs, and vanilla; set aside.
- **Combine** 1 cup flour and pecans, stirring to coat; set aside.
- **Combine** remaining 6 cups flour, sugar, and soda in a large mixing bowl; gradually stir in white chocolate mixture. Fold in pecan mixture.
- **Spoon** 2 cups batter into 6-inch pan, 3½ cups batter into 8-inch pan, and 8

Here's why: Cakes with cream cheese frosting should be stored in the refrigerator. All 3 frosted tiers can be assembled ahead and refrigerated or frozen. (Place cake in freezer until frosting is firm; wrap tightly in heavy-duty aluminum foil or freezer paper. Unwrap cake to thaw.)

cups batter into 12-inch pan. Set remaining 2 cups batter aside.
- **Bake** at 325° for 40 to 45 minutes or until a wooden pick inserted in center comes out clean. Cool in pans on wire racks 10 minutes; remove from pans, and let cool completely on wire racks.
- **Spoon** 2 cups remaining batter into a greased and floured (6-inch) round cakepan, and bake according to above directions.
- **Wrap** layers in plastic wrap and then in aluminum foil; refrigerate up to 2 days or freeze up to 2 months, if desired. Unwrap and thaw layers at room temperature about 2 hours. (It's easier to frost cold layers.) **Yield:** two 6-inch layers, one 8-inch layer, and one 12-inch layer.

White Chocolate-Cream Cheeese Tiered Cake Frosting

2 (4-ounce) bars white chocolate, broken into pieces
2 (8-ounce) packages cream cheese, softened
2 (3-ounce) packages cream cheese, softened
⅔ cup butter or margarine, softened
13 cups sifted powdered sugar
1 tablespoon vanilla extract

- **Melt** white chocolate in a heavy saucepan over low heat, stirring constantly. Remove from heat; cool 10 minutes, stirring occasionally.

Here's how: Bake the 6-inch and 8-inch layers; stagger the pans on the same rack in the middle of the oven so they don't touch each other or the oven sides. Bake the 12-inch layer on the middle rack in a separate oven. Use the extra oven rack for cooling the 12-inch layer. If you don't have a double oven, set aside batter for 12-inch layer with batter for second 6-inch layer. Bake both layers in same oven after 6- and 8-inch layers are baked.

- **Beat** cream cheese and butter at medium speed with an electric mixer until creamy. Gradually add white chocolate, beating constantly, until blended. Gradually add powdered sugar, beating until smooth. Stir in vanilla. Use immediately, or cover and refrigerate up to 2 days. Let stand at room temperature until softened to spreading consistency. **Yield:** about 10 cups.

CHEERS FOR SUMMER

This menu is perfect for spring and summer celebrations. It's light enough for lunch and pretty enough for company. It can also be adjusted to serve just a few people or expanded to accommodate a large group. And not only is it adaptable and attractive, it's delicious, too.

SUMMER CELEBRATION MENU
Serves Eight

Baked Chicken With Tarragon Sauce
Marinated Squash Medley
Bakery Rolls
Iced Tea
Commercial Ice Cream

BAKED CHICKEN WITH TARRAGON SAUCE

8   skinned and boned chicken breast halves
½   teaspoon salt
¼   teaspoon pepper
3   tablespoons lemon juice
½   cup mayonnaise or salad dressing
1   cup finely chopped celery
1   teaspoon dried tarragon
1   pound fresh spinach
3   medium tomatoes, cut into wedges
Garnish: celery leaves

● **Sprinkle** chicken breasts with salt and pepper. Arrange in a lightly greased 13- x 9- x 2-inch pan; sprinkle chicken breasts with lemon juice.
● **Bake** at 375° for 20 minutes or until done. Chill 1 hour.

● **Combine** mayonnaise, celery, and tarragon; set aside.
● **Remove** stems from spinach. Wash leaves thoroughly, and pat dry. Arrange spinach on individual plates. Arrange chicken and tomato wedges on top of spinach. Spoon mayonnaise mixture over chicken. Garnish, if desired. **Yield:** 8 servings.

Note: For chicken salad, cooked chicken may be coarsely chopped and combined with mayonnaise mixture.

Gina Holmes
Andrews, Texas

MARINATED SQUASH MEDLEY

¾   cup olive oil
⅓   cup tarragon-flavored wine vinegar
2   tablespoons finely chopped shallots
1   clove garlic, minced
½   teaspoon salt
¼   teaspoon pepper
¼   teaspoon dried thyme
3   medium-size yellow squash, sliced
3   medium zucchini, sliced

● **Combine** first 7 ingredients in a jar. Cover tightly, and shake vigorously.
● **Pour** dressing over squash; toss gently. Cover and chill 4 hours. To serve toss again, and serve with a slotted spoon. **Yield:** 8 servings.

SUMMER FOOD SAFETY

Keep hot foods HOT...
■ Do not depend on warming units that use small candles to keep foods hot. Use electric skillets, chafing dishes, or hot trays. Always keep hot foods above 140° to avoid the risk of food poisoning.
■ Hot foods being transported should be kept above 140°, too. Take advantage of casserole quilts, baking dish baskets, or cardboard boxes lined with several thicknesses of newspaper to help hold the heat.

Keep cold foods COLD...
■ Serve food in small dishes, refilling frequently from refrigerator. Bacterial growth starts very quickly above 40°.
■ Use an insulated cooler to transport food, and avoid storing it in the trunk of your vehicle.
■ Include a cold source in coolers like ice, commerical ice packs, or frozen water or juice.

JUNE

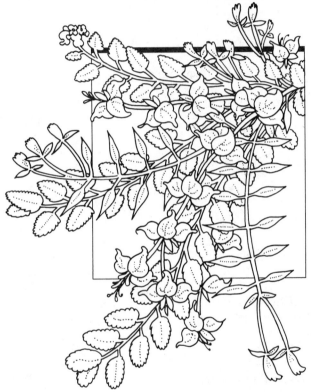

SUPPER BY STARLIGHT

Imagine an early summer evening, the perfect ending to

a sun-warmed day and the beginning of a dinner under the stars. If this

sounds like *your* summer fantasy, then follow our easy plan for a starlit

dinner for two. It includes a dreamy menu that's simple enough

to leave you plenty of time to enjoy the company of someone special

or to think of just the right wish under a star-filled sky.

DINNER UNDER THE STARS
Serves Two

Peppered Goat Cheese
Roasted Peppers With Balsamic Vinaigrette
French Baguettes
Grilled Sirloin Salad
Commercial Breadsticks
Frozen Fruit Cream   Fresh Plum Sauce

A MIDSUMMER NIGHT'S SCHEME

ONE TO FOUR DAYS AHEAD
■ Roast and marinate peppers.
■ Prepare Frozen Fruit Cream; freeze.

EARLY IN THE DAY
■ Marinate sirloin.
■ Prepare and chill Fresh Plum Sauce.
■ Wash salad greens, and pat dry; store in a heavy-duty, zip-top plastic bag in refrigerator.

SEVERAL HOURS AHEAD
■ Grill and slice sirloin for salad. Cover and store in refrigerator.

■ Set table.
■ Chill wine or other beverages, plates, and dessert dishes.

AS THE SUN BEGINS TO SET
■ Prepare Peppered Goat Cheese.
■ Arrange salad on chilled plates; store in refrigerator.
■ Slice French baguettes, and arrange on platter with goat cheese and roasted peppers.
■ To set the mood, select appropriate background music. Light candles, and enjoy the evening.

PEPPERED GOAT CHEESE
(pictured on page 111)

1 (3-ounce) package goat cheese
1 to 2 teaspoons freshly cracked pepper
2 to 3 teaspoons olive oil
Garnishes: fresh rosemary sprigs, fresh oregano sprigs

● **Roll** goat cheese in pepper to coat; drizzle with olive oil. Garnish, if desired, and serve with French baguette slices. **Yield:** 2 to 4 appetizer servings.

Bill Keller
Birmingham, Alabama

ROASTED PEPPERS WITH BALSAMIC VINAIGRETTE
(pictured on page 111)

1 large sweet red pepper
1 large sweet yellow pepper
½ cup olive oil
¼ cup balsamic vinegar
¼ teaspoon salt
¼ teaspoon pepper

● **Wash** and dry peppers; place on a foil-lined baking sheet. Bake at 500° for 20 minutes or until blistered.
● **Place** peppers in a zip-top plastic bag; seal and let stand 10 minutes. Peel peppers; remove and discard membranes

---

SHORTCUTS WHEN YOU HAVE ONLY A FEW HOURS

....

■ Instead of making Frozen Fruit Cream, buy lemon sherbet or lemon sorbet, and serve with Fresh Plum Sauce.

■ To quickly make Roasted Peppers With Balsamic Vinaigrette, buy commercial roasted peppers packed in oil; drain oil, and omit ½ cup olive oil from recipe. Sprinkle peppers with balsamic vinegar and dash of salt and pepper.

and seeds. Cut peppers into thin strips; set aside.

● **Combine** oil and remaining ingredients; pour over pepper strips, and toss gently. Cover mixture, and refrigerate up to 4 days. Serve with French baguette slices or crackers. **Yield:** 2 to 4 appetizer servings.

Jan Downs
Shreveport, Louisiana

GRILLED SIRLOIN SALAD
(pictured on page 111)

½ to 1 fresh jalapeño pepper, unseeded
⅓ cup chopped onion
1 green onion, chopped
2 cloves garlic
1 tablespoon brown sugar
1 teaspoon ground ginger
1 teaspoon lime rind
¼ cup lime juice
¼ cup reduced-sodium soy sauce
1 (1¼-pound) boneless top sirloin steak, trimmed
½ cup peanut oil
1 teaspoon sea or table salt
3 to 4 cups mixed salad greens
½ cup fresh mint leaves, chopped
2 tablespoons coarsely chopped fresh cilantro
6 yellow pear tomatoes, halved
Garnishes: green onion fans, lime slices

● **Place** first 9 ingredients in container of an electric blender. Process until smooth, stopping once to scrape down sides. Set jalapeño pepper mixture aside in blender.
● **Place** steak in a shallow container; pour ¼ cup jalapeño pepper mixture over steak, reserving remaining pepper mixture in blender. Cover steak, and refrigerate 3 hours.
● **Turn** blender on high; gradually add oil to remaining pepper mixture in a slow, steady stream. Cover pepper dressing, and refrigerate.
● **Remove** steak from marinade, discarding marinade. Sprinkle steak with salt. Cook, covered with grill lid, over medium-hot coals (350° to 400°) 8 to 10 minutes on each side. Remove from grill, and let stand 5 minutes.

● **Slice** steak diagonally across grain into ¼-inch-thick slices.
● **Combine** salad greens and next 3 ingredients; arrange on individual plates. Place 5 steak slices on each plate. (Reserve remaining slices for another use.)
● **Serve** salad with pepper dressing. Garnish, if desired. **Yield:** 2 servings.

FROZEN FRUIT CREAM
(pictured on page 111)

1 envelope unflavored gelatin
3 cups sugar
2 cups pineapple juice
2 cups orange juice
⅓ cup lemon juice
2 (8-ounce) packages cream cheese, softened
1 pint whipping cream, whipped
1 teaspoon almond extract
Fresh Plum Sauce (see recipe)

● **Combine** first 3 ingredients in a saucepan; cook over medium heat, stirring constantly, until gelatin dissolves (about 2 minutes). Pour into a bowl.
● **Add** orange juice and lemon juice; set aside.
● **Beat** cream cheese at high speed with an electric mixer until creamy. Gradually stir about one-fourth of juice mixture into cream cheese; add to remaining juice mixture, stirring constantly.

● **Fold** whipped cream and almond extract into juice mixture.
● **Pour** mixture into freezer container of a 1-gallon hand-turned or electric freezer. Freeze according to manufacturer's instructions.
● **Pack** freezer with ice and rock salt, and let stand 1 hour. Serve with Fresh Plum Sauce. **Yield:** 3 quarts.

Rebecca Salisbury Price
Murfreesboro, Tennessee

FRESH PLUM SAUCE
(pictured on page 111)

1 pound ripe plums, pitted and quartered (about 4 plums)
½ cup water
3 tablespoons sugar
¼ teaspoon ground cinnamon
3 tablespoons port or other sweet red wine

● **Combine** first 4 ingredients in a small saucepan; bring to a boil. Reduce heat, and simmer 15 minutes or until plums are soft.
● **Pour** mixture through a fine wire-mesh strainer into a small bowl, pressing mixture against sides of strainer with back of spoon; discard solids, and cool.
● **Stir** in port; cover and refrigerate. Serve sauce over ice cream or fresh fruit. **Yield:** 1¼ cups.

"And what is so rare as a day in June?
Then, if ever, come perfect days..."
—*James Russell Lowell*
The Vision of Sir Launful

Dusk falls softly across the landscape just as crickets begin their nightly chorus. A breeze whispers an invitation to slow down, even stop for a while and savor late afternoon's fading light. Then night drops its inky curtain, and diamonds sprinkle across the heavens.

BERRIES – BURSTING WITH FLAVOR

Pop one of nature's plump bonbons into your mouth, and savor its explosion of sweet juicy freshness. And enjoy the flavor of blackberries, blueberries, strawberries, and raspberries in these easy-to-make sauces. Serve them over fresh fruit, pound cake, angel food cake, waffles, ice cream, or cheesecake – you'll appreciate summer with each bite.

TEA-BERRY SAUCE

1 quart fresh raspberries
½ cup water
1 regular-size tea bag
¾ cup sugar
1 tablespoon cornstarch
2 tablespoons butter or
    margarine
1 teaspoon vanilla extract

• **Combine** raspberries and water in a saucepan; bring to a boil. Reduce heat, and simmer 5 minutes.
• **Add** tea bag; cover and steep 5 minutes; remove tea bag.
• **Pour** mixture through a wire-mesh strainer into a 2-cup measuring cup; press berry mixture against sides of strainer with back of spoon to squeeze out juice. Discard pulp and seeds. Measurement should be 1 cup juice. (If necessary, boil juice to reduce to 1 cup.)
• **Combine** sugar and cornstarch in a small saucepan; gradually add 1 cup juice, stirring until smooth.
• **Bring** to a boil over medium heat, stirring constantly; boil 1 minute. Remove from heat; stir in butter and vanilla. Cover and chill. **Yield:** 1⅓ cups.

OLD-FASHIONED STRAWBERRY SAUCE

4 cups fresh strawberries, hulled
1 cup sugar

• **Place** half of strawberries in a bowl; sprinkle with half of sugar. Repeat layers.
• **Cover** and chill 8 hours.
• **Pour** mixture into a heavy saucepan; bring to a boil over medium heat. Reduce heat, and simmer 15 minutes, stirring often. Cool.
• **Cover** and chill at least 8 hours. **Yield:** 2 cups.

Sibyl White
Woodstock, Georgia

BERRY SAUCE

2 tablespoons sugar
1 tablespoon cornstarch
¼ teaspoon grated orange rind
⅛ teaspoon ground nutmeg
Dash of salt
¼ cup water
¼ cup orange juice
2 cups fresh blueberries,
    blackberries, or raspberries,
    washed and drained

• **Combine** first 5 ingredients in a saucepan; gradually add water and orange juice, stirring until smooth. Gently stir in berries.
• **Bring** mixture to a boil over medium heat, stirring constantly; boil 1 minute. Cover and chill. **Yield:** 1½ cups.

Mildred Bickley
Bristol, Virginia

ALL IN THE FAMILY

. . . .

To awe Dad on Father's Day, help the youngsters create your family in ice cream, using the directions for our Parfait Family as a guide.

The best surprise is that the project is quick; you have to work fast so the ice cream won't melt.

The kids will proudly show their results to Dad on his special day. Help with cleanup is guaranteed. What child can resist the opportunity to sample the leftovers?

PARFAIT FAMILY

Old-Fashioned Strawberry
    Sauce * (see recipe)
Vanilla ice cream or frozen yogurt
1 (7-ounce) can refrigerated
    instant whipped cream
12 semisweet chocolate
    mini-morsels
1 maraschino cherry, cut into thin
    strips
1 cream-filled chocolate sandwich
    cookie
1 ice cream bonbon or chocolate
    drop
1 large gumdrop
3 inches cherry-flavored chewy
    fruit roll by the foot

• **Spoon** a small amount of Old-Fashioned Strawberry Sauce into each parfait glass; top with a scoop of ice cream. Repeat procedure until glasses are filled, ending with ice cream. Freeze.
• **Remove** from freezer one at a time. Decorate as desired, using whipped cream for hair, mini-morsels for eyes and noses, and cherry strips for mouths.
• **Separate** cookie; place one half on dad's head for hat, and top with ice cream bonbon. Crush remaining cookie half; sprinkle crumbs on ice cream for brother's hair.
• **Cut** a small slice from bottom of gumdrop, and place on brother's head. Set top of gumdrop off center to form a baseball cap.
• **Cut** fruit roll into thirds; pinch each third in the middle to make bows.
• **Place** a bow on dad's neck and in hair for sister and mom.
• **Freeze** decorated parfaits. **Yield:** 4 servings.

* You may substitute commercial strawberry sauce.

COOLING INFUSIONS

Steep tea leaves in boiling water, sweeten with sugar, add a squirt of lemon, and you've got a pitcher of Southern tradition. For a flavor twist, try one of our refreshing enhancements of the South's favorite beverage.

FRUITED TEA COOLER

3 cups boiling water
6 Celestial Seasonings Red Zinger tea bags
1 (12-ounce) can frozen pineapple juice concentrate, thawed and undiluted
1 quart water
1 lemon, sliced

• **Pour** boiling water over tea bags; cover and steep 15 minutes.
• **Remove** tea bags from water, squeezing gently.
• **Stir** in pineapple juice concentrate and remaining ingredients, and chill. Serve tea over ice. **Yield:** about 2 quarts.

SPARKLING STRAWBERRY TEA

1 (10-ounce) package frozen strawberries, thawed
1½ quarts boiling water
3 family-size tea bags
½ cup sugar
1 (6-ounce) can frozen lemonade concentrate, thawed and undiluted
1 (2-liter) bottle lemon-lime carbonated beverage, chilled
Garnish: fresh mint sprigs

• **Place** strawberries in container of an electric blender or food processor; process until smooth, stopping once to scrape down sides. Set aside.
• **Pour** boiling water over tea bags; cover and steep 5 minutes.

• **Remove** tea bags, squeezing gently. Stir in sugar, lemonade concentrate, and strawberry puree; chill.
• **Stir** in lemon-lime beverage just before serving; serve tea over ice. Garnish, if desired. **Yield:** about 4 quarts.

Regina Axtell
Buffalo, Texas

GINGER-ALMOND TEA
(pictured on page 152)

1 cup boiling water
5 regular-size tea bags
1½ cups sugar
4 cups water
¾ cup lemon juice
1 tablespoon vanilla extract
1 teaspoon almond extract
1 (1-liter) bottle ginger ale, chilled

• **Pour** boiling water over tea bags; cover and steep 5 minutes.
• **Remove** tea bags, squeezing gently. Stir in sugar and next 4 ingredients; chill.
• **Stir** in ginger ale just before serving. Serve tea over ice. **Yield:** 3 quarts.

Charlene Howard
Crystal Springs, Mississippi

CRANBERRY TEA

2 family-size tea bags
1 teaspoon whole cloves
2 (2½-inch) cinnamon sticks
1 quart boiling water
2 cups sugar
2 quarts water
2 cups cranberry juice cocktail
1 cup orange juice
¼ cup lemon juice

• **Combine** first 3 ingredients in a 1-quart container; add boiling water. Cover and steep 5 minutes.
• **Pour** mixture through a wire-mesh strainer into a large container, discarding tea bags and spices. Stir in sugar and remaining ingredients. Serve tea over ice. **Yield:** 4 quarts.

Karen Elliot
Greenwood, South Carolina

SANGRÍA TEA
(pictured on page 152)

1 (10-ounce) package frozen raspberries, thawed
3 cups water
¾ cup sugar
1 family-size tea bag
2 cups Burgundy or other dry red wine
1 lemon, sliced
1 lime, sliced
1 (16-ounce) bottle orange soda, chilled
Garnishes: lemon slices, lime slices

• **Place** raspberries in container of an electric blender or food processor; process until smooth, stopping once to scrape down sides.
• **Pour** raspberries through a fine wire-mesh strainer into a pitcher, discarding seeds. Set aside.
• **Combine** water and sugar in a saucepan; bring to a boil, stirring often. Remove from heat; add tea bag. Cover and steep 5 minutes.
• **Remove** tea bag, squeezing gently; cool tea.
• **Pour** tea into pitcher; stir in wine and lemon and lime slices. Chill.
• **Stir** in orange soda just before serving. Serve tea over ice. Garnish, if desired. **Yield:** 9 cups.

BREW PERFECT ICED TEA

....

To brew a quart of tea: Place three regular-size tea bags or one family-size bag in a heatproof pitcher. Pour two cups boiling water over bags, and let them steep 3 to 5 minutes. Squeeze the bags when you remove them to extract all the flavor. Stir in ¼ to ½ cup of sugar, if desired, and 2 more cups of water. Pour the tea over ice, and serve each glass with a lemon wedge. Remember, don't refrigerate tea; it will get cloudy.

TRY YOUR LUCK AT POTLUCK

Potluck? What's a potluck? To the uninitiated, a potluck or covered-dish lunch or supper means that each person brings a meat, salad, vegetable, bread, or dessert – with enough extra to share. Typically you don't know what kind of foods people will bring. Here's a sampling of a potluck meal you might like to try for an office lunch.

STRAWBERRY-NUT SALAD

We lightened the original version of this salad by substituting sugar-free or fat-free products for their regular counterparts.

2 (0.3-ounce) packages sugar-
   free strawberry-flavored
   gelatin
1 cup boiling water
1 (16-ounce) package frozen
   whole strawberries, thawed,
   halved, and drained
1 (20-ounce) can crushed
   pineapple, drained
1 cup chopped pecans
3 medium bananas, cut into small
   pieces
1 (8-ounce) carton nonfat sour
   cream
¼ cup fat-free mayonnaise
1½ teaspoons grated orange rind
Garnishes: leaf lettuce, strawberry
   fans

• **Combine** gelatin and boiling water in a large bowl, stirring 2 minutes or until gelatin dissolves. Stir in strawberries, pineapple, and pecans. Set mixture aside.
• **Place** bananas in container of an electric blender; pulse 3 times or until finely chopped, but not mashed. Stir into gelatin mixture.
• **Spoon** half of strawberry mixture into a lightly oiled 11- x 7- x 1½-inch dish; refrigerate until almost set. Set remaining strawberry mixture aside (do not refrigerate).
• **Combine** sour cream, mayonnaise, and orange rind; spread over congealed strawberry layer. Top with remaining strawberry mixture.
• **Cover** and chill 8 hours. Garnish, if desired. **Yield:** 12 servings.

John Floyd
Birmingham, Alabama

BROCCOLI-CHEESE CASSEROLE

To make this recipe healthier, we substituted lighter versions of some ingredients. When using lighter products in recipes, always try them ahead of time. Altering ingredients doesn't always result in success.

1 cup long-grain rice
2 (10-ounce) packages frozen
   chopped broccoli, thawed and
   drained
1 (10¾-ounce) can reduced-
   sodium, reduced-fat cream
   of mushroom soup,
   undiluted
½ cup skim milk
¼ cup butter or margarine
1 tablespoon dry onion soup mix
1 (8-ounce) jar light process
   cheese spread
½ cup cheese cracker crumbs

• **Cook** rice according to package directions, omitting salt and fat. Set rice aside.
• **Combine** broccoli and next 4 ingredients in a large skillet.
• **Bring** mixture to a boil over medium heat. Cover, reduce heat, and simmer 10 minutes.
• **Stir** in rice.
• **Microwave** cheese spread according to package directions, and stir into rice mixture.
• **Spoon** into a lightly greased 2-quart baking dish.
• **Sprinkle** with cracker crumbs.
• **Cover** and bake at 300° for 30 minutes. **Yield:** 8 servings.

Jo Kellum
Birmingham, Alabama

ARTICHOKE-CHICKEN-RICE SALAD

2 (6-ounce) jars marinated
   artichoke hearts, undrained
1 (6.9-ounce) package chicken-
   flavored rice and vermicelli mix
2½ cups chopped cooked chicken
1 (6-ounce) can sliced water
   chestnuts, drained and
   chopped
1 (3-ounce) jar pimiento-stuffed
   olives, drained and sliced
1 cup chopped green onions
1 cup reduced-fat mayonnaise
1½ tablespoons curry powder
1 teaspoon pepper
Lettuce leaves or red cabbage leaves

• **Drain** artichoke hearts, reserving marinade; coarsely chop artichokes.
• **Cook** rice and vermicelli mix according to package directions; stir in reserved marinade, and cool.
• **Combine** artichoke hearts, rice mixture, chicken, and next 3 ingredients.
• **Combine** mayonnaise, curry powder, and pepper; stir into chicken mixture.
• **Cover** and chill 1 to 2 hours. Serve on lettuce leaves. **Yield:** 8 servings.

Mary McWilliams
Birmingham, Alabama

PULL-APART YEAST BREAD

1 (25-ounce) package frozen roll
   dough, thawed
⅓ cup butter or margarine, melted
⅓ cup grated Parmesan cheese

• **Cut** each roll in half; dip in butter, and roll in cheese.
• **Arrange** rolls in a lightly greased 10-inch tube pan.
• **Cover** and let rise in a warm place (85°), free from drafts, 1 hour or until doubled in bulk.
• **Bake** at 325° for 25 to 30 minutes or until golden brown. Remove from pan, and cool on a wire rack. Store in a heavy-duty, zip-top plastic bag. **Yield:** one 10-inch loaf.

Manola Wheeler
Alabaster, Alabama

GRANDMA'S CHOCOLATE CAKE

We varied this recipe slightly with the addition of melted peppermint patties.

2 cups all-purpose flour
2 cups sugar
¼ cup cocoa
1 teaspoon ground cinnamon
1 cup butter or margarine
1 cup water
1 teaspoon baking soda
2 large eggs
½ cup buttermilk
1 teaspoon vanilla extract
1 (14-ounce) package miniature chocolate-covered peppermint patties, unwrapped
Chocolate Frosting

● **Combine** first 4 ingredients, and set aside.
● **Combine** butter and water in a large saucepan; bring to a boil.
● **Remove** from heat; stir in soda. Add flour mixture, stirring well.
● **Stir** in eggs, buttermilk, and vanilla.
● **Spoon** into a greased and floured 13- x 9- x 2-inch pan.
● **Bake** at 350° for 30 minutes. Top with candy; bake 2 additional minutes. Gently spread melted candy over warm cake. Spread Chocolate Frosting over top. Cut into squares. **Yield:** 15 servings.

Chocolate Frosting

½ cup butter or margarine
⅓ cup milk
1 (16-ounce) package powdered sugar, sifted
¼ cup cocoa
1 teaspoon vanilla extract

● **Combine** butter and milk in a large saucepan. Bring mixture to a boil, and remove from heat.
● **Combine** powdered sugar and cocoa; add to butter mixture. Add vanilla, stirring until smooth. **Yield:** 2 cups.

Carol Boker
Birmingham, Alabama

GOOEY PECAN BARS

1 (18-ounce) package butter pecan cake mix
1 large egg, lightly beaten
1 cup butter or margarine, melted and divided
2 large eggs
1 (8-ounce) package cream cheese, softened
1 (16-ounce) package powdered sugar, sifted
1½ cups chopped pecans

● **Combine** cake mix, 1 egg, and ½ cup butter; press into bottom of a lightly greased 13- x 9- x 2-inch pan. Set aside.
● **Combine** 2 eggs, cream cheese, powdered sugar, and remaining ½ cup butter; beat at medium speed with an electric mixer until smooth. Stir in pecans, and pour over cake mix layer.
● **Bake** at 350° for 50 to 55 minutes or until set, covering loosely with aluminum foil after 45 minutes. Cool on a wire rack. Cut into squares. **Yield:** 3 dozen.

Nancy Orr Myers
Birmingham, Alabama

A FRESH APPROACH

For every richly colored fresh fruit or vegetable that beckons to be sampled from roadside produce stands or farmers market stalls, there looms the question, "When I get it home, what do I do with it?"

Georgia Massie, whose Machala Gourmet Farm in Seagoville, Texas, produces more than 100 varieties of vegetables each year, knows the answer. She's taken her vegetable ideas and compiled them in a book entitled *Fresh Ideas for Vegetable Cooking*. Here are a few squash recipes from that book. Try them after your next market visit.

SCALLOPINI PIE

2 cups sliced fresh scallopini or pattypan squash
½ cup chopped onion
½ cup sliced fresh mushrooms
2 tablespoons finely chopped fresh parsley
1 cup (4 ounces) shredded Swiss cheese
½ cup finely chopped cooked ham
¾ cup biscuit mix
1½ cups milk
2 large eggs, lightly beaten
½ teaspoon salt
¼ teaspoon pepper
⅛ teaspoon hot sauce

● **Arrange** squash in a steamer basket; place over boiling water. Cover and steam 4 minutes. Remove from basket; drain between paper towels.
● **Combine** squash and next 5 ingredients in a lightly greased 10-inch pieplate or quiche dish.
● **Combine** biscuit mix and remaining ingredients; pour over vegetables in pieplate.
● **Bake** at 400° for 35 to 40 minutes or until set. **Yield:** 6 servings.

SPAGHETTI SQUASH AND CHICKEN SKILLET CASSEROLE

3 tablespoons butter or margarine
1 cup sliced fresh mushrooms
⅓ cup chopped leeks
¼ cup chopped celery
3 tablespoons chopped sweet red pepper
3 tablespoons finely chopped fresh parsley
2 cups cooked spaghetti squash
4 skinned and boned chicken breast halves, cooked and cut into thin strips
¼ cup crushed seasoned croutons
¼ teaspoon salt
¼ teaspoon seasoned pepper
⅛ teaspoon garlic powder
Pinch of dried summer savory
½ cup sour cream
½ cup (2 ounces) shredded Swiss cheese

● **Melt** butter in a large skillet over medium heat. Add mushrooms and next 4 ingredients; cook, stirring constantly, 5 minutes or until tender.
● **Add** squash and next 6 ingredients; cook, stirring constantly, 4 minutes.
● **Stir** in sour cream; cook, stirring constantly, just until thoroughly heated. Remove from heat.
● **Sprinkle** with cheese. Cover and let stand 1 minute. **Yield:** 3 to 4 servings.

Note: To bake, prepare according to directions, omitting cheese. Spoon into a lightly greased 1½-quart casserole. Cover and bake at 350° for 20 to 25 minutes. Uncover; sprinkle with cheese. Bake 5 additional minutes.

Spaghetti Squash Tortillas: Prepare recipe according to directions; omit chicken and cheese. Spoon onto 8 (6-inch) flour tortillas, and fold. Place, seam side down, in a lightly greased 11- x 7- x 1½-inch baking dish. Cover and bake at 350° for 20 minutes. Uncover; sprinkle with cheese. Bake 5 additional minutes.

GARDEN-FRESH "PASTA"

The flesh of spaghetti squash, when cooked, comes out like strands of cooked spaghetti and makes a great light stand-in for pasta lovers.

● **Prepare** squash by cutting in half lengthwise and removing seeds. Pierce skin several times with a fork, and follow one of these cooking methods.

■ **To bake,** prepare squash, and place, cut side down, in a large baking pan. Bake at 350° for 45 minutes or until skin is tender and strands may be loosened easily with a fork.

■ **To microwave,** prepare squash, and place, cut side down, in a baking dish. Add ¼ cup water; cover with plastic wrap, folding back a small edge of wrap to allow steam to escape. Cook on HIGH 7 to 10 minutes.

■ **To boil,** prepare squash, and place, cut side down, in a Dutch oven; add water to depth of 2 inches. Bring to a boil; cover, reduce heat, and simmer 20 to 25 minutes or until tender. Drain.

● **Cool** cooked squash. Using a fork, remove spaghetti-like strands of pulp. Discard shell. **Yield:** 1 medium spaghetti squash equals about 4 cups cooked.

MARINATED SPAGHETTI SQUASH SALAD

1 (6-ounce) jar marinated artichoke hearts, undrained
4 cups cooked spaghetti squash
1 zucchini, cut into thin strips
1 carrot, scraped and cut into thin strips
⅔ cup chopped sweet red pepper
1 cup (4 ounces) shredded mozzarella cheese
2 tablespoons grated Parmesan cheese
¼ cup rice vinegar
1 tablespoon dry mustard
1 tablespoon chopped fresh oregano
1 tablespoon chopped fresh basil
1 tablespoon chopped fresh parsley
1 tablespoon finely chopped onion
1 tablespoon capers, drained and crushed
2 tablespoons vegetable oil
2 tablespoons red wine vinegar
1 teaspoon dry white wine (optional)
1 clove garlic, minced

● **Drain** artichokes, reserving marinade; coarsely chop artichokes.
● **Combine** artichokes, spaghetti squash, and next 5 ingredients in a large bowl; set aside.
● **Combine** reserved marinade, rice vinegar, and remaining ingredients in a jar. Cover tightly, and shake vigorously. Pour over vegetables.
● **Cover** and chill 8 hours. **Yield:** 8 to 10 servings.

SQUASH SOUP

2 cups chicken broth
2 pounds yellow squash, sliced
2 medium onions, sliced
1 (8-ounce) carton sour cream
1 (8-ounce) carton half-and-half
1½ teaspoons salt
½ teaspoon ground white pepper
Garnishes: paprika, finely chopped fresh dill

- **Combine** first 3 ingredients in a large Dutch oven.
- **Bring** to a boil. Cover, reduce heat, and simmer 8 to 10 minutes or until tender. Remove from heat; let cool 10 minutes.
- **Pour** half of squash mixture into container of an electric blender; process until mixture is smooth, stopping once to scrape down sides. Transfer to a separate container. Repeat the procedure with remaining mixture.
- **Return** squash mixture to Dutch oven; stir in sour cream and next 3 ingredients.
- **Cook** over low heat, stirring constantly, just until thoroughly heated, or cover and chill 2 hours. Serve hot or cold. Garnish, if desired. **Yield:** 2 quarts.

LIGHT, HOT *HEAT*

There's no excess in this Tex-Mex. Assertive seasonings make these spicy dishes the answer to your plea for recipes packed with flavor, not fat. With smoky roasted peppers, sharp cilantro, and tangy tomatillos, you won't notice that a lot of the fat is missing.

SAUTÉED ZUCCHINI WITH MUSHROOMS

1 clove garlic, minced
2 tablespoons sesame oil
2 cups thinly sliced zucchini
1 cup sliced fresh mushrooms
1 tablespoon finely chopped fresh basil
½ teaspoon salt
¼ teaspoon seasoned pepper
1 medium tomato, peeled and finely chopped
⅓ cup freshly grated Parmesan cheese
2 tablespoons crushed croutons

- **Cook** garlic in sesame oil in a large skillet, stirring constantly, until tender.
- **Add** zucchini and next 4 ingredients; cook 4 minutes, stirring constantly.
- **Add** chopped tomato, and cook, stirring constantly, until mixture is thoroughly heated.
- **Sprinkle** with cheese and croutons. Serve immediately. **Yield:** 4 servings.

FILLETS TOMATILLO

1 cup finely chopped fresh tomatillo (4 large tomatillos)
¼ cup finely chopped onion
¼ cup finely chopped celery
2 tablespoons chopped green pepper
1 clove garlic, minced
2 teaspoons olive oil
¼ cup clam juice or chicken broth
2 tablespoons canned chopped green chiles
2 tablespoons lime juice
½ teaspoon chopped fresh cilantro
½ teaspoon ground cumin
¼ teaspoon dried oregano
⅛ teaspoon salt
⅛ teaspoon ground red pepper
4 (4-ounce) orange roughy fillets
Vegetable cooking spray

- **Cook** first 5 ingredients in olive oil in a medium skillet over medium-high heat, stirring constantly, 5 minutes.
- **Add** clam juice and next 7 ingredients; cover, reduce heat, and cook 15 minutes, stirring occasionally. Remove from heat, and keep warm.
- **Arrange** fish in a grill basket coated with cooking spray. Cook, covered with grill lid, over medium-hot coals (350° to 400°) 7 to 8 minutes on each side or until fish flakes easily with a fork. Serve fillets with tomatillo mixture. **Yield:** 4 servings.

Ginny Munsterman
Garland, Texas

♥ Per serving: Calories 124 (27% from fat) Fat 3.7g (0.3g saturated) Cholesterol 23mg Sodium 193mg Carbohydrate 4.8g Fiber 0.5g Protein 17.4g

TEX-MEX SPICE MIX

Make a batch of this spice mix to use in Tortilla Soup, Chicken Taco Salad, and Santa Fe Skinny Dip. Save leftover mix to use in any recipe that needs a little extra zip.

3 tablespoons chili powder
2 tablespoons ground cumin
1 tablespoon ground black pepper
1 tablespoon salt
1 tablespoon garlic powder
1½ teaspoons ground red pepper

- **Combine** all ingredients thoroughly, and store mixture in a sealed container in a cool, dark, dry place up to 3 months. **Yield:** 8½ tablespoons.

Note: Try this spice mix in any recipe that calls for chili powder, or sprinkle it on meat for fabulous fajitas.

TORTILLA SOUP

3 (6-inch) corn tortillas, cut into
    thin strips
2 poblano chile peppers
1 cup chopped onion
2 cloves garlic, minced
Vegetable cooking spray
4 (13¾-ounce) cans ready-to-
    serve, fat-free chicken broth
2 (28-ounce) cans crushed
    tomatoes
2 (8-ounce) cans reduced-sodium
    tomato sauce
2 (6-inch) corn tortillas, quartered
1 tablespoon Tex-Mex Spice Mix
    (see recipe on page 135)
¼ cup chopped fresh cilantro
1 avocado, peeled and finely
    chopped
1 cup (4-ounces) shredded
    reduced-fat Monterey Jack
    cheese
½ cup chopped green onions

• **Place** tortilla strips on a baking sheet; bake at 350° for 10 minutes or until browned, stirring after 5 minutes. Set aside, and cool.

• **Place** peppers on an aluminum foil-lined baking sheet. Bake at 500° for 20 minutes or until skin is blistered.
• **Place** peppers in a large, heavy-duty zip-top plastic bag; seal and let stand 10 minutes to loosen skins. Peel peppers, and remove seeds. Chop and set aside.
• **Cook** onion and garlic in a Dutch oven coated with cooking spray over medium heat, stirring constantly, about 3 minutes. Add peppers, broth, and next 3 ingredients.
• **Bring** to a boil. Reduce heat, and simmer 1 hour, stirring mixture often. Stir in Tex-Mex Spice Mix.
• **Pour** one-fourth of mixture into container of an electric blender; process until smooth, stopping once to scrape down sides. Transfer mixture to a large saucepan; keep warm. Repeat procedure three times. Stir in cilantro.
• **Top** each serving evenly with avocado, cheese, green onions, and baked tortilla strips. **Yield:** 13 cups.

❤ Per 1½-cup serving: Calories 215 (31% from fat)
Fat 7.6g (2.3g saturated) Cholesterol 9mg
Sodium 509mg Carbohydrate 28.1g
Fiber 3.1g Protein 9.3g

CHICKEN TACO SALAD
(pictured on page 146)

Tortilla shells for Chicken Taco Salad are crisped in the microwave.

4 (4-ounce) skinned and boned
    chicken breast halves
1 tablespoon Tex-Mex Spice Mix
    (see recipe on page 135)
Vegetable cooking spray
1 cup chopped mango (1 medium
    mango)
½ cup chopped green pepper
½ cup chopped sweet red pepper
½ cup chopped jicama
1 tablespoon chopped fresh
    cilantro
Spicy Southwestern Dressing
4 (10-inch) flour tortillas
6 cups shredded Bibb lettuce

• **Coat** chicken with Tex-Mex Spice Mix. Cover and chill 8 hours.
• **Cook** chicken in a large nonstick skillet coated with cooking spray over medium heat 4 to 5 minutes on each side. Chill.
• **Chop** chicken, and place in a medium bowl. Add mango and next 4 ingredients; toss with Spicy Southwestern Dressing.
• **Place** each tortilla in a medium-size microwave-safe bowl; microwave at HIGH 1½ minutes or until crisp.
• **Place** lettuce into tortilla shells; top with chicken mixture. **Yield:** 4 servings.

Spicy Southwestern Dressing

1 tablespoon Tex-Mex Spice Mix
    (see recipe on page 135)
2 tablespoons lime juice
1 tablespoon vegetable oil
2 tablespoons water
1 teaspoon sugar

• **Combine** all ingredients in a small bowl. **Yield:** 6 tablespoons.

❤ Per serving: Calories 352 (25% from fat)
Fat 9.9g (1.4g saturated) Cholesterol 70mg
Sodium 690mg Carbohydrate 35.3g
Fiber 3.6g Protein 30.9g

PECULIAR PRODUCE

Cilantro – Pungent parsley. Try cilantro three times before you decide you don't like the distinctive flavor. The taste tends to grow on you.

Tomatillos – If anyone tells you tomatillos are the same as green tomatoes, don't believe them. Raw tomatillos are tart, but when cooked or roasted, their flavor mellows. Don't forget to remove the husk.

Jicama – It's like a turnip with a crisp, water chestnut-type texture, but sweeter. Jicama takes on the flavor of anything you mix it with. Add raw jicama to slaws and salads, or serve sliced as a vegetable for dips.

Poblanos – The heat of these large green chile peppers ranges from mellow to fiery. Roast the chile peppers to add an unmistakable smoky flavor to sauces and soups.

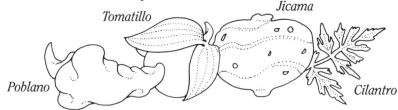

Tomatillo *Jicama*

Poblano *Cilantro*

SANTA FE SKINNY DIP

2 cups broccoli flowerets
1 (15-ounce) can chili-style beans, undrained
Lettuce leaves
1 cup nonfat sour cream
1 tablespoon Tex-Mex Spice Mix (see recipe on page 135)
1 (4.5-ounce) can chopped green chiles
3 tablespoons lime juice
1 clove garlic
1 cup (4 ounces) reduced-fat Cheddar cheese
½ cup sliced green onions
1 cup chopped tomato

● **Cook** broccoli in a small amount of boiling water 3 minutes or until crisp-tender; drain and set aside.
● **Position** knife blade in food processor bowl; add beans, and process until smooth, stopping once to scrape down sides. Spread on a lettuce-lined serving plate.
● **Combine** sour cream and spice mix, spread over bean layer; top with chiles.
● **Position** knife blade in food processor bowl; add broccoli, lime juice, and garlic, and process until smooth, stopping once to scrape down sides.
● **Spread** broccoli mixture over chiles, and top with cheese, green onions, and tomato. Serve with baked tortilla chips. **Yield:** 15 servings.

Janice Elder
Charlotte, North Carolina

♥ Per serving: Calories 69 (23% from fat)
Fat 1.7g (0.9g saturated) Cholesterol 5mg
Sodium 287mg Carbohydrate 7.7g
Fiber 1g Protein 5.6g

FROZEN AVOCADO YOGURT WITH CANDIED LIME STRIPS

2 ripe avocados, peeled and seeded
⅔ cup lime juice
½ cup sugar
1 quart nonfat vanilla frozen yogurt, softened
Candied Lime Strips

● **Position** knife blade in food processor bowl; add first 3 ingredients. Process until smooth, stopping occasionally to scrape down sides.
● **Pour** into a large bowl; add yogurt, stirring until blended. Spoon mixture into an 8-inch square pan.
● **Cover** and freeze. Top each serving evenly with Candied Lime Strips. **Yield:** 4¾ cups.

Candied Lime Strips

¼ cup thinly sliced lime rind strips
¼ cup water
¼ cup sugar

● **Cook** lime strips in boiling water to cover 5 minutes; drain.
● **Combine** ¼ cup water and sugar in a small saucepan; bring to a boil over medium heat. Add lime strips; simmer 2 minutes.
● **Remove** lime strips from heat; chill. **Yield:** ¼ cup.

♥ Per ½-cup serving: Calories 208 (27% from fat)
Fat 6.6g (1g saturated) Cholesterol 0mg
Sodium 40mg Carbohydrate 36.9g
Fiber 1g Protein 3.5g

LIGHTEN UP

■ Don't go overboard with too much regimentation. Vary the foods you eat and your exercise routine.

■ If you really want to exercise, you'll find enough time.

■ Create an eating plan that's comfortable, or you won't stay on it.

■ List your goals for exercise and weight loss, and review them often.

■ Don't feel bad if you gain back a few pounds; just keep in mind what it took to lose those pounds, and get back on track.

GAZPACHO WITH GUSTO

....

You've tried one gazpacho, you've tried them all, right? Wrong. Here's a recipe for gazpacho that's refreshingly different. You'll find shrimp, bites of avocado, and chunks of rich cream cheese in this chilled tomato soup. Each spoonful brings new flavor from an old favorite.

SHRIMP-CREAM CHEESE GAZPACHO

Before adding the cream cheese to Shrimp-Cream Cheese Gazpacho, quickly chill in the freezer; then it will be easy to cube.

5 cups water
1½ pounds unpeeled, small fresh shrimp
2 quarts tomato juice
1 bunch green onions, chopped
2 cucumbers, peeled, seeded, and chopped
4 tomatoes, peeled, seeded, and chopped
1 avocado, peeled and chopped
1 (8-ounce) package cream cheese, cut into ½-inch cubes
¼ cup lemon juice or white wine vinegar
2 tablespoons sugar
½ teaspoon hot sauce
Garnishes: cucumber slices, sour cream, whole shrimp

● **Bring** water to a boil; add shrimp, and cook 3 to 5 minutes or until shrimp turn pink. Drain well; rinse with cold water. Cool.
● **Peel** and devein shrimp. (Set aside about 10 shrimp for garnishing soup, if desired.)
● **Combine** shrimp and next 9 ingredients in a large bowl; cover.
● **Refrigerate** at least 3 hours. Garnish, if desired. **Yield:** 13 cups.

Carol Savage
Charleston, South Carolina

BURGER BLUEPRINTS

Who doesn't remember that first burger – homemade, thick and sizzling, on a fresh bun, topped with a juicy, ripe slice of tomato? However you relish your burger, you'll find this contemporary lineup will lay the foundation for a rebuilding of the Great American Sandwich.

TORTILLA BURGERS

2 pounds lean ground beef
½ cup Italian-seasoned breadcrumbs
1 large egg, lightly beaten
1 (10-ounce) can diced tomatoes and green chiles, drained
1 tablespoon chopped fresh cilantro
¼ teaspoon salt
Vegetable cooking spray
1 (8-ounce) package Monterey Jack cheese, cut into 24 slices
24 (6-inch) corn tortillas
1 (13-ounce) bottle salsa-style ketchup
Garnishes: fresh cilantro sprigs, jalapeño pepper, lime slices

• **Combine** first 6 ingredients; shape into 24 (2½-inch) patties. Place in 2 grill baskets coated with cooking spray.
• **Cook,** without grill lid, over medium-hot coals (350° to 400°) 4 to 5 minutes on each side.
• **Open** basket, and top each burger with cheese. (Do not reclose basket.) Cook until cheese melts.
• **Heat** tortillas according to package directions.
• **Spread** 1 tablespoon salsa-style ketchup on side of each tortilla. Place a burger, cheese side up, near top edge of each tortilla. Fold bottom edge up, and fold opposite sides over. Garnish, if desired. **Yield:** 24 mini burgers.

TERIYAKI HAMBURGERS

1 pound lean ground beef
⅓ cup chopped water chestnuts
¼ cup chopped green pepper
2 green onions, finely chopped
1 tablespoon brown sugar
2 tablespoons water
1 tablespoon lemon juice
1 tablespoon soy sauce
½ teaspoon ground ginger
Vegetable cooking spray
4 sesame seed buns
Hoisin Ketchup
Garnish: green onion brushes

• **Combine** first 9 ingredients; shape into 4 patties.
• **Coat** grill rack with cooking spray; place rack on grill over medium-hot coals (350° to 400°).
• **Place** patties on rack, and cook, without grill lid, 5 minutes on each side or until done. Serve on buns with Hoisin Ketchup. Garnish, if desired. **Yield:** 4 servings.

Hoisin Ketchup

¼ cup ketchup
¼ cup hoisin sauce

• **Combine** ketchup and hoisin sauce. **Yield:** ½ cup.

Elaine McVinney
Alexandria, Virginia

FRIED GREEN TOMATO CHEESEBURGERS

½ cup mayonnaise
1 clove garlic, pressed
1½ pounds lean ground beef
½ pound ground pork sausage
½ cup Italian-seasoned breadcrumbs
2 large eggs
3 tablespoons white wine Worcestershire sauce
1 teaspoon fennel seeds, crushed
3 green tomatoes, cut into ¼-inch slices
½ teaspoon salt
¼ teaspoon pepper
1 cup yellow cornmeal
1 to 4 tablespoons vegetable oil
Vegetable cooking spray
8 Kaiser rolls, split
Lettuce leaves
8 slices sharp Cheddar cheese
Purple onion slices
Garnish: pimiento-stuffed olives

• **Combine** mayonnaise and garlic; cover and chill.
• **Combine** ground beef and next 5 ingredients; shape into 8 patties. Cover and chill.
• **Sprinkle** tomato slices with salt and pepper; let stand 5 minutes. Dredge in cornmeal.
• **Cook** tomato slices in oil in a large skillet over medium heat until golden brown on each side. Drain on paper towels, and keep warm.
• **Place** patties in a grill basket coated with cooking spray.
• **Cook,** covered with grill lid, over medium-hot coals (350° to 400°) 4 to 5 minutes on each side or until done.
• **Spray** cut sides of rolls with cooking spray; place rolls, cut side down, on rack, and grill until lightly browned.
• **Place** a patty on lettuce on bottom half of each roll; top each patty with a cheese slice, green tomatoes, purple onion slices, mayonnaise mixture, and top half of bun. Garnish, if desired. **Yield:** 8 servings.

BURGER SPIRALS

⅓ cup grated Parmesan cheese
1 (4-ounce) can mushroom stems and pieces, drained and finely chopped
3 tablespoons chopped pimiento-stuffed olives
2 tablespoons finely chopped onion
2 tablespoons finely chopped green pepper
1 pound lean ground beef
8 slices bacon
8 whole wheat buns
Mayonnaise or salad dressing
Roma tomato slices
Lettuce leaves

● **Combine** Parmesan cheese, mushrooms, olives, onion, and green pepper; set aside.

● **Shape** beef into a 12- x 7-inch rectangle on wax paper. Sprinkle with Parmesan cheese mixture.
● **Roll** up, jellyroll fashion, starting at the short side. Cut into 8 slices. Wrap each slice with bacon, securing with wooden picks.
● **Cook** patties, without grill lid, over medium-hot coals (350° to 400°) about 5 minutes on each side or until done. Place each patty on a bun with mayonnaise, tomato slice, and lettuce; add top half of bun. **Yield:** 8 servings.

Debie Hayse
Lexington, Kentucky

OPEN-FACED CHICKEN-ONION BURGERS

1½ pounds ground chicken
½ cup finely chopped green pepper
⅓ cup finely chopped fresh mushrooms
10 large pimiento-stuffed green olives, finely chopped
1 (8-ounce) package shredded sharp Cheddar cheese
½ teaspoon salt
½ teaspoon pepper
1 tablespoon butter or margarine
2 medium onions, sliced and separated into rings
8 slices French bread
Garnishes: cherry tomatoes, fresh parsley sprigs

● **Combine** first 7 ingredients in a large bowl; shape chicken mixture into 8 patties. Cover and chill.
● **Melt** butter in a large skillet over medium-low heat. Add onions, and cook until tender and brown, stirring often. Keep warm.
● **Cook** patties, covered with grill lid, over medium-hot coals (350° to 400°) 5 minutes on each side or until done. Place bread slices on grill rack, and cook until lightly browned, if desired. Place patties on bread slices; top patties with onions. Garnish, if desired. **Yield:** 8 servings.

K. Nella Simmons
Cookeville, Tennessee

POTATO-CRUSTED CRAB BURGERS

2 tablespoons butter or margarine
1 sweet red pepper, chopped
1 green pepper, chopped
1 purple onion, chopped
1 clove garlic, minced
1 pound fresh crabmeat, drained and flaked
2 cups soft breadcrumbs
3 large eggs, lightly beaten
¼ cup Dijon mustard
2 cups instant potato flakes
Vegetable oil
6 Kaiser rolls, split
Lettuce leaves
Tomato slices
Rémoulade Sauce
Garnishes: fresh tarragon sprigs, lemon wedges

● **Melt** butter in a large skillet over medium heat. Add red pepper and next 3 ingredients; cook, stirring constantly, 3 minutes or until tender.
● **Combine** cooked vegetables, crabmeat, and next 3 ingredients. Shape into 6 patties, and coat with potato flakes. (Patties will be fragile and difficult to handle.)
● **Cook** patties, two at a time, in oil in a skillet over medium-high heat 2 minutes on each side or until golden. Drain on paper towels, and place on a baking sheet.
● **Bake** at 350° for 15 minutes or until thoroughly heated. Serve each patty on a roll with lettuce, tomato slices, and Rémoulade Sauce; add top half of roll. Garnish, if desired. **Yield:** 6 servings.

Rémoulade Sauce

1½ cups mayonnaise or salad dressing
2 tablespoons Creole mustard
1 tablespoon capers, chopped
1 tablespoon chopped sweet pickle
1 tablespoon chopped fresh parsley
1 teaspoon dried tarragon

● **Combine** all ingredients; cover and chill. **Yield:** 1¾ cups.

Karen Lapidus
Huntsville, Alabama

A BURGER BIO

Although it's known worldwide as a true bite of Americana, the hamburger boasts an international background. Legend has it that German sailors, returning to the seaport of Hamburg during the 1800s, brought with them a Russian recipe for raw shredded beef. A German chef wisely cooked the beef, and the burger was born.

It made its American debut at the 1904 St. Louis Louisiana Purchase Exposition. There German settlers of St. Louis served it in honor of their European origin.

Observes on-the-road journalist Charles Kuralt, "You can find your way across this country using burger joints the way a navigator uses stars."

For tips on beef, see "From Our Kitchen to Yours" on page 140.

FROM OUR KITCHEN TO YOURS

....

Hamburgers top most kids' list of a preferred meal. However, even with new concerns, they can remain loyal to the burger, and you can, too. (For burger recipes, turn to page 138.)

THE BEST BUY ON BEEF FOR BURGERS

Burger lovers agree that lower priced ground beef cooks up juicy and flavorful. And higher priced leaner ground beef makes a less-fatty burger, but is it as flavorful? And which lean-to-fat ratio in ground beef is the best buy?

Looking for a solution, we compared grilled ground beef, ground chuck, and low-fat ground beef. For the money, we preferred the flavor and texture of 80% lean ground chuck (see chart below).

REDUCING THE FAT

No matter which type of ground beef you buy, you *can* further reduce its fat content. According to research information from the National Live Stock and Meat Board, you can reduce the fat in a 3-ounce burger (after cooking) by blotting the patty with white, nonrecycled paper towels. By doing this, you'll decrease the fat content of a 73% lean ground beef patty from 18g to 15.7g and reduce the calories from 248 to 230. The same blotting with an 80% lean ground beef patty reduces fat from 15g to 13.8g and calories from 228 to 217.

BRINGING HOME THE BEEF

■ Refrigerate ground beef up to two days, or freeze in the original packaging up to two weeks. For longer storage, wrap in heavy-duty aluminum foil, plastic wrap, or freezer paper, and freeze up to four months.

■ Wash hands immediately before and after handling raw ground beef.

■ Thaw frozen ground beef in the refrigerator. Allow 24 hours to thaw a 1- to 1½-inch-thick package.

■ To freeze ground beef patties, place uncooked patties in a single layer on a baking sheet, and freeze until firm (about 30 minutes). Stack frozen patties, layering with wax paper; place in an airtight container. Freeze up to four months.

■ Never refreeze thawed, uncooked ground beef.

Ground beef packages are labeled according to USDA standards and by supermarket preference. Lean-to-fat ratios vary; however, if a package is labeled ground beef, it must be at least 70% lean. These figures are based on a burger weighing 3 ounces after cooking.

Beef	Calories	Fat	Our Cost	Insiders' Tips
73% lean (ground beef)	248	18g	$1.69/lb	moist, juicy
80% lean (ground chuck)	228	15g	$1.79/lb	juicy, firm, best flavor
93% lean (low-fat ground beef)	169	8g	$2.49/lb	compact, drier, very firm

STUFFED WITH GOOD TASTE

....

They're back: vine-ripened tomatoes, rich and red and bursting with flavor.

Our four stuffed versions elevate the tomato to main course status with ingredients that really like one another: crab and avocado, chiles and cheese, turkey and dill, and a medley of vegetables. On a warm afternoon or evening, serve your meal in Mother Nature's most luscious bowl – the tomato.

TURKEY STUFFED TOMATOES

6 medium tomatoes
2 cups chopped cooked turkey
1 cup shredded zucchini
½ cup chopped green onions
⅓ cup chopped green pepper
¼ cup chopped celery
3 tablespoons chopped fresh parsley
2 tablespoons chopped fresh dill
¼ teaspoon garlic powder
¼ teaspoon pepper
¼ cup reduced-calorie mayonnaise
Lettuce leaves
Garnish: fresh dill sprigs

●**Cut** tops from tomatoes; scoop out pulp, leaving shells intact. Discard pulp. Place shells upside down on paper towels to drain.
●**Cut** scalloped edges around tomatoes using a sharp paring knife, if desired. Set aside.
●**Combine** chopped turkey and next 9 ingredients.
●**Cover** and chill 1 hour.
●**Spoon** mixture into tomato shells, and serve on lettuce leaves. Garnish, if desired. **Yield:** 6 servings.

Peggy Fowler Revels
Woodruff, South Carolina

CRAB-AND-AVOCADO STUFFED TOMATOES

4 medium tomatoes
1 medium avocado, peeled and finely chopped
1 (6-ounce) can lump crabmeat, drained
2 tablespoons lemon juice
2 large hard-cooked eggs, chopped
3 slices bacon, cooked and crumbled
2 tablespoons finely chopped onion
2 tablespoons chopped fresh parsley
¼ teaspoon pepper
3 tablespoons mayonnaise or salad dressing
Lettuce leaves

● **Cut** tops from tomatoes; scoop out pulp, leaving shells intact. Discard pulp. Place shells upside down on paper towels to drain.
● **Combine** avocado, crabmeat, and lemon juice in a medium bowl.
● **Stir** in eggs and next 5 ingredients.
● **Spoon** into tomatoes, and serve on lettuce leaves. **Yield:** 4 servings.

Doris Garton
Shenandoah, Virginia

VEGETABLE STUFFED TOMATOES

6 medium tomatoes
⅔ cup finely chopped zucchini
⅔ cup finely chopped green pepper
⅔ cup finely chopped onion
2 tablespoons olive oil
1 cup corn cut from cob
1 teaspoon sugar
¼ teaspoon salt
¼ teaspoon pepper
¼ teaspoon hot sauce

● **Cut** tops from tomatoes; chop tops, and set aside. Scoop out pulp, leaving shells intact; chop pulp, and set aside. Place shells upside down on paper towels to drain.
● **Cook** zucchini, green pepper, and onion in oil in a skillet over medium heat, stirring constantly, 5 minutes.

● **Stir** in chopped tomato tops and pulp, corn, and remaining ingredients. Cover, reduce heat, and simmer 20 minutes, stirring often.
● **Spoon** into tomato shells, and place in a shallow baking dish.
● **Bake** at 350° for 20 minutes. **Yield:** 6 servings.

Caroline Wallace Kennedy
Newborn, Georgia

CHILE-CHEESE STUFFED TOMATOES

4 medium tomatoes
½ cup sour cream
2 teaspoons all-purpose flour
1 tablespoon chopped green onions
½ cup (2 ounces) shredded Cheddar cheese
3 tablespoons canned green chiles, drained

● **Cut** tomatoes in half horizontally; scoop out pulp, leaving shells intact. Discard pulp. Place shells upside down on paper towels to drain.
● **Combine** sour cream and remaining ingredients.
● **Spoon** into tomatoes.
● **Place** in a greased 13- x 9- x 2-inch baking pan.
● **Broil** 5½ inches from heat (with electric oven door partially opened) 4 minutes or until thoroughly heated. **Yield:** 8 servings.

Carol Barclay
Portland, Texas

ANY-HOUR BREAKFASTS

Although convention may suggest what's eaten when, food boundaries are as flexible as you are. Don't overlook any of these anytime breakfast dishes for an eye-opening supper.

MASHED POTATO NESTS

3 tablespoons butter or margarine, melted
1 small onion, finely chopped
3 cups cooked, mashed potato
½ teaspoon salt
¼ teaspoon pepper
2 tablespoons chopped fresh parsley
6 large eggs
Paprika
½ cup (2 ounces) shredded Cheddar cheese

● **Melt** butter in a medium saucepan over medium heat. Add onion; cook, stirring constantly, until tender.
● **Stir** in potatoes and next 3 ingredients. Shape potato mixture into 6 mounds on a lightly greased baking sheet; make a 2½-inch indentation in center of each. Carefully break an egg into each; sprinkle with paprika.
● **Bake** at 325° for 15 minutes.
● **Sprinkle** with cheese; bake 5 additional minutes or until eggs are set. **Yield:** 6 servings.

Shelby Adkins
Penhook, Virginia

CHEDDAR EGGS

2 large eggs, lightly beaten
½ cup peeled, chopped tomato
¼ cup (1 ounce) shredded extra-sharp Cheddar cheese
2 tablespoons finely chopped onion
¼ teaspoon salt
⅛ teaspoon pepper
Toast or toasted English muffins

● **Combine** first 6 ingredients; spoon into 3 lightly greased 6-ounce custard cups. Cover loosely with heavy-duty plastic wrap.
● **Microwave** at MEDIUM (50% power) 5 to 6 minutes, giving cups a quarter-turn at 2-minute intervals. Let stand 1 minute.
● **Serve** on toast or English muffins. **Yield:** 3 servings.

Betty Sims
Hiram, Georgia

POTATO-CRUSTED TEXAS TOAST

3 large eggs
½ cup buttermilk
½ teaspoon dried thyme
½ teaspoon salt
⅛ teaspoon pepper
3 green onions, finely chopped
Dash of hot sauce
6 (1-inch-thick) slices white bread,
     cut diagonally in half
2 cups instant potato flakes
6 tablespoons butter or margarine

• **Combine** first 7 ingredients; dip bread triangles in mixture, and dredge in potato flakes.
• **Melt** 2 tablespoons butter in a large skillet; add 4 bread triangles, and cook over medium-low heat until golden brown. Remove from pan; keep warm. Repeat procedure twice. Serve immediately. **Yield:** 4 servings.

Ina Mae Denham
Forestburg, Texas

CALLING ALL CHEESECAKE LOVERS

....

If you're a cheesecake lover, you know why this creamy, melt-in-your-mouth dessert has become a favorite. Add these new flavors to your recipe collection.

PEANUT BUTTER CHEESECAKE

1½ cups salted pretzel crumbs
⅓ cup butter or margarine, melted
5 (8-ounce) packages cream
     cheese, softened
1½ cups sugar
¾ cup creamy peanut butter
3 large eggs
2 teaspoons vanilla extract
1 (8-ounce) carton sour cream
3 tablespoons creamy peanut
     butter
½ cup sugar

• **Combine** pretzel crumbs and butter; firmly press onto bottom and 1 inch up sides of a 10-inch springform pan.
• **Bake** at 350° for 5 minutes. Set prepared pan aside.
• **Beat** cream cheese at medium speed with an electric mixer until fluffy; gradually add 1½ cups sugar, beating mixture well. Add ¾ cup peanut butter, beating well. Add eggs, one at a time, beating after each addition. Stir in vanilla. Pour into prepared pan.
• **Bake** at 350° for 40 minutes; turn oven off, and partially open door. Leave cheesecake in oven 30 minutes.
• **Combine** sour cream, 3 tablespoons peanut butter, and ½ cup sugar, stirring until sugar dissolves. Spread sour cream mixture over warm cheesecake. Cool completely on a wire rack.
• **Cover** and chill 8 hours. **Yield:** one 10-inch cheesecake.

Jill Goldblatt
Pelham, Alabama

CHOCOLATE-MINT BAKED ALASKA CHEESECAKE

1 cup chocolate wafer crumbs
2 tablespoons sugar
3 tablespoons butter or margarine,
     melted
1 cup mint chocolate morsels
3 (8-ounce) packages cream
     cheese, softened
⅔ cup sugar
3 large eggs
1 teaspoon vanilla extract
3 egg whites
1 (7-ounce) jar marshmallow
     cream

• **Combine** first 3 ingredients; firmly press onto bottom of a 9-inch springform pan.
• **Bake** at 350° for 10 minutes. Set prepared pan aside.
• **Melt** chocolate morsels in a small heavy saucepan over low heat, stirring constantly. Set aside.
• **Beat** cream cheese at medium speed with an electric mixer until fluffy; gradually add ⅔ cup sugar, beating well. Add eggs, one at a time, beating after each addition. Stir in melted chocolate and vanilla. Pour into prepared pan.

• **Bake** at 350° for 50 minutes.
• **Remove** from oven; immediately run a knife around sides of cheesecake to loosen, and cool completely in pan on a wire rack.
• **Cover** and chill 8 hours.
• **Beat** egg whites at high speed with an electric mixer until soft peaks form. Gradually add marshmallow cream, beating until stiff peaks form. Remove sides of pan from cheesecake. Carefully spread egg white mixture over top and sides of cake.
• **Bake** at 325° for 25 to 30 minutes or until golden brown. Serve immediately. **Yield:** one 9-inch cheesecake.

Erma Jackson
Huntsville, Alabama

MARGARITA CHEESECAKE

To prevent cracking, try running a knife around the edge of the cheesecake as soon as it comes out of the oven. This allows the cake to pull toward the middle of the pan as it cools.

1¼ cups salted pretzel crumbs
1 tablespoon sugar
½ cup butter or margarine, melted
2 (8-ounce) packages cream
     cheese, softened
½ cup sugar
2 individual-size envelopes instant
     margarita mix *
4 large eggs
⅓ cup tequila
1 teaspoon grated lime rind
½ teaspoon vanilla extract
1 (16-ounce) carton sour cream
¼ cup sugar
½ teaspoon grated lime rind
1 tablespoon fresh lime juice
Garnishes: lime slices, grated lime
     rind

• **Combine** first 3 ingredients; firmly press onto bottom and 1 inch up sides of a 9-inch springform pan.
• **Bake** at 375° for 6 to 8 minutes. Set prepared pan aside.
• **Beat** cream cheese at medium speed with an electric mixer until fluffy; gradually add ½ cup sugar and margarita mix, beating well. Add eggs, one at a time, beating after each addition.

Stir in tequila, 1 teaspoon grated lime rind, and vanilla. Pour into pan.

- **Bake** at 375° for 25 to 30 minutes or until center is almost set.
- **Remove** from oven; cool on a wire rack 30 minutes.
- **Combine** sour cream and next 3 ingredients; spread mixture over top of cheesecake.
- **Bake** at 425° for 10 minutes. Remove from oven, and cool completely on a wire rack.
- **Cover** and chill at least 8 hours. Garnish, if desired. **Yield:** one 9-inch cheesecake.

* Substitute 2½ teaspoons lemon- or lime-flavored presweetened drink mix for each envelope of margarita mix. In some areas the drink mix may be called lemonade or limeade.

Carol Barclay
Portland, Texas

FROZEN PEPPERMINT CHEESECAKE

1½ cups chocolate wafer crumbs
¼ cup sugar
¼ cup butter or margarine, melted
1 (8-ounce) package cream cheese, softened
1 (14-ounce) can sweetened condensed milk
1 cup crushed hard peppermint candy
3 drops of red liquid food coloring
2 cups whipping cream, whipped
Garnishes: whipped cream, crushed and whole hard peppermint candy

- **Combine** first 3 ingredients; firmly press onto bottom and 1 inch up sides of a 9-inch springform pan. Chill.
- **Beat** cream cheese at high speed with an electric mixer until fluffy. Add condensed milk, 1 cup crushed candy, and food coloring; beat well.
- **Fold** in whipping cream. Pour into prepared pan.
- **Cover** and freeze until firm. Garnish, if desired. **Yield:** one 9-inch cheesecake.
Rublelene Singleton
Scotts Hill, Tennessee

FREEZE SOME FUN

We've gotten a little crazy with a few of our flavor combinations for these pops. Some are definitely for kids. We've kept them healthy, adding fruit juices – or even milk. We offer great adult versions, as well – spiked.

We've given the yield in cups, so you can adapt the recipes to whatever freezing container you have. If the mixture you're freezing is too thin to allow wooden craft sticks or cocktail picks to stand up, partially freeze the pops for an hour and then insert sticks. Return pops to freezer to finish freezing.

TEXAS TORNADOES FOR GROWN-UPS

Try these tequila-laced pops as a starter at your next Tex-Mex party.

1 (6-ounce) can frozen limeade concentrate, thawed and undiluted
1½ cups orange juice
¾ cup water
¼ cup tequila
1 tablespoon chopped canned jalapeño peppers, drained

- **Combine** all ingredients in container of an electric blender; process until smooth. Pour into 2 ice cube trays.
- **Freeze** 1 hour or until partially frozen. Insert plastic cocktail forks in center of each cube. Freeze until firm. **Yield:** 3¼ cups.

DEEP BLUE SEA POPS

2 cups sugar
2 cups milk
2 cups half-and-half
1 cup lemon juice
12 drops of blue liquid food coloring
Bite-size, fish-shaped, chewy real fruit snacks

- **Combine** first 5 ingredients. Spoon mixture into paper cups or pop molds. Drop snacks into each cup or mold.
- **Freeze** 1 hour.
- **Insert** a wooden craft stick into each paper cup; freeze until firm. For molds, insert base of mold into pop immediately. Freeze until firm. **Yield:** 5½ cups.

Note: Here's a rainy-day idea. Let kids draw or paste fish on outside of cups. Fill cups, and freeze as directed.

CRAN-ORANGE SURPRISE

1 quart orange sherbet, softened
2 cups cranberry juice cocktail
1 cup lemon-lime carbonated beverage

- **Combine** all ingredients. Spoon mixture into paper cups or pop molds.
- **Freeze** 1 hour.
- **Insert** a wooden craft stick into each paper cup; freeze until firm. For molds, insert base of mold into pop immediately. Freeze until firm. **Yield:** 6 cups.

Note: To make pops for adults only, substitute ¼ cup Grand Marnier for 1 cup lemon-lime beverage, and freeze as directed. **Yield:** about 5 cups.

HAWAIIAN ORANGE-PINEAPPLE POPS

2 cups orange juice
1 (15¼-ounce) can crushed pineapple, undrained
¼ cup flaked coconut
2 tablespoons honey
1 teaspoon vanilla extract

- **Combine** all ingredients. Spoon mixture into paper cups or pop molds.
- **Freeze** 1 hour.
- **Insert** a wooden craft stick into each paper cup; freeze until firm. For molds, insert base of mold into pop immediately. Freeze until firm. **Yield:** 4½ cups.

Note: To make pops for adults only, add ½ cup light rum to the Hawaiian Orange-Pineapple mixture, and freeze as directed. **Yield:** 5 cups.

NO-BIG-DEAL MEALS

Ever get tired of the old "meat-vegetable-starch" rule of menu planning? Sometimes it's just too hard to be *that* organized. Come summer, it's hot, and your whole family is busy, so forget the "big meal" idea. Instead, try these lighter, brighter dishes that, with a crusty loaf of bread and a salad from the deli, make super summer meals.

SALSA-TOPPED CHICKEN BREASTS

Don't let the long list of ingredients fool you. The first 10 are simply tossed together to make the salsa topping.

1 (15-ounce) can black beans,
   rinsed and drained
1¼ cups frozen whole kernel corn,
   thawed
¾ cup finely chopped purple
   onion
¾ cup finely chopped sweet red
   pepper
2 jalapeño peppers, seeded and
   finely chopped
½ cup balsamic vinegar
¼ cup olive oil
1½ tablespoons Dijon mustard
¼ teaspoon salt
⅛ teaspoon pepper
1 tablespoon chili powder
1 teaspoon ground cumin
¼ teaspoon salt
⅛ teaspoon pepper
4 skinned and boned chicken
   breast halves *
1 tablespoon butter or margarine
¼ cup chopped fresh cilantro

• **Combine** first 10 ingredients; cover and chill at least 2 hours.
• **Combine** chili powder and next 3 ingredients; sprinkle over chicken.

• **Melt** butter in a nonstick skillet. Add chicken, and cook 5 to 7 minutes on each side or until done.
• **Stir** cilantro into black bean mixture. Serve over chicken. **Yield:** 4 servings.

* 4 (4-ounce) orange roughy fillets may be substituted. Cook 5 minutes on each side or until fish flakes easily when tested with a fork.

Margot Hahn
Washington, D.C.

BOILED SHRIMP WITH GREEN PEPPERCORN TARTAR SAUCE

1 cup mayonnaise or salad
   dressing
1 (3-ounce) jar green peppercorns
   in liquid, drained
2 cloves garlic, pressed
2 tablespoons Dijon mustard
4½ cups water
1 teaspoon liquid shrimp-and-crab
   boil seasoning
1½ pounds unpeeled, medium-size
   fresh shrimp

• **Combine** first 4 ingredients in container of an electric blender; process until smooth, stopping once to scrape down sides. Set aside.

• **Combine** water and shrimp-and-crab seasoning in a Dutch oven.
• **Bring** to a boil. Add shrimp, and cook 3 to 5 minutes or until shrimp turn pink. Drain well; serve immediately with peppercorn tartar sauce or chill, if desired. **Yield:** 4 servings.

Becky Davidson
Nashville, Tennessee

ANTIPASTO KABOBS
(pictured on facing page)

Choose this recipe that serves 10 if you're having company, or make it to feed your family a couple of times. Even quicker – skip the skewers, and toss ingredients in a bowl, instead.

1 (9-ounce) package refrigerated
   cheese-filled tortellini
1 (14-ounce) can quartered
   artichoke hearts, drained
1 (6-ounce) jar pitted ripe olives,
   drained
½ pound (2-inch-round) thin
   pepperoni slices
1 (8-ounce) bottle reduced-fat
   Parmesan Italian salad
   dressing

• **Cook** tortellini according to package directions, omitting salt. Drain and cool.
• **Thread** tortellini and next 3 ingredients onto 25 (6-inch) wooden skewers. Place in a 13- x 9- x 2-inch dish; drizzle with salad dressing, turning to coat.
• **Cover** and chill at least 4 hours. Drain before serving. **Yield:** 10 to 12 servings.

Right: Thread tortellini, pepperoni, olives, and artichoke hearts onto skewers. Then marinate them a few hours in commercial salad dressing for a simple supper of Antipasto Kabobs (recipe above).

Above: *Let the black beans and barley marinate separately overnight to soak up the spicy dressing for Black Bean-and-Barley Salad (recipe, page 174).*

Right: *Tortilla shells for Chicken Taco Salad (recipe, page 136) are crisped in the microwave.*

Left: *Packing food for a long weekend? Consider taking make-ahead Marinated Bean Salad and Flavored Mayonnaise. Then the only step left for dinner is preparing Grilled Chicken and slicing fresh tomatoes. (Recipes begin on page 167.)*

Below: *A lemon Dijon dressing accompanies a bounty of vegetables in Brown Rice Confetti Salad (recipe, page 174).*

Above: *Share summer's harvest of fresh tomatoes and basil with friends at a Backyard Summer Buffet. (Menu begins on page 157.)*

Left: *Blueberry-Peach Pie (recipe, page 158) isn't just for summer. In winter, substitute frozen blackberries and peaches for a sweet remembrance of warm breezes.*

Far left: *Family favorites such as Black Bean Salsa, Creamy Texas Dip, a basketful of tortilla chips, and Fresh Corn Salad help kick off a Fourth of July celebration. (Recipes begin on page 161.)*

Above: *Cut the colorful vegetables for Grilled Vegetable Skewers (recipe, page 160) into ¾-inch slices to ensure stability and even cooking.*

Right: *Showstoppers Yellowfin Tuna With Corn, Pepper, and Tomato Salsa (foreground) and Balsamic Caramelized Florida Sweet Onions need no special equipment – a cast-iron skillet and an outdoor grill are all it takes for a delectable meal. (Recipes begin on page 163.)*

Far right: *Vintage tablecloths, bouquets of summer wildflowers, and brightly colored tableware provide the perfect backdrop for supper's fresh-market menu of Grilled Pork Tenderloins, Kentucky Wonder Green Beans Vinaigrette, sliced tomatoes with fresh basil, Fried Corn, and Raspberry-Walnut Salad. (Menu begins on page 157.)*

When summer's thirst calls for a new brew, steep some Ginger-Almond Tea (left) or Sangría Tea (recipes, page 131).

JULY

TOP FLIGHT BBQ

Everyone loves a cookout. We sniff the alluring aroma. We see the slightly charred surfaces. We savor the results. How can you come up with an applause-provoking barbecue sauce? And just what gives that crusty-on-the-outside, juicy-on-the-inside result? We've consulted with some of the fiercest barbecue fanatics we know. They all agreed there are three important elements to great barbecuing: smoke, fire, and spice.

HERBED LEMON BARBECUE SAUCE

¾ cup lemon juice
2 cloves garlic, peeled
1 tablespoon onion powder
1½ teaspoons salt
1½ teaspoons paprika
1½ cups vegetable oil
1 tablespoon dried basil
1 teaspoon dried thyme, crushed

● **Combine** lemon juice, garlic, onion powder, salt, and paprika in container of an electric blender; process on high 1 minute. With blender on high, add oil in a slow, steady stream; process 1 minute. Add basil and thyme; process mixture on low 30 seconds.
● **Remove** 1 cup sauce for basting; cover and chill.
● **Pour** remaining sauce over chicken; cover and chill 8 hours. Drain and blot off excess sauce.
● **Brush** 1 cup sauce frequently over chicken the last 30 minutes of cooking time. (Discard any remaining basting sauce.) **Yield:** 2 cups.

Millie Givens
Savannah, Georgia

MAPLE SYRUP BARBECUE SAUCE

1 cup maple syrup
1 cup ketchup
1 cup finely chopped onion
¼ cup firmly packed brown sugar
¼ cup apple cider vinegar
¼ cup lemon juice
¼ cup water
2 tablespoons olive oil
2 tablespoons Worcestershire sauce
2 teaspoons minced garlic
2 teaspoons grated lemon rind
1 teaspoon salt
¼ teaspoon hot sauce

● **Combine** all ingredients in a saucepan.
● **Bring** to a boil; reduce heat, and simmer 20 minutes. Cool.
● **Pour** mixture into container of an electric blender; process until smooth.
● **Remove** 1 cup sauce for basting, and brush sauce frequently over chicken the last 30 minutes of cooking time. (Discard any remaining basting sauce.) Serve chicken with remaining sauce. Refrigerate sauce up to 1 month. **Yield:** 3½ cups.

Barbara Evans
Hendersonville, Tennessee

SPICY SOUTHWEST BARBECUE SAUCE

6 cloves garlic, unpeeled
2 cups ketchup
2 stalks celery, chopped
1 cup water
½ cup chopped onion
½ cup firmly packed brown sugar
½ cup butter or margarine
½ cup Worcestershire sauce
½ cup cider vinegar
3 tablespoons chili powder
2 teaspoons instant coffee granules
1½ to 2 teaspoons dried crushed red pepper
½ teaspoon salt
½ teaspoon ground cloves

● **Bake** garlic in a small baking pan at 350° for 20 to 30 minutes or until lightly browned. Cool and peel.
● **Combine** garlic and remaining ingredients in a saucepan.
● **Bring** to a boil; reduce heat, and simmer 20 minutes. Cool.
● **Pour** mixture into container of an electric blender; process until smooth, stopping once to scrape down sides.
● **Remove** 1 cup sauce for basting, and brush sauce frequently over chicken the last 30 minutes of cooking time. (Discard any remaining basting sauce.) Serve chicken with remaining sauce. Refrigerate sauce up to 1 month. **Yield:** 4½ cups.

> *"Barbecuing chicken is as much about the process as it is about the recipe."*
>
> —*Peggy Smith*
> *Assistant Test Kitchens Director*
> Southern Living *magazine*

WHAT TO DO WHEN YOU BARBECUE CHICKEN

These tips from barbecue experts promise sure-fire success at your next cookout. For more sizzling information on barbecue, see "From Our Kitchen to Yours" on this page.

■ **Place** 2 cups hickory or mesquite chips in center of a large square of heavy-duty aluminum foil; fold into a rectangle, and seal. Punch several holes in top of packet.

■ **Prepare** fire by piling charcoal or lava rocks on each side of grill, leaving center empty. Place packet on one side of coals or rocks, and ignite. Let charcoal burn 30 minutes or until flames disappear and coals turn white. If using a gas grill, preheat grill for 15 minutes. Place a drip pan in center. Coat food rack with cooking spray, and place rack on grill.

■ **Trim** any excess skin off chicken halves, quarters, or pieces.

■ **Arrange** chicken, skin side up, on rack directly over medium-hot coals (350° to 400°); cook, covered with grill lid, 15 minutes.

■ **Turn** chicken, and cook, covered with grill lid, 10 to 15 minutes or until golden. Move chicken over drip pan; cook, covered with grill lid, over indirect heat 25 to 35 minutes, brushing frequently with sauce and turning chicken, skin side up, after 5 minutes.

FROM OUR KITCHEN TO YOURS

....

The subjects of smoke and fire are near and dear to Assistant Test Kitchens Director Peggy Smith, our barbecue mentor. Peggy's barbecue knowledge comes from her family, who owned and operated a barbecue restaurant in Birmingham, Alabama, for more than 40 years. For our story "Top Flight BBQ" (on facing page), she tried several different grilling techniques until she achieved the perfect barbecued chicken. She kept detailed notes while searching for just the right cooking method. Here, we share a peek inside her journal.

BARBECUE CHICKEN TEST 1

Cooking 10 pounds of large chickens over three fires (gas, wood chunks, and charcoal) topped with foil wood chip packets, while juggling three sauces, tongs, basting brushes, and an instant-read thermometer in a cool, drizzling rain is a challenge. There are three fires to test the cooking times and the flavor of the different methods. The fires are too hot. I have basted the chicken too soon, and the sauces drip on the hot fires, causing continuous flames. The chicken burns. (The spray bottle I usually use to put out flare-ups isn't enough. I need a fire hose.) The chicken chars before it's done. With smoke-scented hair and red eyes, I serve tough, stringy, overcooked chicken to the Foods staff. It's difficult to compare the flavors of the sauces with the flavors imparted by the fuel products.

BARBECUE CHICKEN TEST 2

I once again light three fires topped with the foil packets of mesquite or hickory chips. This time I stack the hot coals on either side of the grill, and place a drip pan in the middle. I also add an oven thermometer inside the grill to be sure that the temperature isn't too hot.

Smaller chickens (weighing a total of 7½ pounds), trimmed of excess skin, are arranged directly above the medium-hot coals (350° to 400°) on food racks coated with vegetable cooking spray. The chickens have been marinated in Herbed Lemon Barbecue Sauce and drained and blotted with paper towels before grilling.

The chicken sears (browns) on the food racks directly over medium-hot coals, developing an outside crust. After I turn the pieces once and grill them 30 minutes, I rearranged them over the drip pans, away from the coals. Now, having basted the half-cooked chicken with the sauces over the drip pans, I prevent flare-ups and charring.

The combination of direct and indirect cooking methods has caramelized the sauces on the outside of the chicken, encrusting a juicy, tender inside. The smoke from both mesquite and hickory wood chip packets adds dimension to the barbecue flavor. The pieces of chicken smoked with mesquite have a sweet, rich, woody flavor, while the chicken smoked with hickory is filled with a strong, pungent, smoky flavor.

PEGGY'S HOT TIPS FOR COOL BARBECUES

"Barbecuing is long, slow cooking, because the real point is flavor," Peggy advises. "First you sear chicken directly over medium-hot coals to achieve a browned, caramelized outside crust. After turning once and grilling 30 minutes, place the chicken over the drip pan to finish the grilling with indirect heat."

You'll find the following hints on grilling chicken to be helpful.

■ Sauces containing ketchup, maple syrup, brown sugar, vegetable oil, or butter cause flare-ups when basted on chicken that's directly over the heat source.

■ Adding the packet of wood chips before lighting the fire starts the smoking process.

■ Let the charcoal burn 30 minutes or until the flames disappear and the coals turn white. If you're using a gas grill, close the lid, and allow the grill to preheat for 15 minutes. For a wood fire, close the lid when at least half the chunks are burning, and the flames will subside.

■ Drain marinated chicken, discarding marinade; blot chicken with paper towels before grilling.

■ As a rule of thumb, chicken parts, quarters, and halves are ready to eat in approximately one hour. However, using a meat thermometer is a foolproof way to tell when the chicken parts are safely cooked to 170°. Be sure the thermometer, when inserted, doesn't touch bone.

■ Cooking time lengthens when the day is cold or windy.

■ When exposed to too much woodsmoke or when overcooked, foods become tough, dry, and stringy and impart a bitter, burned flavor.

SUMMER SUPPERS®

GOOD FRIENDS, GOOD FOOD

Southern farmers markets and produce stands are brimming with the season's freshest treasures.

Summer's slow pace and a basketful of the season's best produce inspire Kelli and Jim Silliman of

Dallas, Texas, to host a get-together of neighborhood families. "We are not formal people,"

says Kelli. "We do a lot of potluck dinners. Whatever the menu, we always enjoy being together,"

says Kelli. And that, after all, is what's best about summer.

BACKYARD SUMMER BUFFET
Serves 12

Fruit 'Ritas
Summer Dip   Assorted Fresh Vegetables
Grilled Pork Tenderloins
Kentucky Wonder Green Beans Vinaigrette
Fried Corn
Raspberry-Walnut Salad
Sliced Tomatoes With Fresh Basil   Easy Cornbread
Blueberry-Peach Pie

FRUIT 'RITAS

1 (6-ounce) can frozen limeade
    concentrate, thawed and
    undiluted
¾ cup tequila
⅓ cup Triple Sec or other
    orange-flavored liqueur
2 medium nectarines or
    peaches, peeled, seeded,
    and sliced
Ice cubes
Garnish: fresh mint sprigs

● **Combine** first 4 ingredients in container of an electric blender; add enough ice cubes to bring limeade mixture to 5-cup level.
● **Process** 30 seconds or until mixture is slushy, stopping once to scrape down sides. Garnish, if desired. **Yield:** about 5 cups.

Note: For a nonalcoholic version, omit tequila and Triple Sec, and add ¾ cup lemon-lime carbonated beverage. Prepare as directed.

SUMMER DIP

1 (8-ounce) carton reduced-fat
    sour cream
1 cup plain nonfat yogurt
1 (1.4-ounce) envelope vegetable
    soup mix
2 teaspoons minced fresh dill

● **Combine** all ingredients in a medium bowl. Cover; refrigerate at least 6 hours. Serve with assorted fresh vegetables. **Yield:** 2¼ cups.

GRILLED PORK TENDERLOINS

(pictured on page 151)

½ cup teriyaki sauce
½ cup soy sauce
3 tablespoons brown sugar
2 green onions, chopped
1 clove garlic, pressed
1 tablespoon sesame seeds
½ teaspoon ground ginger
½ teaspoon pepper
1 tablespoon vegetable oil
3 (1½-pound) packages pork
   tenderloins

● **Combine** first 9 ingredients in a shallow dish. Add pork, and turn to coat.
● **Cover** and refrigerate 2 to 4 hours.
● **Cook** tenderloins, covered with grill lid, over medium-hot coals (350° to 400°) 20 minutes or until a meat thermometer inserted in thickest portion registers 160°, turning once. **Yield:** 12 to 16 servings.

KENTUCKY WONDER GREEN BEANS VINAIGRETTE

(pictured on page 151)

2 pounds fresh Kentucky Wonder
   green beans *
1 large sweet red pepper, seeded
   and chopped
1 large sweet yellow pepper,
   seeded and chopped
½ cup commercial fat-free Italian
   salad dressing
½ teaspoon freshly ground pepper

● **Wash** green beans, and trim ends. Arrange beans in a steamer basket, and place over boiling water.
● **Cover** and steam 8 to 10 minutes or until crisp-tender.
● **Plunge** beans into cold water to stop cooking process; drain.
● **Combine** beans, peppers, and salad dressing; sprinkle with pepper.
● **Cover** and chill 2 hours. **Yield:** 10 to 12 servings.

* 2 pounds any type fresh green beans may be substituted.

FRIED CORN

(pictured on page 151)

12 ears fresh corn
8 slices bacon, uncooked
½ cup butter or margarine
2 to 4 tablespoons sugar
2 teaspoons salt
½ teaspoon pepper

● **Cut** off tips of corn kernels into a large bowl; scrape milk and remaining pulp from cob with a paring knife. Set aside.
● **Cook** bacon in a large skillet until crisp; remove bacon, reserving about ¼ cup drippings in skillet. Crumble bacon, and set aside. Add corn, butter, and remaining ingredients to drippings in skillet.
● **Cook** over medium heat 20 minutes, stirring frequently. Spoon corn mixture into a serving dish, and sprinkle with crumbled bacon. **Yield:** 12 servings.

RASPBERRY-WALNUT SALAD

(pictured on page 151)

4 cups torn Boston lettuce
4 cups torn red leaf lettuce
¾ cup walnuts, chopped and
   toasted
1 cup fresh raspberries
1 avocado, peeled and cubed
1 kiwifruit, peeled and
   sliced
Raspberry Salad Dressing

● **Combine** first 6 ingredients in a large bowl; toss gently. Serve with Raspberry Salad Dressing. **Yield:** 12 servings.

Raspberry Salad Dressing

⅓ cup seedless raspberry jam
⅓ cup raspberry vinegar
1 cup vegetable oil
1 tablespoon poppy seeds

● **Combine** jam and vinegar in container of an electric blender; process 20 seconds. With blender on high, gradually add oil in a slow, steady stream.
● **Stir** in poppy seeds. **Yield:** 1½ cups.

EASY CORNBREAD

2 (8.5-ounce) packages corn
   muffin mix
1 (8-ounce) can cream-style corn
2 large eggs
½ cup plain nonfat yogurt
½ cup (2 ounces) shredded
   reduced-fat Cheddar cheese
¼ to ½ cup milk

● **Combine** all ingredients in a bowl; stir just until moistened. Pour batter into a lightly greased 13- x 9- x 2-inch pan.
● **Bake** at 400° for 17 to 20 minutes or until golden. **Yield:** 15 servings.

BLUEBERRY-PEACH PIE

(pictured on page 149)

1 cup sugar
3 tablespoons cornstarch
1 cup water
¼ cup lemon-flavored gelatin
4 cups unpeeled sliced fresh or
   frozen peaches, thawed
¾ cup fresh or frozen blueberries,
   thawed
Pastry Shell
Sweetened whipped cream

● **Combine** first 3 ingredients in a saucepan. Bring to a boil over medium heat; cook 1 minute, stirring constantly. Remove from heat; add gelatin, stirring until gelatin dissolves. Cool.
● **Combine** peaches and blueberries in a large bowl. Add gelatin mixture; toss gently.
● **Spoon** into prepared Pastry Shell.
● **Cover** and chill 1 hour or until set. Serve with sweetened whipped cream. **Yield:** one 9-inch pie.

Pastry Shell

1¼ cups all-purpose flour
1 teaspoon sugar
½ teaspoon salt
½ cup slivered almonds, coarsely
   chopped
⅓ cup vegetable oil
3 to 4 tablespoons water

●**Combine** all ingredients in a medium bowl, stirring until dry ingredients are moistened. Press into a 9-inch pieplate.
●**Bake** at 375° for 20 minutes; cool on a wire rack. **Yield:** one 9-inch pastry shell.

RIGHT IN THEIR OWN BACKYARD

....

Jim and Jane Bowyer enjoy the freshest and finest produce at their home in Maitland, Florida, thanks to nearby farmers markets – and they bring home plenty to prepare a feast for a group of friends.

A FEAST OF FLORIDA FRESHNESS
Serves 10

Appetizers
Garlic-Cheese Logs
Crabmeat Mousse
Mullet Spread

Dinner by the Pool
Greek Salad
Garlic-Basil Marinated Grouper
Grilled Vegetable Skewers
Corn on the Grill
Tropical Rainbow Salsa

GARLIC-CHEESE LOGS

2 (3-ounce) packages cream cheese, softened
1 tablespoon mayonnaise
1 tablespoon Worcestershire sauce
1 clove garlic, pressed
1 teaspoon dry mustard
¼ teaspoon salt
3 dashes of hot sauce
4 cups (16 ounces) shredded sharp Cheddar cheese
2 teaspoons paprika
1 teaspoon chili powder

●**Combine** first 7 ingredients in a large mixing bowl; beat at medium speed with an electric mixer until creamy. Gradually add Cheddar cheese, mixing until blended.
●**Divide** mixture in half, and shape each portion into a log.
●**Combine** paprika and chili powder; roll logs in mixture.
●**Cover** and refrigerate 8 hours. Serve with assorted crackers. **Yield:** 2 logs.

CRABMEAT MOUSSE

1 envelope unflavored gelatin
3 tablespoons cold water
¼ cup mayonnaise or salad dressing
2 tablespoons lime juice
2 tablespoons lemon juice
1 tablespoon chopped fresh parsley
1 tablespoon chopped fresh or frozen chives
1 tablespoon prepared mustard
¼ teaspoon salt
¼ teaspoon pepper
2 cups fresh lump crabmeat, drained
¾ cup whipping cream, whipped
2 to 3 limes, thinly sliced
2 avocados, peeled and mashed
2 tablespoons lime juice
1 tablespoon chopped fresh or frozen chives

●**Sprinkle** gelatin over cold water in a small saucepan; let stand 1 minute. Cook over low heat, stirring until gelatin dissolves, about 2 minutes.
●**Combine** gelatin mixture, mayonnaise, and next 7 ingredients in a large bowl. Fold in crabmeat and whipped cream; spoon into a lightly greased 4-cup (8-inch) ring mold.
●**Cover** and chill until set.
●**Unmold** onto a serving plate, and arrange lime slices around edge.
●**Combine** avocado and 2 tablespoons lime juice; spoon into center of mousse, and sprinkle with 1 tablespoon chives. Serve with assorted crackers. **Yield:** 20 to 25 appetizer servings.

MULLET SPREAD

Jane uses mullet, a plentiful Florida fish, in this appetizer spread, but you can substitute mackerel or any other smoked fish.

1 (8-ounce) package cream cheese, softened
2 tablespoons lemon juice
1 tablespoon prepared horseradish
¼ teaspoon salt
¼ teaspoon hot sauce
1 small onion, finely chopped
¾ pound smoked mullet or mackerel, flaked

●**Combine** first 5 ingredients in a medium bowl; stir in onion and fish.
●**Cover** and chill. Serve spread with assorted crackers or melba rounds. **Yield:** 2¼ cups.

TO MARKET, TO MARKET

■ Prices of fresh fruits and vegetables change with the seasons. It's best to buy seasonal produce when it's most plentiful and at peak quality.

■ The young leaves of all types of greens are the most tender. Don't buy greens with wilted or yellowing leaves.

■ When buying fresh citrus, look for fruit with smooth, blemish-free skins. Select firm fruits that are heavy for their size and yield to slight pressure. They have a high juice content generally.

■ When purchasing fresh produce for two people, select small-size items. Produce is the one food in which small items usually don't cost more per serving than large ones.

GREEK SALAD

Jane adapted this salad from one of her favorite Florida books, The Gasparilla Cookbook. *If you dig to the bottom of the mound of vegetables, you'll discover creamy potato salad.*

2 cups water
½ pound unpeeled, medium-size fresh shrimp
1 large head leaf lettuce
Potato Salad
1 bunch watercress, chopped
3 tomatoes, cut into wedges
1 to 2 cucumbers, peeled and cut into spears
½ cup feta cheese
2 avocados, peeled and cut into wedges
1 green pepper, cut into rings
1 sweet red pepper, cut into rings
1 (16-ounce) jar sliced beets, drained
12 pitted ripe olives
8 radishes
8 green onions
6 to 8 Greek pickled peppers
¾ cup olive oil
¼ cup red wine vinegar
2 teaspoons dry mustard
1 teaspoon dried oregano

• **Bring** water to a boil; add shrimp, and cook 3 to 5 minutes or until shrimp turn pink. Drain well, and rinse with cold water. Chill. Peel shrimp, and devein, if desired.
• **Remove** large outer leaves from lettuce, and line a large platter. Shred remaining lettuce, and arrange on lettuce-lined platter.
• **Spoon** Potato Salad in center; sprinkle with watercress. Arrange tomato and cucumber alternately around edge. Sprinkle with cheese. Top with shrimp, avocado, and next 7 ingredients.
• **Combine** olive oil and remaining ingredients in a jar; cover tightly, and shake vigorously. Drizzle over salad, and serve immediately. **Yield:** 20 servings.

Note: Increase shrimp to two pounds for eight main-dish servings.

Potato Salad

2 pounds medium-size round red potatoes
1 cup finely chopped purple onion
3 tablespoons red wine vinegar
¾ to 1 cup mayonnaise
2 teaspoons salt

• **Cook** potatoes in boiling water to cover 25 to 30 minutes or until tender; drain. Let cool to touch; peel and cut into ¾-inch cubes.
• **Combine** onion and vinegar; let stand 10 minutes. Stir in mayonnaise and salt; pour over potatoes, tossing gently. Cover and chill. **Yield:** about 6 cups.

GARLIC-BASIL MARINATED GROUPER

5 pounds grouper fillets
Garlic-Basil Marinade
Vegetable cooking spray
Garnish: fresh parsley

• **Arrange** fish in a large shallow dish; pour Garlic-Basil Marinade over fish. Cover and chill 1 hour.
• **Remove** fish from marinade, discarding marinade. Arrange fish in a grill basket coated with cooking spray.
• **Cook,** covered with grill lid, over medium coals (300° to 350°) 9 minutes on each side. Garnish, if desired, and serve immediately. **Yield:** 10 servings.

Garlic-Basil Marinade

¾ cup olive oil
½ cup tomato sauce
¼ cup balsamic vinegar
4 cloves garlic, crushed
¼ cup chopped fresh basil
1 teaspoon salt
1 teaspoon ground red pepper

• **Combine** all ingredients in a small bowl. **Yield:** 1⅔ cups.

GRILLED VEGETABLE SKEWERS
(pictured on page 150)

2 large yellow squash, cut into ¾-inch slices
1 large zucchini, cut into ¾-inch slices
1 large green pepper, cut into 1-inch squares
1 large sweet yellow pepper, cut into 1-inch squares
1 large sweet red pepper, cut into 1-inch squares
¼ cup olive oil
2 tablespoons tarragon vinegar *
1 clove garlic, crushed
¼ teaspoon dried thyme
¼ teaspoon salt
¼ teaspoon pepper
¾ pound medium-size fresh mushrooms

• **Combine** first 5 ingredients; cook in boiling water to cover 1 to 2 minutes. Drain vegetables; plunge into cold water to stop the cooking process. Set aside.
• **Combine** oil and next 5 ingredients in a large bowl, stirring with a wire whisk. Add cooked vegetables and mushrooms to oil mixture; toss gently. Let stand 1 hour, tossing occasionally.
• **Drain** vegetables, and alternate on skewers.
• **Cook,** covered with grill lid, over medium-hot coals (350° to 400°) for 10 minutes or until tender, turning once. **Yield:** 10 servings.

* 2 tablespoons white wine vinegar and ¼ teaspoon dried tarragon may be substituted for 2 tablespoons tarragon vinegar.

CORN ON THE GRILL

12 ears fresh corn in husks
½ cup butter
½ teaspoon salt
½ teaspoon freshly ground
   pepper

- **Pull** back husk from corn (do not remove). Remove silks.
- **Rub** corn with butter; sprinkle with salt and pepper. Pull husk over corn, and tie top with heavy string.
- **Cook,** covered with grill lid, over medium-hot coals (350° to 400°) 15 to 20 minutes, turning occasionally.
- **Remove** strings, and serve immediately. **Yield:** 12 servings.

TROPICAL RAINBOW SALSA

1 large sweet onion, quartered and
   sliced
¼ cup balsamic vinegar
2 tomatoes, peeled, seeded, and
   coarsely chopped
2 yellow tomatoes, peeled,
   seeded, and coarsely
   chopped
1 sweet red pepper, seeded and
   chopped
1 green pepper, seeded and
   chopped
1 sweet yellow pepper, seeded and
   chopped
½ cup chopped fresh
   cilantro
1 mango, peeled, seeded, and
   coarsely chopped
Garnish: fresh cilantro

- **Cook** onion in a heavy nonstick skillet over medium heat, stirring constantly, until tender and golden, adding water if necessary to prevent scorching.
- **Add** vinegar; cook 2 to 3 minutes. Add tomato and pepper; cook 2 to 3 minutes. Remove from heat.
- **Stir** in cilantro and mango; cover and chill. Garnish, if desired, and serve with fish. **Yield:** 6 cups.

COME HOME TO SUMMER FAVORITES

Rebecca and Don Farris of Dallas, Texas, look forward to every holiday as a chance to host a family celebration. Their Stars and Stripes supper on the Fourth of July features seasonal finds from the local farmers market. Dessert by the pool and fireworks cap the patriotic evening.

FOURTH OF JULY FAMILY-STYLE SUPPER
Serves 12

Creamy Texas Dip
Black Bean Salsa
Tortilla Chips
Deviled Eggs
Spicy Fried Chicken
Fresh Asparagus and Tomatoes
Fresh Corn Salad
New Potato Salad
Strawberry Shortcake

CREAMY TEXAS DIP
(pictured on page 148)

2 (8-ounce) jars chunky picante
   sauce
1 (16-ounce) carton sour cream
Garnishes: paprika, fresh cilantro

- **Drain** picante sauce, reserving ¼ cup liquid.
- **Combine** picante sauce and sour cream. Stir in 2 to 4 tablespoons reserved liquid. Cover and chill. Garnish, if desired; serve with tortilla chips. **Yield:** 2¼ cups.

♥ To reduce fat and calories, substitute reduced-fat sour cream.

BLACK BEAN SALSA
(pictured on page 148)

2 (15-ounce) cans black beans,
   rinsed and drained
1 (17-ounce) can whole kernel
   corn, drained
2 large tomatoes, seeded and
   chopped
1 large avocado, peeled and
   chopped
1 purple onion, chopped
⅛ to ¼ cup chopped fresh
   cilantro
3 to 4 tablespoons lime juice
2 tablespoons olive oil
1 tablespoon red wine
   vinegar
1 teaspoon salt
½ teaspoon pepper
Garnishes: avocado slices, fresh
   cilantro

- **Combine** first 11 ingredients in a large bowl. Cover and chill. Garnish, if desired, and serve with tortilla chips. **Yield:** 6 cups.

DEVILED EGGS

12 hard-cooked eggs
⅓ cup mayonnaise
2 tablespoons sweet pickle
   relish
1 teaspoon dry mustard
1 teaspoon red wine vinegar
¼ teaspoon salt
⅛ teaspoon pepper
Paprika

- **Slice** eggs in half lengthwise, and carefully remove yolks.
- **Mash** yolks; stir in mayonnaise and next 5 ingredients. Spoon into cooked egg whites. Sprinkle with paprika. **Yield:** 12 servings.

SPICY FRIED CHICKEN

1 quart buttermilk
½ teaspoon salt
½ teaspoon ground red pepper
1 teaspoon freshly ground black pepper
4 cloves garlic, minced
9 pounds chicken pieces
2½ cups all-purpose flour
2 teaspoons salt
2 teaspoons freshly ground black pepper
2 teaspoons ground red pepper
1 teaspoon paprika
Vegetable oil
Garnishes: corn salad-filled sweet peppers, fresh cilantro sprigs

• **Combine** first 5 ingredients in a large bowl. Add chicken pieces, turning to coat. Cover and refrigerate at least 8 hours.
• **Drain** chicken, discarding buttermilk mixture.
• **Combine** flour and next 4 ingredients in a shallow dish.
• **Dredge** chicken in flour mixture, shaking off any excess. Let stand in refrigerator 30 minutes.
• **Pour** oil to depth of ½ inch into a large skillet; heat to 350°. Add one-third of chicken, and fry 20 to 25 minutes, turning once. Drain on paper towels. Repeat procedure with remaining chicken. Garnish, if desired. **Yield:** 18 servings.

FRESH ASPARAGUS AND TOMATOES

2 pounds fresh asparagus
6 medium tomatoes, thinly sliced
⅓ cup (1.3 ounces) shredded mozzarella cheese
2 to 3 tablespoons chopped fresh basil
3 to 4 tablespoons balsamic vinegar

• **Snap** off tough ends of asparagus; remove scales from stalks with a knife or vegetable peeler, if desired.

• **Cook** asparagus, covered, in a small amount of boiling water 4 to 6 minutes or until crisp-tender; drain. Plunge asparagus into ice water to stop the cooking process; drain and set aside.
• **Arrange** tomato slices around outside edge of a large platter.
• **Sprinkle** slices with cheese and basil; drizzle with vinegar.
• **Arrange** asparagus in center. **Yield:** 12 servings.

FRESH CORN SALAD
(pictured on page 148)

8 to 10 ears fresh white corn
4 cups water
½ to 1 teaspoon sugar
⅓ cup finely chopped purple onion
1 large green pepper, seeded and chopped
1 large sweet red pepper, seeded and chopped
1 (8-ounce) package Monterey Jack cheese, cut into small cubes
2 tablespoons olive oil
½ teaspoon salt
¼ teaspoon ground cumin
¼ teaspoon ground black pepper
⅛ teaspoon ground red pepper

• **Cut** off corn kernels; set aside.
• **Combine** water and sugar in a large saucepan; bring to a boil. Add corn, and return to a boil. Reduce heat, and simmer 10 to 12 minutes. Drain and rinse with cold water. Drain on paper towels, patting dry.
• **Combine** corn, onion, and remaining ingredients. Let stand 30 minutes, or cover and refrigerate 8 hours. **Yield:** 12 servings.

NEW POTATO SALAD

3 pounds new potatoes, unpeeled
⅓ cup finely chopped purple onion
⅓ cup olive oil
⅓ cup red wine vinegar
¼ cup stone-ground mustard
2 teaspoons sugar
½ teaspoon salt
½ teaspoon freshly ground pepper
½ pound thick-sliced bacon, cooked and crumbled
1 cup chopped fresh parsley

• **Cook** potatoes in boiling water to cover 15 minutes or until tender. Drain and cool slightly. Cut into ¼-inch slices. Combine potato and onion in a large bowl; set aside.
• **Combine** olive oil and next 5 ingredients; mix well with a wire whisk. Pour dressing over potato mixture; toss gently. Cover and chill.
• **Add** bacon and parsley just before serving; toss. **Yield:** 12 servings.

STRAWBERRY SHORTCAKE

1 quart strawberries, sliced
½ cup sugar
2 cups all-purpose flour
1 teaspoon baking powder
½ teaspoon salt
1 cup sugar
½ cup butter or margarine
2 large eggs
1 cup whipping cream
¼ cup sifted powdered sugar
Garnishes: whole strawberry, fresh mint sprigs

• **Combine** 1 quart strawberries and ½ cup sugar; set aside.
• **Combine** flour and next 3 ingredients; cut in butter with pastry blender until mixture is crumbly. Add eggs, stirring until moistened.
• **Turn** dough out onto a lightly floured surface. Knead lightly several times to

form a ball. (Dough will be grainy.) Press into a wax paper-lined 8-inch round cakepan.

- **Bake** at 350° for 35 minutes or until golden. Cool in pan on a wire rack 10 minutes; remove from pan, and peel off wax paper. Cool on wire rack.
- **Beat** whipping cream at low speed with an electric mixer until foamy; gradually add powdered sugar, beating at medium speed until soft peaks form.
- **Split** shortcake crosswise into 2 layers. Place 1 layer on a serving plate; drizzle with 2 tablespoons liquid from strawberry mixture. Spread with half of whipped cream, and arrange half of strawberries on top. Place remaining shortcake layer over strawberries, and top with remaining whipped cream and strawberries. Garnish, if desired. **Yield:** one 2-layer shortcake.

DINING AT "THE IMPROV"

When funny guy Mark Rodriguez, chef/owner of Jordan's Grove in Maitland, Florida, hits the kitchen, it's serious business.

The stunning results of Mark's zany approach to cooking keep his culinary audience coming back for more. His delivery of both witty one-liners and fabulous Florida flavors to a happy audience proves his talent for "improv." Throw him any subject, he'll ad-lib. Same with his cooking. Give him the day's freshest ingredients, and he'll produce a mouthwatering menu in nothing flat.

Although your kitchen may not be as professional as a chef's, these recipes will still work well for you at home. Mark uses equipment you probably already have on hand – a cast-iron skillet, an outdoor grill, a smoker, and – most important – a sense of humor.

SMOKED PORTABELLO MUSHROOM TART

When smoked or grilled, the saucer-size portabello mushrooms taste like a steak, which may justify their expense. Filled with a blend of smoked vegetables, goat cheese, and mascarpone (a mild, creamy Italian cheese), this one dish is plenty for dinner on its own.

Hickory chips
8 (6-inch) fresh portabello
    mushrooms
8 cloves garlic, peeled
1 medium tomato
1 medium-size sweet red pepper
8 ounces goat cheese
½ cup mascarpone *
1½ teaspoons freshly ground
    pepper
Garnishes: fresh rosemary sprigs,
    chopped fresh parsley,
    tomato wedges, mascarpone

- **Soak** hickory chips in water for 30 minutes.
- **Prepare** charcoal fire in smoker; let burn 20 minutes.
- **Drain** hickory chips, and place on coals. Place water pan in smoker, and add water to pan.
- **Remove** stems from portabello mushrooms. (Reserve stems for another use.) Rinse mushrooms thoroughly; pat dry.
- **Thread** garlic cloves on a wooden skewer.
- **Arrange** mushrooms, garlic, tomato, and sweet red pepper on food rack. Cover with smoker lid.
- **Cook** 2 to 3 hours or until vegetables are tender, removing vegetables as they become tender.
- **Core** tomato, and remove stem from pepper.
- **Place** garlic, tomato, and sweet red pepper in container of an electric blender; process until smooth, stopping once to scrape down sides. Add goat cheese, mascarpone, and pepper; process until smooth.
- **Place** 4 mushrooms on a baking sheet, stem side up. Spoon pureed mixture evenly on mushrooms; top with remaining mushrooms, stem side down.

- **Bake** at 350° for 10 minutes or until thoroughly heated. Garnish, if desired. **Yield:** 4 servings.

* ¼ cup sour cream and 4 ounces cream cheese may be substituted.

BALSAMIC CARAMELIZED FLORIDA SWEET ONIONS
(pictured on page 150)

"Caramelize" means to heat sugar until it becomes liquid or syrupy. In this recipe, the onions' natural sugar becomes caramelized while they're baking.

1 cup balsamic vinegar
2 large sweet onions, skinned and
    cut in half crosswise (about
    1½ pounds)
2 tablespoons butter or
    margarine
1 cup walnut halves
¼ cup firmly packed brown
    sugar
¼ cup chopped sweet red pepper
¼ cup chopped sweet yellow
    pepper
1 to 1½ teaspoons ground red
    pepper
Garnish: fresh pineapple sage
    sprig

- **Bring** vinegar to a boil in a cast-iron skillet over medium-high heat.
- **Remove** from heat; place onions, cut side down, in skillet.
- **Bake** at 400° for 55 to 60 minutes or until onions are tender and vinegar turns the color of dark chocolate.
- **Melt** butter in a skillet over medium heat. Add walnuts; cook 2 minutes, stirring often. Add sugar and next 3 ingredients; cook until bubbly, stirring often.
- **Place** an onion half, cut side up, on each plate. Sprinkle walnut mixture evenly around onions; drizzle onions with vinegar. Garnish, if desired. Serve immediately. **Yield:** 4 servings.

Note: Balsamic (dark, aged) vinegar is found next to the more common vinegars at your grocer.

YELLOWFIN TUNA WITH CORN, PEPPER, AND TOMATO SALSA
(pictured on page 150)

Spice up sweet peppers, corn, tomatoes, and tuna with Scotch bonnet peppers. They look like tiny bell peppers, but zowee, they pack a powerful punch.

1 sweet red pepper
1 sweet yellow pepper
4 ears fresh corn
2 large tomatoes, seeded and chopped
1 Scotch bonnet pepper, seeded and chopped *
2 tablespoons ground cumin
½ teaspoon salt
¼ teaspoon ground white pepper
Hickory chips
4 tuna steaks (about 2 pounds)
1 tablespoon olive oil
2 to 3 teaspoons cracked black pepper
½ to 1 teaspoon dried thyme
Garnishes: mixed greens, whole chile peppers

• **Place** sweet peppers on a baking sheet; bake at 425° for 5 minutes. Cool; remove seeds, and chop peppers.
• **Cut** corn from cob. Cook corn in boiling water to cover 3 minutes. Drain corn, and cool.
• **Combine** chopped sweet pepper, corn, tomato, and next 4 ingredients. Cover and chill.
• **Soak** hickory chips in water 30 minutes. Prepare charcoal fire on 1 side of grill; let burn until coals are white. Drain hickory chips, and place on hot coals.
• **Brush** tuna steaks with oil; sprinkle with black pepper and thyme.
• **Cook** tuna steaks, without grill lid, directly over coals 2 minutes on each side. Move tuna steaks to opposite side of grill, and cook indirectly, covered with grill lid, 5 to 7 minutes or until done.
• **Spoon** salsa onto serving plates, and top with tuna steaks. Garnish, if desired. Serve immediately. **Yield:** 4 servings.

* Substitute your favorite hot chiles or skip the pepper altogether.

A PEEK BEHIND THE STANDS

So, you've gathered a rainbow of fruits and vegetables. You only wish your recipes were as fresh as the produce itself. Here's a hint: Strike up a conversation with the people who staff the produce stand. They're usually passionate about their work, and you can bet they've discovered lots of flavor combinations in their own kitchens. Go ahead and ask them for some of their favorite recipes.

From the staff of International Produce in Winter Park, Florida, we learned about something as simple as potato salad with a zing from fresh thyme and as involved as a pasta dish with exotic ingredients. Enjoy these recipes from these pros who really know their fruits and vegetables.

HERBED POTATO SALAD

5 pounds new potatoes, unpeeled
1 cup chopped celery
1 cup chopped onion
2 teaspoons chopped fresh or ¾ teaspoon dried thyme
1⅓ cups mayonnaise or salad dressing
1½ teaspoons salt
¼ teaspoon pepper

• **Cook** potatoes in boiling salted water to cover 12 to 15 minutes or until tender; drain and cool.
• **Cut** potatoes into quarters, and place in a large bowl.
• **Add** celery and remaining ingredients; toss gently. Cover and chill. **Yield:** 12 servings.

Sue Bone
Winter Park, Florida

PEPPERY PASTA

3 pounds ripe plum tomatoes, peeled and quartered
8 green onions, thinly sliced
8 cloves garlic, minced
1 tablespoon olive oil
2 small sweet banana peppers, thinly sliced
⅓ cup chopped fresh or 2 tablespoons dried oregano
¼ cup chopped fresh or 1½ teaspoons dried basil
½ teaspoon sea or table salt
8 green onions, thinly sliced
3 sweet yellow peppers, cut into thin strips
3 sweet red or orange peppers, cut into thin strips
3 tablespoons chopped fresh or 1 tablespoon dried oregano
1 tablespoon olive oil
10 to 12 cremini or button mushrooms, coarsely chopped
1 teaspoon sea or table salt
1 teaspoon dried crushed red pepper
1 pound hot cooked mostaccioli pasta
8 ounces fontina or mozzarella cheese, shredded

• **Position** knife blade in food processor bowl; add one-third of tomato. Pulse 5 or 6 times or until finely chopped. Remove tomato from bowl, and set aside. Repeat procedure twice.
• **Cook** 8 green onions and garlic in 1 tablespoon olive oil in a large, heavy saucepan, stirring constantly, 10 minutes or until tender.
• **Stir** in tomato, banana peppers, and next 3 ingredients.
• **Bring** mixture to a boil over medium heat, stirring constantly; reduce heat, and simmer, uncovered, 1 hour, stirring occasionally. Remove from heat; keep tomato mixture warm.
• **Cook** 8 green onions, sweet pepper strips, and 3 tablespoons fresh oregano in 1 tablespoon olive oil in a large skillet over medium heat, stirring constantly,

12 to 15 minutes or until vegetables are crisp-tender. Add mushrooms, 1 teaspoon salt, and crushed red pepper; cook about 7 minutes or until mushrooms are tender, stirring often.
● **Place** hot cooked pasta on a large serving platter.
● **Pour** tomato mixture over pasta; spoon mushroom mixture over sauce, and sprinkle with shredded cheese. **Yield:** 8 servings.

Joelle Diorio
Orlando, Florida

GREEK GREEN BEANS

1 tablespoon butter or
   margarine
1 medium onion, chopped
¼ teaspoon ground cinnamon
1½ pounds fresh green
   beans
¾ cup chicken broth
½ teaspoon salt
¼ teaspoon pepper
2 tablespoons tomato paste

● **Melt** butter in a large saucepan; add chopped onion and cinnamon, and cook 4 minutes or until onion is tender, stirring often.
● **Add** green beans, chicken broth, salt, and pepper.
● **Bring** mixture to a boil. Cover, reduce heat, and simmer 15 to 20 minutes or until green beans are tender, stirring occasionally.
● **Remove** from heat, and stir in tomato paste. **Yield:** 6 servings.

Lynda Venens
Winter Park, Florida

PICK A PECK OF PEPPERS

Roadside produce stands and farmers markets

brimming with bumper crops give inspiration to create this

hot look for your summer table.

WHAT YOU'LL NEED...

STEP 1:
2 pieces natural-colored burlap
   (Each piece should measure
   2 times height of the table +
   diameter of table + 12
   inches.)
1 square contrasting color
   burlap (We used a 54-inch
   square for a 48-inch round
   table.)

STEP 2:
18-inch plastic foam cone
8-inch terra-cotta flowerpot
Hot-glue gun
Wooden picks
5 dozen assorted peppers
   (for pepper topiary)
1 cluster small peppers
   (for top)
Florist pick
2 yards raffia twine or raffia

STEP 3:
Metal garden markers
Grease pencil
3-inch terra-cotta flowerpots
Florist vials
Seasonal bedding plants

1: Cover the table by overlapping 2 pieces of natural-colored burlap. Don't worry about hemming; just tuck under the unfinished edges, and allow excess cloth to puddle on the floor. A 54-inch square of burlap in a contrasting color tops a 48-inch round table. Pull threads around the edge of the square to create a 1-inch fringed border.

2: Create a topiary centerpiece by wedging an 18-inch plastic foam cone into an 8-inch terra-cotta flowerpot. (Use a hot-glue gun to secure the cone.) Allow vegetables to hang over the edge of the pot. The subsequent rows of vegetables should overlap preceding row. Cut off point of cone, if desired, and attach a cluster of peppers to the top; secure with hot glue, if desired. For a finishing touch, use a florist pick to attach a raffia bow with streamers.

3: Welcome guests with a collection of garden items at each place setting. Metal garden markers labeled with a grease pencil become place cards. Small terra-cotta flowerpots hold each guest's flatware and napkins, along with a small bouquet of bright summer blossoms. (We used 3-inch pots.) Keep flowers looking fresh by placing the stems in water-filled florist vials, which are available at garden and crafts stores. (We used lantana for our table because the blooms of this bedding plant won't wilt easily in the heat.)

Meals Go Far in Jars

Packing food for a long weekend at the beach is standard operating procedure for some vacationers. But this year you can make some changes. A few jars filled with combinations of basic ingredients and a small cooler will replace the many coolers and boxes that used to take up more room than the luggage. These recipes quickly assemble into multiple meals in minutes. So, spend your weekend on the beach, not in the kitchen. Our meal plan shows you how.

Menus for the Weekend

For the meal plan to work for all three days, follow this schedule.

DAY 1

Breakfast
Coffee Cake
Fresh Fruit

Lunch
Take the family out.

Supper
Grilled Chicken
Marinated Bean Salad
Sliced Fresh Tomatoes
French Bread

DAY 2

Breakfast
Peanut Butter-Chocolate
Chip Muffins
Fresh Fruit

Lunch
Marinated Bean-Pasta Salad
Grilled Cheese Sandwiches
Rainy Day Cookies

Supper
Toasted Appetizers
Shrimp-and-Chicken Paella
Green Salad
Fruit Crisp With
Frozen Vanilla Yogurt
or Ice Cream

DAY 3

Breakfast
Granola Mix With Milk
Scrambled Eggs
Fresh Fruit

PANTRY LIST

· · · · · · · · · · · · · · ·

Before you leave home, pack up these odds and ends that you'll probably have on hand in your pantry:

- Spiral pasta, 4 ounces
- Sugar, 2 tablespoons
- Creamy peanut butter, 2 tablespoons
- Commercial salad dressing, 1 bottle
- Vegetable cooking spray

PRODUCE LIST

Stop at a roadside produce stand on the way, and purchase a few fresh fruits and vegetables.

- Fresh peaches, 4 large
- Fresh blackberries or blueberries, ½ pint
- Assorted fresh fruits (enough for three breakfasts)
- Leaf lettuce, 1 head
- Fresh tomatoes, 3

GROCERY LIST

When you arrive at your destination, zip to the local grocery store to pick up the following items:

- French bread, 1 (16-ounce) unsliced loaf
- Sandwich bread, 1 loaf
- Mozzarella cheese slices, 2 (6-ounce) packages
- Milk
- Butter or margarine
- Eggs, 1 dozen
- Chicken, 1 (3-pound) broiler-fryer plus 2 bone-in chicken breast halves
- Unpeeled, medium-size fresh shrimp, 1 pound
- Frozen vanilla yogurt or ice cream

QUICK MIX

3 cups all-purpose flour
1½ cups sugar
⅔ cup firmly packed brown
  sugar
1¼ teaspoons baking powder
1¼ teaspoons baking soda
½ teaspoon salt
¼ cup cultured buttermilk
  powder
1 cup butter-flavored shortening
½ cup regular oats, uncooked
¼ cup semisweet chocolate
  mini-morsels
½ teaspoon ground cinnamon
¼ cup raisins

• **Combine** first 7 ingredients; cut in shortening with pastry blender until mixture is crumbly.
• **Remove** 1½ cups mixture, and add oats and mini-morsels; store mixture in an airtight container, and label mixture for Peanut Butter-Chocolate Chip Muffins.
• **Remove** 1½ cups mixture; store in an airtight container, and label for Rainy Day Cookies.
• **Measure** 3¼ cups mixture, and add cinnamon and raisins; store in an airtight container, and label for Coffee Cake. **Yield:** about 7 cups.

Coffee Cake: Combine Quick Mix with raisins, 1 lightly beaten large egg, and ½ cup water. Spoon into a 9-inch round cakepan coated with cooking spray. Bake at 350° for 25 to 30 minutes or until a wooden pick inserted in center comes out clean. **Yield:** 8 servings.

Peanut Butter-Chocolate Chip Muffins: Combine 1 lightly beaten large egg, ½ cup water, and 2 tablespoons creamy peanut butter; stir in Quick Mix with oats. Spoon into greased and floured or paper-lined muffin pan, filling two-thirds full. Bake at 400° for 14 minutes or until golden. Remove from pan immediately. **Yield:** 10 muffins.

FLAVORED MAYONNAISE

1 cup reduced-fat mayonnaise
2 tablespoons lime juice
2 cloves garlic, pressed
½ to 1 teaspoon ground red pepper
½ teaspoon dry mustard

• **Combine** all ingredients; spoon into an airtight container. Refrigerate. Transport chilled in a cooler. **Yield:** 1 cup.

Grilled Chicken: (Pictured on page 147) Cut up and skin 1 (3-pound) broiler-fryer, and skin 2 bone-in chicken breast halves. Brush chicken pieces with ¼ cup Flavored Mayonnaise. Place chicken on grill rack; cook, without grill lid, over medium-hot coals (350° to 400°) 20 minutes or until done, turning once. Serve immediately, reserving 2 chicken breast halves for Shrimp-and-Chicken Paella (on the next page). **Yield:** 4 servings.

Grilled Cheese Sandwiches: Remove ¼ cup Flavored Mayonnaise. Spread mayonnaise on 1 side of 4 slices of sandwich bread. Top each with a mozzarella cheese slice, a tomato slice, and another bread slice. Spread mayonnaise on outside of sandwiches on both sides. Brown sandwiches in a hot skillet coated with cooking spray. Serve immediately. **Yield:** 4 servings.

MAKING TIME FOR FUN

■ Granola, Quick Mix, and Paella Rice Mix can be prepared in advance and require no refrigeration.

■ Marinated Beans and Flavored Mayonnaise are best made the day before departure and refrigerated until it's time to go. Transport them in a small cooler.

■ A visit to a roadside produce stand and a stop at the grocery store complete the necessities.

MARINATED BEAN SALAD
(pictured on page 147)

This salad is best made the day before you leave. Refrigerate it until it's time to go.

1 (15.8-ounce) can great Northern beans, drained and rinsed
1 (15-ounce) can black beans, drained and rinsed
1 (15-ounce) can kidney beans, drained and rinsed
1 (8¾-ounce) can whole kernel corn, drained and rinsed
1 (2-ounce) jar diced pimiento, drained
1 carrot, scraped and chopped
½ cup olive oil
½ cup cider vinegar
1 clove garlic, pressed
½ teaspoon salt
½ teaspoon pepper
½ teaspoon chili powder

• **Combine** first 6 ingredients in a large bowl. Set aside.
• **Combine** olive oil and remaining ingredients; pour over bean mixture. Spoon into an airtight container, and refrigerate up to 4 days. Transport chilled in a cooler. **Yield:** 5½ cups.

Marinated Bean-Pasta Salad: Toss 2 cups Marinated Bean Salad with 4 ounces spiral pasta, cooked according to package directions; stir in ¼ cup Flavored Mayonnaise. Serve pasta salad on lettuce-lined plates with Grilled Cheese Sandwiches. (Cooked shrimp or chunks of cheese may be added; spoon into a tomato shell, if desired.) **Yield:** 4½ cups.

Toasted Appetizers: Place 1 cup Marinated Bean Salad into container of an electric blender; process until smooth, adding 1 to 2 tablespoons marinating liquid, if necessary. Spread evenly on 10 thin slices of toasted French bread; top with thin slices of mozzarella or goat cheese. Bake at 350° for 3 to 5 minutes. **Yield:** 4 servings.

PAELLA RICE MIX

1 (5-ounce) package saffron rice
   (¾ cup)
2 tablespoons dried green onions
1½ teaspoons dried parsley
   flakes
½ teaspoon dried oregano
½ teaspoon ground cumin
½ teaspoon garlic powder

•**Combine** all ingredients; store in an airtight container. **Yield:** about 1 cup.

Shrimp-and-Chicken Paella: Peel 1 pound medium-size fresh shrimp, and devein, if desired. Bone and chop reserved Grilled Chicken (recipe on page 167). Combine Paella Rice Mix and 2½ cups water in a 3-quart saucepan. Bring to a boil. Cover, reduce heat, and simmer 15 minutes. Stir in shrimp, and cook 5 minutes. Add chicken, and cook until thoroughly heated and shrimp turn pink. **Yield:** 4 servings.

GRANOLA MIX

2 (3-ounce) packages ramen
   noodles
4 cups regular oats, uncooked
1 (2⅛-ounce) jar sesame seeds
   (⅓ cup)
1 (3.75-ounce) package sunflower
   kernels (¾ cup)
½ cup dry-roasted peanuts
⅓ cup firmly packed brown
   sugar
¼ cup honey
¼ cup vegetable oil
1 teaspoon vanilla extract
½ cup raisins (optional)

•**Remove** seasoning packets from noodles, and discard; break noodles into small pieces.
•**Combine** noodles and next 4 ingredients in a large bowl; set aside.
•**Combine** brown sugar and next 3 ingredients; pour over noodle mixture, and stir well. Spread mixture evenly in a 15- x 10- x 1-inch jellyroll pan.
•**Bake** at 325° for 30 minutes or until golden brown, stirring mixture every 10 minutes.

•**Stir** in raisins, if desired. Cool and store mixture in an airtight container. Serve with milk or over frozen yogurt. **Yield:** 8½ cups.

Rainy Day Cookies: Combine 1½ cups Quick Mix (recipe on page 167), 1½ cups Granola Mix, 1 lightly beaten large egg, and 3 tablespoons water. Drop by rounded teaspoonfuls 1 inch apart onto greased baking sheets. Bake at 375° for 9 minutes or until browned. Cool on wire racks. **Yield:** 2½ dozen.

Fruit Crisp: Combine 4 cups sliced fresh peaches and 1 cup fresh or frozen blackberries or blueberries, thawed, in a 9-inch round cakepan; sprinkle with 2 tablespoons sugar and 1 cup Granola Mix. Bake at 375° for 35 minutes. Serve with frozen yogurt or ice cream. **Yield:** 6 servings.

CREATE WITH CANDY BARS

Indulgent is the only word for these decadent chocolate desserts made with candy bars. They promise to be hits at potluck suppers or any dessert table. So the next time you're lingering in line at the grocery checkout, pick up a few candy bars and enjoy the flavor they add to a trifle, pie, and cookies.

TOFFEE TRIFLE

6 (1.4-ounce) English toffee-
   flavored candy bars, frozen
1 (18.25-ounce) package chocolate
   cake mix
2 (3.9-ounce) packages chocolate
   instant pudding mix
1 (8-ounce) container frozen
   whipped topping, thawed and
   divided

•**Place** unwrapped candy bars in a heavy-duty, zip-top plastic bag. Coarsely crush, using a rolling pin or meat mallet; set side.
•**Prepare** cake mix according to package directions; spoon batter into a greased and floured 13- x 9- x 2-inch pan. Bake according to package directions. Cool cake in pan on a wire rack.
•**Break** into bite-size pieces; set aside.
•**Prepare** pudding mix according to package directions in a large bowl; omit chilling. Gently fold in cake pieces.
•**Place** half of mixture in bottom of a 4-quart trifle bowl; top with half each of whipped topping and crushed candy bars. Repeat layers, ending with crushed candy bars.
•**Cover** and refrigerate at least 2 hours. **Yield:** 16 to 18 servings.

Note: For English toffee-flavored candy bars, we used Skor.

Jerry Lipka
Annapolis, Maryland

MOCHA PIE

1 (11.75-ounce) jar hot fudge
   sauce, divided
1 (6-ounce) chocolate-flavored
   crumb crust
1 pint coffee ice cream, softened
3 (2.07-ounce) chocolate-coated
   caramel-peanut nougat bars,
   chopped and divided
1 pint chocolate ice cream, softened
¼ cup slivered almonds, toasted

•**Spread** half of fudge sauce into crumb crust; carefully spread coffee ice cream over sauce. Top with half of chopped candy bars.
•**Freeze** 2 hours.
•**Spread** chocolate ice cream over candy bars; carefully spread remaining fudge sauce over ice cream. Top with remaining candy, and sprinkle with almonds.
•**Cover** and freeze until firm. **Yield:** one 9-inch pie.

Note: For chocolate-coated caramel-peanut nougat bars, we used Snickers.

Sharon Dorris
Nashville, Tennessee

PEANUT BUTTER AND CHOCOLATE CHUNK COOKIES

½ cup butter or margarine, softened
¾ cup sugar
⅔ cup firmly packed brown sugar
2 egg whites
1¼ cups chunky peanut butter
1½ teaspoons vanilla extract
1 cup all-purpose flour
½ teaspoon baking soda
¼ teaspoon salt
5 (2.1-ounce) chocolate-covered crispy peanut-buttery candy bars, cut into ½-inch pieces

• **Beat** butter at medium speed with an electric mixer until creamy; gradually add sugars, beating well. Add egg whites, beating well. Stir in peanut butter and vanilla. Set aside.
• **Combine** flour, soda, and salt; gradually add to butter mixture, mixing well. Stir in candy.
• **Shape** dough into 1½-inch balls, and place 2 inches apart on lightly greased baking sheets.
• **Bake** at 350° for 11 minutes or until browned. Cool 3 minutes on baking sheets; transfer to wire racks to cool completely. **Yield:** 4 dozen.

Note: For chocolate-covered crispy peanut-buttery candy bars, we used Butterfinger.

Linda Magers
Clemmons, North Carolina

CAN-DO COOKIE DOUGH

■ Cookie doughs make great pie crust – and there's no rolling. Press dough into pan, and refrigerate before baking.

■ To freeze drop-cookie dough, place drops on a baking sheet; freeze until firm. Remove from baking sheet, and place dough in freezer-proof plastic bag; return to freezer. Thaw before baking.

CORNBREAD: A TASTE OF THE SOUTH

It's hot outside. The just-poured glasses of iced tea and cold milk are already leaving puddles on the table. As garden-fresh vegetables steam in their serving dishes, a hand with a pot holder reaches into the oven to pull out the cornbread. Now that's supper in the South!

For garden-fresh vegetable recipes to serve with cornbread, see our "Summer Suppers" special section that begins on page 157.

PECAN CORNBREAD

1½ cups yellow cornmeal
1 cup unbleached flour
1 tablespoon baking powder
1 teaspoon salt
¼ cup sugar
1½ cups half-and-half
¾ cup butter or margarine, melted
2 large eggs, lightly beaten
½ cup chopped pecans

• **Combine** first 5 ingredients in a large bowl; make a well in center of mixture. Set aside.
• **Combine** half-and-half and remaining ingredients. Add to dry ingredients; stir just until moistened. Pour batter into a well-greased 9- x 5- x 3-inch loafpan.
• **Bake** at 375° for 45 to 50 minutes or until golden. Remove from pan, and serve immediately or cool on a wire rack. **Yield:** one 9-inch loaf.

Thelma Peedin
Newport News, Virginia

PICANTE CORNBREAD

1 cup all-purpose flour
¾ cup yellow cornmeal
1½ teaspoons baking powder
½ teaspoon baking soda
½ teaspoon salt
1 cup buttermilk
2 large eggs
⅓ cup picante sauce
¼ cup butter or margarine

• **Heat** an 8-inch cast-iron skillet at 425° for 5 minutes.
• **Combine** first 5 ingredients in a large bowl; make a well in center of mixture. Set aside.
• **Combine** buttermilk, eggs, and picante sauce. Add to dry ingredients, stirring just until moistened.
• **Remove** skillet from oven. Add butter, and return to oven 1 minute or until butter melts.
• **Pour** melted butter into batter; stir until blended. Pour into hot skillet.
• **Bake** at 425° for 20 minutes or until golden. Serve immediately. **Yield:** 6 to 8 servings.

Cindy Ditmars
Tulsa, Oklahoma

CONFETTI CORNBREAD

(pictured on page 187)

3   tablespoons vegetable oil
1   cup yellow cornmeal
¾   cup all-purpose flour
2   teaspoons baking powder
½   teaspoon baking soda
½   teaspoon salt
1 to 2 tablespoons sugar
½   teaspoon chili powder
¼   teaspoon ground cumin
2   tablespoons chopped green
    onions
1   cup plain nonfat yogurt
1   large egg
1   (2-ounce) jar diced pimiento,
    drained

● **Heat** oil in an 8-inch cast-iron skillet or 8-inch square pan in a 400° oven for 5 minutes.
● **Combine** cornmeal and next 8 ingredients in a large bowl; make a well in center of mixture. Set aside.
● **Combine** yogurt, egg, and pimiento; add to dry ingredients, stirring just until moistened.
● **Remove** skillet from oven. Pour oil into batter, stirring until blended; pour batter into hot skillet.
● **Bake** at 400° for 20 to 25 minutes or until golden. Serve immediately. **Yield:** 6 servings.

Charlotte Pierce
Greensburg, Kentucky

UMMM...CORNBREAD!

■ The proportion of cornmeal to flour in cornbreads determines the texture – more flour results in a softer, lighter texture.

■ Fats such as butter or margarine added to cornmeal help make cornbread tender. Eggs add lightness and volume.

■ Sugar, used in small amounts in cornbread, helps bring out the sweet, nutlike flavor of cornmeal.

GRILLED CHEESE IN A BREEZE

This innovative grilled cheese lineup presents some grown-up variations of the single-slice version of your youth. And to tuck you in, we've created a *dessert* grilled cheese sandwich, using pound cake and flavored cream cheese.

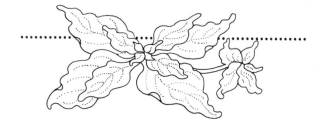

WAFFLE-GRILLED TURKEY SANDWICH

⅓   cup commercial chili sauce
1½ tablespoons Worcestershire
    sauce, divided
8   slices whole wheat bread
4   slices process American
    cheese
8   tomato slices
8   slices deli-style smoked turkey
    breast
¼   cup butter or margarine,
    melted

● **Combine** chili sauce and 1½ teaspoons Worcestershire sauce; spread on 1 side of each slice of bread.
● **Arrange** cheese, tomato, and turkey evenly on half of bread slices; top with remaining bread slices.
● **Combine** butter and remaining Worcestershire sauce, and brush on outside of sandwiches.
● **Bake** in a preheated waffle iron 3 to 4 minutes or until cheese melts. **Yield:** 4 servings.

Erma Jackson
Huntsville, Alabama

GRILLED ITALIAN PESTO SANDWICH

1   (6-ounce) package sliced
    mozzarella cheese, cut into
    thirds
8   (1-inch-thick) slices Italian
    bread
¼   cup commercial pizza sauce
¼   cup commercial pesto sauce
20 slices pepperoni
2   tablespoons butter or margarine,
    softened

● **Arrange** 1 cheese slice on each of 4 bread slices; spread evenly with pizza sauce. Top each with a cheese slice, and spread evenly with pesto sauce. Arrange pepperoni on top; cover with remaining cheese slices, and top with remaining bread slices.
● **Spread** half of butter on outside of 1 side of each sandwich. Invert sandwiches onto a hot nonstick skillet or griddle.
● **Cook** over medium heat until browned.
● **Spread** remaining butter on ungrilled side; turn and cook until browned. **Yield:** 4 servings.

GRILLED SPINACH FONDUE SANDWICH

1   (10-ounce) package frozen chopped spinach, partially thawed
½   cup dry sherry
1½ cups (6 ounces) shredded Swiss cheese
1   teaspoon ground nutmeg, divided
2   tablespoons mayonnaise or salad dressing
¼   teaspoon salt
¼   teaspoon pepper
12 (1-inch-thick) slices French bread
2   tablespoons butter or margarine, softened

• **Combine** spinach and sherry in a small saucepan, and cook 4½ minutes; drain.
• **Combine** spinach, cheese, ½ teaspoon nutmeg, and next 3 ingredients. Spoon evenly onto half of bread; top with remaining bread slices.
• **Spread** half of butter on outside of 1 side of each sandwich; sprinkle with half of remaining nutmeg. Invert sandwiches onto a hot nonstick skillet or griddle. Cook sandwiches over medium heat until golden.
• **Spread** remaining butter on ungrilled side, and sprinkle with remaining nutmeg. Turn and cook until golden. **Yield:** 6 servings.

GRILLED POUND CAKE DESSERT SANDWICH

¼   cup strawberry-flavored cream cheese *
1   tablespoon chopped sliced almonds, toasted
4   (½-inch-thick) slices frozen pound cake, thawed
2   teaspoons butter or margarine, softened
1   tablespoon powdered sugar

• **Combine** cream cheese and almonds.
• **Spread** on 1 side of half of pound cake slices. Top with remaining cake slices.
• **Spread** half of butter evenly on outside of 1 side of each sandwich. Invert

sandwiches onto a hot nonstick skillet or griddle. Cook over medium heat until golden.
• **Spread** remaining butter on ungrilled side; turn and cook until browned.
• **Sprinkle** with powdered sugar. **Yield:** 2 servings.

* ¼ cup fruit- or sweet-flavored cream cheese may be substituted.

PLAIN AND FANCY FISH

Catch a new fish recipe. For a family supper or a formal dinner – from simple to involved – here are some fish ideas swimming your way. Fish may soon become one of your family's favorites.

WINE-HERB HALIBUT STEAK

3   tablespoons butter or margarine
4   (1-inch-thick) halibut steaks
½   cup Chablis or other dry white wine
1   tablespoon lemon juice
¼   teaspoon dried basil
¼   teaspoon dried oregano
¼   teaspoon salt
¼   teaspoon pepper
¼   teaspoon paprika

• **Melt** butter in a large skillet over medium heat. Arrange halibut steaks in a single layer, and cook 3 to 4 minutes on each side.
• **Add** wine and lemon juice; sprinkle basil and remaining ingredients over steaks. Cover, reduce heat, and simmer 8 to 10 minutes. Serve with pan drippings. **Yield:** 4 servings.

Carrie Treichel
Johnson City, Tennessee

CATFISH PILAF

1½ pounds catfish fillets
2   tablespoons butter or margarine, melted
2   teaspoons lemon juice
8   slices bacon (about ½ pound)
1   cup chopped green pepper
¾   cup chopped onion
1   (28-ounce) can tomatoes, chopped and undrained
1½ cups water
1½ cups long-grain rice, uncooked
1   (2-ounce) jar diced pimiento, undrained
1   teaspoon salt

• **Place** catfish fillets in a lightly greased 13- x 9- x 2-inch baking dish. Drizzle with butter and lemon juice.
• **Bake** at 350° for 20 to 25 minutes or until fish flakes easily when tested with a fork; drain and flake. Set aside.
• **Cook** bacon in a large skillet until crisp; remove bacon, reserving 2 tablespoons drippings in skillet. Crumble bacon, and set aside.
• **Cook** green pepper and onion in drippings, stirring constantly, until tender. Stir in bacon, tomatoes, and next 4 ingredients; bring to a boil. Cover, reduce heat, and simmer 25 minutes or until most of liquid is absorbed. Stir in catfish; cover and let stand 5 minutes before serving. **Yield:** 6 servings.

Reba Thompson
Greenville, Mississippi

FISH TIPS

■ When buying whole fish, keep the head and tail; they make good stock for sauces and soups.

■ Thawed fish should not be kept longer than one day before cooking; the flavor is better if cooked immediately after thawing.

■ The process of smoking fish is done for flavor, not preservation. Smoked fish should be refrigerated.

OVEN-FRIED FISH

¼ cup cornmeal
¼ cup fine, dry breadcrumbs
½ teaspoon salt
½ teaspoon paprika
¼ teaspoon dillweed
⅛ teaspoon pepper
1 pound fish fillets, cut into
   1-inch strips
⅓ cup milk
3 tablespoons butter or
   margarine, melted
Garnishes: lemon halves tied in
   cheesecloth, flat-leaf parsley
   sprigs

• **Combine** first 6 ingredients in a shallow dish. Dip fillets in milk, and dredge in cornmeal mixture. Place in a lightly greased 13- x 9- x 2-inch pan, and drizzle with butter.
• **Bake** fillets at 450° for 10 minutes or until fish flakes easily when tested with a fork. Garnish, if desired. **Yield:** 4 to 6 servings.

Note: For fish fillets, we used grouper and orange roughy.

Louise Ellis
Talbott, Tennessee

ORDER IN THE KITCHEN

Federal Administrative Judge Jean Cooper of Washington, D.C., possesses two working uniforms – a flowing black robe and a plastic-coated apron. Both perfectly express who she is.

As a first-year law student, her only kitchen tool was a can opener. "One day I had to face the fact that I really couldn't feed myself," she says. Some friends came to her rescue with a book that changed her diet – and her life.

"I started with the poultry section of *River Road Recipes* and made the first recipe about 14 times," she laughs. "Today if I wet the page and run my finger over it, I can still taste the sauce." By the time she finished that first cookbook, she considered cooking to be "therapy."

In 1982, a dessert contest entry won her a course at L'Academie de Cuisine in Bethesda, Maryland. When the course ended, she signed up for more cooking classes. In 1985, she was invited to teach at the school. Today she divides her time between the courtroom and the classroom.

WHOLE ONIONS WITH WARM VINEGAR SAUCE

8 large onions, unpeeled
4 slices pancetta or bacon, cut into
   pieces
¼ cup olive oil
¼ cup balsamic vinegar
3 tablespoons butter or margarine
½ teaspoon salt
½ teaspoon pepper

• **Remove** tops from onions; place in a lightly greased baking pan.
• **Bake** at 425° for 35 to 40 minutes or until tender. Remove from oven. Peel onions, and make shallow diagonal cuts in top of each; set aside.
• **Cook** pancetta in olive oil in a small skillet until lightly browned; stir in vinegar and next 3 ingredients, stirring until butter melts. Spoon over onions. **Yield:** 8 servings.

CORN-CHIVE FLAN

2½ cups fresh or frozen whole
   kernel corn, thawed
1½ cups whipping cream
4 large eggs
¾ teaspoon salt
¼ teaspoon hot sauce
3 tablespoons shredded Monterey
   Jack cheese
⅓ cup chopped fresh or frozen
   chives
Garnishes: corn kernels, fresh
   chives

• **Combine** first 5 ingredients in container of an electric blender; process until smooth, stopping once to scrape down sides.
• **Stir** in cheese and chives.
• **Pour** mixture into 6 lightly greased 8-ounce ramekins. Place in a large pan. Add hot water to pan to depth of 1 inch. Cover with foil.
• **Bake** at 325° for 45 to 50 minutes or until a knife inserted in center comes out clean. Unmold and garnish, if desired. **Yield:** 6 servings.

SALMON SCALOPPINE WITH VEGETABLE CONFETTI AND PERNOD SAUCE

⅓ cup all-purpose flour
¼ teaspoon salt
¼ teaspoon pepper
1 pound salmon fillet, cut
   diagonally into ½-inch strips
1 leek
¼ cup butter or margarine,
   divided
1 carrot, scraped and cut into
   2-inch thin strips
¼ cup Chablis or other dry white
   wine
¼ cup chicken broth
½ cup whipping cream
¼ teaspoon salt
⅓ cup finely chopped tomato
1½ tablespoons Pernod

• **Combine** first 3 ingredients; dredge salmon strips in flour mixture. Set aside.
• **Wash** leek. Remove root, tough outer leaves, and dark-green leaves. Cut white part of leek into 2-inch thin strips.
• **Melt** 2 tablespoons butter in a large skillet. Add leek and carrot, and cook over medium heat, stirring constantly, 2 minutes or until crisp-tender. Remove vegetables from skillet; set aside.
• **Melt** remaining 2 tablespoons butter in skillet; add salmon, and cook 2 minutes on each side. Remove from skillet, and place in a 250° oven to keep warm.
• **Add** wine and chicken broth to skillet; cook over high heat 5 minutes or until reduced to about ¼ cup.
• **Stir** in whipping cream and salt. Cook over medium-high heat 4 minutes or

until sauce is thickened. Add chopped tomato and Pernod; cook 1 minute.
- **Place** salmon on serving plates; drizzle with sauce, and sprinkle with vegetables. **Yield:** 2 main-dish servings or 4 appetizer servings.

QUESADILLAS WITH SHRIMP AND BRIE

1 medium-size purple onion, sliced
2 tablespoons vegetable oil, divided
6 (6-inch) flour tortillas
1 (15-ounce) Brie
½ pound cooked shrimp, peeled, deveined, and coarsely chopped
Papaya Salsa

- **Cook** onion in 1 tablespoon oil in a skillet over medium-high heat, stirring constantly, until tender. Set aside.
- **Heat** tortillas according to package directions.
- **Remove** outer casing from Brie, and discard; thinly slice Brie. Place Brie slices on half of each tortilla. Top evenly with onion and shrimp; fold in half, and set aside.
- **Brush** skillet with remaining oil; place 2 quesadillas in skillet at a time. Cook over medium heat about 1 minute or until lightly browned, turning once. Remove from skillet, and keep warm.
- **Cut** each into 4 wedges; serve with Papaya Salsa. **Yield:** 6 servings.

Papaya Salsa

1 ripe papaya, peeled, seeded, and chopped
1 small ripe avocado, peeled, seeded, and chopped
3 scallions, chopped
½ sweet red pepper, finely chopped
½ jalapeño pepper, seeded and finely chopped
2 tablespoons chopped fresh cilantro
Juice of 1 lime

- **Combine** all ingredients; cover and chill. **Yield:** 2½ cups.

SALAD FOUNDATION

Most people have the notion that grains rate right up there in flavor with a cardboard box. And, that unless you want white rice, shopping for grains is like looking for candy canes in August. Wrong. We've selected grains that are readily available in most supermarkets and paired them with delicious combinations of summer's freshest vegetables and herbs. And when summer get-togethers call for a make-ahead salad that won't wilt on the buffet table, try any of these recipes. They all multiply easily to serve a crowd.

ORIENTAL SALMON-AND-WILD RICE SALAD

1 (8-ounce) fillet fresh salmon
⅓ cup rice wine vinegar
¼ cup orange marmalade
2 tablespoons teriyaki sauce
1 tablespoon grated fresh gingerroot
2 teaspoons sesame oil
1 (6-ounce) package wild rice, cooked without salt
¾ cup fresh snow pea pods
½ cup sliced green onions
½ cup finely chopped sweet red pepper
Bibb lettuce leaves

- **Place** salmon in an 8-inch square dish; set aside.
- **Combine** vinegar and next 4 ingredients in a jar; cover tightly, and shake vigorously. Pour half of mixture over salmon, turning to coat well. Set remaining vinegar mixture aside.
- **Cover** salmon and chill 1 hour.
- **Drain** salmon, discarding marinade; place salmon on a rack in broiler pan.
- **Broil** 5½ inches from heat (with electric oven door partially opened) 3 to 5 minutes on each side or until fish flakes easily when tested with a fork.
- **Separate** salmon into chunks. Cool.
- **Combine** salmon, rice, and next 3 ingredients in a large bowl; drizzle with remaining vinegar mixture, tossing gently.
- **Cover** and chill at least 3 hours. Serve on lettuce leaves. **Yield:** 5 cups.

♥ Per 1-cup serving: Calories 323 (18% from fat) Fat 6.5g (1g saturated) Cholesterol 31mg Sodium 389mg Carbohydrate 48.9g Fiber 3.5g Protein 19.1g

TABBOULEH SALAD

2 cups hot water
1 cup bulgur wheat, uncooked
1 cup chopped fresh parsley
½ cup chopped fresh mint
½ cup chopped onion
⅓ cup lemon juice
2 tablespoons olive oil
½ teaspoon salt
½ teaspoon pepper
2 medium tomatoes, finely
    chopped
Lettuce leaves

• **Pour** hot water over bulgur; let stand 30 minutes. Drain well, and press between layers of paper towels.
• **Combine** bulgur and next 7 ingredients in a large bowl.
• **Cover** and chill 8 hours.
• **Stir** in tomato. Serve on lettuce leaves. **Yield:** 6 cups.

Sara Cairns
Cullman, Alabama

♥ Per 1-cup serving: Calories 141 (30% from fat)
Fat 5.1g (0.7g saturated) Cholesterol 0mg
Sodium 209mg Carbohydrate 22.8g
Fiber 5.5g Protein 3.8g

BLACK BEAN-AND-BARLEY SALAD
(pictured on page 146)

¾ cup barley, uncooked
¼ cup lime juice
2 tablespoons water
1 tablespoon vegetable oil
1 teaspoon sugar
½ teaspoon garlic powder
¼ teaspoon salt
¼ teaspoon ground black pepper
¼ teaspoon ground cumin
¼ teaspoon ground red pepper
1 (15-ounce) can black beans,
    rinsed and drained
Leaf lettuce
1 cup chopped tomato
¼ cup (2 ounces) shredded
    reduced-fat Cheddar
    cheese
¼ cup sliced green onions

• **Cook** barley according to package directions; drain and set aside.
• **Combine** lime juice and next 8 ingredients in a jar. Cover tightly, and shake vigorously.
• **Pour** half of dressing over barley; cover and refrigerate 8 hours, stirring mixture occasionally.
• **Combine** beans and remaining dressing; cover and refrigerate 8 hours, stirring occasionally.
• **Spoon** barley mixture evenly onto lettuce-lined plates. Top evenly with black beans, tomato, cheese, and green onions. **Yield:** 4 servings.

♥ Per serving: Calories 342 (20% from fat)
Fat 7.6g (0.3g saturated) Cholesterol 10mg
Sodium 260mg Carbohydrate 53.7g
Fiber 10.8g Protein 17.4g

BROWN RICE CONFETTI SALAD
(pictured on page 147)

2¼ cups water
1 cup brown rice, uncooked
½ teaspoon salt
1 cup thin yellow squash
    strips
1 cup small broccoli flowerets
1 cup sliced radishes
½ cup sliced green onions
¼ cup chopped fresh dill
3 tablespoons chopped fresh
    parsley
1 teaspoon grated lemon rind
⅓ cup lemon juice
2 tablespoons olive oil
2 teaspoons Dijon mustard
½ teaspoon freshly ground
    pepper
Garnishes: fresh dill sprigs, sliced
    yellow squash

• **Combine** first 3 ingredients in a saucepan; cook rice according to package directions. Remove rice from heat, and cool.
• **Combine** rice, squash strips, and next 6 ingredients. Set aside.
• **Combine** lemon juice and next 3 ingredients in a jar; cover tightly, and shake vigorously. Pour over rice mixture; toss gently.
• **Cover** and chill 1 to 2 hours. Garnish, if desired. **Yield:** 6 cups.

Mary Seale
Plano, Texas

♥ Per 1-cup serving: Calories 174 (29% from fat)
Fat 5.8g (0.8g saturated) Cholesterol 0mg
Sodium 259mg Carbohydrate 28.1g
Fiber 2.3g Protein 3.5g

GRAIN GLOSSARY

Barley – This beady grain tastes as good in salads as it does in soups.

Whole grain wheat – Also called wheat berries, these whole, unprocessed kernels of wheat are packed with fiber and have a rich, earthy flavor.

Bulgur wheat – These tender, chewy kernels of wheat are steamed, dried, and crushed.

Wild rice – This expensive marsh grass takes almost an hour to cook, but the nutty flavor makes it worth the price and the wait.

Couscous – The tiny grains of couscous are made from coarse ground semolina flour, the same flour used to make pasta.

Brown rice – Only the inedible outer husk has been removed. The bran layers remaining give the rice more flavor, fiber, and texture than white rice.

BASIL-AND-TOMATO COUSCOUS SALAD

1¼ cups boiling water
1¼ cups couscous, uncooked
2 cups chopped tomato
1 cup finely chopped fresh basil
⅓ cup finely chopped purple onion
3 slices bacon, cooked and crumbled
¼ cup apple cider vinegar
2 tablespoons olive oil
¼ teaspoon salt
¼ teaspoon pepper

● **Combine** boiling water and couscous. Cover and let stand 5 minutes. Uncover and fluff with a fork; cool.
● **Combine** couscous, tomato, and next 3 ingredients; set aside.
● **Combine** vinegar and remaining ingredients in a jar; cover tightly, and shake vigorously. Drizzle over salad, and toss gently.
● **Cover** and chill. Toss before serving. **Yield:** 6 cups.

Constance Ober
Port Haywood, Virginia

❤ Per 1-cup serving: Calories 216 (25% from fat)
Fat 6g (0.7g saturated)   Cholesterol 2mg
Sodium 149mg   Carbohydrate 34.3g
Fiber 1.6g   Protein 6.5g

WHEAT BERRY-AND-ROASTED CORN SALAD

1 cup whole grain wheat
2 cups water
2 ears fresh yellow corn
½ cup finely chopped green pepper
½ cup finely chopped sweet red pepper
¼ cup sliced celery
¼ cup finely chopped onion
¼ cup chopped fresh cilantro
¼ cup lime juice
1 tablespoon vegetable oil
1 tablespoon honey
2 teaspoons chili powder
1 teaspoon ground cumin
⅛ teaspoon ground red pepper
¼ teaspoon salt

● **Combine** wheat and water; cover and refrigerate 8 hours.
● **Transfer** to a saucepan; bring to a boil. Cover, reduce heat, and simmer 40 to 45 minutes or until tender. Drain, if necessary. Set aside.
● **Cook** corn in boiling water to cover 5 minutes. Drain; cool 10 minutes.
● **Cut** kernels from cob, and place kernels in a shallow baking pan. Broil kernels 5½ inches from heat (with electric oven door partially opened) 5 to 10 minutes or until edges begin to brown, stirring occasionally. Cool.
● **Combine** wheat mixture, corn, chopped green pepper, and next 4 ingredients; set aside.
● **Combine** lime juice and remaining ingredients in a jar; cover tightly, and shake vigorously. Pour over salad; toss gently.
● **Cover** and chill at least 3 hours. **Yield:** 4¾ cups.

❤ Per 1-cup serving: Calories 212 (18% from fat)
Fat 4.3g (0.2g saturated)   Cholesterol 0mg
Sodium 148mg   Carbohydrate 42.5g
Fiber 18.6g   Protein 5.4g

FITNESS AND FAT FREE CAN BE FUN

■ Do fun things that keep you fit: Ski, skate, ride a bike, go for long walks. Use exercise time as thinking time – dream about your next vacation or ponder tomorrow's schedule as you pedal up a hill.

■ Hold yourself back at the supermarket. If you don't buy high-fat foods, you can't cook high-fat meals.

■ When you're cooking something you know you shouldn't eat – treats for the kids or a birthday cake for a friend – chew gum while you cook. The gum will diminish any temptation to lick the bowl.

■ Use red wine, flavored vinegars, or even fruit juices instead of oil for marinating meats.

■ Cook at home. If you make it yourself, you know what's in it.

■ Put food on plates in the kitchen, not in bowls on the dining table. If it's not sitting in front of you, you'll be less tempted to have seconds.

■ Stop eating desserts; you'll see results in no time.

■ Don't fool yourself into thinking you can eat all the reduced-fat and fat-free products you want. If you're tempted to eat 10 fat-free cookies, remember they may not have any fat, but they still have calories.

■ Whole grain breads have more flavor than white bread, so if you eat whole grains you'll be less tempted to use butter.

■ Don't starve yourself; it doesn't work. Cut back on fat intake instead.

■ If you find it impossible to eat bread without butter, go without bread for a week. Replace the bread with grains and beans.

■ You'll eat less salad dressing if you pour some into a small dish and dip the tines of your fork into the dressing and then into the salad greens.

■ Forgo cream and sugar in your coffee. It's the little things that add up to pounds.

THRU THE GRAPEVINE

Elmira, New York, is an area known for its vineyards. So when the Junior League

members of Greater Elmira-Corning decided to produce a fund-raising cookbook,

Thru the Grapevine, they included a section on wine.

....

CREAM OF CARROT-AND-TOMATO SOUP
(pictured on page 187)

4 cups peeled, chopped fresh
    tomato (3 large)
2 pounds carrots, scraped and
    cut into ¼-inch slices
¼ cup water
¾ teaspoon salt, divided
3 tablespoons butter or
    margarine
3 tablespoons all-purpose flour
1 (14½-ounce) can ready-to-
    serve chicken broth
3 cups milk
1 cup whipping cream
¼ teaspoon freshly ground
    pepper
¼ teaspoon hot sauce
¼ cup chopped fresh dill, divided
1 cup sour cream
Garnish: fresh dill sprigs

• **Place** tomato in a saucepan. Bring to a boil over medium heat; reduce heat, and simmer 30 minutes.
• **Combine** carrot, water, and ¼ teaspoon salt in a saucepan. Bring to a boil over medium-high heat; cover, reduce heat, and simmer 30 minutes. (Do not drain.)
• **Melt** butter in a heavy saucepan over low heat; add flour, stirring until smooth. Cook 1 minute, stirring constantly. Gradually add chicken broth; cook over medium heat, stirring constantly, until mixture is thickened and bubbly (about 15 minutes).
• **Combine** half of tomato, carrot mixture, and broth mixture in container of an electric blender or food processor. Process until smooth, stopping once to scrape down sides, if necessary. Pour into a Dutch oven. Repeat procedure.
• **Stir** milk and whipping cream into tomato mixture.
• **Cook** over medium heat, stirring constantly, until thoroughly heated. Stir in remaining ½ teaspoon salt, pepper, hot sauce, and 2 tablespoons dill. Serve hot or cold.
• **Combine** remaining 2 tablespoons dill and sour cream; dollop on individual servings. Garnish, if desired. **Yield:** 2½ quarts.

PARTY PASTA WITH PROSCIUTTO

½ cup butter or margarine,
    divided
2 cups thin prosciutto strips
    (about ⅓ pound) *
1 (12-ounce) package spinach
    fettuccine, uncooked
1½ cups whipping cream
½ cup freshly grated Parmesan
    cheese
1 (14-ounce) can artichoke
    hearts, drained and halved
½ cup chopped fresh or frozen
    chives, divided

• **Melt** ¼ cup butter in a skillet. Add prosciutto, and cook over medium heat until browned, stirring often; drain. Set aside.
• **Cook** pasta according to package directions; drain.
• **Melt** remaining butter in a Dutch oven over medium heat. Add pasta, whipping cream, cheese, artichoke hearts, and ¼ cup chives; toss gently. Arrange on a serving platter.
• **Sprinkle** with prosciutto and remaining chives. Serve immediately. **Yield:** 6 servings.

* If prosciutto isn't available, substitute cooked, crumbled bacon and reduce butter to ¼ cup.

LEMON CHAMPAGNE PUNCH

1 (12-ounce) can frozen
    lemonade concentrate,
    thawed and undiluted
1 (46-ounce) can unsweetened
    pineapple juice, chilled
1 (750-milliliter) bottle Rhine
    wine
Strawberry Ice Ring
2 (750-milliliter) bottles
    champagne, chilled

• **Combine** first 3 ingredients in a punch bowl. Place Strawberry Ice Ring in bowl.
• **Stir** in champagne, and serve immediately. **Yield:** 17 cups.

Strawberry Ice Ring

Whole strawberries

• **Fill** a 6-cup mold two-thirds full with water, and freeze.
• **Arrange** whole strawberries on top; freeze 30 minutes. Slowly add enough water to fill mold, and freeze.
• **Let** stand at room temperature 5 minutes or until loosened to unmold. **Yield:** 1 ring mold.

VERSATILE GARLIC

Garlic has a split personality. Raw or slightly cooked, it brings a hot, pungent overtone to dishes. But when it's roasted, garlic's booming flavor softens to a whisper. These contradictory qualities allow you to become a kitchen magician.

TOMATO-GARLIC PASTA

12 ounces angel hair pasta, uncooked
20 cloves garlic, coarsely chopped
2 tablespoons olive oil
3 large tomatoes, peeled, seeded, and diced
¼ cup fresh basil, cut into ¼-inch strips
½ cup Chablis or other dry white wine
3 to 4 tablespoons balsamic vinegar
1 teaspoon pepper
1 cup grated Parmesan or Romano cheese

• **Cook** pasta according to package directions; drain. Keep warm.
• **Cook** garlic in olive oil in a large skillet over medium-high heat until lightly browned; add tomato and next 4 ingredients. Cook until thoroughly heated.
• **Spoon** tomato mixture over pasta; sprinkle with cheese. Serve immediately. **Yield:** 4 main-dish servings or 6 side-dish servings.

Caroline Wallace Kennedy
Newborn, Georgia

GARLICKY HAM-AND-SPINACH GRITS

1 head garlic
2 to 3 teaspoons olive oil
4 ounces thinly sliced country ham, cut into ¼-inch strips
1 tablespoon peanut or vegetable oil
3 cups chicken broth
1 cup quick-cooking grits
½ cup butter or margarine
¼ teaspoon salt
¼ teaspoon pepper
1 cup milk
4 large eggs
1 cup (4 ounces) shredded Swiss cheese
1 (10-ounce) package frozen chopped spinach, thawed and well drained
¼ cup grated Parmesan cheese

• **Cut** off flat end of garlic head, and spread apart whole cloves, leaving tight outer covering intact. Trim pointed end so head will sit flat. Place garlic head, trimmed end down, in a garlic roaster or on a sheet of aluminum foil.
• **Drizzle** with olive oil; cover with lid or wrap in aluminum foil.
• **Bake** at 350° for 1 hour or until golden. Cool.
• **Squeeze** out pulp from each clove.
• **Position** knife blade in food processor bowl, and add garlic pulp. Process until smooth, stopping often to scrape down sides. Set aside.

• **Cook** ham in peanut oil in a skillet over medium-high heat, stirring constantly, until browned. Drain on paper towels, and set aside.
• **Bring** broth to a boil in a large saucepan; stir in grits. Cook over medium heat 3 to 5 minutes or until thick, stirring frequently. Remove from heat.
• **Stir** in butter, salt, pepper, and garlic puree.
• **Combine** milk and eggs; add to grits mixture, mixing well. Fold in Swiss cheese, spinach, and ham.
• **Grease** an 11- x 7- x 1½-inch baking dish or 8 (10-ounce) custard cups. Sprinkle bottom and sides with Parmesan cheese, coating well. Spoon grits mixture into baking dish or cups.
• **Bake** at 350° for 45 minutes (35 minutes for cups) or until puffed and firm. Serve immediately. **Yield:** 8 servings.

Note: To freeze Garlicky Ham-and-Spinach Grits, prepare as directed, but do not bake. Cover unbaked grits with aluminum foil, and freeze. To serve, thaw in refrigerator; remove from refrigerator, and let stand 30 minutes. Bake as directed.

ROASTED GARLIC

3 large heads garlic
2 to 3 tablespoons olive oil
Freshly ground pepper

• **Cut** off flat end of each garlic head, and spread apart whole cloves, leaving tight outer covering intact. Trim pointed end so heads will sit flat. Place heads, trimmed end down, in a garlic roaster or on a sheet of aluminum foil.
• **Drizzle** with olive oil, and sprinkle with pepper. Cover garlic with lid or wrap in foil.
• **Bake** at 350° for 1 hour or until golden. Cool.
• **Squeeze** out pulp from each clove, and spread on slices of toasted French bread. **Yield:** 3 garlic heads.

Herbed Roasted Garlic: Assemble garlic head, and sprinkle with ¼ teaspoon dried rosemary, dried thyme, or dried oregano. Bake as directed. **Yield:** 3 garlic heads.

Pep up Potato Salad

. . . .

Take potato salad from common to kingly with these updated ideas that transform an old favorite. Add some basil or dill to give it a fresh, new taste, or throw in a little chili powder and hot sauce to make South-of-the-Border Potato Salad.

SOUTH-OF-THE-BORDER POTATO SALAD

4 large round red potatoes (about 2 pounds)
⅓ cup salad or vegetable oil
¼ cup white vinegar
1 tablespoon sugar
1½ teaspoons chili powder
1 teaspoon seasoned salt
⅛ teaspoon hot sauce
1 (8¾-ounce) can whole kernel corn, drained
½ cup shredded carrot
½ cup chopped green pepper
½ cup sliced pitted ripe olives
1 small onion, thinly sliced and separated into rings
Leaf lettuce

• **Cook** potatoes in boiling water to cover 20 to 30 minutes or until tender.
• **Drain** potatoes, and let cool to touch. Peel and cut into ½-inch cubes; place in a large bowl.
• **Combine** oil and next 5 ingredients; pour over potatoes, tossing gently. Cover with aluminum foil.
• **Refrigerate** 1 hour.
• **Uncover** potato mixture, and stir in corn and next 4 ingredients. Serve potato salad in a lettuce-lined bowl. **Yield:** 8 to 10 servings.

Cathy Williams
Vale, North Carolina

IRISH TURNIP SALAD

2 potatoes (about ¾ pound)
2 turnips, peeled and shredded (about ¾ pound)
1 small purple onion, chopped
1 stalk celery, sliced
½ cup sour cream
¼ cup mayonnaise or salad dressing
½ teaspoon salt
⅛ teaspoon pepper

• **Cook** potatoes in boiling water to cover 25 minutes or until tender.
• **Drain** potatoes, and let cool to touch. Peel and cut into ½-inch cubes.
• **Combine** potato, shredded turnip, onion, and celery in a large bowl; set aside.
• **Combine** sour cream and remaining ingredients; pour over potato mixture, tossing gently. Cover and chill. **Yield:** 4 to 6 servings.

Mrs. Thomas Lee Adams
Kingsport, Tennessee

BASIL POTATO SALAD

3 pounds new potatoes
3 hard-cooked eggs, chopped
¾ cup chopped celery
4 to 5 green onions, chopped
1 tablespoon chopped fresh basil or 1 teaspoon dried basil
2 tablespoons chopped fresh parsley
Vinaigrette (see recipe on next page)

• **Cook** potatoes in boiling salted water to cover 15 minutes or until tender.
• **Drain** potatoes, and let cool to touch. Cut into quarters, leaving skins on, if desired.
• **Combine** potato and next 5 ingredients in a large bowl.
• **Pour** Vinaigrette over potato mixture, tossing gently, and cover bowl with aluminum foil.
• **Refrigerate** 3 to 4 hours. **Yield:** 12 servings.

SAVOR POTATO SALAD

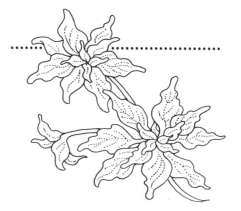

■ New and round red potatoes are the best to use for potato salad. These potatoes keep their shape and texture when sliced or cubed, and when the peel is left on, they add color to the salad. Long white potatoes are our second choice.

■ Potatoes that are cooked and then peeled and cut hold their shape better and retain more nutrients than those that are peeled and cut before cooking. Most importantly, don't overcook the potatoes.

Vinaigrette

¼ cup mayonnaise or salad
   dressing
¼ cup vegetable oil
3 tablespoons red wine vinegar
1 tablespoon Dijon mustard
½ teaspoon salt
¼ teaspoon pepper
2 cloves garlic, minced

• **Combine** all ingredients in a small
bowl. **Yield:** 1¼ cups.

DILL POTATO SALAD

7 medium-size round red potatoes
   (about 3 pounds)
¼ cup vegetable oil
2 tablespoons white vinegar
1 teaspoon garlic powder
1 teaspoon onion powder
1 teaspoon salt
Dash of pepper
4 hard-cooked eggs, chopped
¾ cup chopped celery
⅓ cup sliced green onions with
   tops
½ cup mayonnaise or salad
   dressing
½ cup sour cream
1 tablespoon chopped fresh dill

• **Cook** potatoes in boiling water to
cover 30 minutes or until tender.
• **Drain** potatoes, and let cool to touch.
Peel and cut into ¼-inch slices; place in
large bowl.
• **Combine** oil and next 5 ingredients;
pour over potato, and cover with aluminum foil.
• **Refrigerate** at least 1 hour.
• **Uncover** potato mixture, and stir in
chopped egg, celery, and green onions;
set aside.
• **Combine** mayonnaise and remaining
ingredients; gently stir into potato mixture. Cover and chill. **Yield:** 8 servings.
Lula Bell Hawks
Newport, Arkansas

GINGERBREAD REDO

We're hardly ready to rid Southern kitchens of warm,

traditional gingerbread. So we added to ordinary desserts some

pizzazz for flavors that dance across your tongue.

APPLESAUCE GINGERBREAD

1 (16-ounce) can applesauce
1 cup molasses
2 teaspoons baking soda
4 large eggs
1⅓ cups sugar
⅔ cup vegetable oil
3 cups all-purpose flour
½ teaspoon salt
1 teaspoon ground ginger
1 teaspoon ground cinnamon
½ teaspoon ground cloves
1 cup sifted powdered sugar
2 tablespoons hot water
½ teaspoon vanilla extract

• **Bring** applesauce to a boil in a saucepan; stir in molasses and soda (mixture
will bubble). Remove from heat; cool.
• **Beat** eggs at high speed with an electric mixer until thick and pale; gradually
add sugar, beating well. Stir in oil.
• **Combine** flour and next 4 ingredients;
add flour mixture to egg mixture alternately with applesauce mixture, beginning and ending with flour mixture.
Mix after each addition. Pour batter into
a greased and floured 10-inch tube pan.
• **Bake** at 325° for 1 hour and 15 minutes or until a wooden pick inserted in
center of cake comes out clean. Cool
cake in pan on a wire rack 15 minutes.
Remove from pan; let cool completely
on wire rack.
• **Combine** powdered sugar, water, and
vanilla; drizzle over cake. **Yield:** one
10-inch cake.
Louise Smith
Columbus, Georgia

GINGER SHORTCAKES

2 tablespoons butter or
   margarine
2 tablespoons brown sugar
4 pears, peeled, cored, and sliced
⅓ cup apple jelly
2 cups all-purpose flour
1 tablespoon baking powder
½ teaspoon salt
½ cup firmly packed brown sugar
1 teaspoon ground cinnamon
1 teaspoon ground ginger
⅓ cup butter or margarine
¾ cup buttermilk
Sweetened whipped cream
Ground ginger

• **Combine** 2 tablespoons butter and
2 tablespoons brown sugar in a skillet;
cook over medium heat, stirring constantly, until butter melts.
• **Add** pear; cook 3 minutes or until
softened, stirring occasionally. Stir in
jelly; set aside.
• **Combine** flour and next 5 ingredients.
Cut in ⅓ cup butter with pastry blender
until mixture is crumbly. Add buttermilk; stir with a fork until dry ingredients are moistened.
• **Turn** dough out onto a lightly floured
surface, and knead lightly 4 or 5 times.
Roll dough to ¾-inch thickness; cut
with a 3-inch round cutter. Place rounds
on a lightly greased baking sheet.
• **Bake** at 425° for 10 to 13 minutes or
until golden. Cool slightly; split and fill
with warm pear mixture. (Cut pear slices
in half if too long.) Top with whipped
cream and ginger. **Yield:** 6 servings.

APPLE-GINGER UPSIDE-DOWN CAKE

3 tablespoons butter or
    margarine
¼ cup firmly packed brown sugar
2 tablespoons finely chopped
    crystallized ginger
2 Granny Smith apples, peeled,
    cored, and thinly sliced
1 tablespoon lemon juice
½ cup butter or margarine,
    softened
1 cup sugar
2 large eggs
1½ cups all-purpose flour
2 teaspoons baking powder
½ teaspoon salt
½ teaspoon ground cinnamon
½ cup milk
½ teaspoon vanilla extract

● **Melt** 3 tablespoons butter in a 10-inch cast-iron skillet. Remove from heat, and sprinkle skillet with brown sugar and ginger; set aside.
● **Toss** sliced apple with lemon juice to prevent browning, and arrange on brown sugar mixture; set aside.
● **Beat** ½ cup butter at medium speed with an electric mixer until creamy; gradually add sugar, beating well. Add eggs, one at a time, mixing after each addition.
● **Combine** flour and next 3 ingredients; add to butter mixture alternately with milk, beginning and ending with flour mixture. Stir in vanilla. Spoon evenly over apples.
● **Bake** at 350° for 35 to 40 minutes or until a wooden pick inserted in center comes out clean. Cool in skillet on a wire rack 5 minutes; invert onto serving plate. **Yield:** one 10-inch cake.

WHAT CAN I BRING?

Whether you're assigned an appetizer, salad, or dessert for a potluck supper, pick from these unusual reader favorites. They're not difficult to make, but these showstopping accompaniments won't be lost in the glory of the entrée.

ARTICHOKE-PASTA SALAD

Orzo, rice-shaped pasta, is tossed with artichoke hearts, vinaigrette, and basil, and then topped with prosciutto, an Italian salt-cured ham. (If your deli doesn't carry it, ask for a good smoked ham, sliced paper thin.)

2 tablespoons white wine vinegar
2 tablespoons lemon juice
1 teaspoon Dijon mustard
⅓ cup olive oil
¼ cup chopped fresh parsley
2 tablespoons chopped fresh basil
1½ cups orzo, uncooked
1 (14-ounce) can artichoke hearts,
    drained and quartered
⅔ cup grated Parmesan cheese
Lettuce leaves
4 ounces prosciutto, cut into
    ½-inch strips
4 green onions, thinly sliced

● **Combine** first 3 ingredients in container of an electric blender or food processor; process until blended. With blender or processor still running, add oil in a slow, steady stream; process until blended. Stir in parsley and basil. Set dressing aside.
● **Cook** orzo according to package directions; drain and rinse with cold water.
● **Combine** orzo, artichoke hearts, Parmesan cheese, and dressing; toss gently. Cover and chill.
● **Arrange** orzo mixture on a lettuce-lined platter; sprinkle with prosciutto and green onions. **Yield:** 6 servings.
Fran Baker
Rockledge, Florida

CURRIED SHRIMP BALLS

How easy could it get? Just five ingredients. Traditional goes tropical when creamy shrimp balls are rolled in toasted, curried coconut.

1 cup flaked coconut
1 teaspoon curry powder
2 (8-ounce) packages cream
    cheese, softened
1 (4¼-ounce) can shrimp, rinsed,
    drained, and chopped
2 tablespoons finely chopped
    onion

● **Combine** coconut and curry powder; place on a baking sheet, and bake at 325° for 5 minutes or until golden. Set coconut mixture aside.
● **Combine** cream cheese and remaining ingredients; shape into 1-inch balls, and roll in coconut mixture. Cover and chill. **Yield:** 3 dozen.
Janet Filer
Arlington, Virginia

WHITE CHOCOLATE CHEESECAKE

Much easier than traditional cheesecake, this one does not use eggs. Simply mix the ingredients, pour them over a "crust" of pound cake crumbs, and bake for just 30 minutes.

1¼ cups commercial pound cake
    crumbs
3 (4-ounce) bars white chocolate
3 (8-ounce) packages cream
    cheese, softened
1 cup sugar
1 (16-ounce) carton sour cream
1 tablespoon apricot brandy
    (optional)
1 teaspoon vanilla extract
Garnishes: sliced strawberries,
    kiwifruit, mint sprig

● **Press** crumbs on bottom of a lightly greased 9-inch springform pan.
● **Bake** at 350° for 5 minutes. Cool on a wire rack.
● **Melt** white chocolate in a heavy saucepan over low heat, stirring it constantly. Cool.

- **Beat** cream cheese at medium speed with an electric mixer 3 minutes or until fluffy; add sugar, beating 5 minutes. Add chocolate; beat 5 minutes. Add sour cream, brandy, if desired, and vanilla, mixing until blended. Pour over prepared crust.
- **Bake** at 350° for 30 to 35 minutes. Cool 10 minutes on wire rack. Gently run a knife around edge of pan to release sides. Let cool in pan on wire rack. Cover and chill 8 hours. Remove cake from pan, and garnish, if desired. **Yield:** one 9-inch cheesecake.

Margot Hahn
Washington, D.C.

SHAPE UP GROCERY SHOPPING

- Set a weekly grocery budget and stick to it.

- Plan weekly menus to fit your budget. Look for advertised specials and coupons in your newspapers. Work them into your menus, if possible.

- Make your grocery list from your meals plans. Never go shopping without a list; you'll end up spending too much.

- Organize your list so that it corresponds to the layout of your grocery store. For example, if the produce section is at the front of the store, start your shopping list with produce.

- The more times you go to the store, the more you'll spend. Plan on one major grocery trip a week. You may need to plan on a second trip later to pick up fresh vegetables, fruit, and milk.

- Don't go shopping when you're hungry. Everything looks good, and it's easy to go over your budget.

EXCEPTIONAL EGG SALADS

·················

Egg salad strikes many memory notes. Mom made it. The school cafeteria made it. And *you* even made it – right after you learned to hard cook an egg. (You say you never learned how? See "Don't Call Me Hard-Boiled!" on the next page.) But have you tried adding salsa, shrimp, or horseradish to egg salad? Here's your chance. These recipes take egg salad up an octave.

YOLKLESS EGG SALAD

When we tasted this recipe in our test kitchens, only two people knew the ingredients. Labeled "Egg Salad Number 3," it received strong votes of approval. Only then was it announced that "Egg Salad Number 3" was a yolkless egg salad, made with mashed potatoes. It's the ideal salad for anyone on a low-cholesterol diet.

6 large hard-cooked eggs
3 tablespoons sweet pickle relish
2 tablespoons finely chopped green onions
1 tablespoon diced pimiento, undrained (optional)
½ cup cooked, mashed potatoes
3 tablespoons mayonnaise or salad dressing
1 tablespoon creamy mustard
½ teaspoon salt
¼ teaspoon pepper
2 teaspoons curry powder (optional)

- **Remove** yolks from eggs; discard or reserve for another use. Chop egg whites. Combine egg white, pickle relish, green onions, and pimiento, if desired; set aside.
- **Combine** mashed potatoes and next 4 ingredients; stir in curry powder, if desired. Fold into egg mixture. Serve as a salad, sandwich filling, or stuffing for vegetables. **Yield:** 1¾ cups.

BACON-HORSERADISH EGG SALAD

6 large hard-cooked eggs, chopped
1 cup chopped celery
¼ cup chopped green onions
7 slices bacon, cooked and crumbled
½ cup mayonnaise or salad dressing
1½ tablespoons prepared horseradish
1 tablespoon caraway seeds
¼ teaspoon salt
¼ teaspoon pepper
2 tablespoons chopped fresh parsley

- **Combine** first 4 ingredients in a large bowl; set aside.
- **Combine** mayonnaise and next 4 ingredients; fold into egg mixture. Sprinkle with parsley. Serve as a salad or sandwich filling. **Yield:** 3 cups.

Mrs. James Todd
Savannah, Georgia

MEXICAN EGG SALAD TACOS

4 large hard-cooked eggs, chopped
¼ cup (2 ounces) shredded sharp Cheddar cheese
1 tablespoon chopped green onions
2 tablespoons mayonnaise or salad dressing
2 tablespoons salsa
1 tablespoon sour cream
⅛ teaspoon salt
⅛ teaspoon pepper
6 taco shells
Lettuce leaves
Garnishes: shredded Cheddar cheese, avocado slices

- **Combine** first 3 ingredients in a bowl; set aside.
- **Combine** mayonnaise and next 4 ingredients; fold into egg mixture.
- **Line** taco shells with lettuce. Spoon egg salad evenly into taco shells. Garnish, if desired, and serve with salsa. **Yield:** 6 servings.

Edith Evans
Edgewood, Maryland

DON'T CALL ME HARD-BOILED!

Just what is the best way to boil an egg? Home Economist Jane Cairns of our Test Kitchens staff chooses to call them *hard-cooked eggs* – not hard-boiled. "You should not allow them to boil hard," she says. Here is Jane's recipe for the perfect "hard-cooked" egg.

■ Place eggs in a single layer in a saucepan. Add enough cold water to measure at least 1 inch over eggs. Bring *just* to a boil. Cover, remove saucepan from heat, and let stand 15 minutes for small eggs, 16 minutes for medium eggs, and 17 minutes for large eggs. Pour off water. Immediately run cold water over eggs, and gently tap eggs all over to help loosen the shells. Hold eggs under cold running water as you peel off the shell.

SHRIMP-AND-EGG SALAD SANDWICHES

2 cups water
½ pound unpeeled, medium-size fresh shrimp
6 large hard-cooked eggs, chopped
¼ cup finely chopped green onions
2 tablespoons finely chopped celery
1 tablespoon chopped fresh parsley
2 tablespoons capers (optional)
2 teaspoons chopped fresh dill (optional)
3 tablespoons mayonnaise or salad dressing
1 teaspoon lemon juice
1 teaspoon prepared mustard
¼ teaspoon salt
¼ teaspoon hot sauce
3 English muffins, split and toasted
Garnishes: fresh dill, whole shrimp, lemon slices

• **Bring** water to a boil; add shrimp, and cook 3 to 5 minutes or until shrimp turn pink. Drain well, and rinse with cold water. Peel shrimp, and devein, if desired. Coarsely chop shrimp.
• **Combine** chopped shrimp, eggs, and next 3 ingredients; if desired, stir in capers and dill. Set mixture aside.
• **Combine** mayonnaise and next 4 ingredients, and gently fold into egg mixture.
• **Spoon** onto English muffins; garnish, if desired. **Yield:** 6 servings.

Virginia J. MacMillan
Summerland Key, Florida

PRESTO ANTIPASTO

Antipasto makes a bountiful appetizer buffet, whether it's on a platter for two or a tray for 20. Assemble the ingredients in minutes and you'll have the perfect hors d'oeuvre to serve before an Italian meal or with refreshments for a casual get-together.

Add a special touch to deli cold cuts and cheeses with a few of our homemade antipasto offerings. Finish the presentation with an assortment of fresh and pickled vegetables. Add some crusty loaves and a cruet of Italian dressing for a setting that'll transport you to sunny Italy.

PICKLED SHRIMP

4 cups water
½ cup celery leaves
¼ cup pickling spice
1 tablespoon salt
1½ pounds unpeeled, medium-size fresh shrimp
2 small onions, sliced
7 bay leaves
¾ cup vegetable oil
¼ cup white vinegar
3 tablespoons capers
2½ teaspoons celery seeds
1 teaspoon salt
3 to 4 drops of hot sauce
Lettuce leaves

• **Bring** first 4 ingredients to a boil in a Dutch oven; add shrimp, and cook 3 to 5 minutes or until shrimp turn pink. Drain shrimp well, and rinse with cold water. Peel shrimp, and devein, if desired.
• **Combine** shrimp, onion, and bay leaves in a large heavy-duty, zip-top plastic bag. Set aside.
• **Combine** vegetable oil and next 5 ingredients in a jar. Close tightly, and shake vigorously. Pour over shrimp.

Seal bag, and refrigerate 24 hours, turning bag occasionally.

• **Drain** shrimp; remove and discard bay leaves. Serve shrimp on a lettuce-lined plate. **Yield:** 6 to 8 appetizer servings.

Nancy L. Greco
Mars Hill, North Carolina

MARINATED VEGETABLES

1 (8-ounce) container small fresh
   mushrooms
1 (14-ounce) can artichoke hearts,
   drained
1 (6-ounce) can pitted ripe olives,
   drained
½ cup vegetable oil
¼ cup olive oil
½ cup lemon juice
⅓ cup finely chopped onion
1 teaspoon salt
¼ teaspoon pepper
3 bay leaves
1 tablespoon chopped fresh
   parsley

• **Clean** mushrooms with damp paper towels; trim ends from stems. Combine mushrooms, artichokes, and olives. Set aside.
• **Combine** vegetable oil and remaining ingredients in a jar. Close tightly, and shake vigorously.
• **Pour** marinade over vegetable mixture. Cover and refrigerate at least 12 hours. Drain vegetables, and remove and discard bay leaves. **Yield:** 8 appetizer servings.

Cindy Horlander
Plantation, Florida

PICKLED CAULIFLOWER

1 large head cauliflower, broken
   into flowerets
3 carrots, scraped and sliced
6 jalapeño peppers, sliced
1 large onion, sliced
1 (6-ounce) can pitted ripe olives,
   drained
6 cloves garlic
4 cups white vinegar (5% acidity)
2 cups water
¼ cup pickling spice
1½ teaspoons salt

• **Combine** cauliflower and carrots in a large Dutch oven; add water to cover. Bring to a boil; cover and cook 3 minutes. Drain.
• **Combine** cooked vegetables, jalapeño peppers, onion, olives, and garlic in a large bowl; toss gently, and set aside.
• **Combine** vinegar, water, pickling spice, and salt in a large saucepan.
• **Bring** vinegar mixture to a boil. Pour mixture over vegetables. Cover and refrigerate for 24 hours. **Yield:** 12 cups.

ANTIPASTO ELEMENTS

Choose all or just a few of these ingredients to make your antipasto as elaborate as you'd like.

Line a plate or platter with radicchio, leaf lettuce, or kale. Add colorful sweet pepper slices, cherry tomatoes, and steamed green beans.

Gorgonzola: If you like blue or Roquefort cheese, you'll love this full, pungent-flavored, blue-veined cheese.

Mortadella: A step above regular bologna, this delicious garlic version is studded with pork fat.

Mozzarella, fresh: Softer and more delicately flavored than the mozzarella used on pizza, it's usually sold in irregularly shaped spheres that can be rolled in fresh or dried basil or oregano for a wonderful flavor combination.

Parmesan: Not just for grating, this hard cheese with its rich, nutty flavor marries perfectly with crusty bread.

Prosciutto: A salt-cured ham, similar to our Southern salt-cured country ham, prosciutto is pressed, creating a dense texture that is best enjoyed in paper-thin slices.

Provolone: Thin slices of this mild-flavored, firm-textured cheese are ideal for joining with salami on a chunk of bread.

Salami: Choose Genoa salami, flecked with white peppercorns, or cotto salami, flecked with black peppercorns.

Other easy antipasto additions from a jar include pimiento-stuffed olives, pickled pepperoncini peppers, whole ripe olives, and pickled okra.

FAST FIXES

Do you ever have one of those days when making dinner is stuck at the bottom of your priority list? If you're as busy as we think you are, that happens more often than not. These recipes are for those supper-in-a-pinch weeknights. They taste like you spent plenty of time putting them together and they rely on ingredients you probably have in your refrigerator or pantry.

THE SEBASTIAN

Serve this grilled ham-and-cheese sandwich with gazpacho from the deli or your favorite tomato soup.

3 cups shredded cabbage
⅔ cup mayonnaise
⅓ cup commercial chutney
1 tablespoon curry powder
⅛ teaspoon salt
12 (1-ounce) slices ham
6 (¾-ounce) slices Cheddar
      cheese
12 slices rye bread
¼ cup butter, softened

● **Combine** first 5 ingredients; set slaw aside.
● **Place** 2 ham slices, ½ cup slaw, and 1 cheese slice onto 6 bread slices; top with remaining slices of bread.
● **Spread** half of butter on outside of 1 side of each sandwich. Place sandwiches, buttered side down, onto a hot griddle or skillet.
● **Cook** 1 minute or until golden.
● **Spread** remaining butter on ungrilled side of sandwich, and cook, buttered side down, until golden and cheese begins to melt.
● **Serve** immediately. **Yield:** 6 servings.
The Williamsburg Lodge
Williamsburg, Virginia

RANCH-STYLE TURKEY 'N' PASTA SALAD

The Ranch-style dressing lends a mild flavor to this salad. For more oomph, sprinkle on lemon-pepper seasoning or your choice of herbs.

2 cups penne pasta, uncooked
2 cups chopped cooked
      turkey
1 small zucchini, sliced
2 small yellow squash, sliced
1 small green pepper, chopped
1 small sweet red pepper,
      chopped
¼ cup grated Parmesan cheese
¾ cup commercial Ranch-style
      dressing

● **Cook** pasta according to package directions; drain. Rinse with cold water; drain.
● **Combine** pasta and remaining ingredients in a large bowl. Cover and chill at least 2 hours. Toss before serving.
Yield: 6 to 8 servings.
Adelyne Smith
Dunnville, Kentucky

BRAISED CHICKEN BREAST IN LEMON CREAM SAUCE

For the broth in this recipe, use canned chicken broth or water and a chicken-flavored bouillon cube.

⅓ cup butter or margarine,
      divided
1 (12-ounce) package fresh
      mushrooms, sliced
6 skinned and boned chicken
      breast halves
½ teaspoon salt
½ teaspoon ground white pepper
½ cup all-purpose flour
1 cup chicken broth
1 cup whipping cream
3 tablespoons lemon juice

● **Melt** 3 tablespoons butter in a large skillet over medium heat. Add sliced mushrooms, and cook until browned, stirring often. Drain mushrooms, and set aside.

● **Sprinkle** chicken breasts with salt and pepper; dredge in flour, shaking off excess.
● **Melt** remaining butter in skillet over medium heat; add chicken, and cook about 8 minutes on each side. Remove chicken from skillet, reserving 1 tablespoon drippings in skillet. Add broth.
● **Bring** broth mixture to a boil. Cook mixture over high heat about 15 minutes or until broth mixture is reduced to ⅓ cup.
● **Combine** whipping cream and lemon juice; add to broth mixture. Cook over medium heat about 5 minutes. Add mushrooms and chicken breasts.
● **Bring** sauce to a boil; reduce heat, and simmer 4 to 5 minutes or until chicken is thoroughly heated, spooning sauce over chicken as it cooks.
Yield: 6 servings.
Freida Merrell
Magnolia, Arkansas

QUICK TIPS FOR FAST FIXES

■ Many foods such as cheese, pasta, rice, and fresh vegetables can be prepared ahead of time. Simply chop, grate, or cook in advance, and refrigerate for later use.

■ Turn on the oven when you enter the kitchen so it can preheat while you begin meal preparations.

■ Start preparing a meal by beginning with the dish that takes the longest. That way, it can be cooking while you prepare other foods.

■ No time for a centerpiece? You can create instant atmosphere with candles – just don't forget to light them.

■ Assemble food on plates in the kitchen to eliminate the need for serving pieces.

Elegance with ease – the chicken in Basil-Stuffed Chicken With Tomato-Basil Pasta (recipe, page 204) can be grilled ahead of time and microwaved just before serving.

Left: *Kissed with a pat of butter, melt-in-your-mouth Confetti Cornbread (recipe, page 170) is a true taste of the South.*

Far left: *Grilled Vegetable Salad, with its blend of molasses and white balsamic vinegar, is the best light recipe we've tried in years (recipe, page 203).*

Above: *We found that we could easily reduce the six tablespoons of butter in the original Cream of Carrot-and-Tomato Soup (recipe, page 176) to three, without affecting the recipe's taste or texture.*

Tarragon Vinaigrette drizzled on fresh vegetables makes Summer Tomato Salad high in taste appeal. (Recipes begin on page 201.)

AUGUST

COOL! TAMALES

You may have savored more traditional tamales – bundles steaming with spicy fillings of cheese, chicken, or pork. "Not all tamales have to be flavored with fire and brimstone," says Mark Miller, a pioneer of the southwestern cuisine and chef and owner of Red Sage restaurant in Washington, D.C.

As proof, Mark and Red Sage pastry chef Kim Peoples introduce Blackberry and Mango Dessert Tamales. They're delectable combinations of familiar and exotic ingredients. If you already have a passion for tamales, you'll find these unique fruit-filled versions the perfect ending to any meal.

FRUIT PUREE

5 pints fresh blackberries or
  6 mangoes, peeled and seeded

• **Position** knife blade in food processor bowl; add half of blackberries or mangoes. Process until smooth, stopping once to scrape down sides.
• **Pour** blended fruit through a large wire-mesh strainer into a bowl, discarding seeds, if necessary. Repeat procedure with remaining fruit.
• **Refrigerate** puree until ready to use. Use as a sauce, and add to fillings for Mango or Blackberry Dessert Tamales. **Yield:** about 5 cups.

FRESH FRUIT COMPOTE

1 cup peeled, chopped fresh
  mango
1 cup chopped fresh pineapple
1 cup chopped fresh strawberries
2 tablespoons sugar
1 teaspoon lemon juice

• **Combine** all ingredients, stirring gently until sugar dissolves. Serve with either Mango or Blackberry Dessert Tamales or over pound cake or ice cream. **Yield:** 3 cups.

MANGO DESSERT TAMALES

13 large dried cornhusks
1¼ cups unsalted butter,
  softened
4¼ cups masa harina
1 tablespoon baking powder
Mango Fruit Puree, divided (see
  recipe)
1 (7-ounce) can flaked coconut,
  divided
4 egg whites
½ cup sugar
⅛ teaspoon salt
2 tablespoons unsalted butter,
  softened
¼ teaspoon vanilla extract
Fresh Fruit Compote (see
  recipe)
Grated nutmeg (optional)

• **Cover** husks with hot water, and let stand 1 hour or until softened.
• **Drain** cornhusks, and pat dry. Tear 1 cornhusk lengthwise into thin strips to make ties; set aside.
• **Place** butter in a large bowl; beat at medium speed with an electric mixer until creamy. Gradually add masa harina and baking powder, beating after each addition. (Mixture will be crumbly.)
• **Stir** 2 cups mango Fruit Puree and 1 cup coconut into mixture. (Mixture should not be sticky. If it is, stir in a small amount of masa harina.)
• **Divide** mango mixture evenly onto 12 cornhusks. Pat each portion into a 5½- x 4½-inch rectangle, leaving at least a ½-inch border on 3 sides of husks and a greater margin at pointed ends.
• **Combine** egg whites and next 4 ingredients; stir in remaining coconut. Spoon evenly down center of mango mixture.
• **Bring** long sides of husk together, pressing mango mixture to seal in coconut mixture. Twist pointed end closed, and tie with a cornhusk strip. Leave opposite end untied.
• **Place** a cup in center of a steamer basket or metal colander in a Dutch oven, and add enough water to fill below basket. Bring water to a boil. Stand tamales, pointed (closed) end down, around cup. Cover and steam 10 minutes. Let stand 5 minutes. Trim open end of each tamale to allow filling to show.
• **Spoon** remaining Fruit Puree and Fresh Fruit Compote onto each plate just before serving. Top with tamales. Sprinkle grated nutmeg on rim of plate, if desired. **Yield:** 12 tamales or 6 servings.

BLACKBERRY DESSERT TAMALES

13 large dried cornhusks
1¼ cups unsalted butter,
  softened
4¼ cups masa harina
1 tablespoon baking powder
Blackberry Fruit Puree, divided
  (see recipe)
½ cup honey
2 cups finely chopped pecans
¼ cup praline paste *
3 tablespoons corn oil
½ pint fresh blackberries
Fresh Fruit Compote (see
  recipe)
Grated nutmeg (optional)

- **Cover** husks with hot water, and let stand 1 hour or until softened.
- **Drain** cornhusks, and pat dry. Tear 1 cornhusk lengthwise into thin strips to make ties; set aside.
- **Place** butter in a large bowl; beat at medium speed with an electric mixer until creamy. Gradually add masa harina and baking powder, beating after each addition. (Mixture will be crumbly.)
- **Stir** 2 cups blackberry Fruit Puree and honey into mixture. (Mixture should not be sticky. If it is, stir in a small amount of masa harina.)
- **Divide** blackberry mixture evenly onto 12 cornhusks. Pat each portion into a 5½- x 4½-inch rectangle, leaving at least a ½-inch border on 3 sides of husks and a greater margin at pointed ends.
- **Combine** pecans, praline paste, and oil. Spoon evenly down center of blackberry mixture; top each with 5 or 6 blackberries.
- **Bring** long sides of husk together, pressing to seal. Twist pointed end closed; tie with a cornhusk strip. Leave opposite end untied.
- **Place** a cup in center of a steamer basket or metal colander in a Dutch oven. Add enough water to fill below basket. Bring water to a boil. Stand tamales, pointed (closed) end down, around cup. Cover and steam 10 minutes. Let stand 5 minutes. Trim open end of each to allow filling to show.
- **Spoon** remaining Fruit Puree and Fresh Fruit Compote onto each plate. Top with tamales. Sprinkle grated nutmeg on rim of plate, if desired. **Yield:** 12 tamales or 6 servings.

* ½ cup skinned, toasted hazelnuts, processed in food processor 3 to 5 minutes, may be substituted.

"Don't let tamales intimidate you. When it comes down to it, there are only three steps: the masa (corn mixture), the filling, and the assembly."

—*Mark Miller*
Owner, Red Sage restaurant
Washington, D.C.

If this is your first attempt at making tamales, see Mark's quick step-by-step lesson below. You'll be surprised at how simple it is to assemble these fresh summer treats.

If you're working solo, break the tamale recipe down into smaller tasks. Better still, gather recipe ingredients and a group of friends and turn tamale-making into a party. Make double batches so everyone can take home some of the desserts.

"Tamales hold well, so you can make a large amount ahead of time and refrigerate or freeze them. Thaw and steam when you're ready to eat," Mark advises.

A LESSON WITH MARK
- Divide masa among cornhusks; pat evenly over husks to form ⅛-inch-thick rectangle.
- Leave a ½-inch margin along three straight edges and a greater margin at pointed end of husk for tying.
- Bring long sides of cornhusk together, pressing masa mixture to seal. Twist or fold over pointed end to close.
- Tie one or both ends closed with a narrow strip of cornhusk or a piece of heavy string.
- Steam tamales, seam side down, in a steamer basket, bamboo steamer, or metal colander.

SERVE IT LIKE A PRO
- To serve the dessert tamales in style, spoon both flavors of Fruit Puree onto a plate along with Fresh Fruit Compote. Place one of each flavor dessert tamale on the sauces, and serve. Two tamales equal one serving.
- For a simple dessert, make only one flavor of tamale, and rely on the easy Fruit Puree to make your dessert plate special.
- Dress up the tamales by coloring the cornhusks. First cover them with hot water for 15 minutes. Drain and pat dry. Then combine 1 cup of the desired flavor Fruit Puree with 1 cup water in a large dish. Place the husks in the fruit mixture, coating evenly; cover and refrigerate 8 hours.

When you're ready to make the tamales, remove the husks from the puree, drain, and pat dry. Now you're ready to assemble them. Use the husks soaked in mango Fruit Puree for the Blackberry Dessert Tamales and husks soaked in blackberry Fruit Puree for the Mango Dessert Tamales.

FROM OUR KITCHEN TO YOURS

....

When testing the tamale recipes on the last two pages, we made several discoveries. For example, homemade tamales served in steamy wrappings, which you unfold to eat, taste twice as good as the mass-produced ones.

Masa harina swells with the addition of liquid. Fresh young corn makes a moist, creamy tamale dough; old corn past its peak of freshness produces a drier dough. And making tamale dough is easy; it's the spreading and folding that's time-consuming. Invite a friend to help with the task and share in the rewards.

Traditional tamales consist of a filling surrounded with corn dough and wrapped in fresh or dried cornhusks. You can also wrap and steam tamales in banana leaves (found at Oriental markets), aluminum foil, or oiled parchment paper. Don't try wax paper. We did, and it doesn't work very well.

After filling the wrapper, fold the long sides together, and choose the tying technique that's easiest for you. Secure the wrapper with thin strips of cornhusk or pieces of heavy string. The speediest method ties only one end. (Steam these bundles with the tied end down.) Tying the wrapper at both ends to resemble hard candy is also quick. The most familiar, but slower, method is to fold up both ends and wrap the tamale like a gift package tied up with ribbon. (See photo on page 221.) Many of the ingredients for the recipes can be purchased at large supermarkets.

Mango (MANG-goh): Called the "apple" of the tropics, the oval fruit tastes like a blend of peach, apricot, and pineapple. For a sweet flavor choose a ripe mango. Unripe fruit is bitter.

Masa harina (MAH-sah ah-REE-nah): This flour is made from specially processed corn. Labeled "corn masa mix" by brands like Quaker, masa harina can be found in the flour section of many supermarkets or in specialty stores. Cornmeal is *not* a substitute.

TEXAS WINES

On a thirsty landscape that's home to lizards and rattlesnakes, grapevines cast a long shadow on the Texas horizon. They don't look like they belong there. But, as surely as sagebrush, they do belong.

Half of the 26 grape species that grow worldwide were described as native to Texas by the legendary T. V. Munson of Denison, Texas, the man who saved the vineyards of France from a devastating insect called phylloxera. In the 1880s, he sent French vintners disease-resistant Texas rootstocks for grafting to European grapevines. Today, Texans can proudly raise a glass – of Texas wine – to the many French grapes grown on Texas rootstocks.

In the 1970s, pioneer growers across Texas planted test plots. They cultivated different grape varieties, including *vitis vinifera*, the mother vine of European wine, but one foreign to Texas soil. Challenges were enormous. One of the greatest was for water.

Drip irrigation was the breakthrough that revolutionized the Texas wine industry. The prolific *vinifera* grape took hold – Texas wines had been reborn.

TEXAS WINE INDUSTRY TAKES OFF

A decade ago, cynical comments at a Texas wine tasting could uncork a vintner's heart. "A slight bouquet of Texas crude," sneered haughty wine connoisseurs. "By the turn of the century, Texas wine will be as good as *any* in California, and we'll be the number two wine producer nationally," says Texas Commissioner of Agriculture Rick Perry. Texas now

ranks fifth, behind California, New York, Washington, and Oregon.

Texas's industry has grown from 50,000 gallons in 1982 to 1.5 million gallons 10 years later. The selection includes Cabernets, Merlots, Chenin Blancs, Chardonnays, Rieslings, Gewürztraminers, and Ports.

It seems the people with the opinion of Texes wines are people who have *never* tasted them.

AWARDS SWEETEN THE VINTAGE

What will ultimately put to rest any misgivings about Texas wines is the number of awards the state's 20-plus wineries are winning.

At the 1986 San Francisco National Wine Competition, two Texas wineries won gold medals.

In 1991, the victory was sweeter still when a Texas Chardonnay placed second in a Texas versus France Chardonnay competition in Dijon, France, an event the French brazenly expected to sweep. French judges recalculated the results dozens of times and finally, humbled, saluted the Texas Chardonnays.

Since 1986, six other Texas wineries have won national or international gold medals.

When the wine is from Texas, you are looking at blazing red sunsets, swirling pale tumbleweeds, inhaling heat thick as honey, and you are tasting bottled sunlight, the liquid wonder born of Texas tenacity.

WHISKS & WHIMSY

So it's back-to-school time...cooking school, that is. Take a lesson

from the professional chefs and instructors on these pages, and then

whip up some recipe fun with your kids.

We traveled to Jackson, Mississippi, and Memphis to visit cooking classes designed for inquiring young minds. We wanted to experience the classes through the eyes of a child. In each location, we tied on aprons and put on chef's hats. While working side by side with the kids, we witnessed the concentration, determination, and squeals of glee that accompany the thrill of accomplishment.

Join us in our look at two masterful teachers who are stirring up lots of fun. They've shared their quick and easy ideas for snacks and such. You'll learn, as we did, that kids in the kitchen – with just a bit of assistance – make the most wonderful sort of child's play.

FOR THE LOVE OF COOKING

At the Memphis Children's Museum, the animated chef in command is Dolores Katsotis.

The creativity and endless energy which Chef Dough-Dough, as she is known to her students, brings to each of her sessions springs from a love of cooking that crosses several generations. Dolores's father, John Grisanti, taught his daughter the basics of cooking in the

kitchen of the Memphis restaurant that bears his name.

From there Dolores formally trained at the Culinary Institute of America. Today she shares her knowledge and passion by conducting children's cooking camps and classes.

PITA PIZZA SNACK

Let your child create his favorite topping for this make-and-bake quick supper or after-school snack.

1 tablespoon tomato paste
1 pita bread round
2 tablespoons shredded mozzarella cheese
Toppings: chopped ham, shredded carrot, sliced olives, chopped green pepper, cooked sausage, grated Parmesan cheese

• **Spread** tomato paste on pita round; place on a baking sheet.
• **Sprinkle** evenly with cheese and desired toppings.
• **Bake** at 350° for 8 to 10 minutes. **Yield:** 1 serving.

RECIPE FOR DISCOVERY

1 teacher
8 to 12 young minds
1 to 2 cups curiosity
4 to 5 spoonfuls fun
Hands-on participation
Patience
Laughter
Enthusiasm

• **Combine** talented teacher and eager young minds; add cupfuls of curiosity and spoonfuls of fun.
• **Blend** in generous amounts of hands-on participation mixed with patience.
• **Sprinkle** with laughter, and serve with enthusiasm. **Yield:** Learning at its best.

GRISANTI SPAGHETTI SAUCE

Here's a great chance for your child to practice measuring, chopping, and stirring.

½ pound Italian sausage
½ cup butter or margarine
1⅓ cups chopped onion
½ cup all-purpose flour
2 tablespoons minced garlic
1 pound ground beef
1 (6-ounce) can tomato paste
1 (14-ounce) can ready-to-serve chicken broth
1 cup water
1 cup sliced fresh mushrooms
1 tablespoon chopped fresh rosemary
1 tablespoon chopped fresh parsley
1 bay leaf
¼ teaspoon salt
¼ teaspoon pepper
¼ teaspoon rubbed sage
Hot cooked spaghetti

• **Remove** sausage from casing; set sausage aside.
• **Melt** butter in a large skillet over medium heat; add onion, and cook, stirring constantly, until tender. Stir in flour; cook, stirring constantly, 1 minute. Add garlic; cook, stirring constantly, 1 minute.
• **Add** beef and sausage, and cook, stirring until meat crumbles; drain. Stir in tomato paste and next 9 ingredients.
• **Bring** to a boil. Reduce heat, and simmer 2 hours, stirring often. Remove and discard bay leaf.
• **Serve** over pasta. **Yield:** 6 servings.

INSPIRATION FOR IMAGINATION

"And he huffed, and he puffed, and he blew the house down!"

Not a creature stirs as Cheryl Welch continues her reading of the "Three Little Pigs." For a moment, the 5- and 6-year-olds forget they're seated in the cookbook corner of the Everyday Gourmet, a kitchen store in Jackson, Mississippi.

"It's fun to read and then use our imaginations. And we're going to use our imaginations today as we cook together," Cheryl explains.

With words and gestures the former preschool educator deftly transports the youngsters to her land of make-believe. The children are then seated at scaled-down tables to await their next surprise.

With guidance from Cheryl and three teaching assistants, the students work in small groups, creating Piggy Apples. "Through cooking, children learn to use their senses as they touch, taste, and smell each ingredient," Cheryl says. "They learn to share as they take turns stirring and helping with different steps in each recipe.

"Concentrate on having fun at first. Introduce cooking to younger children as an enjoyable experience. The goal is to instill a love of cooking and to have fun in the kitchen," Cheryl says.

PIGGY APPLE

Beginning cooks will have fun making this incredible edible.

1 small Red Delicious apple
1½ tablespoons creamy peanut butter
2 raisins
1 miniature marshmallow
1 carrot stick
2 small turnip or apple triangles
5 wooden picks

• **Core** apple; fill with peanut butter.
• **Attach** raisins for eyes, marshmallow for nose, carrot stick for tail, and turnip triangles for ears, using wooden picks. **Yield:** 1 serving.

LOLLAPALOOZA

This crazy, mixed-up name perfectly describes this fudge sundae that begins with an awesome brownie.

¼ cup butter or margarine
1 cup semisweet chocolate morsels
¾ cup sugar
⅔ cup all-purpose flour
¼ teaspoon baking powder
¼ teaspoon salt
2 large eggs, lightly beaten
½ teaspoon vanilla extract
½ cup chopped pecans
½ cup semisweet chocolate morsels
Ice cream
Easy Hot Fudge Sauce

• **Combine** butter and 1 cup chocolate morsels in a heavy saucepan. Cook over low heat, stirring constantly, until chocolate and butter melt. Remove from heat.
• **Add** sugar and next 5 ingredients, stirring until blended. Stir in pecans and ½ cup chocolate morsels.
• **Spread** mixture into a lightly greased 8-inch square pan.
• **Bake** at 350° for 30 minutes or until center is set. Cool brownies in pan on a wire rack.
• **Cut** into squares, and serve with ice cream and warm Easy Hot Fudge Sauce. **Yield:** 16 servings.

Easy Hot Fudge Sauce

1 (12-ounce) package semisweet chocolate morsels
1 (12-ounce) can evaporated milk
1 cup sugar
1 tablespoon butter or margarine
1 teaspoon vanilla extract

• **Combine** first 3 ingredients in a heavy saucepan.
• **Cook** over medium heat, stirring constantly, until chocolate melts and mixture comes to a boil.
• **Stir** in butter and vanilla. **Yield:** 3 cups.

WHEN YOU WISH UPON A CHEF...

...your dreams come true. Disney dreams, that is. Can you imagine your child's excitement if Chef Mickey came to *your* hometown? Mickey Mouse and a team of culinary cohorts took a magic carpet ride to Lafayette, Louisiana, to judge a kids' cooking competition, bringing the sparkle of the Magic Kingdom to bayou country.

As part of the decade-old annual Acadiana Culinary Classic for local professional chefs, the kids' contest – Le Petit Classique – aims to interest children in creative food early on and perhaps a culinary career down the road. Try some of the winning recipes, and cast your vote for the best future "whisker."

SEAFOOD MANICOTTI

1 quart whipping cream
½ teaspoon salt
¼ teaspoon ground black pepper
¼ teaspoon ground red pepper
14 manicotti shells
2 pounds unpeeled, large fresh shrimp
3 tablespoons butter or margarine
1 cup chopped onion
1 cup chopped green pepper
¼ cup chopped celery
1 clove garlic, minced
1 pound fresh crabmeat, drained and flaked
½ cup (2 ounces) shredded Cheddar cheese
½ cup (2 ounces) shredded Monterey Jack with peppers

• **Combine** first 4 ingredients in a saucepan; cook over medium-high heat 30 minutes or until thickened and reduced to 2 cups. Set aside.

• **Cook** manicotti according to package directions. Drain and set aside.
• **Peel** shrimp, and devein, if desired. Chop and set aside.
• **Heat** butter in a large Dutch oven over medium-high heat; add onion and next 3 ingredients. Cook, stirring constantly, 5 minutes or until tender.
• **Add** shrimp and crabmeat, and cook, stirring constantly, 5 minutes or until shrimp turn pink.
• **Cool** 10 minutes, and drain well.
• **Combine** seafood mixture and whipping cream mixture.
• **Fill** manicotti shells, and place in 2 lightly greased 11- x 7- x 1½-inch baking dishes. Sprinkle with cheeses, and cover with foil.
• **Bake** at 350° for 15 minutes.
• **Uncover** and bake 10 additional minutes. Serve immediately. **Yield:** 6 to 8 servings.

Aimee Biessenberger, age 11
Lafayette, Louisiana

SHRIMP C'EST BON

3 pounds unpeeled, large fresh shrimp
1 (16-ounce) loaf French bread, cut in half lengthwise
1 cup butter
2 onions, chopped
1½ teaspoons minced garlic
1 teaspoon Creole seasoning

• **Peel** shrimp, and devein, if desired. Set aside.
• **Place** bread on a baking sheet, and bake at 350° for 5 minutes or until lightly browned. Cut each half into 3 pieces, and set aside.
• **Melt** butter in a Dutch oven. Add onion, garlic, and seasoning. Cook over medium heat until tender. Add shrimp.
• **Cover** and cook 8 minutes or until shrimp turn pink. Serve over bread. **Yield:** 6 servings.

Justin Boswell, age 10
Lafayette, Louisiana

PIE PAN SPINACH

1 unbaked 9-inch pastry shell
1 (10-ounce) package frozen chopped spinach, thawed
3 slices bacon
½ cup chopped onion
1¾ cups cottage cheese
¼ cup grated Parmesan cheese
3 large eggs, lightly beaten
½ teaspoon salt
¼ teaspoon pepper
⅛ teaspoon ground nutmeg
Garnishes: lemon slices and red chile peppers

• **Prick** bottom and sides of pastry with a fork. Bake at 400° for 3 minutes; remove from oven, and gently prick with fork. Bake 5 additional minutes. Set aside.
• **Drain** spinach well, pressing between paper towels, and set aside.
• **Cook** bacon in a large skillet until crisp; remove bacon, reserving 1 tablespoon drippings in skillet. Crumble bacon, and set aside.
• **Cook** onion in drippings over medium-high heat, stirring constantly, until tender. Stir in spinach, and remove from heat.
• **Combine** cottage cheese and next 5 ingredients in a bowl; stir in spinach mixture and bacon. Pour into pastry shell. Bake at 350° for 30 to 35 minutes or until set. Let stand 5 minutes. Garnish, if desired. Yield: 6 to 8 servings.

Adam Trahan, age 8
Lafayette, Louisiana

KIDS COOK UP SOME FUN

Why not try a new kids summer activity – *cooking class*? Along with the excitement of learning to cook and making new friends, students develop confidence. Measuring ingredients and working with recipes allow children to sharpen their creativity and math skills.

SWEET POTATO SUPREME

2 (14½-ounce) cans or 3⅔ cups
   cooked, mashed sweet
   potatoes
½ cup sugar
2 large eggs
¼ cup milk
3 tablespoons butter or margarine,
   melted
1 teaspoon vanilla extract
½ teaspoon salt
3 tablespoons butter or margarine,
   softened
1 cup firmly packed brown
   sugar
1 cup chopped pecans
1 cup flaked coconut
⅓ cup all-purpose flour

• **Combine** first 7 ingredients; beat at
medium speed with an electric mixer
until smooth. Pour batter into a
greased 11- x 7- x 1½-inch baking
dish; set aside.
• **Combine** 3 tablespoons butter and
remaining ingredients, stirring with a
fork; sprinkle over potato mixture.
• **Bake** at 350° for 35 minutes. **Yield:**
8 servings.

Molly Reid, age 10
Lafayette, Louisiana

CAJUN FIG COBBLER

¼ cup butter or margarine
1 cup all-purpose flour
1 cup sugar
2 teaspoons baking powder
1 cup milk
1 large egg
1 teaspoon vanilla extract
2 (11-ounce) jars fig
   preserves

• **Place** butter in a 2-quart baking dish.
Bake at 375° until butter melts. Remove from oven, and set aside.
• **Combine** flour, sugar, and baking
powder in a large bowl. Add milk, egg,
and vanilla, stirring until smooth. Pour
batter into baking dish; spoon preserves over batter.

• **Bake** at 375° for 40 minutes, covering dish with aluminum foil after 20
minutes. Serve warm with vanilla ice
cream or whipped cream. **Yield:** 8
servings.

Joshua Pucheu, age 8
Ville Platte, Louisiana

SNACKS ONSTAGE

. . . .

Did you know that our traveling *South-*
ern Living Cooking School brings the
pages of our Foods section to life in
hometowns across the region each year?
For nearly two decades, our talented
team has demonstrated recipes on stages
in civic centers and auditoriums
throughout the South.

The show's theme changes annually,
and cooking with kids has become an
important focus in recent years. Here
we share some of the cooking school's
favorite snacks to make with your kids.

CRUNCHY MUNCHIES

6 cups corn-and-rice cereal
1½ cups pecan pieces or peanuts
½ cup light corn syrup
⅓ cup butter or margarine,
   melted
½ cup sifted powdered sugar

• **Combine** cereal and pecans in a large
bowl; set aside.
• **Combine** corn syrup, butter, and
powdered sugar, stirring mixture until
smooth. Pour over cereal mixture, stirring to coat. Pour mixture into a
lightly greased 15- x 10- x 1-inch jellyroll pan.
• **Bake** at 250° for 1 hour, stirring
every 15 minutes.
• **Stir** mixture carefully to loosen from
pan; cool completely, and break into
pieces. Store in an airtight container.
Yield: 7 cups.

LOLLIPOP COOKIES

½ cup butter or margarine,
   softened
1 egg yolk
2 teaspoons vanilla extract
1¼ cups all-purpose flour
1 teaspoon baking powder
¼ teaspoon salt
1 cup sifted powdered sugar
18 wooden craft sticks
Assorted 4½-ounce tubes
   decorating frosting
Assorted candies and sprinkles

• **Combine** first 3 ingredients in a large
mixing bowl; beat at medium speed
with an electric mixer until blended.
Set aside.
• **Combine** flour and next 3 ingredients; add gradually to butter mixture,
beating after each addition.
• **Shape** dough into 1-inch balls, and
place on ungreased baking sheets. Dip
a flat-bottomed glass in granulated
sugar and use to flatten each ball. Insert a wooden stick into each to resemble a lollipop.
• **Bake** at 350° for 11 to 12 minutes.
• **Cool** completely on baking sheets;
remove carefully.
• **Decorate** cookies, as desired. **Yield:**
1½ dozen.

Lollipop
Cookies

TACO-CHEESE ANIMAL CRACKERS

1 cup all-purpose flour
1½ cups (6 ounces) shredded taco-flavored Cheddar cheese
½ cup butter or margarine, softened
Paprika (optional)

• **Position** knife blade in food processor bowl; add flour, shredded cheese, and butter. Process until mixture forms a ball, stopping once to scrape down sides.
• **Wrap** dough in heavy-duty plastic wrap; chill 30 minutes.
• **Unwrap** dough, and roll to ¼-inch thickness on a lightly floured surface. Cut with 2½-inch animal-shaped cookie cutters; place on ungreased baking sheets. Sprinkle with paprika, if desired.
• **Bake** at 375° for 10 to 12 minutes or until lightly browned; cool on wire racks. **Yield:** 3 dozen.

NO-BAKE PEANUT BUTTER COOKIES

1½ cups quick-cooking oats, uncooked
½ cup flaked coconut
⅓ cup chopped peanuts
⅓ cup sugar
¼ cup creamy peanut butter
¼ cup vegetable oil
1 (10-ounce) package peanut butter morsels

• **Combine** first 3 ingredients in a large bowl; set aside.
• **Combine** sugar, peanut butter, and oil in a large saucepan; bring to a boil, stirring constantly until sugar melts. Remove from heat.
• **Add** peanut butter morsels to saucepan, stirring until morsels melt. Add to oat mixture, stirring mixture until dry ingredients are moistened.
• **Drop** by rounded teaspoonfuls onto wax paper. Chill about 30 minutes or until set. **Yield:** 5 dozen.

BANANA-CHOCOLATE MUFFINS

You don't have to tell the kids (they'll never guess), but this one's light. For all they know, they're getting away with eating gooey rich-tasting, chocolate muffins between meals.

1¼ cups all-purpose flour
1 teaspoon baking powder
½ teaspoon baking soda
¼ teaspoon salt
¾ cup sugar
¼ cup cocoa
3 small ripe bananas, mashed
½ cup egg substitute
2 tablespoons vegetable oil
2 tablespoons buttermilk
1 teaspoon vanilla extract

• **Combine** first 6 ingredients in a large bowl; make a well in center of mixture. Set aside.
• **Combine** bananas and remaining ingredients; add to dry ingredients, stirring just until moistened. Spoon batter into greased muffins pans, filling two-thirds full.
• **Bake** at 400° for 15 minutes. Cool in pans 5 minutes. Remove and serve warm or at room temperature. **Yield:** 1 dozen.

DIG THESE DINO-MITE MUFFINS

· · · · · · · · · · · · · · · ·

Here's a Stone Age snack that's "yabba! dabba! doable!" with dino-mad youngsters in your house. These muffins are delicious and sure to be extinct from the table in no time.

Children will enjoy making and decorating the edible stegosaurus, triceratops, tyrannosaurus, and other fossil favorites.

DINO-MITE MUFFINS

2 cups all-purpose flour
1 tablespoon baking powder
½ teaspoon salt
⅔ cup sugar
2 large eggs
1 cup milk
½ cup butter or margarine, melted
Vegetable cooking spray
Chewy fruit rolls by the foot
Plastic straw

• **Combine** first 4 ingredients in a large bowl; make a well in center.
• **Combine** eggs, milk, and butter; add to flour mixture, stirring just until moistened.
• **Spoon** into dinosaur-shaped muffin pans coated with cooking spray, filling two-thirds full.
• **Bake** at 375° for 20 to 22 minutes. Remove from pans immediately; let cool on wire racks.
• **Cut** angular spikes with a knife along 1 side of fruit roll to create jagged edges. Slice along top ridge of muffins. Carefully insert fruit-roll "backbone." Create eyes by using a plastic straw to cut out a dot from fruit roll. Affix "eye" to muffin. **Yield:** 1 dozen.

Using chewy fruit rolls, make the backbone by cutting angular spikes with a knife.

After making a slit along the top of the muffin, gently insert the fruit roll for the backbone.

Dino-Mite Muffin

Easy, Creamy Desserts

If the thought of baking a dessert in August makes you want to swoon, you'll love these sweet endings. The only cooking required is the few minutes it takes to melt peppermint candy, chocolate squares, or gelatin.

For a treat that won't overheat the kitchen or the cook, these creamy, make-ahead desserts are the answer.

ORANGE MOUSSE

1 envelope unflavored gelatin
¼ cup cold water
¾ cup orange or tangerine juice
⅓ cup sugar
1 tablespoon grated orange rind
1 tablespoon lemon juice
1½ cups whipping cream, whipped

● **Sprinkle** gelatin over cold water in a small nonaluminum saucepan; let stand 1 minute. Add orange juice and next 3 ingredients.
● **Cook** over low heat, stirring until gelatin and sugar dissolve (about 2 minutes). Pour into a large bowl.
● **Chill** until the consistency of unbeaten egg white.
● **Fold** in whipped cream, and chill. To serve, pipe or spoon into serving dishes. **Yield:** 4 cups.

Orange Cream Parfaits: Prepare Orange Mousse as directed. Fold in 1 (11-ounce) can mandarin oranges, drained. Layer mousse and 1 cup vanilla wafer crumbs into 8 (4-ounce) parfait glasses; chill 2 hours. Top with whipped cream, if desired. **Yield:** 8 servings.

PEPPERMINT CANDY MOUSSE

8 ounces hard red-and-white peppermint candies (2 cups)
½ cup half-and-half
1 envelope unflavored gelatin
1 tablespoon cold water
1½ cups whipping cream
Commercial chocolate sauce

● **Place** candies in a heavy-duty, zip-top plastic bag; seal bag, and crush, using a mallet or rolling pin until the consistency of powder.
● **Combine** crushed candies and half-and-half in a small saucepan. Cook mixture over low heat, stirring constantly, about 10 minutes or until candies dissolve. (Remove and discard any lumps of undissolved candy.) Set peppermint mixture aside.
● **Sprinkle** gelatin over 1 tablespoon cold water in a large bowl; let stand 1 minute. Add peppermint mixture, stirring until gelatin dissolves (about 2 minutes). Set peppermint mixture aside to cool to room temperature.

● **Beat** whipping cream until soft peaks form. Gently fold into peppermint mixture. Pour mixture into a lightly oiled 4-cup mold.
● **Cover** and chill at least 8 hours. Unmold onto a serving plate. Serve with chocolate sauce. **Yield:** 6 to 8 servings.
Rublelene Singleton
Scotts Hill, Tennessee

COCONUT-PINEAPPLE MOUSSE

3 envelopes unflavored gelatin
2 cups pineapple juice, divided
½ cup sugar
¼ teaspoon salt
2 cups whipping cream, divided
3 tablespoons lemon juice
1 teaspoon almond extract
2 cups flaked coconut, divided
Fresh strawberries or other fresh fruit (optional)

● **Sprinkle** gelatin over ½ cup pineapple juice in a large bowl; let stand 1 minute.
● **Bring** remaining 1½ cups pineapple juice to a boil; pour over gelatin mixture. Stir until gelatin dissolves (about 2 minutes). Add sugar and salt; cool to room temperature.
● **Stir** in 1 cup whipping cream, lemon juice, almond extract, and 1 cup coconut. Chill until the consistency of unbeaten egg white.
● **Beat** remaining 1 cup whipping cream until soft peaks form; fold into coconut mixture.
● **Pour** into a lightly oiled 6-cup ring mold. Cover and chill until firm.
● **Unmold** onto a serving plate; sprinkle with remaining 1 cup coconut. Arrange strawberries in center of mold, if desired. **Yield:** 10 servings.
Lynne Chatellier
Summerville, South Carolina

LEMON SOUFFLÉ

We used Wilton meringue powder in this soufflé. Look for it in crafts stores, cake-decorating supply stores, or at Wal-Mart.

1 tablespoon butter or margarine
2 tablespoons sugar
2 envelopes unflavored gelatin
½ cup cold water
1 teaspoon sugar
1 tablespoon grated lemon rind
¾ cup lemon juice
⅓ cup meringue powder
1½ cups sugar
1 cup water
2 cups whipping cream
1 (2-ounce) package slivered almonds, toasted and chopped
Garnish: Candied Lemon Peel

• **Cut** a piece of wax paper long enough to fit around a 2-quart soufflé dish, allowing a 1-inch overlap; fold paper lengthwise into thirds. Lightly butter 1 side of paper and soufflé dish. Wrap paper around outside of dish, buttered side against dish, allowing it to extend 3 inches above rim; secure with tape. Sprinkle sides of dish with 2 tablespoons sugar.
• **Sprinkle** gelatin over cold water in a saucepan; let stand 1 minute. Add 1 teaspoon sugar; cook over low heat, stirring until gelatin dissolves. Stir in lemon rind and juice. Set aside.
• **Combine** meringue powder, 1 cup sugar, and water in a large bowl. Beat at high speed with an electric mixer 5 minutes. Gradually add remaining ½ cup sugar, and beat at high speed 5 minutes or until stiff peaks form. Fold in gelatin mixture.
• **Beat** whipping cream until soft peaks form. Fold into gelatin mixture.
• **Pour** into prepared dish, and refrigerate 8 hours.
• **Remove** collar, gently pat chopped almonds around sides. Garnish, if desired. **Yield:** 8 to 10 servings.

Candied Lemon Peel

1 large lemon
2 tablespoons light corn syrup
1 tablespoon sugar

• **Peel** the lemon, and cut rind into ¼-inch-wide strips. (Reserve lemon for another use.)
• **Combine** lemon rind and corn syrup in a small saucepan; bring to a boil over medium heat; reduce heat, and cook 3 to 4 minutes.
• **Toss** lemon rind with sugar to coat; spread on wax paper to dry. **Yield:** about ⅓ cup.

Barbara Crowe
Birmingham, Alabama

CINNAMON-CHOCOLATE CREAM

3 egg yolks, lightly beaten
2 cups whipping cream, divided
16 (1-ounce) squares semisweet chocolate
½ cup light corn syrup
½ cup butter or margarine
¼ cup sifted powdered sugar
¼ to ½ teaspoon ground cinnamon
1 teaspoon vanilla extract
Sweetened whipped cream (optional)

• **Combine** egg yolks and ½ cup whipping cream; set aside.
• **Combine** chocolate, corn syrup, and butter in a heavy saucepan; cook over low heat, stirring constantly, until chocolate melts. Gradually stir chocolate mixture into egg mixture. Return to saucepan.
• **Cook** over medium heat, stirring constantly, 3 to 5 minutes or until mixture reaches 160°. Cool.
• **Beat** remaining 1½ cups whipping cream until foamy; gradually add powdered sugar and cinnamon, beating until soft peaks form. Stir in vanilla. Stir 1 cup whipped cream mixture into chocolate mixture.
• **Fold** remaining whipped cream mixture into chocolate mixture. Pour into individual serving dishes.
• **Cover** and refrigerate 8 hours. Serve each with a dollop of sweetened whipped cream, if desired. **Yield:** 10 to 12 servings.

Becky Griffin
Woodstock, Georgia

YOU'RE INVITED TO A RECIPE SWAP

All of us are looking for good recipes for special occasions as well as weeknight meals. The hunt is over. Here we offer recipes versatile enough for company and your family.

CHICKEN-ALMOND CASSEROLE

4 cups chopped, cooked chicken
2 cups finely chopped celery
¼ cup finely chopped onion
2 hard-cooked eggs, chopped
½ cup slivered almonds, toasted
2 (10¾-ounce) cans cream of chicken soup, undiluted
½ to 1 cup mayonnaise
½ cup chicken broth
¼ cup lemon juice
½ teaspoon salt
¼ teaspoon pepper
1 cup crushed round buttery crackers

• **Combine** first 11 ingredients. Spoon into a 13- x 9- x 2-inch lightly greased baking dish. Sprinkle with cracker crumbs.
• **Bake** at 350° for 40 minutes. **Yield:** 8 to 10 servings.

♥ To reduce fat and cholesterol, you can substitute reduced-sodium, reduced-fat cream of chicken soup and reduced-fat mayonnaise.

Louise N. Mayer
Richmond, Virginia

BOILED SHRIMP SUPPER

3 quarts water
2 (6-ounce) packages dry shrimp-
    and-crab boil seasoning
1½ pounds new potatoes,
    unpeeled
1 pound boiling onions (about
    1-inch diameter)
4 ears fresh corn, halved
1½ pounds unpeeled, large fresh
    shrimp
Lemon wedges
Commercial cocktail sauce

• **Combine** water and seasoning bags
in a Dutch oven.
• **Bring** to a boil. Add vegetables; return to a boil, and cook for 10 to 15
minutes or until potatoes are tender.
• **Add** shrimp; cook, stirring constantly, 3 to 5 minutes or until shrimp
turn pink.
• **Drain** mixture; remove and discard
seasoning bags. Serve immediately
with lemon and cocktail sauce. **Yield:**
4 servings.

Lauren Salter
Alpharetta, Georgia

ARABIC RICE

1½ pounds lean ground beef
3 tablespoons garlic powder
2 tablespoons ground cinnamon
1 tablespoon ground allspice
2 cups long-grain rice, uncooked
1 tablespoon beef-flavored
    bouillon granules
4 cups water
¼ cup pine nuts, toasted
Rice wine vinegar or lemon juice

• **Combine** first 4 ingredients in a large
skillet; cook over medium heat until
meat is browned, stirring until it crumbles. Stir in rice, bouillon granules, and
water.
• **Bring** to a boil. Cover, reduce heat,
and cook 20 minutes or until rice is
tender and liquid is absorbed.
• **Sprinkle** with pine nuts, and serve
with vinegar. **Yield:** 6 servings.

Van Chaplin
Birmingham, Alabama

VIVA VINEGARS

Jewel-toned vinegars sparkle in Cindie Hackney's kitchen
in Longview, Texas. The liquid hues of rose, deep gold, and pale yellow
transform decorative bottles into works of art to delight both the eye
and the taste buds. Garden-fresh herbs combine with the robust bite of
assorted vinegars, creating a tingling, slightly mysterious flavor.
These creative home-bottled concoctions give a personal touch to
everything from salads and marinades to salsas and sauces.

SOUTHWEST VINEGAR

1 large bunch fresh cilantro
10 to 12 fresh jalapeño peppers,
    unseeded and cut in half
    lengthwise
10 to 12 cloves garlic, cut in half
    lengthwise
1 lime, thinly sliced
10 to 12 dried tomato halves
1 teaspoon black peppercorns
5 (17-ounce) bottles white wine
    vinegar
Fresh cilantro sprigs and lime
    slices (optional)

• **Twist** cilantro stems gently. Place
cilantro and next 5 ingredients in a
large glass container.
• **Bring** vinegar to a boil, and pour
over cilantro mixture. Cover and let
stand at room temperature 2 weeks.
• **Pour** mixture through a large wire-
mesh strainer into decorative bottles,
discarding solids. Thread additional
cilantro sprigs and lime slices onto
wooden skewers, if desired, and place
in bottles. Seal bottles, and store in a
cool, dark place. **Yield:** 10 cups.

TOMATO-HERB VINEGAR

10 large sprigs fresh rosemary
6 large sprigs fresh basil
4 large sprigs fresh oregano
12 cloves garlic, peeled and
    halved
10 dried tomato halves
1 teaspoon black peppercorns
3 (32-ounce) bottles red wine
    vinegar
Fresh rosemary sprigs
    (optional)

• **Twist** stems of herbs gently, and
press garlic with back of spoon. Place
herbs and garlic in a large glass container. Add tomatoes and peppercorns.
Set aside.
• **Bring** vinegar to a boil, and pour
over herb mixture. Cover vinegar mixture and let stand at room temperature
2 weeks.
• **Pour** vinegar mixture through a large
wire-mesh strainer into decorative bottles, discarding solids. Add additional
rosemary sprigs, if desired. Seal bottles,
and store in a cool, dark place. **Yield:**
11 cups.

TARRAGON VINEGAR

1 bunch fresh tarragon (about 14 sprigs)
7 (17-ounce) bottles champagne wine vinegar
Fresh tarragon sprigs (optional)

● **Twist** tarragon gently, and place in a large glass container. Set aside.
● **Bring** vinegar to a boil, and pour over tarragon. Cover and let stand at room temperature 2 weeks.
● **Pour** vinegar mixture through a wire-mesh strainer into decorative bottles, discarding solids. Add additional tarragon sprigs, if desired. Seal bottles, and store in a cool, dark place. **Yield:** about 16 cups.

LEMON-ROSEMARY CHICKEN

Just marinating the chicken for one hour adds flavor. Serve it with risotto and a Caesar salad.

4 skinned and boned chicken breast halves *
1 cup olive oil
⅓ cup lemon juice
⅓ cup Tomato-Herb Vinegar (see recipe on facing page)
4 or 5 sprigs fresh rosemary

● **Place** chicken in a shallow dish, and set aside.
● **Combine** olive oil, lemon juice, and Tomato-Herb Vinegar, stirring with a wire whisk. Divide olive oil mixture in half, reserving 1 portion.
● **Pour** remaining olive oil mixture over chicken, turning to coat. Add rosemary. Cover and refrigerate 1 hour. Drain chicken, discarding olive oil mixture and rosemary.
● **Cook** chicken, without grill lid, over medium coals (300° to 350°) 10 minutes on each side or until done, basting with reserved olive oil mixture. **Yield:** 4 servings.

* Bone-in chicken breast halves may be substituted; grill 45 minutes or until chicken is done.

SUMMER TOMATO SALAD

(pictured on page 188)

2 medium-size ripe tomatoes, sliced
8 ounces fresh mozzarella cheese or goat cheese, thinly sliced
6 large fresh basil leaves, finely chopped and divided
½ teaspoon freshly ground pepper, divided
Tarragon Vinaigrette
1 medium cucumber, thinly sliced
1 sweet onion, thinly sliced
Fresh basil leaves (optional)

● **Layer** tomato and cheese slices in a shallow dish; sprinkle with half of chopped basil and ¼ teaspoon pepper. Drizzle with ¼ cup Tarragon Vinaigrette. Top with cucumber and onion slices; sprinkle with remaining chopped basil and pepper, and drizzle with remaining ¼ cup vinaigrette.
● **Cover** and chill 4 hours. Serve on a basil leaf-lined plate, if desired. **Yield:** 4 to 6 servings.

Note: Fresh mozzarella cheese is available at gourmet grocery stores and large supermarkets.

Tarragon Vinaigrette

¼ cup Tarragon Vinegar (see recipe)
¼ cup olive oil
1 tablespoon chopped fresh basil
½ teaspoon lemon juice
½ teaspoon finely chopped green onions
½ teaspoon honey
¼ teaspoon Dijon mustard

● **Combine** all ingredients in container of an electric blender; process until smooth. **Yield:** ½ cup.

AVOCADO-CORN SALSA

This salsa makes a clever topper for tortilla soup.

4 ears fresh yellow corn
1 jalapeño pepper, seeded and chopped
1 medium tomato, chopped
¼ cup chopped sweet red pepper
¼ cup chopped purple onion
¼ cup finely chopped fresh cilantro
⅓ cup Southwest Vinegar (see recipe on facing page)
2 tablespoons lime juice
½ teaspoon salt
1 large avocado, peeled and chopped

● **Cook** corn 5 minutes in boiling water; drain. Cut kernels from cob.
● **Combine** corn and remaining ingredients. Cover and refrigerate up to 8 hours, if desired. Serve with tortilla chips or grilled fish or chicken. **Yield:** 4 cups.

Note: If you need a recipe for Tortilla Soup, see *1993 Southern Living Annual Recipes,* page 274.

CINDIE'S TIPS

■ Wash decorative bottles in a hot wash cycle, and dry completely.
■ Give fresh herbs a spin in a salad spinner to remove moisture.
■ To speed the steeping process, pour hot vinegar over herbs. For maximum flavor, steep twice.
■ Anchor lime slices, garlic cloves, or jalapeño peppers on wooden skewers for garnish.
■ Remove herbs used for garnish when they are no longer submerged in the vinegar.
■ Sediment naturally occurs in vinegar and doesn't impair flavor.
■ Store vinegars in a cool, dark place up to six months.

WE'VE A HEAD FOR LETTUCE

. . . .

If you find yourself confused by specialty lettuces, such as arugula, sorrel, and escarole, then we have just the recipes for you. All are made from iceberg – that familiar round, light-green head of lettuce.

MEXICAN SALAD

½ head iceberg lettuce, torn
1 (16-ounce) can black beans or
    chili hot beans, drained
1 large tomato, chopped
½ cup chopped onion
2 cups (8 ounces) shredded
    Cheddar cheese
Commercial spicy-sweet French
    dressing
Corn chips

• **Combine** first 5 ingredients; toss gently. Drizzle with dressing; sprinkle with corn chips. Serve immediately. **Yield:** 6 servings.

Rubye Bailey
Knoxville, Tennessee

GREEK SALAD

1 head iceberg lettuce,
    shredded
1 small purple onion, thinly
    sliced
½ cup pepperoncini salad
    peppers
½ cup kalamata olives
4 ounces crumbled feta cheese
½ cup commercial red wine
    vinaigrette

• **Combine** all ingredients in a large bowl; toss gently, and serve immediately. **Yield:** 6 servings.

Greg Dowling
Montgomery, Alabama

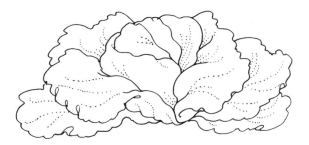

TIP OF THE ICEBERG

■ Look for springy-firm heads of iceberg lettuce. Don't worry about rust spots; they're just a harmless discoloration.

■ It's easy to core lettuce. Tap the core end of the head firmly against a counter or tabletop. Then pull or twist out the core. If tapping doesn't do it, simply remove the core with a knife.

■ Rinse lettuce, core end up, with cool running water, spreading the cut edges of the leaves so water runs between them. Then, with core end down, shake gently, and continue to drain in a colander or dish drainer.

BLUE CHEESE-STUFFED LETTUCE SALAD

1 head iceberg lettuce
2 (3-ounce) packages cream
    cheese, softened
⅓ cup crumbled blue cheese
2 tablespoons milk
¼ teaspoon dry mustard
Dash of ground red pepper
Dash of salt
Dash of black pepper
Commercial Italian salad dressing
Garnish: fresh parsley sprigs

• **Hold** lettuce, core end down, and tap core on countertop; twist and remove core. Rinse lettuce, and drain. Set aside.
• **Combine** cream cheese and next 6 ingredients in a bowl; spoon into cavity of lettuce. Wrap in plastic wrap.
• **Refrigerate** 8 hours. Cut into 6 wedges, and serve with dressing. Garnish, if desired. **Yield:** 6 servings.

Elizabeth Andress
Arlington, Virginia

DATE-NUT LETTUCE SANDWICH

1 (8-ounce) package cream cheese,
    softened
2 tablespoons chopped dates
2 tablespoons chopped walnuts,
    toasted
1 tablespoon sour cream
¼ teaspoon grated orange rind
8 slices whole wheat bread
1 cup shredded iceberg lettuce

• **Combine** first 5 ingredients.
• **Spread** date mixture evenly on 1 side of bread slices.
• **Sprinkle** lettuce evenly on 4 slices, and top with remaining slices. **Yield:** 4 servings.

Karen Marlow
Birmingham, Alabama

GRILL ONCE, *EAT TWICE*

As long as you're firing up the coals tonight, why not get a head start

on another meal? If impromptu grilling is more your style, don't despair.

You can easily grill and serve these dishes the same day.

GRILLED VEGETABLE SALAD
(pictured on page 186)

⅓ cup white balsamic vinegar
2 tablespoons olive oil
2 shallots, finely chopped
1 teaspoon dried Italian seasoning
¼ teaspoon salt
¼ teaspoon pepper
1½ teaspoons molasses
½ pound carrots, scraped
1 sweet red pepper, seeded
1 sweet yellow pepper, seeded
2 zucchini
2 yellow squash
1 large onion

• **Combine** first 7 ingredients in a large bowl. Set aside.
• **Cut** carrots and remaining vegetables into large pieces.
• **Add** vegetables to vinegar mixture, tossing to coat. Let stand 30 minutes, stirring occasionally.
• **Drain** vegetables, reserving vinegar mixture. Arrange vegetables in a grill basket.
• **Cook,** covered with grill lid, over medium-hot coals (350° to 400°) 15 to 20 minutes, turning occasionally.
• **Return** vegetables to reserved vinegar mixture, tossing gently.
• **Cover** and refrigerate at least 8 hours. **Yield:** 6 cups.

Margaret Jordan
Birmingham, Alabama

♥ Per 1-cup serving: Calories 103 (40% from fat)
Fat 4.9g (0.7g saturated) Cholesterol 0mg
Sodium 116mg Carbohydrate 14.6g
Fiber 3g Protein 2.3g

ROASTED CHILES RELLENOS WITH TOMATILLO SAUCE

8 Anaheim chile peppers
10 tomatillos, husked
1 small onion, sliced
2 cloves garlic, minced
¼ teaspoon salt
¼ teaspoon pepper
¼ teaspoon ground cumin
2 tablespoons chopped fresh cilantro
¾ cup canned black beans, drained and rinsed
1 cup (4 ounces) shredded reduced-fat Monterey Jack cheese
1 egg white
¼ cup egg substitute
¾ cup all-purpose flour
1 teaspoon vegetable oil
Vegetable cooking spray

• **Place** chile peppers, tomatillos, and onion on food rack of grill. Cook, covered with grill lid, over hot coals (400° to 500°) about 5 minutes on each side or until peppers look blistered, and tomatillos and onion are lightly browned.
• **Place** peppers immediately in a heavy-duty, zip-top plastic bag; seal and refrigerate at least 8 hours.
• **Place** grilled vegetables in an airtight container; refrigerate at least 8 hours.
• **Peel** peppers, and remove seeds; set aside.
• **Combine** tomatillos, onion, garlic, and next 3 ingredients in container of an electric blender. Process until smooth. Stir in cilantro; set tomatillo sauce aside.
• **Combine** black beans and cheese; spoon into peppers (some peppers may split). Set aside.
• **Beat** egg white at high speed with an electric mixer until stiff peaks form; gradually beat in egg substitute. Set aside.
• **Coat** stuffed peppers with flour; dip in egg white mixture, and lightly re-coat peppers with flour.
• **Add** oil to a large nonstick skillet coated with cooking spray. Cook chiles in hot oil on both sides until lightly browned. Serve immediately with tomatillo sauce. **Yield:** 4 servings.

Note: Instead of grilling 8 Anaheim chile peppers, substitute 3 (4-ounce) cans whole green chiles, drained.

♥ Per serving: Calories 311 (23% from fat)
Fat 8.3g (3.2g saturated) Cholesterol 19mg
Sodium 523mg Carbohydrate 42.8g
Fiber 8.2g Protein 18.9g

KICK THE COUCH POTATO ROUTINE

....

■ Your body will respond to exercise, if you nudge it gently. If 10 minutes is all the exercise you can handle, then start with that and gradually increase it.

■ Tired of nibbling on salad while your friends order everything on the menu? Here's how to have four courses under 400 calories: Start with a consommé or vegetable-based soup and follow with a green salad and low-calorie dressing. For an entrée, order shrimp cocktail and an à la carte vegetable. Have fresh fruit for dessert.

■ Don't be fat phobic. Use fats, but select those with lots of flavor and use less. Use real butter, try sesame oil for stir-frying, and keep walnut oil for salad dressings.

BASIL-STUFFED CHICKEN WITH TOMATO-BASIL PASTA
(pictured on page 185)

4 (4-ounce) skinned and boned
   chicken breast halves
¼ teaspoon salt
¼ teaspoon garlic powder
2 bunches fresh basil (about 20
   large basil leaves)
Tomato-Basil Pasta
Garnish: fresh basil sprigs

● **Place** each piece of chicken between 2 sheets of heavy-duty plastic wrap; flatten to ¼-inch thickness, using a rolling pin or meat mallet.
● **Sprinkle** chicken breasts evenly with salt and garlic powder.
● **Arrange** basil leaves in a single layer over chicken breasts. Starting at short end, roll up 2 chicken breasts. Place each roll on top of a remaining chicken breast, and roll up, forming two larger rolls. Secure chicken with wooden picks.
● **Cook,** covered with grill lid, over medium-hot coals (350° to 400°) 18 to 20 minutes, turning once.
● **Wrap** in aluminum foil, and refrigerate at least 8 hours.
● **Remove** chicken rolls from refrigerator, and unwrap. Place chicken rolls on a microwave-safe plate, and cover with wax paper.
● **Microwave** at MEDIUM-HIGH (70% power) 1½ minutes, turning once. Remove wooden picks.
● **Cut** each chicken roll into thin slices. Serve on individual plates with tomato-Basil Pasta. Garnish, if desired. **Yield:** 4 servings.

♥ Per serving: Calories 387 (13% from fat)
Fat 5.4g (1.2g saturated) Cholesterol 70mg
Sodium 252mg Carbohydrate 46.7g
Fiber 2g Protein 33.7g

Tomato-Basil Pasta

1 tablespoon reduced-calorie
   margarine
2 cloves garlic, minced
¼ cup lemon juice
¼ cup Chablis or other dry white
   wine
¼ cup chopped fresh basil
1 cup peeled, seeded, and finely
   chopped tomato
8 ounces thin spaghetti, cooked
   without salt or fat

● **Melt** margarine in a large saucepan over medium heat; add minced garlic, and cook 1 minute, stirring constantly. Add the lemon juice and remaining ingredients; toss gently. **Yield:** 4 servings.

♥ Per serving: Calories 249 (9% from fat)
Fat 2.5g (0.4g saturated) Cholesterol 0mg
Sodium 44mg Carbohydrate 46.5g
Fiber 2g Protein 7.9g

GRILL SKILLS

■ When grilling two meals at once, make tomorrow's dinner first – that way you'll be sure tonight's dinner is served hot. If your grill is big enough, cook both at once.

■ When the coals are covered with a gray ash, it's time to get dinner on the grill. The coals will stay hot enough to cook for about an hour.

■ Reduce fat by coating the food rack with cooking spray before placing food over the fire instead of brushing oil on it. Food won't stick, and cleanup will be easier.

■ Soak wood chips in water for 30 minutes. Drain the chips, and toss them on the coals just before lighting the coals. You'll get flavor, without adding fat.

■ Hinged grill baskets prevent small pieces of food from falling through the food rack. Another advantage is that you don't have to turn the foods individually.

■ Everything tastes better when it's cooked on a grill – even low-fat food like fish.

■ Don't throw away dried herbs that have been sitting on your kitchen shelves for years. Instead, moisten a handful, and sprinkle them over hot coals before grilling to add extra flavor.

■ Spray water on a flare-up only as a last resort; it could damage the finish of the grill while it's hot.

SEARED TUNA STEAKS ON MIXED GREENS WITH LEMON-BASIL VINAIGRETTE

This recipe works with shrimp, too.

4 (4-ounce) tuna steaks
1 tablespoon reduced-sodium Cajun seasoning
Vegetable cooking spray
8 cups mixed salad greens
Lemon-Basil Vinaigrette
Garnish: finely chopped sweet red pepper

• **Sprinkle** tuna steaks evenly with seasoning.
• **Coat** food rack with cooking spray; place on grill over medium-hot coals (350° to 400°). Place tuna on rack.
• **Cook,** covered with grill lid, 5 minutes on each side or until done.
• **Cover** and refrigerate at least 8 hours.
• **Combine** salad greens and half of Lemon-Basil Vinaigrette; arrange on 4 plates. Top each with a tuna steak, and drizzle evenly with remaining vinaigrette. Garnish, if desired. **Yield:** 4 servings.

♥ Per serving: Calories 189 (24% from fat)
Fat 5.1g (0.3g saturated) Cholesterol 51mg
Sodium 59mg Carbohydrate 7.7g
Fiber 2.4g Protein 28.4g

Lemon-Basil Vinaigrette

2 lemons, peeled, sectioned, and finely chopped
2 tablespoons white wine vinegar
1 tablespoon vegetable oil
1 tablespoon fresh basil, finely chopped
¼ teaspoon cracked black pepper
¼ teaspoon hot sauce

• **Combine** all ingredients in a jar. Cover tightly, and shake vigorously. **Yield:** ½ cup.

Sally Koch
Metairie, Louisiana

♥ Per 2 tablespoons: Calories 40 (72% from fat)
Fat 3.5g (0g saturated) Cholesterol 0mg
Sodium 4mg Carbohydrate 2.7g
Fiber 0.1g Protein 0.3g

WEEKDAY WAFFLES

If the only waffle you've ever known comes from your grocer's freezer case, you're in for a delightful surprise. We've got waffles in flavors that will chase the sleep from your eyes in the morning and satisfy your sweet tooth after dinner.

FUDGE WAFFLES

2 large eggs
¼ cup butter or margarine, melted
1 teaspoon vanilla extract
1 cup buttermilk
1 cup all-purpose flour
½ teaspoon baking powder
½ teaspoon baking soda
¼ teaspoon salt
¼ teaspoon ground nutmeg
¾ cup sugar
½ cup cocoa
½ cup chopped walnuts (optional)
¼ cup semisweet chocolate mini-morsels (optional)
Vanilla ice cream
Chocolate-Peppermint Sauce (see recipe)
Garnish: crushed hard peppermint candy

• **Combine** first 3 ingredients in a large mixing bowl; beat at medium speed with an electric mixer until foamy (about 2 minutes). Add buttermilk, mixing well. Set aside.
• **Combine** flour and next 6 ingredients; gradually add to egg mixture, beating at low speed just until blended.
• **Stir** in walnuts and mini-morsels, if desired.

• **Bake** in a preheated, oiled waffle iron until done. Serve with vanilla ice cream and warm Chocolate-Peppermint Sauce. Garnish, if desired. **Yield:** 18 (4-inch) waffles.

Priscilla A. Nackley
Marietta, Georgia

CHOCOLATE-PEPPERMINT SAUCE

1 cup semisweet chocolate morsels
½ to ⅔ cup half-and-half, divided
¼ cup finely crushed hard peppermint candy

• **Combine** chocolate morsels, ½ cup half-and-half, and candy in a small saucepan; cook over low heat about 10 minutes or until candy melts, stirring occasionally.
• **Stir** in enough of remaining half-and-half for desired consistency. Serve over waffles, pound cake, or ice cream. Store sauce in refrigerator up to 2 weeks. **Yield:** 1¼ cups.

Marsha Littrell
Sheffield, Alabama

HONEY-BUTTERED PEANUT BUTTER WAFFLES

⅓ cup chunky peanut butter
1 cup pancake mix
2 tablespoons sugar
1 (5-ounce) can evaporated milk
½ cup water
1 large egg
Honey Butter

• **Place** peanut butter in a 1-quart glass bowl. Microwave at HIGH 20 to 30 seconds.
• **Add** pancake mix and next 4 ingredients; beat at medium speed with an electric mixer just until smooth.
• **Bake** in a preheated, oiled waffle iron until golden. Serve with Honey Butter. **Yield:** 8 (4-inch) waffles.

Honey Butter

¼ cup butter or margarine, softened
2 tablespoons honey

• **Combine** butter and honey, stirring until blended. **Yield:** ⅓ cup.

Valerie G. Stutsman
Norfolk, Virginia

BANANA-OATMEAL WAFFLES

1¼ cups all-purpose flour
1 tablespoon baking powder
½ teaspoon baking soda
¾ cup regular oats, uncooked
3 tablespoons brown sugar
¼ teaspoon ground cinnamon
Pinch of ground nutmeg
1½ cups buttermilk
2 large eggs
¼ cup butter or margarine, melted
2 medium bananas, sliced
Praline Sauce (see recipe)

• **Position** knife blade in food processor bowl; add first 10 ingredients. Process until smooth, stopping once to scrape down sides.
• **Add** bananas; pulse 3 or 4 times.
• **Bake** in a preheated, oiled waffle iron until golden. (Waffles will be slightly

soft.) Serve with warm Praline Sauce or syrup. **Yield:** 12 (4-inch) waffles.

Becky Bradshaw
North Richland Hills, Texas

PRALINE SAUCE

1 cup firmly packed brown sugar
½ cup chopped pecans
½ cup light corn syrup
¼ cup water
Dash of salt
1 tablespoon butter or margarine
1 teaspoon vanilla extract

• **Combine** first 5 ingredients in a small saucepan; bring to a boil, stirring constantly, until sugar dissolves. Remove from heat.
• **Stir** in butter and vanilla. Serve sauce over waffles or ice cream. Store sauce in refrigerator up to 2 weeks. **Yield:** 1½ cups.

LaJuan Coward
Jasper, Texas

BELGIAN WAFFLES

4 large eggs, separated
3 tablespoons butter or margarine, melted
½ teaspoon vanilla extract
1 cup all-purpose flour
½ teaspoon salt
1 cup milk
Sweetened whipped cream
Sliced fresh strawberries

• **Beat** egg yolks at medium speed with an electric mixer until thick and pale. Add butter and vanilla, beating until blended. Set aside.
• **Combine** flour and salt. Add flour mixture and milk to egg mixture, beating until smooth. Set aside.
• **Beat** egg whites until stiff peaks form; fold into batter.
• **Bake** in a preheated, oiled Belgian waffle iron until golden. Serve with sweetened whipped cream and strawberries. **Yield:** 8 (4-inch) waffles.

Jane Maloy
Wilmington, North Carolina

CORN-CHILE WAFFLES

For a change of pace, try these waffles in place of traditional cornbread.

1½ cups yellow cornmeal
1½ cups all-purpose flour
1½ teaspoons baking soda
¼ teaspoon salt
½ teaspoon chili powder
3 large eggs, separated
1 (8¾-ounce) can cream-style corn
2¼ cups buttermilk
⅓ cup butter or margarine, melted
1 (4½-ounce) can chopped green chiles, drained

• **Combine** first 5 ingredients in a large bowl; make a well in center of mixture. Set aside.
• **Combine** egg yolks and next 4 ingredients; add to dry ingredients, stirring just until moistened. Set aside.
• **Beat** egg whites until stiff peaks form; fold into batter.
• **Bake** in a preheated, oiled waffle iron until golden. Serve with butter or salsa. **Yield:** 16 (4-inch) waffles.

CLUB SODA WAFFLES

2¼ cups biscuit mix
3 tablespoons vegetable oil
1 large egg
1 (10-ounce) bottle club soda
Garnish: fresh strawberries

• **Combine** first 3 ingredients in a large mixing bowl; beat at medium speed with an electric mixer until smooth. Slowly add club soda, beating until smooth.
• **Bake** in a preheated, oiled waffle iron until golden. Garnish, if desired, and serve with maple syrup. **Yield:** 14 (4-inch) waffles.

Mrs. Robert L. Humphrey
Palestine, Texas

SEPTEMBER

DREAM PIES

These shivery drifts of Southern tradition are the ethereal

sweets of the dessert world. When a billowy wedge lands on

your dessert plate, dinner ends on a blissful note.

CHOCOLATE CREAM PIE

1¼ cups sugar
½ cup all-purpose flour
¼ cup cocoa
Dash of salt
4 egg yolks
2 cups milk
¼ cup butter or margarine
1 teaspoon vanilla extract
1 baked 9-inch pastry shell
Meringue (see recipe)

• **Combine** first 4 ingredients in a large heavy saucepan; set sugar mixture aside.
• **Combine** egg yolks and milk; stir into sugar mixture. Add butter.
• **Cook** over medium heat, stirring constantly, until mixture thickens and boils. Remove from heat. Stir in vanilla. Spoon into pastry shell.
• **Spread** Meringue over hot filling, sealing to edge of pastry.
• **Bake** at 325° for 25 to 28 minutes. **Yield:** one 9-inch pie.

Maryanne I. Kachelhofer
Birmingham, Alabama

BEST-EVER LEMON MERINGUE PIE

(pictured on page 1)

1½ cups sugar
½ cup cornstarch
⅛ teaspoon salt
4 egg yolks
1¾ cups water
½ cup lemon juice
3 tablespoons butter or margarine
1 teaspoon grated lemon rind
1 baked 9-inch pastry shell
Meringue (see recipe)

• **Combine** first 3 ingredients in a large heavy saucepan; set sugar mixture aside.
• **Combine** egg yolks, water, and juice; stir into sugar mixture. Cook over medium heat, stirring constantly, until mixture thickens and boils. Boil 1 minute, stirring constantly. Remove from heat. Stir in butter and lemon rind. Spoon into pastry shell.
• **Spread** Meringue over hot filling, sealing to edge of pastry.
• **Bake** at 325° for 25 to 28 minutes. **Yield:** one 9-inch pie.

Anne Galbraith
Knoxville, Tennessee

Note: This pie is very firm with a bright yellow color. If you prefer a less firm pie with a more translucent color, substitute ⅓ cup cornstarch for ½ cup cornstarch and cook as directed.

ORANGE-COCONUT CREAM PIE

1 cup sugar
3 tablespoons all-purpose flour
3 tablespoons cornstarch
¼ teaspoon salt
3 egg yolks
1½ cups water
¾ cup orange juice
2 tablespoons lemon juice
¾ cup flaked coconut
1 tablespoon grated orange rind
1 baked 9-inch pastry shell
Meringue (see recipe)
1 to 2 tablespoons flaked coconut (optional)

• **Combine** first 4 ingredients in a large, heavy saucepan; set mixture aside.
• **Combine** egg yolks and next 3 ingredients. Gradually stir egg yolk mixture into sugar mixture.
• **Cook** over medium heat, stirring constantly, until mixture thickens and boils. Remove from heat.
• **Stir** in ¾ cup coconut and orange rind. Spoon into pastry shell.
• **Spread** Meringue over hot filling, sealing to edge of pastry. Sprinkle top of pie with 1 to 2 tablespoons coconut, if desired.
• **Bake** at 325° for 25 to 28 minutes. **Yield:** one 9-inch pie.

Ruth Sams
Covington, Georgia

MERINGUE

(pictured on page 1)

4 to 6 egg whites
½ to ¾ teaspoon cream of tartar
½ cup sugar
½ teaspoon vanilla extract

• **Beat** egg whites and cream of tartar at high speed with an electric mixer just until foamy.
• **Gradually** add sugar, 1 tablespoon at a time, beating until stiff peaks form and sugar dissolves (2 to 4 minutes). Add vanilla, beating well. **Yield:** enough for one 9-inch pie.

RASPBERRY CREAM PIE

(pictured on page 1)

1 cup sugar
⅓ cup all-purpose flour
2 large eggs, lightly beaten
1⅓ cups sour cream
1 teaspoon vanilla extract
3 cups fresh raspberries
1 unbaked 9-inch pastry shell
⅓ cup all-purpose flour
⅓ cup firmly packed brown sugar
⅓ cup chopped pecans
3 tablespoons butter, softened
Garnishes: whipped cream, fresh
   raspberries

● **Combine** first 5 ingredients in a large bowl, stirring until smooth. Gradually fold in raspberries. Spoon into pastry shell.
● **Bake** at 400° for 30 to 35 minutes or until a knife inserted in center comes out clean.
● **Combine** ⅓ cup flour and next 3 ingredients; sprinkle over hot pie.
● **Bake** at 400° for 10 minutes or until golden. Garnish, if desired. **Yield:** one 9-inch pie.

Nell Hamm
Louisville, Mississippi

Note: Do not substitute frozen raspberries in this pie.

COFFEE CREAM PIE

(pictured on page 1)

¼ cup butter or margarine
⅔ cup semisweet chocolate
   morsels
1⅓ cups graham cracker crumbs
½ cup sugar
3 tablespoons cornstarch
1 teaspoon instant coffee
   granules
¼ cup boiling water
1¼ cups milk
5 egg yolks, lightly beaten
1¾ cups whipping cream
¼ cup sifted powdered sugar
Garnish: chocolate-covered coffee
   beans

● **Melt** butter and chocolate morsels in a heavy saucepan over low heat. Stir in graham cracker crumbs. Firmly press into a lightly greased 9-inch pieplate. Bake at 375° for 8 minutes. Cool pie shell completely on a wire rack.
● **Combine** ½ cup sugar and cornstarch in a large heavy saucepan; set sugar mixture aside.
● **Combine** coffee granules and boiling water, stirring until coffee granules dissolve. Gradually stir coffee, milk, and egg yolks into sugar mixture.
● **Cook** over medium heat, stirring constantly, until mixture thickens and boils. Boil 1 minute, stirring constantly. Remove from heat; whisk until smooth. Place plastic wrap directly on surface of mixture; chill 1 hour.
● **Beat** whipping cream at low speed with an electric mixer until foamy; gradually add powdered sugar, beating until soft peaks form.
● **Fold** 1½ cups whipped cream into coffee mixture, reserving remaining whipped cream for topping. Spoon filling into baked pie shell.
● **Pipe** or dollop remaining cream on top of pie. Chill up to 8 hours. Garnish, if desired. **Yield:** one 9-inch pie.

Agnes L. Stone
Ocala, Florida

"They sit up so tall. People see them through the glass and try to resist them, but they just can't."

—*Richard Lawrence*
Bryce's Cafeteria
Texarkana, Texas

Richard Lawrence who, with his brother, Bryce, owns Bryce's Cafeteria, knows very well why he sells more than 4,800 slices of cream and meringue pies each week at the Texas Eatery.

Because they stand so high and mighty, meringue-topped pies are intimidating to some beginning cooks. But they're really as easy as they are airy. Our four-ingredient Meringue recipe (on the facing page) will raise your confidence to majestic heights. The more egg whites you use, the higher the meringue will be.

Some pies, such as lemon meringue, are a delicious collision of tart and sweet tastes. Others are sublimely sweet, the stuff great bowl-licking is made of.

MAGNOLIA PIE

1½ cups sugar
¼ cup all-purpose flour
⅓ cup butter or margarine,
  softened
3 large eggs
1 cup buttermilk
1 teaspoon vanilla extract
½ teaspoon lemon extract
1 unbaked 9-inch pastry shell
Garnishes: whipped cream, lemon
  slices

• **Combine** first 3 ingredients; beat at medium speed with an electric mixer until blended. Add eggs, buttermilk, and flavorings. Beat at low speed until blended. Pour into pastry shell.
• **Bake** at 325° for 1 hour or until a knife inserted in center comes out clean. Cool on a wire rack. Garnish, if desired. **Yield:** one 9-inch pie.

Mrs. H. W. Walker
Richmond, Virginia

A PIE IN YOUR FACE

Since silent film days, cream pies as ballistic instruments have been one of Hollywood's favorite comic props. It all began in the 1913 film *A Noise From the Deep*, when actress Mabel Normand sent a pie flying into Fatty Arbuckle's face.

In the 1927 film, *The Battle of the Century*, Laurel and Hardy threw 3,000 cream pies, a Hollywood record. Later, the Three Stooges were launching pies and falling on banana peels in classic slapstick routines.

More recently, pies have been thrown with malice rather than wild abandon. A Key lime pie was sacrificed in the film *Heartburn* when actress Meryl Streep slapped it to Jack Nicholson's forehead. Contrary to Hollywood tradition, Jack didn't think it was funny.

CHOCOLATE-BANANA-PECAN
CREAM PIE

¼ cup butter or margarine,
  softened
1 (3-ounce) package cream cheese,
  softened
1½ cups sifted powdered sugar
¼ cup whipping cream
½ teaspoon vanilla extract
3 bananas, sliced
1 (6-ounce) can pineapple juice
1 baked 9-inch pastry shell
½ cup chopped pecans,
  toasted
2 (1-ounce) squares semisweet
  chocolate
1 cup whipping cream
3 tablespoons powdered sugar

• **Beat** butter and cream cheese at medium speed with an electric mixer until creamy; gradually add 1½ cups powdered sugar alternately with ¼ cup whipping cream, beginning and ending with powdered sugar. Stir in vanilla. Set filling aside.
• **Toss** banana slices in pineapple juice; drain. Pat slices dry with paper towels.
• **Spoon** half of filling into baked pastry shell. Arrange banana slices over top of filling. Top with remaining filling, and sprinkle with pecans. Set pie aside.
• **Melt** chocolate in a heavy saucepan over low heat. Spoon into a small heavy-duty, zip-top plastic bag. Snip a tiny hole from corner of bag; drizzle melted chocolate over pecans and filling. Set aside.
• **Beat** 1 cup whipping cream at low speed with an electric mixer until foamy; gradually add 3 tablespoons powdered sugar, beating until soft peaks form.
• **Spoon** whipped cream into a large heavy-duty, zip-top plastic bag. Snip ½ inch from corner of bag. Pipe dollops around outside edge of pie. **Yield:** one 9-inch pie.

Joel Allard
San Antonio, Texas

FROM OUR
KITCHEN TO YOURS

Homemade pies – prized, but not often baked – *are* easy. Here we offer beginning bakers a basic pastry recipe with easy-to-follow steps to accompany our "Dream Pies" story beginning on page 208. With our pastry recipe and tips, you no longer have to travel to Grandma's or the local diner for a piece of your favorite pie. All you need is a little patient practice. The pastry stirs together in 5 minutes, chills in the freezer, and is ready to roll in 35 minutes.

BASIC PASTRY

1¼ cups all-purpose flour
½ teaspoon salt
½ cup shortening
3 to 4 tablespoons cold water

• **Combine** flour and salt in a medium bowl; cut in shortening with pastry blender until crumbly.
• **Sprinkle** cold water, 1 tablespoon at a time, evenly over surface; stir mixture with a fork just until dry ingredients are moistened.
• **Shape** dough into a flattened disk; wrap in plastic wrap, and chill 2 hours or freeze 30 minutes.
• **Roll** dough out to ⅛-inch thickness on a lightly floured surface.
• **Place** in a 9-inch pieplate; trim off excess pastry along edges. Fold edges under, and crimp.
• **Prick** bottom and sides of pastry shell generously with a fork for a baked pastry shell. (Do not prick if the pastry shell is to be filled before baking.)
• **Bake** at 450° for 10 to 12 minutes or until golden brown. Cool on a wire rack. **Yield:** one 9-inch pastry shell.

PASTRY THAT'S EASY AS PIE

Here are our secrets to success for the pastry recipe on facing page.

■ For a flaky crust, the crumbly mixture needs to have irregular-size pieces of shortening as small as dried peas and as large as English peas.

■ Cold water is important; add ice to water before measuring. Add 3 tablespoons water, tossing mixture gently with a fork. To make sure you've added enough water, squeeze the dough between your fingers. If it falls apart, gradually add the remaining 1 tablespoon water. (Don't overstir because it will toughen dough.)

■ Chilling dough gives the flour time to absorb the water.

■ Before rolling the dough, let it stand at room temperature 5 minutes to help soften the fat. Using a cloth-covered rolling pin minimizes the amount of flour needed during rolling. Roll dough from the center into a 12-inch circle.

■ To transfer pastry to a pieplate, fold dough in half; place in center of pieplate, and unfold. Or loosely roll the dough around the rolling pin; then starting at one side of the pieplate, unroll the dough over it. Press dough gently, without stretching, into the bottom and onto sides of the pieplate, using your fingertips. (Stretching the dough causes it to shrink during baking.) If the pastry tears, dampen the dough, and press on a scrap of rolled-out dough to repair break.

■ Trim pastry so that it extends over the pieplate rim by about one inch. Fold edge under to form a ridge, pinch the inner rim of the dough with the thumb and forefinger of one hand while pushing against the outer rim of the dough with the forefinger of the other hand. (To keep from poking holes in the pastry, bend your fingers and press with the knuckles.) To help prevent shrinking, use one of these methods: Lightly press the outer points of pastry under the rim of the pieplate; or freeze until rock hard, and bake without thawing.

■ Pricking the bottom and sides keeps the pastry from puffing during baking. If it does begin to puff, reprick the crust. (Omit for pastry that bakes with a filling.)

No-Fuss Crust

Use purchased piecrusts as a shortcut. There are several forms of commercial piecrusts available – piecrust mixes, piecrust sticks, refrigerated piecrusts, and frozen ready-to-bake pastry shells. We prefer the flavor, texture, appearance, and convenience of the refrigerated piecrust. It's closest to homemade.

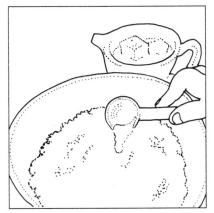

Step 1: Sprinkle cold water (1 tablespoon at a time) over crumbly mixture. Stir just until moistened.

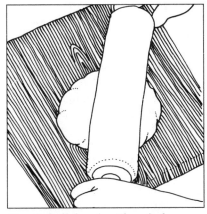

Step 2: Roll dough with a cloth-covered rolling pin to $1/8$-inch thickness on a lightly floured surface.

Step 3: Trim and fold edge of pastry; pinch edge of pastry with your fingers to crimp.

A Fresh Look At Fall

Try a seasonal menu with surprising combinations.

Chicken breasts filled with a savory sausage-pecan stuffing compose

a harmony of flavors. On another note, the unexpected pairing of apples and

pears sautéed with onions is worthy of an encore.

FALL FEAST
Serves Four

Chicken Breasts With Pecan-Sausage Stuffing
Sautéed Apples, Onions, and Pears Over Spinach
Golden Cornbread Sticks

CHICKEN BREASTS WITH PECAN-SAUSAGE STUFFING
(pictured on page 258)

⅓ pound ground pork sausage
⅓ cup butter or margarine
⅓ cup finely chopped celery
⅓ cup finely chopped green pepper
1 small onion, finely chopped
½ cup chopped pecans, divided
¼ teaspoon pepper
⅛ teaspoon salt
3 cups dry bread cubes (¼-inch pieces)
1 large egg, lightly beaten
1½ tablespoons milk
4 skinned and boned whole chicken breasts
1½ tablespoons butter or margarine, melted
3 tablespoons fine, dry breadcrumbs
Garnish: chopped fresh parsley

• **Brown** sausage in a Dutch oven, stirring until it crumbles. Remove from pan, and set aside; discard drippings.
• **Melt** ⅓ cup butter in Dutch oven over medium-high heat; add celery, green pepper, and onion. Cook, stirring constantly, until vegetables are tender.
• **Add** ⅓ cup pecans, pepper, and salt; cook 3 minutes, stirring constantly. Remove from heat; stir in sausage, bread cubes, egg, and milk. Set aside.
• **Place** each chicken breast between 2 sheets of heavy-duty plastic wrap or wax paper. Flatten chicken breasts to ¼-inch thickness, using a meat mallet or rolling pin.
• **Place** chicken breasts on a flat surface. Spoon sausage mixture evenly into center of each chicken breast. Fold long sides over filling, and secure with wooden picks. Place chicken, seam side down, in a baking pan lined with aluminum foil.

• **Combine** 1½ tablespoons melted butter, remaining pecans, and breadcrumbs; press evenly onto chicken breasts.
• **Bake** at 350° for 30 minutes or until golden brown. Garnish, if desired. **Yield:** 4 servings.

Jeanne S. Hotaling
Augusta, Georgia

SAUTÉED APPLES, ONIONS, AND PEARS OVER SPINACH
(pictured on page 258)

2 tablespoons honey
¼ cup white wine vinegar
¼ cup dry sherry or apple juice
1 tablespoon lemon juice
⅛ teaspoon salt
⅛ teaspoon ground white pepper
⅛ teaspoon dried thyme (optional)
1 small onion, sliced and separated into rings
1 tablespoon olive oil
1 pear, cored and sliced
1 cooking apple, cored and sliced
1 (10-ounce) package fresh spinach, washed and trimmed

• **Combine** first 6 ingredients; add thyme, if desired. Set aside.
• **Cook** onion in olive oil in a large skillet over medium-high heat, stirring constantly, until tender. Add pear, cooking apple, and honey mixture.
• **Cook** 5 to 6 minutes or until fruit is tender and liquid is slightly thickened, stirring often. Serve over fresh spinach. **Yield:** 4 servings.

Helen H. Maurer
Christmas, Florida

GOLDEN CORNBREAD STICKS

(pictured on page 258)

2 cups self-rising cornmeal
¼ teaspoon baking soda
1 (10¾-ounce) can golden corn
    soup, undiluted
1 cup buttermilk
2 large eggs
⅓ cup vegetable oil
1 tablespoon chopped green
    chiles
1½ cups (6 ounces) shredded
    Cheddar cheese
Vegetable cooking spray

• **Combine** cornmeal and soda in a large bowl; make a well in center.
• **Combine** soup and next 5 ingredients; add to dry ingredients, stirring just until moistened.
• **Heat** cast-iron breadstick or corn stick pans in a 450° oven 5 minutes or until hot. Remove pans from oven, and coat with cooking spray. Spoon batter into hot pans.
• **Bake** at 350° for 15 minutes or until browned. Remove from pans; cool on a wire rack. **Yield:** 2 dozen.

Ginger Spurrier
Birmingham, Alabama

FASHIONABLY MASHED

Mashed vegetables are one of the first foods we eat as children. But any notion of babyhood blandness ends with these mashed combinations. These mashed veggies will make you glad to be a grown-up.

Traditional mashed potatoes are light-years away from the flash of flavors found in Thunderbolt Potatoes. And humble turnips turn up in grand form in Sunset Orange Carrots and Turnips.

THUNDERBOLT POTATOES

(pictured on page 259)

1 cup fresh yellow corn, cut from
    cob (about 2 ears)
2 cloves garlic, minced
2 tablespoons butter, melted
4 large baking potatoes, peeled
    and quartered (about 2¾
    pounds)
½ to ¾ cup warm milk
1 teaspoon salt
⅛ teaspoon pepper
2 teaspoons chili powder
½ teaspoon ground cumin
1 (4½-ounce) can chopped
    green chiles
Garnish: chili powder

• **Cook** corn and garlic in butter in a skillet over medium-high heat, stirring constantly, until tender; set aside.
• **Cook** potato in boiling water to cover 20 minutes or until tender; drain.
• **Combine** potato and next 5 ingredients in a large mixing bowl; beat at medium speed with an electric mixer until smooth. Stir in corn mixture and chiles. Garnish, if desired. **Yield:** 4 to 6 servings.

Thunderbolt Potato Patties: (pictured on page 259) Combine 2 cups leftover Thunderbolt Potatoes, 1 large egg, and 2 tablespoons all-purpose flour. Shape mixture into eight 3-inch patties, and dredge in ½ cup cornmeal. Cook patties in ½ cup hot vegetable oil in a large skillet until golden brown, turning once. **Yield:** 8 patties.

SUNSET ORANGE CARROTS AND TURNIPS

1½ pounds carrots, scraped and
    cut into chunks
2 small fresh turnips, peeled and
    quartered *
¼ cup firmly packed brown sugar
¼ cup frozen orange juice
    concentrate, undiluted
2 tablespoons butter, melted
⅛ teaspoon ground nutmeg
Garnish: chopped parsley

• **Cook** carrot in boiling, salted water 20 minutes or until tender; drain and mash. Set aside. Repeat procedure with turnip.
• **Combine** mashed carrot and turnip in a large bowl. Stir in brown sugar and next 3 ingredients. Serve immediately. Garnish, if desired. **Yield:** 4 to 6 servings.

* 1 (1¾-pound) rutabaga may be substituted.

Laura Mobley
Boonsboro, Maryland

TURNIP PUDDING

8 fresh turnips, peeled and sliced
    (about 2½ pounds)
1 cup water
½ teaspoon salt
¼ cup chopped onion
2 tablespoons butter, melted
¼ cup milk
2 large eggs, lightly beaten
½ teaspoon salt
¼ teaspoon pepper

• **Combine** first 3 ingredients in a saucepan; bring to a boil. Cover and cook over medium heat 40 minutes or until tender. Drain well.
• **Beat** turnip at medium speed with an electric mixer 5 minutes. Set aside.
• **Cook** onion in butter in a saucepan over medium-high heat, stirring constantly, until tender. Remove from heat; stir in turnip, milk, and remaining ingredients.
• **Spoon** mixture into a greased 8-inch square baking dish.
• **Bake** at 350° for 35 to 40 minutes or until set. Serve immediately. **Yield:** 6 servings.

Louise Holmes
Winchester, Tennessee

EGGPLANT CASSEROLE

1 eggplant, peeled and
      chopped
4 slices white bread, torn
1 (5-ounce) can evaporated
      milk
1 medium onion, chopped
2 cloves garlic, minced
¼ cup butter or margarine,
      melted
2 large eggs, separated
½ teaspoon salt
¼ teaspoon pepper
¼ cup grated Parmesan
      cheese

• **Cook** eggplant in boiling water to cover 10 minutes or until tender; drain well. Mash eggplant; set aside.
• **Combine** bread and milk; let stand 10 minutes.
• **Cook** onion and garlic in butter in a large skillet over medium-high heat, stirring constantly, until tender. Add bread mixture, eggplant, egg yolks, salt, and pepper. Set aside.
• **Beat** egg whites at high speed with an electric mixer until stiff peaks form; fold into eggplant mixture. Pour into a well-greased 1½-quart baking dish; sprinkle with Parmesan cheese.
• **Bake** at 350° for 30 minutes or until set. Serve immediately. **Yield:** 4 to 6 servings.

Tad Cairns
Birmingham, Alabama

TWO FOR ONE

....

As the leaves turn and cool weather arrives, the craving for hot and spicy food begins, and Cavatini, a pasta casserole, hits the spot. The pepperoni slices and pepperoncini salad peppers lend a zesty flavor. There is something else you'll love about this recipe: It makes two casseroles. So serve one tonight, and freeze the other one for later.

CAVATINI

1 pound ground beef
1 pound mild ground pork
      sausage
1 medium onion, chopped
1 green pepper, chopped
1 (3½-ounce) package pepperoni
      slices, chopped
1 (28-ounce) can crushed
      tomatoes, undrained
1 (26½-ounce) can spaghetti
      sauce
1 (16-ounce) jar mild salsa
1 (4-ounce) can sliced mushrooms,
      drained
1 (10-ounce) jar pepperoncini
      salad peppers, drained and
      sliced
1 (16-ounce) package shell
      macaroni, cooked
1 cup grated Parmesan cheese
4 cups (16 ounces) shredded
      mozzarella cheese

• **Cook** first 4 ingredients in a large skillet over medium heat, stirring until meat browns and crumbles. Drain well; set aside.
• **Combine** chopped pepperoni and next 5 ingredients in a large bowl; stir in meat mixture and pasta shells.
• **Spoon** half of pasta mixture into 2 lightly greased 11- x 7- x 1½-inch baking dishes; sprinkle each casserole with ¼ cup Parmesan and 1 cup mozzarella cheeses. Top with remaining pasta mixture.
• **Bake** at 350° for 30 minutes or until heated; top with remaining cheeses. Bake 5 additional minutes. **Yield:** 6 servings per casserole.

Note: Unbaked casseroles may be frozen up to three months (freeze cheeses for topping separately). Thaw casseroles in refrigerator 24 hours; let stand at room temperature 30 minutes. Bake at 350° for 40 minutes; sprinkle with cheeses. Bake 5 additional minutes.

Debbie Forrest
Hartford, Kentucky

BETTER BISCUITS

When you hold a biscuit in your hand and pull it apart to release a butter-scented cloud of steam and reveal a hundred flaky layers, you know life is good.

For a biscuit recipe that's as easy as one-two-three, try this three-ingredient recipe. Once you've mastered the basics, try the variations. They're as good as the original.

BASIC BUTTERMILK BISCUITS
(pictured on page 264)

⅓ cup butter or margarine
2 cups self-rising soft-wheat flour
¾ cup buttermilk
Butter or margarine, melted

• **Cut** ⅓ cup butter into flour with pastry blender until mixture is crumbly. Add buttermilk, stirring until dry ingredients are moistened.
• **Turn** dough out onto a lightly floured surface; knead 3 or 4 times.
• **Roll** dough to ¾-inch thickness; cut with a 2½-inch round cutter, and place on a baking sheet.
• **Bake** biscuits at 425° for 12 to 14 minutes. Brush with melted butter. **Yield:** 10 biscuits.

Cornmeal-Jalapeño Biscuits: Substitute 1 cup self-rising cornmeal for 1 cup self-rising flour. Add 1 cup (4 ounces) shredded Monterey Jack cheese with peppers or 1 cup shredded sharp Cheddar cheese and 1 unseeded, chopped jalapeño pepper. Bake as directed. **Yield:** 10 biscuits.

Potato-Bacon Biscuits: (pictured on page 264) Substitute 1 cup instant potato flakes for 1 cup self-rising flour. Add 8 slices cooked and crumbled bacon and ½ cup (4 ounces) shredded Colby cheese. Bake as directed. **Yield:** 10 biscuits.

Tomato-Herb Biscuits: Substitute ⅓ cup olive oil for butter. Stir in ½ cup grated Parmesan cheese, ¼ cup chopped oil-packed dried tomatoes, 1 teaspoon dried Italian seasoning, and ¼ teaspoon pepper. Bake as directed. **Yield:** 10 biscuits.

Country Ham Biscuits: Reduce butter to ¼ cup and buttermilk to ¼ cup. Add 1 (8-ounce) carton sour cream and 1 cup finely chopped cooked country ham. Bake as directed. **Yield:** 10 biscuits.

Beer-and-Cheese Biscuits: Add 1 cup (4 ounces) shredded Swiss cheese and 1 teaspoon dried whole-leaf or rubbed sage. Substitute ¾ cup beer for buttermilk. Bake biscuits as directed. **Yield:** 10 biscuits.

Orange-Pecan Scones: (pictured on page 264) Add 3 tablespoons sugar, 1 teaspoon grated orange rind, 1 teaspoon vanilla extract, and ½ cup chopped pecans. Divide dough in half; roll each portion into a 7-inch circle, and place on a lightly greased baking sheet. Cut each circle into 8 wedges. Bake as directed. **Yield:** 16 scones.

PEAR SHORTCAKES

2 cups apple juice, divided
6 firm ripe pears, peeled and chopped
1 cup sugar
3 tablespoons lemon juice
½ teaspoon ground nutmeg
¼ teaspoon ground cinnamon
⅛ teaspoon ground cloves
1½ tablespoons cornstarch
½ cup slivered almonds, toasted
2 teaspoons grated lemon rind
8 Orange-Pecan Scones (see recipe)
1 cup whipping cream, whipped

● **Combine** 1¾ cups apple juice and next 6 ingredients in a large saucepan;

bring to a boil. Cook 10 to 12 minutes or until pears are tender. Remove pears from liquid, reserving liquid. Set pears aside. Bring liquid to a boil; reduce heat, and cook until liquid is reduced to 1 cup.
● **Combine** remaining apple juice and cornstarch; stir into reduced mixture. Bring to a boil, stirring constantly. Boil 1 minute, stirring constantly. Remove from heat. Stir in almonds, lemon rind, and pears; cool.
● **Split** scones; place bottom half on serving plates, and top with pear mixture, half of whipped cream, and remaining scone halves. Dollop each with remaining whipped cream. **Yield:** 8 servings.

CHOCOLATE BISCUIT BREAD PUDDING

2 cups half-and-half
½ cup butter or margarine
3 large eggs
1 cup sugar
¼ cup cocoa
10 Basic Buttermilk Biscuits (see recipe on facing page)
Whipped cream

● **Combine** half-and-half and butter in a heavy saucepan; cook over medium heat until butter melts. Cool.
● **Combine** eggs, sugar, and cocoa; beat at medium speed of an electric mixer 1 minute. Gradually stir in half-and-half mixture; set aside.
● **Crumble** biscuits into a lightly greased 2-quart shallow baking dish; add egg mixture.
● **Bake** at 350° for 45 minutes or until a knife inserted in center comes out clean, covering with aluminum foil after 35 minutes to prevent over-browning. Serve warm with whipped cream. **Yield:** 8 to 10 servings.

Raisin Bread Pudding: Omit cocoa and add ½ cup raisins.

A BISCUIT BAKING PRIMER

■ The first rule of making prize-winning biscuits is to start with self-rising soft-wheat flour like Martha White or White Lily. Work butter into flour quickly, so butter will stay cold. If butter is too warm, the biscuits won't rise as high during baking.

■ Pour the buttermilk into the flour, and stir just until the flour becomes moist. Too much stirring makes the biscuits tough.

■ Starting from the center, roll the dough out in all directions. A back and forth rolling motion makes the biscuits tough.

■ Plunge the cutter into the dough, and pull it back out without twisting. If you twist the cutter, the biscuits won't rise as high.

■ Biscuits are the exception to the rule of etiquette that says bread should be broken into small pieces before buttering. Pull the biscuit apart crosswise, and butter both halves immediately so the butter can melt into the layers while the biscuit's hot. Etiquette experts still insist that the biscuit be held over a plate, rather than flat in your palm, when you do the buttering.

■ To store leftover biscuits, wrap in foil. Store at room temperature up to three days or wrap in heavy-duty, zip-top, plastic bags, and freeze up to three months.

THE LAST STRAW

The last ordinary *cheese* straw, that is. Try these fresh little squiggles of flavor at your next party. Or you can make these recipes ahead and store the cheese straws in airtight containers up to a week or freeze them up to three months.

(For tips on making them in a cookie press or shaping them by hand, see "Pressing Matters" on the facing page.)

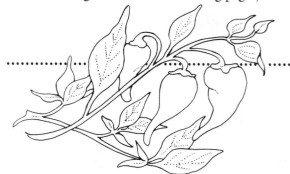

EASY-AS-PIE CHEESE STRAWS

If only Grandma had it this easy: a pie crust mix, a jar of cheese (no shredding), and a food processor.

1 (11-ounce) package pie crust mix
1 (5-ounce) jar sharp process cheese spread
¼ teaspoon ground red pepper (optional)

• **Position** knife blade in food processor bowl; add all ingredients, and process about 30 seconds or until mixture forms a ball, stopping often to scrape down sides.
• **Use** a cookie press fitted with a bar-shaped disk to shape dough into 2½-inch straws, following manufacturer's instructions. Or divide dough in half, and shape each portion into a 7-inch log; wrap in plastic wrap, and chill 1 hour. Cut into ¼-inch slices. Place on lightly greased baking sheets.
• **Bake** at 375° for 8 minutes or until lightly browned. Transfer to wire racks to cool. **Yield:** 5 dozen.

Laurie McKim
Richmond, Virginia

CHILI-CHEESE STRAWS

2 cups (8 ounces) shredded Monterey Jack cheese with peppers, softened
½ cup butter or margarine, softened
1 cup all-purpose flour
½ cup yellow cornmeal
1 teaspoon chili powder
½ teaspoon salt
½ teaspoon ground cumin

• **Combine** softened cheese and butter, stirring until mixture is blended. Gradually add flour and remaining ingredients, stirring until mixture is no longer crumbly and will shape into a ball.
• **Use** a cookie press fitted with a star-shaped disk to shape dough into straws, following manufacturer's instructions. Or divide dough into fourths, and roll each portion into a ¼-inch-thick rectangle on wax paper. Cut into 2- x ½-inch strips with a knife or pastry wheel. Place on ungreased baking sheets.
• **Bake** at 375° for 8 minutes or until lightly browned. Transfer to wire racks to cool. **Yield:** about 8 dozen.

PARMESAN CHEESE STRAWS

A twist on the wine-and-cheese theme, these elegant appetizers are great paired with your favorite vino.

⅔ cup refrigerated preshredded Parmesan cheese *
½ cup butter or margarine, softened
1 cup all-purpose flour
¼ teaspoon salt
¼ teaspoon ground red pepper
¼ cup milk
Pecan halves (optional)

• **Position** knife blade in food processor bowl; add cheese and butter. Process until blended. Add flour, salt, and red pepper; process about 30 seconds or until mixture forms a ball, stopping often to scrape down sides.
• **Divide** dough in half; roll each portion into a ⅛-inch-thick rectangle, and cut into 2- x ½-inch strips. Or shape dough into ¾-inch balls; flatten each ball to about ⅛-inch thickness. Place on ungreased baking sheets; brush with milk. Top with pecan halves, if desired.
• **Bake** at 350° for 7 minutes for strips and 10 minutes for rounds or until lightly browned. Transfer to wire racks to cool. **Yield:** 5 dozen cheese straws or 3 dozen wafers.

* ⅔ cup freshly grated Parmesan cheese plus an additional ¼ cup all-purpose flour may be substituted for the preshredded Parmesan cheese.

Sue-Sue Hartstern
Louisville, Kentucky

BRIE CHEESE STRAWS

½ pound Brie, softened
½ cup butter, softened
2 cups all-purpose flour
¼ teaspoon salt
¼ teaspoon ground red pepper
¼ teaspoon Worcestershire sauce

• **Position** knife blade in food processor bowl; add Brie (with rind) and butter. Process until blended, stopping often to scrape down sides. Add flour and remaining ingredients, pulsing until a soft dough forms.

● **Use** a cookie press fitted with a star-shaped disk to shape dough into straws, following manufacturer's instructions. Or divide dough in half, and shape each portion into an 8-inch log; wrap in plastic wrap, and chill 8 hours. Cut chilled dough into ¼-inch slices. Place the cheese straws on ungreased baking sheets.

● **Bake** at 375° for 8 minutes or until lightly browned. Transfer to wire racks to cool. **Yield:** 7 dozen cheese straws or 5 dozen wafers.

Mike Singleton
Memphis, Tennessee

ITALIAN CHEESE STRAWS

Move these from the party table to the dinner table, alongside a great salad.

2 cups (8 ounces) shredded
    mozzarella cheese, softened
½ cup butter, softened
1½ cups all-purpose flour
2 teaspoons dried Italian
    seasoning
½ teaspoon salt
¼ teaspoon ground white pepper

● **Combine** cheese and butter, stirring until blended. Gradually add remaining ingredients, stirring until mixture is no longer crumbly and will shape into a ball.

● **Use** a cookie press fitted with a bar-shaped disk to shape into straws, following manufacturer's instructions. Or roll dough into a ¼-inch-thick rectangle on floured wax paper. Cut into 2- x ½-inch strips with a knife or pastry wheel. Place on ungreased baking sheets.

● **Bake** at 375° for 8 minutes or until lightly browned. Transfer to wire racks to cool. **Yield:** about 8 dozen.

PRESSING MATTERS

....

Any good cook in Dixie knows the ever-popular cheese straws are just flour, butter, cheese, and a little red pepper pushed through a cookie press and baked to a delicate crunch. But you don't have to use a cookie press to make all the cheese straws in "The Last Straw," on facing page; we give you easy directions for shaping them by hand as well. But a cookie press will speed things along, and even be fun, if you know how to use one. Here we tell you how.

■ Pick a star-shaped disk for "fingers" or a bar-shaped one for flat "ribbons." Then put disk into tip of cookie press. Screw onto canister.

■ Load dough into canister until about three-fourths full. (Don't chill dough beforehand or it may be too stiff to go through press.) Screw the lid (with turning handle attached) onto the canister.

■ Hold press at a 45-degree angle to baking sheet. Starting at one end of the baking sheet, turn the handle clockwise to extract dough, slowly pulling the press across the baking sheet and continuing to turn the handle.

■ Stop pulling and turning when there is a continuous ribbon of dough on baking sheet. Repeat to make more rows until baking sheet is filled.

■ With a knife, cut across rows every couple of inches to make individual cheese straws. (You do not need to separate them; they will bake individually.) Trim ragged edges before baking, if desired.

■ To form a narrow, flat ribbon shape, place tape across part of the opening on bar-shaped disk to make the opening smaller.

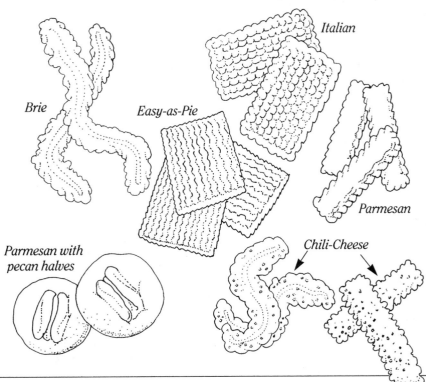

Brie

Easy-as-Pie

Italian

Parmesan

Parmesan with pecan halves

Chili-Cheese

living light
FIX & FREEZE

Keep these low-fat entrée selections in your freezer for a head start on from-scratch dinners for hectic days. Every fat watcher needs an occasional "fudge" factor, so we end the entrée ideas with Chocolate Cream Log.

SKILLET PIZZA CRUSTS
(pictured on page 224)

3 packages active dry yeast
1 teaspoon sugar
¾ cup warm water (105° to 115°)
3 cups all-purpose flour
1 teaspoon salt
½ cup warm water (105° to 115°)
2 tablespoons olive oil
Vegetable cooking spray

• **Combine** first 3 ingredients in a 2-cup glass measuring cup; let stand 5 minutes.
• **Combine** yeast mixture, flour, and next 3 ingredients in a large bowl, stirring until well blended.
• **Turn** dough out onto a lightly floured surface, and knead 5 minutes. Place in a bowl coated with cooking spray, turning to grease top. Cover and let rise in a warm place (85°), free from drafts, 30 minutes or until dough is doubled in bulk.
• **Punch** dough down, and knead lightly 4 or 5 times. Divide dough into 6 equal portions; roll each portion into an 8-inch circle.
• **Cook** each round on 1 side in a nonstick 8-inch skillet coated with cooking spray over medium heat about 2 minutes or until dough rounds are lightly browned. Cool crusts, and freeze in an airtight container up to 6 months. **Yield:** 6 (8-inch) pizza crusts.

Kathy Piques
Knoxville, Tennessee

♥ Per crust: Calories 286 (19% from fat)
Fat 5.9g (0.7g saturated) Cholesterol 0mg
Sodium 392mg Carbohydrate 49.7g
Fiber 2.7g Protein 7.8g

VEGETABLE PIZZA
(pictured on page 224)

6 (8-inch) Skillet Pizza Crusts
     (see recipe)
1½ cups commercial reduced-fat
      pasta sauce
1 cup sliced fresh mushrooms
1 cup (4 ounces) shredded
      part-skim mozzarella cheese
¾ cup chopped green pepper
½ cup chopped onion
¼ cup sliced ripe olives

• **Place** frozen pizza crusts on baking sheets. Spread each crust with ¼ cup pasta sauce, and sprinkle evenly with toppings.
• **Bake** at 425° for 12 to 15 minutes or until edges are lightly browned and cheese melts. Cut into wedges. **Yield:** 6 servings.

Kathy Piques
Knoxville, Tennessee

♥ Per pizza: Calories 391 (24% from fat)
Fat 10.3g (2.8g saturated) Cholesterol 11mg
Sodium 607mg Carbohydrate 59.9g
Fiber 3.5g Protein 14.3g

PERFECT PIZZAS

• • • • • • • • • • • • • • •

The Skillet Pizza Crusts with vegetable toppings inspired us to create several variations. All bake at 425° for 12 to 15 minutes.

■ **Mexican Pizza:** Spread crusts with salsa, and sprinkle with sliced green onions, sliced ripe olives, and shredded reduced-fat Monterey Jack cheese. Bake as directed. Top with shredded lettuce and chopped tomato.

■ **Pesto Pizza:** Spread crusts with commercial pesto; top with sliced Roma tomatoes and grated Parmesan cheese. Bake as directed. Garnish pizza with fresh basil leaves.

■ **Roasted Pepper Pizza:** Top crusts with commercial chopped roasted red peppers and chopped purple onion; sprinkle with minced fresh garlic and shredded part-skim mozzarella cheese. Bake as directed.

■ **Chicken Pizza:** Top crusts with cooked thinly sliced chicken, sliced Roma tomatoes, and thinly sliced purple onion. Sprinkle with shredded part-skim mozzarella cheese. Bake as directed.

CARNE GUISADA

Nutrients in this meat stew will vary depending on which condiments you use.

2 pounds boneless sirloin steak, trimmed and cubed
2 tablespoons cornstarch
Vegetable cooking spray
2 (14-ounce) cans whole tomatoes, undrained and chopped
1 cup water
3 cloves garlic, minced
1 jalapeño pepper, unseeded and chopped
2 tablespoons ground cumin
2 teaspoons pepper
½ teaspoon salt
24 (6-inch) flour tortillas
Condiments: shredded lettuce, chopped tomato, shredded reduced-fat Monterey Jack cheese, reduced-fat sour cream, salsa

• **Combine** steak and cornstarch in a plastic bag, and toss until lightly coated. Cook steak in a large nonstick skillet coated with cooking spray over medium-high heat, stirring constantly, until browned. Drain on paper towels.
• **Rinse** skillet; return steak to skillet, and add tomatoes and next 6 ingredients. Bring to a boil; cover, reduce heat, and cook 30 minutes, stirring often.
• **Remove** beef mixture from heat, and cool. Place desired amount of meat mixture into airtight containers, and freeze up to 6 months.
• **Thaw** in refrigerator overnight. Cook beef mixture over medium heat until thoroughly heated.
• **Spread** beef mixture evenly down center of tortillas, and top with desired condiments. Fold up tortillas burrito style. **Yield:** 12 servings.

Becky Villarreal
San Angelo, Texas

❤ Per serving (does not include condiments):
Calories 370 (23% from fat)
Fat 9.4g (2.4g saturated) Cholesterol 53mg
Sodium 617mg Carbohydrate 45.3g
Fiber 2.4g Protein 25g

DO-AHEAD IDEAS

Take-out can mean taking dinner out of the freezer, not out of a drive-through window. Learn to maximize your time by freezing ahead. Try these tips for cooking in advance.

■ Become a weekend cook. With a few meals in the freezer, all you'll need to do during the week is thaw and reheat.

■ Always follow proper storage instructions and food safety rules when freezing and thawing foods. Never thaw dishes that contain meat, fish, eggs, or poultry at room temperature; always thaw in the refrigerator.

■ Don't tie up all your baking pans in the freezer. Use disposable aluminum pans. Or freeze casseroles in aluminum foil-lined pans until firm, remove them from the pans, and wrap well with foil. To serve, unwrap the frozen casserole, and put it back in the pan to thaw and heat.

■ Freeze single servings of soup, stew, chili, and spaghetti sauce in individual microwave-safe containers or freezer bags for fast help-yourself convenience. Thawing will take less time, and you'll thaw only as much as you need.

■ Be sure to note on the label the number of servings as well as any ingredients that need to be added to the frozen item once it's thawed.

■ When taking your lunch to work, make and freeze several sandwiches ahead. Just pull a sandwich from the freezer in the morning, and by lunchtime, it'll be perfect for eating. Avoid freezing sandwiches made with fresh vegetables or mayonnaise. Spread the bread with nonfat cream cheese or margarine instead.

■ Doubling a recipe can be the most straightforward time-saver. If you decide to put twice the amount of food in one pot, as with a soup, you'll need a pot large enough so that food will brown quickly and liquids can simmer without boiling over. The larger quantity of food will probably take longer to cook, so you'll have to rely on signs of doneness rather than timing.

■ Put your electric slow cooker to use. Let batches of stew or soup simmer while you're at work. When you get home, dinner will be ready with enough left over to freeze.

■ While the food processor is out, chop an extra batch of peppers and onions and store in the freezer.

BEAN AND PASTA SOUP

1½ pounds low-fat ground beef
Vegetable cooking spray
3 (13¾-ounce) cans fat-free
    beef broth
2 (5½-ounce) cans tomato-
    vegetable juice
1 (28-ounce) can crushed
    tomatoes, undrained
1 (6-ounce) can tomato paste
1½ cups chopped onion
1½ cups chopped celery with
    leaves
1½ cups shredded carrot
1 (15-ounce) can kidney beans,
    rinsed and drained
1 (15-ounce) can Northern beans,
    rinsed and drained
¼ cup lemon juice
1½ teaspoons minced garlic
2 teaspoons dried Italian
    seasoning
2 teaspoons ground red pepper
½ teaspoon salt
Wagon-wheel pasta, cooked
    without salt or fat

• **Brown** ground beef in a large Dutch oven coated with cooking spray, stirring until it crumbles. Drain and pat dry with paper towels.

• **Wipe** pan drippings from Dutch oven with a paper towel; recoat with cooking spray. Return beef to Dutch oven; add beef broth and next 13 ingredients.

• **Bring** to a boil. Reduce heat, and simmer, uncovered, 45 minutes.

• **Remove** from heat, and cool. Place desired amount of soup into airtight containers; freeze up to 6 months.

• **Thaw** soup in refrigerator overnight. Cook over medium heat until thoroughly heated. Stir in ⅔ cup cooked pasta per 3 cups soup mixture. **Yield:** 14 cups.

Frances Walker
Broken Arrow, Oklahoma

♥ Per 1½-cup serving:
Calories 342 (17% from fat)
Fat 6.8g (3.7g saturated) Cholesterol 37mg
Sodium 446mg Carbohydrate 46.9g
Fiber 5.3g Protein 26.2g

30-MINUTE CHICKEN DINNERS

....

Freeze boneless, skinless chicken breast halves on a baking sheet. When they're frozen solid, wrap them individually, and freeze up to nine months. Thaw before using.

■ **Crisp Oven-Fried Chicken:** Combine 1 cup cornflake crumbs, 2 teaspoons dried parsley flakes, ½ teaspoon garlic salt, ½ teaspoon poultry seasoning, and ¼ teaspoon pepper. Dip 4 boneless, skinless chicken breast halves into 1 beaten egg white, and dredge in crumb mixture. Place on a baking sheet, and bake at 400° for 30 minutes.

Jo Wallers
Miami, Florida

■ **Spicy Skillet Chicken:** Combine 4 boneless, skinless chicken breast halves and 1 (10-ounce) can diced tomatoes and green chiles in a skillet. Bring to a boil; cover, reduce heat, and cook 10 minutes, turning chicken once. Remove chicken, and cook tomato mixture until thickened. Spoon over chicken, sprinkle evenly with ½ cup reduced-fat sharp Cheddar cheese, and dollop with reduced-fat sour cream.

Mary Burdine
Pearland, Texas

CHOCOLATE CREAM LOG

Vegetable cooking spray
⅔ cup sifted cake flour
1 teaspoon baking powder
3 tablespoons unsweetened cocoa
3 large eggs
1 egg white
½ cup sugar
2¼ cups low-fat vanilla ice cream,
    softened
¾ cup chocolate syrup
¾ cup reduced-fat frozen whipped
    topping, thawed

• **Coat** a 15- x 10- x 1-inch jellyroll pan with cooking spray; line with wax paper, and coat with cooking spray. Set aside.

• **Combine** flour, baking powder, and cocoa; set aside.

• **Combine** eggs, egg white, and sugar; beat mixture at high speed with an electric mixer 8 minutes.

• **Fold** in flour mixture. Spread batter evenly into prepared pan.

• **Bake** cake at 400° for 8 minutes or until a wooden pick inserted in center comes out clean.

• **Loosen** cake immediately from sides of pan, and turn out onto a towel. Peel off wax paper. Starting at narrow end, roll up cake and towel together; cool cake completely on a wire rack, seam side down.

• **Unroll** cake. Spread with ice cream; reroll cake. Cover and freeze up to 1 month. Cut roll into 10 slices; spoon chocolate syrup evenly onto dessert plates. Top each with a cake slice and a dollop of whipped topping. **Yield:** 10 servings.

Sandra Ackman
Dunwoody, Georgia

♥ Per serving: Calories 206 (18% from fat)
Fat 4.1g (1.3g saturated) Cholesterol 71mg
Sodium 67mg Carbohydrate 37.3g
Fiber 0g Protein 5.1g

Choose the tying technique that's easiest for you. Then, steam tamales in a bamboo steamer (shown), steamer basket, or metal colander. (See "From Our Kitchen to Yours," page 192.)

Sausage-Stuffed Pork Rib Roast (recipe, page 240)

Grillades and Baked Cheese Grits (recipe, page 240)

Sweet Potato Bread Pudding (recipe, page 241)

Oak Alley, a Louisiana River Road Plantation

Skip buying expensive Italian pizza crusts. With a little effort in the kitchen, you can stock your freezer with the Skillet Pizza Crusts for Vegetable Pizza (recipes, page 218).

CAN-DO SOUPS

....

September's return to car pools, class-rooms, and living by the clock needn't be an uphill climb. If you can operate a can opener, you've practically mastered these super speedy soups.

TACO SOUP

1 pound lean ground beef
1 large onion, chopped
3 (16-ounce) cans Mexican-style chili beans, undrained
1 (16-ounce) can whole kernel corn, undrained
1 (16-ounce) can chopped tomatoes, undrained
1 (15-ounce) can tomato sauce
1½ cups water
1 (4½-ounce) can chopped green chiles
1 (1¼-ounce) package taco seasoning mix
1 (1-ounce) envelope Ranch-style salad dressing mix
Toppings: tortilla chips, shredded cheese, shredded lettuce, chopped tomatoes, sour cream, chopped avocado

• **Cook** ground beef and onion in a large Dutch oven over medium-high heat until meat is browned, stirring until it crumbles; drain. Stir in beans and next 7 ingredients. Bring to a boil; reduce heat, and simmer, uncovered, 15 minutes. Serve with desired toppings. **Yield:** 3½ quarts.

Note: Taco Soup may be frozen up to three months.

Bette Stevens
Texarkana, Texas

SPICY WHITE BEAN SOUP

1 large onion, chopped
2 tablespoons butter or margarine, melted
2 (15½-ounce) cans Great Northern beans, rinsed and drained
2 (15½-ounce) cans yellow hominy, rinsed and drained
2 (14½-ounce) cans chili-style chopped tomatoes, undrained
2 (14½-ounce) cans ready-to-serve vegetable broth
1 teaspoon sugar
½ teaspoon ground cumin
¼ to ½ teaspoon ground red pepper
¼ teaspoon ground cloves
2 tablespoons chopped fresh cilantro

• **Cook** onion in butter in a Dutch oven over medium heat until tender. Add beans and remaining ingredients.
• **Bring** to a boil; reduce heat, and simmer, uncovered, 20 minutes. **Yield:** 3½ quarts.

Wendy V. Kitchens
Charlotte, North Carolina

SUPER SOUPS

■ Use the cooking liquid from vegetables or meats as a flavorful base for soups or stews.

■ Refrigerate soups to allow any fat to float to the surface and harden. This makes it easy to remove the fat before reheating the soup.

CREAMY ASPARAGUS SOUP

You can prepare the vegetable puree base ahead and refrigerate up to three days or freeze up to six months. Dilute with milk, and heat to serve.

½ cup chopped onion
1 cup sliced celery
3 cloves garlic, pressed
3 tablespoons butter or margarine, melted
2 (14½-ounce) cans cut asparagus, undrained
1 (16-ounce) can sliced potatoes, drained *
1 (14½-ounce) can ready-to-serve chicken broth
1 teaspoon white vinegar
1 teaspoon salt
½ teaspoon ground black pepper
¼ teaspoon ground red pepper
½ teaspoon dried basil
1 cup milk
½ cup sour cream (optional)
Garnish: celery leaves

• **Cook** first 3 ingredients in butter in a Dutch oven over medium-high heat, stirring constantly, until tender. Stir in asparagus and next 7 ingredients.
• **Bring** to a boil, stirring often. Reduce heat, and simmer, uncovered, 10 minutes, stirring often. Cool slightly.
• **Pour** half of mixture into container of an electric blender; process until smooth, stopping once to scrape down sides. Transfer mixture to another container. Repeat procedure.
• **Return** asparagus mixture to Dutch oven. Stir in milk; cook just until thoroughly heated (do not boil). Dollop each serving with sour cream; garnish, if desired. **Yield:** 2 quarts.

* 2 medium potatoes, cooked, peeled, and sliced, may be substituted.

Sider Krison
Shreveport, Louisiana

FIRST-STRING SNACKS

Football season's here. If you can't make it to the game in person, then invite a few friends over to cheer with you at home. As for fare, serve the fans Onion Blossom, the fried onion appetizer like the one some restaurants serve, or Bean Burrito Appetizers. Try either recipe or both for a kick-off party that's as exciting as the game.

ONION BLOSSOM

Purchase more than one onion. You'll need to practice the cutting technique. If you mess up, you can chop that onion for another use and start again with a new one.

1 large Vidalia or other sweet
    onion
2 tablespoons all-purpose
    flour
1 large egg, lightly beaten
1 cup crushed saltine crackers
Vegetable oil
½ teaspoon salt (optional)
Commercial dark honey-mustard
    or Ranch-style salad
    dressing

• **Peel** onion, leaving root end intact. Cut onion vertically into quarters, cutting to within ½ inch of root end. Cut each quarter vertically into thirds.
• **Place** onion in boiling water 1 minute; remove and place in ice water 5 minutes. Loosen "petals" if necessary. Drain onion, cut side down.
• **Place** flour in a heavy-duty, zip-top plastic bag; add onion, shaking to coat. Dip onion in egg.
• **Place** crushed crackers in plastic bag; add onion, tossing to coat. Chill onion 1 hour.

• **Pour** oil to depth of 3 inches into an electric fryer or heavy saucepan, and heat to 375°.
• **Fry** onion 5 to 7 minutes or until golden brown; drain on paper towels. Sprinkle with salt, if desired. Serve with honey-mustard or salad dressing. **Yield:** 2 appetizer servings.

Jean Scott
Floyd, Virginia

BEAN BURRITO APPETIZERS

½ cup chopped onion
Vegetable cooking spray
1 (15-ounce) can kidney beans or
    pinto beans, drained and
    mashed
⅓ cup mild salsa
1 tablespoon chili powder
⅛ teaspoon garlic powder
⅛ teaspoon salt
⅛ teaspoon pepper
¼ cup reduced-fat cream cheese
½ cup cubed avocado
1½ teaspoons lemon juice
1 (8½-ounce) package 6-inch
    flour tortillas
1 medium-size sweet red pepper,
    cut into thin strips
Commercial salsa
Nonfat sour cream

• **Cook** onion in a nonstick skillet coated with cooking spray over medium heat, stirring constantly, until tender. Stir in mashed beans and next 5 ingredients. Set aside.
• **Combine** cream cheese, avocado, and lemon juice; spread about 2½ teaspoons over 1 side of each tortilla, leaving a ½-inch border around edge. Spread 2 tablespoons bean mixture over avocado mixture. Top with 2 or 3 pepper strips, and roll up.
• **Cut** each tortilla roll into fourths; insert a wooden pick into each appetizer. Serve with salsa and sour cream. **Yield:** 40 appetizers.

LIQUID ASSETS

For game-time gatherings, try a change from the usual beer, wine, or soft drinks. It's easy with these recipes. Most can be made ahead of time.

For a conversation piece, as well as a crowd-pleaser, try the Blue Woo-Woo. Gary Klepak, the creator of this recipe, says he arrived at its name because "too many of these might make you woo-woozy!"

If a Blue Woo-Woo is not your style, then try any of our other first-string refreshments, and you're sure to become a winning host.

BLUE WOO-WOO

1 cup tropical schnapps
½ cup Blue Curaçao
¼ cup light rum
1½ cups pineapple juice

• **Combine** all ingredients in a pitcher, and chill. Serve over crushed ice. **Yield:** 3¼ cups.

Gary Klepak
Columbus, Georgia

MULLED CIDER

1 quart apple cider
⅓ cup firmly packed brown
   sugar
½ teaspoon whole allspice
2 (3-inch) sticks cinnamon
6 whole cloves
Garnish: cinnamon sticks

• **Combine** first 5 ingredients in a Dutch oven, and bring to a boil. Reduce heat; cover and simmer 15 minutes. Remove and discard spices. Serve hot. Garnish each serving, if desired. **Yield:** 4 cups.

ST. PETE SUNRISE

Let guests add the grenadine to their drinks – and watch it create a sunrise in a glass.

4 cups fresh pink grapefruit juice
¼ cup firmly packed brown
   sugar
½ cup cream sherry
¼ cup grenadine

• **Combine** grapefruit juice and brown sugar in a saucepan; bring to a boil, stirring occasionally. Remove from heat, and cool.
• **Add** sherry. Pour into clear glasses; add 1 tablespoon grenadine to each glass. **Yield:** 4 servings.

Ronn Johnson
St. Petersburg, Florida

LEMON-LIME MARGARITAS

2 tablespoons fresh lime juice
Margarita salt
1 cup tequila
¼ cup Triple Sec
¼ cup fresh lime juice
¼ cup fresh lemon juice
¼ cup sugar
Crushed ice

• **Place** 2 tablespoons lime juice and margarita salt in separate saucers. Dip

rims of 6 widemouthed glasses into lime juice and then salt. Set aside.
• **Combine** tequila and next 4 ingredients in container of an electric blender; add enough ice to mixture to measure 4 cups. Process until frothy. Pour into prepared glasses. Serve immediately. **Yield:** 4 cups.

GRAPE-LIME COOLER

3 cups white grape juice
¼ cup lime juice

• **Combine** juices, and chill. Serve over ice. **Yield:** 3¼ cups.

Linda Giar
Garland, Texas

BOURBON-CITRUS PUNCH

The ice ring requires at least four hours to freeze, so plan ahead.

1 (10-ounce) jar red maraschino
   cherries, undrained
1 lemon, sliced
1 orange, sliced
2 (6-ounce) cans frozen lemonade
   concentrate, thawed and
   undiluted
2 (6-ounce) cans frozen orange
   juice concentrate, thawed
   and undiluted
2 (1-liter) bottles sparkling
   water
2 cups bourbon

• **Drain** cherries, reserving juice.
• **Arrange** cherries, lemon slices, and orange slices in bottom of a 6-cup ring mold, and add just enough water to cover fruit mixture; freeze until firm. Fill ring mold with water, and freeze until firm.
• **Combine** reserved cherry juice, lemonade concentrate, orange juice concentrate, sparkling water, and bourbon in a punch bowl.
• **Unmold** ice ring, and place in punch. **Yield:** 3½ quarts.

Margaret Hanley
Palm Harbor, Florida

PINEAPPLE-STRAWBERRY SLUSH

1 (46-ounce) can unsweetened
   pineapple juice
1 (6-ounce) can frozen orange
   juice concentrate, thawed and
   undiluted
2½ cups gin, vodka, or rum
1½ cups sugar
2 tablespoons lemon juice
⅔ cup strawberry-flavored syrup
1 (3-liter) bottle lemon-lime
   carbonated beverage, chilled

• **Combine** first 6 ingredients in a 4-quart plastic container; cover and freeze.
• **Remove** mixture from freezer; let stand 10 minutes.
• **Spoon** ½ cup mixture into each glass; add ½ cup carbonated beverage to each. **Yield:** 22 servings.

Nancy Matthews
Grayson, Georgia

PEPPY TOMATO SIPPER

4 cups tomato juice
¼ cup lime or lemon juice
2 teaspoons Worcestershire sauce
1 to 2 teaspoons prepared
   horseradish
⅛ to ¼ teaspoon hot sauce
½ cup vodka (optional)
Garnishes: celery stalks, coarse
   ground pepper

• **Combine** first 5 ingredients in a large pitcher, stirring well. Stir in vodka, if desired. Chill the beverage, or serve over ice. Garnish, if desired. **Yield:** 4¼ cups.

Mike Singleton
Memphis, Tennessee

THREE RIVERS COOKBOOK I

Everything you'd want to know about a recipe and more – that's what you'll find in *Three Rivers Cookbook I*. The members of the Child Health Association of Sewickley, Pennsylvania, have created a cookbook that people will use and recommend to their friends. While testing the entries, they recorded preparation and baking times and listed them with each recipe. As a bonus, most of the recipes have a tip or descriptive quote from someone who has tried it. Sales of the cookbook have raised more than $1.5 million to benefit the southwestern Pennsylvania-area children in need.

RAISIN BARS

1 cup all-purpose flour
¼ cup sugar
⅓ cup butter or margarine
2 large eggs
1 cup sugar
2 tablespoons all-purpose flour
½ teaspoon baking powder
¼ teaspoon salt
1 tablespoon grated orange rind
2 tablespoons orange juice
¾ cup raisins, chopped
½ cup flaked coconut
2 teaspoons orange juice
2 teaspoons lemon juice
1½ teaspoons butter or
        margarine, softened
1 cup sifted powdered sugar

● **Combine** 1 cup flour and ¼ cup sugar; cut in ⅓ cup butter with pastry blender until mixture is crumbly. Press into bottom of a lightly greased 9-inch square pan.
● **Bake** at 350° for 15 minutes.
● **Combine** eggs and next 8 ingredients, stirring until blended. Pour over crust.
● **Bake** at 350° for 20 to 25 minutes.
● **Combine** 2 teaspoons orange juice, lemon juice, and 1½ teaspoons

butter in a small bowl; beat at medium speed with an electric mixer until smooth. Gradually add powdered sugar, beating until smooth. Pour mixture over hot layer. Cool on a wire rack. Cut into bars. Freeze in an airtight container up to 3 months, if desired. **Yield:** about 3 dozen.

UNCLE ED'S FAVORITE CHEESE SOUP

5 slices bacon
½ cup grated carrot
½ cup finely chopped celery
½ cup finely chopped onion
½ cup finely chopped green
        pepper
¼ cup all-purpose flour
4 cups chicken or beef broth
3 cups shredded sharp process
        cheese loaf
2 cups milk
2 tablespoons dry sherry
1 cup pimiento-stuffed olives,
        rinsed and sliced
¼ teaspoon coarsely ground
        pepper
Garnish: chopped fresh parsley

● **Cook** bacon in a Dutch oven until crisp; remove bacon, reserving 1 tablespoon drippings in Dutch oven. Crumble bacon, and set aside.
● **Cook** carrot and next 3 ingredients in drippings over low heat, stirring vegetables constantly, about 3 minutes or until vegetables are tender, but not browned.
● **Add** flour, stirring to blend; cook 1 minute, stirring constantly. Gradually add broth, stirring constantly.
● **Bring** to a boil over medium heat; reduce heat, and simmer 8 minutes or until thickened.
● **Add** cheese, stirring until melted. Stir in milk and next 3 ingredients; cook over medium heat until thoroughly heated. Sprinkle with bacon. Garnish, if desired. **Yield:** 9 cups.

The Kosher Kitchen, Southern Style

....

Myth: Jewish food is basically chicken soup, latkes, and matzo balls.

Fact: "There are Jewish people all over the South, and we cook just like everyone else," says Mildred Covert of her latest work, *Kosher Southern-Style Cookbook.*

Her coauthor, Sylvia Gerson, adds, "When you think of way down Dixie, you don't think kosher." Thanks to these New Orleanians, more folks will.

A crash course in "kosher" for those who need it: The ingredients and procedures of Jewish cooking are dictated by biblical laws. Although these fill volumes, the basics prohibit combining meat and dairy products, and eating shellfish, fish without scales, and pork.

So that rules out some favorite Southern flavors like bacon, ham, and oysters, right? Not exactly. The authors have tweaked old recipes into clever imitations and given old Jewish standbys Southern twists.

NU AWLINS KUGEL

This traditional Jewish noodle pudding takes on local flavor with the addition of pralines.

3 large eggs, lightly beaten
1 (8-ounce) package cream cheese, softened
1 (8-ounce) carton sour cream
½ cup butter, melted
¼ cup sugar
1 teaspoon vanilla extract
⅛ teaspoon salt
1 (8-ounce) package ½-inch-wide noodles, cooked without salt or fat
4 pecan pralines, finely crumbled *

● **Combine** first 7 ingredients in a large bowl, and stir in cooked noodles. Pour mixture into a buttered 8-inch square baking dish.
● **Bake** at 350° for 35 minutes.
● **Sprinkle** with praline crumbs, and bake 12 additional minutes. Let stand about 10 minutes; cut into squares. Serve warm. **Yield:** 6 to 8 servings.

* ¼ cup firmly packed brown sugar and 2 tablespoons chopped pecans may be substituted.

BIRMING "HAM"

It's cooked like a ham. But it's corned beef, instead. If you can't find one labeled "kosher" from your butcher, try a specialty food store.

1 (6- to 7-pound) cooked corned beef roast
1 (10-ounce) jar red maraschino cherries, undrained
1 cup firmly packed brown sugar
½ cup orange juice
½ teaspoon whole cloves
1 medium orange, sliced

● **Place** beef roast in a lightly greased 13- x 9- x 2-inch pan; cover.
● **Bake** at 325° for 30 minutes.
● **Drain** cherries, reserving syrup. Set cherries aside.
● **Combine** cherry syrup, brown sugar, orange juice, and cloves in a saucepan; bring to a boil. Reduce heat, and simmer 5 minutes, stirring occasionally. Set aside.
● **Make** shallow cuts in roast in diamond designs, and brush with cherry syrup mixture. Secure orange slices and cherries on roast with wooden picks. Brush fruit with cherry syrup mixture.
● **Cover** and bake 30 minutes, brushing every 10 minutes with remaining cherry syrup mixture. **Yield:** 10 to 12 servings.

MY-AMI'S MEAT LOAF

The authors avoid mixing milk or cream with meat by substituting non-dairy creamer in many recipes. This ingredient change is beneficial for those who are lactose intolerant.

2 pounds lean ground beef
1 cup soft breadcrumbs
½ cup finely chopped onion
½ cup powdered nondairy coffee creamer
¼ cup ketchup
2 large eggs, lightly beaten
2 teaspoons salt
1 teaspoon dried oregano
¼ teaspoon freshly ground pepper
1 tomato, sliced

● **Combine** first 9 ingredients; shape into an 8-inch loaf. Place on a lightly greased rack; place rack in broiler pan, and top with tomato slices.
● **Bake** at 350° for 1 hour and 20 minutes. Let stand 5 minutes. **Yield:** 6 to 8 servings.

TRADITIONAL JEWISH HOLIDAY FOODS

■ **Hanukkah:** Dairy foods, sugar cookies in different shapes representing Hanukkah traditions, and potato latkes (potato pancakes) are basics.

■ **Passover:** Crackers or unleavened bread such as matzo are staples. No foods are allowed that include yeast as an ingredient.

■ **Rosh Hashanah:** Apples dipped in honey express wishes for a good, sweet new year as does the custom of serving sweet dishes like Tzimmes (carrots, honey, and sweet potato casserole), Honey Cake, or seasonal fruit in honor of the Jewish New Year.

PASTA ENCORE

When the pasta water's boiling, it's just as easy to cook a lot of pasta as a little – so go ahead and cook enough for two nights. But how do you transform yesterday's leftover pasta into a distinctly different dish?

Each of these two-in-one recipes begins with a pound of dried pasta. With a few additions, each main-dish recipe turns around to become a new and different meal: Penne pasta becomes a soup, spaghetti becomes a frittata, and bow-tie pasta becomes a casserole.

To round out the meal, add a salad and some crusty bread, and don't expect to hear any complaints about the "leftovers."

CHORIZO CARBONARA

½ pound chorizo sausage, crumbled
1 cup half-and-half
2 cups (8 ounces) shredded Monterey Jack cheese with peppers
1 (4½-ounce) can chopped green chiles
½ teaspoon ground cumin
1 (16-ounce) package spaghetti, cooked

● **Brown** sausage in a nonstick skillet over medium heat; drain well on paper towels. Set aside.
● **Heat** half-and-half in a small saucepan.
● **Combine** half-and-half, sausage, cheese, and remaining ingredients in a large bowl, tossing until cheese melts. Serve immediately. **Yield:** 8 servings (12 cups).

PASTA WITH COLLARDS AND SAUSAGE

1 pound spicy smoked sausage, sliced
1 (8-ounce) package sliced fresh mushrooms
2 cloves garlic, minced
3 tablespoons olive oil
2 (10-ounce) packages frozen chopped collard greens, thawed and well drained
1 tablespoon dried Italian seasoning
2 (14½-ounce) cans chunky Italian-seasoned tomatoes, undrained
1 pound penne or rigatoni, cooked
Freshly grated Parmesan cheese

● **Brown** sausage in a Dutch oven; remove from pan, drain on paper towels, and discard drippings. Set sausage aside.
● **Wipe** drippings from Dutch oven with a paper towel.
● **Cook** mushrooms and garlic in olive oil in Dutch oven over medium heat, stirring constantly, until mushrooms are tender. Add sausage, collard greens, Italian seasoning, and tomatoes. Cook 10 minutes.
● **Add** pasta, and toss well. Serve with grated Parmesan cheese. **Yield:** 8 servings (16 cups).

Caroline Weiler
Apalachicola, Florida

FIRECRACKER PASTA FRITTATA

6 cups Chorizo Carbonara (see recipe)
4 large eggs, lightly beaten
1 cup half-and-half
½ teaspoon salt
½ teaspoon pepper
⅛ teaspoon hot sauce
1 tablespoon butter-flavored shortening
1 tablespoon grated Parmesan cheese
Garnishes: sour cream, ground cumin, tomato wedges, pickled jalapeño pepper slices

● **Combine** first 6 ingredients. Set carbonara mixture aside.
● **Heat** a 10-inch cast-iron skillet in a 375° oven for 15 minutes.
● **Remove** skillet from oven, and add shortening; let stand until melted.
● **Add** carbonara mixture.
● **Bake** at 375° for 20 minutes. Sprinkle with cheese; bake 5 additional minutes or until lightly browned. Garnish, if desired. **Yield:** 6 servings.

DIXIE MINESTRONE

4 (16-ounce) cans reduced-sodium chicken broth
1 (15½-ounce) can black-eyed peas, rinsed and drained
2 (14½-ounce) cans chunky-style tomato sauce
1 (10-ounce) package frozen corn
8 cups Pasta With Collards and Sausage (see recipe)
Freshly grated Parmesan cheese

● **Combine** first 5 ingredients in a large Dutch oven.
● **Cook** over medium heat 25 minutes or until heated. Serve with Parmesan cheese. **Yield:** 8 servings (16 cups).

BOW-TIE PESTO

2 cups tightly packed fresh basil
1½ cups freshly grated Parmesan
   cheese
1 (1¾-ounce) jar pine nuts
3 cloves garlic, halved
⅔ cup olive oil
1 (16-ounce) package bow-tie
   pasta, cooked
1 (14-ounce) can artichoke
   hearts, rinsed, drained, and
   quartered
½ cup oil-packed dried tomatoes,
   cut into thin strips

• **Position** knife blade in food processor bowl; add first 4 ingredients. Process until smooth, stopping once to scrape down sides.
• **Pour** olive oil through food chute with processor running; process until smooth. Set pesto mixture aside.
• **Place** pasta in a large bowl. Add 1½ cups pesto mixture and artichoke hearts. (Reserve remaining pesto mixture for another use.)
• **Sprinkle** pasta with tomatoes, and serve hot or cold. **Yield:** 8 servings (12 cups).

Marie A. Davis
Charlotte, North Carolina

PESTO-CHICKEN CASSEROLE

2½ cups chopped, cooked
   chicken
1 (10¾-ounce) can cream of
   chicken soup, undiluted
1 (4-ounce) jar diced pimiento,
   drained (optional)
6 cups Bow-Tie Pesto (see recipe)
⅓ to ½ cup freshly grated
   Parmesan cheese

• **Combine** first 4 ingredients; spoon into a lightly greased 1½-quart baking dish. Sprinkle with cheese.
• **Bake** at 350° for 35 to 40 minutes. Serve immediately. **Yield:** 4 servings.

SCHOOL'S IN– LET'S PARTY

....

School's in session. So go ahead and choose your reason to celebrate.
   1. "Come over to our house for a get-together after the football game."
   2. "Our children will be in school together for the next 12 years; let's get to know each other."
   3. "We're inviting friends over before Ann leaves for college."
   4. "Hallelujah, I don't have to drive the car pool until 3 o'clock, let's *really* enjoy lunch."
   No matter why you decide to have folks over, try Chicken Enchiladas With Tomatillo Sauce and Orange Sherbet With Blackberry Sauce. Complete the menu with store-bought items (see the Suggested Sides on the next page).

CHICKEN ENCHILADAS WITH TOMATILLO SAUCE

5 chicken breast halves, skinned
2 (3-ounce) packages cream
   cheese, softened
⅓ cup half-and-half
¾ cup finely chopped onion
½ teaspoon salt
Tomatillo Sauce
12 (6-inch) corn tortillas
¾ cup (3 ounces) shredded
   Cheddar cheese
¾ cup (3 ounces) shredded
   Monterey Jack cheese
Garnish: chopped fresh cilantro
Condiments: shredded lettuce,
   chopped tomato, sliced ripe
   olives, sour cream

• **Place** chicken in a Dutch oven; add water to cover. Bring to a boil; cover, reduce heat, and simmer 40 minutes or until tender.
• **Remove** chicken, reserving 2½ cups broth for Tomatillo Sauce. Bone and chop chicken; set aside.
• **Beat** cream cheese and half-and-half at medium speed with an electric mixer until mixture is smooth. Stir in chopped chicken, onion, and salt. Set aside.
• **Spread** ¾ cup Tomatillo Sauce in a lightly greased 13- x 9- x 2-inch baking dish; set aside.
• **Soften** tortillas according to the package directions.
• **Spoon** about 1½ tablespoons Tomatillo Sauce evenly over each tortilla, spreading to edge of tortilla; spoon ¼ cup chicken mixture evenly down center of each tortilla. Roll up tortillas, and place, seam side down, in baking dish.
• **Cover** and bake enchiladas at 350° for 25 minutes.
• **Sprinkle** with cheddar and Monterey Jack cheeses. Garnish, if desired. Serve with remaining Tomatillo Sauce and desired condiments. **Yield:** 6 servings.

Tomatillo Sauce

½ pound fresh tomatillos *
4 to 6 jalapeño peppers, seeded
   and finely chopped
2½ cups reserved chicken broth
2 tablespoons cornstarch
2 tablespoons water
2 tablespoons chopped fresh
   cilantro or parsley
1 teaspoon salt

• **Remove** husks from tomatillos; rinse tomatillos.
• **Combine** tomatillos, peppers, and broth in a saucepan. Bring to a boil; reduce heat, and simmer 6 minutes.
• **Combine** cornstarch and water; stir into tomatillo mixture. Add cilantro and salt.
• **Bring** to a boil; let boil 1 minute, stirring constantly. Cool slightly.
• **Pour** into container of an electric blender or food processor; process until smooth, stopping once to scrape down sides. **Yield:** 3 cups.

* 2 (11-ounce) cans tomatillos, drained and chopped, may be substituted.

Note: To spice up Tomatillo Sauce, seed only half of the jalapeño peppers.

Carol Barclay
Portland, Texas

ORANGE SHERBET WITH BLACKBERRY SAUCE

2 cups orange juice
¾ cup sugar
½ cup orange marmalade
1 cup half-and-half
1 cup sour cream
Blackberry Sauce

• **Combine** first 3 ingredients in a medium bowl, stirring until sugar dissolves. Stir in half-and-half and sour cream. Pour into a 9- x 5- x 3-inch loafpan.
• **Freeze** mixture for 2 hours or until almost firm.
• **Remove** from freezer, and place in a medium mixing bowl. Beat at medium speed with an electric mixer 1 to 2 minutes or until mixture is fluffy but not thawed.
• **Return** to loafpan; freeze 2 hours or until firm. Serve with Blackberry Sauce. **Yield:** 6 servings.

Blackberry Sauce

1 pint fresh blackberries *
¼ cup sugar
1 tablespoon crème de cassis (optional)

• **Position** knife blade in food processor bowl; add blackberries. Process 30 seconds or until smooth, stopping once to scrape down sides.
• **Pour** through a fine wire-mesh strainer into a small bowl, pressing with back of spoon. Discard seeds.
• **Add** sugar and crème de cassis, if desired, stirring until sugar dissolves. Cover and refrigerate. **Yield:** ¾ cup.

* 1 (12-ounce) package frozen blackberries, thawed, may be substituted.
Louise Bodziony
Gladstone, Missouri

AFTER-DINNER COFFEE

········

After the dishes are cleared, make room for coffee – coffee dessert that is. These sumptuous treats satisfy a coffee craving and a sweet tooth.

MOCHA MOUSSE

1 cup whipping cream, divided
1 egg yolk, lightly beaten
8 (1-ounce) squares semisweet chocolate
¼ cup light corn syrup
¼ cup butter or margarine
1 tablespoon instant coffee granules
¼ cup sifted powdered sugar
1 tablespoon Kahlúa
Garnishes: sweetened whipped cream, chocolate curls

• **Combine** ¼ cup whipping cream and egg yolk in a medium bowl, and set aside.

• **Combine** chocolate squares and next 3 ingredients in a heavy saucepan; cook over low heat, stirring constantly, until chocolate melts. Gradually stir into egg yolk mixture. Return mixture to saucepan.
• **Cook** over medium heat, stirring constantly, 3 to 5 minutes or until mixture reaches 160°. Cool.
• **Beat** remaining ¾ cup whipping cream until foamy; gradually add powdered sugar, beating until soft peaks form. Fold in Kahlúa.
• **Fold** whipped cream mixture into chocolate mixture. Pipe or spoon into coffee cups. Garnish, if desired. **Yield:** 4 to 6 servings.

WHITE CHOCOLATE-COFFEE FUDGE

2 cups sugar
⅔ cup evaporated milk
½ cup butter or margarine
12 large marshmallows
1 tablespoon instant coffee granules
Pinch of salt
1 (6-ounce) package white chocolate-flavored baking bar, chopped
1 cup chopped pecans or walnuts
1 teaspoon vanilla extract

• **Combine** first 6 ingredients in a large saucepan. Cook over medium-low heat, stirring constantly, until mixture comes to a boil.
• **Cover,** reduce heat, and simmer 5 minutes; remove from heat.
• **Add** baking bar and remaining ingredients; stir until chocolate melts. Spoon into a buttered 8-inch square pan, spreading evenly. Cool and cut into squares. **Yield:** 2 pounds.

HAZELNUT-COFFEE ICE

4 cups cold brewed coffee
½ cup Frangelico or other
 hazelnut-flavored liqueur
Sweetened whipped cream

● **Freeze** coffee in ice cube trays or small paper cups.
● **Position** knife blade in food processor bowl; add coffee cubes and liqueur. Process until thoroughly blended. Serve with sweetened whipped cream. **Yield:** 4½ cups.

Note: If a sweeter coffee flavor is desired, add sugar to taste before freezing.

COFFEE COMPLEMENTS

If there's not time to prepare dessert, try a coffee bar instead. Make a pot of coffee, and let guests choose from an array of add-ins. Here are our favorites.

■ White, milk, or mint chocolate chips
■ Toffee bits
■ Cinnamon sticks
■ Chocolate-covered caramels
■ Candy canes
■ Vanilla- or almond-flavored whipped cream
■ Piece of a favorite candy bar
■ Maple-, praline-, or cinnamon-flavored syrup
■ Few drops of vanilla or almond extract
■ Chocolate-covered peppermints
■ Butter-pecan ice cream
■ Brown sugar

JAVA SHORTBREAD COOKIES

1 cup butter or margarine,
 softened
2 teaspoons instant coffee
 granules
½ cup sifted powdered sugar
2 cups all-purpose flour
3 ounces vanilla-flavored candy
 coating, melted
½ cup chopped pecans

● **Beat** butter and coffee granules at medium speed with an electric mixer until creamy; gradually add powdered sugar, beating well. Stir in flour.
● **Shape** dough into 3-inch logs; place on ungreased baking sheet.
● **Bake** at 350° for 8 minutes or until lightly browned. Transfer to wire racks to cool.
● **Dip** both ends of cookies into candy coating, and then into chopped pecans. Place on wax paper until set. **Yield:** 2½ dozen.

Wendy V. Kitchens
Charlotte, North Carolina

MEET SALLY LUNN

....

Even though Sally Lunn is more than 200 years old, the slightly sweet, briochelike yeast bread has remained popular through the centuries and a favorite in the South because of its versatility. Eat it fresh from the oven, serve it with jam for breakfast or tea, or cover it with fresh berries and whipped cream for dessert.

Although there are several stories behind the origin of the bread's name, most believe the delicate, cakelike bread was named for baker Sally Lunn, who baked and sold the bread as large buns in Bath, England, in the late 18th century. Brought to the Colonies from England, the bread is still selling well today.

SALLY LUNN

1 package dry yeast
¼ cup warm water (105° to 115°)
¾ cup milk
¼ cup sugar
¼ cup shortening
½ teaspoon salt
1 large egg
2½ cups all-purpose flour

● **Combine** yeast and warm water in a 1-cup glass measuring cup; let stand 5 minutes.
● **Combine** milk and next 3 ingredients in a saucepan; heat until shortening melts. Cool to 105° to 115°.
● **Combine** yeast mixture, milk mixture, and egg in a large mixing bowl; beat at medium speed with an electric mixer until well blended. Gradually add flour, beating at lowest speed until blended. (Mixture will be a sticky, soft dough.)
● **Cover** and let rise in a warm place (85°), free from drafts, 1 hour or until dough is doubled in bulk.
● **Stir** dough down; cover and let rise in a warm place (85°), free from drafts, 30 minutes or until dough is doubled in bulk.
● **Stir** dough down, and spoon into a well-greased, 6-cup Bundt pan. Cover and let rise in a warm place (85°), free from drafts, 20 to 30 minutes or until doubled in bulk.
● **Bake** at 350° for 25 to 30 minutes or until golden brown. Remove from pan immediately. **Yield:** 1 loaf.

Note: Bread may also be baked in a well-greased 9-inch square pan for 30 minutes.

Clara Martin
Gadsden, Alabama

SIMPLY CHOCOLATE

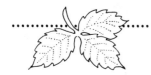

Easy chocolate recipes can satisfy just as much as the more difficult ones. In each of these recipes, the predominant flavor is chocolate, with the exception of Chocolate-Pecan Tart With Caramel Sauce. We included it because you get excellent returns from the short time invested; there's no crust to handle, and the Caramel Sauce requires only three ingredients.

EASY CHOCOLATE CHEWIES

1 (18.25-ounce) package devil's food cake mix
½ cup vegetable shortening
2 large eggs, lightly beaten
1 tablespoon water
½ cup sifted powdered sugar

● **Combine** first 4 ingredients in a large bowl, stirring until smooth.
● **Shape** dough into 1-inch balls, and roll in powdered sugar. Place balls 2 inches apart on lightly greased baking sheets.
● **Bake** at 375° for 10 minutes. Cool about 10 minutes on baking sheets; remove to wire racks to cool completely. **Yield:** 4 dozen.

Mrs. Chris Bryant
Johnson City, Tennessee

DARK CHOCOLATE SAUCE

¾ cup cocoa
½ cup sugar
½ cup light corn syrup
¼ cup vegetable oil
¼ cup butter or margarine
¼ cup water
1 teaspoon vanilla extract

● **Combine** cocoa and sugar in a medium saucepan; stir in corn syrup and vegetable oil.
● **Cook** over low heat 8 to 10 minutes, stirring constantly, or until sugar dissolves. Add butter, water, and vanilla; cook, stirring constantly, just until butter melts. Serve warm over ice cream. **Yield:** 1⅔ cups.

Note: Sauce may be reheated.

Anne Fowler Newell
Johnsonville, South Carolina

CHOCOLATE POTS DE CRÈME

Luscious Chocolate Pots de Crème, served in dainty cups, boast just four ingredients and require only a saucepan and measuring utensils to make.

1 cup semisweet chocolate morsels
1 cup whipping cream
½ cup half-and-half
2 egg yolks

● **Combine** first 3 ingredients in a heavy saucepan; cook over low heat, stirring constantly, until chocolate melts.
● **Beat** egg yolks until thick and pale. Gradually stir about one-fourth of hot mixture into yolks; add to remaining hot mixture, stirring constantly.
● **Cook** over low heat, stirring constantly, 2 minutes or until mixture thickens slightly. Spoon into individual serving containers.
● **Cover** custard and chill. **Yield:** 4 to 6 servings.

Mrs. C. M. Conklin II
Dallas, Texas

CHOCOLATE-PECAN TART WITH CARAMEL SAUCE

2 cups pecan pieces
¼ cup firmly packed brown sugar
¼ teaspoon ground cinnamon
2 tablespoons butter or margarine, softened
1 (12-ounce) package semisweet chocolate morsels
½ cup half-and-half
Caramel Sauce

● **Position** knife blade in food processor bowl; add pecans, and pulse 5 or 6 times or until finely chopped. Add brown sugar, cinnamon, and butter; process 30 seconds, stopping once to scrape down sides.
● **Press** mixture evenly onto bottom and about ½ inch up sides of a 9-inch tart pan.
● **Bake** at 325° for about 25 minutes; set aside.
● **Combine** chocolate morsels and half-and-half in a saucepan; cook over medium heat, stirring constantly, until chocolate melts and mixture is smooth. Pour into tart shell.
● **Cover** and chill at least 2 hours. Serve with warm Caramel Sauce. **Yield:** one 9-inch tart.

Caramel Sauce

½ cup butter or margarine
1¼ cups sugar
2 cups half-and-half

● **Melt** butter in a heavy saucepan over medium heat; add sugar, and cook, stirring constantly with a whisk, about 10 minutes or until mixture is a deep golden brown.
● **Add** half-and-half (mixture will lump), and cook, stirring constantly, until mixture is smooth and reduced to 2¼ cups (about 10 minutes). **Yield:** 2¼ cups.

Louise Bodziony
Gladstone, Missouri

OCTOBER

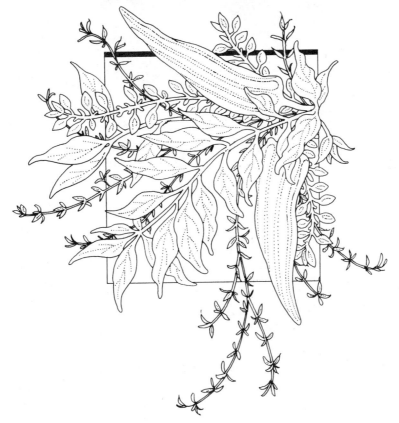

Cajun or Creole?

The flavors of south Louisiana change as you travel across the state. From Lake Charles in the southwest corner east to New Orleans, we give you a few samples, including everything from appetizers to desserts. Bon appétit, cher.

CRABMEAT HORS D'OEUVRE

Wilder Selman adds a few ingredients to plentiful fresh crabmeat. (She always makes her own mayonnaise, but for ease, we substituted commercial.) Wilder serves this appetizer in her living room before laying out a Creole buffet in her dining room.

3 tablespoons mayonnaise
¼ teaspoon Dijon mustard
1½ teaspoons lime juice
Dash of ground red pepper
½ cup chopped green onions
1 pound fresh lump crabmeat, drained
½ to 1 bunch fresh watercress
2 to 3 tablespoons capers

• **Combine** first 5 ingredients; fold in crabmeat.
• **Arrange** watercress on a serving plate; top with crabmeat mixture, and sprinkle with capers. Serve with assorted crackers. **Yield:** 8 appetizer servings.

Wilder Selman
New Orleans, Louisiana

SQUASH NICHOLAS

Jude Theriot's grandfather, Nicholas, grew plenty of squash as a truck farmer. So what in the world do you do with all that wonderful produce? Here's Jude's answer.

1½ pounds medium-size yellow squash
3 slices bacon, cut into 1-inch pieces
¼ cup butter or margarine
1 large onion, chopped
½ cup chopped green pepper
¼ cup finely chopped celery
2 tablespoons finely chopped fresh parsley
1 clove garlic, minced
1 teaspoon Worcestershire sauce
½ teaspoon hot sauce
1½ cups crushed round buttery crackers
½ teaspoon pepper
¼ teaspoon salt
¼ teaspoon garlic powder
¼ teaspoon onion powder
2 tablespoons Italian-seasoned breadcrumbs
1 tablespoon butter or margarine, cut into small pieces

• **Arrange** squash in a steamer basket over boiling water. Cover and steam 3 minutes. Cool squash to touch, and cut crosswise into ¼-inch slices; set aside.
• **Cook** bacon pieces in a large skillet over medium heat until crisp. Add ¼ cup butter, stirring until it melts. Stir in chopped onion and next 4 ingredients; cook until tender. Add squash, and cook 5 minutes, stirring mixture occasionally. Stir in Worcestershire sauce and hot sauce. Set squash mixture aside.
• **Combine** cracker crumbs and next 4 ingredients; stir into squash mixture. Spoon mixture into a lightly greased 2-quart casserole.
• **Sprinkle** with breadcrumbs and butter pieces.
• **Bake** at 350° for 30 minutes. **Yield:** 6 servings.

Jude Theriot
Lake Charles, Louisiana

MACQUE CHOUX (SMOTHERED CORN)

Jude Theriot's hometown of Lake Charles sits in Calcasieu Parish, which takes its name from the Indians who once inhabited the area. This dish gives corn a Cajun twist.

12 ears fresh corn
2 tablespoons vegetable oil
1 tablespoon butter or margarine
2 large tomatoes, peeled and chopped
1 large onion, chopped
1 medium-size green pepper, chopped
1 clove garlic, minced
1 tablespoon sugar
1 teaspoon salt
¼ teaspoon pepper
¼ teaspoon hot sauce

• **Cut** off tips of corn kernels into a bowl; scrape milk and remaining pulp from cob with a knife. Set aside.
• **Combine** oil and butter in a large skillet; heat until butter melts. Add corn, chopped tomato, and remaining

ingredients, and cook, stirring constantly, 5 minutes. Cover, reduce heat, and simmer 20 minutes, stirring often. **Yield:** 8 servings.

Jude Theriot
Lake Charles, Louisiana

SPINACH SALAD
WITH SAUTÉED PEARS

1 (10-ounce) package fresh
    spinach
1 cup water
¼ cup lemon juice
2 Bosc pears
4 slices bacon, chopped
¼ cup olive oil
1 medium onion, sliced
1 medium-size sweet red or yellow
    pepper, seeded and sliced
1 cup white wine or red wine
    vinegar
2 tablespoons sugar
1 teaspoon grated orange rind
1 teaspoon dried thyme
½ teaspoon dried basil
1 teaspoon salt
½ teaspoon cracked pepper
½ to 1 teaspoon hot sauce

• **Wash** spinach, and remove and discard stems; set spinach aside.
• **Combine** water and lemon juice in a bowl; peel, core, and chop pears. Place in lemon-water mixture, and set aside.
• **Cook** bacon in olive oil over medium-high heat in a large skillet until crisp. Add onion and pepper slices; cook 3 minutes or until tender.
• **Drain** pears; add to skillet, and cook just until tender.
• **Add** vinegar, sugar, and orange rind; bring to a boil. Remove mixture from heat, and stir in thyme and next 4 ingredients.
• **Place** spinach in a large bowl; add hot mixture, and toss gently. Serve immediately with a slotted spoon. **Yield:** 6 to 8 servings.

Chef John Folse
Lafitte's Landing
Donaldsonville, Louisiana

"Cajun food is Louisiana country food, and Creole food is New Orleans city food."

—*Chef Paul Prudhomme,*
born in Opelousas, Louisiana,
in the heart of Cajun country

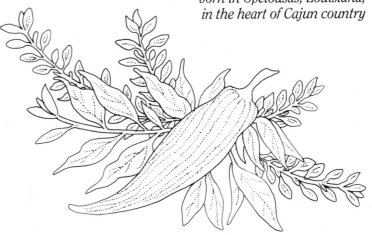

Cajun and Creole are similar – they both use filé powder and the culinary "holy trinity" of celery, onions, and green peppers generously. But they differ, too, in wonderful ways.

Cajun cooking is a combination of French and Southern cooking, tracing its roots to the French-speaking Acadians exiled from Nova Scotia for religious reasons in the 1700s. They carved a new home from the rough, isolated swamplands of southwest Louisiana.

In contrast, the Creoles' ancestors flocked to the progressive port city of New Orleans from France, Spain, Africa, and the Caribbean.

The hearty, robust style of Cajun cooking makes use of a dark roux and – many believe – spices with a kick. And nowhere is this move evident than in the Cajun classics of gumbo and jambalaya.

"Gumbo. That says it all," says Joe Broussard of Lafayette,

Louisiana. "It uses all the natural products of the area. I don't know any dish that typifies Cajun cooking better." Chef Wayne Jean of Charley G's in Lafayette, describes the differences between country and city or Cajuns and Creoles, and refers to the friendly in-state rivalry over spice levels. Teasingly, he notes, "They [the Creoles] basically don't season it over there."

Grillades and grits is a traditional Creole dish that contains tomatoes, a mainstay of Creole cooking. "When I was a little girl I never heard it called 'grillades' until I started going to brunch. At home, we always called it 'Steak à la Creole,'" says Wilder Selman of New Orleans.

Much has happened in two centuries to blur the lines of distinction between Cajun and Creole. But as Jude Theriot of Lake Charles remembers his grandmother's words, " 'Mais, cher [but, dear], you put your heart in the pot, and it all comes out okay.' "

SWEET POTATO VELOUTÉ

A velouté is technically a sauce thickened with a roux (flour cooked in fat), but the chefs at Juban's restaurant in Baton Rouge have turned it into a rich, smooth soup of sweet potatoes. Unlike Louisiana's medium to dark roux, this one is blond, making it easier and faster.

9 to 10 cups chicken broth
1¼ pounds sweet potatoes, peeled and finely chopped
1 bay leaf
1 teaspoon dried Italian seasoning
½ teaspoon ground white pepper
Dash of ground red pepper
Dash of ground nutmeg
½ cup butter or margarine
½ cup all-purpose flour
Garnishes: crème fraîche or sour cream, chopped fresh parsley
Fried Sweet Potato Strips

• **Combine** first 3 ingredients in a Dutch oven; bring to a boil over high heat. Reduce heat; simmer 20 minutes or until potatoes are tender. Remove from heat; stir in Italian seasoning and next 3 ingredients. Remove and discard bay leaf. Set aside.
• **Melt** butter in a heavy skillet over medium-high heat. Add flour, and cook, stirring constantly, 5 minutes or until light golden, and stir into potato mixture.
• **Place** about one-fourth of potato mixture into container of an electric blender or food processor; process until smooth. Pour into a large bowl. Repeat procedure with remaining mixture. Return mixture to Dutch oven, and cook until thoroughly heated and slightly thickened.
• **Spoon** into soup bowls. Garnish, if desired. Top each with Fried Sweet Potato Strips just before serving. **Yield:** 11 cups.

Note: To make lines on soup with crème fraîche or sour cream, spoon it into a zip-top plastic bag. Snip a small hole in one corner of bag, and squeeze in straight lines onto soup. Pull a wooden pick through lines in opposite directions at intervals to create design.

Fried Sweet Potato Strips

1 large sweet potato, peeled and grated into long strips
1 cup vegetable oil

• **Fry** potato in hot oil in a skillet until lightly browned. (Watch carefully – the thin strips brown quickly.) Remove with a slotted spoon, and drain on paper towels. (Strips will be crisp when cooled.) **Yield:** about 1 cup.
Chefs Gary Schenk and William Wells
Juban's
Baton Rouge, Louisiana

CAJUN SEAFOOD GUMBO

Joe Broussard makes seafood stock for the gumbo. But you can substitute fish bouillon. Joe begins with a roux, and then chills it. He pours off excess oil and adds the chilled roux to the gumbo.

⅓ cup vegetable oil
⅓ cup all-purpose flour
2½ pounds unpeeled, medium-size fresh shrimp
1½ quarts Seafood Stock *
1 large onion, chopped
1 large green pepper, chopped
3 stalks celery, chopped
¼ cup vegetable oil
6 cloves garlic, minced
1 teaspoon ground red pepper
½ teaspoon ground white pepper
½ teaspoon dried thyme
½ teaspoon gumbo filé
¼ teaspoon ground black pepper
1 bay leaf
½ pound fresh crabmeat, drained and flaked
1 (12-ounce) container Standard oysters, undrained
½ teaspoon salt
Hot cooked rice
Garnishes: chopped green onions and fresh parsley

• **Combine** ⅓ cup oil and flour in a small skillet; cook over medium heat, stirring constantly, 15 minutes or until roux is caramel colored. Remove from heat, and chill the roux up to 24 hours.

• **Peel** shrimp, and devein, if desired, reserving shrimp shells and tails for Seafood Stock. Refrigerate shrimp. Make Seafood Stock.
• **Remove** roux from refrigerator, and discard excess oil.
• **Cook** onion, green pepper, and celery in ¼ cup oil in a Dutch oven over medium-high heat until tender, stirring often. Add garlic and next 5 ingredients; cook until garlic is tender, stirring often.
• **Add** about ¼ cup hot Seafood Stock to roux, stirring until blended. Add roux mixture, remaining Seafood Stock, and bay leaf to Dutch oven, stirring until blended.
• **Bring** to a boil; reduce heat, and simmer 1 hour, stirring occasionally.
• **Skim** fat from surface, if desired. Return mixture to a full boil; add shrimp, and cook 3 minutes, stirring often.
• **Add** crabmeat; cook 3 minutes, stirring often.
• **Add** oysters; cook 2 minutes, stirring often. Add salt.
• **Remove** and discard bay leaf. Serve gumbo over rice. Garnish, if desired. **Yield:** 12 servings.

* 2 tablespoons fish-flavored bouillon granules and 1½ quarts water may be substituted for Seafood Stock.

Seafood Stock

Reserved shrimp shells and tails from gumbo
2½ quarts water
2 carrots, halved
2 stalks celery with leaves, halved
1 large onion, halved
6 whole black peppercorns
1 bay leaf
3 sprigs fresh parsley
3 small cooked crabs, cut in half

• **Combine** all ingredients in a Dutch oven, and bring to a boil over high heat. Reduce heat, and simmer 2 hours.
• **Pour** mixture through a wire-mesh strainer into a container, discarding solids. **Yield:** 1½ quarts.

Joe Broussard
Lafayette, Louisiana

GUMBO Z' HERBES

Everything but the kitchen sink is in this Creole gumbo of greens. Chef Leah Chase of New Orleans' Dooky Chase's restaurant uses a meat grinder to finely chop the greens, but we sped up the preparation with a food processor.

1 (5-pound) bunch fresh turnip greens with turnips (about 14 cups)
1 (6-pound) bunch fresh collard greens (about 24 cups)
1 (3-pound) bunch fresh mustard greens (about 24 cups)
1 bunch fresh watercress (about 1½ cups)
1 bunch fresh beet greens (about 2 cups)
1 bunch fresh carrot greens (about 1 cup)
1 (10-ounce) bag fresh spinach
3 quarts water
2 medium onions, chopped
4 cloves garlic, pressed
½ head lettuce, chopped (about 4 cups)
½ head cabbage, chopped (about 6 cups)
2 pounds smoked sausage, sliced and divided
1 pound smoked ham, cubed
1 pound beef stew meat
1 pound boneless brisket, cut into pieces
⅓ cup all-purpose flour
1 tablespoon salt
1 teaspoon dried thyme
1 teaspoon ground red pepper
1 tablespoon gumbo filé
Hot cooked rice

• **Remove** turnips from turnip greens. (Reserve turnips for another use.)
• **Wash** turnip greens and next 6 ingredients thoroughly. Remove tough stems from greens, and discard.
• **Bring** 3 quarts water to a boil in a large Dutch oven, and gradually add greens, onion, garlic, chopped lettuce, and chopped cabbage. Return to a boil; reduce heat, and cook 30 minutes, stirring occasionally. Drain greens mixture, reserving 2½ quarts liquid.

• **Position** knife blade in food processor bowl; add about one-third of greens mixture, processing until smooth. Transfer pureed greens to another container, and set aside. Repeat procedure twice with remaining greens mixture. Set pureed greens aside.
• **Combine** 1 pound smoked sausage and smoked ham, beef stew meat, and brisket pieces in a 12-quart stockpot; add 2 cups reserved liquid, and cook 15 minutes. Stir in pureed greens; set greens mixture aside.
• **Brown** remaining 1 pound smoked sausage in a heavy skillet over medium heat, stirring constantly; remove sausage from skillet with a slotted spoon, reserving drippings in skillet. Set cooked sausage aside.
• **Stir** flour into reserved drippings; cook over medium heat, stirring constantly, 5 minutes. Add flour mixture (roux) to greens mixture in stockpot. Stir in remaining 2 quarts of reserved liquid. Simmer 20 minutes, stirring occasionally.
• **Stir** in cooked sausage, salt, thyme, and red pepper. Simmer 40 minutes, stirring occasionally.
• **Stir** in filé, and remove from heat; serve gumbo over rice. **Yield:** 6½ quarts.

Note: Beet and carrot greens are the leaves that grow out of the top of beets and carrots.

Chef Leah Chase
Dooky Chase's
New Orleans, Louisiana

CRAWFISH ÉTOUFFÉE

Seafood markets sell frozen, peeled crawfish tails harvested in Louisiana or China. You can substitute peeled shrimp, but the color won't be as intense.

½ cup butter or margarine
1 large onion, chopped
¼ cup finely chopped celery
¼ cup chopped green pepper
2 cloves garlic, minced
1 pound peeled crawfish tails
1 teaspoon salt
½ teaspoon ground black pepper
½ teaspoon onion powder
¼ teaspoon ground white pepper
½ teaspoon hot sauce
1½ tablespoons all-purpose flour
¾ cup water
½ cup finely chopped green onions
¼ cup finely chopped fresh parsley
Hot cooked rice

• **Melt** butter in a large skillet over medium heat. Add onion and next 3 ingredients; cook, stirring constantly, 5 minutes.
• **Stir** in crawfish and next 5 ingredients; cook 5 minutes. Stir in flour; cook, stirring constantly, 2 minutes.
• **Stir** in water gradually; cook over low heat 20 minutes, stirring mixture occasionally.
• **Stir** in green onions and parsley; cook 3 minutes. Serve over rice. **Yield:** 4 to 6 servings.

Jude Theriot
Lake Charles, Louisiana

"Creole is a more sophisticated cooking. Cajun is divine, but it's one-pot cooking. It's like, if you're in France, and you're eating either in Paris or in the provinces."

—Ella Brennan,
New Orleans native
and "grande dame"
of the Brennan family restaurants

SAUSAGE-STUFFED PORK RIB ROAST
(pictured on page 222)

1 (3- to 5-pound) center-cut pork rib roast (8 bone)
½ to 1 pound smoked sausage
¼ cup butter, softened
2 tablespoons red port
2 tablespoons cane syrup
2 tablespoons muscadine jelly
¼ cup minced garlic
1 tablespoon chopped fresh tarragon
1 tablespoon chopped fresh thyme
1 tablespoon chopped fresh basil
1 tablespoon chopped fresh rosemary
1 teaspoon salt
1 teaspoon pepper
10 pearl onions
1 cup chicken broth
Brown Sauce
Muscadine jelly
Garnish: fresh rosemary sprigs

• **Push** a boning knife through center of pork roast, making a slit from end to end. Cut sausage the length of the roast; prick sausage at ½-inch intervals, and insert into slit in roast. Place the stuffed roast in a lightly greased roasting pan.
• **Combine** softened butter and next 3 ingredients; spread over roast.
• **Combine** garlic and next 6 ingredients; sprinkle over roast. Add onions and chicken broth to roasting pan; cover.
• **Bake** at 350° for 45 minutes. Uncover and bake 15 to 20 additional minutes. Remove roast, reserving 1 cup pan drippings for Brown Sauce. Serve roast with Brown Sauce and muscadine jelly. **Yield:** 8 servings.

Brown Sauce

2 tablespoons butter
2 tablespoons all-purpose flour
2½ cups beef broth
1 cup reserved pan drippings
2 tablespoons muscadine jelly
1 tablespoon tomato sauce
¼ cup red port

• **Melt** butter in a heavy saucepan over medium heat, and add flour, stirring mixture constantly. Cook 1 minute, stirring constantly. Gradually stir in broth and 1 cup reserved drippings.
• **Bring** to a boil, stirring constantly, and cook until slightly thickened. Stir in jelly, tomato sauce, and port.
• **Pour** through a fine wire-mesh strainer into a container for a smoother consistency, if desired. **Yield:** 3½ cups.

Chef John Folse
Lafitte's Landing
Donaldsonville, Louisiana

GRILLADES AND BAKED CHEESE GRITS
(pictured on page 222)

4½ pounds round steak
2 teaspoons salt
2 teaspoons pepper
Vegetable oil
⅔ cup all-purpose flour
2 cups chopped onion
1½ cups chopped green pepper
½ cup chopped green onions
½ cup chopped celery
½ cup chopped fresh parsley
4 cloves garlic, minced
2 (14½-ounce) cans stewed tomatoes, undrained
1 teaspoon dried thyme
3 bay leaves
2 cups water
Garnish: fresh parsley
Baked Cheese Grits

• **Cut** meat into serving-size pieces; sprinkle with salt and pepper.
• **Pour** ½ cup oil into a Dutch oven. Fry steak in hot oil over medium-high heat until browned (about 2 minutes on each side). Remove to platter, and repeat until all meat is browned.
• **Measure** pan drippings; add enough oil to drippings to measure ⅔ cup, and return to Dutch oven. Add flour; cook over medium heat, stirring constantly, 10 minutes or until roux is caramel colored.
• **Stir** in onion and next 5 ingredients; cook until tender. Add tomatoes and next 3 ingredients, stirring well.

• **Return** meat to Dutch oven. Bring to a boil; cover, reduce heat, and simmer 1½ hours, stirring occasionally. Remove and discard bay leaves.
• **Transfer** mixture to a serving dish; garnish, if desired. Serve with Baked Cheese Grits. **Yield:** 12 servings.

Baked Cheese Grits

5 cups boiling water
1 teaspoon salt
⅔ cup uncooked quick-cooking yellow grits
⅔ cup uncooked quick-cooking white grits
1 (15½-ounce) can yellow hominy
½ cup butter or margarine
2 cups (8 ounces) shredded sharp Cheddar cheese
½ cup grated Parmesan cheese

• **Bring** water and salt to a boil in a heavy Dutch oven; stir in grits. Return to a boil; reduce heat, and cook 4 to 5 minutes, stirring occasionally.
• **Stir** in hominy, butter, and Cheddar cheese; spoon into a lightly greased 13- x 9- x 2-inch baking dish. Sprinkle with Parmesan cheese.
• **Bake** at 350° for 45 minutes or until set. **Yield:** 12 servings.

Wilder Selman
New Orleans, Louisiana

GLORIOUS GRILLADES

Grillades (gree-YAHDS) and grits, like salt and pepper or bread and butter, are an assumed pair in New Orleans.

A Louisiana twist on smothered steak grillades are thinly pounded pieces of beef or veal round served in a tomato gravy over grits. It sounds like dinner, and sometimes it is, but brunch is the most popular menu spot for this Creole dish.

SWEET POTATO BREAD PUDDING

(pictured on page 223)

This recipe comes from cane syrup country, so that's what it calls for. If you don't like the strong flavor of cane syrup, you can substitute molasses.

1¼ pounds sweet potatoes, peeled and finely chopped
2 cups raisins
¼ cup dark rum
5 large eggs, lightly beaten
½ cup sugar
1 quart whipping cream
2 cups half-and-half
2 tablespoons cane syrup
1 tablespoon ground cinnamon
½ (16-ounce) loaf French bread, torn into 1-inch pieces
Rum Sauce
Whipped cream

• **Arrange** sweet potato in a steamer basket over boiling water. Cover and steam 10 minutes or until tender. Set sweet potato aside.
• **Combine** raisins and rum, and set aside.
• **Combine** eggs and next 5 ingredients in a bowl; add bread pieces, sweet potato, and raisin mixture. Spoon mixture evenly into 2 lightly greased 11- x 7- x 1½-inch baking dishes.
• **Bake** at 350° for 1 hour or until set, covering with aluminum foil to prevent overbrowning, if necessary. Serve warm with Rum Sauce and whipped cream. **Yield:** 16 servings.

Rum Sauce

1½ cups butter
¼ to ⅓ cup dark rum
3 cups sifted powdered sugar
1 egg yolk

• **Melt** butter in a heavy saucepan over low heat; stir in rum. Add powdered sugar; stir with a whisk until smooth. Stir in egg yolk; cook, stirring constantly, 5 minutes or until mixture reaches 160°. **Yield:** about 2½ cups.
Chefs Gary Schenk and William Wells
Juban's
Baton Rouge, Louisiana

VANILLA: IT'S NOT JUST FOR ICE CREAM ANYMORE

Vanilla works as well in savory dishes as it does in sweet ones.

Surprised? There's nothing plain and ordinary about our vanilla-spiked fish or

vinaigrette. The vanilla deliciously heightens the flavors to extraordinary.

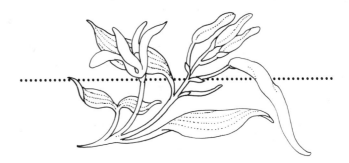

PAN-FRIED GROUPER WITH VANILLA WINE SAUCE

(pictured on pages 260 and 261)

1 cup boiling water
1 fish-flavored bouillon cube
1 cup dry white wine
2 tablespoons chopped onion
1 vanilla bean, cut in half lengthwise and divided
⅓ cup all-purpose flour
¼ teaspoon salt
¼ teaspoon pepper
1 (2½-pound) grouper fillet
¼ cup butter or margarine, divided
2 tablespoons all-purpose flour
⅓ cup whipping cream
⅛ teaspoon salt
Garnish: chopped fresh chives

• **Combine** first 4 ingredients and half of the vanilla bean in a saucepan; bring to a boil, stirring until bouillon cube dissolves. Boil 10 minutes or until mixture is reduced to ¾ cup. Pour mixture through a wire-mesh strainer into a 1-cup glass measuring cup, discarding solids, and set broth mixture aside.

• **Position** knife blade in food processor bowl; add remaining half of vanilla bean. Process until finely chopped. Add ⅓ cup flour, ¼ teaspoon salt, and pepper; process 10 seconds.
• **Cut** fillet into 6 portions. Coat each portion evenly with flour mixture; shake off excess.
• **Melt** 2 tablespoons butter in a heavy skillet; add fish, and cook 3 minutes on each side or until fish flakes easily when tested with a fork. Remove fish to a serving platter, and keep warm.
• **Melt** remaining 2 tablespoons butter in a heavy saucepan over low heat; add 2 tablespoons flour, stirring until smooth. Cook 1 minute, stirring constantly. Gradually add reduced broth mixture; cook over medium heat, stirring constantly, until mixture thickens.
• **Stir** in whipping cream and ⅛ teaspoon salt; cook over medium heat until thoroughly heated.
• **Pour** sauce over grouper. Garnish, if desired. Serve grouper with steamed vegetables. **Yield:** 6 servings.
Kim McCully
Knoxville, Tennessee

VANILLA VINAIGRETTE

¼ cup sugar
2 tablespoons white wine vinegar
2 teaspoons grated onion
½ teaspoon dry mustard
¼ teaspoon salt
¼ vanilla bean or 2 teaspoons vanilla extract
½ cup vegetable oil

• **Combine** first 6 ingredients in container of an electric blender; process mixture until smooth, stopping once to scrape down sides. With blender on high, add oil in a slow, steady stream. Serve with fresh fruit or salad greens. **Yield:** ⅔ cup.

Note: ½ cup Vanilla Oil may be substituted for vegetable oil, omitting the vanilla bean or extract.

Carol Lundy
New Tazewell, Tennessee

APPLE-WALNUT CAKE
(pictured on page 260)

1 cup butter or margarine, softened
2 cups sugar
2 large eggs
1 tablespoon vanilla extract
2 cups sifted cake flour
1 teaspoon baking powder
¼ teaspoon salt
1 (8-ounce) carton sour cream
1 cup peeled, finely chopped apple
1 cup finely chopped walnuts
2 tablespoons brown sugar
½ teaspoon ground cinnamon
Cream Cheese Glaze

• **Beat** butter at medium speed with an electric mixer until creamy; gradually add 2 cups sugar, beating well. Add eggs, one at a time, beating after each addition. Stir in vanilla.
• **Combine** flour, baking powder, and salt. Add flour mixture to butter mixture alternately with the sour cream, beginning and ending with flour mixture. Mix at low speed after each addition, just until blended. Pour half of

the batter into a greased and floured 12-cup Bundt pan.
• **Combine** apple and next 3 ingredients; spoon over batter in pan, leaving a ½-inch border around center and outer edges. Add remaining batter.
• **Bake** at 350° for 50 to 55 minutes or until a wooden pick inserted in center comes out clean. Cool in pan on a wire rack 10 minutes. Remove from pan; cool completely on wire rack.
• **Drizzle** with Cream Cheese Glaze. Store cake in refrigerator. **Yield:** one 10-inch cake.

Cream Cheese Glaze

1 (3-ounce) package cream cheese, softened
2 to 2½ teaspoons milk
1 teaspoon vanilla extract
Dash of salt
1½ cups sifted powdered sugar

• **Beat** cream cheese at medium speed with an electric mixer until fluffy. Add milk, vanilla, and salt; beat until smooth. Add powdered sugar gradually, beating mixture until smooth. **Yield:** 1 cup.

Note: 2 cups granulated Vanilla Sugar may be substituted for granulated sugar in the cake, omitting the vanilla extract. In the glaze, 1½ cups powdered Vanilla Sugar may be substituted for powdered sugar, omitting the vanilla extract.

Mrs. A. Mayer
Richmond, Virginia

SCOTTISH SHORTBREAD

1 pound butter, softened
1 cup sugar
2 teaspoons vanilla extract
3 cups all-purpose flour
½ cup cornstarch

• **Place** softened butter in a large mixing bowl. Beat at medium speed with an electric mixer until creamy; gradually add sugar, beating well. Stir in vanilla.
• **Combine** flour and cornstarch; gradually add to butter mixture, beating at

lowest speed after each addition. Press into a 15- x 10- x 1-inch jellyroll pan.
• **Bake** at 350° for 15 minutes. Reduce heat to 325°, and bake 20 additional minutes or until top is lightly browned.
• **Cool** in pan on a wire rack 5 minutes; cut shortbread into 1-inch squares. Store in an airtight container at room temperature up to 1 week or freeze up to 3 months. **Yield:** 12½ dozen.

Note: 1 cup Vanilla Sugar may be substituted for sugar, omitting the vanilla extract.

Amy L. Halverson
Atlanta, Georgia

VANILLA SOUFFLÉS WITH VANILLA CRÈME SAUCE
(pictured on page 260)

Butter
Sugar
3 tablespoons butter or margarine
3 tablespoons all-purpose flour
¾ cup half-and-half
¼ cup sugar
4 large eggs, separated
2 tablespoons vanilla extract
2 tablespoons sugar
Sifted powdered sugar
Vanilla Crème Sauce

• **Coat** the bottom and sides of 8 (4-ounce) baking dishes with butter; sprinkle with sugar. Set aside.
• **Melt** 3 tablespoons butter in a large saucepan over medium heat; add flour, stirring until smooth. Cook 1 minute, stirring constantly. Add half-and-half, stirring constantly. Stir in ¼ cup sugar. Cook over medium heat, stirring constantly, until thickened. Remove from heat, and set hot mixture aside.
• **Beat** egg yolks until thick and pale. Gradually stir about one-fourth of hot mixture into yolks; add to remaining hot mixture, stirring constantly. Cook 2 minutes; stir in vanilla. Cool 15 to 20 minutes.
• **Beat** egg whites in a large bowl at high speed with an electric mixer until foamy. Gradually add 2 tablespoons

sugar, 1 tablespoon at a time, beating until soft peaks form. Gently fold about one-fourth of egg whites into half-and-half mixture; fold in remaining whites. Spoon into prepared dishes.
● **Bake** at 350° for 20 minutes or until puffed and set. Sprinkle with powdered sugar. Serve soufflés immediately with Vanilla Crème Sauce. **Yield:** 8 servings.

Vanilla Crème Sauce

½ vanilla bean
1 cup sugar
2 teaspoons cornstarch
2 cups whipping cream
7 egg yolks

● **Position** knife blade in food processor bowl; add vanilla bean and sugar; process until bean is finely chopped.
● **Combine** sugar mixture and cornstarch in a heavy saucepan; gradually add whipping cream. Cook over low heat until sugar dissolves. Set hot mixture aside.
● **Beat** egg yolks until thick and pale; gradually stir about one-fourth of hot mixture into yolks. Add to remaining mixture, stirring constantly.
● **Cook** over medium heat, stirring constantly, until thickened. Pour through a wire-mesh strainer into a 1-quart bowl, discarding solids. Refrigerate up to 3 days. Serve leftover sauce over fresh fruit, pound cake, or ice cream. **Yield:** 3 cups.

Note: ¼ cup plus 2 tablespoons granulated Vanilla Sugar may be substituted for sugar in the soufflés, omitting the vanilla extract. One cup granulated Vanilla Sugar may be substituted for sugar in the Vanilla Crème Sauce, omitting the vanilla bean.

Nicholas Rutyna
San Antonio, Texas

SPILLING THE BEANS

If you really want to start from scratch, make your own vanilla-flavored sugar, oil, and extract. Begin a big batch of Vanilla Sugar or Vanilla Extract in early fall to give as Christmas gifts. Add a personal touch by including your favorite vanilla-inspired recipe.

Vanilla Sugar: Cut 2 vanilla beans in half lengthwise. Cut each half crosswise into 4 pieces. Combine beans and 2 (16-ounce) packages sifted powdered sugar or 6 cups granulated sugar in a container with a tight-fitting lid.

Shake container daily for one week to loosen the seeds from the beans. Remove sugar as needed, being careful to leave beans in container. Replenish container with additional sugar. The two beans will add flavor to several batches of sugar. The sugar can be stored indefinitely. Use vanilla sugar for baking, stirring into tea, coffee, or lemonade, or sprinkling over fruit or baked desserts. After you've used the vanilla beans to flavor a few batches of sugar, remove the beans, and place a piece of bean in the drip basket of your coffeemaker to add a touch of vanilla to your java.

Vanilla Oil: Cut 2 vanilla beans in half lengthwise. Cut each half crosswise into 4 pieces. Combine vanilla beans and 2 cups light olive oil in a small saucepan. Warm oil over low heat for 30 minutes. Cool slightly; pour oil through a wire-mesh strainer into a container, discarding beans. Use the oil immediately or store in a sealed container in refrigerator up to one month. Let oil return to room temperature, and shake well before using. (Clouding in refrigerator is normal.) Use oil for making salad dressing.

Vanilla Extract: Cut 4 vanilla beans in half lengthwise. Cut each half crosswise into 4 pieces. Combine vanilla beans and 1 cup vodka in a jar; seal and store at room temperature for one month. Pour mixture through a wire-mesh strainer into a clean jar, discarding beans. Extract may be stored indefinitely. Use in any recipe that calls for vanilla extract.

Bargain Hunters, Beware

Don't think you're getting a bargain if you buy synthetic Mexican vanilla extract when you visit Mexico. It's made from coumarin, a substance which can cause internal bleeding and liver damage. The Food and Drug Administration banned its use in 1954. However, Mexican vanilla sold in the United States is pure vanilla extract.

COOKIES 'N' CREAM

If there's anything that can improve plain ice cream, it's those cream-filled chocolate sandwich cookies. Start with cookies and ice cream; then get creative with nuts, chopped candy bars, coconut, ice cream toppings … you get the idea.

These frozen desserts aren't difficult to prepare and are perfect make-ahead finales. Serve them on chilled plates for a frosty look, and return any leftovers to the freezer.

CARAMEL-NUT CRUNCH PIE

Use a squeeze bottle to drizzle the hot fudge and caramel toppings on this pie. The tip of a teaspoon or a zip-top plastic bag with a corner snipped off will also work.

2 cups cream-filled chocolate sandwich cookie crumbs (about 20 cookies, crushed)
½ cup unsalted, dry-roasted peanuts, coarsely chopped
¼ cup butter or margarine, melted
6 (2.07-ounce) chocolate-coated caramel-peanut nougat bars
1½ quarts vanilla ice cream, slightly softened
1 (11.75-ounce) jar hot fudge sauce, divided
1 (12-ounce) jar hot caramel sauce, divided

• **Combine** first 3 ingredients; press into bottom and up sides of a 9-inch deep-dish pieplate.
• **Bake** at 350° for 10 minutes; set aside to cool completely.
• **Chop** candy bars into small pieces, and reserve 2 tablespoons. Fold remaining candy into ice cream, and spread evenly into crust.
• **Drizzle** with 2 tablespoons fudge sauce and 2 tablespoons caramel sauce; sprinkle with reserved candy.
• **Freeze** until firm. Cover and return to freezer.
• **Remove** pie from freezer 20 minutes before serving. Serve pie with remaining fudge and caramel sauce. **Yield:** 8 servings.

Note: For chocolate-coated caramel-peanut nougat bars we used Snickers.

Lilann Taylor
Savannah, Georgia

TRIPLE CREAM DESSERT

2½ cups cream-filled chocolate sandwich cookie crumbs (about 25 cookies, crushed)
⅓ cup butter or margarine, melted
1 quart chocolate-mint ice cream, slightly softened
½ gallon vanilla ice cream, slightly softened
3 (1-ounce) squares unsweetened chocolate
¼ cup butter or margarine
⅔ cup evaporated milk
¾ cup sugar
⅛ teaspoon salt
¾ cup chopped pecans
Sweetened whipped cream

• **Combine** cookie crumbs and ⅓ cup melted butter; press into bottom of a 13- x 9- x 2-inch dish or pan. Set aside.
• **Cut** chocolate-mint ice cream into slices, and arrange evenly (cutting to fit) over crust; freeze 1 hour. Repeat procedure with vanilla ice cream.
• **Combine** chocolate and next 4 ingredients in a saucepan; bring to a boil over medium heat, stirring occasionally. Reduce heat, and simmer, stirring constantly, 2 minutes or until thickened. Set saucepan in ice, stirring constantly, until mixture cools. Spoon over ice cream; sprinkle with pecans.
• **Freeze** until firm. Cover and return to freezer.
• **Remove** dessert from freezer 20 minutes before serving. Serve with sweetened whipped cream. **Yield:** 12 to 15 servings.

Anita M. Peck
Penfield, New York

ICE CREAM SUNDAE PIE

2 cups chocolate cookie crumbs
2 cups chopped pecans, toasted and divided
½ cup sugar
½ cup butter or margarine, melted
½ gallon vanilla ice cream, slightly softened
1 cup flaked coconut
1 (11.75-ounce) jar chocolate sauce, divided
2 ripe bananas, sliced
1 cup whipping cream, whipped

• **Combine** cookie crumbs, 1 cup pecans, sugar, and butter. Reserve ¼ cup mixture. Press remaining crumb mixture into bottom of a 9-inch springform pan; set aside.
• **Cut** ice cream in half. Return 1 portion to freezer; cut remaining portion into slices, and arrange evenly (cutting to fit) over crumb crust.
• **Sprinkle** coconut and remaining 1 cup pecans over ice cream; drizzle with half of chocolate sauce. Freeze pie until firm.
• **Cut** remaining portion of ice cream into slices. Arrange over chocolate sauce; top with bananas, and drizzle with remaining chocolate sauce. Top with whipped cream; sprinkle with reserved crumb mixture.
• **Freeze** until firm. Cover and return to freezer.
• **Remove** pie from freezer 20 minutes before serving. **Yield:** 10 to 12 servings.

Note: For chocolate cookie crumbs, we used Oreo brand crumbs, available in a 15-ounce package where baking items are sold.

Cindy Zager
Ellijay, Georgia

SUNRISE, SUNSET

From sunup to sundown, this easy stuffed bread with three variations shines with flavors ideal for both breakfast and dinner or anytime in between. No from-scratch baking skills are required. It starts with a roll mix and adds an assortment of ingredients for fillings.

ALMOND SUNBURST

1 (16-ounce) package hot roll mix
Vegetable cooking spray
Cornmeal
Fruit Filling
Glaze
Garnish: toasted sliced almonds

● **Prepare** roll mix according to directions up to point of shaping dough.
● **Coat** a 12-inch pizza pan with cooking spray; sprinkle with cornmeal.
● **Turn** dough out onto a lightly floured surface, and knead 4 or 5 times. Roll dough into a 15- x 10-inch rectangle; sprinkle evenly with Fruit Filling to within 1 inch from edge.
● **Roll** up, jellyroll fashion, starting at long side; moisten edge with water, and pinch seam to seal. Place, seam side down, on prepared pan. Shape into a ring; moisten ends with water, and pinch together to seal.
● **Make** cuts in dough at 1-inch intervals, using kitchen shears, cutting from outside edge to, but not through, inside edge. Gently turn each slice on its side, slightly overlapping slices.
● **Cover** and let rise in a warm place (85°), free from drafts, 30 minutes or until doubled in bulk.
● **Bake** at 350° for 25 minutes or until golden. Remove to a wire rack; cool 15 minutes. Drizzle warm coffee cake with Glaze, and garnish, if desired. **Yield:** 1 coffee cake.

Fruit Filling

½ cup raisins *
½ cup chopped dried apricots *
½ cup dried cherries *
½ cup chopped almonds
2 teaspoons ground cinnamon
2 teaspoons grated orange rind
1 teaspoon grated lemon rind
⅓ cup firmly packed brown sugar

● **Combine** all ingredients, stirring well. **Yield:** 2 cups.

* 1 (6-ounce) package dried tropical fruit medley may be substituted for the raisins, dried apricots, and dried cherries.

Glaze

1 cup sifted powdered sugar
2 tablespoons milk
1 teaspoon almond extract

● **Combine** all ingredients. **Yield:** ⅓ cup.

Greek Sunburst: Combine 1 (10-ounce) package frozen chopped spinach, thawed and well drained, 1 (4-ounce) package crumbled basil-tomato feta cheese blend, and ¼ teaspoon salt, stirring well. Spread spinach mixture over the dough. Shape dough, and let rise as directed. Sprinkle dough with 3 tablespoons grated Parmesan cheese, and bake as directed.

Pizza Sunburst: Spread ½ cup pizza sauce over dough. Brown ½ pound ground pork sausage in a small skillet, stirring until it crumbles; drain. Sprinkle sausage and 1 cup (4 ounces) shredded Cheddar cheese over pizza sauce. Shape dough, and let rise as directed. Sprinkle with 2 tablespoons grated Parmesan cheese, and bake as directed.

Blue Cheese-Apple Sunburst: Sprinkle dough with 1 (4-ounce) package crumbled blue cheese, 1 (2-ounce) package chopped walnuts, and 1 peeled, cored, finely chopped apple. Shape dough, let rise, and bake as directed.

EASY DOES IT

....

In Huntsville, Alabama, Barbara and Tommy Glenn's supper club takes the easy way out. The only thing the host has to make is dinner reservations. Afterward, the group often heads to one couple's home for dessert and coffee.

These make-ahead recipes are perfect for entertaining, eliminating last-minute fuss. Put on the coffee, slice the dessert, and sit back and enjoy the company.

MINT-CHOCOLATE CHIP ICE CREAM SQUARES

3 cups cream-filled chocolate sandwich cookie crumbs (about 30 cookies, crushed)
¼ cup butter or margarine, melted
½ gallon mint-chocolate chip ice cream, slightly softened
1 (5-ounce) can evaporated milk
½ cup sugar
1½ (1-ounce) squares unsweetened chocolate
1 tablespoon butter or margarine
1 (12-ounce) carton frozen whipped topping, thawed
1 cup chopped pecans, toasted
Garnish: fresh mint sprigs

● **Combine** cookie crumbs and ¼ cup butter. Press into a lightly greased 13- x 9- x 2-inch pan; freeze.
● **Spread** ice cream evenly over crust; freeze until firm.
● **Combine** evaporated milk and next 3 ingredients in a small heavy saucepan. Bring to a boil over low heat, stirring constantly with a wire whisk. Cook, stirring constantly, 3 to 4 minutes or until mixture thickens. Cool to room temperature.
● **Spread** chocolate mixture over ice cream; top with whipped topping, and sprinkle with pecans. Freeze until firm. To serve, let stand 10 minutes at room temperature, and cut into squares. Garnish, if desired. **Yield:** 15 servings.

BUTTERMILK-COCONUT PIE

3 large eggs, lightly beaten
1½ cups sugar
½ cup flaked coconut
½ cup buttermilk
½ cup butter or margarine,
   melted
2 tablespoons all-purpose flour
1 teaspoon vanilla extract
1 unbaked (9-inch) deep-dish
   frozen pastry shell

• **Combine** first 7 ingredients; pour into pastry shell.
• **Bake** at 350° for 45 minutes; shield with aluminum foil after 25 minutes to prevent excessive browing, if necessary. **Yield:** one 9-inch pie.

FLUFFY PEANUT BUTTER PIE

1 (8-ounce) package cream cheese,
   softened
1 cup sifted powdered sugar
½ cup creamy peanut butter
½ cup milk
1 (8-ounce) carton frozen
   whipped topping, thawed
1 (6-ounce) chocolate-flavored
   crumb crust
¼ cup finely chopped peanuts

• **Beat** cream cheese at medium speed with an electric mixer until smooth; add sugar and peanut butter, beating well. Gradually add milk, beating until smooth.
• **Fold** in whipped topping, and spoon into chocolate crust.
• **Sprinkle** with peanuts; freeze until firm. **Yield:** one 9-inch pie.

GREAT GREENS

The Southern tradition of serving greens with plenty of cornbread

for sopping up the "pot likker" takes a creative turn with these recipes.

The results are outstanding.

TURNIP GREENS AND WHITE BEAN BAKE

4 slices bacon
1½ pounds fresh turnip greens,
   trimmed
1 large onion, chopped
3 cloves garlic, minced
1 tablespoon minced fresh ginger
¼ to ½ teaspoon dried crushed
   red pepper
1 (14½-ounce) can Italian-
   seasoned tomatoes, undrained
1 (15-ounce) can Great Northern
   beans, drained
1 cup crumbled cornbread
2 tablespoons butter or margarine,
   melted

• **Cook** bacon in a large skillet until crisp; remove bacon, reserving 1½ tablespoons drippings in skillet. Drain bacon on paper towels, crumble, and set aside.
• **Remove** and discard stems and any discolored spots from greens. Wash greens thoroughly; drain and cut into 1-inch strips. Set aside.
• **Cook** chopped onion and next 3 ingredients in reserved drippings over medium-high heat 3 minutes or until crisp-tender, stirring often. Add tomatoes; bring to a boil. Gradually add greens, stirring after each addition until leaves wilt. Cover and cook over medium-low heat 10 minutes or until tender, stirring occasionally. Stir in beans. Spoon mixture into a lightly greased shallow 1½-quart baking dish.

• **Combine** cornbread and butter; sprinkle over casserole.
• **Bake** at 350° for 25 minutes. Sprinkle with bacon, and bake 3 additional minutes. **Yield:** 4 servings.

SOUTHWEST KALE WITH SALSA

1 cup finely chopped tomato
½ cup finely chopped sweet yellow
   pepper
2 tablespoons finely chopped
   jalapeño
1 clove garlic, minced
2 tablespoons balsamic vinegar
¼ cup olive oil, divided
2 pounds fresh kale
1 cup finely chopped onion
½ cup water
¼ teaspoon salt

• **Combine** first 5 ingredients and 1 tablespoon olive oil; cover and refrigerate salsa about 1 hour.
• **Remove** and discard stems, thick center ribs, and any discolored spots from kale. Wash kale thoroughly, drain, and cut into bite-size pieces. Set aside.
• **Cook** onion in remaining 3 tablespoons olive oil in a large Dutch oven over medium heat until tender. Gradually add kale, stirring after each addition until leaves wilt. Add water. Cover and cook 10 minutes or until tender, stirring occasionally; stir in salt. Serve with salsa. **Yield:** 6 servings.

SPINACH FETTUCCINE WITH MUSTARD GREENS

1½ pounds fresh mustard greens
10 ounces spinach fettuccine,
       uncooked *
1 cup whipping cream
4 ounces goat cheese
¼ teaspoon salt
½ teaspoon freshly ground
       pepper
2 tablespoons butter or
       margarine
2 cloves garlic, minced
¼ cup water
½ cup coarsely chopped walnuts,
       toasted

● **Remove** and discard stems and any discolored spots from greens. Wash greens thoroughly, drain, and cut into 1-inch strips; set aside.
● **Cook** fettuccine according to package directions; drain and set aside.

● **Bring** whipping cream to a boil in a heavy saucepan; boil until cream is reduced to ¾ cup. Remove from heat; add goat cheese, salt, and pepper, stirring with a spoon or wire whisk until smooth. Set aside.
● **Melt** butter in a large heavy skillet over medium heat; add garlic, and cook 1 minute. Gradually add greens, stirring after each addition until leaves wilt. Add water; cover and cook 10 minutes or until tender, stirring occasionally. Drain.
● **Return** greens to skillet; add cream mixture. Cook over medium heat, stirring constantly, 1 minute or until thoroughly heated.
● **Combine** greens mixture, fettuccine, and walnuts; toss gently. Serve immediately. **Yield:** 6 to 8 side-dish servings or 3 to 4 main-dish servings.

* Regular spaghetti noodles may be substituted.

A GREENS SUCCESS STORY

■ **Selection:** Leaves should look vibrant and crisp, with no wilted, decayed, or blemished spots. (The peppery taste of greens becomes bitter with age.) Stems on loose greens should appear freshly cut.

■ **Storing:** Remove any wilted or decayed leaves and bands or ties that bind greens together. Place greens in storage bags; perforated plastic bags are ideal because they retain moisture while allowing air circulation. Store in the crisper drawer of the refrigerator.

■ **Cleaning:** When ready to prepare, cut away stems, roots, or cores if they're tough. Leaves should be washed in a large basin of cold water so they have room to swim freely. Use your hands to gently agitate the water. Greens that are especially gritty or have deep ridges may need to be washed several times. Lift the greens from the water, allowing the grit to remain at the bottom of the basin. Dry in a salad spinner or pat dry with paper towels. (Do not fill the salad spinner more than half full or the leaves may bruise.)

SLAW THAT'LL TICKLE YOU PINK

....

The pinkness in "Think Pink" Slaw comes from richly colored beets releasing their rosiness into the creamy dressing. The leaf lettuce garnish showcases the pears' green skin and helps this side dish take the beauty contest tiara from most entrées.

But "Think Pink" Slaw isn't all glamour and good looks. Its flavor and crunch make it the hands-down winner of the talent competition as well. And by using a food processor, you can trim the shredding time to mere minutes.

"THINK PINK" SLAW

Tuck leaf lettuce under individual servings of this slaw for colorful contrast.

3 medium-size firm pears,
       unpeeled and cored
1 (16-ounce) can whole beets,
       drained *
⅓ cup mayonnaise or salad
       dressing
⅓ cup sour cream
1 tablespoon raspberry
       vinegar
1 tablespoon honey
Garnish: leaf lettuce

● **Position** medium-size shredding disk in food processor bowl; process pears and beets until shredded. Place in a large bowl.
● **Combine** mayonnaise and next 3 ingredients; add to pear mixture, tossing to coat. Cover slaw, and chill at least 1 hour. Toss before serving. Garnish, if desired. **Yield:** 8 servings.

* 2 medium-size fresh beets, peeled, may be substituted.

Note: Pears and beets may be shredded with a hand-held grater instead of using a food processor.

SPRUNG BEANS: GUILTY OF GOOD TASTE

Patty Renwick is known for her outstanding Barbecued Beans. She has been charged with successfully reducing the time it takes to make baked beans by using canned goods. Other accomplices appear to be working in coordination with Patty, suggesting an underground of cooks who rely on canned products. Here the accused share several dangerously delicious recipes.

BARBECUED BEANS
(pictured on page 263)

½   pound ground beef
½   cup chopped onion
⅓   cup sugar
⅓   cup firmly packed brown sugar
½   cup barbecue sauce
¼   cup ketchup
½   teaspoon salt
½   teaspoon pepper
½   teaspoon chili powder
2   tablespoons molasses
2   teaspoons Dijon mustard
1   (15-ounce) can kidney beans, drained
1   (15-ounce) can butter beans, drained
1   (16-ounce) can pork and beans, undrained
10 slices bacon, cooked and crumbled

• **Cook** ground beef and onion in a Dutch oven, stirring until meat crumbles; drain and place in a large bowl.
• **Stir** sugar and remaining ingredients into mixture. Spoon into a lightly greased 2½-quart baking dish.
• **Bake,** uncovered, at 350° for 1 hour, stirring once. **Yield:** 8 to 10 servings.

Patty Renwick
Mount Airy, Maryland

GREEN BEAN ITALIANO

1   (4½-ounce) package brown and wild rice mix
2   tablespoons butter or margarine
1   medium onion, chopped
1   (16-ounce) carton sour cream
1   (8-ounce) package cream cheese, softened
3   (16-ounce) cans French-style green beans, drained
1   (4-ounce) jar diced pimiento, drained
1   (2¼-ounce) can sliced ripe olives
1   teaspoon dried Italian seasoning
1   (8-ounce) package (2 cups) shredded mozzarella cheese
¼   cup grated Parmesan cheese
½   cup Italian-seasoned dried breadcrumbs

• **Cook** rice mix according to package directions, and set aside.
• **Melt** butter in a Dutch oven over medium-high heat. Add onion, and cook until tender, stirring often. Stir in rice, sour cream, and next 5 ingredients. Spoon mixture into a greased 13- x 9- x 2-inch baking dish.
• **Sprinkle** with mozzarella cheese and Parmesan cheeses; top with breadcrumbs.
• **Bake** at 350° for 20 to 25 minutes until cheese is bubbly and lightly browned. **Yield:** 12 servings.

Note: For the rice, we used Success Boil-in-Bag Rice Mix for brown and wild rice mix.

Louise W. Mayer
Richmond, Virginia

CANNED BEANS

■ Always drain and rinse canned beans to remove excess salt.

■ Check canned foods closely as you're shopping to be sure they aren't spoiled. Do not buy cans that are dented, leaking, or bulging at the ends.

BEANOLLA SOUP

1   tablespoon butter or margarine
1   tablespoon olive oil
1   pound boneless pork loin chops, cut into cubes
2   medium onions, chopped
3   cloves garlic, minced
3   (14½-ounce) cans ready-to-serve chicken broth
3   (16-ounce) cans pinto beans, rinsed and drained
1¼ teaspoons dried oregano
¾   teaspoon cumin seeds
½   teaspoon pepper
Vegetable oil
12 (6-inch) corn tortillas, cut into 2- x ¼-inch strips
2   (3-ounce) packages cream cheese, cut into ¼-inch cubes
Condiments: shredded lettuce, chopped tomato, sliced green onions, chopped fresh cilantro (optional)

• **Melt** butter in a Dutch oven, and add olive oil; add pork, and cook over medium-high heat until browned. Remove pork with a slotted spoon, reserving drippings in Dutch oven. Drain pork on paper towels; set aside.
• **Cook** onion and garlic in reserved drippings over medium heat, stirring constantly, 3 to 5 minutes or until onion is tender. Add pork, chicken broth, and next 4 ingredients.
• **Bring** to a boil; cover, reduce heat, and simmer 20 to 30 minutes.
• **Pour** oil to depth of 1 inch into a heavy skillet. Fry one-fourth of tortilla strips in hot oil over medium heat until browned. Remove strips; drain on paper towels. Repeat procedure with remaining tortilla strips.
• **Ladle** soup into bowls; top with tortilla strips and cream cheese cubes. Serve with condiments, if desired. **Yield:** 11 cups.

Joni Mosher
Arlington, Texas

GET SAUCED

We've got a sauce for every schedule. If you have extra time, invest in one that needs to simmer. When you're in a hurry, throw a few ingredients into the blender for an instant meal. You can double any of these recipes to have an extra batch to freeze for a shortcut on the busy days ahead. These sauces are versatile, too. Spoon them over plain meats, fish, or pasta, or try them in the accompanying recipes.

DRIED TOMATO PESTO

Use this sauce chilled as a dip for raw vegetables or steamed shrimp, or serve it hot, tossed with pasta.

½ cup dried tomatoes
1 cup ready-to-serve vegetable broth, divided
½ cup fresh basil leaves
1 clove garlic
¼ cup grated reduced-fat Parmesan cheese
2 tablespoons pine nuts
1 tablespoon olive oil
¼ teaspoon salt
¼ teaspoon ground white pepper
1 teaspoon cornstarch

• **Combine** tomatoes and ½ cup vegetable broth in a small saucepan, and bring mixture to a boil. Remove from heat; let stand 10 minutes.
• **Position** knife blade in food processor bowl; add tomato mixture, fresh basil, and next 6 ingredients. Process until smooth, stopping twice to scrape down sides. Set tomato mixture aside.
• **Combine** remaining ½ cup broth and cornstarch in a saucepan; bring to a boil over medium heat, stirring constantly. Cook mixture 1 minute, stirring constantly. Stir in tomato mixture.

Refrigerate up to 3 days or freeze up to 3 months. **Yield:** 1 cup.

❤ Per ¼-cup serving: Calories 106 (62% from fat)
Fat 7.9g (1.8g saturated) Cholesterol 4mg
Sodium 390mg Carbohydrate 6.5g
Fiber 1g Protein 4.6g

FETTUCCINE AND SHRIMP WITH DRIED TOMATO PESTO

8 ounces fettuccine, uncooked
1½ pounds unpeeled, medium-size fresh shrimp
2 cloves garlic, minced
2 teaspoons olive oil
¼ cup Chablis or other dry white wine
1 cup Dried Tomato Pesto (see recipe)
¼ cup freshly grated Parmesan cheese
Garnish: fresh basil sprigs

• **Cook** fettuccine according to package directions, omitting salt or fat. Set aside, and keep warm.
• **Peel** shrimp, and devein, if desired.
• **Cook** garlic in olive oil in a large skillet over medium heat, stirring constantly, until tender; add shrimp, and cook, stirring constantly, about 1 minute. Add wine, and cook, stirring constantly, until shrimp turn pink.
• **Stir** in Dried Tomato Pesto; cook until thoroughly heated. Spoon over fettuccine, and sprinkle with cheese. Garnish, if desired. **Yield:** 4 servings.

❤ Per serving: Calories 458 (28% from fat)
Fat 14.1g (3.5g saturated) Cholesterol 144mg
Sodium 622mg Carbohydrate 50.6g
Fiber 2.4g Protein 32.3g

DRESS WITH FINESSE

These fat-free recipes are variations on our Basic Vinaigrette and are a snap with a hand-held blender. Toss them with the salad ingredients so that the flavors will distribute evenly.

Basic Vinaigrette: Bring ½ cup ready-to-serve vegetable broth to a boil in a saucepan. Combine an additional ¼ cup vegetable broth and 1 tablespoon cornstarch; gradually stir cornstarch mixture into broth, and boil 1 minute, stirring constantly. Remove from heat; let cool. Blend in ¼ cup white wine vinegar. **Yield:** 1 cup.

Honey-Mustard Vinaigrette: Blend 2 tablespoons honey and 1 tablespoon Dijon mustard into 1 cup Basic Vinaigrette. Toss with a spinach salad.

Raspberry Vinaigrette: Blend 3 tablespoons seedless raspberry jam; 1 clove garlic, minced; ⅛ teaspoon dry mustard; and ⅛ teaspoon pepper into 1 cup Basic Vinaigrette. Toss with fruit or salad greens.

Poppy Seed Vinaigrette: Blend 2 tablespoons sugar, 1 teaspoon poppy seeds, 2 teaspoons grated onion, and ⅛ teaspoon dry mustard into 1 cup Basic Vinaigrette. Toss with a fruit salad.

RED WINE GARLIC SAUCE

Serve this slow-simmered, fat-free sauce over cooked mushrooms, beef, chicken, pork, or firm-fleshed fish like tuna or swordfish.

1 (750-milliliter) bottle Burgundy or other dry red wine
1 head of garlic, crushed (about 12 cloves)

• **Combine** wine and garlic in a large saucepan; simmer 45 minutes or until mixture is reduced to about 1 cup.
• **Pour** mixture through a wire-mesh strainer into a small container, discarding garlic. Store sauce in refrigerator up to 1 week or freeze up to 3 months. **Yield:** 1 cup.

♥ Per ½-cup serving: Calories 48 (2% from fat) Fat 0.1g (0g saturated) Cholesterol 0mg Sodium 33mg Carbohydrate 11.2g Fiber 0g Protein 1.9g

50 FOODS UNDER 50 CALORIES

40 small pretzel sticks	2 sweet peppers
1 tangerine	½ cup skim milk
2 tomatoes	1 tablespoon whipped cream
1 cup bean sprouts	8 stalks celery
1½ cups sliced zucchini	4 saltine crackers
8 dill pickles	1 teaspoon regular mayonnaise
1 rice cake	¼ cup nonfat mayonnaise
1 cup tomato juice	2 cups broccoli
12 mushrooms	5 brussels sprouts
4 potato chips	½ head iceberg lettuce
1 carrot	1 tablespoon cream cheese
1 cup sauerkraut	2 tablespoons fat-free cream cheese product
¾ cup cooked spinach	1 teaspoon butter
1 slice bacon	1 teaspoon margarine
¾ cup raspberries	1 tablespoon sour cream
2 tablespoons chocolate ice cream	¼ cup nonfat sour cream
⅓ cup nonfat frozen yogurt	1 tablespoon grape jelly
1 gingersnap	1 slice wheat bread
12 strawberries	1 kiwifruit
⅓ cup nonfat yogurt	2 apricots
1 tablespoon sour cream	½ cup blueberries
1 cup green beans	10 ripe olives
1 teaspoon vegetable oil	½ cup orange juice
60 radishes	16 asparagus spears
3 graham crackers	1 teaspoon peanut butter

SALMON FILLETS WITH RED WINE GARLIC SAUCE

1 teaspoon fish-flavored bouillon granules
½ cup water
½ cup Red Wine Garlic Sauce (see recipe)
1 tablespoon no-salt-added tomato paste
⅛ teaspoon pepper
4 (4-ounce) salmon steaks
Vegetable cooking spray

• **Combine** first 5 ingredients in a medium saucepan.
• **Cook** bouillon mixture over medium heat until thoroughly heated, stirring often. Remove saucepan from heat, and keep sauce warm.
• **Place** salmon steaks on a rack coated with cooking spray; place rack in broiler pan. Broil 5½ inches from heat (with electric oven door partially opened) 5 minutes or until fish flakes easily when tested with a fork. Serve salmon with warm sauce. **Yield:** 4 servings.

♥ Per serving: Calories 177 (38% from fat) Fat 7.2g (1.1g saturated) Cholesterol 63mg Sodium 288mg Carbohydrate 3.6g Fiber 0.1g Protein 23.3g

FILET MIGNON WITH MUSHROOM SAUCE

4 (4-ounce) beef tenderloin steaks
½ teaspoon dried thyme
¼ teaspoon salt
¼ teaspoon freshly ground pepper
Vegetable cooking spray
2 shallots, finely chopped
1 cup sliced fresh mushrooms
½ cup Red Wine Garlic Sauce (see recipe)
¼ cup canned ready-to-serve, no-salt-added, fat-free beef broth
¼ teaspoon salt

• **Sprinkle** steaks with thyme, ¼ teaspoon salt, and pepper. Place steaks on a rack coated with cooking spray; place rack in broiler pan.

• **Broil** steaks 5½ inches from heat (with electric oven door partially opened) 2 to 3 minutes on each side or until desired degree of doneness. Remove steaks from oven, and wrap in aluminum foil to keep warm; set aside.
• **Cook** shallot in a large skillet coated with cooking spray over medium heat, stirring constantly, until tender. Stir in mushrooms, and cook 1 to 2 minutes. Add Red Wine Garlic Sauce, beef broth, and ¼ teaspoon salt; cook mushroom mixture 2 to 3 minutes. Serve over steaks. **Yield:** 4 servings.

♥ Per serving: Calories 214 (36% from fat)
Fat 8.4g (3.1g saturated) Cholesterol 71mg
Sodium 366mg Carbohydrate 8.4g
Fiber 0.5g Protein 25.6g

RED CHILE SAUCE

Use a few spoonfuls of this sauce to spice up salsa, Spanish rice, gazpacho, tacos, refried beans, or vegetable soup.

4 ounces dried Anaheim chile
    peppers *
2 cloves garlic, minced
1 tablespoon vegetable oil
2 tablespoons all-purpose flour
2 cups water
1½ teaspoons ground cumin
¾ teaspoon salt

• **Remove** pepper stems and seeds. (Wear rubber gloves when handling peppers.) Cover peppers with boiling water; let stand 30 minutes. Drain, reserving 1 cup liquid.
• **Position** knife blade in food processor bowl; add peppers and reserved liquid. Process until smooth, stopping twice to scrape down sides. Set aside.
• **Cook** garlic in oil in a heavy saucepan until tender. Gradually stir in flour, and cook over medium heat, stirring constantly, until caramel colored (about 6 minutes). Gradually add 2 cups water, stirring constantly. Stir in pepper mixture, and cook until slightly thickened.
• **Pour** mixture through a wire-mesh strainer into a bowl, discarding solids. Return to saucepan; add cumin and salt, and cook over medium heat until

thickened. Sauce may be refrigerated up to 3 days or frozen up to 3 months. **Yield:** 2¾ cups.

* 4 ounces dried ancho or chipotle chiles may be substituted.

♥ Per ¼-cup serving: Calories 42 (30% from fat)
Fat 1.5g (0g saturated) Cholesterol 0mg
Sodium 175mg Carbohydrate 6.7g
Fiber 1.3g Protein 1.6g

CHILE-BEEF KABOBS
(pictured on page 263)

16 (1½-inch) onions
1 pound lean boneless sirloin, cut
    into 16 pieces
16 medium-size fresh
    mushrooms
2 sweet red peppers, each cut into
    8 pieces
2 sweet yellow peppers, each cut
    into 8 pieces
1 cup Red Chile Sauce, divided
    (see recipe)
½ cup Burgundy or other dry
    red wine
1 cup nonfat sour cream
Garnishes: jalapeño peppers,
    kale leaves

• **Cook** onions in boiling water to cover 8 minutes; drain.
• **Alternate** meat, onions, mushrooms, and the remaining vegetables on 8 (14-inch) skewers; place skewers in a shallow dish.
• **Combine** ½ cup Red Chile Sauce and wine. Pour over kabobs, turning to coat. Cover and refrigerate 4 hours.
• **Remove** kabobs from marinade, discarding marinade. Place kabobs on a rack; place rack in broiler pan.
• **Broil** 5½ inches from heat (with electric oven door partially opened) 8 to 10 minutes, turning occasionally.
• **Combine** sour cream and remaining ½ cup Red Chile Sauce. Serve with kabobs. Garnish, if desired. **Yield:** 4 servings.

Note: The Red Chile Sauce and sour cream mixture makes a spicy dip for raw vegetables or baked tortilla chips.

♥ Per 2 kabobs and ⅓ cup sauce:
Calories 372 (22% from fat)
Fat 8.5g (2.6g saturated) Cholesterol 80mg
Sodium 244mg Carbohydrate 32.6g
Fiber 5.1g Protein 36.8g

YOU CAN TURN BACK TIME

••••••••••••••••••••••••••••

Want to be as fit at 50 as at 29? Whether you're pushing 30 or 70, these tips will work for you.

■ Start an exercise program, and commit yourself to sticking with it for at least two months. If you can hang in that long, it will become routine.
■ Munch on fat-free snacks, such as fresh fruit or raw vegetables, in midmorning and midafternoon to keep yourself from overeating at mealtime.
■ Recruit a dependable fitness friend to help talk you out of eating all those fattening foods.
■ Life is too short to do exercises you don't like. Find something you enjoy, and do it five times a week.
■ When you're craving something you know you shouldn't have, think about how long it takes to eat it, and balance that with how long it takes to burn those calories.

Spare Parts

Poultry Principle #1: When a recipe calls for chicken, it's best to use chicken breasts.

Not necessarily. Here are some options we share using other pieces of chicken. For terrific flavor and great value, these recipes are unsurpassed. (For tips on cutting up a whole chicken, see "From Our Kitchen to Yours" on the facing page.)

SKILLET CHICKEN IN ORANGE SAUCE

⅓ cup butter or margarine
3 pounds chicken thighs
¼ cup all-purpose flour
2 tablespoons brown sugar
1 teaspoon salt
½ teaspoon ground ginger
⅛ teaspoon pepper
1 cup orange juice
¼ cup water
2 medium oranges, peeled and sliced
Hot cooked rice

• **Melt** butter in a large skillet over medium heat.
• **Add** chicken to skillet, and brown on all sides. Remove chicken from skillet, and set aside; reserve drippings in skillet.
• **Combine** flour and the next 4 ingredients, and stir into pan drippings. Cook over medium-high heat, stirring mixture constantly, for 1 minute. Gradually stir in orange juice and water.
• **Bring** mixture to a boil; add chicken. Cover and simmer 25 minutes.
• **Place** orange slices on top of chicken. Cover and simmer 10 minutes or until chicken is done. Serve over rice. **Yield:** 4 servings.

Ella Turner
Arlington, Texas

COUNTRY CAPTAIN CHICKEN

¾ cup all-purpose flour
½ teaspoon paprika
¼ teaspoon ground red pepper
12 chicken legs
¼ cup butter or margarine, divided
2 tablespoons vegetable oil
½ cup chopped fresh parsley
2 to 3 medium onions, chopped
3 to 4 medium-size green peppers, chopped
2 cloves garlic, minced
1½ tablespoons curry powder
½ to 1 teaspoon salt
½ to 1 teaspoon black pepper
½ teaspoon ground nutmeg
2 (14.5-ounce) cans chopped tomatoes, undrained
½ cup raisins
6 cups hot cooked rice
Garnishes: toasted slivered almonds, chopped fresh parsley

• **Combine** first 3 ingredients in a large, heavy-duty, zip-top plastic bag; set aside.
• **Place** chicken, a few pieces at a time, in bag of flour mixture, shaking to coat. Melt 2 tablespoons butter in a large Dutch oven over medium heat. Add oil.
• **Brown** chicken on all sides in hot butter mixture. Remove pieces as they brown; set chicken aside, reserving pan drippings.
• **Add** remaining 2 tablespoons butter, parsley, and next 7 ingredients to pan drippings; cook until onion is tender, stirring often. Stir in tomatoes and raisins.
• **Bring** mixture to a boil; reduce heat, and add chicken. Cover and simmer 15 minutes; uncover and cook 15 additional minutes or until done. Serve over rice. Garnish, if desired. **Yield:** 6 to 8 servings.

Julie Bernard
Shreveport, Louisiana

PRETZEL-CRUSTED CHICKEN

1 (6.5-ounce) container pretzel twists
5 slices bacon, cooked
½ cup grated Parmesan cheese
2 teaspoons dried parsley flakes
⅓ cup all-purpose flour
1 teaspoon paprika
1 teaspoon salt
¼ teaspoon pepper
¼ teaspoon ground ginger
½ cup beer
1 large egg, lightly beaten
3 pounds chicken pieces

• **Position** knife blade in food processor bowl; add first 4 ingredients. Process until pretzels resemble fine crumbs. Place in a large, heavy-duty, zip-top plastic bag; set aside.
• **Combine** flour and next 4 ingredients in a medium bowl. Stir in beer and egg.
• **Dip** chicken pieces, one at a time, in batter; place in bag of pretzel mixture, shaking to coat. Place on a lightly greased baking sheet.
• **Bake** at 350° for 1 hour or until done. **Yield:** 4 servings.

Janice M. France
Louisville, Kentucky

BOURBON CHICKEN WITH GRAVY

¼ cup butter or margarine
4 pounds chicken pieces, skinned
¾ cup bourbon, divided
1 medium onion, finely chopped
2 tablespoons dried parsley flakes
1 teaspoon dried thyme
½ teaspoon salt
⅛ teaspoon pepper
¼ cup whipping cream

• **Melt** butter in a large heavy skillet over medium heat; add chicken, and brown on all sides. Add ¼ cup bourbon to skillet. Carefully ignite bourbon with a long match, and let burn until flames die.

- **Add** onion and next 4 ingredients. Stir in remaining ½ cup bourbon, stirring until blended. Bring to a boil; cover, reduce heat, and simmer 30 minutes or until chicken is done. Remove to serving plate, reserving liquid in skillet.
- **Add** whipping cream to skillet; bring to a boil, stirring constantly. Cook over medium heat until thickened. Serve with chicken. **Yield:** 4 servings.

Hazel Sellers
Albany, Georgia

FROM OUR KITCHEN TO YOURS

Why learn how to cut up a chicken? Money. You can buy a whole fryer for a lot less per pound, cut it up in 10 minutes (15 minutes if it's your first time), serve three extra pieces (wings and wishbone), and make stock for the freezer with the giblets and back. Or you can spend more per pound for a cut-up chicken and lots more per pound for a package of pick-of-the-chick pieces (breasts, legs, and thighs). A sharp knife makes the process easier. Follow this step-by-step guide.

Step 1: Remove giblets and excess fat from the cavity; reserve giblets to make broth, if desired. Discard fat. Rinse chicken, and place, breast side up, on a cutting board. To remove drumstick and thigh, grasp leg, and pull away from the body; slice through skin between the leg and body to expose the joint where the thigh connects to the back. If you push on the leg to open the joint, the knife easily cuts through it. Repeat procedure with remaining leg.

Step 2: To separate drumstick and thigh, locate the leg-thigh joint by placing your finger where the leg and thigh

meet. You'll feel a slight indentation. Cut through the skin, and bend the drumstick back gently. Sever the two pieces at this joint.

Step 3: To remove wing, pull it away from the body. Cut through the skin into the hollow between wing and body. Pull wing away from the body, exposing the joint, and sever. Repeat with remaining wing.

Step 4: Using kitchen shears, separate the breast from the back by cutting along each side of backbone between rib joints. Bend breast and back halves apart, cutting through neck joints. (If someone is partial to the back pieces, hold the back at each end. Bend the ends toward the skin side until the bones break, and cut the back in half where the bones are broken; cut off the tail. Or send the back along with the giblets to the stockpot.)

Step 5: To split the breast, cut lengthwise along each side of the large white breastbone. (Fond of the wishbone piece? To remove it, start at the tail end, and cut straight down through the breastbone until you hit the wishbone at the neck end of the bird. Cut straight down about 1½ inches; turn the knife toward the neck end at a slight angle, cutting to sever the piece.)

THE OOMPH IN OOMPAH

....

Oktoberfest, the 16-day festival that takes place in Munich each October, is replicated in many Southern cities and towns. We think the robust fare of Germany is reason enough for a celebration. Because no German menu worthy of its name is complete without sauerkraut, we offer an appetizer and – believe it or not – dessert options for this "oompah" necessity.

GRILLED BRATWURST

4 cups water
2 pounds bratwurst
Coarse-grained Dijon mustard

- **Bring** water to a boil; add sausage, and return to a boil. Cover, reduce heat, and simmer 5 minutes. Remove sausage, and pat dry.
- **Cut** sausage lengthwise to, but not through, other side.
- **Cook** sausage, covered with grill lid, over hot coals (400° to 500°) 4 to 5 minutes on each side. Serve with coarse-grained mustard. **Yield:** 4 to 6 servings.

Birgitt Lopez
Dallas, Texas

REUBEN TURNOVERS

2 (8-ounce) cans refrigerated crescent rolls
1 (12-ounce) can corned beef, flaked
1 (16-ounce) can sauerkraut, drained
1 (4-ounce) package shredded Swiss cheese
½ cup commercial Russian dressing
2 tablespoons butter or margarine, melted
Poppy seeds

- **Separate** crescent rolls into 8 rectangles on ungreased baking sheets, pressing perforations to seal.
- **Layer** equal portions of corned beef, sauerkraut, and cheese in center of each rectangle; top evenly with dressing. Moisten edges with water; fold dough in half, pressing edges with a fork to seal.
- **Brush** tops with butter; sprinkle lightly with poppy seeds.
- **Bake** at 400° for 12 minutes or until golden brown. Serve immediately. **Yield:** 8 servings.

Janice M. France
Louisville, Kentucky

GERMAN RED CABBAGE

¼ cup sugar
¼ cup firmly packed brown sugar
½ cup apple cider vinegar
1 medium-size red cabbage, shredded (about 2½ pounds)
2 slices bacon
1 medium Granny Smith apple, chopped
½ cup chopped onion
¼ cup water
2 tablespoons white wine vinegar
½ teaspoon salt
¼ teaspoon pepper
¼ teaspoon ground cloves

• Combine first 3 ingredients, stirring until sugar dissolves. Pour over cabbage; toss to coat. Let stand 5 to 10 minutes.
• Cook bacon in a skillet until crisp; remove bacon, reserving drippings in skillet. Crumble bacon, and set aside.
• Cook apple and onion in reserved drippings, stirring constantly, until tender. Add cabbage mixture and water; bring to a boil. Cover, reduce heat, and simmer 10 minutes.
• Add wine vinegar and next 3 ingredients; simmer, uncovered, 5 minutes. Spoon into a serving dish, and sprinkle with bacon. **Yield:** 6 to 8 servings.

Cindie Hackney
Longview, Texas

HOT GERMAN POTATO SALAD

9 medium-size round red potatoes, scrubbed (about 4¼ pounds)
6 slices bacon
1 medium onion, chopped
2 tablespoons all-purpose flour
2 tablespoons sugar
2 to 3 teaspoons salt
⅛ teaspoon pepper
½ teaspoon celery seeds
¾ cup water
⅓ cup apple cider vinegar

• Cook potatoes in boiling water to cover 25 to 30 minutes or until tender. Drain and cool 10 minutes. Cut potatoes into ½-inch-thick slices; set aside.

• Cook bacon in a large skillet until crisp, and remove bacon, reserving drippings in skillet. Crumble bacon, and set aside.
• Cook onion in reserved drippings, stirring constantly, until tender. Add flour and next 4 ingredients, stirring until blended. Cook 1 minute over medium heat, stirring constantly. Gradually stir in ¾ cup water and vinegar; cook until sauce is thickened and bubbly.
• Layer one-third each of potato and bacon in a 2½-quart serving bowl; drizzle with one-third of sauce mixture. Repeat procedure twice; serve immediately. **Yield:** 8 servings.

Theresa Sheldon
Ponca City, Oklahoma

SAUERKRAUT CAKE

⅔ cup shortening
1½ cups sugar
3 large eggs
2¼ cups all-purpose flour
1 teaspoon baking powder
1 teaspoon baking soda
¼ teaspoon salt
½ cup cocoa
1 cup water
1¼ teaspoons vanilla extract
½ cup sauerkraut, drained
Cream Cheese Frosting

• Beat shortening at medium speed with an electric mixer until fluffy; gradually add sugar, beating well. Add eggs, one at a time, beating until blended after each addition.
• Combine flour and next 4 ingredients, and add to shortening mixture alternately with water, beginning and ending with flour mixture. Beat at low speed until blended after each addition. Stir in vanilla; fold in sauerkraut. Pour batter into a greased and floured 13- x 9- x 2-inch pan.
• Bake at 350° for 25 to 30 minutes or until a wooden pick inserted in center comes out clean. Cool completely in pan on a wire rack.
• Spread cooled cake with Cream Cheese Frosting. Cut into squares. **Yield:** one 13- x 9- x 2-inch cake.

Cream Cheese Frosting

1 (8-ounce) package cream cheese, softened
¼ cup butter or margarine, softened
1 (16-ounce) package powdered sugar, sifted
1 teaspoon vanilla extract

• Beat cream cheese and butter at medium speed with an electric mixer until creamy. Gradually add sugar, beating until blended after each addition. Add vanilla; beat until blended. **Yield:** about 3 cups.

Becky Duncan
Leming, Texas

RECIPES THE KIDS WILL LOVE

....

We know the challenge of planning nutritious meals that kids will eat. The parents who submitted these recipes assured us that kids love them.

CHEESY FISH AND VEGETABLES

If your kids won't eat parsley, omit it or use it as a garnish.

1 (10-ounce) package frozen broccoli, cauliflower, and carrots in cheese sauce
1 pound farm-raised catfish fillets or orange roughy fillets
¼ teaspoon lemon-pepper seasoning
¼ cup chicken broth
1 tablespoon chopped fresh parsley

• Cook vegetables according to the package directions; set aside.
• Sprinkle fish with lemon-pepper seasoning; place in a single layer in a large skillet. Add broth. Bring to a boil. Cover, reduce heat, and simmer 10 minutes or until fish flakes easily when

tested with a fork. Remove to a serving platter with a slotted spoon, reserving drippings; keep warm.
- **Cut** open bag of cooked broccoli, cauliflower, and carrots; pour into skillet with reserved drippings. Cook over medium heat until heated.
- **Spoon** vegetables and sauce over fish; sprinkle with parsley. **Yield:** 4 servings.

Judi Grigoraci
Charleston, West Virginia

TUNA CHOPSTICKS

Slice celery in large pieces so your children can push it aside if they don't like it.

1 (10¾-ounce) can cream of
   mushroom soup, undiluted
¼ cup water
2 cups chow mein noodles, divided
1 (6½-ounce) can tuna packed in
   water, drained
½ cup sliced celery
½ cup cashews, toasted
¼ cup chopped onion
⅛ teaspoon pepper

- **Combine** soup and water in a bowl; stir in 1 cup noodles and remaining ingredients. Spoon into a lightly greased 11- x 7- x 1½-inch baking dish; sprinkle with remaining noodles.
- **Bake** at 350° for 30 minutes or until thoroughly heated. **Yield:** 4 servings.

Ida Loe
Pelham, Alabama

BEEF-MACARONI BAKE

1 pound ground chuck
1¼ cups water
1 (⅞-ounce) package onion
   gravy mix
1 (8-ounce) can tomato sauce
1 cup elbow macaroni,
   uncooked
1 cup (4 ounces) shredded
   mozzarella cheese

- **Brown** meat in a large skillet, stirring until it crumbles; drain and return to skillet. Add water and next 3 ingredients. Bring to a boil. Cover, reduce heat, and simmer 20 minutes or until macaroni is tender.
- **Sprinkle** with cheese; cover and let stand 5 minutes. **Yield:** 4 servings.

QUICK TAMALE CASSEROLE

1 (29-ounce) can hot tamales,
   undrained
1 (15-ounce) can chili with
   beans
1½ cups (6 ounces) shredded
   Cheddar cheese
2 cups crushed corn chips

- **Remove** tamales from can, reserving liquid. Remove husks from tamales. Cut tamales in half crosswise; place in a lightly greased 8-inch square baking dish. Spoon reserved liquid over tamales. Spread chili over tamales, and sprinkle with cheese. Top with crushed corn chips.
- **Bake** at 350° for 30 minutes or until thoroughly heated. **Yield:** 4 servings.

♥ To reduce fat and calories in this recipe, use fat-free chili and reduced-fat Cheddar cheese.

Sheila L. Deere
Mountain Home, Arkansas

PASS IT ON

....

Looking for a casserole to bring to a casual supper? Here's the answer. And be prepared to share this rave-getter from Lynn Lloyd, a former *Southern Living* Test Kitchens director.

PORK CHOP CASSEROLE

1 (6-ounce) package long-grain
   and wild rice mix
2 cups hot water
6 (½-inch-thick) bone-in pork
   loin chops, trimmed
¼ teaspoon pepper
1 (10¾-ounce) can condensed
   cream of celery soup,
   undiluted
½ cup milk

- **Combine** rice, seasoning packet from rice mix, and hot water; place in a lightly greased 13- x 9- x 2-inch baking dish. Set aside.
- **Sprinkle** pork chops with pepper, and place over rice mixture.
- **Cover** and bake at 350° for 1 hour.
- **Uncover** casserole; combine cream of celery soup and milk, and pour over casserole. Bake casserole, uncovered, 15 minutes or until thoroughly heated. **Yield:** 6 servings.

Lynn Lloyd
Birmingham, Alabama

KID-APPROVED SWITCH-HITS

If your children don't like...
- Chili with beans
- Corn chips
- Tuna
- Onions
- Cream of mushroom soup
- Broccoli, cauliflower, and carrots in cheese sauce

Try using...
- Chili without beans
- Tortilla chips
- Chicken
- Onion powder
- Cream of chicken or celery soup
- Any 10-ounce package of their favorite frozen vegetables and ⅓ cup pasteurized process cheese spread

Haunting for Treats?

When little gremlins and goblins come calling on Halloween, greet them with one of our fun-to-fix goodies.

Jan Downs of Shreveport, Louisiana, shares her ideas for transforming two recipes and a popular popcorn snack mix into festive treats that all creatures – great and small – are sure to pronounce a Halloween success.

CANDY APPLE CREATIONS

Assorted candies and nuts can be used to change apples and pears into a gallery of goblins.

5 small Red Delicious apples or Bartlett pears
5 wooden craft sticks
1 (14-ounce) package caramels, unwrapped
2 tablespoons water
Decorations: 4 to 5 (2-ounce) squares chocolate-flavored candy coating, melted; 4 to 5 (2-ounce) squares vanilla-flavored candy coating, melted; assorted chopped nuts; white chocolate morsels; semisweet chocolate morsels; raffia or ribbon; assorted candies; raisins; marshmallows; cookies

● **Wash** apples; dry. Insert craft sticks into stem ends of apples, and set aside.
● **Line** a baking sheet with wax paper; lightly grease wax paper, and set aside.
● **Combine** caramels and water in top of a double boiler; bring water to a boil. Reduce heat to low, and cook until caramels melt, stirring often. Remove caramel mixture from heat.
● **Dip** apples in caramel mixture, covering completely. (Spoon mixture over bare spots, if necessary.) Place apples on prepared baking sheet, allowing excess to drain; cool. Chill 1 hour. Scrape off excess caramel with a knife or metal spatula, if necessary. Decorate, if desired. **Yield:** 5 apples.

Jan's Tips: Decorate Halloween apples by drizzling them with melted candy coatings and/or dipping apples in nuts and/or chocolate morsels. Wrap apples individually in plastic wrap; tie with raffia or ribbon.

Apple Goblins: Use chocolate-flavored candy coating, vanilla-flavored candy coating, assorted candies, assorted nuts, raisins, chocolate morsels, marshmallows, or cookies for goblin eyes, noses, ears, teeth, and hats.

GHOUL'S HANDS

Jan's creativity turns popcorn snack mix into frightful fun.

Commercial caramel-coated popcorn snack mix
75 pieces candy corn
5 clear industrial food handler's gloves
5 rubber bands
Orange ribbon
Black ribbon
5 plastic spider rings

● **Package** popcorn snack mix as desired, using the suggestions that follow. **Yield:** 5 favors.

Jan's Tips: To create hand-shaped favors for the kids, place three pieces candy corn into ends of each glove finger. Fill gloves tightly with popcorn snack mix; close securely at wrist with a rubber band, and tie orange and black ribbons over rubber band. Place a ring on one finger of each hand.

To create adult favors: Place about 4 cups popcorn snack mix into each of 5 (1-gallon) zip-top bags, and seal bags securely. Wrap plastic bags in black or orange tissue paper, and tie with orange and black ribbons.

MONSTER MUFFINS

Save a few undecorated muffins to serve for breakfast on Halloween morning.

1½ cups all-purpose flour
2 teaspoons baking powder
¾ teaspoon salt
⅔ cup sugar
¼ cup firmly packed brown sugar
½ teaspoon ground cinnamon
½ teaspoon ground nutmeg
1 large egg, lightly beaten
1 (8-ounce) can crushed pineapple, drained
½ cup canned pumpkin
½ cup milk
¼ cup butter or margarine, melted
Creamy peanut butter
Decorations: assorted candies, pretzels, mints, pipe cleaners

● **Combine** first 7 ingredients in a large bowl; make a well in center of mixture.
● **Combine** egg and next 4 ingredients; add to dry ingredients, stirring just until moistened. (Batter will be stiff.) Place paper baking cups in muffin pans; spoon batter into cups, filling each two-thirds full.
● **Bake** at 425° for 20 minutes or until golden. Remove from pan immediately, and cool on wire racks. Decorate, if desired. **Yield:** 1 dozen.

*Mary Francis Gibson
Birmingham, Alabama*

Jan's Tips: Spread muffins with peanut butter, and decorate as desired. Use assorted candies, pretzels, mints, and pipe cleaners to transform these snacks into devils, cats, spiders, and aliens.

Winter squash paints a palette of color and flavor in Cream of Acorn Squash Soup and Acorn Squash Puppies (recipes, page 268).

Above: *Chili powder sprinkled through a zigzag paper stencil sparks the top of Thunderbolt Potatoes* (top, left). *Leftovers turn into cornmeal-coated Thunderbolt Potato Patties (recipes, page 213).*

Left: *Try a seasonal menu with surprising combinations – Chicken Breasts With Pecan-Sausage Stuffing, Sautéed Apples, Onions, and Pears Over Spinach, and Golden Cornbread Sticks. (Recipes begin on page 212.)*

*Vanilla isn't just for ice cream.
Right: Vanilla Soufflés With Vanilla Crème Sauce;
Far Right: Pan-Fried Grouper
With Vanilla Wine Sauce; Below: Apple-Walnut
Cake. (Recipes begin on page 241.)*

Above: *Barbecued Beans (recipe, page 248) are so good, everyone will want the recipe.*

Top of page: *Toss greens with baked tortilla chips and reduced-fat Cheddar cheese for a quick salad to serve with Chile-Beef Kabobs (recipe, page 251).*

Left: *Ham-and-Cheese Sandwich Round showcases the versatility of ham (recipe, page 326).*

You'll enjoy sampling our bounty of biscuits: (clockwise from top right) Potato-Bacon Biscuits, Orange-Pecan Scones, and Basic Buttermilk Biscuits. (Recipes begin on page 214.)

NOVEMBER

Winter Squash

Hardy winter squash are the tough guys of the vegetable

patch – stocky, rugged, some with craggy hides and rippled bodies.

But those resilient surfaces protect an interior that turns soft

and mellow when it's cooked and mirrors the color

of sunbeams, from hazy yellow to brilliant orange.

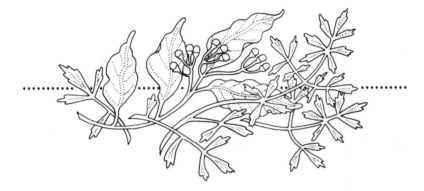

TURBAN CHICKEN CURRY

1 (7¾-pound) turban squash
3½ cups chicken broth, divided
1 cup long-grain rice, uncooked
1 (6-ounce) package chopped
    dried tropical fruit mix
3 green onions, cut into ½-inch
    slices
2 tablespoons vegetable oil
1½ tablespoons all-purpose flour
1 tablespoon curry powder
½ teaspoon salt
¼ teaspoon ground red pepper
½ cup unsweetened coconut milk
3 cups chopped cooked chicken
¼ cup flaked coconut, toasted
½ cup cashews, toasted
Garnish: fresh cilantro sprigs

• **Remove** squash crown by cutting around it with a sharp knife angled toward the center; set crown aside. Remove and discard fiber and seeds.
• **Place** base and crown, cut sides down, in a large baking pan. Add water to pan to depth of 1 inch.
• **Bake** at 350° for 1 hour or until tender. Remove from water, reserving pan of water.
• **Bring** 2½ cups chicken broth to a boil in a medium saucepan; add rice. Cover, reduce heat, and cook 20 minutes or until rice is tender. Stir in fruit mix; cover and set aside.
• **Cook** green onions in oil in a large skillet 3 minutes; stir in flour and next 3 ingredients. Cook 1 minute, stirring constantly. Gradually add remaining 1 cup chicken broth; cook 1 minute or until mixture is slightly thickened. Stir in coconut milk.
• **Add** rice mixture and chicken to skillet, stirring just until blended. Spoon into squash base; top with crown. Place in pan with water.
• **Bake** at 350° for 20 minutes or until thoroughly heated.
• **Set** crown to the side, and sprinkle rice mixture with coconut and cashews before serving. Garnish, if desired. **Yield:** 6 servings.

Kinsey Mills
Birmingham, Alabama

ACORN SQUASH-AND-BOURBON BUTTER

1 (2-pound) acorn squash
1 cup apple cider
¼ cup bourbon
¾ cup firmly packed brown sugar
½ teaspoon ground ginger
½ teaspoon ground allspice
¼ teaspoon ground nutmeg

• **Cut** squash in half crosswise; remove seeds. Place squash, cut side down, in a shallow baking dish or pan. Add water to dish to depth of ½ inch.
• **Bake** at 375° for 45 minutes or until tender. Drain and cool slightly.
• **Scoop** out pulp, discarding shells. Place pulp in container of an electric blender or food processor. Process until smooth, stopping once to scrape down sides.
• **Combine** pulp, cider, and bourbon in a heavy saucepan. Bring to a boil; reduce heat to low, and cook 35 minutes, stirring often. Stir in brown sugar and remaining ingredients.
• **Cook** 10 minutes or until mixture reaches spreading consistency. Serve with biscuits, English muffins, or toast; or serve as a relish with pork or ham. Store in refrigerator up to 1 month or freeze up to 6 months. **Yield:** 2 cups.

BAKED SWEET DUMPLING SQUASH

2 sweet dumpling squash or acorn
    squash (about 3 pounds total)
¼ teaspoon salt
2 tablespoons butter or margarine,
    cut into small pieces
¼ cup firmly packed brown sugar

• **Cut** squash in half crosswise; remove seeds. Place squash, cut side down, in a shallow baking dish or pan. Add water to dish to depth of ½ inch.
• **Bake** at 375° for 30 minutes or until tender. Drain.
• **Turn** squash cut side up; sprinkle with salt. Dot with butter and sprinkle brown sugar equally into each cavity.
• **Bake** at 350° for 10 minutes or until sugar bubbles. Serve immediately. **Yield:** 4 servings.

BASIC ACORN SQUASH PUREE

3 (1¼-pound) acorn squash
3 tablespoons butter or margarine
½ teaspoon salt
¾ teaspoon ground allspice

• **Cut** squash in half crosswise; remove seeds. Place squash, cut side down, in a shallow baking dish or pan. Add water to dish to depth of ½ inch.
• **Bake** at 375° for 45 minutes or until tender. Drain and cool slightly.
• **Scoop** out pulp; discarding shells.
• **Place** pulp and remaining ingredients in container of an electric blender or food processor; process until smooth, stopping once to scrape down sides. Use pureed mixture in Granola-Squash Pancakes and Orange-Squash Brûlée. Freeze acorn squash puree up to 3 months, if desired. **Yield:** 4 cups.

GRANOLA-SQUASH PANCAKES

These pancakes are very fragile. Handle gingerly, and they will be well worth the effort.

2½ cups reduced-fat granola cereal without raisins
1 cup finely chopped pecans
1¼ cups all-purpose flour
½ teaspoon baking powder
¼ teaspoon salt
¾ teaspoon ground nutmeg
1 cup Basic Acorn Squash Puree (see recipe)
2 large eggs, lightly beaten
Vegetable oil

• **Position** knife blade in food processor bowl; add granola. Pulse 5 times or until granola is the consistency of dry breadcrumbs.
• **Combine** granola and pecans in a pieplate. Set granola mixture aside.
• **Combine** flour and next 3 ingredients; make a well in center of mixture. Set aside.
• **Combine** squash puree and eggs; add to flour mixture, stirring just until blended.
• **Spoon** about 2 tablespoons batter onto granola mixture in pieplate.

Using a 3-inch-wide spatula, turn batter over to coat the other side. Flatten batter into a ¼-inch-thick pancake. Set pancake aside, and repeat procedure with remaining batter.
• **Pour** oil to depth of ¼ inch into a large skillet. Fry pancakes in hot oil about 2 minutes on each side or until golden brown. Drain on paper towels. Serve with syrup or applesauce. **Yield:** 12 pancakes.

ORANGE-SQUASH BRÛLÉE

2 cups whipping cream
2 tablespoons Cointreau or other orange-flavored liqueur
6 egg yolks
1 cup Basic Acorn Squash Puree (see recipe)
¼ cup sugar
2 tablespoons orange marmalade
1 teaspoon cornstarch
⅛ teaspoon salt
¼ cup firmly packed brown sugar

• **Combine** whipping cream and Cointreau in a small saucepan; bring to a boil. Remove from heat, and set aside.
• **Combine** egg yolks and next 5 ingredients in container of an electric blender; process until smooth. Turn blender on high; gradually add hot mixture. Pour into 6 (8-ounce) ramekins. Place ramekins in a large baking pan. Add water to pan to reach halfway up sides of ramekins.
• **Bake** at 350° for 35 minutes or until center is almost set. Remove from water; cool completely.
• **Cover** and chill at least 3 hours. Remove ramekins from refrigerator 30 minutes before preparing brown sugar topping.
• **Place** brown sugar in container of an electric blender; process until very fine. Sprinkle 2 teaspoons sugar onto each custard. Set ramekins on a baking sheet.
• **Broil** 3 inches from heat (with electric oven door partially opened) 1 minute or until sugar bubbles. **Yield:** 6 servings.

Bountiful and bodacious, these versatile vegetables reveal unexpected talents.

Sturdy winter squash are as varied in shape and color as jigsaw puzzle pieces: club-shaped butternuts, wavy acorns, oval-shaped spaghetti squash, and regal turbans. They grow slowly and can be stored for three to four months in a cool, dry place.

Their smaller summer cousins, pattypans, crooknecks, and zucchini, grow more rapidly, but are much more fragile and best eaten soon after harvesting.

Summer squash, with their tender skin, are very perishable and can be refrigerated in a plastic bag no more than five days.

Versatile winter squash show up in a variety of recipes. Baked squash halves are roly-poly side dishes. Cooked spaghetti squash is a great pasta impersonator. And when pureed, winter's most stalwart vegetables offer comfort in dishes from soup to pancakes.

HARVEST SQUASH MEDLEY

1 (1½-pound) butternut squash, peeled and seeded
2 sweet potatoes (about ¾ pound total), peeled
3 tablespoons butter or margarine
¼ cup honey
¼ cup orange juice
½ teaspoon ground cinnamon
⅛ teaspoon ground nutmeg
1 tablespoon grated orange rind
2 small cooking apples, peeled, cored, and sliced
½ cup chopped walnuts, toasted

● Cut squash and sweet potatoes into ¾-inch chunks. Place in a lightly greased 11- x 7- x 1½-inch baking dish; set aside.
● Combine butter and next 5 ingredients in a small saucepan. Bring to a boil over medium heat, stirring constantly; pour over squash and sweet potato. Cover.
● Bake at 350° for 30 minutes.
● Uncover and stir in apples. Bake, uncovered, at 350° for 30 additional minutes or until tender. Sprinkle with walnuts. **Yield:** 6 to 8 servings.

Valerie Stutsman
Norfolk, Virginia

ASIAN SPAGHETTI SQUASH

2 (2¼-pound) spaghetti squash
1 clove garlic
2 tablespoons sesame or olive oil
2 tablespoons vegetable oil
2 tablespoons rice wine vinegar
2 tablespoons soy sauce
1 teaspoon sugar
½ to 1 teaspoon dried crushed red pepper
½ cup sliced green onions
½ cup grated carrot
½ cup snow pea pods, cut lengthwise into thin strips
2 tablespoons sesame seeds, toasted

● Cut squash in half lengthwise; remove seeds. Place squash, cut side down, in a shallow baking dish or pan. Add water to dish to depth of ½ inch.

● Bake at 375° for 45 minutes or until skin is tender and strands may be easily loosened with a fork. Drain and cool slightly.
● Position knife blade in food processor bowl; add garlic, and process until finely chopped, scraping down sides, if nesessary. Add sesame oil and next 5 ingredients. Process until blended, stopping once to scrape down sides; set garlic mixture aside.
● Remove spaghetti-like strands of squash, using a fork; discard shells. Combine squash, green onions, carrot, and snow peas in a large bowl. Add garlic mixture; toss gently. Sprinkle with sesame seeds. Serve immediately. **Yield:** 6 to 8 servings.

ACORN SQUASH PUPPIES
(pictured on page 257)

1 (1¾-pound) acorn squash
2 cups self-rising cornmeal
¼ cup all-purpose flour
1 large egg, lightly beaten
½ cup milk
½ cup finely chopped onion
Vegetable oil

● Cut squash in half crosswise; remove seeds. Place squash, cut side down, in a shallow baking dish or pan. Add water to dish to depth of ½ inch.
● Bake at 375° for 45 minutes or until tender. Drain and cool slightly.
● Scoop out pulp, discarding shells. Place pulp in container of an electric blender or food processor; process until smooth. Measure 1¼ cups squash puree; set aside. (Reserve any additional puree for another use.)
● Combine cornmeal and flour in a large bowl; make a well in center of mixture. Set aside.
● Combine squash puree, egg, milk, and onion. Add to dry ingredients, stirring just until moistened.
● Pour oil to depth of 2 inches into a Dutch oven; heat to 360°. Drop by tablespoonfuls into hot oil. Cook 2 minutes or until golden, turning once. Drain on paper towels. **Yield:** 2 dozen.

Mary Horton
Moulton, Alabama

CREAM OF ACORN SQUASH SOUP
(pictured on page 257)

2 large acorn squash (about 3¾ pounds)
¼ cup butter or margarine
1 cup chopped onion
6 cups chicken broth
1½ cups Chablis or other dry white wine
2 teaspoons grated lime rind
2 tablespoons lime juice
¼ teaspoon pepper
1 cup whipping cream
Garnish: chopped chives

● Cut squash in half crosswise; remove seeds. Place squash, cut side down, in a shallow baking dish or pan. Add water to dish to a depth of ½ inch.
● Bake at 375° for 45 minutes or until tender. Drain and cool slightly.
● Scoop out pulp, discarding shells. Chop pulp; set aside.
● Melt butter in a Dutch oven over medium-high heat; add onion, and cook, stirring constantly, until tender. Add chicken broth, wine, and chopped pulp. Bring to a boil; reduce heat, and simmer 10 minutes. Add lime rind, juice, and pepper; cool.
● Pour half of broth mixture into container of an electric blender; process until smooth. Pour pureed mixture into a large container. Repeat procedure with remaining broth mixture. Return both portions to Dutch oven. Stir in whipping cream.
● Cook over low heat, stirring constantly, until thoroughly heated. Serve hot or cold. Garnish, if desired. **Yield:** 11½ cups.

Mrs. Joel Allard
San Antonio, Texas

HOLIDAY DINNERS®

MAKING AND BREAKING TRADITION

We love "possibility thinking." You know, the "What if ..." and "If only ..." thoughts

so many of us have this time of year that tap into dreams. As you think of ways to make the coming

holiday weeks truly special, remember a bit of advice: "Don't try hard; try easy."

HOLIDAY COUNTDOWN

The simplicity of our two holiday menus comes in trying a different approach. Take a look at our Thanksgiving Made Easy menu (on page 272), a feast that surprises – classic turkey, cranberries, and cornbread dressing with flavors of the Southwest. Using convenience products will help you to streamline preparations. They help get you out of the kitchen quicker so you can spend more time with your guests.

Or to break the turkey tradition this holiday season, proclaim this the year to beef up the celebration with some new customs. Our Festive Holiday Dinner menu (on page 270) offers a crowd-pleasing beef tenderloin and an easy and elegant make-ahead dessert.

As you make your plans, be sure to look over "Holiday Countdown" (on this page). We guarantee you'll be humming a carol or two as you move with ease through the busy days ahead.

ONE MONTH AHEAD
- Plan menu.
- Check supply of staples.
- Make shopping list of perishables and nonperishables. Purchase items needed as grocery specials occur.

TWO WEEKS AHEAD
- Check all serving dishes, silverware, and glassware.
- Check table linens to see if pressing or cleaning is needed.
- Invite guests.
- Make place cards, and plan table centerpiece.

ONE WEEK AHEAD
- Shop for nonperishables.
- Start stockpiling ice if you don't have an ice-maker.

FOUR TO FIVE DAYS AHEAD
- Polish silverware.

TWO DAYS AHEAD
- Shop for perishables.
- Clean fresh vegetables, and refrigerate them.
- Chill beverages.
- Set the table.

ONE DAY AHEAD
- Review recipes; make a list of temperatures and cooking times, and prepare cooking schedule.
- If using place cards, decide seating arrangements.
- Make centerpiece for table.

SEVERAL HOURS BEFORE PARTY
- Review cooking schedule.

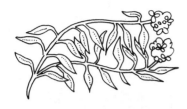

FESTIVE HOLIDAY DINNER
Serves 12

Chutneyed Beef Tenderloin
Baked Rice
Brussels Sprouts
Ambrosia Salad
Gold-Dusted Cookies 'n'
Cream Dessert
Sugar-and-Spice Pecans

FESTIVE HOLIDAY DINNER COUNTDOWN

TWO WEEKS AHEAD
■ Order beef tenderloin at your local supermarket.

FOUR TO FIVE DAYS AHEAD
■ Bake Sugar Cookies and Chocolate-Gingerbread Cookies; freeze.
■ Prepare Sugar-and-Spice Pecans; store in an airtight container.

TWO DAYS AHEAD
■ Thaw beef, if frozen.
■ Drizzle dessert goblets with melted candy coating.
■ Soak rice for Baked Rice.

ONE DAY AHEAD
■ Prepare Baked Rice.
■ Prepare Ambrosia Salad.
■ Prepare beef broth reduction and Wine Reduction Sauce for tenderloin.

SEVERAL HOURS BEFORE PARTY
■ Thaw cookies.
■ Unmold salad.
■ Bake tenderloin, and assemble and reheat items according to your schedule of cooking times.

FINAL COUNTDOWN
■ Prepare brussels sprouts.

CHUTNEYED BEEF TENDERLOIN

4   cups ready-to-serve, reduced-sodium beef broth
1   carrot, scraped and chopped
1   onion, quartered
1   stalk celery, chopped
1   (8-ounce) jar chutney, finely chopped
1   teaspoon salt
½   teaspoon coarsely ground pepper
1   tablespoon butter or margarine, softened
1   (5- to 6-pound) beef tenderloin, trimmed
    Wine Reduction Sauce
3   tablespoons butter
½   teaspoon chopped fresh thyme or ¼ teaspoon dried thyme

● **Combine** first 4 ingredients in a saucepan; bring to a boil over medium heat. Reduce heat, and simmer 40 minutes or until mixture is reduced to about 1½ cups. Pour mixture through a wire-mesh strainer into a bowl, reserving the vegetables; set beef broth reduction mixture aside.
● **Position** knife blade in food processor bowl; add reserved vegetables. Process until smooth. Set vegetable mixture aside.
● **Combine** chutney and next 3 ingredients, stirring until smooth. Spread half of chutney mixture over all surfaces of tenderloin. Place tenderloin on a rack in a shallow roasting pan.
● **Bake** at 450° for 20 minutes. Remove from oven, and spread remaining chutney mixture on tenderloin. Bake 10 to 20 additional minutes or until a meat thermometer inserted in thickest portion registers 145° for rare, 160° for medium. Remove meat from pan, and let stand 15 minutes before slicing.
● **Remove** rack from pan.
● **Add** beef broth reduction to pan; place pan over burners. Bring to a boil over medium heat, stirring to loosen browned particles. Pour broth mixture into a saucepan; add Wine Reduction Sauce and vegetable mixture.

● **Bring** mixture to a boil; reduce heat, and simmer 5 minutes, stirring frequently. Whisk in 3 tablespoons butter, 1 tablespoon at a time. Stir in thyme. Serve sauce with tenderloin. **Yield:** 12 servings.

Wine Reduction Sauce

1   (750-milliliter) bottle Cabernet Sauvignon
3   cloves shallots, minced
1   bay leaf
3 to 4 sprigs fresh thyme

● **Combine** all ingredients in a large saucepan. Bring mixture to a boil over medium heat; reduce heat, and simmer until liquid is reduced to about 1 cup (about 40 minutes). Pour mixture through a wire-mesh strainer into a measuring cup, pressing with back of a spoon against sides of strainer to remove all juices. Discard solids. **Yield:** 1 cup.

Jan Downs
Shreveport, Louisiana

BAKED RICE

1   cup wild rice, uncooked
1½ cups brown rice
1   tablespoon butter or margarine
1   (10½-ounce) can condensed beef broth, undiluted
2½ to 3 cups water
3   tablespoons butter or margarine
1   (8-ounce) package mushrooms, sliced
2   carrots, scraped and finely chopped
1   bunch green onions, sliced
1   (8-ounce) can sliced water chestnuts, drained
¼   teaspoon salt (optional)
¼   cup dry white vermouth (optional)
2   tablespoons cold butter or margarine, cut into small pieces

- **Place** wild rice in a bowl; add water to depth of 1 inch above rice. Cover and let stand at least 8 hours.
- **Drain** rice. Rinse and drain again.
- **Combine** wild rice, brown rice, 1 tablespoon butter, beef broth, and 2½ cups water in a large heavy saucepan.
- **Bring** to a boil; cover, reduce heat, and simmer about 45 minutes or until water is absorbed and rice is tender. (Add additional water, if necessary to prevent sticking or burning.)
- **Melt** 3 tablespoons butter in a large heavy skillet. Add mushrooms and next 3 ingredients; cook over medium heat until all liquid is absorbed (about 3 minutes), stirring often.
- **Stir** vegetables and salt, if desired, into rice mixture, and spoon into a lightly greased 13- x 9- x 2-inch baking dish.
- **Drizzle** with vermouth, if desired, and dot with butter; cover.
- **Bake** at 350° for 40 minutes or until thoroughly heated. **Yield:** 12 servings.

Note: To make ahead, prepare casserole, omitting vermouth and butter. Cover and refrigerate overnight. Remove from refrigerator, and let stand at room temperature 30 minutes. To serve, add vermouth, if desired, and butter, and bake at 350° for 50 minutes or until thoroughly heated. To prepare casserole without soaking wild rice, cook wild rice as directed on package.

UNMOLDING THE SALAD

· · · · · · · · · · · · · · · · ·

After your shaped salad has completely congealed, carefully unmold. To break the suction, run a knife around the edge of the mold. If the mold has fluted sides, press the edge of the salad lightly with your finger, and gently pull away from the sides of mold.

AMBROSIA SALAD

Rosé wine and sliced strawberries add the festive ruby color to this congealed version of a holiday favorite.

2 (6-ounce) packages apricot-flavored gelatin
2 cups boiling water
1 cup rosé wine or dry white wine, chilled
¾ cup cold water
1 (10-ounce) package frozen sliced strawberries, thawed and undrained
1 (8-ounce) can crushed pineapple, undrained
2 bananas, peeled, cut in half lengthwise, and sliced
1 (8-ounce) carton sour cream
2 tablespoons brown sugar
1 to 2 tablespoons coconut, toasted
Lettuce leaves

- **Combine** gelatin and boiling water in a large bowl; stir 2 minutes or until gelatin dissolves. Add wine and cold water; chill until the consistency of unbeaten egg white.
- **Stir** in strawberries, pineapple, and banana; pour into a lightly oiled 6-cup mold.
- **Cover** and chill at least 8 hours.
- **Combine** sour cream and brown sugar; spoon into a serving dish. Sprinkle with toasted coconut.
- **Unmold** salad onto lettuce leaves; serve with sour cream mixture. **Yield:** 12 servings.

Martha Myers
Manchester, Maryland

GOLD-DUSTED COOKIES 'N' CREAM DESSERT
(pictured on page 300)

½ gallon vanilla ice cream
8 ounces chocolate-flavored candy coating, melted
½ cup finely chopped Sugar-and-Spice Pecans (see recipe on page 272)
½ teaspoon edible gold-leaf powder
12 Sugar Cookies
12 Chocolate-Gingerbread Cookies (see recipe on page 293)

- **Scoop** ice cream into 12 balls. Place on a baking sheet in freezer until ready to use.
- **Place** melted candy coating in a small heavy-duty, zip-top plastic bag. Snip a small hole in 1 corner of bag; drizzle inside of 12 goblets to decorate. Set aside in a cool, dry place. (Do not store glasses in refrigerator.)
- **Place** an ice cream ball in each glass. Sprinkle ice cream with Sugar-and-Spice Pecans and gold-leaf powder; top with cookies. Serve with additional cookies and pecans, if desired. **Yield:** 12 servings.

Note: Edible gold-leaf powder can be purchased at most cooking specialty stores.

Sugar Cookies

1 (20-ounce) package refrigerated sliceable sugar cookie dough
All-purpose flour
Garnish: edible gold-leaf powder (see note above)

- **Roll** dough to ⅛-inch thickness on a lightly floured surface. Dip star-shaped cookie cutter into flour; cut dough into desired sizes with cutters; place on greased baking sheets.
- **Bake** at 350° for 7 minutes or until lightly browned. Cool 1 minute; remove to wire racks to cool. Garnish, if desired. **Yield:** about 5 dozen cookies.

SUGAR-AND-SPICE PECANS
(pictured on page 300)

Crumble these gold-dusted pecans, and use to crown Gold-Dusted Cookies 'n' Cream Dessert (on page 271). Package leftovers for gifts or party favors.

¾ cup sugar
1 teaspoon ground cinnamon
½ teaspoon salt
¼ teaspoon ground nutmeg
¼ teaspoon ground allspice
¼ teaspoon ground cloves
1 egg white
2½ tablespoons water
8 cups pecan halves
¾ teaspoon edible gold-leaf powder (see note on page 271)

• **Combine** first 8 ingredients in a bowl; stir well. Add pecans; stir until evenly coated. Spread in a lightly greased, foil-lined 15- x 10- x 1-inch jellyroll pan. Bake at 275° for 50 to 55 minutes, stirring occasionally.
• **Remove** from pan, and cool on wax paper. Place in a heavy-duty, zip-top plastic bag; sprinkle with gold-leaf powder, shaking bag gently to coat pecans. Store pecans in an airtight container. **Yield:** 8 cups.

THANKSGIVING MADE EASY
Serves Eight

Shrimp-Chile Bisque
Citrus-Marinated Turkey Breast
Mexican Cranberries
Southwestern-Style
Spoonbread Dressing
Garlic Green Beans
Brandied Yams
Commercial Rolls
Frozen Almond Crunch (see recipe on page 283)

THANKSGIVING MADE EASY COUNTDOWN

TWO WEEKS AHEAD
■ Order turkey breast at supermarket.

FOUR TO FIVE DAYS AHEAD
■ Thaw turkey breast, if frozen.
■ Prepare marinade, and refrigerate.
■ Prepare Frozen Almond Crunch (see recipe on page 283); freeze.
■ Bake cornbread; cool, crumble, and store in refrigerator.
■ Prepare Mexican Cranberries.

ONE DAY AHEAD
■ Prepare Shrimp-Chile Bisque.
■ Marinate turkey breast.
■ Prepare spoonbread dressing.
■ Prepare Brandied Yams and Garlic Green Beans.

SEVERAL HOURS BEFORE PARTY
■ Transfer dessert to a serving platter; remove sides of springform pan.
■ Grill turkey and bake dressing; assemble and reheat items according to your schedule of cooking times.

SHRIMP-CHILE BISQUE
(pictured on page 298)

2 (10¾-ounce) cans cream of shrimp soup, undiluted
3 cups milk
½ (16-ounce) loaf mild Mexican-style process cheese spread, cubed
1 (14-ounce) can artichoke hearts, drained and chopped
¼ teaspoon seasoned salt
¼ teaspoon ground white pepper
½ teaspoon Beau Monde seasoning (optional)
1 (5-ounce) package frozen cooked small shrimp
Garnishes: sweet red pepper slices, fresh parsley sprigs

• **Combine** first 7 ingredients in a Dutch oven; cook over low heat until cheese melts and mixture is hot, stirring often.

• **Add** shrimp; cook 1 minute or until thoroughly heated, stirring often. Spoon into serving bowls, and garnish, if desired. **Yield:** 2 quarts.

Note: Bisque may be prepared a day ahead except for adding shrimp. Reheat over low heat, stirring often. Stir in shrimp as directed.

Candy Stevens Smith
Texarkana, Texas

CITRUS-MARINATED TURKEY BREAST
(pictured on page 299)

Most grocery store meat departments will gladly bone turkey breasts.

1 (6- to 7-pound) turkey breast
1 cup orange juice
¼ cup lime juice
¼ cup olive oil
3 tablespoons apple cider vinegar
2 teaspoons salt
2 teaspoons dried oregano
1 teaspoon pepper
Garnishes: fresh sage, oregano, rosemary sprigs

• **Remove** and discard skin and breast bone from turkey. Place breast halves in a jumbo, heavy-duty, zip-top plastic bag; set aside.
• **Combine** orange juice and next 6 ingredients in a jar; close tightly, and shake vigorously. Set ½ cup marinade in refrigerator. Pour remaining marinade over turkey; seal bag. Chill 8 hours, turning bag occasionally.
• **Remove** turkey from marinade; discard marinade.
• **Cook** turkey, covered with grill lid, over hot coals (400° to 500°) for 18 minutes on each side or until a meat thermometer registers 170°, brushing occasionally with reserved marinade. Let stand 10 minutes before slicing. **Yield:** 8 servings.

Note: To cook turkey in oven, place on a rack in a roasting pan; bake at

325° for 1 hour and 10 minutes or until a meat thermometer registers 170°, brushing turkey occasionally with reserved marinade.

Carolyn Gaskins
Cherryville, North Carolina

MEXICAN CRANBERRIES
(pictured on page 299)

1 (16-ounce) can whole-berry cranberry sauce
1 (10½-ounce) jar jalapeño pepper jelly
2 tablespoons chopped fresh cilantro

• **Combine** all ingredients in a small saucepan; cook over low heat until the jelly melts, stirring often. Cool. Serve immediately or chill. **Yield:** 2½ cups.

Carolyn Gaskins
Cherryville, North Carolina

SOUTHWESTERN-STYLE SPOONBREAD DRESSING
(pictured on page 299)

2 (8½-ounce) packages cornbread mix
2 to 3 teaspoons cumin seeds
¼ cup butter or margarine
2 cups finely chopped celery
½ cup chopped onion
½ cup chopped sweet red pepper
½ cup chopped green pepper
1 (8-ounce) package herb-seasoned stuffing mix
2 (10½-ounce) cans condensed chicken broth, undiluted
2¼ cups water
2 large eggs
½ teaspoon salt
½ teaspoon ground red pepper
Garnishes: sweet red pepper strips, celery leaves

• **Prepare** cornbread according to package directions; cool and crumble into a large bowl. Set aside.

• **Cook** cumin seeds in a large heavy skillet over medium heat, stirring constantly, 3 minutes or until seeds are more fragrant and lightly browned. Cool seeds and crush; set aside.
• **Melt** butter in skillet over medium heat; add celery and next 3 ingredients, and cook, stirring constantly, until tender.
• **Stir** celery mixture, crushed cumin, stuffing mix, and next 5 ingredients into crumbled cornbread.
• **Spoon** mixture into a lightly greased 13- x 9- x 2-inch baking dish.
• **Bake** at 350° for 1 hour and 15 minutes or until lightly browned. Garnish, if desired. **Yield:** 8 servings.

♥ To save 51 calories and 8.1 fat grams per serving, prepare cornbread mix using egg substitute and nonfat buttermilk. Substitute 2 tablespoons reduced-calorie margarine for butter. Substitute 5 cups plus 2 tablespoons reduced-sodium, ready-to-serve, fat-free chicken broth for condensed chicken broth and water, and ½ cup egg substitute for eggs. Instead of greasing the baking dish, coat it with vegetable cooking spray. Bake dressing at 350° for 1 hour and 5 minutes. This version makes a firmer textured dressing than the original recipe.

GARLIC GREEN BEANS
(pictured on page 299)

2 pounds fresh green beans
1 cup water
¼ cup butter or margarine
4 cloves garlic, minced
¼ teaspoon lemon-pepper seasoning
¼ teaspoon salt-free herb seasoning
⅓ cup chopped fresh parsley

• **Wash** beans; and remove ends.
• **Bring** water to a boil in a Dutch oven. Add beans; return to a boil, cover, and simmer 10 minutes or until crisp-tender. Drain and keep warm.

• **Melt** butter in Dutch oven over medium heat; add garlic, and cook until tender, stirring occasionally. Stir in seasonings. Add green beans; cook, stirring occasionally, 3 minutes or until thoroughly heated. Spoon into a serving dish; sprinkle with parsley. **Yield:** 8 servings.

BRANDIED YAMS
(pictured on page 299)

5 large sweet potatoes (about 4¼ pounds)
¼ cup sugar
¼ to ⅓ cup brandy
3 tablespoons butter or margarine, melted
1 teaspoon salt
½ teaspoon ground nutmeg
½ teaspoon ground ginger
⅛ teaspoon pepper
1 tablespoon butter or margarine, melted
1 tablespoon grated orange rind
Garnish: orange slices

• **Cook** sweet potatoes in boiling water to cover 45 minutes or until tender; cool to touch. Peel and mash.
• **Stir** in sugar and next 6 ingredients; spoon mixture into a lightly greased 11- x 7- x 1½-inch baking dish. Brush top with 1 tablespoon melted butter; sprinkle with orange rind.
• **Bake** at 350° for 25 to 30 minutes. Garnish, if desired. **Yield:** 8 servings.

Phyllis Taylor
Gillham, Arkansas

FROM OUR KITCHEN TO YOURS

....

With one bite of the Chutneyed Beef Tenderloin from "Making and Breaking Tradition" (beginning on page 269), you're suddenly transported to a linen cloth-covered table in a French restaurant in New Orleans. The secret of this exceptional entrée from Jan Downs of Shreveport, Louisiana, is making reductions and using them as a foundation for building flavor.

Professional chefs have used reductions for centuries to decrease liquid and increase flavor. It's as easy as boiling water. Broth or wine cooks rapidly over high heat to evaporate some of the liquid, intensify and enrich the flavor, and thicken the mixture. And these lower fat

---

REDUCTION REVIEW

■ Reductions can't be rushed. They can take a few minutes to an hour or more, depending on the amount of ingredients used.

■ Plan to make the reductions ahead; refrigerate up to three days, or freeze up to six months.

■ Just simmer the liquid; a full boil may cause the sauce to become cloudy.

■ To speed evaporation of the liquid, keep the pot uncovered during the reduction process.

■ When substituting canned broth for a homemade version, use the no-salt-added version. Reducing the broth intensifies the flavor of sodium.

---

sauces are as richly flavored as the ones laden with butter and cream.

Jan's mouth-watering beef tenderloin combines two reductions. The beef broth reduction starts with simple ingredients. (Using canned broth is a timesaving step for the home cook.) After 40 minutes, the mixture reduces from 4 cups to 1½ cups. She then removes the aromatic vegetables, purees them in a food processor, and returns them to the reduction mixture. (This step adds extra thickness to the mixture.) For the Red Wine Reduction, she simmers savory herbs and shallots in red wine for 40 minutes. As the volume reduces to 1 cup, the flavors become concentrated and some of the alcohol content evaporates.

Another outstanding recipe that builds flavor with reductions is Game Pot Pie With Parmesan Crust (on page 304). Executive Chef David Everett at the Dining Room at Ford's Colony in Williamsburg, Virginia, layers on intense flavor beginning with his from-scratch Venison Stock.

Both Jan and David share an easy way to add concentrated flavor to meat. When you serve their recipes, your family or guests might also "travel" to New Orleans. Regardless, they'll be impressed that the magician in the kitchen is you.

FAMILIAR BUT FABULOUS

Turn an everyday dinner classic into a festive meal. All it takes is a few savory additions and an enticing presentation.

Dinner begins with the flavors of apricot, pecans, and thyme rolled up in succulent pork. Bourbon serves as the foundation for the robust sauce. Oven-roasted vegetables, instead of the usual baked potato, are the perfect complement to pork.

The sweet-tart vinaigrette for the spinach salad keeps bites of apple white and crisp. Plump rolls, adorned with a mosaic of herbs and savory seasonings, round out the menu. Bake the dough with sides touching for a sensational centerpiece or in clusters to be passed around the table.

FAMILIAR BUT FABULOUS MENU
Serves 10

Apricot-Pecan Stuffed Pork Loin
Roasted Potatoes, Carrots,
And Leeks
Spinach Salad With
Apple-Onion Vinaigrette
Centerpiece Rolls

APRICOT-PECAN STUFFED PORK LOIN

The bourbon sauce for this roast requires "flaming" on the cooktop before pouring over the pork and baking. This is to burn off the alcohol and to prevent the sauce from flaming in the oven. (Beware: Skipping this step could mean a call to the fire department.)

1½ cups dried apricot halves
½ cup pecans
1 clove garlic
½ teaspoon salt
¼ teaspoon pepper
2 tablespoons dried thyme, divided
¼ cup molasses, divided
¼ cup peanut or vegetable oil, divided
1 (5-pound) boneless rolled pork loin roast, well trimmed
1 cup bourbon
1 cup chicken broth
¼ cup whipping cream
¼ teaspoon salt

• **Position** knife blade in food processor bowl; add the first 5 ingredients, and process until coarsely chopped. Add 1 tablespoon thyme, 1 tablespoon molasses, and 2 tablespoons oil; process until mixture is finely chopped, but not smooth.

● **Remove** pork loin halves from elastic net. (There should be 2 pieces.) Trim excess fat. Make a cut lengthwise down the center of each piece, cutting to, but not through, bottom. Starting from center cut, slice horizontally toward 1 side, stopping ½ inch from edge. Repeat on opposite side. Unfold meat so that it's flat. Repeat with other loin half.

● **Flatten** to ½-inch thickness, using a meat mallet or rolling pin. Repeat with remaining loin half.

● **Spread** apricot mixture evenly on top of pork. Roll each loin half, separately, jellyroll fashion, starting with long side. Secure with string, and place, seam side down, in a shallow roasting pan. Brush with remaining 2 tablespoons oil; sprinkle with remaining 1 tablespoon thyme.

● **Bring** bourbon, chicken broth, and remaining 3 tablespoons molasses to a boil in a large saucepan. Remove from heat. Carefully ignite bourbon mixture with a long match. When flames die, pour over pork roasts.

● **Bake** at 350° for 1 to 1½ hours or until meat thermometer inserted in thickest portion registers 160°. Remove pork from pan, reserving drippings in pan, and keep pork warm.

● **Add** whipping cream and salt to pan drippings; cook over medium-high heat, stirring constantly, until slightly thickened.

● **Slice** pork, and serve with sauce.
Yield: 10 servings.

Note: Here's how to flame the not-to-be-missed bourbon sauce. Heat bourbon mixture in a saucepan over medium-high heat until hot; remove from heat. Carefully ignite mixture with a long (fireplace) match, and allow to burn until extinguished.

STUFFING PORK LOIN

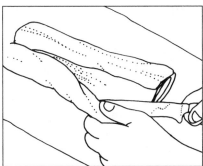

Step 1: To "butterfly" pork loin halves, cut an inverted "T" down the length of each half, and open it out flat. (Or ask a butcher to butterfly it for you.)

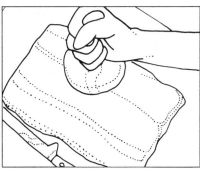

Step 2: With a meat mallet or rolling pin, pound the pork to an even thickness. (The filling spreads smoother and the loin rolls uniformly.)

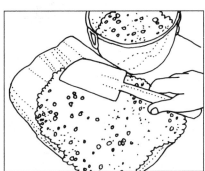

Step 3: Spread the apricot filling evenly over pork.

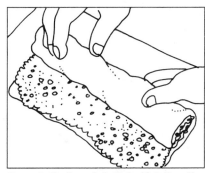

Step 4: Roll each loin half, jellyroll fashion, starting with long side.

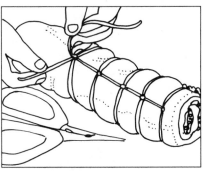

Step 5: With kitchen twine, tie the rolls at even intervals to keep them rolled while cooking. (Baking the loin halves, seam side down, seals them better and also keeps them from unrolling after untying and slicing.)

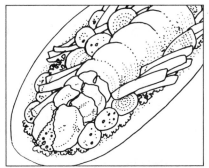

Step 6: For a change, arrange roasted potatoes, carrots, and leeks on the serving plate before placing the sliced pork loin on the serving plate.

ROASTED POTATOES, CARROTS, AND LEEKS

Roast the vegetables on the bottom oven rack while pork cooks on the top rack. Vegetables will finish cooking while you make the bourbon sauce for the pork just before serving.

3 medium leeks (about 2 pounds)
1 (16-ounce) package baby carrots
2 pounds new potatoes, thinly
    sliced
3 tablespoons butter or margarine,
    melted
1 tablespoon olive oil
1 clove garlic, pressed
¼ teaspoon salt
¼ teaspoon pepper

• **Remove** roots, tough outer leaves, and tops from leeks, leaving about 4 inches of dark leaves. Cut diagonally into 1-inch slices; wash well.
• **Trim** tops of carrots. Place leeks, carrots, and potato in a 15- x 10- x 1-inch jellyroll pan lined with aluminum foil. Set aside.
• **Combine** butter and the remaining ingredients. Drizzle over vegetables, stirring gently to coat.
• **Bake** at 350° for 1½ hours or until tender, stirring occasionally. **Yield:** 10 servings.

SPINACH SALAD WITH APPLE-ONION VINAIGRETTE

Slice spinach leaves into emerald ribbons. They're not only pretty, but easier to eat.

2 (10-ounce) packages fresh
    spinach
½ cup sugar
½ cup apple cider vinegar
1 teaspoon grated purple
    onion
½ teaspoon dry mustard
½ teaspoon salt
¼ cup vegetable oil
¾ cup finely chopped, unpeeled
    red apple
Garnish: purple onion
    slices

• **Remove** stems from spinach; wash leaves thoroughly, and pat dry. Set aside.
• **Combine** sugar and next 4 ingredients, stirring with a wire whisk. Gradually add oil, whisking rapidly until thoroughly blended. Stir in chopped apple.
• **Stack** several spinach leaves together; roll tightly. Slice at ¼-inch intervals, forming "ribbons." Repeat with remaining leaves.

• **Arrange** spinach on individual plates; drizzle with dressing. Garnish, if desired. **Yield:** 10 servings.

*Rebecca Crowder
Birmingham, Alabama*

♥ Per serving: Calories 87 (28.6% from fat)
Fat 3g (0g saturated) Cholesterol 0mg
Sodium 150mg Carbohydrate 15g
Fiber 0.9g Protein 1.8g

♥ To save 25 calories and 2.7 fat grams per serving, decrease vegetable oil to 2 tablespoons.

CENTERPIECE ROLLS

1 large egg, lightly beaten
1 tablespoon water
1 (25-ounce) package frozen roll
    dough, thawed
Toppings: poppy seeds, caraway
    seeds, dillseeds, dried basil,
    dried thyme, dried
    marjoram, cornmeal, oats

• **Combine** egg and water. Brush top of each unbaked roll with egg mixture, and sprinkle with desired toppings.
• **Arrange** all but 5 unbaked rolls in a cluster with sides touching on a lightly greased baking sheet. Knead remaining 5 rolls together, and divide dough in half. With hands, form each portion into a rope long enough to go around the cluster. Twist the ropes together, and wrap around cluster, pressing edges to seal.
• **Let** rise in a warm place (85°), free from drafts, 1 hour or until dough is doubled in bulk.
• **Bake** at 350° for 15 minutes or until lightly browned. **Yield:** 1 loaf.

Note: Rolls may also be baked individually or in clusters of two or three. Bake at 350° for 12 minutes or until lightly browned.

*Greg Dowling
Montgomery, Alabama*

SIMPLE SHORTCUTS

Here's how to prepare a show-stopping meal and still have time to relax.

■ Assemble pork loin the night before. Prepare basting liquid just before baking the pork.

■ Wash and store spinach in a plastic bag in the refrigerator the day before. The apple vinaigrette can also be made a day ahead.

■ Cut vegetables in advance, and place in a bowl of water to prevent discoloration. Drain before baking.

■ Bake and freeze Centerpiece Rolls up to one month ahead. Thaw and reheat in aluminum foil at 350° for 15 minutes or until hot.

SHORTCUT CHEFS

Let's face it – your holiday schedule is going to get crazy. With all the baking to be done, the potluck parties to cook for, and the daily meals you still have to think about, you can't just close down the kitchen for the month. But you *can* take some shortcuts.

We've gone to Southern "chefs" (loosely defined here as anyone who tastefully wields a wooden spoon) for their time-trimming tips.

■ Although free-lance Foods Editor **Phyllis Young Cordell** of Gadsden, Alabama, isn't officially on the *Southern Living* Foods staff, she isn't far away and helps with projects. After years on stage with the *Southern Living* Cooking School, she's good at thinking fast on her feet. For a shortcut, she created a cream soup, cutting out the step of starting with a white sauce. Instead, she just unwraps packages of cream cheese for rich flavor. (We offer a light version, too.)

CREAM WITH GREENS SOUP

¾ pound fresh spinach
2 (14½-ounce) cans ready-to-serve chicken broth
1 (8-ounce) package cream cheese, softened
1 (3-ounce) package cream cheese, softened
1 tablespoon lemon juice
½ teaspoon fines herbes
⅛ teaspoon freshly ground pepper
5 tablespoons freshly grated Parmesan cheese

• **Remove** stems from spinach; wash leaves thoroughly, and pat dry. Tightly roll leaves lengthwise, and cut into very thin strips or shreds. Set aside.

• **Combine** chicken broth and cream cheese in a large saucepan; cook mixture, stirring constantly, over low heat until cream cheese melts. Add lemon juice, fines herbes, and pepper.
• **Remove** from heat. Stir in spinach. Sprinkle each serving with Parmesan cheese. **Yield:** about 5 cups.

♥ Per serving: Calories 202 (60% from fat) Fat 13.2g (7.9g saturated) Cholesterol 43mg Sodium 535mg Carbohydrate 8.6g Fiber 2.8g Protein 11.5g

♥ To save 102 calories and 14.7 fat grams per 1-cup serving, substitute reduced-fat cream cheese, and 2 (16-ounce) cans ready-to-serve, reduced-sodium, fat-free chicken broth.

■ The holiday challenge for **Chef Jim Napolitano** at the Cumberland Club in Nashville, Tennessee, is the multitude of cocktail parties that requires lots of attractive nibbles. So he has created an assortment of what he refers to as "puffs": sheets of commercial puff pastry that are cut into squares, stuffed with fillings, and then baked. His Cajun Hot Puffs, with just four ingredients, are easy and elegant.

"I can knock out hundreds of bite-size appetizers in no time," Jim says. "Not like my mother and grandmother, who started cooking three days before a party. Times change. You don't have to do that anymore. People like simple things."

CAJUN HOT PUFFS

1 (17¼-ounce) package frozen puff pastry, thawed
Cornmeal
½ pound hot smoked link sausage
1 (4½-ounce) can sliced pickled jalapeño peppers, drained

• **Roll** 1 pastry sheet into a 15- x 12-inch rectangle on a surface lightly sprinkled with cornmeal. Cut into 3-inch squares.

• **Cut** sausage into ¼-inch slices. Cut each slice in half crosswise. Place 1 piece of sausage and 1 jalapeño slice in center of each square. Fold corners to center, slightly overlapping edges.
• **Place** filled pastries, seam side down, on greased baking sheets sprinkled with cornmeal. Repeat procedure with remaining pastry, sausage, and jalapeño peppers.
• **Bake** at 400° for 12 to 15 minutes. Serve immediately. **Yield:** 40 appetizer servings.

Note: Unbaked Cajun Hot Puffs may be frozen up to three months. Let thaw, and bake according to directions.

■ Author **Linda Gassenheimer** of Miami, Florida, has turned 25 years of family life and a professional food career into a "complete package" of kitchen help. Her book, *Dinner in Minutes,* offers more than 80 menus (doable in 45 minutes) with shopping lists, schedules for efficient preparation, shortcuts, and the fat and calorie content of each menu. Here are some of Linda's favorites.

BLACK BEAN GUACAMOLE

¼ small onion
1 (15-ounce) can black beans, rinsed and drained
2 tablespoons fresh lime juice
2 tablespoons orange juice
2 cloves garlic, pressed
⅛ teaspoon salt
¼ teaspoon freshly ground pepper

• **Position** knife blade in food processor bowl; add onion. Process until chopped. Add beans and remaining ingredients. Pulse 3 times or until chopped, stopping to scrape down sides between pulses. Serve with tortilla chips. **Yield:** 1⅓ cups.

KEY WEST SHRIMP

1¾ pounds unpeeled, large fresh
   shrimp
3 (12-ounce) cans beer
2 tablespoons Old Bay seasoning
   or dry shrimp-and-crab-boil
   seasoning
Key Lime Mustard

• **Rinse** and drain shrimp.
• **Bring** beer and seasoning to a boil in
a large Dutch oven; add shrimp, and
cook 3 to 5 minutes or until shrimp
turn pink. Drain shrimp well. Serve
immediately with Key Lime Mustard.
Yield: 4 main-dish servings or 12
appetizer servings.

Key Lime Mustard

¾ cup nonfat mayonnaise
¼ cup Dijon mustard
¼ cup bottled Key lime juice or
   fresh lime juice
⅛ teaspoon freshly ground
   pepper

• **Combine** all ingredients in a small
bowl. **Yield:** 1¼ cups.

■ As the *Southern Living* Foods Staff
gathers daily for taste-testing in the
test kitchens, the brainstorming really
gets going. We find that we often take
ideas and recipes from work into our
home kitchens. Editorial Coordinator
Susan Nash and Test Kitchens Staff
Member **Julia Dowling** created this
seafood recipe and presentation together on a day when one of Susan's
out-of-town friends was arriving in
time for dinner.

Wanting something simple but elegant, they thought of grilled salmon.
Knowing that a salmon steak just laid
on the plate was too plain, they
thought to tuck a lemon half into the
steak's natural empty spot and top it
with a sprig of fresh dill. Sautéed zucchini strips add the finishing touch. It
was so easy; Susan wasn't stressed, and
her visitor was impressed.

GRILLED SALMON STEAKS

2 tablespoons mayonnaise
½ teaspoon chopped fresh dill
   or ⅛ teaspoon dried
   dillweed
2 (1-inch-thick) salmon steaks
Garnishes: lemon halves, fresh dill
   sprigs

• **Combine** mayonnaise and dill;
spread on both sides of salmon.
• **Cook,** covered with grill lid, over
medium-hot coals (350° to 400°) 5 to
6 minutes on each side or until done.
Garnish, if desired. **Yield:** 2 servings.

■ With this easy recipe, Associate
Foods Editor **Kaye Mabry Adams**
just pours a bottle of salad dressing
over chicken and lets it marinate while
she's at work. At day's end, all that's
left to do is coat the chicken and bake.

SEASONED
CHICKEN BAKE

8 skinned and boned chicken
   breast halves
1 (8-ounce) bottle Italian salad
   dressing
¾ cup herb-seasoned stuffing mix,
   crushed
¼ cup grated Parmesan cheese
1 teaspoon dried parsley
   flakes
¼ teaspoon salt
⅛ teaspoon pepper

• **Combine** chicken and salad dressing
in a shallow dish; cover and refrigerate
8 hours.
• **Remove** chicken, discarding marinade. Set chicken aside.
• **Combine** stuffing mix and remaining
ingredients; coat chicken with mixture.
• **Arrange** chicken in a lightly greased
15- x 10- x 2-inch baking dish.
• **Bake** at 350° for 30 minutes or until
chicken is done.
• **Broil** 4 to 6 inches from heat (with
electric oven door partially opened) 2
minutes. **Yield:** 8 servings.

■ While eating out saves time, it costs
calories, and many find themselves a
few pounds heavier by the end of the
holiday season. Not **Nan Jacobs** of
Birmingham, Alabama. She plans
ahead and pulls out some of her easiest
and healthiest recipes, like Southwestern Pasta Salad. (For more health
pointers, see "Slimming Secrets" on
page 294.)

SOUTHWESTERN PASTA SALAD

1 (16-ounce) package penne or
   mostaccioli pasta, uncooked
Creamy Southwestern Salad
   Dressing
Lettuce leaves
1 (15-ounce) can black beans,
   rinsed and drained
1 (8¾-ounce) can whole kernel
   corn, rinsed and drained
1 sweet red pepper, chopped
3 green onions, sliced
¼ cup chopped fresh cilantro
Garnish: fresh cilantro sprigs

• **Cook** pasta according to package directions; drain. Rinse with cold water,
and drain.
• **Combine** pasta and 1¾ cups Creamy
Southwestern Salad Dressing; toss
gently. Chill.
• **Spoon** pasta mixture onto a lettuce-
lined serving platter. Top with black
beans and next 4 ingredients. Garnish,
if desired. Serve with remaining dressing. **Yield:** 6 servings.

Creamy Southwestern Salad Dressing

1 (8-ounce) carton nonfat sour
   cream
1 (16-ounce) jar mild thick-and-
   chunky salsa
½ teaspoon ground cumin
2 cloves garlic, minced

• **Combine** all ingredients; chill. **Yield:**
2¾ cups.

♥ Per serving: Calories 463 (5% from fat)
Fat 2.2g (0g saturated) Cholesterol 0mg
Sodium 1,026mg Carbohydrate 84.1g
   Fiber 4.8g Protein 18.8g

■ When **Dorsella Utter** of Louisville, Kentucky, serves her fruit compote, no one guesses it's an easy recipe. Just open some cans, add a few ingredients, stir, and bake.

FESTIVE FRUIT COMPOTE

1 (8-ounce) package mixed dried fruits
1 (16-ounce) can cherry pie filling
1 (11-ounce) can mandarin oranges, drained
⅓ cup firmly packed brown sugar
½ teaspoon ground cinnamon
½ teaspoon ground nutmeg
½ cup bourbon *

• **Combine** first 3 ingredients in a lightly greased 1½-quart casserole; set aside.
• **Combine** brown sugar and the remaining ingredients, stirring until sugar dissolves; pour over fruit mixture, and cover.
• **Bake** at 350° for 45 minutes. Serve warm. **Yield:** 8 to 10 servings.

* ½ cup apple juice may be substituted.

CHRISTMAS DINNER: GIVE MOM A BREAK

Remember childhood Christmases, gazing across a seemingly endless buffet of food? Mom always prepared everyone's favorite, with more than enough for leftovers. She also spent many hours in the kitchen cooking the feast.

But times have changed. These days, many mothers divide hectic schedules among family, work, and a host of other activities. Give her a break this year by divvying up the Christmas menu.

FESTIVE CHEESE BALL

3 (8-ounce) packages cream cheese, softened
1 (4-ounce) package crumbled blue cheese
1 cup (4 ounces) shredded sharp Cheddar cheese
1 (8-ounce) package chopped dates
1 cup golden raisins
½ cup chopped pecans, toasted

• **Combine** first 5 ingredients; divide in half. Shape each portion into a ball; roll in pecans. Cover and chill. Serve with gingersnaps or apple slices. **Yield:** 2 (4-inch) cheese balls.

Linda Crowson
Oxford, Mississippi

CARROT-POTATO PUDDING

8 carrots, peeled and sliced (about 1¼ pounds)
2 medium potatoes, peeled and chopped (about 1½ pounds)
1 large egg, lightly beaten
2 tablespoons grated onion
2 tablespoons sour cream
½ to ¾ teaspoon salt
¼ teaspoon pepper
½ cup (2 ounces) Cheddar cheese, cut into small pieces
1 tablespoon cold butter or margarine, cut into pieces
Garnishes: carrot strips, fresh parsley sprigs

• **Cook** carrot in boiling water to cover 10 minutes. Add potato and cook 10 additional minutes or until vegetables are tender; drain and mash. Set aside.
• **Combine** egg and next 4 ingredients; add carrot mixture, mixing well. Fold in cheese. Spoon into a greased 1½-quart casserole. Bake at 350° for 30 minutes. Dot with butter; broil 8 inches from heat (with electric oven door partially opened) 5 minutes. Garnish, if desired. **Yield:** 6 servings.

Louise Holmes
Winchester, Tennessee

BRUSSELS SPROUTS-AND-ARTICHOKE CASSEROLE

1 (10-ounce) package frozen brussels sprouts in butter sauce
1 (14-ounce) can artichoke hearts, drained
½ cup mayonnaise
2 teaspoons lemon juice
¼ teaspoon celery salt
¼ cup grated Parmesan cheese
¼ cup sliced almonds

• **Cook** brussels sprouts according to package directions.
• **Arrange** brussels sprouts and artichoke hearts in a lightly greased 1-quart casserole. Set aside.
• **Combine** mayonnaise, lemon juice, and celery salt; spoon over vegetables, and sprinkle with Parmesan cheese and almonds.
• **Bake** at 325° for 20 minutes or until thoroughly heated. **Yield:** 4 servings.

Brenda H. Rohe
Charlotte, North Carolina

GREEN BEANS WITH WALNUT DRESSING

2 pounds fresh green beans
3 quarts water
½ cup finely chopped green onions
⅓ cup olive oil
¼ cup cider vinegar
¼ cup chopped fresh parsley
¼ cup chopped fresh dill
½ teaspoon salt
¼ teaspoon pepper
¾ cup coarsely chopped walnuts, toasted

• **Wash** beans; trim ends.
• **Bring** water to a boil in a Dutch oven; add beans, and cook 10 minutes or until tender. Drain and set aside.
• **Combine** green onions and next 6 ingredients; pour over green beans, and toss gently. Sprinkle with walnuts; serve hot or cold. **Yield:** 8 servings.

Charlotte Pierce
Greensburg, Kentucky

HAVE FOOD, WILL TRAVEL

From turkey to dessert, here are some tips for a portable Christmas dinner:

■ If you live nearby, do your cooking at home and bring the finished dish in your own serving pieces. (For a no-spills delivery, nestle the dishes among an abundance of cloth napkins on a wicker or bamboo tray.) If you're crossing the country for a holiday homecoming, we're sure Mom would be happy to step aside and let you make your part of the feast in her kitchen upon arrival.

■ Rely on zip-top plastic bags and disposable baking pans to eliminate making a return trip with empty dishes.

■ Smoke or roast a whole turkey up to one month in advance. Wrap it securely in heavy-duty aluminum foil, and freeze. Packed frozen, it helps keep other foods in the ice chest cold.

■ Prepare cornbread dressing and vegetable casseroles up to the point of baking. Pack in air-tight plastic bags, and freeze. When you arrive at your destination, they will have thawed in the ice chest and will be ready to spoon into a casserole dish for baking.

■ Marinate fruit or vegetable salads in zip-top plastic bags a day before traveling. The filled bags conform to crushed ice in the ice chest, making them space-efficient.

■ Bar cookies keep nicely in shirt boxes and slide easily under car seats.

WINTER BROCCOLI CASSEROLE

2 (10-ounce) packages frozen broccoli spears
1 cup (4 ounces) shredded Cheddar cheese
2 large eggs, lightly beaten
1 (10¾-ounce) can cream of mushroom soup, undiluted
½ cup mayonnaise
½ cup finely chopped onion
¾ cup herb-seasoned stuffing mix
2 tablespoons butter or margarine, melted

• **Cook** broccoli according to package directions; drain well.
• **Arrange** broccoli in a lightly greased 11- x 7- x 1½-inch baking dish. Sprinkle with cheese, and set aside.
• **Combine** eggs and the next 3 ingredients; spread over cheese. Set aside.
• **Combine** stuffing mix and butter; sprinkle over casserole.
• **Bake** at 350° for 30 minutes or until thoroughly heated. **Yield:** 8 servings.
Sharon McClatchey
Muskogee, Oklahoma

❤ Per serving: Calories 151 (49% from fat)
Fat 8.4g (2.2g saturated) Cholesterol 17mg
Sodium 414mg Carbohydrate 11g
Fiber 1g Protein 8.9g

❤ If you want to save 121 calories and 14 fat grams per serving, substitute ½ cup egg substitute, reduced-fat Cheddar cheese, mushroom soup, and vegetable cooking spray.

SWEET POTATO-AND-APPLE CASSEROLE

3 medium-size sweet potatoes
½ cup firmly packed brown sugar
1 teaspoon ground cinnamon
1 teaspoon ground nutmeg
2 large Winesap or other cooking apples, peeled and cut into ¼-inch rings
Streusel Topping

• **Cook** unpeeled sweet potatoes in water to cover in a Dutch oven 25 minutes or until tender (do not over-cook). Drain and cool; peel and slice into ¼-inch rounds.
• **Combine** brown sugar, cinnamon, and nutmeg.
• **Layer** sweet potato, apples, and brown sugar mixture in a lightly greased 11- x 7- x 1½-inch baking dish, beginning and ending with sweet potato. Sprinkle sweet potato with Streusel Topping.
• **Bake** at 350° for 30 minutes. **Yield:** 8 servings.

Streusel Topping

¼ cup all-purpose flour
¼ cup firmly packed brown sugar
¼ cup butter or margarine
¼ cup chopped pecans

• **Combine** all ingredients. **Yield:** about 1 cup.
Lu Clark
Ste. Genevieve, Missouri

SPICY ORANGE BEETS

2 pounds small fresh beets *
¼ cup firmly packed brown sugar
1 tablespoon grated orange rind
2 teaspoons cornstarch
¼ teaspoon salt
¼ teaspoon ground allspice
⅛ teaspoon pepper
⅔ cup orange juice
2 tablespoons butter or margarine
1 tablespoon chopped fresh chives

• **Leave** root and 1 inch of stem on beets; scrub with a vegetable brush.
• **Cook** beets in boiling water to cover 30 minutes or until tender. Drain. Pour cold water over beets, and drain. Trim off roots and stems; rub off skins. Cut beets into ¼-inch slices; set aside.
• **Combine** sugar and next 5 ingredients in a saucepan; gradually add juice, stirring until smooth. Stir in butter; bring to a boil, stirring constantly. Boil 1 minute, stirring constantly. Add

beets; cook until thoroughly heated. Sprinkle with chives before serving. **Yield:** 4 to 6 servings.

* To save time, substitute 2 (16-ounce) cans sliced beets for fresh, and omit precooking them. Add beets to orange sauce mixture, and cook until thoroughly heated; sprinkle with chives.

Hilda Marshall
Front Royal, Virginia

SWEET ON SALADS

Only devout Southerners could turn something that's healthy such as a salad into something decadent and sweet. When it comes to holiday salads, we bear that guilt with glee.

What traditional feast is complete without plump mandarin oranges? Salads with apples are also classic candidates for the sweet treatment, paired perfectly with tangy vinegar and a pinch of sugar. And the greens? Oooh, we almost forgot. Well, Sugar, just throw in what's handy.

SWEET-AND-SOUR GREEN SALAD

½ medium head iceberg lettuce, torn
½ medium head red-tipped leaf lettuce, torn
1 head Bibb or Boston lettuce, torn
½ purple onion, thinly sliced
1 (11-ounce) can mandarin oranges, drained
½ cup walnut pieces, toasted
Sweet-and-Sour Dressing

● **Combine** first 6 ingredients in a large salad bowl. Pour Sweet-and-Sour Dressing over top; toss to coat. Serve immediately. **Yield:** 8 servings.

Sweet-and-Sour Dressing

½ cup vegetable oil
¼ cup tarragon vinegar
¼ cup sugar
¾ teaspoon salt
Dash of pepper
⅛ teaspoon hot sauce

● **Combine** all ingredients in a jar. Cover tightly, and shake vigorously. **Yield:** about 1 cup.

Dana W. Yeatman
Brandon, Mississippi

BROCCOLI-ORANGE SALAD

Cyndi Christensen says this salad is better made a day before serving.

4 cups fresh broccoli flowerets (about 1½ pounds fresh broccoli)
1 small purple onion, thinly sliced and separated into rings
½ cup raisins
½ cup pecan pieces, toasted
¾ cup mayonnaise or salad dressing
¼ cup sugar
1½ tablespoons white vinegar
1 (11-ounce) can mandarin oranges, drained

● **Combine** first 4 ingredients in a bowl; set aside.
● **Combine** mayonnaise, sugar, and vinegar; add to broccoli mixture, stirring to coat. Gently stir in mandarin oranges.
● **Cover** and refrigerate at least 3 hours. **Yield:** 6 servings.

Cyndi Christensen
Virginia Beach, Virginia

❤ Per serving: Calories 268 (51% from fat) Fat 16.1g (2g saturated) Cholesterol 11mg Sodium 196mg Carbohydrate 31.3g Fiber 3.7g Protein 3.7g

❤ To save 121 calories and 14 fat grams per salad serving, substitute reduced-fat mayonnaise.

WILTED CABBAGE SALAD

1 tablespoon sugar
2 tablespoons white vinegar
2 tablespoons water
½ teaspoon salt
⅛ teaspoon pepper
2 slices bacon
¼ cup chopped onion
½ medium cabbage, shredded (about 4½ cups)
1 Red Delicious apple, cored and finely chopped

● **Combine** first 5 ingredients; set vinegar mixture aside.
● **Cook** bacon in a large skillet until crisp; remove bacon, reserving drippings in skillet. Crumble bacon; set aside.
● **Cook** onion in reserved drippings over medium heat, stirring constantly, until tender. Stir in vinegar mixture; bring to a boil. Add cabbage and apple, tossing gently to coat. Cover and cook 5 minutes or until cabbage is wilted. Sprinkle with bacon, and serve immediately. **Yield:** 4 servings

Valerie Stutsman
Norfolk, Virginia

SALAD "DRESSINGS"

■ Arrange Belgian endive leaves around the outside of the salad bowl in a spoke fashion or center the salad with a nest of fluted mushrooms or tomato roses for an eye-catching arrangement.

■ Dress up plain chicken or seafood salad for company by serving it in a fruit or vegetable cup. A shell made from tomato, green pepper, avocado, melon, or pineapple makes an attractive and colorful presentation for a salad.

MINCEMEAT SALAD

2 (3-ounce) packages
    orange-flavored gelatin
1½ cups boiling water
2 cups commercial mincemeat
½ cup chopped walnuts or pecans
Lettuce leaves
½ cup sour cream
2 teaspoons maraschino cherry
    juice
1 tablespoon finely chopped
    walnuts or pecans

• **Combine** gelatin and boiling water in a large bowl, stirring 2 minutes or until gelatin dissolves. Chill until mixture is the consistency of unbeaten egg white.
• **Fold** mincemeat and ½ cup walnuts into gelatin mixture. Spoon into lightly oiled individual molds; chill until firm.
• **Unmold** onto lettuce-lined plates. Set aside.
• **Combine** sour cream and maraschino cherry juice. Dollop onto each salad, and sprinkle with finely chopped walnuts. **Yield:** 7 servings.

Jean Jordan
Oviedo, Florida

THE GIFT OF TIME

Give yourself and a few close friends a true gift this holiday season – time. Make a pact. Instead of buying each other gifts, gather for a relaxing evening. We've suggested a timesaving menu with lots of options, easy enough for the hostess to prepare, and even easier if a friend pitches in to help.

Have guests bring shopping finds for their families, along with paper, ribbon, scissors, and tape. After dinner, turn on some Christmas music, wrap your gifts, and enjoy the company.

HOLIDAY GIFT-OF-TIME MENU
Serves Four

Hot Crab-and-Cheese Dip
Mixed Salad Greens With
Dijon Dressing
Pecan-Crusted Turkey Cutlets
Or Swiss Chicken Thighs
Long-Grain-and-Wild Rice Mix
Or Quick Potatoes
Sautéed Sweet Peppers
Or Steamed Broccoli
Bacon Monkey Bread
Frozen Almond Crunch

HOT CRAB-AND-CHEESE DIP

1 (8-ounce) package cream cheese,
    softened
3 tablespoons milk
1 tablespoon finely chopped onion
¼ teaspoon prepared
    horseradish
Dash of garlic powder
1 (4¼-ounce) can lump crabmeat,
    rinsed and drained
2 tablespoons grated Parmesan
    cheese

• **Combine** first 5 ingredients; fold in crabmeat. Spoon into a lightly greased 2-cup baking dish.
• **Bake** at 400° for 20 minutes. Sprinkle with grated Parmesan cheese, and serve with assorted crackers or chips. **Yield:** 1⅔ cups.

DIJON DRESSING

½ cup Dijon mustard
½ cup vegetable oil
½ cup white wine vinegar
2 tablespoons grated Parmesan
    cheese
2 tablespoons light corn syrup
1 tablespoon chopped fresh or
    1 teaspoon dried oregano
1 teaspoon garlic powder
½ teaspoon celery seeds
¼ teaspoon salt
⅛ teaspoon pepper

• **Combine** all ingredients; stir with a wire whisk until blended. Cover; chill at least 1 hour. Serve over salad greens. **Yield:** 1⅔ cups.

Pat Boschen
Ashland, Virginia

PECAN-CRUSTED TURKEY CUTLETS

¾ cup soft breadcrumbs,
    toasted
½ cup finely chopped pecans
½ teaspoon dried sage
¼ teaspoon salt
¼ teaspoon pepper
1 egg white, lightly beaten
1 tablespoon water
4 (4-ounce) turkey breast
    cutlets
Butter-flavored cooking spray

• **Combine** first 5 ingredients in a shallow dish; set aside.
• **Combine** egg white and water. Dip turkey cutlets in egg mixture; coat with breadcrumb mixture. Place on a baking sheet coated with cooking spray. Coat cutlets with cooking spray.
• **Bake** at 350° for 12 minutes or until juices run clear when cut with a knife. **Yield:** 4 servings.

♥ Per serving: Calories 293 (37% from fat)
Fat 12g (1g saturated) Cholesterol 70mg
Sodium 341mg Carbohydrate 16.7g
Fiber 1.8g Protein 29.3g

SWISS CHICKEN THIGHS

8 chicken thighs, skinned (about 3
    pounds)
4 slices Swiss cheese, cut in
    half
1 (10¾-ounce) can cream of
    mushroom soup, undiluted
¼ cup skim milk
8 thin slices green pepper
¾ cup herb-seasoned stuffing mix,
    crushed
3 tablespoons butter, melted

- **Arrange** chicken thighs in an 8-inch square baking dish. Top each thigh with Swiss cheese.
- **Combine** soup and milk; pour over cheese. Top evenly with green pepper slices.
- **Combine** stuffing mix and butter; sprinkle over casserole.
- **Bake** at 400° for 1 hour or until juices run clear when cut with a knife. **Yield:** 4 servings.

Linda A. Bowman
Cordele, Georgia

♥ Per serving: Calories 529 (39% from fat)
Fat 22.4g (6.5g saturated) Cholesterol 236mg
Sodium 769mg Carbohydrate 12.2g
Fiber 0.3g Protein 65.6g

♥ To save 100 calories and 12 fat grams per serving, substitute reduced-fat Swiss cheese, reduced-sodium, reduced-fat cream of mushroom soup, and reduced-calorie margarine.

QUICK POTATOES

1 tablespoon olive oil
1 large onion, chopped
2 cloves garlic, minced
½ cup chopped sweet red pepper
½ teaspoon salt
¼ teaspoon pepper
¼ teaspoon hot sauce
3 cups unpeeled cubed potatoes
2 tablespoons butter or margarine

- **Heat** olive oil in a 10-inch cast-iron skillet. Add onion and garlic; cook over medium heat, stirring constantly, until tender. Stir in red pepper and next 3 ingredients; cook 2 minutes, stirring constantly. Add potato and butter, stirring well.
- **Bake** at 400° for 20 to 30 minutes. **Yield:** 4 servings.

Pam Floyd
Birmingham, Alabama

BACON MONKEY BREAD

11 slices bacon, cooked and crumbled
½ cup grated Parmesan cheese
1 small onion, chopped
3 (10-ounce) cans refrigerated buttermilk biscuits
½ cup butter or margarine, melted

- **Combine** first 3 ingredients; set aside.
- **Cut** biscuits into fourths; dip each piece in butter, and layer one-third in a lightly greased 10-inch Bundt pan.
- **Sprinkle** half of bacon mixture over biscuits; repeat procedure, ending with biscuits.
- **Bake** at 350° for 40 minutes or until golden. Cool 10 minutes in pan; invert onto a serving platter, and serve immediately. **Yield:** one 10-inch ring.

Elizabeth Thompson
Connelly Springs, North Carolina

FROZEN ALMOND CRUNCH

⅔ cup sliced almonds
½ cup sugar
½ cup butter or margarine
1 tablespoon all-purpose flour
2 tablespoons milk
½ gallon vanilla ice cream, softened
Dark Chocolate Sauce

- **Combine** first 5 ingredients in a heavy saucepan; bring to a boil over medium heat, stirring constantly. Remove from heat, and set aside.
- **Line** a 15- x 10- x 1-inch jellyroll pan with aluminum foil; spread almond mixture onto foil in a thin layer.
- **Bake** at 350° for 7 minutes or until light golden brown (do not overbake). Cool; remove from foil, and crumble.
- **Sprinkle** half of almond mixture in bottom of a 10-inch springform pan. Spoon ice cream evenly on top; sprinkle with remaining almond mixture, gently pressing down slightly with back of a spoon.

- **Freeze** 8 hours or until firm. Serve with Dark Chocolate Sauce. **Yield:** 12 servings.

Dark Chocolate Sauce

½ cup butter
4 (1-ounce) squares unsweetened chocolate
1½ cups sugar
½ cup cocoa
Pinch of salt
1 cup milk
1 teaspoon vanilla extract *

- **Melt** butter and chocolate in a heavy saucepan over low heat, stirring often.
- **Combine** sugar, cocoa, and salt; stir sugar mixture and milk into chocolate mixture.
- **Bring** just to a boil over medium heat, stirring constantly; remove from heat, and stir in vanilla. Cool, stirring occasionally. Sauce may be refrigerated up to 1 week. **Yield:** 3 cups.

* 1 to 2 tablespoons Kahlúa may be substituted.

Note: Sauce thickens when refrigerated. To serve, microwave at HIGH, stirring at 30-second intervals, until drizzling consistency.

Peggy W. Feist
Eatonton, Georgia

FUN GIFTS OF LOVE

For a gift almost as precious as time, draw names with your friends, and ask each person to buy a child's gift to match the personality of the name drawn: a tiara for the Miss America wannabe or a barrel of monkeys for the humorous one in the group. You'll have lots of laughs opening the gifts. Then simply rewrap, and give them to a local charity for children.

CROWD-PLEASING CASSEROLES

....

Looking for a simple way to casually entertain a holiday crowd? Here's the answer. We took three great casserole recipes that originally served eight and expanded them to serve 16, 24, and 32. We've tested them for each number of servings, so you can rest assured that they will work at your house.

To make three or more casseroles, you'll need more than one oven. Call on a neighbor for help, or if your gathering is in a rented space, make sure there's more than one oven available at the site to bake the casseroles. The casseroles will fill your oven, so plan on serving chilled side dishes or hot ones that cook on a cooktop.

And, if you're making more than one casserole, simplify cleanup by using disposable aluminum pans. Make the holidays as easy as possible on yourself, even if you're expecting a crowd of carolers at your door.

SAUSAGE-AND-EGG CASSEROLE

Serve fresh fruit and juice with this make-ahead casserole for a hearty breakfast or brunch.

Ingredients	For 8	For 16	For 24	For 32
12-ounce package(s) link sausage, cut into ¼-inch slices	1	2	3	4
Sandwich bread, cut into 1-inch pieces	8 slices	16 slices	24 slices	32 slices
Shredded sharp Cheddar cheese	2 cups (8 ounces)	4 cups (16 ounces)	6 cups (24 ounces)	8 cups (32 ounces)
Milk	2½ cups, divided	5 cups, divided	7½ cups, divided	10 cups, divided
Large eggs, lightly beaten	6	12	18	24
Dry mustard	¾ teaspoon	1½ teaspoons	2½ teaspoons	3 teaspoons
Dried marjoram	½ teaspoon	1 teaspoon	1½ teaspoons	2 teaspoons
Dried basil	½ teaspoon	1 teaspoon	1½ teaspoons	2 teaspoons
10¾-ounce can(s) cream of mushroom soup, undiluted	1	2	3	4

• **Brown** sausage in a large skillet; drain well, and set aside.
• **Place** bread in a greased 13- x 9- x 2-inch baking dish or disposable aluminum foil pan. Top with cheese and sausage.
• **Combine** 2 cups milk and next 4 ingredients in a bowl, and pour over bread mixture.
• **Cover** and chill 8 hours.

• **Combine** soup and remaining ½ cup milk, and pour over casserole.
• **Bake** at 350° for 1 hour. Serve casserole immediately. **Yield:** 8 servings.

Note: To serve 16, prepare Sausage-and-Egg Casserole twice using two 13- x 9- x 2-inch baking dishes; to serve 24, use three baking dishes, and bake in two ovens. To serve 32, use four baking dishes, and bake in two ovens. Bake casserole at 350° for 1 hour and 15 to 25 minutes.

Fran Pointer
Kansas City, Missouri

TEXAS TORTILLA BAKE

Tortilla chips and commercial salsa, along with Spanish rice made from a commercial mix, will carry out the southwestern theme of this Tex-Mex casserole.

Ingredients	For 8	For 16	For 24	For 32
Lean ground beef	1½ pounds	3 pounds	4½ pounds	6 pounds
Large onion(s) chopped	1	2	3	4
14½-ounce can(s) Mexican-style stewed tomatoes, undrained	1	2	3	4
10-ounce can(s) mild enchilada sauce	1	2	3	4
16-ounce loaf (loaves) process cheese spread, sliced	½	1	1½	2
Ground cumin	2 teaspoons	4 teaspoons	6 teaspoons	8 teaspoons
Salt	½ teaspoon	1 teaspoon	1½ teaspoons	2 teaspoons
Pepper	½ teaspoon	1 teaspoon	1½ teaspoons	2 teaspoons
Crushed tortilla chips	2 cups	4 cups	6 cups	8 cups
3-ounce package(s) cream cheese softened	1	2	3	4
8-inch flour tortillas	8	16	24	32
4½ ounce can(s) chopped green chiles	1	2	3	4
Shredded Monterey Jack cheese	1 cup (4 ounces)	2 cups (8 ounces)	3 cups (12 ounces)	4 cups (16 ounces)

- **Brown** ground beef and onion in a large skillet or Dutch oven, stirring until meat crumbles. Drain.
- **Stir** in tomatoes, enchilada sauce, sliced cheese spread, cumin, salt, and pepper; cook mixture over low heat, stirring constantly, until cheese melts. Set aside.
- **Place** crushed tortilla chips in a greased 13- x 9- x 2-inch baking dish or disposable aluminum foil pan. Spoon two-thirds of beef mixture over tortilla chips.
- **Spread** cream cheese evenly on 1 side of tortillas, and sprinkle evenly

with chiles. Fold tortillas in half, and arrange on beef mixture. Spoon remaining beef mixture on top of tortillas, and cover.
- **Bake** at 350° for 20 minutes. Uncover casserole, and sprinkle with Monterey Jack cheese. Bake 5 additional minutes to melt cheese, if desired. **Yield:** 8 servings.

Note: To serve 16, divide tortilla chips, beef mixture, and remaining ingredients into two 13- x 9- x 2-inch baking dishes. To serve 24, divide into three baking dishes, and bake casseroles

in two ovens. To serve 32, divide into four baking dishes, and bake casseroles in two ovens.

❤ Per serving: Calories 445 (36% from fat) Fat 17.6g (7.1g saturated) Cholesterol 53mg Sodium 1,206mg Carbohydrate 42.9g Fiber 3.7g Protein 30.9g

❤ To save 105 calories and 8.9 fat grams per serving, substitute no-oil tortilla chips, reduced-fat loaf process cheese spread, reduced-fat cream cheese, and reduced-fat Monterey Jack cheese.

CHICKEN-NOODLE CASSEROLE

Warm up the crowd with Chicken-Noodle Casserole, a classic comfort dish. All you need to add to this rich and hearty dish is a crisp salad, and dinner is complete.

Ingredients	For 8	For 16	For 24	For 32
Butter	1½ tablespoons	3 tablespoons	4½ tablespoons	6 tablespoons
All-purpose flour	1½ tablespoons	3 tablespoons	4½ tablespoons	6 tablespoons
Half-and-half	1½ cups	3 cups	4½ cups	6 cups
14½-ounce can(s) ready-to-serve chicken broth	1	2	3	4
8-ounce package(s) cream cheese, cut into pieces	2	4	6	8
Cooked chopped chicken or turkey	6 cups	12 cups	18 cups	24 cups
Salt	1 teaspoon	2 teaspoons	3 teaspoons	4 teaspoons
Pepper	1 teaspoon	2 teaspoons	3 teaspoons	4 teaspoons
2¼-ounce can(s) sliced ripe olives, drained	1	2	3	4
2½-ounce can(s) sliced mushrooms, drained	1	2	3	4
2-ounce jar(s) diced pimiento, drained	1	2	3	4
6-ounce package(s) medium egg noodles, cooked	1	2	3	4
Dry breadcrumbs	2 tablespoons	4 tablespoons	6 tablespoons	8 tablespoons
Vegetable cooking spray				

• **Melt** butter in a Dutch oven over low heat; add flour, stirring until smooth. Cook 1 minute, stirring constantly. Gradually add half-and-half and broth; cook over medium heat, stirring constantly, until mixture is slightly thickened.

• **Remove** from heat; add cheese, stirring until melted. Stir in chicken and next 5 ingredients.

• **Fold** noodles into mixture, and place in a lightly greased 13- x 9- x 2-inch baking dish. Top with breadcrumbs; coat with cooking spray, and cover.

• **Bake** at 350° for 15 minutes. Uncover and bake 15 additional minutes. **Yield:** 8 servings.

Note: Two 3½-pound broiler-fryers or 12 chicken breast halves, cooked, equal 6 cups of chopped chicken. To serve 16, divide mixture into two baking dishes. For 24, prepare it twice, in separate Dutch ovens, using the recipe for 8 servings and 16 servings; bake in two ovens. To serve 32, prepare it twice, in separate Dutch ovens, using the recipe for 16. Bake in two ovens.

Lisa Green
Edmond, Oklahoma

TASTEFUL TREASURES

So many Southerners count old family recipes among their blessings. Many were scribbled on whatever pieces of paper were handy, while others were carefully penned in books. All grew into revered family documents.

Shirley Hall proudly displays an old family treasure. Rummaging around recently in the bottom of a trunk, she discovered a recipe book that belonged to her great-great grandmother, Louisa Ann Akers. Dated March 12, 1860, the recipes are written in sweeping, swirling penmanship in now-faded ink. We tested a recipe simply entitled "Chili Sauce" and found it a piquant, zesty addition to black-eyed peas.

Family recipes may appear on bonded paper, business stationery, scratch pad pages, even in the back of a Bible. Louise Floyd copied her recipes into a spiral-bound composition book. The pages are filled with recipes like Lazy Woman's Pie, Mrs. Bean's Coconut Cake, and Millionaire Salad. The pages, as Louise says, are "all spattered up" from preparations of meals past.

Her Chocolate Pound Cake has long been the sweet ending of meals of fried chicken, creamed potatoes, sliced tomatoes, butter beans, salad, cornbread muffins, and iced tea.

Mama Cle's Special Coffee Cake is a hand-me-down recipe that Carolanne Griffith-Roberts treasures. As she stands in her kitchen, adrift in the aromas of her grandmother's recipe, Carolanne remembers an earlier kitchen, that of Mama Cle's in Beckley, West Virginia.

Another special recipe is Mom Ford's Chocolate Chip Cookies first made soon after Nestlé introduced chocolate morsels in 1939. Son Gary has preserved it in high-tech fashion – on his personal computer.

CHILI SAUCE

4 quarts chopped fresh tomatoes (about 7½ pounds)
2 cups chopped onion
3 green peppers, chopped
2 cups white vinegar
½ cup firmly packed brown sugar
2 tablespoons salt
1½ teaspoons dry mustard
1½ teaspoons ground cloves
1½ teaspoons ground allspice
1½ teaspoons pepper

● **Combine** all ingredients in a large Dutch oven; bring to a boil. Cover, reduce heat, and simmer, 1 hour, stirring occasionally.
● **Pour** hot mixture into hot half-pint jars, filling to ½ inch from top. Remove air bubbles; wipe jar rims. Cover at once with metal lids, and screw on bands.
● **Process** in boiling-water bath 15 minutes. **Yield:** 11 half pints.

Shirley Hall
Ocean City, Maryland

MAMA CLE'S SPECIAL COFFEE CAKE

½ cup butter or margarine, softened
½ cup shortening
1¼ cups sugar
2 large eggs
1 (8-ounce) carton sour cream
2 cups all-purpose flour
1 teaspoon baking powder
½ teaspoon baking soda
½ teaspoon salt
1 teaspoon vanilla extract
½ cup chopped pecans
2 tablespoons sugar
1 teaspoon ground cinnamon
Sifted powdered sugar

● **Beat** butter and shortening at medium speed with an electric mixer about 2 minutes or until creamy. Gradually add 1¼ cups sugar, beating at medium speed 5 to 7 minutes. Add eggs, one at a time, beating just until yellow disappears. Add sour cream, mixing until blended.
● **Combine** flour and next 3 ingredients; gradually add to butter mixture, mixing until blended. Stir in vanilla. Spoon half of batter into a greased and floured 8-inch tube pan.
● **Combine** chopped pecans, 2 tablespoons sugar, and cinnamon; sprinkle half of mixture over batter. Repeat procedure with remaining batter and pecan mixture.
● **Bake** at 350° for 55 minutes. Cool in pan on a wire rack 10 to 15 minutes; remove from pan, and let cool completely on wire rack. Sprinkle with powdered sugar. **Yield:** one 8-inch coffee cake.

Carolanne Griffith-Roberts
Birmingham, Alabama

MOM FORD'S CHOCOLATE CHIP COOKIES

½ cup shortening
⅓ cup sugar
⅓ cup firmly packed brown sugar
1 large egg
½ teaspoon vanilla extract
1 cup all-purpose flour
½ teaspoon baking soda
¼ teaspoon salt
1 cup (6 ounces) semisweet chocolate morsels
½ cup chopped pecans

● **Beat** shortening at medium speed with an electric mixer until fluffy. Gradually add sugars, beating mixture well. Add egg and vanilla, beating until blended.
● **Combine** flour, soda, and salt; add to shortening mixture, mixing well. Stir in chocolate morsels and pecans.
● **Drop** dough by tablespoonfuls onto ungreased baking sheets.
● **Bake** at 350° for 10 to 12 minutes. Transfer to wire racks to cool. **Yield:** 2½ dozen.

Gary Ford
Birmingham, Alabama

CHOCOLATE POUND CAKE

1 cup butter or margarine,
   softened
1 cup shortening
3 cups sugar
5 large eggs
3 cups all-purpose flour
½ teaspoon baking powder
½ teaspoon salt
¼ cup cocoa
1 cup milk
1 tablespoon vanilla extract

• **Beat** butter and shortening at medium speed with an electric mixer about 2 minutes or until soft and creamy. Gradually add sugar, beating at medium speed 5 to 7 minutes. Add eggs, one at a time, beating just until yellow disappears.
• **Combine** flour and next 3 ingredients; add to butter mixture alternately with milk, beginning and ending with flour mixture. Mix at low speed just until blended after each addition. Stir in vanilla. Pour batter into a greased and floured 10-inch tube pan.
• **Bake** at 325° for 1 hour and 30 minutes or until a wooden pick inserted in center of cake comes out clean. Cool in pan on a wire rack 10 to 15 minutes; remove from pan, and let cool completely on wire rack. **Yield:** one 10-inch cake.

Louise Floyd
Potters Station, Alabama

TAKING CARE OF A TREASURE

Often, old family recipes are handled without care – stuffed in recipe books, shoved in kitchen drawers, and torn each time they're handled. To protect them, you should cook from a copy, and store your originals, or even frame them for kitchen decor. Stacy Rusch, conservator of books and paper at the Virginia Historical Society in Richmond, offers these suggestions for preserving the culinary heirlooms.

■ If you frame the recipes, ask your framing shop to use only archival backing materials.

■ Don't laminate or dry mount recipes, and don't trim torn edges. Preserve the entire paper.

■ Be careful where you display your recipes; don't put them in direct sunlight or any other harsh light. Frame more than one recipe and rotate recipes on your wall, storing them in a cool, dark place when not displayed.

■ If you really love that recipe, frame a copy, and keep the original recipe in an acid-free paper folder in a cool, dark place.

GIFTS THAT PACK A PUNCH

....

Have a friend who's hosting a party this month? You can help. Drop by to RSVP in person with a timesaving gift: a punch bowl or clever container filled with ingredients and instructions for the bash's beverage. We've trimmed minutes from *your* holiday schedule as well, by picking four recipes for different occasions and creating packaging ideas for you.

CHERRY CIDER

Perfect for a small afternoon tea or gathering around the fire, Cherry Cider delivered in a wicker basket with mugs for serving will set the mood. Add some natural touches to the gift basket with a dried fruit potpourri, beeswax candles, or cinnamon sticks tied with raffia.

2 quarts apple cider
1 (3-inch) stick cinnamon
1 (3-ounce) package cherry-
   flavored gelatin

• **Assemble** all ingredients in a gift container.
• **Attach** a recipe card to gift with the following directions: Combine apple cider and cinnamon stick in a saucepan; bring to a boil. Reduce heat, and simmer 15 minutes. Add gelatin, stirring 2 minutes or until gelatin dissolves. Serve beverage hot. **Yield:** 2 quarts.

Nancy M. Skillman
Asheville, North Carolina

FESTIVE PUNCH

This punch is fun packed with tissue paper, ribbons, stickers, and paint pens. For even more pizzazz, include colorful plastic cups from the grocery store and whimsical stirrers or straws found at party or import stores. If the occasion is New Year's Eve, add a few hats and party horns.

1 (48-ounce) bottle cranberry-
   apple juice drink
1 (46-ounce) can unsweetened
   pineapple juice
½ cup sugar
1 (1-pint) bottle vodka
1 (2-liter) bottle ginger ale

● **Assemble** all ingredients in a gift container.
● **Attach** a recipe card to gift with the following directions: Combine juices and sugar in a large punch bowl, stirring until sugar dissolves. Add vodka, and chill. Stir in chilled ginger ale just before serving. **Yield:** about 5 quarts.

Marge Killmon
Annandale, Virginia

PARTY PUNCH IN A PAIL

Who says you have to wait till summer for a beach party? This sugar-sweet punch for kids is great fun delivered in sand pails. Add shredded tissue paper, leis, and playful sipping straws. Decorate the pails and plastic cups with stickers.

1 (0.17-ounce) package
   unsweetened, tropical
   punch-flavored drink mix
1 (3-ounce) package cherry-
   flavored gelatin
1 cup sugar
1 (46-ounce) can unsweetened
   pineapple juice
1 (2-liter) bottle ginger ale

● **Assemble** all ingredients in a gift container.
● **Attach** a recipe card to gift with the following directions: Combine drink

mix, gelatin, and sugar in a large bowl. Add 1 cup boiling water; stir until sugar dissolves. Stir in pineapple juice and 2 quarts cold water; freeze. Remove from freezer 1 to 2 hours before serving or until mixture can be broken into chunks. Add chilled ginger ale; stir until slushy. **Yield:** 1½ gallons.

Casey Clark
Yukon, Oklahoma

WHITE SANGRÍA

Bright colors fit the mood of sangría, so line a punch bowl with tissue paper, and add ribbon to the fruit and bottles. Include stickers and paint pens so the host, or even guests, can dress up disposable, plastic wine glasses. Put any items that don't fit in the bowl into a gift bag. (If you don't want to splurge on a punch bowl, rent one, lend the host your own, or look for one at a garage sale.)

2 lemons
2 limes
2 large Red Delicious apples
2 (750-milliliter) bottles Chablis
   or other dry white wine
1½ cups sugar
1 cup brandy
2 (1-liter) bottles club soda

● **Assemble** all ingredients in a punch bowl or other gift container.
● **Attach** a recipe card to gift with the following directions: Slice lemons, limes, and apples. Combine sliced fruit, wine, sugar, and brandy; chill mixture at least 2 hours. Gently stir in chilled club soda, and serve sangría over ice. **Yield:** 3¾ quarts.

Kathy Bowes
Metairie, Louisiana

TO ALL A GOOD NIGHT

When the word "stress" crops up too frequently in your vocabulary, it's time to put the kids to bed early and plan a night of relaxation.

But first, here are bedtime snacks for both you and the kids that need little preparation or can be made ahead. Light a fire in the fireplace, and let the children enjoy their snacks. Meanwhile, one of you can prepare your appetizers in the kitchen. Tuck the children in bed, kiss them good-night, and you're ready to kick off your shoes, wiggle your toes, and finally relax.

TOASTED PESTO ROUNDS

½ cup thinly sliced fresh basil
   leaves (about 1½ bunches)
½ cup grated Parmesan cheese
1 clove garlic, minced
⅓ cup mayonnaise
24 (¼-inch) slices French
   baguette

● **Combine** first 4 ingredients; set aside. (Or refrigerate up to 8 hours.)
● **Arrange** bread slices in a single layer on a 15- x 10- x 1-inch jellyroll pan. Broil 4 to 6 inches from heat (with electric oven door partially opened) about 1 minute.
● **Remove** from oven; turn bread slices over, and spread untoasted sides evenly with basil mixture.
● **Broil** 4 to 6 inches from heat (with electric oven door partially opened) 2 minutes or until lightly browned. **Yield:** 2 dozen.

Janice Elder
Charlotte, North Carolina

BACON-ONION APPETIZERS

⅓ cup butter or margarine, softened
½ cup finely chopped onion
6 slices bacon, cooked and crumbled
2 tablespoons chopped fresh parsley
2 (8-ounce) cans refrigerated crescent rolls

• **Combine** first 4 ingredients.
• **Unroll** crescent rolls, and separate into 8 rectangles; firmly press diagonal perforations to seal.
• **Spread** butter mixture evenly over dough. Roll up each rectangle, beginning with short side; pinch seam to seal. Cut each into 4 slices. Place pinwheels on ungreased baking sheets; flatten slightly.
• **Bake** at 375° for 15 minutes or until golden. **Yield:** 32 appetizers.

Note: To freeze, bake Bacon-Onion Appetizers 10 minutes or until lightly browned; cool and freeze up to three months. To serve, thaw and place on a baking sheet; bake at 375° for 5 minutes.

Sandra Russell
Gainesville, Florida

HONEY-AND-SPICE CRUNCH

3 quarts popcorn, popped
Vegetable cooking spray
3 tablespoons butter or margarine
¼ cup honey
¼ cup light corn syrup
3 tablespoons sugar
⅛ teaspoon salt
½ teaspoon ground cinnamon
¼ teaspoon baking soda
½ teaspoon vanilla extract
2 (0.9-ounce) packages dried fruit bits (about ½ cup)

• **Pour** popcorn into a bowl coated with cooking spray; set aside.

• **Melt** butter in a saucepan over low heat; stir in honey and next 3 ingredients. Bring to a boil over medium heat, stirring constantly. Boil mixture, without stirring, 7 minutes or until a candy thermometer reaches 250°.
• **Remove** from heat; stir in cinnamon, soda, and vanilla; pour over popcorn, stirring to coat. Spoon mixture into a lightly greased 15- x 10- x 1-inch jelly-roll pan.
• **Bake** at 250° for 25 minutes or until golden, stirring every 5 minutes. Stir in dried fruit. Cool. Store in airtight containers. **Yield:** 3 quarts.

Peggy Fowler Revels
Woodruff, South Carolina

CHOCOLATE BRICKLE SQUARES

Vegetable cooking spray
12 (4¾- x 2½-inch) graham crackers
1 cup butter or margarine
1 cup sugar
2 cups (12 ounces) semisweet chocolate morsels
1 cup (6 ounces) brickle chips

• **Line** a 15- x 10- x 1-inch jellyroll pan with aluminum foil, and coat foil with cooking spray.
• **Place** graham crackers in a single layer in prepared pan. Set aside.
• **Combine** butter and sugar in a saucepan; bring to a boil over medium heat, stirring often. Boil 1½ to 2 minutes without stirring. Pour mixture over graham crackers.
• **Bake** at 350° for 5 minutes.
• **Remove** from oven, and sprinkle with chocolate morsels. Let stand until morsels are soft enough to spread. Spread smoothly over top.
• **Sprinkle** with brickle chips; press gently into chocolate.
• **Cool** and cut into squares. **Yield:** 5 dozen.

Kerrin H. Parris
Fort Worth, Texas

HOT CHOCOLATE

4 cups milk
¾ cup semisweet chocolate morsels
1 teaspoon vanilla extract
½ cup miniature marshmallows

• **Combine** milk and chocolate morsels in a heavy 2-quart saucepan; cook over low heat, stirring constantly, until chocolate melts. Stir in vanilla.
• **Pour** into mugs; sprinkle evenly with marshmallows. **Yield:** 4 cups.

COME FOR COOKIES AND COFFEE... *AFTER* CHRISTMAS

If you're like some, you look forward to hosting that perfect Christmas party or open house. But when the holiday season finally arrives, life is a whirlwind. There's baking to do, gifts to buy, and parties to attend. As a result, you do what some do and put it off until "next year."

This year, resolve to have your party *and* enjoy it. As you bake holiday cookies for other occasions or to give to several of your closest neighbors or busiest hostesses, prepare extra batches to freeze. (All that we've suggested freeze well.) When you're ready to entertain, thaw the baked cookies, and brew a pot of coffee.

You choose the best time, between Christmas and New Year's Day or in mid-January when you and your friends aren't "get-togethered" out.

APRICOT KOLACHES

1 (12-ounce) jar apricot preserves
   (about 1 cup)
½ cup finely chopped walnuts or
   pecans
¼ teaspoon ground cinnamon
¼ teaspoon ground nutmeg
¼ teaspoon ground cloves
1 cup butter or margarine,
   softened
1 (8-ounce) package cream cheese,
   softened
2 tablespoons sugar
2 cups all-purpose flour
1 large egg, lightly beaten
1 tablespoon water
Sifted powdered sugar

● **Combine** first 5 ingredients in a small bowl; set filling aside.
● **Beat** butter and cream cheese at medium speed with an electric mixer until creamy; add sugar, beating well. Add flour, mixing at low speed until well blended.
● **Divide** dough into thirds; roll each portion to ⅛-inch thickness on a lightly floured surface, and cut with a 3-inch round cutter. Spoon ½ teaspoon filling in center of each round. Combine egg and water; brush on edges. Fold opposite sides to center, slightly overlapping edges; pinch to seal. Place on lightly greased baking sheets.
● **Bake** at 350° for 12 minutes or until golden. Remove to wire racks to cool. Sprinkle with powdered sugar. **Yield:** 5 dozen.

JoAnn Ritmiller
Baltimore, Maryland

PEANUT BUTTER-JAM BARS

½ cup butter or margarine,
   softened
½ cup sugar
½ cup firmly packed brown sugar
½ cup chunky peanut butter
1 large egg
1 teaspoon vanilla extract
1¼ cups all-purpose flour
¾ teaspoon baking soda
½ teaspoon baking powder
2 cups peanut butter morsels,
   divided
1 cup strawberry jam

● **Beat** butter at medium speed with an electric mixer until creamy; gradually add sugars, beating well. Add peanut butter, egg, and vanilla, mixing well.
● **Combine** flour, soda, and baking powder; gradually add to butter mixture, mixing well. Reserve 1 cup of dough.
● **Stir** 1 cup peanut butter morsels into remaining dough; press into bottom of a 13- x 9- x 2-inch pan. Spread jam evenly over dough. Crumble reserved dough over jam, and sprinkle with remaining peanut butter morsels.
● **Bake** at 325° for 40 minutes or until golden brown. Cool completely and cut into bars. Cookies may be frozen up to 3 months. **Yield:** about 3 dozen.

Patty Flowers
Midland, Texas

BREWING BASICS

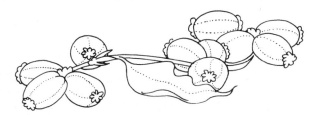

■ Remove any residual coffee oils by cleaning and rinsing your coffeemaker with hot water before each use.

■ Start coffee with fresh, cold water. Water that is high in minerals or chlorine or that has been treated with chemical softeners won't make as flavorful coffee. Use bottled water to make coffee if you don't like the way your water tastes.

■ When possible, buy fresh coffee beans and grind them just before use. (Grinders just right for home kitchens are available at gourmet coffee and kitchen shops.) Store the beans in an airtight container, in the refrigerator for two to three weeks, or in the freezer for two to three months.

■ Grind the beans (either at home or in the grocery store's grinder) as directed for your coffeemaker. If the grind is too coarse or too fine, you won't get the best flavor.

■ Use about two level tablespoons (one standard coffee measure) for each six ounces of water. Adjust the amount of coffee to your taste.

■ Drink coffee within 30 minutes after it's brewed, or store it for a short time in an insulated carafe or thermos. Coffee loses flavor quickly, and reheated coffee never tastes as good as fresh perked.

HoLIDAY DINNERS

BROWNIES WITH MOCHA FROSTING

½ cup butter or margarine
½ cup shortening
1 cup water
⅓ cup cocoa
1 tablespoon instant coffee granules
2 cups sugar
2 cups all-purpose flour
2 large eggs, lightly beaten
½ cup buttermilk
1 teaspoon baking soda
1 teaspoon vanilla extract
Mocha Frosting

• **Combine** first 5 ingredients in a large heavy saucepan; bring to a boil over medium heat, stirring often. Remove from heat. Gradually stir in sugar and flour. Add eggs and next 3 ingredients; stir until blended. Spread into a greased 15- x 10- x 1-inch jellyroll pan.
• **Bake** at 400° for 18 to 20 minutes or until a wooden pick inserted in center comes out clean.
• **Spread** Mocha Frosting over warm brownies. Cool on a wire rack; cut into squares. Store in an airtight container in the refrigerator up to 1 week or freeze up to 8 months. **Yield:** 5 dozen.

Mocha Frosting

½ cup butter or margarine
3 tablespoons cocoa
1 teaspoon instant coffee granules
¼ cup milk
1 teaspoon vanilla extract
1 (16-ounce) package powdered sugar, sifted

• **Combine** first 4 ingredients in a heavy saucepan; cook over low heat until butter melts, stirring often. Remove from heat.
• **Stir** in vanilla; gradually add sugar, stirring until smooth. **Yield:** 2 cups.

Linda Lowry Gerbode
Houston, Texas

FUDGE PUDDLES

½ cup butter or margarine, softened
½ cup creamy peanut butter
½ cup sugar
½ cup firmly packed brown sugar
1 large egg
½ teaspoon vanilla extract
1¼ cups all-purpose flour
¾ teaspoon baking soda
½ teaspoon salt
Fudge Filling
2 tablespoons chopped peanuts

• **Beat** butter and peanut butter at medium speed with an electric mixer until creamy; gradually add sugars, beating well. Add egg and vanilla, mixing well. Combine flour, baking soda, and salt; add to butter mixture, mixing well. Cover and refrigerate 1 hour.
• **Roll** into 48 (1-inch) balls. Place in lightly greased miniature (1¾-inch) muffin pans. Bake at 325° for 12 to 14 minutes or until lightly browned. Cool in pans on wire racks 5 minutes. Carefully remove cookies to racks to cool.
• **Spoon** warm Fudge Filling into a heavy-duty, zip-top plastic bag; seal. Snip a tiny hole in 1 corner of bag; pipe a small amount of filling in center of each cookie. Sprinkle with peanuts. Cool. Filled cookies may be frozen up to 8 months. **Yield:** 4 dozen.

Fudge Filling

1 cup (6 ounces) milk chocolate morsels
1 cup (6 ounces) semisweet chocolate morsels
1 (14-ounce) can sweetened condensed milk
1 teaspoon vanilla extract

• **Combine** all ingredients in a heavy saucepan, and cook over low heat until morsels melt, stirring often. **Yield:** 2 cups.

Note: Remaining Fudge Filling can be heated and served over pound cake.

Barbara Ritchie
Waynesboro, Virginia

OATMEAL-CARROT COOKIES

1¼ cups butter or margarine, softened
¾ cup firmly packed brown sugar
½ cup sugar
1 large egg
1 teaspoon vanilla extract
1½ cups all-purpose flour
1 teaspoon baking soda
½ teaspoon salt
1 teaspoon ground cinnamon
2 cups regular oats, uncooked
1 cup grated carrot
1 cup chopped pecans

• **Beat** butter at medium speed with an electric mixer until creamy; gradually add sugars, beating well. Add egg and vanilla, mixing well.
• **Combine** flour and next 3 ingredients; add to butter mixture, mixing well. Stir in oats, carrot, and pecans.
• **Drop** dough by level tablespoonfuls onto ungreased baking sheets.
• **Bake** at 350° for 10 minutes. Remove to wire racks to cool. Store in an airtight container up to 3 weeks or freeze up to 8 months. **Yield:** 4 dozen.

COOKIES THAT MAKE THE CUT

■ Unless otherwise specified, always preheat the oven at least 10 minutes before baking.

■ Use shiny baking sheets for baking. Dark ones absorb more heat and cause cookies to overbrown.

■ Let cookies cool completely before storing. To keep cookies fresh, store soft and chewy ones in an airtight container, and crisp cookies in a jar with a loose-fitting lid.

OH MY STARS

....

If the busy holiday season has you seeing stars, go with it. The celestial look is in, and what an easy way to decorate.

You can create a galaxy of simply stunning ideas to set your table twinkling. For the table, arrange gilt candlesticks and blue serving pieces against lengths of metallic fabric. Accent the table accessories with wired tinsel and metallic ribbon.

FUDGE CAKE

Hanukkah dessert takes on star proportions in this adaptation from Kosher Southern-Style Cookbook, by Mildred Covert and Sylvia Gerson.

¼ cup shortening
4 (1-ounce) squares unsweetened chocolate
¼ cup milk
2 cups sugar
2 large eggs, lightly beaten
1 teaspoon vanilla extract
2 cups all-purpose flour
2 teaspoons baking powder
¼ teaspoon baking soda
¼ teaspoon salt
2 (8-ounce) cartons sour cream
Garnish: sifted powdered sugar

● **Place** shortening and chocolate in a 2-quart glass bowl; microwave at MEDIUM (50% power) 2 minutes, stirring after 1 minute. Stir in milk and next 3 ingredients; set aside.
● **Combine** flour and next 3 ingredients. Stir half of flour mixture and 1 carton sour cream into chocolate mixture. Repeat procedure.
● **Spoon** batter into a greased and floured 11-inch star-shaped pan or 10-inch round cakepan.

● **Bake** at 350° for 30 minutes; cover with aluminum foil to prevent excessive browning. Bake 20 additional minutes. Cool cake in pan on a wire rack 10 to 15 minutes; remove cake from pan, and cool completely on wire rack. Garnish, if desired. **Yield:** one 10-inch cake.

Note: Star-shaped baking pans may be purchased at most craft and cooking specialty stores.

CHOCOLATE-GINGERBREAD COOKIES
(pictured on page 300)

To gild these cookies, lightly brush edible gold-leaf powder onto the cookies, using a small, dry paintbrush.

½ cup butter or margarine, softened
¾ cup sugar
1 large egg
½ cup molasses
3 cups all-purpose flour
2 tablespoons cocoa
1 teaspoon baking soda
1 teaspoon ground cinnamon
½ teaspoon salt
½ teaspoon baking powder
Garnish: edible gold-leaf powder

● **Beat** butter at medium speed with an electric mixer until creamy; gradually add sugar, beating well. Add egg and molasses, beating well.
● **Combine** flour and next 5 ingredients. Gradually add to butter mixture, beating until blended.
● **Divide** dough in half; wrap each portion in plastic wrap, and refrigerate dough 1 hour.
● **Roll** each portion of dough to ⅛-inch thickness on a lightly floured surface. Cut into desired sizes with star-shaped cutters; place on lightly greased baking sheets.
● **Bake** at 350° for 5 to 7 minutes. Remove cookies to wire racks to cool.

Garnish, if desired. **Yield:** about 5 dozen cookies.

Note: Edible gold-leaf powder adds shine to baked goods. The stardust powder may be purchased at most cooking specialty stores.

SET FOR THE SEASON

Wishing for a way to light up your holiday table? Just look to the stars.

Bright Star in the Kitchen
■ Our Fudge Cake takes on stellar proportions baked in a star-shaped pan. It's also great for ice cream cakes and gelatin desserts or salads.

Child Stars
■ Kids love the kitchen, especially during the holidays. Set aside some time during the holidays for baking cookies with your aspiring cooks. Using Hanukkah or Christmas cookie cutters, they'll become baking stars.

Starlight Express
■ Edible gold-leaf powder comes in one-ounce vials at cooking specialty stores. (A little goes a long way.) The decorative product also comes in a glitter form.

SURPRISINGLY LIGHT

These low-fat desserts only taste sinful. Delicately sweet angel food cake goes from simple to spectacular when layered with rich-tasting puddings or floated in a pool of luscious berry sauce. No one will be able to resist the temptation of these heavenly delights.

SLIMMING SECRETS

■ Lose weight for *yourself*. If you do it for anyone else, you won't have much chance of success.

■ If you take away all the foods you love, your healthy lifestyle will be sabotaged. Think of indulgences such as nuts or chocolate as just detours along the way.

■ Reward yourself, but do so in moderation. Two cookies are a treat; a dozen are devastating.

■ Never skip meals. Skip breakfast, and by 10 a.m. the vending machine will be your mecca. You'll eat twice as much dinner if you skip lunch.

■ Don't be afraid to ask for restaurant meals to be prepared without extra fat. Most waiters and chefs are happy to help you in your effort to watch what you eat.

■ For a quick and easy light recipe, see Southwestern Pasta Salad on page 278.

ORANGE-COCONUT ANGEL FOOD CAKE

Celebrate the holiday season with a coconut cake that has less than five fat grams per slice.

1 (14.5-ounce) package angel food cake mix
1 cup water
⅓ cup freshly squeezed orange juice
2 teaspoons orange extract, divided
1 (3-ounce) package vanilla pudding mix
2 cups skim milk
1 tablespoon grated orange rind
2 cups flaked coconut, divided
2½ cups reduced-fat frozen whipped topping, thawed and divided

● **Prepare** cake mix according to package directions, using 1 cup water and ⅓ cup orange juice instead of liquid called for on package. Stir in 1 teaspoon orange extract. Spoon evenly into an ungreased 10-inch tube pan.
● **Bake** at 375° on lowest oven rack for 30 minutes or until cake springs back when lightly touched. Invert pan; cool completely. Loosen cake from sides of pan, using a narrow metal spatula; remove from pan, and slice horizontally into 4 equal layers; set aside.
● **Combine** pudding mix and skim milk in a large saucepan; bring to a boil over medium heat, stirring constantly. Remove from heat, and stir in remaining 1 teaspoon orange extract and orange rind. Cool mixture. Fold 1 cup coconut and 1 cup whipped topping into pudding mixture.
● **Place** bottom cake layer on a serving plate; spread top of layer with one-third pudding mixture. Repeat procedure with remaining cake layers and pudding mixture, ending with top cake layer.
● **Spread** remaining 1½ cups whipped topping on top and sides of cake; sprinkle with remaining 1 cup coconut. Store in refrigerator. **Yield:** 16 servings.

Carol Lundy
New Tazewell, Tennessee

♥ Per serving: Calories 193 (21% from fat)
Fat 4.5g (2.5g saturated) Cholesterol 1mg
Sodium 301mg Carbohydrate 33.8g
Fiber 0.2g Protein 4g

LEMON ANGEL ROLLS WITH RASPBERRY SAUCE

Remove the crust of an angel food cake before slicing it to make these rolls. Gently rub the cake with your fingers and the brown crumbs will easily flake off. Even with the lemon curd, this dessert has less than seven fat grams per serving.

1 angel food cake loaf
¼ cup Key Largo liqueur *
1 (11¼-ounce) jar lemon curd
Sifted powdered sugar
Raspberry Sauce
Garnishes: lemon twist, fresh mint sprigs

- **Remove** crust from cake. Cut cake horizontally into 8 slices; flatten each slice slightly with a rolling pin. Brush cake slices with liqueur. Spread each cake slice with about 1½ tablespoons lemon curd. Starting from the narrow end, roll up cake jellyroll fashion.
- **Wrap** filled cake rolls in wax paper; chill several hours.
- **Cut** each roll into thirds; sprinkle with powdered sugar.
- **Spoon** 1 tablespoon Raspberry Sauce onto dessert plates; arrange 3 cake roll slices on sauce. Garnish, if desired. **Yield:** 8 servings.

* ¼ cup tropical fruit schnapps may be substituted.

♥ Per serving: Calories 331 (19% from fat)
Fat 6.9g (1.5g saturated) Cholesterol 65mg
Sodium 168mg Carbohydrate 60.7g
Fiber 2.5g Protein 4.3g

Raspberry Sauce

1 (10-ounce) container frozen raspberries in light syrup, thawed
2 teaspoons cornstarch

- **Place** raspberries in container of an electric blender; process until smooth. Pour mixture through a wire-mesh strainer into a small saucepan. Stir in cornstarch; place over medium heat, stirring constantly, until mixture thickens and boils. Boil 1 minute, stirring constantly. Remove from heat, and let cool. **Yield:** ½ cup.

Barbara Rutyna
Louisville, Kentucky

♥ Per tablespoon: Calories 39 (0% from fat)
Fat 0g (0g saturated) Cholesterol 0mg
Sodium 0mg Carbohydrate 9.9g
Fiber 0g Protein 0.2g

TIRAMISÙ

Tiramisù literally means "pick me up" in Italian. Try it with mascarpone or with our reduced-fat substitute.

1 (3-ounce) package vanilla pudding mix
2 cups skim milk
1 cup mascarpone cheese *
2¾ cups reduced-fat frozen whipped topping, thawed and divided
1 angel food cake loaf
1½ teaspoons instant coffee granules
½ cup hot water
¼ cup brandy
¼ cup Kahlúa or other coffee-flavored liqueur
Garnish: cocoa

- **Combine** pudding mix and milk in a saucepan; bring to a boil over medium heat, stirring constantly. Remove from heat; cool.
- **Add** mascarpone cheese; beat at low speed with an electric mixer until smooth. Fold in 1¾ cups whipped topping, and set aside.
- **Slice** cake in half horizontally. Cut each layer into 16 equal rectangles, and set aside.
- **Dissolve** coffee granules in hot water; stir in brandy and Kahlúa. Brush coffee mixture over tops and bottoms of cake pieces.
- **Line** bottom and sides of a 3-quart trifle bowl or soufflé dish with half of cake pieces; cover with half of pudding mixture. Repeat procedure with remaining cake and pudding mixture, ending with pudding mixture. Cover and refrigerate 8 hours.
- **Spread** remaining 1 cup whipped topping over Tiramisu, and garnish, if desired. Refrigerate. **Yield:** 12 servings.

* 1 (8-ounce) package reduced-fat cream cheese, 3 tablespoons reduced-fat sour cream, and 2 tablespoons skim milk may be substituted. With this substitution, you'll save 5.4 fat grams and 46 calories per serving.

Note: Mascarpone cheese is a soft, rich, buttery Italian cheese made from fresh

cream. You can find it in the gourmet section at large supermarkets.
Lucy Susan Barrett
Birmingham, Alabama

♥ Per serving: Calories 257 (42% from fat)
Fat 11.1g (4.7g saturated) Cholesterol 18mg
Sodium 174mg Carbohydrate 29.5g
Fiber 0g Protein 4.6g

SWEET SAUCES

To make any commercial fat-free pound cake, angel food cake, or nonfat frozen yogurt special, spoon on one of these easy-to-make toppings.

Rum-Raisin Sauce: Combine 1 tablespoon light-colored rum and 1½ teaspoons Irish whiskey; stir in 3 tablespoons raisins. Let stand 1 hour. Combine 1 (8-ounce) carton reduced-fat sour cream and ¼ cup firmly packed brown sugar. Stir in raisin mixture. Chill. **Yield:** 1¼ cups.

La Juan Coward
Jasper, Texas

Orange-Mallow Cream: Beat 1 (8-ounce) package reduced-fat cream cheese and ½ cup reduced-fat sour cream at medium speed with an electric mixer until smooth. Stir in 1 (7-ounce) jar marshmallow cream and 2 tablespoons Grand Marnier or other orange-flavored liqueur. Garnish with orange rind strips, if desired. **Yield:** 2⅓ cups.

Fay Redding
Gastonia, North Carolina

PLEASE PASS THE DRESSING

For many folks, cornbread dressing is the soul of Thanksgiving dinner. This side dish rich with butter and broth, made fragrant with onions and herbs, stands out among holiday pleasures. Whether moist or dry, cornbread- or white bread-based, dressing is often the most popular part of the harvest feast. We added variation to the tradition with apples, and even green chiles.

Our dishes are perfect partners for traditional roast turkey, but they would also be a great match for baked chicken, crown roast pork, beef tenderloin, Cornish hens, or wild game. If dressing is the hands-down favorite at your Thanksgiving table, surprise your guests with a couple of these treats.

Each of the recipes here is a dressing, not a stuffing. They are baked separately from the turkey in a casserole dish. For safety's sake, we recommend this baking method.

GREEN CHILE-CORNBREAD DRESSING

¼ cup butter or margarine
2 cups chopped onion
1 cup sliced celery
1 (14½-ounce) can ready-to-serve chicken broth
1 (17-ounce) can whole kernel corn, drained
2 (4½-ounce) cans chopped green chiles, drained
3 tablespoons chopped fresh parsley
½ teaspoon salt
½ teaspoon poultry seasoning
¼ teaspoon dried oregano
¼ teaspoon pepper
6 cups cornbread crumbs
½ cup chopped pecans, toasted

• **Melt** butter in a large Dutch oven; add onion and celery, and cook over medium-high heat, stirring constantly, until tender.
• **Stir** in broth and next 7 ingredients. Add cornbread crumbs and pecans, tossing until moistened; spoon into a greased 13- x 9- x 2-inch baking dish, and cover with aluminum foil.
• **Bake** at 350° for 30 minutes or until thoroughly heated. **Yield:** 8 to 10 servings.

Charlotte Pierce
Greensburg, Kentucky

SAUSAGE-APPLE DRESSING

1 (1-pound) loaf thick-sliced bread, cut into 1-inch cubes
1 pound ground mild pork sausage
6 slices bacon, chopped
1 large onion, chopped
1 cup chopped celery
1 (8-ounce) package fresh mushrooms, sliced
2 Granny Smith apples, peeled, cored, and chopped
2 cups chicken broth
1 cup chopped fresh parsley
1 teaspoon rubbed sage
1 teaspoon dried thyme
½ teaspoon pepper
¼ teaspoon salt

• **Place** bread cubes on a baking sheet. Bake at 225° for 1 hour, stirring occasionally. Set aside.
• **Cook** pork sausage and bacon in a Dutch oven, stirring until sausage crumbles; drain, reserving 3 tablespoons drippings in Dutch oven.
• **Cook** onion and next 3 ingredients in drippings over medium-high heat, stirring constantly, until tender (about 5 minutes). Remove from heat.
• **Add** sausage mixture, bread cubes, broth, and remaining ingredients to onion mixture; spoon mixture into a greased 13- x 9- x 2-inch baking dish, and cover with aluminum foil.
• **Bake** at 350° for 30 minutes. Uncover and bake 30 additional minutes. **Yield:** 8 to 10 servings.

Marguerite Morgan
Horse Shoe, North Carolina

GRITS DRESSING

3 cups regular grits, uncooked
1 cup all-purpose flour
1 teaspoon baking powder
¼ teaspoon baking soda
2 large eggs
4 cups buttermilk
2 tablespoons vegetable oil
1 large onion, chopped
1 cup chopped celery
2 to 4 tablespoons leaf sage, crumbled
1 teaspoon baking powder
2 large eggs, lightly beaten
1 (12-ounce) can evaporated milk
2 (14½-ounce) cans ready-to-serve chicken broth

• **Heat** a well-greased, 10-inch cast-iron skillet in a 325° oven 5 minutes or until hot.
• **Combine** first 4 ingredients in a large bowl; make a well in center of mixture. Combine 2 eggs, buttermilk, and oil; add to grits mixture, stirring just until moistened.
• **Remove** skillet from oven, and pour batter into skillet. Bake at 325° for 1 hour or until firm in center, but not browned. Cool and crumble.
• **Combine** crumbled bread, onion, and remaining ingredients; pour mixture into a greased 13- x 9- x 2-inch baking dish. Bake at 325° for 50 minutes or until dressing is firm. **Yield:** 10 servings.

Right: *You'll appreciate a contrast of textures between crispy fried oysters and tender greens in Spinach Salad With Oysters and Red Wine Vinaigrette (recipe, page 327).*

Tradition takes a turn toward the Southwest in this Thanksgiving feast. Above: *Citrus-Marinated Turkey Breast, Garlic Green Beans, Brandied Yams, commercial roll, Southwestern-Style Spoonbread Dressing, and Mexican Cranberries.* Left: *Shrimp-Chile Bisque. (Recipes begin on page 272.)*

Trim your holiday menu with Chocolate-Gingerbread Cookies (recipe, page 293) and Sugar-and-Spice Pecans (recipe, page 272) in our five-star dessert, Gold-Dusted Cookies 'n' Cream Dessert (recipe, page 271).

BOURSIN THAT WON'T BUST YOUR BUDGET

. . . .

If you've ever noticed this French herbed cheese spread at the deli, you likely recoiled with sticker shock. A small container, a mere half cup, is pretty pricey. And let's say you need a quick but impressive appetizer to take to a fairly large party.

We've solved the dilemma for you with one exception: You can't pick it up on the way to the gathering. But if you stop by the grocery store that afternoon, and then spend a few minutes in the kitchen with your food processor, you're in business, for a fraction of the cost.

GARLIC BOURSIN CHEESE SPREAD

1 or 2 cloves garlic
½ cup cottage cheese
2 (3-ounce) packages cream cheese, softened
2 teaspoons freeze-dried chives
2 teaspoons dried parsley flakes
⅛ teaspoon salt
⅛ teaspoon ground red pepper

• **Position** knife blade in food processor bowl; add garlic. Process until finely chopped, stopping once to scrape down sides. Add cottage cheese and remaining ingredients; process until smooth, stopping twice to scrape down sides. **Yield:** 1 cup.

Mary Pappas
Richmond, Virginia

♥ To reduce fat and calories, substitute reduced-fat cottage cheese and reduced-fat cream cheese. Do not pipe this softer mixture.

BUTTERY BOURSIN CHEESE SPREAD

1 clove garlic
2 (8-ounce) packages cream cheese, softened
1 cup butter or margarine, softened
1 teaspoon dried oregano
¼ teaspoon dried basil
¼ teaspoon dried dillweed
¼ teaspoon dried marjoram
¼ teaspoon dried thyme
¼ teaspoon pepper

• **Position** knife blade in food processor bowl; add garlic. Process until finely chopped, stopping once to scrape down sides. Add cream cheese and remaining ingredients; process until smooth, stopping twice to scrape down sides. **Yield:** about 3 cups.

Note: Cheese mixture may be refrigerated up to one week or frozen up to three months.

Brenda H. Rohe
Charlotte, North Carolina

SO, WHAT DO I DO WITH BOURSIN?

The easiest and most popular answer is to spread Boursin cheese on bread or crackers and indulge, but we found other possibilities.

■ Spread on Roma or plum tomato halves. Serve cold, or bake at 350° for 15 minutes; then broil until bubbly.

■ Spoon into fresh mushroom caps. Serve cold, or bake at 350° for 12 to 15 minutes.

■ Combine 1 cup Boursin and ½ cup milk. Toss with 12 ounces hot cooked pasta.

■ Spoon Boursin (not the low-fat version) into a pastry bag, and pipe onto cucumber slices, Belgian endive leaves, or into commercial canapé shells.

■ Spread 1 tablespoon under skin of chicken breast or 1 teaspoon over boneless, skinless chicken breast before baking.

■ Spoon onto baked potatoes instead of sour cream, or stir into mashed potatoes.

■ Use as a sandwich spread in place of mayonnaise.

NEW GAME IN TOWN

Several sporting folks who know wild game best share their bounty

of recipes. Some are traditional; some will surprise you. And all are exquisite.

Enjoy a feast with these rewards from a hunt.

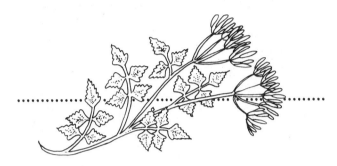

MUSHROOM-CRUSTED VENISON LOIN

*Allow venison loin to rest five to
10 minutes before carving. Serve venison
with Whipped Butternut Squash,
Venison Reduction Sauce, and Roasted
Shallot-Garlic Confit.*

1 (3¼-ounce) package fresh
   shiitake mushrooms
1 (8-ounce) package fresh cremini
   mushrooms
¼ cup olive oil
1 teaspoon sea or table salt
½ teaspoon pepper
1 pound skinned and boned
   chicken breast halves
¼ cup loosely packed fresh
   parsley leaves
¼ cup loosely packed fresh
   chervil leaves
1 (20-ounce) boneless
   venison loin *
Garnishes: grilled purple onion
   strip, asparagus spears, sweet
   red pepper strips

● **Wash** mushrooms thoroughly;
remove and discard shiitake stems.
● **Place** oil in a large skillet; add mushrooms, salt, and pepper. Cover and
cook until mushrooms are tender.
Drain and set mushrooms aside.

● **Position** knife blade in food processor bowl; add chicken, and process
until finely chopped, stopping occasionally to scrape down sides. Add
mushrooms, parsley, and chervil;
process until mixture is thoroughly
blended, stopping occasionally to
scrape down sides.
● **Cut** 2 sheets of heavy-duty plastic
wrap long enough to fit around venison loin. Place chicken mixture on 1
sheet, and top with remaining sheet.
Roll mixture to about ¼-inch thickness, covering entire sheet. Remove
top layer of plastic wrap.
● **Place** venison in center of chicken
mixture. Using plastic wrap to lift
chicken mixture, cover entire venison
with chicken mixture; remove plastic
wrap, and place venison, seam side
down, on a greased baking sheet.
● **Bake** at 350° until a meat thermometer registers at least 150° (medium-
rare), checking temperature after first
10 minutes. Garnish, if desired. **Yield:**
8 servings.

* 1 (20-ounce) beef tenderloin,
trimmed, may be substituted. Bake as
directed.

Chef David Everett
Williamsburg, Virginia

WHIPPED BUTTERNUT SQUASH

1 (4-pound) butternut squash
¾ cup instant potato flakes
½ cup firmly packed brown sugar
½ cup butter, softened
¼ teaspoon salt
¼ teaspoon freshly ground pepper
⅛ teaspoon ground nutmeg

● **Cut** butternut squash in half lengthwise, and remove and discard seeds.
Place squash halves, cut sides down, in
a shallow baking dish or pan. Add
water to dish to depth of ½ inch.
● **Bake** squash at 350° for 45 minutes
or until squash is tender. Cool slightly.
● **Remove** pulp from squash, discarding shells. Combine squash, potato
flakes, and remaining ingredients in a
large mixing bowl; beat at medium-
high speed with an electric mixer until
smooth. Pipe or spoon onto individual
plates. **Yield:** 6 cups.

Note: For instant potato flakes, we used
Idahoan brand.

Chef David Everett
Williamsburg, Virginia

VENISON STOCK

*Ask your butcher or game processor to
cut leg bones into smaller pieces.*

5 pounds venison bones
2 (10¾-ounce) cans tomato
   puree
2 large carrots, scraped and
   coarsely chopped
4 stalks celery, coarsely chopped
2 large onions, coarsely
   chopped
2 cups Burgundy or other dry
   red wine
3 quarts water
¼ teaspoon pepper
1 bay leaf
4 sprigs of fresh thyme
8 sprigs of fresh parsley

● **Place** first 5 ingredients in a roasting
pan; bake at 500° for 1 hour or until
bones are well browned, turning bones
over to prevent burning, if necessary.

Transfer mixture to a large stockpot; set aside.

• **Add** wine to roasting pan; bring to a boil, stirring to loosen browned particles. Pour into stockpot. Add water and remaining ingredients.

• **Bring** to a boil; reduce heat, and simmer at least 3 hours.

• **Line** a large wire-mesh strainer or colander with a double layer of cheesecloth; place over a large bowl. Pour stock through strainer, discarding solids in strainer. Cool stock slightly.

• **Cover** loosely and refrigerate; remove and discard solidified fat from top of stock. Cover and refrigerate up to 2 days or freeze up to 1 month. **Yield:** about 2 quarts.

VENISON REDUCTION SAUCE

For more on how to make reduction sauces, turn to "From Our Kitchen to Yours" on page 274.

1 tablespoon olive oil
2 cloves shallot, minced
1 clove garlic, minced
½ cup Burgundy or other dry red wine
2 cups Venison Stock ∗ (see recipe on facing page)
½ teaspoon chopped fresh parsley or chopped fresh chervil

• **Heat** olive oil in a small saucepan; add shallot and garlic, and cook over medium-high heat, stirring constantly, until tender. Add wine and Venison Stock.

• **Bring** to a boil. Reduce heat, and simmer 20 minutes. Stir in chopped parsley. **Yield:** 1½ cups.

∗ 2 cups no-salt-added beef broth may be substituted for Venison Stock. If you substitute beef broth, add 1 tablespoon all-purpose flour while cooking shallot and garlic.

Chef David Everett
Williamsburg, Virginia

ROASTED SHALLOT-GARLIC CONFIT

This aromatic dish takes its name, (kohn-FEE), from an old method of preserving.

8 cloves garlic, unpeeled
8 cloves shallot, unpeeled
4 sprigs fresh thyme
¼ cup butter, cut into pieces
2 tablespoons coarse sea salt

• **Combine** garlic, shallot, thyme sprigs, butter, and sea salt in a small ovenproof skillet or pan; cover with aluminum foil.

• **Bake** at 350° for 35 minutes or until garlic and shallot are tender.

• **Remove** garlic and shallot, discarding thyme and salt.

• **Peel** and chop garlic and shallot. **Yield:** 1 cup.

Chef David Everett
Williamsburg, Virginia

CHEF TARGETS GAME

"When I became executive chef at the Dining Room at Ford's Colony in Williamsburg, Virginia, I decided it wasn't enough to have creative ideas for the preparation of a dish. My goal was also to introduce new foods and flavors utilizing the freshest native ingredients," explains **David Everett**, while discussing his inventive use of wild game on the restaurant menu.

David continues, "I knew I couldn't raise my own game, but I realized there were wonderful local purveyors eager to harvest venison, rabbit, and boar to order."

In his four years at the resort community, David has built a reputation on serving sensational dishes created from the region's finest ingredients.

Much of his inspiration comes from his herb and vegetable garden. At least a dozen varieties of herbs, tomatoes, and peppers, as well as an arbor of Concord grapes, provide David with the premium ingredients necessary for creating his intensely flavored game dishes.

"Game is not what it used to be," David says. "It's no longer strong or overbearing. Sportsmen and chefs alike now know that proper handling and creative use of stocks, sauces, and herbs can enhance its richness."

Although his recipes are often long on ingredients, David's preparation and presentation techniques are always doable. Try them in your own kitchen and you'll be rewarded with layers of intense flavor.

GAME POT PIE WITH PARMESAN CRUST

This stew works just as well spooned over hot biscuits or cornbread.

4   cloves garlic, minced
2   cloves shallot, minced
¼   cup olive oil
1   pound boneless venison, cut into
      1-inch pieces
1   pound boneless rabbit, cut into
      1-inch pieces
1   pound boneless duck breasts, cut
      into 1-inch pieces
1   cup Burgundy or other dry red
      wine
1   cup crème de cassis or other
      black currant-flavored liqueur
½   cup dried apricot halves,
      chopped
¼   teaspoon salt
¼   teaspoon pepper
1   bay leaf
4   cups Venison Stock (see recipe
      on page 302)
1   small turnip, peeled and
      chopped
1   medium carrot, scraped and
      chopped
1   cup chopped rutabaga
1   cup pearl onions, peeled
1   medium potato, cut into ½-inch
      cubes
½   cup fresh shiitake mushrooms,
      sliced (3 whole)
1   (15½-ounce) can white beans,
      rinsed and drained
1½ teaspoons fresh thyme leaves
1½ teaspoons chopped fresh
      chives
1½ teaspoons chopped fresh
      parsley
Whipped Celery Potatoes
      (see recipe on facing page)
Parmesan Crust

● **Cook** garlic and shallot in oil in a Dutch oven over medium-high heat, stirring constantly, until tender. Add venison, rabbit, and duck; cook, stirring constantly, until browned. Stir in wine and next 5 ingredients. Bring mixture to a boil; reduce heat, and simmer 30 minutes.
● **Stir** in Venison Stock and next 6 ingredients. Bring to a boil; reduce

heat, and simmer 30 minutes or until vegetables are tender. Add beans and next 3 ingredients, stirring until thoroughly heated. Discard bay leaf.
● **Ladle** into bowls. Pipe or dollop Whipped Celery Potatoes into 4 rosettes evenly spaced around rim of each bowl. Top each with Parmesan Crust. **Yield:** 8 servings.

Parmesan Crust

12 sheets frozen phyllo pastry,
      thawed
½   cup butter or margarine,
      melted
¾   cup grated Parmesan cheese

● **Place** 1 sheet of pastry on a large cutting board, keeping remaining pastry covered with a slightly damp towel to prevent it from drying out. Brush pastry sheet with butter, and sprinkle with 1 tablespoon Parmesan cheese. Repeat procedure 2 times, layering pastry, butter, and cheese.
● **Cut** out 2 (6- to 8-inch) circles from pastry, and place on a lightly greased baking sheet. Lightly grease bottom of a second baking sheet, and place on top of circles to keep phyllo flat during baking.
● **Bake** at 350° for 10 minutes or until golden brown. Cool on baking sheet on a wire rack.
● **Repeat** procedure 3 times using remaining pastry, butter, and cheese. **Yield:** 8 crusts.

Chef David Everett
Williamsburg, Virginia

FOR THE LOVE OF THE LAND

Most people in Nashville know **Bill Hall** as a popular television personality. But the jovial weather forecaster gives more than just updates on what the next day's weather might bring. He also offers tips on where to find and how to cook the wild game of the region.

Bill's hunting memories began 35 years ago as a young boy growing up near Springhill, Tennessee. "My family sharecropped on the land where the Saturn manufacturing plant now stands," says Bill. "I loved to explore in the woods. I also loved to cook and eat. Hunting was a means of putting a good meal on the table. I had to account for every shotgun shell I fired. If I missed, we didn't eat."

Hearing his mother admonish, "Don't waste things," Bill developed a reverence for the land and respect for its wildlife. His commitment to take only as much as his family and friends will consume remains steadfast.

Bill exchanges recipes and ideas with viewers through the station's weekly outdoor show that features a cooking segment.

After being diagnosed as a diabetic, Bill was challenged to come up with some healthy recipes. This spurred him to publish *Land and Lakes Cookbook,* a collection of recipes that makes use of the earth's goodness in a fresh, new fashion.

WHIPPED CELERY POTATOES

2 pounds Yukon Gold or red
   potatoes
3½ cups water
1½ teaspoons salt
1 cup butter or margarine,
   divided
1 cup finely chopped celery
¼ cup finely chopped onion
¼ cup milk
¼ teaspoon salt
⅛ teaspoon pepper
⅛ teaspoon ground nutmeg

• **Combine** first 3 ingredients in a large saucepan; bring to a boil. Cover and simmer 30 to 35 minutes or until tender; drain potatoes. Cool 5 minutes; peel and place potatoes in a large mixing bowl.
• **Melt** 2 tablespoons butter in a skillet; add celery and onion. Cook, stirring constantly, 3 to 4 minutes, or until tender.
• **Add** celery mixture to potatoes; beat at low speed with an electric mixer until potatoes are mashed. Add butter, milk, and remaining ingredients; beat at high speed until whipped. Serve immediately. **Yield:** 6 to 8 servings.

Chef David Everett
Williamsburg, Virginia

GRILLED DUCK WITH ORANGE SAUCE

3 wild duck breasts
1½ teaspoons garlic powder
1½ teaspoons onion powder
1½ teaspoons pepper
3 lemons, cut in half
3 oranges, cut in half
¼ cup butter or margarine
¼ cup frozen orange juice
   concentrate, thawed and
   undiluted
¼ cup firmly packed brown
   sugar
1 tablespoon grated orange
   rind

• **Place** each duck breast on a large sheet of heavy-duty aluminum foil. Sprinkle each with ½ teaspoon garlic powder, onion powder, and pepper. Squeeze juice of half a lemon and half an orange over each. Place remaining lemon and orange halves inside duck cavities; wrap tightly with several layers of foil.
• **Cook,** covered with grill lid, over medium-hot coals (350° to 400°) 40 minutes or until a meat thermometer inserted in thickest part of duck registers 180°.
• **Combine** butter and remaining ingredients in a saucepan. Cook over medium heat, stirring constantly, until thickened. Serve over duck. **Yield:** 6 servings.

Bill Hall
Nashville, Tennessee

BAKED QUAIL WITH CORNBREAD STUFFING

The recipe for Cornbread Stuffing from Jill Fortney's grandmother merits a favored place on the table for this side dish.

12 quail
Cornbread Stuffing
12 slices bacon
¼ cup Worcestershire sauce
1 (14½-ounce) can ready-to-serve
   beef broth, divided

• **Cut** a pocket on each side of quail backbone, measuring about 2 inches long and 1½ inches deep.
• **Stuff** quail pockets with unbaked Cornbread Stuffing, spooning about 1 tablespoon into each pocket. Reserve remaining stuffing for baking.
• **Wrap** a bacon slice around each bird; place in a roasting pan, breast side down, and drizzle evenly with Worcestershire sauce.
• **Reserve** 1¼ cups beef broth.
• **Cover** quail and bake at 350° for 1 hour, uncovering and basting birds with remaining beef broth every 10 minutes during the first 30 minutes of cooking time.
• **Uncover** and turn birds, breast side up. Brush with pan drippings.
• **Broil** quail, uncovered, 5 inches from heat (with electric oven door partially opened) 3 to 5 minutes or until birds are browned. Remove quail from the roasting pan, reserving drippings in a pan. Keep quail warm.
• **Add** reserved 1¼ cups beef broth to drippings, stirring to loosen browned particles. Cook over high heat about 15 minutes or until liquid is reduced by one-third; skim fat from liquid. Serve sauce with quail and additional baked Cornbread Stuffing. **Yield:** 6 servings.

Cornbread Stuffing

2 (8½-ounce) packages cornbread
   muffin mix
1 pound ground pork sausage
¼ cup butter or margarine
3 cups finely chopped celery
½ cup chopped onion
½ cup chopped green onions
1 (8-ounce) package herb-
   seasoned stuffing mix
2 (14½-ounce) cans ready-to-serve
   chicken broth
3 large eggs, lightly beaten

• **Prepare** cornbread mix according to package directions; cool and crumble in a large bowl. Set aside.
• **Brown** sausage in a large skillet, stirring until it crumbles. Drain well, and stir into cornbread.
• **Melt** butter in a large skillet, and add celery and onions. Cook over medium-high heat, stirring constantly, until tender. Stir vegetables into cornbread mixture.
• **Stir** stuffing mix and remaining ingredients into cornbread mixture. Remove 1½ cups for stuffing quail. Spoon remaining mixture into a greased 13- x 9- x 2-inch baking dish.
• **Bake** at 350° for 1 hour or until golden. **Yield:** 6 to 8 servings.

Jill Fortney
Fort Worth, Texas

GAME BIRDS IN WINE MARINADE

12 skinned dove breasts
¾ cup Burgundy or other dry red wine
¼ cup vegetable oil
¼ cup soy sauce
1 tablespoon brown sugar
2 tablespoons water
1 teaspoon dried oregano
1 teaspoon ground ginger
1 clove garlic, pressed
1 (8-ounce) can sliced mushrooms, undrained
1 tablespoon vegetable oil
Hot cooked rice
Garnishes: chopped fresh parsley, fresh mushrooms

● **Place** dove breasts in a large shallow dish or heavy-duty, zip-top plastic bag.
● **Combine** Burgundy and next 8 ingredients; pour over dove, turning to coat. Cover dish, or seal bag. Refrigerate 8 hours, turning dove occasionally. Drain, reserving marinade.
● **Brown** dove in 1 tablespoon hot oil in a small Dutch oven. Add reserved marinade. Bring to a boil; cover, reduce heat, and simmer 1 hour.
● **Remove** dove from Dutch oven, reserving liquid in Dutch oven; cool slightly. Remove and discard bone; return meat to Dutch oven.
● **Bring** mixture to a boil; reduce heat, and simmer 3 minutes or until mixture is thoroughly heated. Serve over rice. Garnish, if desired. **Yield:** 4 servings.

Jill Fortney
Fort Worth, Texas

COUNTRY-FRIED WILD TURKEY

An overnight soak in milk adds tenderness to strips of wild turkey.

3 pounds boneless wild turkey breast
2 to 2½ cups milk
1½ cups all-purpose flour
1 to 1¼ teaspoons salt
½ teaspoon pepper
Vegetable oil
Turkey Gravy

● **Cut** turkey into 1-inch slices; cut each slice into 3- x ½-inch strips, and place in an 11- x 7- x 1½-inch baking dish. Pour milk over strips; cover. Refrigerate 8 hours. Drain turkey, discarding milk, and set aside.
● **Combine** flour, salt, and pepper in a large, heavy-duty, zip-top plastic bag. Add 6 to 8 turkey strips; close bag, and shake to coat. Place turkey strips in a single layer on wax paper; repeat procedure with remaining turkey.
● **Pour** oil to depth of 2 to 3 inches in a large Dutch oven; heat to 350°. Cook turkey strips, 8 to 10 at a time, until golden brown. Drain on paper towels, and keep warm. Repeat procedure with remaining turkey. Reserve ⅓ cup drippings for Turkey Gravy. Serve turkey strips with gravy. **Yield:** 16 to 18 appetizer servings or 8 to 10 main-dish servings.

Turkey Gravy

⅓ cup reserved turkey drippings
⅓ cup all-purpose flour
2 cups milk
½ teaspoon salt
½ teaspoon pepper

● **Pour** reserved drippings into a heavy skillet. Stir in flour; cook over medium heat, stirring constantly, until dark golden brown. Gradually stir in milk; cook, stirring constantly, until mixture is thickened. Stir in salt and pepper. **Yield:** 2 cups.

Jill Fortney
Fort Worth, Texas

SANTA FE SPANISH RABBIT

A rich tomato sauce tenderizes and flavors extra-lean rabbit. Bill Hall serves this game dish with black beans and rice.

¼ cup all-purpose flour
¼ teaspoon freshly ground
  pepper
1 (3-pound) rabbit, cleaned and
  cut into pieces
2 to 4 tablespoons olive oil
1 small onion, chopped
1 stalk celery, chopped
2 cloves garlic, minced
1 cup Chablis or other dry white
  wine
1 (10¾-ounce) can condensed
  beef broth, undiluted
4 medium tomatoes, coarsely
  chopped
⅓ cup ripe olives, cut in
  half
⅓ cup green olives, cut in
  half
1 to 2 tablespoons chopped fresh
  oregano
Garnish: roasted sweet red pepper
  slices

• **Combine** flour and pepper in a large, heavy-duty, zip-top plastic bag; add rabbit, shaking to coat.
• **Brown** rabbit in olive oil in a large Dutch oven over medium-high heat; remove rabbit, reserving drippings in Dutch oven.
• **Cook** onion, celery, and garlic in drippings over medium heat, stirring constantly, 3 minutes or until tender. Add wine, and simmer until liquid is reduced by half (about 15 minutes).
• **Stir** in beef broth; bring to a boil. Reduce heat; add rabbit, tomato, olives, and oregano.
• **Simmer**, stirring occasionally, 30 minutes or until rabbit is tender. (For a thicker sauce, remove rabbit, and keep warm. Continue simmering sauce until thickened.) Garnish, if desired. **Yield:** 4 servings.

Bill Hall
Nashville, Tennessee

GAME PLAN

■ Good game begins in the field with proper dressing of the animal or bird. Rinse out body cavities thoroughly, and cool down meat as quickly as possible.

■ Game generally has less fat than other meats. The secret to preparing it well is adding moisture during cooking.

■ Some commercial game processors add fat while grinding venison to improve flavor and texture.

■ Game should first be properly butchered by a commercial processor and then adequately wrapped for freezing.

■ Venison recipes work well for beef, but not all beef recipes work for venison. Venison is frequently leaner, tougher, and has a stronger flavor than beef. So venison may benefit from special handling and seasoning.

■ Use frozen game within six months.

■ If you bag more game than you can use, check with local food banks; many will hold processed frozen game for distribution to those persons in need.

■ Game is best cooked to a medium-rare to medium degree of doneness.

■ The flavor of duck, goose, and other wild fowl is drastically affected by what the bird eats. Fish-eating fowl will often have a stronger flavor than grain-or vegetation-fed birds.

■ Leave skin intact on most game birds during storage to act as a natural protection against freezer burn.

■ If birds are skinned, store in water in freezer-safe containers to prevent freezer burn.

GREAT GRAVY

Beef, pork, or poultry – you name it, you can make a gravy from it. And the basic ingredients are so simple – meat drippings, broth or another liquid, and flour or cornstarch.

Try these recipes, or create your own gravy recipe. Keep in mind that 1 tablespoon of cornstarch or 2 tablespoons of all-purpose flour will thicken 1 cup of liquid.

ROAST TURKEY AND GIBLET GRAVY

1 (12-pound) turkey
¼ teaspoon salt
1 medium onion, chopped
1 stalk celery, sliced
1 carrot, scraped and sliced
1 teaspoon salt
2 tablespoons butter or margarine, melted
¼ cup cornstarch
½ cup water
¾ teaspoon salt
½ teaspoon pepper

• **Combine** giblets and neck from turkey, ¼ teaspoon salt, and next 3 ingredients in a medium saucepan; add water to cover. Bring to a boil over medium heat; cover, reduce heat, and simmer 45 minutes or until giblets and neck are tender. Drain mixture, reserving broth; cover and refrigerate. Coarsely chop neck meat and giblets; refrigerate.
• **Rinse** turkey with cold water; drain and pat dry. Sprinkle cavity with 1 teaspoon salt. Tie ends of legs together with string. Lift wingtips up and over back, and tuck under bird. Place turkey, breast side up, on a rack in a shallow roasting pan; brush entire bird with melted butter.
• **Bake** at 325° until meat thermometer reaches 180° (about 3½ to 4

hours). (To prevent overcooking turkey, begin checking for doneness 1 hour before shortest estimated time.) If turkey starts to brown too much, cover loosely with aluminum foil. Remove turkey and rack from roasting pan, reserving drippings in pan; let the turkey stand 15 minutes before carving.
• **Remove** and discard fat from drippings; return drippings to roasting pan. Add reserved broth and enough water, if necessary, to equal 3 cups. Stir to loosen browned particles.
• **Combine** cornstarch and ½ cup water in a medium saucepan; stir until smooth. Add broth mixture; cook over medium heat, stirring constantly, until thickened. Stir in neck meat and giblets, ¾ teaspoon salt, and pepper. Serve with turkey. **Yield:** 12 servings.

Denise Cooper
Sparta, North Carolina

BAKED HEN WITH CRANBERRY PAN GRAVY

1 (5½- to 6-pound) hen
5 cups water
1 large onion, quartered
Celery leaves from 3 stalks celery
1 teaspoon salt
⅛ teaspoon dried thyme
1 cup frozen cranberry juice cocktail concentrate, thawed and undiluted
½ cup fresh cranberries, finely chopped
2½ tablespoons cornstarch
3 tablespoons water
Garnishes: fresh rosemary, oregano, thyme, fresh cranberries

• **Combine** giblets and neck from hen, 5 cups water, and next 4 ingredients in a 3-quart saucepan. Bring to a boil; cover, reduce heat, and simmer 1½ hours. Pour mixture through a wire-mesh strainer into a container, reserving broth and discarding solids in strainer. Cover and refrigerate broth.
• **Rinse** hen with cold water; drain and pat dry. Tie ends of legs together with

string. Lift wingtips up and over back, and tuck under bird. Place hen, breast side up, in a 15- x 10- x 2-inch baking dish. Cover dish with foil.
• **Bake** at 325° for 3 hours; uncover and bake 30 minutes or until a meat thermometer reaches 180°. Remove hen from dish, reserving drippings.
• **Remove** and discard fat from drippings in dish; return 2 tablespoons drippings to dish.
• **Add** water to reserved broth to equal 1½ cups. Add broth to drippings in a dish. Stir to loosen browned particles; add cranberry juice concentrate and chopped cranberries.
• **Bring** mixture to a boil; reduce heat, and cook, stirring occasionally, 3 to 5 minutes.
• **Combine** cornstarch and water, stirring until mixture smooth. Stir into gravy mixture; return to a boil. Cook 1 minute, stirring constantly. Serve with hen. Garnish hen, if desired. **Yield:** 8 to 10 servings.

Estelle Gilbert
Stanardsville, Virginia

COUNTRY-STYLE POT ROAST AND GRAVY

1 (4- to 5-pound) boneless chuck roast
1 tablespoon vegetable oil
1 (1-ounce) envelope onion soup mix
2 cups water
4 potatoes, peeled and cut into 1-inch cubes
4 carrots, scraped and cut into 1-inch slices
2 tablespoons all-purpose flour
½ cup water
¼ teaspoon salt
¼ teaspoon pepper

• **Brown** roast in hot oil in a Dutch oven. Add soup mix and 2 cups water; bring to a boil. Cover, reduce heat, and simmer 2 hours.
• **Add** vegetables; return to a boil. Cover, reduce heat, and simmer 30 minutes. Remove roast and vegetables to a serving platter; keep warm.

● **Remove** and discard fat from pan drippings; return 1 cup drippings to Dutch oven.

● **Combine** flour and ½ cup water, stirring until smooth. Add to drippings, stirring constantly. Bring to a boil over medium heat, stirring constantly, until thickened. Stir in salt and pepper. Serve with roast. **Yield:** 8 to 10 servings.

Ethel C. Jernegan
Savannah, Georgia

IT'S ALL IN THE DRIPPINGS

■ Gravies rely on the drippings from meat for their rich flavor and color. The drippings called for in recipes may be extended with bouillon or milk if the volume is too low; keep the proportions of liquid to thickening agents the same as in the recipe.

■ Make Pan Gravy from the natural drippings left in the skillet or roasting pan by roasts, steaks, chops, or other meats.

■ Make Pot Roast Gravy from the liquid in which pot roast has simmered.

■ If your sauce is not dark enough in color, add a few splashes of commercial browning and seasoning sauce. Be sure to add it before you add your other seasonings, as it does add flavor as well as color. You may want to reduce the other seasonings.

■ Cream Gravy is the typical accompaniment to Southern fried chicken. In many homes, one is never served without the other. This gravy can also be made from drippings of meat other than fried chicken.

AND THE WINNER IS...

Watching 13 young chef hopefuls flex their culinary muscles is nothing short of amazing.

It's not often that we get to sample 13 interpretations of one recipe. Our visit to Norfolk's Careers Through Culinary Arts Program (C-CAP) scholarship competition in Virginia allowed us to observe a talented group of future chefs.

Each of them prepared classic Poached Chicken Breast with Turned Vegetables and Chive Sauce during the timed exercise.

Here is our adaptation of their chicken dish, ready for you to test for your own panel of judges.

POACHED CHICKEN BREAST WITH TURNED VEGETABLES AND CHIVE SAUCE

"Turned" vegetables, pieces of carrot and zucchini trimmed into small football shapes, give this dish a chef's signature.

2 (6-inch-long) zucchini, cut into 2-inch pieces
4 (8-inch-long) carrots, scraped and cut into 2-inch pieces
3 (10½-ounce) cans ready-to-serve reduced-sodium chicken broth
2¼ cups water
½ teaspoon salt
½ teaspoon freshly ground pepper
4 (4- to 5-ounce) skinned and boned chicken breast halves
1 teaspoon chicken-flavored bouillon granules
1½ tablespoons cornstarch
3 tablespoons unsalted butter, cut into ½-inch pieces and chilled
1 teaspoon lemon juice
1 tablespoon finely chopped fresh chives
⅛ teaspoon freshly ground pepper
Garnishes: lemon twist, fresh chives

● **Cut** each zucchini piece in half lengthwise.

● **Trim** zucchini and carrot pieces to resemble football shapes, using a paring knife, and set aside.

● **Place** carrots in boiling water to cover; remove from heat, cover, and let stand 10 minutes. Add zucchini; cover, and let stand 5 minutes. Drain and set aside.

● **Reserve** 2 tablespoons chicken broth; set aside.

● **Combine** remaining chicken broth, water, salt, and ½ teaspoon pepper in a large Dutch oven; bring to a boil. Add chicken; reduce heat to low, and cook 5 minutes. Turn chicken over; cook 5 minutes.

● **Remove** 2 cups chicken broth mixture from Dutch oven; set aside.

● **Add** carrots and zucchini to Dutch oven; cover and let stand while making sauce.

● **Place** 2 cups chicken broth mixture in a 2-quart saucepan; bring to a boil over medium heat, and cook 6 to 8 minutes or until liquid is reduced to 1 cup; reduce heat. Add bouillon granules, stirring until granules dissolve.

● **Combine** cornstarch and reserved 2 tablespoons chicken broth; gradually stir into reduced liquid. Return to a boil, and cook 1 minute, stirring constantly, or until thickened. Remove from heat; add butter pieces, one at a time, and stir with a wire whisk until butter melts. (Do not boil mixture after butter is added.)

● **Stir** in lemon juice, chopped chives, and ⅛ teaspoon pepper. Set aside.

● **Drain** chicken and vegetables; cut chicken diagonally into ½-inch wide slices. Arrange with vegetables on serving plates; spoon sauce over chicken. Garnish, if desired. **Yield:** 4 servings.

A TASTE OF GEORGIA

Not only does *A Taste of Georgia* have 500 pages of triple-tested recipes, but this *Southern Living* Community Cookbook Hall of Fame winner includes tips on garnishing, decorating cakes, and substitutions. If that's not enough, the cookbook features cooking hints on almost every page. You'll want to join the more than 250,000 people who rely on the Junior Service League of Newnan's *A Taste of Georgia*.

EASY CHICKEN DIVAN

We liked this casserole just as well without dotting the top with two tablespoons of butter, as recommended in the original recipe.

1 (3½- to 4-pound) broiler-
    fryer, cut in half
2 (10-ounce) packages frozen
    broccoli spears, thawed and
    coarsely chopped
2 (10¾-ounce) cans cream of
    chicken soup, undiluted
1 cup mayonnaise
1½ teaspoons lemon juice
¾ teaspoon curry powder
½ cup (2 ounces) shredded sharp
    Cheddar cheese
¾ cup herb-seasoned stuffing
    mix

• **Combine** chicken and enough water to cover in a Dutch oven; bring to a boil. Cover, reduce heat, and simmer 40 minutes or until tender. Remove chicken, reserving broth for another use. Let chicken cool. Skin, bone, and cut chicken into bite-size pieces. Set aside.
• **Place** broccoli in a lightly greased 11- x 7- x 1½-inch baking dish. Top with chicken.
• **Combine** soup and next 3 ingredients; spoon over chicken. Sprinkle with cheese and stuffing mix.

• **Bake** at 400° for 25 to 30 minutes or until thoroughly heated. **Yield:** 6 to 8 servings.

♥ To reduce fat and calories, substitute reduced-sodium, reduced-fat cream of chicken soup and reduced-fat mayonnaise.

LEMON PARFAIT PIE

We used meringue powder instead of raw egg whites because the safety of uncooked meringues has become questionable since A Taste of Georgia was written.

1 cup sugar
2 tablespoons cornstarch
¼ teaspoon salt
1 tablespoon grated lemon rind
⅓ cup lemon juice
3 egg yolks, lightly beaten
¼ cup butter or margarine
2 pints vanilla ice cream,
    softened
Graham Cracker Crust
¾ cup sugar
½ cup boiling water
¼ cup meringue powder

• **Combine** first 5 ingredients in a heavy saucepan, stirring until mixture is smooth. Add egg yolks and butter. Bring mixture to a boil over medium heat, stirring constantly. Boil 1 minute; cool.
• **Spread** half of ice cream in Graham Cracker Crust, and top with half of lemon mixture. Freeze until firm. Repeat procedure with remaining ice cream and lemon mixture, and freeze until firm.
• **Combine** ¾ cup sugar and boiling water, stirring until sugar dissolves. Cool.
• **Add** meringue powder; beat at high speed with an electric mixer until stiff peaks form. Spread meringue over filling, sealing to edge of crust.
• **Bake** at 425° for 5 to 7 minutes or until golden brown. Serve pie immediately or return to freezer. **Yield:** one 9-inch pie.

Note: For meringue powder, we used Country Kitchen brand.

Graham Cracker Crust

1¼ cups graham cracker crumbs
¼ cup sugar
⅓ cup butter or margarine,
    melted

• **Combine** all ingredients, and press mixture evenly on bottom and sides of a 9-inch pieplate.
• **Bake** at 375° for 6 to 8 minutes. Cool. **Yield:** one 9-inch crust.

DECEMBER

ROLL CALL

We've developed show-stopping holiday variations of *roulage*

(ru-LAZH), a classic rolled cake dessert, that may remind you of

a jellyroll.Each of our never-fail cakes wraps around a flavored whipped

cream filling. We've eliminated involved techniques and lengthy

preparation. Our recipes start with a commercial cake mix, and there's

a quick sauce to complement each version.

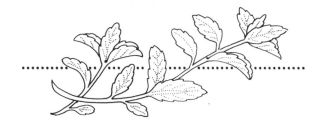

TOFFEE-PECAN ROULAGE
(pictured on front cover)

Vegetable cooking spray
4 large eggs
½ cup water
1 (18.25- or 18.5-ounce) package
   yellow cake mix
¼ cup almond brickle chips
¼ cup finely chopped pecans,
   toasted
2 to 4 tablespoons powdered
   sugar
2 cups whipping cream
2 tablespoons powdered
   sugar
4 to 6 tablespoons praline liqueur,
   divided *
Additional powdered sugar
Praline Sauce
Garnishes: whipped cream, toasted
   pecan halves

● **Coat** 2 (15- x 10- x 1-inch) jellyroll pans with cooking spray; line with wax paper, and coat with cooking spray. Set aside.
● **Beat** eggs in a mixing bowl at medium-high speed with an electric mixer 5 minutes. Add water, beating at low speed to blend. Gradually add cake mix, beating at low speed until moistened. Beat at medium-high speed 2 minutes. Fold in brickle chips and chopped pecans. Divide batter in half, and spread evenly into prepared pans. (Layers will be thin.)
● **Bake** each cake at 350° on the middle rack in separate ovens for 13 minutes or until cake springs back when lightly touched in the center. (If you don't have a double oven, set 1 pan aside.)
● **Sift** 1 to 2 tablespoons powdered sugar in a 15- x 10-inch rectangle on a cloth towel; repeat with second towel. When cakes are done, immediately loosen from sides of pans, and turn each out onto a sugared towel. Peel off wax paper. Starting at narrow end, roll up each cake and towel together; place, seam side down, on wire racks to cool completely.
● **Beat** whipping cream at medium-high speed with an electric mixer until foamy; gradually add 2 tablespoons powdered sugar, beating until soft peaks form. Fold in 2 to 3 tablespoons praline liqueur.
● **Unroll** cakes; brush each lightly, using remaining 2 to 3 tablespoons liqueur. Spread each cake with half of whipped cream mixture. Reroll cakes without towels; place, seam side down, on a baking sheet. Cover and freeze at least 1 hour or up to 3 months.
● **Dust** cakes with additional powdered sugar. Cut into 1- to 2-inch slices; spoon warm Praline Sauce evenly onto dessert plates. Top each with a cake slice. Garnish, if desired. **Yield:** 2 filled cake rolls (5 to 6 servings each).

* 2 tablespoons vanilla extract may be substituted. Use 1 tablespoon in whipped cream, and brush cakes with a mixture of 1 tablespoon vanilla plus 2 teaspoons water.

Praline Sauce

1 cup firmly packed brown
   sugar
½ cup half-and-half
½ cup butter or margarine
½ cup finely chopped pecans,
   toasted
½ teaspoon vanilla extract

● **Combine** first 3 ingredients in a small saucepan; bring to a boil over medium heat, stirring constantly. Boil 1 minute, stirring constantly. Remove from heat; stir in pecans and vanilla. **Yield:** about 2 cups.

CHOCOLATE CAKE ROLLS

Vegetable cooking spray
4 large eggs
½ cup water
1 (18.25- or 18.5-ounce) package
   Swiss chocolate, devil's food,
   or fudge cake mix
2 to 4 tablespoons cocoa

● **Coat** 2 (15- x 10- x 1-inch) jellyroll pans with cooking spray; line with wax paper, and coat with cooking spray. Set aside.
● **Beat** eggs in a large mixing bowl at medium-high speed with an electric mixer 5 minutes. Add water, beating at low speed to blend. Gradually add

cake mix, beating at low speed until moistened. Beat at medium-high speed 2 minutes. Divide batter in half, and spread batter evenly into prepared pans. (Layers will be thin.)
● **Bake** each cake at 350° on the middle rack in separate ovens for 13 minutes or until cake springs back when lightly touched in the center. (If you don't have a double oven, set 1 pan aside.)
● **Sift** 1 to 2 tablespoons cocoa in a 15- x 10-inch rectangle on a cloth towel; repeat with second towel. When cakes are done, immediately loosen from sides of pans, and turn each out onto a prepared towel. Peel off wax paper. Starting at narrow end, roll up each cake and towel together; place cakes, seam side down, on wire racks. Cool cakes completely. Use cake rolls for Chocolate-Cranberry Roulage, Chocolate-Orange Roulage, or Mint-Chocolate Roulage. **Yield:** 2 cake rolls.

CHOCOLATE-CRANBERRY ROULAGE
(pictured on page 336)

1 (12-ounce) carton cranberry-raspberry crushed fruit
¾ cup cranberry juice cocktail
2 tablespoons powdered sugar
1½ tablespoons cornstarch
4 to 5 tablespoons crème de cassis or other black currant-flavored liqueur, divided *
2 cups whipping cream
Chocolate Cake Rolls (see recipe on facing page)
Cocoa
Garnishes: fresh cranberries, fresh mint sprigs

● **Combine** first 4 ingredients in container of an electric blender or food processor; process until smooth, stopping several times to scrape down sides.
● **Pour** mixture into a small saucepan; bring to a boil over medium heat, stirring constantly. Boil 1 minute, stirring constantly. Stir in 2 tablespoons crème de cassis. Cool cranberry mixture.

● **Beat** whipping cream at medium-high speed with an electric mixer until soft peaks form. Fold in ⅔ cup cranberry mixture; cover and refrigerate the remaining cranberry mixture to use as a garnish.
● **Unroll** cake rolls; brush each lightly with remaining 2 to 3 tablespoons crème de cassis. Spread each cake with half of whipped cream mixture. Reroll cakes without towels; place, seam side down, on a baking sheet. Cover and

freeze cakes at least 1 hour or up to 3 months.
● **Dust** cakes with cocoa, and cut into 1- to 2-inch slices. Spoon remaining cranberry mixture evenly onto dessert plates. Top each with a cake slice. Garnish, if desired. **Yield:** 2 filled cake rolls (5 to 6 servings each).

* 4 to 5 tablespoons cranberry juice cocktail may be substituted for crème de cassis.

Don't let the fancy name fool you; these elegant desserts aren't difficult to prepare.

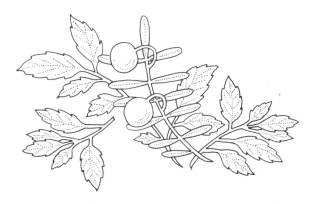

To get you started, we've compiled a short list of hints.

And, best of all, each recipe makes two cakes, a real bonus at this time of year when friends stop by or you need a last-minute gift.

For a roulage that's picture perfect:

■ Spray jellyroll pans with cooking spray; then line with wax paper. Spray wax paper with cooking spray.

■ When cakes are done, immediately loosen from sides of pans and turn out onto cloth towels dusted with cocoa or powdered sugar.

■ While cakes are warm, roll up each cake and towel together, beginning at narrow end.

■ Cool the cakes on wire racks, seam side down.

■ Gently unroll cooled cakes, brush with liqueur, and spread with filling.

■ Reroll cakes without towels; cover and freeze until ready to serve. The cakes thaw almost as quickly as you can slice them.

■ Dust filled cakes with additional cocoa or powdered sugar before slicing and serving.

MINT-CHOCOLATE ROULAGE

2 cups whipping cream
5 to 6 tablespoons green crème de menthe, divided *
Chocolate Cake Rolls (see recipe on page 312)
Cocoa
Garnishes: whipped cream, fresh mint sprigs
Chocolate-Mint Sauce

● **Beat** whipping cream at medium-high speed with an electric mixer until soft peaks form. Fold in 2 to 3 tablespoons crème de menthe; set aside.
● **Unroll** cake rolls; brush each lightly with 3 tablespoons crème de menthe. Spread each cake with half of whipped cream mixture. Reroll cakes without towels; place, seam side down, on a baking sheet. Cover and freeze at least 1 hour or up to 3 months.
● **Dust** cakes with cocoa, and cut into slices. Garnish, if desired. Serve with Chocolate-Mint Sauce. **Yield:** 2 filled cake rolls (5 to 6 servings each).

* 1½ teaspoons mint extract and 5 drops of green food coloring may be substituted. Omit brushing cake rolls.

Chocolate-Mint Sauce

¾ cup half-and-half
1 (10-ounce) package mint chocolate morsels
1½ cups miniature marshmallows
¼ teaspoon salt
1 teaspoon vanilla extract

● **Heat** half-and-half in a heavy saucepan over low heat. Stir in chocolate morsels, marshmallows, and salt; cook over low heat, stirring constantly, until chocolate and marshmallows melt. Remove from heat, and stir in vanilla. **Yield:** 2 cups.

CHOCOLATE-ORANGE ROULAGE
(pictured on front cover)

2 cups whipping cream
5 to 6 tablespoons Grand Marnier or other orange-flavored liqueur, divided *
1 tablespoon finely grated orange rind
Chocolate Cake Rolls (see recipe on page 312)
Cocoa
Garnish: orange rind curls
Chocolate-Orange Sauce

● **Beat** whipping cream at medium-high speed with an electric mixer until soft peaks form. Fold in 2 to 3 tablespoons Grand Marnier and orange rind; set aside.
● **Unroll** cake rolls; brush each lightly with remaining 3 tablespoons Grand Marnier. Spread each cake with half of whipped cream mixture. Reroll cakes without towels; place, seam side down, on a baking sheet. Cover and freeze at least 1 hour or up to 3 months.
● **Dust** cakes with cocoa, and cut into slices. Garnish, if desired. Serve with Chocolate-Orange Sauce. **Yield:** 2 filled cake rolls (5 to 6 servings each).

* 5 to 6 tablespoons frozen orange juice concentrate, thawed and undiluted, may be substituted.

Chocolate-Orange Sauce

¾ cup half-and-half
2 cups (12 ounces) semisweet chocolate morsels
1½ cups miniature marshmallows
¼ teaspoon salt
¼ cup Grand Marnier or other orange-flavored liqueur *

● **Heat** half-and-half in a heavy saucepan over low heat. Stir in chocolate morsels, marshmallows, and salt. Cook over low heat, stirring constantly, until chocolate and marshmallows melt. Remove from heat; stir in Grand Marnier. **Yield:** 2 cups.

* ¼ cup frozen orange juice concentrate, thawed and undiluted, may be substituted.

TIME FOR AMERICA'S BEST DESSERT

This year the prestigious James Beard Foundation has named the White Chocolate-Banana Cream Pie at Atlanta's Buckhead Diner "America's Best Dessert."

Crowned with a snowy mound of white chocolate curls, the pie is by far the most popular dessert on the restaurant's menu. More than 35,000 slices are sold each year.

"People often have a slice for dessert and end up ordering a whole pie to go," says the restaurant's executive sous chef Gregg McCarthy.

The Buckhead Diner's famous pie has captured the attention of a number of celebrities, including Elizabeth Taylor, Donald Trump, and Elton John.

Here is our streamlined version of the diner's prize-winning recipe.

WHITE CHOCOLATE-BANANA CREAM PIE

1 (4-ounce) white chocolate bar, finely chopped and divided
1 cup milk
½ vanilla bean
3 tablespoons sugar
2 tablespoons cornstarch
3 egg yolks
1 tablespoon butter or margarine
1 cup whipping cream
2 tablespoons white crème de cacao
2 tablespoons crème de bananes
2 to 3 bananas, sliced
3 tablespoons lemon juice
1 baked 9-inch pastry shell
Cocoa
Garnish: strawberry fan

● **Place** half of white chocolate in top of a double boiler; place over boiling water. Cook until chocolate melts, stirring often. Pour onto an aluminum foil-lined baking sheet. Let stand at room temperature until chocolate cools and feels slightly tacky but is not firm. (If chocolate is too hard, curls will break; if too soft, chocolate will not curl.) Pull a cheese plane across chocolate until curl forms. Repeat until chocolate is curled. Refrigerate curls.

● **Combine** milk and vanilla bean in a small saucepan; bring to a boil. Remove and discard vanilla bean. Set hot milk aside.

● **Combine** sugar, cornstarch, and egg yolks in a heavy saucepan; gradually stir in hot milk.

● **Cook** over medium heat, stirring constantly, until mixture comes to a boil. Boil 1 minute. Remove from heat. Add butter and remaining white chocolate, stirring until chocolate melts. Place plastic wrap directly over surface of white chocolate mixture, and let cool.

● **Beat** whipping cream until soft peaks form; fold into white chocolate mixture. Stir in liqueurs.

● **Coat** banana slices with lemon juice; drain. Pat banana slices dry with paper towels. Gently stir into white chocolate mixture. Spoon into baked pastry shell. Top with white chocolate curls, and dust lightly with cocoa. Garnish, if desired. **Yield:** one 9-inch pie.

SWEET MEMORIES

One of Jean Liles's fondest Christmas memories of the *Southern Living* Foods Staff (see story at right) is the Christmas cookie swap.

"Each of us would bake enough to share, and we would have an enormous selection of the very best holiday cookies," Jean remembers.

Over the years, she has tasted hundreds of cookie recipes. Her favorite is at right.

GIFTS IN GOOD TASTE

Jean Wickstrom Liles, former head of the *Southern Living* Foods Department, says that during her 20-year tenure she could tell when the holiday season was near. Her phone would ring incessantly with callers requesting copies of misplaced holiday recipes. So Oxmoor House, our book division, asked her to select recipes for the cookbook, *Our Best Christmas Recipes*. Here's a sampling of our favorite gift recipes from the new book.

WHITE CHOCOLATE-MACADAMIA NUT COOKIES

½ cup butter or margarine, softened
½ cup shortening
¾ cup firmly packed brown sugar
½ cup sugar
1 large egg
1½ teaspoons vanilla extract
2 cups all-purpose flour
1 teaspoon baking soda
½ teaspoon salt
1 (6-ounce) package white chocolate-flavored baking bars, cut into chunks
1 (7-ounce) jar macadamia nuts, coarsely chopped

● **Beat** butter and shortening at medium speed with an electric mixer until soft and creamy; gradually add sugars, beating well. Add egg and vanilla; beat well. Combine flour, soda, and salt; gradually add to butter mixture, beating well. Stir in the white chocolate and nuts.

● **Drop** dough by rounded teaspoonfuls 2 inches apart onto lightly greased baking sheets.

● **Bake** at 350° for 8 to 10 minutes or until lightly browned. Cool slightly on baking sheets; remove to wire racks, and let cool completely. **Yield:** 5 dozen.

LEMON CURD
(pictured on page 334)

2 cups sugar
1 cup butter or margarine
¼ cup grated lemon rind
⅔ cup fresh lemon juice
4 large eggs, lightly beaten

● **Combine** first 4 ingredients in top of a double boiler; bring water to a boil. Reduce heat to low; cook until butter melts.

● **Stir** about one-fourth of hot mixture into eggs; add to remaining hot mixture, stirring constantly.

● **Cook,** stirring constantly, over medium-low heat until the mixture thickens and coats a spoon (about 15 minutes). Remove from heat; cool.

● **Cover** and refrigerate up to 2 weeks. Serve with pound cake, angel food cake, or gingerbread. **Yield:** 3¼ cups.

EDIBLE ORNAMENTS
(pictured on page 334)

¼ cup butter or margarine,
 softened
⅓ cup light corn syrup
1 teaspoon vanilla extract
1 (16-ounce) package powdered
 sugar, sifted
5 to 7 drops of green liquid food
 coloring
Powdered sugar
1 drinking straw
1 (4¼-ounce) tube white
 decorator frosting
Red cinnamon candies
3 to 4 yards ⅛- or ¼-inch-wide
 ribbon

● **Combine** first 3 ingredients in a large mixing bowl; beat at medium speed with an electric mixer until blended. Gradually add half of powdered sugar, beating until smooth. Stir in remaining powdered sugar to make a stiff dough. Knead with hands until smooth. Divide dough in half; wrap 1 portion in plastic wrap, and set aside. Knead food coloring into remaining portion.
● **Roll** green portion to ⅛-inch thickness on a surface lightly sprinkled with powdered sugar. Cut into desired shapes with assorted 3-inch cutters; transfer to wax paper. Repeat procedure with remaining white dough.
● **Punch** a hole in top of ornaments with a drinking straw. Decorate, as desired, with decorator frosting and cinnamon candies. Let stand 4 hours or until partially dry. Remove from wax paper, and transfer to wire racks. Let stand at least 24 hours.
● **Insert** ribbon through holes, and tie to hang. **Yield:** 20 ornaments.

FIRE-AND-ICE PICKLES
(pictured on page 335)

2 (32-ounce) jars medium-size
 whole dill pickles, drained
4 cups sugar
2 tablespoons hot sauce
½ to ¾ teaspoon dried crushed
 red pepper
3 cloves garlic, peeled

● **Cut** pickles into ¼-inch-thick slices. Combine pickles, sugar, hot sauce, and red pepper in a bowl; stir well. Cover and let stand 2 hours, stirring often.
● **Spoon** into 3 (1-pint) jars; add 1 clove garlic clove to each. Cover and refrigerate up to 1 month. For best flavor, wait 1 week before eating. **Yield:** 3 pints.

JEWELED PEPPER CHUTNEY
(pictured on page 335)

2 cups sugar
2 cups firmly packed brown
 sugar
2 cups golden raisins
2½ cups cider vinegar
8 large sweet red peppers,
 seeded and cut into ¼-inch
 cubes
8 cloves garlic, finely chopped
4 jalapeño peppers, seeded and
 finely chopped
1 (2-ounce) jar crystallized
 ginger, finely chopped

● **Combine** all ingredients in a large Dutch oven; bring to a boil. Reduce

---

"Going through all the holiday recipes we've had over the years brought back fond memories of how much we loved them at taste-testing and gave me a chance to recall the favorites of the staff."

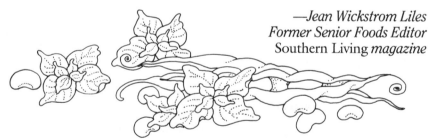

—*Jean Wickstrom Liles*
Former Senior Foods Editor
Southern Living *magazine*

Oxmoor House Assistant Foods Editor Lisa Hooper, who edited *Our Best Christmas Recipes*, says it's not just for Christmas.

"You won't pack this book up with the ornaments," Lisa says. "You'll use it all year long for dinner parties, showers, weddings – anytime you need a delicious recipe for a special occasion."

The book genuinely reflects the "best of the best" holiday recipes

from *Southern Living.* Jean went all the way back to the first Christmas issue, from 1966, searching for the best recipes we've ever published.

"We're proud that *Our Best Christmas Recipes* continues a tradition started by *Southern Living* magazine almost three decades ago – that of helping our readers all across the South celebrate the holiday season with delicious recipes and gracious entertaining ideas," Jean says.

heat, and simmer, uncovered, 1 hour and 45 minutes, stirring occasionally.
● **Pack** hot mixture into hot jars, filling to ½-inch from top. Remove air bubbles; wipe jar rims. Cover at once with metal lids, and screw on bands.
● **Process** in boiling-water bath 10 minutes. Refrigerate after opening. Serve with pork or poultry. **Yield:** 6 half pints.

CHEESE BALLS WITH SUN-DRIED TOMATOES
(pictured on page 335)

3 (8-ounce) packages cream cheese, softened
1 (8-ounce) jar oil-packed sun-dried tomatoes, drained
2 teaspoons dried basil
1 clove garlic, peeled and halved
½ cup coarsely chopped almonds or pine nuts, toasted

● **Position** knife blade in food processor bowl; add first 4 ingredients. Process until smooth. Cover and chill.
● **Divide** cheese mixture into 6 equal portions; shape each portion into a ball. Dip each ball in almonds, lightly pressing almonds into cheese.
● **Wrap** each cheese ball in plastic wrap; refrigerate up to 5 days. Serve with crackers. **Yield:** 6 (3-inch) cheese balls.

FRENCH MARKET SOUP MIX
(pictured on page 334)

1 pound dried black beans
1 pound dried great Northern beans
1 pound dried navy beans
1 pound dried pinto beans
1 pound dried red beans
1 pound dried black-eyed peas
1 pound dried green split peas
1 pound dried yellow split peas
1 pound dried lentils
1 pound dried baby limas
1 pound dried large limas
1 pound barley pearls

● **Combine** all ingredients in a very large bowl. Divide mixture evenly into 13 (2-cup) packages to give with recipe for French Market Soup. **Yield:** 26 cups mix.

FRENCH MARKET SOUP

1 (2-cup) package French Market Soup Mix (see recipe)
2 quarts water
1 large ham hock
1 (16-ounce) can whole tomatoes, undrained and coarsely chopped
1½ cups chopped onion
3 tablespoons lemon juice
1 chile pepper, coarsely chopped
1 clove garlic, minced
1¼ teaspoons salt
¼ teaspoon pepper

● **Sort** and wash soup mix; place in a Dutch oven. Cover with water 2 inches above soup mix; let soak 8 hours.
● **Drain** soup mix, and return to pan; add 2 quarts water and ham hock.
● **Bring** to a boil; cover, reduce heat, and simmer 1½ hours or until beans are tender.
● **Stir** in tomatoes and next 4 ingredients. Bring to a boil, reduce heat, and simmer, uncovered, 30 minutes.
● **Remove** ham hock; remove meat from bone. Chop meat, and return to soup. Stir in salt and pepper. **Yield:** 3 quarts.

Note: To speed soaking time, boil 2 quarts water. Add bean mixture, and boil 3 minutes. Remove from heat; cover and let stand 1 hour. Drain and proceed as directed.

Spicy Bean Soup: Substitute 2 (10-ounce) cans diced tomatoes and green chiles for whole tomatoes, and 2 ham-flavored bouillon cubes for ham hock; reduce salt to ½ teaspoon.

CHRISTMAS POTPOURRI
(pictured on page 335)

Don't try to eat this recipe, but do make it to scent your home for the holiday season.

Bark pieces
Bay, eucalyptus, and patchouli leaves
Beechnut husks
Cinnamon sticks, broken into 2- or 3-inch pieces
Coriander seeds
Dried acorns and chestnuts
Dried rose hips and red strawflower petals
Gingerroot pieces
Lotus pods
Sandalwood pieces
Small pinecones and pine needles
Star anise
Sweet gum balls
Tulip wings
Whole cloves
Whole nutmegs, cracked
Evergreen oil
Patchouli oil
Pine or spruce oil
Sandalwood oil

● **Combine** desired amounts of first 16 ingredients in a large glass bowl. For every 4 cups of mixture, add 2 drops of each oil, tossing gently to distribute oils evenly.
● **Place** mixture in an airtight container, and let it stand at room temperature 4 to 6 weeks. To preserve scent, place potpourri in a glass container with a lid, and uncover only to freshen the air.

CROSTINI: "LITTLE CRUSTS"

Maybe you've seen "crostini" (meaning "little crusts") listed on posh restaurant menus lately. This popular Italian menu item is simply an appetizer of toasted bread crowned with wonderfully gooey cheese and surprising bits of flavor and color.

To make your own crostini, slice a long loaf of French or Italian bread, bake quickly to crisp, and top with anything you can imagine. You can either stop there for cold appetizers or warm them in the oven if you like melted cheese.

For an easy holiday cocktail party, assemble these ahead of time (they won't take long), and pop them in the oven when guests arrive.

CHRISTMAS CROSTINI
(pictured on back cover)

1 French baguette
1 (8-ounce) package cream cheese, softened
½ cup mayonnaise or salad dressing
1 (0.7-ounce) package Italian salad dressing mix
½ cup (2 ounces) shredded Swiss cheese
Garnishes: quartered cucumber slices, finely chopped sweet red pepper

● **Slice** baguette into 36 (¼- to ½-inch) slices; place, cut side down, on an aluminum foil-lined baking sheet.
● **Bake** at 400° for 5 minutes or until lightly browned.
● **Combine** cream cheese and next 3 ingredients; spread mixture evenly on bread slices.
● **Bake** at 400° for 5 minutes or until cheese melts. Garnish, if desired, and serve immediately. **Yield:** 3 dozen.

❤ To reduce fat and calories, substitute reduced-fat mayonnaise and light process cream cheese product.

Maia L. Artman
Norman, Oklahoma

SWISS-BLUE CHEESE CROSTINI

1 (16-ounce) loaf unsliced French bread
4 cloves garlic, pressed
¼ cup olive oil
12 commercial oil-packed dried tomatoes, halved (optional)
1 cup (4 ounces) shredded Swiss cheese
1 (4-ounce) package crumbled blue cheese
¼ cup chopped fresh parsley

● **Slice** bread into 24 (¼- to ½-inch) slices; place, cut side down, on an aluminum foil-lined baking sheet.
● **Bake** at 400° for 5 minutes or until lightly browned.
● **Combine** garlic and olive oil; brush on bread slices. Top each with a tomato half, if desired. Set aside.
● **Combine** cheeses and parsley; spoon on top of bread slices.
● **Bake** at 400° for 5 minutes or until cheese melts. Serve immediately. **Yield:** 2 dozen.

Helen Maurer
Christmas, Florida

ALMOND-BACON-CHEESE CROSTINI
(pictured on back cover)

1 French baguette
2 slices bacon, cooked and crumbled
1 cup (4 ounces) shredded Monterey Jack cheese
⅓ cup mayonnaise or salad dressing
¼ cup sliced almonds, toasted
1 tablespoon chopped green onions
¼ teaspoon salt
Garnish: toasted sliced almonds

● **Slice** baguette into 36 (¼- to ½-inch) slices; place, cut side down, on an aluminum foil-lined baking sheet.
● **Bake** at 400° for 5 minutes or until lightly browned.

- **Combine** bacon and next 5 ingredients; spread on bread slices.
- **Bake** at 400° for 5 minutes or until cheese melts. Garnish, if desired, and serve immediately. **Yield:** 3 dozen.

Valerie Gail Stutsman
Norfolk, Virginia

HOT ARTICHOKE CROSTINI

1 French baguette
1 cup mayonnaise or salad dressing
1 cup grated Parmesan cheese
1 (14-ounce) can artichoke hearts, drained and chopped
1 (4½-ounce) can chopped green chiles, drained
2 cloves garlic, minced
Garnishes: chopped green onions, chopped tomato, crumbled bacon

- **Slice** baguette into 36 (¼- to ½-inch) slices; place, cut side down, on an aluminum foil-lined baking sheet.
- **Bake** at 400° for 5 minutes or until lightly browned.
- **Combine** mayonnaise and next 4 ingredients; spread on bread slices.
- **Bake** at 400° for 5 minutes or until cheese melts. Garnish, if desired, and serve immediately. **Yield:** 3 dozen.

♥ To reduce fat and calories, substitute reduced-fat mayonnaise.

Johnnie Capone
Baton Rouge, Louisiana

MOZZARELLA CROSTINI
(pictured on back cover)

1 (16-ounce) loaf unsliced Italian bread
⅓ cup olive oil
1 clove garlic, finely chopped
¼ teaspoon salt
¼ teaspoon pepper
½ cup sliced green onions
5 to 7 Roma tomatoes, cut into 36 slices
1½ cups (6 ounces) shredded mozzarella cheese
Garnish: sliced green onions

- **Slice** bread into 36 (¼- to ½-inch) slices; place, cut side down, on an aluminum foil-lined baking sheet.
- **Bake** at 400° for 5 minutes or until lightly browned.
- **Combine** olive oil and next 3 ingredients. Brush on bread slices. Top each with green onions and a tomato slice. Sprinkle with cheese.
- **Bake** at 400° for 5 to 7 minutes or until cheese melts. Garnish, if desired, and serve immediately. **Yield:** 3 dozen.

Mrs. E. W. Hanley
Palm Harbor, Florida

BANK ON BAGUETTES

You can use any long, round loaf of bread for crostini, but baguettes are best. These French loaves are longer and skinnier than most, usually just two inches in diameter. You'll get more slices from them, and the size is just right for easy-to-eat bites.

BEIGNETS FOR BREAKFAST

....

Warning: Never wear black while eating beignets. The powdered sugar will dust your clothes. But these traditional New Orleans yeast pastries served warm are definitely worth the floating cloud of sugar that sifts onto your lap. With the first bite, a puff of warm air escapes. With the last bite, lick the sugar from your fingers.

Invite some friends to join you. Make some café au lait. And, most importantly, be sure you all wear white.

FRENCH MARKET BEIGNETS

1 package active dry yeast
1 cup warm water (105° to 115°)
¾ cup canned evaporated milk
¼ cup sugar
1 teaspoon salt
1 large egg, lightly beaten
4 to 4½ cups all-purpose flour
Vegetable oil
Sifted powdered sugar

- **Combine** yeast and warm water in a 2-cup glass measuring cup; let stand 5 minutes.
- **Combine** yeast mixture, evaporated milk, and next 3 ingredients. Gradually stir in enough flour to make a soft dough. Cover dough and refrigerate 8 hours.
- **Turn** dough out onto a well-floured surface; knead 5 or 6 times. Roll dough into a 15- x 12½-inch rectangle; cut into 2½-inch squares.
- **Pour** oil to depth of 3 to 4 inches into a Dutch oven; heat to 375°. Fry 3 or 4 beignets at a time, 1 minute on each side or until golden. Drain on paper towels; sprinkle with powdered sugar. **Yield:** 2½ dozen.

NEW PLATE FOR THE NINETIES

Remember those special-occasion dinners mom used to make? We've updated some of those favorites with fresh flavor and presentation. One step better than home style, each of these recipes is surprisingly easy.

PAN-ROASTED FILLET OF BEEF WITH BLUE CHEESE SAUCE

Though not for the calorie conscious, a splurge of Blue Cheese Sauce is a great way to add pizzazz to your favorite steak.

1 (2-pound) trimmed beef
    tenderloin
½ teaspoon salt
½ teaspoon freshly ground
    pepper
1 tablespoon vegetable oil
Vegetable cooking spray
Blue Cheese Sauce

• **Sprinkle** tenderloin with salt and pepper; rub with oil. Cover and refrigerate up to 8 hours.
• **Brown** tenderloin in a hot cast-iron skillet coated with cooking spray about 1 minute on each side. Transfer tenderloin to a rack coated with cooking spray, reserving drippings in skillet; place rack in broiler pan. (Set skillet aside to make sauce.)
• **Bake** at 450° for 18 minutes or until a meat thermometer registers 145° (medium-rare) or 160° (medium).
• **Remove** tenderloin from oven, and let it stand 5 minutes. Cut tenderloin into 4 equal portions.
• **Spoon** Blue Cheese Sauce evenly onto 4 serving plates, and top each with a portion of tenderloin. **Yield:** 4 servings.

Blue Cheese Sauce

3 tablespoons unsalted butter,
    softened
2 ounces crumbled blue cheese
2 cups beef broth
1 carrot, scraped and coarsely
    chopped
1 stalk celery, coarsely chopped
3 cloves garlic, chopped
3 tablespoons Madeira or port
    wine
⅓ cup half-and-half

• **Combine** butter and blue cheese; shape into 4 portions, and refrigerate until firm.
• **Combine** beef broth, carrot, and celery in a small saucepan. Bring to a boil; reduce heat, and simmer 5 to 7 minutes or until broth is reduced to ½ cup. Remove and discard vegetables; set broth aside.
• **Cook** garlic and Madeira in skillet over medium heat 2 minutes. Add broth, and cook 3 to 5 minutes or until mixture is reduced to ½ cup. Gradually stir in half-and-half, and cook 5 minutes or until sauce is light brown. Remove from heat; set aside up to 1 hour, if desired. Just before serving, heat sauce over low heat.
• **Add** blue cheese mixture to warm sauce, 1 portion at a time, stirring until smooth. Pour through a wire-mesh strainer into a bowl, pressing cheese through strainer with back of a spoon. **Yield:** about 1 cup.

SAGE POTATOES

Fresh sage leaves sandwiched between slices of potato create a mosaic look and provide a flavorful punch.

3 large baking potatoes, peeled
⅓ cup butter or margarine, melted
24 fresh sage leaves
Salt

• **Cut** each potato crosswise into 16 thin slices. Dip each slice into butter; place 24 slices on a lightly greased 15- x 10- x 1-inch jellyroll pan. Arrange a sage leaf in center of each slice, and top with remaining potato slices. Sprinkle with salt.
• **Preheat** oven to 450°. Place potatoes in oven; reduce heat to 350°, and bake 15 minutes or until edges begin to brown, removing potatoes from pan as they begin to brown. Serve potatoes immediately. **Yield:** 4 servings.

BOW-TIE GREEN BEANS

A brief plunge in boiling water renders carrot strips pliable enough to knot and tie green beans in neat bundles. Ice-cold water quickly cools the beans after they're cooked, capturing their just-picked freshness and color.

1 pound fresh green beans
1 large carrot, scraped
8 cups water
2 teaspoons salt
Butter-flavored cooking spray

• **Wash** beans; trim 1 end. Set aside.
• **Remove** 8 long, thin narrow strips from carrot with a vegetable peeler. (Reserve remaining carrot for another use.) Set aside.
• **Bring** water and salt to a boil in a large saucepan; add carrot strips, and cook 10 seconds; remove from water, and immediately rinse with cold water. Set aside.
• **Add** beans to water; bring to a boil, and cook 5 to 7 minutes or until crisp-tender. Drain and immediately rinse with cold water.
• **Divide** beans into 4 portions. Overlap ends of 2 carrot strips on a baking sheet; place 1 portion of beans across strips. Tie strips, securing with a double knot. Repeat procedure with remaining carrot strips and green beans. Spray bundles with cooking spray, and cover with aluminum foil.
• **Bake** at 350° until thoroughly heated. Serve immediately. **Yield:** 4 servings.

Note: To make Bow-Tie Green Beans ahead, assemble bundles, cover, and refrigerate up to 4 hours. Bake according to directions.

VEGETABLES IN COLORS OF THE SEASON

Let these colorful side dishes sparkle on your holiday table. They'll glitter like glass ornaments alongside the turkey or ham on that special day.

SPINACH-TOPPED TOMATOES

1 (10-ounce) package frozen
   chopped spinach
2 teaspoons chicken-flavored
   bouillon granules
3 large tomatoes, cut in half
   crosswise
1 teaspoon salt
⅓ cup freshly grated Parmesan
   cheese
1 cup cornbread stuffing mix
½ cup butter or margarine,
   melted
1 large egg, lightly beaten
⅓ cup chopped onion
1 clove garlic, minced
¼ teaspoon pepper
Additional freshly grated Parmesan
   cheese

• **Cook** spinach according to package directions, adding chicken bouillon granules to cooking water; drain well.
• **Sprinkle** tomato with salt; place, cut side down, on paper towels, and let stand 15 minutes.
• **Combine** spinach, ⅓ cup Parmesan cheese, and next 6 ingredients; set aside.
• **Place** tomato, cut side up, on a baking sheet. Top each tomato evenly with spinach mixture.
• **Bake** at 350° for 15 minutes. Sprinkle with additional Parmesan cheese; bake 5 additional minutes. **Yield:** 6 servings.

Kathy Zenor-Horine
Louisville, Kentucky

SPINACH SALAD WITH RASPBERRY CREAM DRESSING

1 (10-ounce) package fresh
   spinach
2 kiwifruit, peeled and sliced
1 (11-ounce) can mandarin
   oranges, drained
1 purple onion, sliced and
   separated into rings
Raspberry Cream Dressing

• **Remove** stems from spinach; wash thoroughly, and pat dry. Tear into bite-size pieces.
• **Combine** spinach and next 3 ingredients in a large bowl; cover and chill. Serve with Raspberry Cream Dressing. **Yield:** 6 to 8 servings.

Raspberry Cream Dressing

1 (10-ounce) package frozen
   raspberries, thawed and
   well drained
¼ cup plus 2 tablespoons olive oil
¼ cup whipping cream
2 tablespoons sherry wine
   vinegar
½ teaspoon salt

• **Place** raspberries in an electric blender; process until smooth. Pour through a wire-mesh strainer into a bowl; press mixture with back of a spoon against sides of strainer to squeeze out liquid. Discard seeds.
• **Combine** raspberry puree, olive oil, and remaining ingredients, whisking until smooth. Chill. Serve with salad. **Yield:** 1⅔ cups.

Louise Bodziony
Gladstone, Missouri

GREEN BEANS EXCELLENT

1 pound fresh green beans *
1 small onion, thinly sliced
1 tablespoon vegetable oil
1 (4-ounce) jar sliced pimiento,
   undrained
¼ cup apple cider vinegar
¼ cup vegetable oil
2 tablespoons sugar
1 teaspoon salt

• **Wash** beans; remove ends. Cook in boiling water to cover 8 minutes or until crisp-tender; drain. Plunge into ice water; drain and set aside.
• **Cook** onion in 1 tablespoon oil in a large skillet over medium heat, stirring constantly, until tender. Drain on a paper towel; set aside.
• **Drain** pimiento, reserving 2 tablespoons liquid. Combine reserved pimiento liquid, vinegar, and next 3 ingredients, whisking until blended. Set dressing aside.
• **Combine** green beans, onion, and pimiento; add dressing, tossing to coat. Cover and refrigerate 2 hours. **Yield:** 4 servings.

Nora Henshaw
Okemah, Oklahoma

* 2 (9-ounce) packages frozen whole green beans cooked according to package directions may be substituted.

PEAS TO PERFECTION

½ cup butter or margarine
1 cup chopped onion
1 cup chopped celery
1 large sweet red pepper,
   chopped
4 cups frozen English peas
1 (8-ounce) can sliced water
   chestnuts, drained
1 (10¾-ounce) can condensed
   cream of celery soup,
   undiluted
¼ teaspoon salt
¼ teaspoon pepper
1 cup chow mein noodles

• **Melt** butter in a large skillet over medium heat; add onion, celery, and chopped sweet red pepper. Cook until tender, stirring constantly.
• **Stir** in peas and next 4 ingredients. Spoon into a lightly greased 2-quart baking dish; sprinkle with noodles.
• **Bake** at 350° for 30 minutes. **Yield:** 6 servings.

Leslie Genszler
Roswell, Georgia

BROCCOLI IN SWEET RED PEPPER RINGS

1½ pounds fresh broccoli
2 large sweet red peppers, seeded and cut into ½-inch-thick rings
½ cup Italian salad dressing

● **Remove** broccoli leaves, and cut off tough ends of stalks; discard. Cut into 2-inch-long flowerets.
● **Arrange** broccoli and sweet red pepper rings in a steamer basket over boiling water. Cover and steam 5 to 7 minutes or until crisp-tender.
● **Arrange** pepper rings on a plate. Top with broccoli; drizzle evenly with dressing. Serve immediately. **Yield:** 6 to 8 servings.

Barbara Davis
Lilburn, Georgia

KITCHEN CLEANUP

■ For easy cleanup, fill your blender container with warm water, add a few drops of liquid detergent, and blend 30 seconds; rinse well.

■ Before using your broiler pan, lightly spray pan and rack with vegetable cooking spray. After broiling, cleanup is easy.

■ Stains or discolorations inside aluminum cookware can be removed by boiling a solution of 2 to 3 tablespoons of cream of tartar, lemon juice, or vinegar to each quart of water in the cookware 5 to 10 minutes.

■ Pour a strong solution of salt and hot water down the sink to help eliminate odors and remove grease from drains.

■ Wash sharp knives by hand rather than in the dishwasher.

---

living light

A SIMMER OF HOPE

It's that time of year when we all cook too much and eat too much, only to find that come January, we weigh too much. Keep eating under control now, for a guiltless New Year.

■ Just when you thought you'd never finish all the holiday shopping, gift wrapping, and decorating, *and* get dinner ready for your family, these healthy, hearty soups and stews deliver hope. They all need to cook at least an hour – just long enough for you to take a well-deserved respite while your dinner simmers.

SPICY HAM-AND-BEAN SOUP

1 pound dried great Northern beans
4 quarts water
1 pound reduced-salt lean ham, trimmed and cubed
2 stalks celery, chopped
2 carrots, scraped and chopped
2 medium-size red potatoes, finely chopped
1 large onion, finely chopped
1 tablespoon chopped pickled jalapeño pepper
1 tablespoon pickled jalapeño pepper juice
1 (6-ounce) can spicy tomato-vegetable juice
1 (4½-ounce) can chopped green chiles, undrained
1 tablespoon Worcestershire sauce
½ teaspoon chili powder
½ teaspoon garlic powder

● **Sort** and wash beans; place in a Dutch oven. Add water, and let stand 2 hours. Bring to a boil; reduce heat, and simmer 1 hour.
● **Add** ham and next 4 ingredients; simmer 1 hour.
● **Add** jalapeño pepper and remaining ingredients; simmer 1 hour or until the beans are tender and soup is thickened. **Yield:** 14 cups.

Posie Thompson
Edgewood, Maryland

❤ Per 1½-cup serving: Calories 297 (10% from fat) Fat 3.2g (0.9g saturated) Cholesterol 25mg Sodium 528mg Carbohydrate 46.8g Fiber 22.1g Protein 21.9g

SPLIT PEA SOUP

1 pound dried green split peas
4 (16-ounce) cans ready-to-serve, reduced-sodium, fat-free chicken broth
4 stalks celery, chopped
4 carrots, scraped and chopped
1 medium onion, chopped
1 tablespoon olive oil
½ teaspoon salt
¼ teaspoon pepper
1 bay leaf

● **Sort** and wash peas; place in a Dutch oven. Add chicken broth and remaining ingredients.

• **Bring** mixture to a boil; reduce heat, and simmer 2 hours, stirring often. Remove and discard bay leaf. **Yield:** 8 cups.

Janice Lautier
Knightdale, North Carolina

♥ Per 1½-cup serving: Calories 407 (9% from fat)
Fat 4g (0.5g saturated) Cholesterol 0mg
Sodium 304mg Carbohydrate 67.2g
Fiber 8g Protein 24.2g

VEGETABLE-BEEF STEW

1 pound lean beef tips, cut into
   ½-inch cubes
1 tablespoon vegetable oil
2 (10½-ounce) cans low-sodium,
   fat-free beef broth
4 carrots, scraped and
   sliced
4 medium onions, quartered
2 pounds red potatoes, peeled and
   cubed
2 (16-ounce) cans low-sodium
   whole tomatoes, undrained
   and chopped
1 (17-ounce) can whole kernel
   corn, drained
1 (16-ounce) can English peas,
   drained
1 (10-ounce) package frozen lima
   beans
1 tablespoon sugar
1 teaspoon garlic powder
½ teaspoon salt
½ teaspoon pepper

• **Cook** beef in oil in a Dutch oven over medium heat, stirring constantly, until browned. Drain in a colander, and pat meat dry with paper towels. Wipe drippings from Dutch oven. Return meat to Dutch oven. Add beef broth and remaining ingredients.
• **Bring** to a boil over high heat. Reduce heat, and simmer 1 hour, stirring occasionally. **Yield:** 16 cups.

Sue-Sue Hartstern
Louisville, Kentucky

♥ Per 1½-cup serving: Calories 284 (12% from fat)
Fat 4g (0.7g saturated) Cholesterol 18mg
Sodium 334mg Carbohydrate 45.8g
Fiber 6.3g Protein 17.7g

LIGHTEN UP

■ Don't try to lose weight during the holidays. With all the temptations, you'll be doing well just to maintain your weight.

■ If you go to a party hungry, you'll be a human bulldozer at the buffet. Eat a low-fat, high-carbohydrate snack like a bagel and a glass of mineral water beforehand.

■ Cut yourself some slack. No one can survive the holidays without a little eggnog and a few cookies.

■ Stop circling the mall looking for a parking space 20 feet from the door. It's not going to happen in December. Calm your nerves and slim your hips by parking in a space at the end of the lot.

■ Don't break your tradition of holiday baking. Time spent in the kitchen can be therapeutic during the hectic season. Just make sure that others end up with more of the fruits of your labor than you do.

OKRA-AND-SHRIMP SOUP

2 medium onions, chopped
1 large green pepper, chopped
1 jalapeño pepper, chopped
1 tablespoon olive oil
1 large tomato, peeled and
   chopped
3 cloves garlic, minced
2 (6-ounce) cans no-salt-added
   tomato paste
1 fish-flavored bouillon cube
3 quarts water
2 (12-ounce) packages frozen,
   peeled and deveined
   medium-size shrimp, thawed
2 (10-ounce) packages frozen
   sliced okra, thawed
2 teaspoons dried oregano
2 teaspoons dried basil
1 teaspoon dried thyme
1 teaspoon reduced-salt Cajun
   seasoning
1 teaspoon pepper
½ teaspoon salt
⅛ teaspoon hot sauce

• **Cook** first 3 ingredients in olive oil in a large Dutch oven over medium heat, stirring constantly, 2 minutes. Add tomato and garlic; cook 2 minutes, stirring often. Stir in tomato paste, bouillon cube, and water.
• **Bring** to a boil; reduce heat, and simmer 1 hour, stirring occasionally.
• **Stir** in shrimp and remaining ingredients; cook mixture 15 minutes or until shrimp turn pink, stirring often. **Yield:** 15 cups.

Note: For reduced-salt Cajun seasoning, we used Tony Cachere's More Spice Less Salt blend of spices.

Charlene Denoux
Baton Rouge, Louisiana

♥ Per 1½-cup serving: Calories 149 (17% from fat)
Fat 2.9g (0.5g saturated) Cholesterol 104mg
Sodium 470mg Carbohydrate 15.2g
Fiber 1.4g Protein 16.8g

HINTS FOR A HEALTHY FAMILY

Make a commitment to begin early to teach your family healthy eating habits.

■ Expose young children to an abundance of foods that taste good and that are good for them. It lays the groundwork for them to make healthy eating choices on their own.

■ Introduce your family to low-fat versions of their favorite dishes, but don't mention that it's good for them. Chances are they'll enjoy it as much as the original, and then you can tell them it's healthy.

■ Don't turn nutritious foods into high-fat disasters. Low-fat, high-carbohydrate foods, such as grains, rice, beans, and potatoes, are nearly perfect, unless you add loads of butter or other high-fat condiments.

■ If a food label says there are more than 3 grams of fat per 100 calories, leave the package on the grocery store shelf.

■ Don't wait until you're in jeopardy of losing your health to make a healthy lifestyle an everyday habit.

■ Here's a biscuit recipe perfect with any of the soups on the previous page. The Cheese-Chive Biscuits from *River Roads Recipes III: A Healthy Collection* have just 130 calories and fewer than five fat grams each. Lightened versions of traditional Louisiana recipes and healthy new creations make up this collection of more than 300 recipes.

CHEESE-CHIVE BISCUITS

2 cups all-purpose flour
1 tablespoon baking powder
¾ teaspoon salt
¼ cup margarine
½ cup (2 ounces) shredded reduced-fat sharp Cheddar cheese
¼ cup chopped fresh chives
1 cup skim milk
1 tablespoon margarine, melted
2 teaspoons water

• **Combine** first 3 ingredients; cut in ¼ cup margarine with a pastry blender until mixture is crumbly. Stir in cheese and chives. Add milk gradually, stirring just until moistened.
• **Shape** into a ball. Roll dough to ¾-inch thickness on a floured surface. Cut with a 2½-inch round cutter; place on an ungreased baking sheet.
• **Combine** melted margarine and water; brush over tops of biscuits.
• **Bake** at 450° for 12 minutes or until golden brown. **Yield:** 1 dozen.

SOURDOUGH MADE SIMPLE

. . . .

If you've ever wanted to bake sourdough bread but didn't because you were intimidated by the procedure, it's time to reconsider. We share several recipes from Marie Davis of Charlotte, North Carolina, that will have you baking in no time.

POTATO SOURDOUGH STARTER

¾ cup sugar
3 tablespoons instant potato flakes
1 package active dry yeast
1 cup warm water (120° to 130°)
Starter Food

• **Combine** first 3 ingredients in a small bowl. Stir in warm water. Cover with plastic wrap; pierce wrap 4 or 5 times with point of a sharp knife. Refrigerate 3 to 5 days.
• **Remove** starter from refrigerator; let stand at room temperature 1 hour.
• **Stir** well. Remove 1 cup starter; use in a recipe or give to a friend.
• **Prepare** 1 recipe Starter Food, and stir into remaining starter; let stand, uncovered, 8 to 12 hours. Cover with plastic wrap; pierce wrap 4 or 5 times with a sharp knife. Refrigerate 3 to 5 days. Each time starter is used, repeat the feeding procedure. Use all starter or discard after 4 feedings. **Yield:** 3½ cups.

Starter Food

¾ cup sugar
3 tablespoons instant potato flakes
1 cup warm water (120° to 130°)

• **Combine** all ingredients, and use to feed starter as directed.

POTATO SOURDOUGH BREAD DOUGH

6 cups bread flour
⅓ cup sugar
1 package active dry yeast
1 tablespoon salt
½ cup vegetable oil
1 cup Potato Sourdough Starter (see recipe)
1½ cups warm water (120° to 130°)

• **Combine** first 4 ingredients in a large bowl; gradually stir in oil and remaining ingredients.
• **Turn** dough out onto a floured surface; knead lightly 4 or 5 times. Place dough in a well-greased bowl, turning to grease top.

• **Cover** and let rise in a warm place (85°), free from drafts, 2 hours or until doubled in bulk. **Yield:** 6 cups.

Potato Sourdough Bread: Punch prepared dough down, and divide in half; shape each portion into a loaf, and place in a greased 9- x 5- x 3-inch loafpan. Brush tops with 2 tablespoons melted butter; cover and let rise in a warm place (85°), free from drafts, 1 hour or until doubled in bulk. Bake at 350° for 25 minutes or until loaves sound hollow when tapped. Remove bread from pans immediately; cool on wire racks. **Yield:** 2 loaves.

Potato Sourdough Rolls: Punch prepared dough down, and divide in half; shape each portion into 12 balls, and place in a greased 8-inch round pan. Brush tops with 2 tablespoons melted butter. Cover and let rise in a warm place (85°), free from drafts, 1 hour or until doubled in bulk. Bake at 350° for 15 minutes or until golden brown. **Yield:** 2 dozen.

POTATO SOURDOUGH CINNAMON ROLLS

1 recipe Potato Sourdough Bread Dough (see recipe on facing page)
½ cup butter or margarine, softened
½ cup firmly packed brown sugar
1 tablespoon ground cinnamon
½ cup raisins
3 cups sifted powdered sugar
1½ teaspoons vanilla extract
5 to 6 tablespoons milk

• **Divide** dough in half. Roll each portion into a 12- x 10-inch rectangle. Spread each rectangle with ¼ cup softened butter to within ½ inch of edge. Sprinkle each with ¼ cup brown sugar, 1½ teaspoons cinnamon, and ¼ cup raisins.
• **Roll** up dough, jellyroll fashion, starting with long side and pressing firmly to eliminate air pockets; pinch seams to seal. Cut each roll into 12 (1-inch) slices; place slices, cut side

down, in 2 greased 13- x 9- x 2-inch baking pans.
• **Cover** and let rise in a warm place (85°), free from drafts, 1 hour or until doubled in bulk.
• **Bake** at 350° for 20 minutes or until golden.
• **Combine** powdered sugar and remaining ingredients; drizzle over rolls. **Yield:** 2 dozen.

TURKEY TIPS WORTH GOBBLING ABOUT

If you would rather skip the big meal and go straight for turkey sandwiches, then you've come to the right place. These recipes make sensational use of leftover turkey.

And if you're a little nervous about roasting the bird in the first place, try our Savory Turkey and Gravy (on the next page). Oven cooking bags ensure a picture-perfect finish every time. For ideas using leftover ham, see our story on the next page.

HOME-STYLE TURKEY TURNOVERS

½ cup quartered fresh mushrooms
½ cup chopped fresh green beans
1 small onion, finely chopped
1 clove garlic, crushed
½ teaspoon dried thyme
½ teaspoon dried rosemary
2 tablespoons vegetable oil
1 tablespoon all-purpose flour
⅓ cup whipping cream
1 cup chopped cooked turkey
¼ teaspoon salt
¼ teaspoon pepper
1 (17¼-ounce) package frozen puff pastry sheets, thawed

• **Cook** first 6 ingredients in oil in a skillet over medium-high heat until crisp-tender, stirring often. Add flour, and cook, stirring constantly, 1 minute; stir in whipping cream.
• **Cook,** stirring constantly, until thickened; remove from heat. Stir in turkey, salt, and pepper; cool 5 minutes.
• **Unfold** pastry sheets, and cut each sheet into 4 squares.
• **Spoon** turkey mixture evenly in center of each square. Brush pastry edges lightly with water; fold in half to form triangles. Press edges to seal; crimp with a fork. Place on an ungreased baking sheet.
• **Bake** at 400° for 15 minutes or until golden brown. **Yield:** 8 servings.

Lilann Taylor
Savannah, Georgia

FRUIT-AND-SPICE TURKEY SALAD

1 cup long-grain basmati brown rice, uncooked
1½ cups chopped cooked turkey breast
2 green onions, sliced
1 small Red Delicious apple, chopped
1 small Granny Smith apple, chopped
½ cup seedless green grape halves
¼ cup pecan halves, toasted
¼ cup raisins
¼ cup white wine vinegar
1½ teaspoons sugar
¼ teaspoon salt
¼ teaspoon ground cinnamon
¼ cup olive oil
Red leaf lettuce

• **Cook** rice according to package directions. Rinse with cold water, and drain well.
• **Combine** rice and next 7 ingredients in a large bowl; set aside.
• **Combine** vinegar and next 3 ingredients. Add olive oil; stir with a wire whisk. Pour over rice mixture; toss gently. Cover and refrigerate at least 2 hours. Serve on lettuce leaves. **Yield:** 4 to 6 servings.

SAVORY TURKEY AND GRAVY

1 (10- to 12-pound) turkey
2 teaspoons salt
2 teaspoons lemon-pepper
   seasoning
1 medium onion
Fresh parsley sprigs
2 teaspoons dried rosemary,
   divided
1 tablespoon all-purpose flour
1 carrot, scraped and sliced
1 stalk celery, sliced
1 large onion, sliced
1½ cups chicken broth
½ cup tomato juice
¼ cup cornstarch
¼ cup whipping cream
1 teaspoon browning-and-
   seasoning sauce

• **Remove** giblets and neck; set giblets aside, and discard neck. Rinse turkey with cold water; pat dry. Sprinkle cavities with salt and lemon-pepper seasoning. Place medium onion into neck cavity. Lift wingtips up and over back, and tuck under bird. Place a handful of parsley and 1 teaspoon rosemary into body cavity. Tie ends of legs together with string.
• **Place** flour in an oven cooking bag; shake to coat. Place bag in a roasting pan at least 2 inches deep. Place turkey in bag; arrange carrot, celery, onion slices, and turkey giblets around turkey. Sprinkle with remaining 1 teaspoon rosemary. Set aside.
• **Combine** chicken broth and tomato juice in a saucepan; bring to a boil. Pour over turkey. Close bag; make 6 (½-inch) slits in top of bag.
• **Bake** at 325° for about 2 hours or until meat thermometer inserted in meaty part of thigh reaches 180°. (Times are estimates. To prevent overcooking, begin checking for doneness before estimated time given.)
• **Remove** from oven; carefully cut a large slit in top of bag. Remove turkey, reserving drippings. Let turkey stand 15 minutes before carving.
• **Pour** drippings through a wire-mesh strainer into a saucepan; discard solids.
• **Combine** cornstarch and whipping cream, stirring until smooth. Gradually stir into drippings. Cook over medium

heat, stirring constantly, until mixture thickens and boils. Boil 1 minute, stirring constantly. Remove from heat. Stir in browning-and-seasoning sauce. Serve with turkey. **Yield:** 10 to 12 servings.

HELPFUL HINTS FOR LEFTOVER HAM

Looking for the perfect ham to serve at the "big" meal – hopefully with some leftovers? Then try Baked Burgundy Ham. If you have leftovers, try them in the other two recipes. They get their flair from everyday convenience products. Round bread loaves and pizza crusts serve as the backdrop for these handy recipes.

BAKED BURGUNDY HAM

1 (6- to 8-pound) smoked fully
   cooked ham half, well trimmed
6 cups water
2 cups cranberry juice cocktail,
   divided
2 cups Burgundy or other dry red
   wine, divided
2 cups firmly packed dark brown
   sugar, divided
2 (3-inch) sticks cinnamon
1 tablespoon whole cloves

• **Place** ham in a large Dutch oven. Add water, 1 cup cranberry juice cocktail, 1 cup Burgundy, 1 cup brown sugar, cinnamon sticks, and cloves.
• **Bring** to a boil; cover, reduce heat, and simmer 20 minutes. Cool.
• **Remove** ham and marinade from Dutch oven, and place in a large nonmetallic bowl. Cover and refrigerate 8 hours, turning once.

• **Remove** ham from marinade; reserve 2 cups marinade. Discard remaining marinade.
• **Place** ham in a lightly greased shallow roasting pan; cover.
• **Bake** at 325° for 1½ hours, basting ham occasionally with reserved marinade. Uncover and bake 15 additional minutes or until meat thermometer registers 140°, basting ham occasionally with pan juices. Remove ham, reserving pan juices.
• **Combine** pan juices, remaining 1 cup cranberry juice, 1 cup Burgundy, and 1 cup brown sugar in a saucepan. Bring to a boil; reduce heat and cook 20 minutes. Serve with ham. **Yield:** 12 to 14 servings.

HAM-AND-CHEESE SANDWICH ROUND
(pictured on pages 262 and 263)

1 (1-pound) round loaf
   sourdough bread *
½ cup mayonnaise or salad
   dressing
2½ teaspoons dried Italian
   seasoning
½ teaspoon pepper
1 large onion, thinly sliced
2 medium-size green or sweet red
   peppers, cut into thin strips
1 stalk celery, sliced
1 tablespoon olive oil
1 pound cooked ham, thinly sliced
   (about 25 slices)
1½ cups (6 ounces) shredded
   Cheddar and mozzarella cheese
   blend

• **Slice** off top third of bread loaf; set top aside. Hollow out bottom section, leaving a ½-inch shell. (Reserve crumbs for another use.)
• **Combine** mayonnaise, Italian seasoning, and pepper. Brush inside of bread shell with half of mixture. Set shell and remaining mixture aside.
• **Cook** onion, pepper strips, and celery in olive oil in a large skillet over medium-high heat until tender, stirring often.
• **Arrange** half of ham in bread shell, and top with half of vegetable mixture;

sprinkle with half of cheese. Spread remaining mayonnaise mixture over cheese. Repeat layers with remaining vegetable mixture, ham, and cheese. Replace bread top. Wrap sandwich in heavy-duty aluminum foil.

• **Bake** at 400° for 30 minutes or until thoroughly heated. Cut sandwich into wedges, and serve immediately. **Yield:** 6 servings.

∗ 6 hoagie rolls may be substituted.

MEXICAN PIZZA

1 cup sliced fresh mushrooms
½ cup chopped green pepper
1 tablespoon vegetable oil
1 cup chopped cooked ham
1 (2¼-ounce) can sliced ripe
    olives, drained
1 (12-inch) commercial pizza crust
1 (16-ounce) jar thick-and-chunky
    salsa, divided
1 (8-ounce) package shredded
    Monterey Jack and Cheddar
    cheese blend
Shredded lettuce
Sour cream

• **Cook** mushrooms and green pepper in oil in a skillet over medium heat, stirring constantly, until crisp-tender; stir in ham and olives. Spoon mixture evenly over pizza crust. Reserve ½ cup salsa; spoon remaining salsa over vegetable mixture.
• **Bake** at 425° for 10 to 12 minutes. Sprinkle with cheese; bake 5 additional minutes. Serve with reserved ½ cup salsa, lettuce, and sour cream. **Yield:** 1 (12-inch) pizza.

Note: For a crispier crust, bake pizza on bottom rack of oven.
Kay C. Regnier
Newbern, North Carolina

OYSTERS
PLAIN AND FANCY

Regarded as an extravagance for most of the year, fresh oysters are as essential to many Southern celebrations as cranberries when the holidays roll around. Whether served plain or fancy, oysters herald the holiday season with a savory taste of the sea.

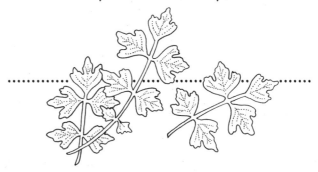

SPINACH SALAD WITH OYSTERS AND RED WINE VINAIGRETTE
(pictured on page 297)

Wolf Hanau, of North Miami, Florida, won the 1991 Buck Briscoe Memorial Award at the National Oyster Cook-Off in Leonardtown, Maryland, with a similar version of this recipe.

1 (10-ounce) package fresh
    spinach
2 (12-ounce) containers fresh
    oysters, drained
2 egg whites, lightly beaten
1½ cups Italian-seasoned
    breadcrumbs
1½ cups vegetable oil
4 large fresh mushrooms, sliced
Red Wine Vinaigrette
1 small purple onion, thinly sliced
4 slices bacon, cooked and
    crumbled

• **Remove** stems from spinach; wash leaves thoroughly, and pat dry. Set aside.
• **Dip** oysters in egg white; coat with breadcrumbs. Set aside.

• **Pour** oil into a large heavy skillet; heat to 350°. Fry oysters about 1 minute on each side or until golden; drain on paper towels.
• **Place** spinach on individual plates. Arrange mushrooms evenly over spinach, and drizzle with half of Red Wine Vinaigrette. Top evenly with oysters, onion slices, and bacon. Serve immediately with remaining Red Wine Vinaigrette. **Yield:** 6 servings.

Red Wine Vinaigrette

¾ cup olive oil
3 tablespoons Burgundy or other
    dry red wine
3 tablespoons red wine
    vinegar
1 tablespoon Dijon mustard
½ teaspoon sugar
½ teaspoon Worcestershire
    sauce
⅛ teaspoon pepper

• **Combine** all ingredients in container of an electric blender or food processor bowl, and process until blended. **Yield:** 1 cup.

CRABMEAT STUFFED OYSTERS

2 dozen fresh oysters in the shell *
1 pound lump crabmeat, drained
½ cup soft breadcrumbs
⅓ cup milk
1 large egg, lightly beaten
¼ cup mayonnaise
½ teaspoon baking powder
2 teaspoons dried onion flakes
2 teaspoons chopped fresh
   parsley
¼ teaspoon garlic salt
¼ teaspoon ground white pepper
2 tablespoons thinly sliced green
   onions
1 (2-ounce) jar sliced pimiento,
   drained

• **Scrub** oyster shells, and open, discarding tops. Arrange shell bottoms containing oysters in a 15- x 10- x 1-inch jellyroll pan. Set aside.
• **Combine** crabmeat and next 9 ingredients. Spoon mixture evenly over each oyster; sprinkle with green onions. Place 1 or 2 pimiento strips on each oyster. (Reserve remaining pimiento for another use.)
• **Bake** at 400° for 15 minutes or until thoroughly heated. **Yield:** 6 appetizer servings.

* 2 (12-ounce) containers fresh oysters may be substituted. (Reserve extra oysters for another use.) Bake according to directions in shell-shaped baking dishes found in kitchen shops.

Roland S. Ormrod
Towson, Maryland

OYSTER-TURNIP SOUP

¼ cup butter or margarine
1 cup sliced green onions
2 stalks celery and leaves, chopped
6 turnips, peeled and cut into
   ¾-inch chunks
1 (14½-ounce) can ready-to-serve
   chicken broth
2 cloves garlic, minced
1½ tablespoons dried parsley
   flakes
1½ teaspoons dried thyme
⅛ teaspoon ground red pepper
2 pints oysters, undrained
3 cups half-and-half
1 cup whipping cream
¾ teaspoon salt
¼ teaspoon ground black
   pepper

• **Melt** butter in a large Dutch oven over medium heat; add green onions and celery, and cook, stirring constantly, until tender.
• **Add** turnips, broth, garlic, parsley flakes, thyme, and red pepper. Bring to a boil; cover, reduce heat, and simmer 15 minutes or until turnips are tender.
• **Drain** oysters, reserving liquid. Cut oysters in half, and add to soup mixture. Cover and cook over medium heat 3 to 5 minutes or until oysters begin to curl.
• **Add** reserved oyster liquid, half-and-half, and remaining ingredients; cook just until thoroughly heated. **Yield:** about 12 cups.

Patsy Powell
Bay St. Louis, Mississippi

ONLY THE BEST WILL DO

This month we celebrate a season when only the best will do. That's why Lona Shealy's Shrimp-and-Rice Casserole is perfect. Lona is gifted in the kitchen and garden, and she generously shares her talents with her family and friends. Her gift to us this month will be enjoyed for years to come.

SHRIMP-AND-RICE CASSEROLE

6 cups water
2 pounds unpeeled, medium-size
   fresh shrimp
2 tablespoons butter or margarine
1 cup chopped celery
1 cup chopped onion
1 cup long-grain rice, cooked
1 cup milk
1 (10¾-ounce) can cream of
   mushroom soup, undiluted
1 (8-ounce) can whole water
   chestnuts, drained and
   chopped
½ cup mayonnaise or salad
   dressing
1 teaspoon dried parsley flakes
¼ teaspoon salt
½ teaspoon pepper
Chopped fresh parsley (optional)

• **Bring** water to a boil; add shrimp, and cook 3 to 5 minutes or until shrimp turn pink. Drain well; rinse with cold water. Peel shrimp, and devein, if desired.
• **Melt** butter in a large skillet over medium-high heat; add celery and onion, and cook, stirring constantly, until tender. Stir in rice and next 7 ingredients. Spoon mixture into a lightly greased 2-quart casserole.
• **Bake** at 350° for 30 minutes or until bubbly. Sprinkle with parsley, if desired. **Yield:** 6 servings.

Lona B. Shealy
Leesville, South Carolina

OYSTER TIPS

■ Select and Standard refer to oyster sizes. Select oysters are medium size. Standard oysters are small.

■ You can purchase oysters live in the shell. The shells should be tightly closed. If shells are open and don't close when you touch them, discard them.

■ To open shells, insert the tip of an oyster knife into the hinge, and twist knife. Scrape knife between the oyster and shell to free meat.

■ Shucked oysters should be plump, uniform in size, have a good color, and smell like the sea. Their liquor (liquid) should be clear.

DINE WITH BARGAIN WINE

Wine snobs, turn the page. You won't find any bottles for your cellar here. These inexpensive wines are for drinking now, and we've given you some ideas on what to drink them with. Don't restrict yourself to these menu suggestions; the best piece of advice is to drink the wine you like with the foods you like.

....

STEAKS, CHOPS, GAME, LAMB, STEWS

Consider the preparation of the dish when choosing one of these wines. A mildly seasoned lamb chop calls for a more delicate red like Pinot Noir. Merlot, a smoother wine than Cabernet Sauvignon, is perfect for broiled steaks, chops, and game. But a rich stew or a grilled steak requires a hearty red, like Zinfandel, Cabernet, or Shiraz. We recommend:

Cabernet Sauvignon –
Marcus James, Brazil 1991

Merlot Eagle Peak –
Fetzer, California 1993

Pinot Noir –
Napa Ridge, North Coast,
California 1992

Shiraz –
Rosemount Estate, Australia 1993

Zinfandel –
Chateau Souverain,
Dry Creek Valley, California 1992

SPICY AND ORIENTAL DISHES

These highly flavored foods are best balanced with medium-dry wines. We recommend:

Gewürztraminer –
Napa Ridge, Central Coast,
California 1993

Johannisberg Riesling –
Hogue, Yakima Valley,
Washington 1993

Pacific Rim Riesling –
Bonny Doon Vineyard,
California 1993

APPETIZERS, CHICKEN, PASTA, SEAFOOD

Serve these dishes with light white wines or a lightly chilled Beaujolais. We recommend:

Le Chamville –
Bouchard Père & Fils,
Beaujolais Villages, France 1990

Blended White –
Black Marlin, Australia 1992

Ca'del Solo Big House White –
Bonny Doon Vineyard
California 1993

Pinot Grigio –
Fontana Candida, Italy 1993

Sauvignon Blanc –
Clos du Bois, California 1993

GO-WITH-ANYTHING SIPPING WINES

We recommend:

Proprietor's Reserve White Zinfandel –
Glen Ellen, California 1993

Vin Gris de Cigare –
Bonny Doon Vineyard,
California 1993

White Zinfandel –
Bel Arbors, California 1993

CHARDONNAY

In a league of its own, Chardonnay can be served as an aperitif with grilled fish or lamb or with rich cream-sauce dishes. We recommend:

Beautour Chardonnay –
Beaulieu Vineyard, California 1992

Macon-Villages Chardonnay –
Georges Duboeuf, France 1993

Select Chardonnay –
Hess, California 1993

Sundial Chardonnay –
Fetzer, California 1993

GOODIES WITHOUT THE HASSLE

Who has time to have goodies ready for any holiday event?
You do – with these quick, no-bake cookies and candies you can
shape while you relax in front of the TV.

NO-BAKE BROWNIES
(pictured on page 333)

2 cups (12 ounces) semisweet
   chocolate morsels
1 (12-ounce) can evaporated
   milk
3 cups vanilla wafer crumbs
2 cups miniature marshmallows
1 cup chopped pecans
1 cup sifted powdered
   sugar
½ teaspoon salt

● **Combine** chocolate morsels and 1 cup evaporated milk in a heavy saucepan; cook over low heat until morsels melt, stirring occasionally. Set chocolate mixture aside.
● **Combine** wafer crumbs and next 4 ingredients in a large bowl; stir until blended. Set ½ cup chocolate mixture aside. Stir remaining chocolate mixture into crumb mixture. Press into a well-greased 9-inch square pan.
● **Combine** reserved ½ cup chocolate mixture and 2 teaspoons evaporated milk; spread over crumb mixture. (Reserve remaining evaporated milk for another use.) Chill. Cut into squares. **Yield:** 3 dozen.

Jane Tutwiler
Birmingham, Alabama

BITTERSWEET TRUFFLES

½ cup butter or margarine
¾ cup cocoa
1 (14-ounce) can sweetened
   condensed milk
1 teaspoon vanilla extract
Cocoa

● **Melt** butter in a heavy saucepan over low heat; stir in ¾ cup cocoa. Gradually add condensed milk, stirring constantly, until smooth. Cook over medium heat, stirring constantly, until thickened and smooth (about 3 minutes). Remove from heat; stir in vanilla. Pour mixture into a lightly greased 8-inch square pan.
● **Cover** and chill 3 hours or until firm.
● **Shape** mixture into 1¼-inch balls; roll in additional cocoa. Place balls in miniature paper baking cups. Store in an airtight container in the refrigerator up to 1 week. **Yield:** 3 dozen.

Rublelene Singleton
Scotts Hill, Tennessee

KEYBOARD COOKIES

12 ounces vanilla-flavored candy
   coating
1 (8.5-ounce) package cream-filled
   sugar wafers
4 ounces chocolate-flavored candy
   coating

● **Place** vanilla-flavored candy coating in a microwave-safe bowl; microwave at MEDIUM (50% power) 2 minutes or until coating melts, stirring at 1-minute intervals.
● **Dip** 1 side of each cookie in melted coating; place cookie, dipped side up, on a wire rack. Carefully remove any excess candy coating on the sides of cookies with a knife. Cool until firm.
● **Place** chocolate-flavored candy coating in a microwave-safe bowl; microwave at MEDIUM (50% power) 1 minute or until coating melts, stirring at 30-second intervals. Using a knife or paintbrush, carefully spread about ½ teaspoon chocolate-flavored coating in a 1- x ¼-inch strip on the upper left-hand corner of half of cookies. Repeat with remaining cookies, spreading chocolate-flavored coating on the upper right-hand corner. Cool cookies completely.
● **Package** cookies, arranging them to resemble a piano keyboard. **Yield:** 6 dozen.

Sandy Whittley
San Angelo, Texas

CHOCOLATE PEANUTTY SWIRLS

8 ounces chocolate-flavored candy
   coating
½ cup peanut butter-flavored
   morsels

● **Place** candy coating in a microwave-safe bowl; microwave at HIGH 1 minute or until coating melts, stirring once. Set aside.
● **Place** peanut butter morsels in a small microwave-safe bowl; microwave at HIGH 45 seconds or until morsels melt, stirring once.
● **Place** miniature paper baking cups in miniature (1¾-inch) muffin pans;

spoon about 1 teaspoon melted coating into each cup. Top each with ½ teaspoon melted peanut butter morsels. Gently swirl mixture with a wooden pick. Tap bottom of pan gently on a flat surface to smooth tops of candies.

● **Chill** 1 hour or until firm. Store in an airtight container in the refrigerator up to 1 week. **Yield:** 2 dozen.

Mildred Bickley
Bristol, Virginia

CHRISTMAS STRAWBERRIES
(pictured on page 333)

1 (2-ounce) package slivered almonds
2 or 3 drops of green liquid food coloring
2 (3-ounce) packages strawberry-flavored gelatin
1 cup finely chopped pecans
1 cup flaked coconut
¾ cup sweetened condensed milk
½ teaspoon vanilla extract
1 (3.25-ounce) jar red decorator sugar crystals
1 (3.25-ounce) jar green decorator sugar crystals

● **Combine** almonds and 2 drops food coloring in a small jar; cover with lid, and shake until almonds are evenly colored. Add additional food coloring, if necessary. Place almonds on paper towels, and set aside.
● **Combine** gelatin, pecans, and coconut. Gradually add condensed milk and vanilla, stirring until blended.
● **Shape** 2 teaspoons mixture to look like a strawberry; roll pointed end in red sugar crystals and large end in green sugar crystals. Press 1 green almond sliver into large end of strawberry to resemble a stem.
● **Repeat** procedure with remaining mixture and almonds. Place on wax paper, and let dry 1 hour. Place in an airtight container, and store in the refrigerator up to 1 week or freeze up to 6 months. **Yield:** about 40 strawberries.

Marie Wiker
Gaithersburg, Maryland

ORANGE BALLS
(pictured on page 333)

1 (12-ounce) package vanilla wafers
1 cup pecan pieces
1 (16-ounce) package powdered sugar, sifted
1 (6-ounce) can frozen orange juice concentrate, thawed and undiluted
½ cup butter or margarine, melted
2 cups flaked coconut or toasted ground pecans

● **Position** knife blade in food processor bowl; add half of vanilla wafers. Process to fine crumbs. Remove crumbs; set aside. Repeat procedure with remaining vanilla wafers; remove crumbs, and set aside.
● **Add** pecan pieces to food processor bowl; process until ground.
● **Combine** wafer crumbs, ground pecans, powdered sugar, orange juice concentrate, and butter in a large bowl; stir until blended. Divide mixture in half. Cover 1 portion with plastic wrap, and set aside.
● **Shape** remaining portion into 1-inch balls, and roll in coconut or toasted ground pecans. (Orange balls dry out quickly; roll immediately after shaping.) Repeat procedure with remaining portion. Store in an airtight container in refrigerator up to 1 week. **Yield:** 7 dozen.

Ruby McCoy
Abilene, Texas

JUST DIP IT!

....

Fondue, the party rage of the sixties, is making a nineties comeback. The idea is age-old: Heat a flavored mixture, dip a bite-size piece of food into it, and enjoy. Fondue pots have been updated, and convenience products make preparation easier.

Want to try the latest fondue revival? Shop for new designs and features in fondue pots and chafing dishes. Or check yard sales for the tried-and-true avocado- or mustard-colored versions. A small Crockpot™ works well, too. Or a saucepan over a burner works fine. For fondue forks, use table forks, wooden picks, or skewers.

CARAMEL FONDUE

3 (14-ounce) packages caramels, unwrapped
⅓ to ½ cup milk
1 (8-ounce) container soft cream cheese

● **Combine** caramels, ⅓ cup milk, and cream cheese in a large Dutch oven; cook over low heat, stirring constantly, until caramels melt and mixture is smooth. Add additional milk if mixture is too thick for dipping. Spoon into a fondue pot or chafing dish. **Yield:** 4 cups.

Carolyn Look
El Paso, Texas

DUNKING MORSELS

Savory:
French or pumpernickel bread cubes
Raw vegetables
Tortilla or corn chips

Sweet:
Angel food cake cubes
Fruit slices or chunks (apple, pear, pineapple, banana)
Marshmallows
Pound cake cubes
Shortbread cookies
Whole small fruits (strawberries, grapes, cherries)

CHOCOLATE PLUNGE

2 cups light corn syrup
1½ cups whipping cream
3 (12-ounce) packages semisweet chocolate morsels

● **Combine** corn syrup and whipping cream in a heavy saucepan; bring mixture to a boil.
● **Remove** from heat; add chocolate morsels, stirring until smooth. Spoon into a fondue pot or chafing dish. **Yield:** 7 cups.

Mary Pappas
Richmond, Virginia

PEPPERMINT FONDUE

1 cup sifted powdered sugar
2 tablespoons cornstarch
2 cups whipping cream
¼ teaspoon peppermint extract
1 or 2 drops of red liquid food coloring

● **Combine** sugar and cornstarch in a heavy saucepan; gradually stir in whipping cream. Bring to a boil over medium heat, stirring constantly.
● **Remove** from heat, and stir in extract and food coloring. Spoon into a fondue pot or chafing dish. **Yield:** 2 cups.

PUB FONDUE

1 (10¾-ounce) can Cheddar cheese soup, undiluted
¾ cup beer
2 cups (8 ounces) shredded mild Cheddar cheese
2 teaspoons prepared mustard
1 teaspoon Worcestershire sauce

● **Combine** soup and beer in a heavy saucepan; bring to a boil over medium heat, stirring constantly. Gradually add shredded cheese and remaining ingredients, stirring constantly, until cheese melts.
● **Spoon** into a fondue pot or chafing dish. **Yield:** 2½ cups.

NACHO FONDUE

3 (11-ounce) cans nacho cheese soup, undiluted
3 cups (12 ounces) shredded Monterey Jack cheese
1½ cups salsa
¾ cup milk

● **Combine** all ingredients in a heavy saucepan; cook over medium heat, stirring constantly, until cheese melts and mixture is smooth. Spoon mixture into a fondue pot or chafing dish. **Yield:** 7½ cups.

Sandra J. Enwright
Winter Park, Florida

FROM OUR KITCHEN TO YOURS

Our Test Kitchens Staff checked out lots of kitchen gadgets in anticipation of the holiday hustle. Here are our best picks for stocking stuffers. Check kitchen shops for availability.

■ With the whirl of a **salad spinner**, leafy greens are washed and dried in a jiffy. A small spinner holds enough for one or two portions, while a larger one cleans three times as much. As an extra bonus, the removable basket can double as a colander. We also found this small gadget handy for washing fresh herbs and berries. (Available at most department and discount stores.)

■ Load a **garlic press and storer** with peeled garlic cloves, and refrigerate. It's odor free and ready to use. With a simple twist, press out exactly the amount you need. It crushes and stores shallots and chopped onions, too.

■ Remove frustrating lids with less muscle power. A **jar-and-bottle opener** adjusts to help you effortlessly unscrew tops from 4-inch jars as well as small caps on extract bottles. The tool also has a built-in cap lifter, can piercer, and lid prier.

■ Filling bottles requires less cleanup when you use a **stainless steel funnel**. One kind comes with an insert to strain any solids from the liquid. It's especially helpful when making flavored vinegars.

■ A **lattice pastry cutter** eliminates cutting and weaving pastry strips in lattice designs. A quick roll with this unique tool cuts the pastry, which is then carefully spread out to create the lattice effect. It's easiest to use for an 8-inch pie.

■ Turning the handle of a **pineapple corer/slicer** peels, cores, and slices whole fruit into a continuous spiral. The juicy pulp separated from its prickly hide is ready to separate into rings, cut, or crush. It's as easy as opening a bottle of wine.

■ Roasting garlic mellows its pungent aroma, creates a sweet, nutty flavor, and softens the texture. The unglazed dome of a **terra-cotta garlic baker** allows steam to escape while the glazed base prevents sticking.

■ To remove offensive onion and garlic odors from your hands, reach for the **NOnion**. This nonallergenic metal bar washes away smelly oils better than any bar of soap.

For an unusual gift, package a few ornaments and an assortment of goodies like Orange Balls, Christmas Strawberries, and No-Bake Brownies in an old ornament box. (Recipes begin on page 330.)

A selection of holiday favorites from
SOUTHERN LIVING Our Best Christmas
Recipes: *(clockwise from bottom left)*
Edible Ornaments, Lemon Curd, French
Market Soup Mix, Jeweled Pepper Chutney,
Fire-and-Ice Pickles, Christmas Potpourri,
and Cheese Ball With Sun-Dried Tomatoes.
(Recipes begin on page 315.)

Your guests will never guess that Chocolate-Cranberry Roulage (recipe, page 313) begins with a cake mix.

APPENDICES

HANDY SUBSTITUTIONS

BAKING PRODUCTS

Ingredient	Substitution
Arrowroot, 1 teaspoon	• 1 tablespoon all-purpose flour • 1½ teaspoons cornstarch
Baking powder, 1 teaspoon	• ½ teaspoon cream of tartar plus ¼ teaspoon baking soda

Chocolate
  semisweet, 1 ounce
  unsweetened, 1 ounce or square
  chips, semisweet, 1 ounce
  chips, semisweet, 6-ounce package, melted
	• 1 ounce unsweetened chocolate plus 1 tablespoon sugar
	• 3 tablespoons cocoa plus 1 tablespoon fat
	• 1 ounce sweet cooking chocolate
	• 2 ounces unsweetened chocolate, 2 tablespoons shortening, plus ½ cup sugar

Cocoa, ¼ cup (4 tablespoons)	• 1 ounce unsweetened chocolate (decrease fat in recipe by ½ tablespoon)

Coconut
  flaked, 1 tablespoon
  cream, 1 cup
  milk, 1 cup
	• 1½ tablespoons grated fresh coconut
	• 1 cup whipping cream
	• 1 cup whole or 2% milk

Corn syrup, light, 1 cup	• 1 cup sugar plus ¼ cup water • 1 cup honey
Cornstarch, 1 tablespoon (for thickening)	• 2 tablespoons all-purpose flour • 2 tablespoons granular tapioca
Cracker crumbs, ¾ cup	• 1 cup dry breadcrumbs

Flour
  all-purpose, 1 tablespoon
 	
  all-purpose, 1 cup sifted
    Note: Specialty flours added to yeast bread will result in a reduced volume and a heavier product.
 	
  cake, 1 cup sifted
  self-rising, 1 cup
	• 1½ teaspoons cornstarch, potato starch, or rice starch
	• 1 teaspoon arrowroot
	• 1 tablespoon granular tapioca
	• 1 tablespoon rice flour or corn flour
	• 1½ tablespoons whole wheat flour
	• ½ tablespoon whole wheat flour plus ½ tablespoon all-purpose flour
	• 1 cup plus 2 tablespoons sifted cake flour
	• 1 cup minus 2 tablespoons all-purpose flour (unsifted)
	• 1½ cups breadcrumbs
	• 1 cup rolled oats
	• ⅓ cup cornmeal or soybean flour plus ⅔ cup all-purpose flour
	• ¾ cup whole wheat flour or bran flour plus ¼ cup all-purpose flour
	• 1 cup rye or rice flour
	• ¼ cup soybean flour plus ¾ cup all-purpose flour
	• 1 cup minus 2 tablespoons all-purpose flour
	• 1 cup all-purpose flour, 1 teaspoon baking powder, plus ½ teaspoon salt

Ingredient	Substitution
Marshmallows, miniature, 1 cup	● 10 large
Marshmallow cream, 1 (7-ounce) jar	● 1 (16-ounce) package marshmallows, melted, plus 3½ tablespoons light corn syrup
Pecans, chopped, 1 cup	● 1 cup regular oats, toasted (in baked products)
Shortening, melted, 1 cup	● 1 cup cooking oil (cooking oil should not be substituted if recipe does not call for *melted* shortening)
Shortening, solid, 1 cup (used in baking)	● 1 cup minus 2 tablespoons lard ● 1⅛ cups butter or margarine (decrease salt called for in recipe by ½ teaspoon)

Sugar
    brown, 1 cup firmly packed
    maple, ½ cup
    powdered, 1 cup
 	
    white, 1 teaspoon
 	
    white, 1 cup
	● 1 cup granulated sugar
	● 1 cup maple syrup
	● 1 cup sugar plus 1 tablespoon cornstarch (processed in food processor)
	● ⅛ teaspoon noncaloric sweetener solution or follow manufacturer's directions
	● 1 cup corn syrup (decrease liquid called for in recipe by ¼ cup)
	● 1⅓ cups molasses (decrease liquid called for in recipe by ⅓ cup)
	● 1 cup firmly packed brown sugar
	● 1 cup honey (decrease liquid called for in recipe by ¼ cup)

Tapioca, granular, 1 tablespoon	● 1½ teaspoons cornstarch ● 1 tablespoon all-purpose flour
Yeast, active dry, 1 tablespoon	● 1 cake yeast, compressed ● 1 (¼-ounce) package active dry yeast

DAIRY PRODUCTS

Ingredient	Substitution
Butter, 1 cup	● ⅞ to 1 cup shortening or lard plus ½ teaspoon salt ● 1 cup margarine

Cream
    heavy (36% to 40% fat), 1 cup
 	
    light (18% to 20% fat), 1 cup
 	
    half-and-half, 1 cup
 	
    whipped
	● ¾ cup milk plus ⅓ cup butter or margarine (for use in cooking and baking; will not whip)
	● ¾ cup milk plus 3 tablespoons butter or margarine (for use in cooking and baking)
	● 1 cup evaporated milk, undiluted
	● ⅞ cup milk plus ½ tablespoon butter or margarine (for use in cooking and baking)
	● 1 cup evaporated milk, undiluted
	● Chill a 13-ounce can of evaporated milk for 12 hours. Add 1 teaspoon lemon juice. Whip until stiff.

Egg
    1 large
 	
    2 large
    white, 1 (2 tablespoons)
 	
    yolk, 1 (1½ tablespoons)
	● 2 egg yolks (for custard and cream fillings)
	● 2 egg yolks plus 1 tablespoon water (for cookies)
	● 3 small eggs
	● 2 tablespoons thawed frozen egg substitute
	● 2 teaspoons sifted, dry egg white powder plus 2 tablespoons warm water
	● 2 tablespoons sifted, dry egg yolk powder plus 2 teaspoons water
	● 1½ tablespoons thawed frozen egg yolk

HANDY SUBSTITUTIONS

Ingredient	Substitution
Milk	
buttermilk, 1 cup	• 1 tablespoon vinegar or lemon juice plus whole milk to equal 1 cup (allow to stand 5 to 10 minutes) • 1 cup plain yogurt • 1 cup whole milk plus 1¾ teaspoons cream of tartar
skim, 1 cup	• 4 to 5 tablespoons nonfat dry milk powder plus enough water to make 1 cup, or follow manufacturer's directions • ½ cup evaporated skim milk plus ½ cup water
whole, 1 cup	• 4 to 5 tablespoons nonfat dry milk powder plus enough water to make 1 cup, or follow manufacturer's directions • ½ cup evaporated milk plus ½ cup water • 1 cup fruit juice or potato water (for use in baking)
sweetened, condensed, 1 (14-ounce) can (about 1⅓ cups)	• Heat the following ingredients until sugar and butter dissolve: ⅓ cup plus 2 tablespoons evaporated milk 1 cup sugar 3 tablespoons butter or margarine
sweetened, condensed, 1 cup	• Heat the following ingredients until sugar and butter dissolve: ⅓ cup evaporated milk ¾ cup sugar 2 tablespoons butter or margarine • Add 1 cup plus 2 tablespoons nonfat dry milk powder to ½ cup warm water. Mix well. Add ¾ cup sugar, and stir until smooth.
Sour cream, 1 cup	• 1 cup yogurt plus 3 tablespoons melted butter • 1 cup yogurt plus 1 tablespoon cornstarch • 1 tablespoon lemon juice plus evaporated milk to equal 1 cup
Yogurt, 1 cup	• 1 cup buttermilk or sour milk

FRUIT AND VEGETABLE PRODUCTS

Ingredient	Substitution
Lemon	
1 medium	• 2 to 3 tablespoons juice and 1 to 2 teaspoons grated rind
juice, 1 teaspoon	• ½ teaspoon vinegar
peel, dried, 1 teaspoon	• 1 to 2 teaspoons grated fresh lemon rind • grated rind of 1 medium lemon • ½ teaspoon lemon extract
Orange	
1 medium	• 6 to 8 tablespoons juice and 2 to 3 tablespoons grated rind
peel, dried, 1 tablespoon	• 1½ teaspoons orange extract • grated rind of 1 medium orange • 1 tablespoon grated fresh orange rind
Mushrooms, 1 pound fresh	• 1 (8-ounce) can sliced mushrooms, drained • 3 ounces dried mushrooms, rehydrated
Onion, chopped, 1 medium	• 1 tablespoon instant minced onion • 1 tablespoon onion powder
Pepper	
sweet red or green, chopped, 3 tablespoons	• 1 tablespoon dried red or green pepper flakes
sweet red, chopped, 3 tablespoons	• 2 tablespoons chopped pimiento
Shallots, chopped, 3 tablespoons	• 2 tablespoons chopped onion plus 1 tablespoon chopped garlic

Ingredient	Substitution

Tomatoes
    fresh, chopped, 2 cups
    juice, 1 cup
	• 1 (16-ounce) can (may need to drain)
	• ½ cup tomato sauce plus ½ cup water

Tomato sauce, 2 cups	• ¾ cup tomato paste plus 1 cup water

MISCELLANEOUS	
Brandy, 1 tablespoon	• ¼ teaspoon brandy extract plus 1 tablespoon water

Broth, beef or chicken
    canned broth, 1 cup
 	
    powdered broth base, 1 teaspoon
    powdered broth base, 1 teaspoon
       dissolved in 1 cup water
	• 1 bouillon cube dissolved in 1 cup boiling water
	• 1 envelope powdered broth base dissolved in 1 cup boiling
	    water
	• 1 teaspoon powdered broth base dissolved in 1 cup boiling
	    water
	• 1 bouillon cube
	• 1 cup canned or homemade broth
	• 1 bouillon cube dissolved in 1 cup boiling water

Chili sauce, 1 cup	• 1 cup tomato sauce, ¼ cup brown sugar, 2 tablespoons
	    vinegar, ¼ teaspoon cinnamon, dash of ground cloves,
	    plus dash of allspice

Gelatin, flavored, 3-ounce package	• 1 tablespoon unflavored gelatin plus 2 cups fruit juice
Honey, 1 cup	• 1¼ cups sugar plus ¼ cup water
Ketchup, 1 cup	• 1 cup tomato sauce, ½ cup sugar, plus 2 tablespoons vinegar (for use in cooking)
Macaroni, uncooked, 2 cups (4 cups, cooked)	• 2 cups spaghetti, uncooked • 4 cups noodles, uncooked
Marsala, ¼ cup	• ¼ cup dry white wine plus 1 teaspoon brandy
Mayonnaise, 1 cup (for salads and dressings)	• ½ cup yogurt plus ½ cup mayonnaise • 1 cup sour cream • 1 cup cottage cheese pureed in a blender
Rennet, 1 tablet	• 1 tablespoon liquid rennet
Rice, uncooked, 1 cup regular (3 cups cooked)	• 1 cup uncooked converted rice • 1 cup uncooked brown rice • 1 cup uncooked wild rice
Vinegar, balsamic, ½ cup	• ½ cup red wine vinegar (slight flavor difference)

SEASONING PRODUCTS	
Allspice, ground, 1 teaspoon	• ½ teaspoon ground cinnamon plus ½ teaspoon ground cloves

Apple pie spice, 1 teaspoon	• ½ teaspoon ground cinnamon, ¼ teaspoon ground
	    nutmeg, plus ⅛ teaspoon ground
	    cardamom

Bay leaf, 1 whole	• ¼ teaspoon crushed bay leaf

HANDY SUBSTITUTIONS

Ingredient	Substitution
Beau Monde seasoning, 1 teaspoon	• 1 teaspoon seasoning or seasoned salt • ½ teaspoon salt • ½ teaspoon Mei Yen seasoning
Chives, chopped, 1 tablespoon	• 1 tablespoon chopped green onion tops
Dill plant, fresh or dried, 3 heads	• 1 tablespoon dill seed
Garlic, 1 clove, small	• ⅛ teaspoon garlic powder or minced dried garlic
Garlic salt, 1 teaspoon	• ⅛ teaspoon garlic powder plus ⅞ teaspoon salt

Ginger
    crystallized, 1 tablespoon
    fresh, grated, 1 tablespoon
    ground, ⅛ teaspoon
	• ⅛ teaspoon ground ginger
	• ⅛ teaspoon ground ginger
	• 1 tablespoon crystallized ginger rinsed in water to remove sugar, and finely cut
	• 1 tablespoon grated fresh ginger

Herbs, fresh, chopped, 1 tablespoon	• 1 teaspoon dried herbs or ¼ teaspoon ground herbs
Horseradish, fresh, grated, 1 tablespoon	• 2 tablespoons prepared horseradish
Mei Yen seasoning, 1 teaspoon	• 1 teaspoon Beau Monde seasoning • ½ teaspoon salt
Mustard, dried, 1 teaspoon	• 1 tablespoon prepared mustard
Onion powder, 1 tablespoon	• 1 medium onion, chopped • 1 tablespoon instant minced onion
Parsley, dried, 1 teaspoon	• 1 tablespoon fresh parsley, chopped
Pimiento, chopped, 2 tablespoons	• rehydrate 1 tablespoon dried sweet red peppers • 2 to 3 tablespoons fresh sweet red pepper, chopped
Pumpkin pie spice, 1 teaspoon	• ½ teaspoon ground cinnamon, ¼ teaspoon ground ginger, ⅛ teaspoon ground allspice, plus ⅛ teaspoon ground nutmeg
Spearmint or peppermint, dried, 1 tablespoon	• ¼ cup chopped fresh mint
Vanilla bean, 1 (1 inch)	• 1 teaspoon vanilla extract
Worcestershire sauce, 1 teaspoon	• 1 teaspoon bottled steak sauce

EQUIVALENT WEIGHTS AND YIELDS

Food	Weight (or Count)		Yield	
Apples	1	pound (3 medium)	3	cups sliced
Bacon	8	slices cooked	½	cup crumbled
Bananas	1	pound (3 medium)	2½	cups sliced or about 2 cups mashed
Bread	1	pound	12	to 16 slices
		About 1½ slices	1	cup soft crumbs
Butter or margarine	1	pound	2	cups
	¼-	pound stick	½	cup
Cabbage	1	pound head	4½	cups shredded
Candied fruit or peels	½	pound	1¼	cups chopped
Carrots	1	pound	3	cups shredded
Cheese, American or Cheddar	1	pound	About 4	cups shredded
cottage	1	pound	2	cups
cream	3-	ounce package	6	tablespoons
Chocolate morsels	6-	ounce package	1	cup
Cocoa	1	pound	4	cups
Coconut, flaked or shredded	1	pound	5	cups
Coffee	1	pound	80	tablespoons (40 cups perked)
Corn	2	medium ears	1	cup kernels
Cornmeal	1	pound	3	cups
Crab, in shell	1	pound	¾	to 1 cup flaked
Crackers, chocolate wafers	19	wafers	1	cup crumbs
graham crackers	14	squares	1	cup fine crumbs
saltine crackers	28	crackers	1	cup finely crushed
vanilla wafers	22	wafers	1	cup finely crushed
Cream, whipping	1	cup (½ pint)	2	cups whipped
Dates, pitted	1	pound	3	cups chopped
	8-	ounce package	1½	cups chopped
Eggs	5	large	1	cup
whites	8	to 11	1	cup
yolks	12	to 14	1	cup
Flour, all-purpose	1	pound	3½	cups
cake	1	pound	4¾	to 5 cups sifted
whole wheat	1	pound	3½	cups unsifted
Green pepper	1	large	1	cup diced
Lemon	1	medium	2	to 3 tablespoons juice; 2 teaspoons grated rind
Lettuce	1-	pound head	6¼	cups torn
Lime	1	medium	1½	to 2 tablespoons juice; 1½ teaspoons grated rind
Macaroni	4	ounces dry (1 cup)	2	cups cooked
Marshmallows	10	large	1	cup
	10	miniature	1	large marshmallow
Marshmallows, miniature	½	pound	4½	cups
Milk, evaporated	5-	ounce can	½	cup
evaporated	12-	ounce can	1½	cups
sweetened, condensed	14-	ounce can	1¼	cups
Mushrooms	3	cups raw (8 ounces)	1	cup sliced cooked

EQUIVALENT WEIGHTS AND YIELDS *(continued)*

Food	Weight (or Count)	Yield
Nuts, almonds	1 pound	1 to 1¾ cups nutmeats
	1 pound shelled	3½ cups nutmeats
peanuts	1 pound	2¼ cups nutmeats
	1 pound shelled	3 cups
pecans	1 pound	2¼ cups nutmeats
	1 pound shelled	4 cups
walnuts	1 pound	1⅔ cups nutmeats
	1 pound shelled	4 cups
Oats, quick cooking	1 cup	1¾ cups cooked
Onion	1 medium	½ cup chopped
Orange	1 medium	½ cup juice; 2 tablespoons grated rind
Peaches	2 medium	1 cup sliced
Pears	2 medium	1 cup sliced
Potatoes, white	3 medium	2 cups cubed cooked or 1¾ cups mashed
sweet	3 medium	3 cups sliced
Raisins, seedless	1 pound	3 cups
Rice, long-grain	1 cup	3 to 4 cups cooked
precooked	1 cup	2 cups cooked
Shrimp, raw in shell	1½ pounds	2 cups (¾ pound) cleaned, cooked
Spaghetti	7 ounces	About 4 cups cooked
Strawberries	1 quart	4 cups sliced
Sugar, brown	1 pound	2⅓ cups firmly packed
powdered	1 pound	3½ cups unsifted
granulated	1 pound	2 cups

EQUIVALENT MEASURES

3	teaspoons	1 tablespoon	2	cups	1	pint (16 fluid ounces)
4	tablespoons	¼ cup	4	cups	1	quart
5⅓	tablespoons	⅓ cup	4	quarts	1	gallon
8	tablespoons	½ cup	⅛	cup	2	tablespoons
16	tablespoons	1 cup	⅓	cup	5	tablespoons plus 1 teaspoon
2	tablespoons (liquid)	1 ounce	⅔	cup	10	tablespoons plus 2 teaspoons
1	cup	8 fluid ounces	¾	cup	12	tablespoons

RECIPE TITLE INDEX

An alphabetical listing of every recipe by exact title

All microwave recipe page numbers are preceded by an "M."

MONTH-BY-MONTH INDEX

An alphabetical listing within the month of every food article and accompanying recipes

All microwave recipe page numbers are preceded by an "M."

GENERAL RECIPE INDEX

A listing of every recipe by food category and/or major ingredient
All microwave recipe page numbers are preceded by an "M."

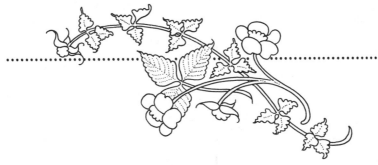

CORNISH HENS
Roasted Cornish Hens with Vegetables, Tarragon, 79
COUSCOUS
Salad, Basil-and-Tomato Couscous, 175
CRAB
Bisque, Crab-and-Leek, 104
Burgers, Potato-Crusted Crab, 139
Cakes, Gulf Coast Crab, 71
Cakes with Tomato Cream, Crab, 70
Dip, Hot Crab-and-Cheese, 282
Hors d'Oeuvre, Crabmeat, 236
Mousse, Crabmeat, 159
Oysters, Crabmeat Stuffed, 328
Stuffing, Crabmeat, 68
Tomatoes, Crab-and-Avocado Stuffed, 141
CRANBERRIES
Apple Berry Sparkler, 100
Gravy, Baked Hen with Cranberry Pan, 308
Mexican Cranberries, 273
Orange Surprise, Cran-, 143
Roulage, Chocolate-Cranberry, 313
Tea, Cranberry, 131
CRÊPES
Crêpes, 116
Fajita Crêpes, 116
CROUTONS
Bread Croutons, Hawaiian, 107
Cornbread Croutons, Honeyed, 106
Egg Roll Fan, Sesame, 107
Pumpernickel Croutons, 62
Tortilla Triangles, 107
CUCUMBERS
Sandwiches, Cucumber, 14
Sauce, Cucumber Dipping, 47
Vichyssoise, Cucumber, 90
CURRY
Chicken, Country Captain, 252
Chicken Curry, Turban, 266
Chowder, Curried Seafood, 103
Sauce, Curry, 54
Shrimp Balls, Curried, 180
CUSTARD
Flan, Corn-Chive, 172

DATES
Cake, Orange-Date, 60
Sandwich, Date-Nut Lettuce, 202
DESSERTS. *SEE ALSO* SPECIFIC TYPES.
Blackberry Dessert Tamales, 190
Brie, Almond-Raspberry, M89
Caramel Fondue, 331
Chocolate
Brickle Squares, Chocolate, 290
Cinnamon-Chocolate Cream, 199
Log, Chocolate Cream, 220
Plunge, Chocolate, 332
Pots de Crème, Chocolate, 234
Roulage, Chocolate-Cranberry, 313
Roulage, Chocolate-Orange, 314
Roulage, Mint-Chocolate, 314
Frozen
Almond Crunch, Frozen, 283
Cookies 'n' Cream Dessert, Gold-Dusted, 271
Cream Dessert, Triple, 244
Fudgy Frozen Dessert, Nutty, 28
Ice, Hazelnut-Coffee, 233
Ice, Mimosa, 24
Pops, Deep Blue Sea, 143
Pops, Hawaiian Orange-Pineapple, 143
Texas Tornadoes for Grown-Ups, 143

Fruit
Compote, Fresh Fruit, 190
Crisp, Fruit, 168
Lemon Angel Rolls with Raspberry Sauce, 294
Lollapalooza, 194
Mango Dessert Tamales, 190
Parfaits
Chocolate Mousse Parfait, 90
Family, Parfait, 130
Orange Cream Parfaits, 198
Pears, Crème de Menthe, 50
Peppermint Fondue, 332
Roulage, Toffee-Pecan, 312
Sauces
Berry Sauce, 130
Blackberry Sauce, 232
Blueberry Sauce, 122
Caramel Sauce, 234
Chocolate-Mint Sauce, 314
Chocolate-Orange Sauce, 314
Chocolate-Peppermint Sauce, 205
Chocolate Sauce, 121
Chocolate Sauce, Dark, 234, 283
Fruit Puree, 190
Fudge Sauce, Easy Hot, 194
Plum Sauce, Fresh, 129
Praline Sauce, 206, 312
Raspberry Sauce, 295
Rum-Raisin Sauce, 295
Rum Sauce, 241
Strawberry Sauce, 121
Strawberry Sauce, Old-Fashioned, 130
Tea-Berry Sauce, 130
Toffee Sauce, 72
Vanilla Crème Sauce, 243
Strawberries, Dipped, 17
Tiramisù, 295
Tortilla Baskets, 97
Trifle, Toffee, 168
DRESSINGS. *SEE* STUFFINGS AND DRESSINGS.
DUCK
Grilled Duck with Orange Sauce, 305
Pot Pie with Parmesan Crust, Game, 304
DUMPLINGS
Cheddar Dumplings, Chicken Ragout with, 44

EGGPLANT
Casserole, Eggplant, 214
Caviar, Homemade Cowboy, 64
EGGS
Casserole, Sausage-and-Egg, 284
Cheddar Eggs, M141
Deviled Eggs, 161
Frittata, Firecracker Pasta, 230
Migas, 26
Omelets
Apple Omelet Stack, 50
Baked Omelets, 50
Olé, Omelet, 31
Potato Omelet, Family-Size, 31
Shrimp-and-Cheese Omelet, 31
Potato Nests, Mashed, 141
Salad, Bacon-Horseradish Egg, 181
Salad Sandwiches, Shrimp-and-Egg, 182
Salad Tacos, Mexican Egg, 181
Salad, Yolkless Egg, 181
ENCHILADAS
Chicken Enchiladas with Tomatillo Sauce, 231
Soup, Shrimp Enchilada, 103

FAJITAS
Crêpes, Fajita, 116
Fettuccine, Fajita, 84
Plum Good Fajitas, 115
FETTUCCINE
Fajita Fettuccine, 84
Ham-and-Asparagus Fettuccine, 84
Primavera, Fettuccine, 85
Shrimp Fettuccine, 84
Shrimp with Dried Tomato Pesto, Fettuccine and, 249
Spinach Fettuccine with Mustard Greens, 247
FIGS
Cobbler, Cajun Fig, 196
FISH. *SEE ALSO* SPECIFIC TYPES AND SEAFOOD.
Catfish, Baked, 67
Catfish Cakes, 70
Catfish Pilaf, 171
Fillets Tomatillo, 135
Flounder, Grand Lagoon Stuffed, 68
Grouper, Garlic-Basil Marinated, 160
Grouper, Hot Spicy, 78
Grouper with Vanilla Wine Sauce, Pan-Fried, 241
Halibut Steak, Wine-Herb, 171
Mullet Spread, 159
Oven-Fried Fish, 172
Snapper Gumbo, Savannah, 105
Snapper with Creamy Dill Sauce, Peppered, 42
Vegetables, Cheesy Fish and, 254
FRENCH TOAST
Potato-Crusted Texas Toast, 142
FRITTERS
Corn Fritters, 22
FROSTINGS, FILLINGS, AND TOPPINGS
Avocado Topping, 96
Chili Topping, 22
Chocolate Cream, 57
Chocolate Frosting, 133
Coffee Frosting, 86
Cream Cheese Frosting, 254
Cream Cheese Glaze, 242
Fruit Filling, 245
Fudge Filling, 292
Fudge Frosting, 51
Hazelnut Whipped Cream, 16
Ketchup, Hoisin, 138
Lemon Curd, 315
Lemon Filling, 122
Mocha Cream, 47
Mocha Frosting, 292
Olive Salad, Doodles, 35
Olive Salad, Italian, 35
Orange-Mallow Cream, 295
Peach Topping, 22
Pecan Topping, 36
Salad Mix, Muffy, 34
Seven-Minute Frosting, 98, 99
Streusel Topping, 280
Teriyaki Glaze, 82
Turkey-Vegetable Topping, 22
Vanilla Buttercream Frosting, 99
White Chocolate-Cream Cheese Tiered Cake Frosting, 125
White Chocolate-Cream Cheese Frosting, 58
FRUIT. *SEE ALSO* SPECIFIC TYPES.
Brie, Tropical Breeze, M18
Compote, Festive Fruit, 279
Compote, Fresh Fruit, 190
Crisp, Fruit, 168
Cup, Mixed Fruit, 60
Filling, Fruit, 245

FRUIT

(continued)

Frozen Fruit Cream, 129
Pizza, Peanut Butter-Fruit, 60
Pork Chops, Fruit-Topped, 41
Punch, Can-Can Fruit, 122
Puree, Fruit, 190
'Ritas, Fruit, 157
Salads
    Citrus-Cilantro Dressing, Fruit Salad
      with, 97
    Turkey Salad, Fruit-and-Spice, 325
Tea Cooler, Fruited, 131

GAME

Birds in Wine Marinade, Game, 306
Duck with Orange Sauce, Grilled, 305
Pot Pie with Parmesan Crust, Game, 304
Quail with Cornbread Stuffing, Baked, 305
Rabbit, Santa Fe Spanish, 307
Turkey, Country-Fried Wild, 306
Venison Loin, Mushroom-Crusted, 302
Venison Reduction Sauce, 303
Venison Stock, 302

GARNISHES
Lemon Peel, Candied, 199

GRANOLA
Mix, Granola, 168
Pancakes, Granola-Squash, 267

GRAPES
Cooler, Grape-Lime, 227

GRAVIES. *SEE ALSO* SAUCES.
Cranberry Pan Gravy, Baked Hen
    with, 308
Giblet Gravy, Roast Turkey and, 308
Sausage Gravy, 20
Turkey Gravy, 306

GREENS
Collards and Sausage, Pasta with, 230
Gumbo z'Herbes, 239
Kale with Salsa, Southwest, 246
Mustard Greens, Spinach Fettuccine
    with, 247
Stir-Fried Greens, 33
Turnip Greens and White Bean Bake, 246

GRITS
Cheese Grits, Baked, 240
Cheese Grits, Grillades and Baked, 240
Dressing, Grits, 296
Ham-and-Spinach Grits, Garlicky, 177
Quiche, Ham-and-Grits Crustless, 89

GUMBOS
Chicken-and-Sausage Gumbo, 20
Seafood Gumbo, Cajun, 238
Snapper Gumbo, Savannah, 105
z'Herbes, Gumbo, 239

HAM. *SEE ALSO* PORK.

Baked Burgundy Ham, 326
Birming "Ham," 229
Biscuits, Country Ham, 215
Fettuccine, Ham-and-Asparagus, 84
Grits, Garlicky Ham-and-Spinach, 177
Muffuletta, Doodles, 35
Prosciutto, Party Pasta with, 176
Quiche, Ham-and-Grits Crustless, 89
Sandwiches, Cheshire Claret Cheese-and-Ham
    Striped Tea, 16
Sandwich Round, Ham-and-Cheese, 326

Sebastian, The, 184
Soup, Spicy Ham-and-Bean, 322

HEARTS OF PALM
Salad with Basil-and-Garlic Dressing, Hearts
    of Palm, 55

HONEY
Butter, Honey, 206
Crunch, Honey-and-Spice, 290
Lemon Honey, 16
Shrimp, Tangy Honeyed, 32
Vinaigrette, Honey-Mustard, 249

HORS D'OEUVRES, *SEE* APPETIZERS

ICE CREAMS AND SHERBETS

Fruit Cream, Frozen, 129
Mint-Chocolate Chip Ice Cream Squares, 245
Orange Sherbet with Blackberry Sauce, 232
Pie, Ice Cream Sundae, 244

JAMS AND JELLIES

Chile Piquín Jelly, 28
Lime Jelly, 23

KABOBS

Antipasto Kabobs, 144
Beef Kabobs, Chile-, 251
Vegetable Skewers, Grilled, 160

KIWIFRUIT
Salsa, Hot Kiwifruit, 82

LAMB

Grape Leaves, Stuffed, 48
Quenelles, Veal-Vermicelli Soup with, 14
Rack of Lamb, Marinated, 55
Stew with Popovers, Lamb, 43

LEEKS
Bisque, Crab-and-Leek, 104
Roasted Potatoes, Carrots, and Leeks, 276

LEMON
Beverages
    Hot Buttered Lemonade, 18
    Margaritas, Lemon-Lime, 227
    Punch, Lemon Champagne, 176
Chicken, Lemon-Rosemary, 201
Curd, Lemon, 315
Desserts
    Candied Lemon Peel, 199
    Filling, Lemon, 122
    Napoleons, Blueberry-Lemon, 122
    Pie, Best-Ever Lemon Meringue, 208
    Pie, Lemon Parfait, 310
    Pops, Deep Blue Sea, 143
    Rolls with Raspberry Sauce, Lemon
      Angel, 294
    Soufflé, Lemon, 199
Honey, Lemon, 16
Olives, Lemon-Garlic, 118
Pork Piccata, 57
Sauces
    Barbecue Sauce, Herbed Lemon, 154
    Cream Sauce, Braised Chicken Breast in
      Lemon, 184
Vinaigrette, Lemon-Basil, 205

LIME
Candied Lime Strips, 137
Cooler, Grape-Lime, 227
Dressing, Spinach Salad with Chili-Lime, 63
Jelly, Lime, 23
Margaritas, Lemon-Lime, 227

Mustard, Key Lime, 278
Sauce, Lime-Saffron, 71
Tornadoes for Grown-Ups, Texas, 143
Vinaigrette, Cilantro-Lime, 77

LIVING LIGHT (*FORMERLY* ON THE LIGHT SIDE)
Breads
    Biscuits and Sausage Gravy, 20
    Biscuits, Cheese-Chive, 324
    Cornbread, Jalapeño, 78
Crust, Whole Wheat, 78
Desserts
    Cake, Orange-Coconut Angel Food, 294
    Cake, Strawberry Yogurt Layer, 85
    Cake with Coffee Frosting, Spice
      Layer, 86
    Cheesecake, Black Forest, 21
    Chocolate Cream Log, 220
    Frosting, Coffee, 86
    Lemon Angel Rolls with Raspberry
      Sauce, 294
    Lime Strips, Candied, 137
    Orange-Mallow Cream, 295
    Sauce, Raspberry, 295
    Sauce, Rum-Raisin, 295
    Tiramisù, 295
    Torte, Chocolate Mint, 86
Dip, Santa Fe Skinny, 137
Glaze, Teriyaki, 82
Main Dishes
    Beef Kabobs, Chile-, 251
    Carne Guisada, 219
    Catfish, Baked, 67
    Chicken à la King, 41
    Chicken Pot Pie, 21
    Chicken with Tomato-Basil Pasta,
      Basil-Stuffed, M204
    Chiles Rellenos with Tomatillo Sauce,
      Roasted, 203
    Cornish Hens with Vegetables, Tarragon
      Roasted, 79
    Fajita Fettuccine, 84
    Fettuccine and Shrimp with Dried
      Tomato Pesto, 249
    Fettuccine, Ham-and-Asparagus, 84
    Fettuccine Primavera, 85
    Fettuccine, Shrimp, 84
    Filet Mignon with Mushroom
      Sauce, 250
    Fillets Tomatillo, 135
    Flank Steak with Black Bean-and-Corn
      Salsa, Grilled, 80
    Grouper, Hot Spicy, 78
    Pizza, Vegetable, 218
    Pizza, Veggie, 78
    Pork Chops, Fruit-Topped, 41
    Pork Tenderloin, Spinach-and-Bacon
      Stuffed, 81
    Salmon Fillets with Red Wine Garlic
      Sauce, 250
    Scallops with Cilantro-Lime Vinaigrette,
      Grilled Orange, 77
    Sirloin, Mustard Marinated, 41
    Snapper with Creamy Dill Sauce,
      Peppered, 42
    Tuna Steaks on Mixed Greens with
      Lemon-Basil Vinaigrette, Seared, 205
Pasta, Tomato-Basil, 204
Pizza Crusts, Skillet, 218
Relish, Papaya-Basil, 82
Salad Dressings
    Cilantro-Lime Vinaigrette, 77
    Spicy Southwestern Dressing, 136
    Vinaigrette, Lemon-Basil, 205

PEANUT BUTTER

Apple, Piggy, 194
Cheesecake, Peanut Butter, 142
Chocolate Peanutty Swirls, M330
"Concrete," All Shook Up, 114
Cookies, No-Bake Peanut Butter, 197
Cookies, Peanut Butter and Chocolate
Chunk, 169
Jam Bars, Peanut Butter-, 291
Muffins, Peanut Butter-Chocolate
Chip, 167
Napoleons, Peanut Butter-and-
Chocolate, 121
Pie, Fluffy Peanut Butter, 246
Pizza, Peanut Butter-Fruit, 60
Waffles, Honey-Buttered Peanut
Butter, M206

PEANUTS

Crunchy Munchies, 196
Pie, Caramel-Nut Crunch, 244

PEARS

Crème de Menthe Pears, 50
Sautéed Apples, Onions, and Pears over
Spinach, 212
Sautéed Pears, Spinach Salad with, 237

PEAS

Black-Eyed Pea Hummus, 123
English
Perfection, Peas to, 321
Soup, Potato-Pea, 90
Soup, French Market, 317
Soup Mix, French Market, 317
Soup, Split Pea, 322

PECANS

Bars, Gooey Pecan, 133
Cornbread, Pecan, 169
Cream Pie, Chocolate-Banana-Pecan, 210
Crunchy Munchies, 196
Dessert, Nutty Fudgy Frozen, 28
Pork Loin, Apricot-Pecan Stuffed, 274
Praline Sauce, 206, 312
Roulage, Toffee-Pecan, 312
Salad, Strawberry-Nut, 132
Scones, Orange-Pecan, 215
Spread, Nutty Carrot, 123
Stuffing, Chicken Breasts with Pecan-
Sausage, 212
Sugar-and-Spice Pecans, 272
Tart with Caramel Sauce, Chocolate-
Pecan, 234
Topping, Pecan, 36
Turkey Cutlets, Pecan-Crusted, 282

PEPPERMINT

Brownies, Pistachio-Mint, 50
Cheesecake, Frozen Peppermint, 143
Fondue, Peppermint, 332
Mousse, Peppermint Candy, 198
Rounds, Peppermint, 19
Sauce, Chocolate-Peppermint, 205

PEPPERS

Chile
Beef Kabobs, Chile-, 251
Jelly, Chile Piquín, 28
Red Chile Sauce, 251
Rellenos with Tomatillo Sauce, Roasted
Chiles, 203
Serrano Chile Blue Cornbread, 114
Waffles, Corn-Chile, 206
Chutney, Jeweled Pepper, 316
Jalapeño
Biscuits, Cornmeal-Jalapeño, 214
Chicken Legs, Jalapeño Oven-Fried, 94
Cornbread, Jalapeño, 78

Puffs, Cajun Hot, 277
Vinegar, Southwest, 200
Pasta, Peppery, 164
Pizza, Roasted Pepper, 218
Roasted Peppers with Balsamic
Vinaigrette, 128
Salsa, Yellowfin Tuna with Corn, Pepper, and
Tomato, 164
Sandwiches, Smoked Turkey-Roasted
Pepper, 66
Spread, Roasted Pepper, 123

PICKLES AND RELISHES

Acorn Squash-and-Bourbon Butter, 266
Chutney, Jeweled Pepper, 316
Confit, Roasted Shallot-Garlic, 303
Fire-and-Ice Pickles, 316
Papaya-Basil Relish, 82

PIES AND PASTRIES

Apple
Fried Apple Pies, 61
Mexican Apple Pie, 97
Apricot Pies, Special, 60
Blueberry-Peach Pie, 158
Buttermilk-Coconut Pie, 246
Caramel-Nut Crunch Pie, 244
Chocolate
Banana-Pecan Cream Pie,
Chocolate-, 210
Coffee Cream Pie, 209
Cream Pie, Chocolate, 208
Mocha Pie, 168
Cobbler, Cajun Fig, 196
Coffee Cream Pie, 209
Empanadas de Calabaza (Pumpkin
Empanadas), 28
Ice Cream Sundae Pie, 244
Lemon Meringue Pie, Best-Ever, 208
Lemon Parfait Pie, 310
Magnolia Pie, 210
Main Dishes
Chicken Pot Pie, 21
Game Pot Pie with Parmesan
Crust, 304
Turkey Turnovers, Home-Style, 325
Orange-Coconut Cream Pie, 208
Pastries and Crusts
Basic Pastry, 210
Graham Cracker Crust, 310
Napoleons, Berry, 120
Napoleons, Blueberry-Lemon, 122
Napoleons, Peanut Butter-and-
Chocolate, 121
Papaya-Pineapple Roll, 18
Parmesan Crust, 304
Paste Pastry, Common, 17
Pastry Shell, 158
Peanut Butter Pie, Fluffy, 246
Raspberry Cream Pie, 209
Tarts
Apple Tart, Creamed, 17
Apricot-Apple Crumb Tart, 60
Chicken Tarts, Deviled, 14
Chocolate-Pecan Tart with Caramel
Sauce, 234
Portabello Mushroom Tart,
Smoked, 163
Turnovers, Reuben, 253
Vegetable
Portabello Mushroom Tart,
Smoked, 163
Scallopini Pie, 133
Spinach, Pie Pan, 195
White Chocolate-Banana Cream Pie, 314

PINEAPPLE

Blue Woo-Woo, 226
Coffee Cake, Pineapple-Coconut, 49
Milk Shake, Pineapple, 113
Mousse, Coconut-Pineapple, 198
Papaya-Pineapple Roll, 18
Pops, Hawaiian Orange-Pineapple, 143
Slaw, Pineapple, 49
Slush, Pineapple-Strawberry, 227

PIZZA

Chicken Pizza, 218
Crusts, Skillet Pizza, 218
Crust, Whole Wheat, 78
Mexican Pizza, 218, 327
Peanut Butter-Fruit Pizza, 60
Pepper Pizza, Roasted, 218
Pesto Pizza, 218
Phyllo Pizza, 91
Pita Pizza Snack, 193
Sunburst, Pizza, 245
Vegetable Pizza, 218
Veggie Pizza, 78

PLUMS

Fajitas, Plum Good, 115
Sauce, Fresh Plum, 129

POPCORN

Ghoul's Hands, 256
Herb-Seasoned Popcorn, 122
Honey-and-Spice Crunch, 290

PORK. SEE ALSO BACON, HAM, SAUSAGE.

Chops
Casserole, Pork Chop, 255
Fruit-Topped Pork Chops, 41
Roasts
Stuffed Pork Loin, Apricot-Pecan, 274
Stuffed Pork Rib Roast,
Sausage, 240
Stew, Pancho Villa, 44
Tenderloin
Grilled Pork Tenderloin, 88
Grilled Pork Tenderloins, 158
Parmigiana, Easy Pork, 57
Piccata, Pork, 57
Scaloppine Marsala, Pork, 57
Stuffed Pork Tenderloin, Spinach-and-
Bacon, 81

POTATOES

Biscuits, Potato-Bacon, 214
Bread Dough, Potato Sourdough, 324
Bread, Potato Sourdough, 325
Chowder, Potato-Corn, 66
Crab Burgers, Potato-Crusted, 139
Mashed Potato Nests, 141
Omelet, Family-Size Potato, 31
Patties, Thunderbolt Potato, 213
Pudding, Carrot-Potato, 279
Quick Potatoes, 283
Roasted Potatoes, Carrots, and Leeks, 276
Rolls, Potato Sourdough, 325
Sage Potatoes, 320
Salads
Basil Potato Salad, 178
Dill-and-Sour Cream Potato
Salad, 100
Dill Potato Salad, 179
German Potato Salad, Hot, 254
Herbed Potato Salad, 164
New Potato Salad, 162
Potato Salad, 160
South-of-the-Border Potato Salad, 178
Soup, Potato-Pea, 90
Sourdough Cinnamon Rolls, Potato, 325
Sourdough Starter, Potato, 324

STEWS. *SEE ALSO* CHILI, GUMBOS, SOUPS.
Chicken Ragout with Cheddar
Dumplings, 44
Game Pot Pie with Parmesan Crust, 304
Lamb Stew with Popovers, 43
Pancho Villa Stew, 44
Veal-and-Artichoke Ragout, 43
Vegetable-Beef Stew, 323
STRAWBERRIES
Cake, Strawberry Yogurt Layer, 85
Christmas Strawberries, 331
Dipped Strawberries, 17
Ice Ring, Strawberry, 176
Milk Shake, Strawberry, 113
Romanoff, Strawberries, 68
Salad, Frozen Strawberry, 119
Salad, Strawberry-Nut, 132
Sauce, Old-Fashioned Strawberry, 130
Sauce, Strawberry, 121
Shortcake, Strawberry, 162
Slush, Pineapple-Strawberry, 227
Tea, Sparkling Strawberry, 131
STUFFINGS AND DRESSINGS
Cornbread Stuffing, 305
Crabmeat Stuffing, 68
Green Chile-Cornbread Dressing, 296
Grits Dressing, 296
Pecan-Sausage Stuffing, Chicken Breasts
with, 212
Sausage-Apple Dressing, 296
Spoonbread Dressing, Southwestern-
Style, 273
SWEET-AND-SOUR
Dressing, Sweet-and-Sour, 281
Salad, Sweet-and-Sour Green, 281
SWISS CHARD
Bundles, Swiss Chard, 48
SYRUP
Barbecue Sauce, Maple Syrup, 154

Tacos
Egg Salad Tacos, Mexican, 181
Salad, Chicken Taco, M136
Sauce, Taco, 30
Soup, Taco, 225
TAMALES
Casserole, Quick Tamale, 255
Mango Dessert Tamales, 190
TEA
Cranberry Tea, 131
Fruited Tea Cooler, 131
Ginger-Almond Tea, 131
Sangría Tea, 131
Sauce, Tea-Berry, 130
Strawberry Tea, Sparkling, 131
TOMATILLOS
Fillets Tomatillo, 135
Sauce, Roasted Chiles Rellenos with
Tomatillo, 203
Sauce, Tomatillo, 231
TOMATOES
Asparagus and Tomatoes, Fresh, 162
Baked Ranch Tomatoes, 72
Biscuits, Tomato-Herb, 215
Bouillon, New Year's Tomato, 24
Cioppino, Gulf Coast, 102
Cream, Tomato, 70
Dried Tomato Focaccia, 65
Dried Tomato Pesto, Fettuccine and
Shrimp with, 249
Green Tomato Cheeseburgers, Fried, 138
Marinara Sauce, 64

Marinara Vinaigrette, 64
Pasta, Tomato-Basil, 204
Pasta, Tomato-Garlic, 177
Pesto, Bow-Tie, 231
Pesto, Dried Tomato, 249
Salad, Basil-and-Tomato Couscous, 175
Salad, Summer Tomato, 201
Salsa, Tomato-Avocado, 83
Salsa, Yellowfin Tuna with Corn, Pepper,
and Tomato, 164
Sauce, Chili, 287
Sauce, Kleberg Hot, 28
Sipper, Peppy Tomato, 227
Soup, Cream of Carrot-and-Tomato, 176
Soup, French Market, 317
Soup, Savory Tomato, 91
Spinach-Topped Tomatoes, 321
Spread, Tomato, 123
Stuffed Tomatoes, Chile-Cheese, 141
Stuffed Tomatoes, Crab-and-Avocado, 141
Stuffed Tomatoes, Turkey, 140
Stuffed Tomatoes, Vegetable, 141
Sun-Dried Tomatoes, Cheese Balls with, 317
Vinegar, Tomato-Herb, 200
TORTILLAS. *SEE ALSO* BURRITOS, ENCHILADAS,
TACOS.
Bake, Texas Tortilla, 285
Baskets, Tortilla, 97
Burgers, Tortilla, 138
Migas, 26
Soup, Tortilla, 136
Triangles, Tortilla, 107
TUNA
Chopsticks, Tuna, 255
Steaks on Mixed Greens with Lemon-Basil
Vinaigrette, Seared Tuna, 205
Yellowfin Tuna with Corn, Pepper, and
Tomato Salsa, 164
TURKEY
Cutlets, Pecan-Crusted Turkey, 282
Gravy, Savory Turkey and, 326
Gravy, Turkey, 306
Marinated Turkey Breast, Citrus-, 272
Roast Turkey and Giblet Gravy, 308
Salad, Fruit-and-Spice Turkey, 325
Salad, Ranch-Style Turkey 'n' Pasta, 184
Sandwiches, Smoked Turkey-Roasted
Pepper, 66
Sandwich, Waffle-Grilled Turkey, 170
Tomatoes, Turkey Stuffed, 140
Topping, Turkey-Vegetable, 22
Turnovers, Home-Style Turkey, 325
Wild Turkey, Country-Fried, 306
TURNIPS
Orange Carrots and Turnips, Sunset, 213
Pudding, Turnip, 213
Salad, Irish Turnip, 178
Soup, Oyster-Turnip, 328

Vanilla
Cookies 'n' Cream Dessert, Gold-Dusted, 271
Extract, Vanilla, 243
Frosting, Vanilla Buttercream, 99
Oil, Vanilla, 243
Sauce, Pan-Fried Grouper with Vanilla
Wine, 241
Sauce, Vanilla Crème, 243
Shortbread, Scottish, 242
Soufflés with Vanilla Crème Sauce,
Vanilla, 242
Sugar, Vanilla, 243
Vinaigrette, Vanilla, 242

VEAL
Ragout, Veal-and-Artichoke, 43
Soup with Quenelles, Veal-Vermicelli, 14
VEGETABLES. *SEE ALSO* SPECIFIC TYPES.
Chicken Breast with Turned Vegetables and
Chive Sauce, Poached, 309
Chinese Vegetable Pouches, 34
Cornish Hens with Vegetables, Tarragon
Roasted, 79
Enchiladas, Vegetable-Cheese, 42
Fettuccine Primavera, 85
Fish and Vegetables, Cheesy, 254
Grilled Vegetable Skewers, 160
Marinated Vegetables, 183
Medley, Masala Vegetable, 56
Pasta Potpourri, 33
Pizza, Vegetable, 218
Pizza, Veggie, 78
Salads
Freezer Salad, 118
Grilled Vegetable Salad, 203
Salmon Scaloppine with Vegetable Confetti
and Pernod Sauce, 172
Soup, Chili Vegetable, 120
Steamed Vegetables with Garlic-Ginger
Butter Sauce, 89
Stew, Vegetable-Beef, 323
Tomatoes, Vegetable Stuffed, 141
Topping, Turkey-Vegetable, 22
VENISON
Loin, Mushroom-Crusted Venison, 302
Pot Pie with Parmesan Crust, Game, 304
Sauce, Venison Reduction, 303
Stock, Venison, 302
VINEGARS
Southwest Vinegar, 200
Tarragon Vinegar, 201
Tomato-Herb Vinegar, 200

Waffles
Banana-Oatmeal Waffles, 206
Belgian Waffles, 206
Club Soda Waffles, 206
Corn-Chile Waffles, 206
Cornmeal Waffles, 22
Fudge Waffles, 205
Peanut Butter Waffles, Honey-
Buttered, M206
WALNUTS
Cake, Apple-Walnut, 242
Dressing, Green Beans with
Walnut, 279
Salad, Raspberry-Walnut, 158
Sandwich, Date-Nut Lettuce, 202
WILD RICE. *SEE* RICE.
WOK COOKING
Chicken Chinese, 33
Greens, Stir-Fried, 33
Pasta Potpourri, 33
Scallop Stir-Fry, 32
Shrimp, Tangy Honeyed, 32
Vegetable Pouches, Chinese, 34

Yogurt
Cake, Strawberry Yogurt Layer, 85
Dip, Yogurt, 21

Zucchini
Marinated Squash Medley, 126
Sautéed Zucchini with Mushrooms, 135

FAVORITE RECIPES

Jot down your family's and *your* favorite recipes for quick and
handy reference. And don't forget to include the dishes that drew rave reviews
when company came for dinner.

RECIPE	SOURCE/PAGE	REMARKS
Appetizers & Beverages		
Breads		
Desserts		

RECIPE	SOURCE/PAGE	REMARKS

Main Dishes

Side Dishes

Soups & Stews

Party Planner

EVENT _____ STYLE/ THEME _____

DATE _____ TIME _____ PLACE _____ NUMBER OF GUESTS _____

GUEST LIST/ R.S.V.P. _____

_____

_____

_____

_____

_____

NOTES _____

_____

MENU	RECIPE SOURCES & GARNISHES	THINGS TO DO
Appetizers:		One Week Before:
Soup/Salad:		
		Three Days Before:
Entree:		
		The Day Before:
Side Dishes:		
Breads:		On the Day:
Dessert:		
Beverages/Wines:		Last Minute: